Lecture Notes in Computer Science 3472

Commenced Publication in 1973
Founding and Former Series Editors:
Gerhard Goos, Juris Hartmanis, and Jan van Leeuwen

Editorial Board

David Hutchison
  Lancaster University, UK
Takeo Kanade
  Carnegie Mellon University, Pittsburgh, PA, USA
Josef Kittler
  University of Surrey, Guildford, UK
Jon M. Kleinberg
  Cornell University, Ithaca, NY, USA
Friedemann Mattern
  ETH Zurich, Switzerland
John C. Mitchell
  Stanford University, CA, USA
Moni Naor
  Weizmann Institute of Science, Rehovot, Israel
Oscar Nierstrasz
  University of Bern, Switzerland
C. Pandu Rangan
  Indian Institute of Technology, Madras, India
Bernhard Steffen
  University of Dortmund, Germany
Madhu Sudan
  Massachusetts Institute of Technology, MA, USA
Demetri Terzopoulos
  New York University, NY, USA
Doug Tygar
  University of California, Berkeley, CA, USA
Moshe Y. Vardi
  Rice University, Houston, TX, USA
Gerhard Weikum
  Max-Planck Institute of Computer Science, Saarbruecken, Germany

Manfred Broy   Bengt Jonsson
Joost-Pieter Katoen   Martin Leucker
Alexander Pretschner (Eds.)

Model-Based Testing of Reactive Systems

Advanced Lectures

 Springer

Volume Editors

Manfred Broy
Martin Leucker
TU Munich
Institute for Informatics I4
Boltzmannstr. 3, 85748 Garching, Germany
E-mail: {broy,leucker}@in.tum.de

Bengt Jonsson
Uppsala University
Department of Computer Systems
Box 337, 751 05 Uppsala, Sweden
E-mail: bengt@it.uu.se

Joost-Pieter Katoen
University of Twente
Department of Computer Science
P.O. Box 271, 7500 AE Enschede, The Netherlands
E-mail: katoen@cs.utwente.nl

Alexander Pretschner
ETH Zurich
D-INFK, Information Security
Haldeneggsteig 4, 8092 Zürich, Switzerland
E-mail: alexander.pretschner@inf.ethz.ch

Library of Congress Control Number: 2005927641

CR Subject Classification (1998): D.2.5, D.2.4, D.2, F.3.1, D.2.11, D.3.1

ISSN   0302-9743
ISBN-10   3-540-26278-4 Springer Berlin Heidelberg New York
ISBN-13   978-3-540-26278-7 Springer Berlin Heidelberg New York

This work is subject to copyright. All rights are reserved, whether the whole or part of the material is concerned, specifically the rights of translation, reprinting, re-use of illustrations, recitation, broadcasting, reproduction on microfilms or in any other way, and storage in data banks. Duplication of this publication or parts thereof is permitted only under the provisions of the German Copyright Law of September 9, 1965, in its current version, and permission for use must always be obtained from Springer. Violations are liable to prosecution under the German Copyright Law.

Springer is a part of Springer Science+Business Media

springeronline.com

© Springer-Verlag Berlin Heidelberg 2005
Printed in Germany

Typesetting: Camera-ready by author, data conversion by Boller Mediendesign
Printed on acid-free paper   SPIN: 11498490   06/3142   5 4 3 2 1 0

Preface

Testing is the primary hardware and software verification technique used by industry today. Usually, it is ad hoc, error prone, and very expensive. In recent years, however, many attempts have been made to develop more sophisticated, formal testing methods. But a comprehensive account of the area of formal testing is missing. The goal of this seminar volume is to provide an in-depth exposure of this emerging area, especially to make it easily accessible to new researchers in this field.

Since testing describes the methodology used to obtain better systems, it is widely used in many scientific and industrial sectors dealing with system development. As such, a book on testing is hardly ever a comprehensive overview on the whole domain of testing, but a selection of important approaches and application domains. In this volume, we focus on testing methods for *reactive systems*. By reactive systems, we understand software and hardware systems with a (usually) non-terminating behavior that interact through visible events, such as Web servers, communication protocols, operating systems, smart cards, processors, etc.

Furthermore, in most chapters of this book, we follow the so-called *model-based* approach. The underlying assumption in the model-based approach is the existence of a precise formal model of the system being developed. This model can be used for studying the system to be. Especially in the testing phase of product development, it can be used to generate *complete test suites* to show *conformance* of the model and the actual implementation, or, just to derive "interesting" *test cases* to check the developed system.

The 19 chapters of the book are grouped into six parts. In the first part, we present the approaches for *testing for finite-state machines*, also called *Mealy machines*. The second part, called *testing of labeled transition systems*, gives an overview of the testing theory due to Hennessy and De Nicola together with its extensions to I/O, timed, and probabilistic systems. In Part III, we focus on methodology, algorithms, and techniques for *model-based test case generation*.

The methods illustrated in the first three parts of the book led to the development of test tools and have been applied in many case studies showing their advantages and drawbacks. Several tools and case studies are presented in Part IV.

While test case generation can be considered the heart of testing, the testing process as a whole is more complicated. The test cases have to executed on the system under test. In several application domains, test suites are used to show conformance to a standard. For this, test cases have to be interchanged among developers. Furthermore, testing should be included in the overall development process. In Part V, called *Standardized Test Notation and Execution Architecture* we cover recent developments.

The last part of the book introduces two extensions of the typical testing approach. It describes methods for the continuous testing effort, also at a later run-time of the system. Furthermore, it recalls essentials of model checking, a different powerful technique to get "better" systems, on the one hand to separate model checking and testing, on the other hand to show possible combination leading to approaches like *black box checking* or *adaptive model checking*. We meaningfully term this last part *Beyond Testing*.

The volume is the outcome of a research seminar that was held in Schloss Dagstuhl in January 2004 and that took place as part of the so-called GI/Research Seminar series. Thirty three young researchers participated in the seminar; each of them prepared a presentation based on one or several recent articles, reshaping the material in form with special emphasis on motivation, examples, and also exercises.

Thanks are due to the International Conference and Research Center of Dagstuhl and the "Gesellschaft für Informatik (GI)" for the support it provided. Further funding was provided by the Research Training Network GAMES financed by the European Commission under the Fifth Framework Programme. We also would like to thank the authors of the tutorial papers as well as their reviewers for their efforts. Last but not least, we would like to thank Britta Liebscher and Springer for substantial help in technical and editorial matters.

The editors hope that this book will help many readers to enter the domain of model-based testing, either to apply the so-far-developed techniques to enhance their product under development, or to improve the current testing techniques to make them even more efficient and effective.

Munich, Uppsala, Enschede, Zurich, January 2005   Manfred Broy
Bengt Jonsson
Joost-Pieter Katoen
Martin Leucker
Alexander Pretschner

Contents

Part I

Testing of Finite State Machines

The first part of the book is devoted to the problem of black-box testing of finite state machines in order to discover properties of their behavior and to check that they conform to given specifications.

Finite state machines is a widely used model for reactive systems. It has been used to model systems in a wide variety of areas, including sequential circuits, communication protocol entities, and embedded controllers. The study of testing of finite state machines has been motivated as fundamental research in computer science, and by applications in the testing of sequential circuits, communication protocols, embedded controllers, etc. For the case of sequential circuits, there were activities in the 60's and 70's. Since the 80's, there has been quite a lot of activity motivated by the problem of conformance testing for communication protocols. This area has generated invaluable insights into the problem of testing the reactive aspects of systems, which can be used in testing today's complex reactive systems.

Although FSM notation is simple, conformance testing for FSMs is very useful in practice. FSMs have been widely used to directly specify many types of systems, including protocols, embedded control systems and digital circuits. Moreover, many formal notations are very similar to finite state machines, or use FSMs to specify some parts of the systems. Such notations include StateCharts [Har87], SDL for communication protocols [BH89], UML state diagrams [RJB99] and ASM [Gur94] for software, and StateFlow [Sta] and SCR [HJL96] for reactive systems. Note that many control or reactive systems are described by an infinite set of states and infinite transitions. However, it is often possible to extract for such systems a system part or a particular system behavior or interaction with the environment, which can be modeled by a finite state machine. In many case this can be done through an abstraction process that allows the designer to ignore some details and focus on the finite part of the system interaction with the environment. This finite part of the specification can be used to derive tests and to test the whole system. To apply these tests to the complete system, we have to assume that we know the input and output finite vocabulary, and that the system produces a response to an input signal within a known, finite amount of time. A state of the system can be defined as a stable condition in which it has produced the expected output and is waiting for a new input. A transition is defined as the consumption of an input, the generation of an output, and the possible move to a new state. In this chapter we consider only deterministic systems, i.e. that produce the outputs and move to the next state in a deterministic way.

Typical problems from applications are as follows.

- *Conformance testing:* Check that a finite state machine conforms to a given specification. Typically the specification is given as a finite machine, and the conformance testing is to check whether the system under test is equivalent to its specification, or that it implements it in the sense of some preorder relation.
- *Property checking:* Check that the behavior of a finite state machine satisfies certain properties. These properties can be formulated, e.g., in some temporal logic.
- *Automata Learning:* Given a finite state machine, determine its behavior. This is a harder problem, which is considered in Section 19.4 of this volume.

In this Chapter, we will focus on the problem of conformance testing. There is a wide literature on conformance testing, especially in the area of communication protocol testing. Most of these algorithms combine techniques for attacking subproblems that investigating particular states or transitions of a finite state machine. We will therefore first consider these subproblems and techniques for their solution in Chapters 1 – 3. Chapter 4 will discuss how they can be combined to the problem of testing conformance.

The contents of the respective chapters are as follows.

- Chapter 1 considers the construction of *Homing and Synchronizing Sequences:* given a finite state machine with known states and transitions, a synchronizing sequence is a sequence of input symbols which takes the machine to a unique final state, independent of the starting state. A homing sequence is a sequence such that the final state (which need not be unique) can be uniquely determined by observing the output.
- Chapter 2 considers the problem of *State Identification:* Given a finite state machine with known states and transitions, identify in which state the machine currently is.
- Chapter 3 considers the problem of *State Verification:* Given a finite state machine with known states and transitions, verify that a machine is in a particular state Björklund (36)

- Chapter 4 considers the problem of *Conformance Testing* is considered: Check that a finite state machine conforms to a given specification, given as a finite state machine.

Many works in the literature on testing of finite state machine assume that systems are be modeled as Mealy machines. Mealy machines allow to model both inputs and outputs as part of their behavior, and are therefore a suitable abstract model of communication protocol entities and other types of reactive systems. An overview of testing finite state machines is given in [LY94, LY96], from which much of the material for this section is taken. Overviews of conformance testing for communication protocols can be found in [SL89, Hol91, Lai02].

The basic concepts of finite states machines used in the following chapters is given in Appendix 21.

1 Homing and Synchronizing Sequences

Sven Sandberg

Department of Information Technology
Uppsala University
svens@it.uu.se

1.1 Introduction

1.1.1 Mealy Machines

This chapter considers two fundamental problems for Mealy machines, i.e., finite-state machines with inputs and outputs. The machines will be used in subsequent chapters as models of a system or program to test. We repeat Definition 21.1 of Chapter 21 here: readers already familiar with Mealy machines can safely skip to Section 1.1.2.

Definition 1.1. A Mealy Machine is a 5-tuple $\mathcal{M} = \langle I, O, S, \delta, \lambda \rangle$, where I, O and S are finite nonempty sets, and $\delta : S \times I \to S$ and $\lambda : S \times I \to O$ are total functions.

The interpretation of a Mealy machine is as follows. The set S consists of "states". At any point in time, the machine is in one state $s \in S$. It is possible to give inputs to the machine, by applying an input letter $a \in I$. The machine responds by giving output $\lambda(s, a)$ and transforming itself to the new state $\delta(s, a)$. We depict Mealy machines as directed edge-labeled graphs, where S is the set of vertices. The outgoing edges from a state $s \in S$ lead to $\delta(s, a)$ for all $a \in I$, and they are labeled "a/b", where a is the input symbol and b is the output symbol $\lambda(s, a)$. See Figure 1.1 for an example.

We say that Mealy machines are *completely specified*, because at every state there is a next state for every input (δ and λ are total). They are also *deterministic*, because only one next state is possible.

Applying a string $a_1 a_2 \cdots a_k \in I^*$ of input symbols starting in a state s_1 gives the sequence of states $s_1, s_2, \ldots, s_{k+1}$ with $s_{j+1} = \delta(s_j, a_j)$. We extend the transition function to $\delta(s_1, a_1 a_2 \cdots a_k) \stackrel{\text{def}}{=} s_{k+1}$ and the output function to $\lambda(s_1, a_1 a_2 \cdots a_k) \stackrel{\text{def}}{=} \lambda(s_1, a_1)\lambda(s_2, a_2) \cdots \lambda(s_k, a_k)$, i.e., the concatenation of all outputs. Moreover, if $Q \subseteq S$ is a set of states then $\delta(Q, x) \stackrel{\text{def}}{=} \{\delta(s, x) : s \in Q\}$. We sometimes use the shorthand $s \xrightarrow{a} t$ for $\delta(s, a) = t$, and if in addition we know that $\lambda(s, a) = b$ then we write $s \xrightarrow{a/b} t$. The number $|S|$ of states is denoted n.

Throughout this chapter we will assume that an explicit Mealy machine $\mathcal{M} = \langle I, O, S, \delta, \lambda \rangle$ is given.

M. Broy et al. (Eds.): Model-Based Testing of Reactive Systems, LNCS 3472, pp. 5-33, 2005.
© Springer-Verlag Berlin Heidelberg 2005

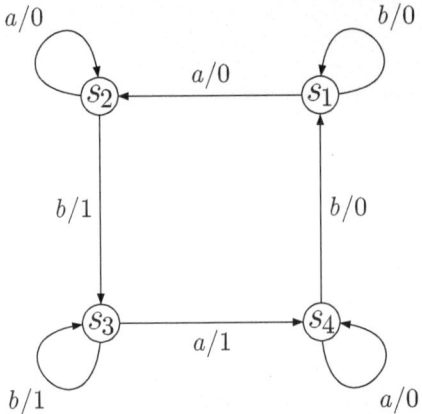

Fig. 1.1. A Mealy machine $\mathcal{M} = \langle I, O, S, \delta, \lambda \rangle$ with states $S = \{s_1, s_2, s_3, s_4\}$, input alphabet $I = \{a, b\}$, and output alphabet $O = \{0, 1\}$. For instance, applying a starting in s produces output $\lambda(s, a) = 0$ and moves to next state $\delta(s, a) = t$.

1.1.2 Synchronizing Sequences

In the problems of this chapter, we do not know the initial state of a Mealy machine and want to apply a sequence of input symbols so that the *final* state becomes known. A **synchronizing sequence** is one that takes the machine to a unique final state, and this state does not depend on where we started. Which particular final state is not specified: it is up to whoever solves the problem to select it. Thus, formally we have:

Definition 1.2. A sequence $x \in I^*$ is **synchronizing** (for a given Mealy machine) if $|\delta(S, x)| = 1$. [1]   □

Note that synchronizing sequences are independent of the output. Consequently, when talking about synchronizing sequences we will sometimes omit stating the output of the machine. For the same reason, it is not meaningful to talk about synchronizing sequences "for minimized machines", because if we ignore the output then all machines are equivalent.

Example. Synchronizing sequences have many surprising and beautiful applications. For instance, robots that grasp and pick up objects, say, in a factory, are often sensitive to the orientation of the object. If objects are fed in a random

---

[1] The literature uses an amazing amount of synonyms (none of which we will use here), including *synchronizing word* [KRS87], *synchronization sequence* [PJH92], *reset sequence* [Epp90], *reset word* [Rys97], *directing word* [ČPR71], *recurrent word* [Rys92], and *initializing word* [Göh98]. Some texts talk about the machine as being a *synchronized* [CKK02], *synchronizing* [KRS87], *synchronizable* [PS01], *resettable* [PJH92], *reset* [Rys97], *directable* [BIĆP99], *recurrent* [Rys92], *initializable* [Göh98], *cofinal* [ID84] or *collapsible* [Fri90] *automaton*.

orientation, the problem arises of how to rotate them from an initially unknown orientation to a known one. Using sensors for this is expensive and complicated. A simple and elegant solution is depicted in Figure 1.2. Two parallel "pushing walls" are placed around the object, and one is moved toward the other so that it starts pushing the object, rotating it until a stable position between the walls is reached. Given the possible directions of these pushing walls, one has to find a sequence of pushes from different directions that takes the object to a known state. This problem can be reduced to finding a synchronizing sequence in a machine where the states are the possible orientations, the input alphabet is the set of possible directions of the walls, and the transition function is given by how a particular way of pushing rotates the object into a new orientation. This problem has been considered by, e.g., Natarajan [Nat86] and Eppstein [Epp90], who relate the problem to automata but use a slightly different way of pushing. Rao and Goldberg [RG95] use our way of pushing and their method works for more generally shaped objects. □

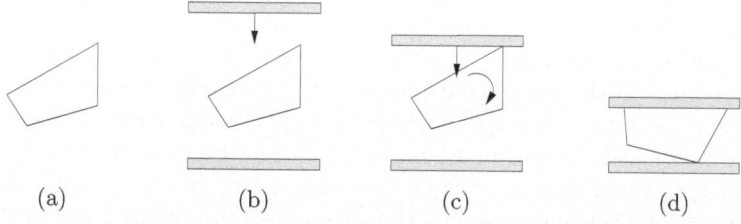

(a)   (b)   (c)   (d)

Fig. 1.2. Two pushing walls rotating the object to a new position. (a) The object. (b) One wall moves toward the object until (c) it hits it and starts pushing it, rotating it to the final stable position (d).

An alternative way to formulate the synchronizing sequence problem is as follows. Let S be a finite set, and $f_1, \ldots, f_k : S \rightarrow S$ total functions. Find a composition of the functions that is constant. Function f_i corresponds to $\delta(\cdot, a_i)$, where a_i is the i'th input symbol.

Example. To see that synchronizing sequences do not always exist, consider the Mealy machine in Figure 1.1. If the same sequence of input symbols is applied to two states that are "opposite corners", then the respective final states will be opposite corners too. So in particular no sequence x satisfies $\delta(s_1, x) = \delta(s_3, x)$ or $\delta(s_2, x) = \delta(s_4, x)$. □

Besides the parts orienting problem in Example 1.1.2, synchronizing sequences have been used to generate test cases for synchronous circuits with no reset [CJSP93], and are also important in theoretical automata theory and structural theory of many-valued functions [Sal02].

1.1.3   Homing Sequences

The second problem of this chapter, **homing sequences**, are sequences of input symbols such that the final state after applying it can be determined by looking at the output:

Definition 1.3. A sequence $x \in I^*$ is **homing** (for a given Mealy machine) if for every pair $s, t \in S$ of states, $\delta(s, x) \neq \delta(t, x) \Rightarrow \lambda(s, x) \neq \lambda(t, x)$. [2]   □

Note that every synchronizing sequence is a homing sequence, but the converse is not true. See Figure 1.1 for an example: we saw earlier that it does not have a synchronizing sequence, but it has a homing sequence. After applying ab, the possible outputs are $\lambda(s_1, ab) = 01$, $\lambda(s_2, ab) = 01$, $\lambda(s_3, ab) = 10$, and $\lambda(s_4, ab) = 00$. Hence, if we observe output 00 or 10, the initial and hence also final state becomes known. For output 01 we only know the initial state was s or t, but in both cases the final state is u. Thus the output uniquely determines the final state, and the sequence is homing.

Homing sequences can be either **preset**[3], as in Definition 1.3, or **adaptive**. While preset sequences are completely determined before the experiment starts, adaptive sequences are applied to the machine as they are constructed, and the next symbol in the sequence depends on the previous outputs. Thus, preset sequences can be seen as a special case of adaptive sequences, where this dependence is not utilized. Formally one can define adaptive homing sequences as decision trees, where each node is labeled with an input symbol and each edge is labeled with an output symbol. The test consists in walking from the root of the tree toward a leaf: apply the input on the node, observe the output and walk to the successor through the edge with the corresponding label. When a leaf is reached, the sequence of outputs determines the final state (but unlike preset sequences, the sequence of *inputs* would not necessarily determine the final state if the initial state had been different).

Homing sequences are typically used as building blocks in testing problems with no reset. Here, a reset is a special input symbol that takes every input to the same state, i.e., it is a synchronizing sequence of length one. They have been used in conformance testing (Section 4.5), and in learning (by Rivest and Schapire [RS93]; see also Chapter 19). For machines with output, homing sequences are often preferable to synchronizing sequences: first, they are usually shorter; second, they always exist if the automaton is minimized (cf. Theorem 1.20), a natural criterion that is often required anyway.

1.1.4   Chapter Outline

Section 1.2 introduces the important notion of current state uncertainty, used when computing homing sequences. Section 1.3 presents algorithms for several

---

[2] Synonyms (not used here) are *homing word* [Rys83], *terminal state experiment* [Hib61], *Identification experiment of the second kind (IE 2)* [Sta72] and *experiment which distinguishes the terminal state of a machine* [Gin58].

[3] A synonym is *uniform* [Gin58].

versions of the homing and synchronizing sequences problems: first an algorithm to compute homing sequences for minimized Mealy machines (Section 1.3.1), then an algorithm to compute synchronizing sequences (Section 1.3.2). Section 1.3.3 unifies these algorithms into one for computing homing sequences for general (not necessarily minimized) machines – this algorithm can be used both to compute homing and synchronizing sequences. The two algorithms for computing homing sequences are then modified to compute *adaptive* homing sequences in Section 1.3.4. Finally, Section 1.3.5 gives exponential algorithms to compute minimal length homing and synchronizing sequences.

Section 1.4 turns from algorithms to complexity. First, Section 1.4.1 shows that it is NP-hard to find the *shortest* homing or synchronizing sequence. Second, Section 1.4.2 shows that it is PSPACE-complete to determine if a machine has a homing or synchronizing sequence, if it is known that the initial state is in a particular subset $Q \subseteq S$. In both cases it means that polynomial algorithms for the problems are unlikely to exist.

Section 1.5 gives an overview of research in the area and mentions some related areas, and Section 1.6 summarizes the most important ideas in the chapter.

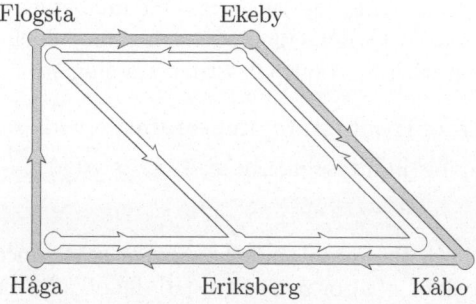

Fig. 1.3. The subway map of Uppsala. The five stations are connected by two one-way lines: white and grey.

Exercise 1.4. The schematic map of the subway in Uppsala looks as in Figure 1.3. You do not know at which station you are, and there are no signs or other characteristics that reveal the current station, but you have to get to Flogsta by moving from station to station, in each step taking either the white or the grey line. What type of sequence does this correspond to? Find a sequence if one exists.

(Hint: use that if you are in Flogsta or Håga, the white line takes you to Eriksberg for sure.)

1.2 Initial and Current State Uncertainty

Consider a Mealy machine to which we apply some input string and receive an output string. Even if the input string was not homing, we may still draw some

partial conclusions from the output. The *initial state uncertainty* describes what
we know about the initial state, and the *current state uncertainty* describes what
we know about the final state. Current state uncertainty is crucial when computing homing sequences, and the definition relies on initial state uncertainty.

Definition 1.5. The **initial state uncertainty** (with respect to a Mealy machine) after applying input sequence $x \in I^*$ is a partition

$$\pi(x) \stackrel{\text{def}}{=} \{B_1, B_2, \ldots, B_r\} \subset \mathcal{P}(S)$$

of the states. Two states s, t are in the same block B_i if and only if $\lambda(s, x) = \lambda(t, x)$. □

Thus, after applying input x, for a certain output we know the initial state
was in B_1, for another output we know it was in B_2, and so on. Although initial
state uncertainty will not be used explicitly until Sections 2 and 3.4.3, it provides
intuitions that will be useful here, and we also need it to define the current state
uncertainty.

The *current* state uncertainty is a data structure that, given an input string,
describes for each output string the set of possible final states. Thus, computing
a homing sequence means to find an input string for which the current state
uncertainty associated with each output string is a singleton.

Definition 1.6. The **current state uncertainty** (with respect to a Mealy
machine) after applying input sequence $x \in I^*$ is $\sigma(x) \stackrel{\text{def}}{=} \{\delta(B_i, x) : B_i \in \pi(x)\} \subset \mathcal{P}(S)$. □

The elements of both the initial and the current state uncertainty are called
blocks. If B is a block of $\pi(x)$ or $\sigma(x)$ then $|B|$ denotes its size, whereas $|\pi(x)|$
and $|\sigma(x)|$ denote the number of blocks. While the initial state uncertainty is
a partition (i.e., any two blocks are disjoint, and the union of all blocks is the
entire set of states), Example 1.2 will show that the current state uncertainty
does not need to be one: a state may belong to several different blocks, and the
union of all blocks does not need to be the whole set of states.

We will frequently take the viewpoint that the current state uncertainty
evolves as more input symbols are applied. Namely, the current state uncertainty
$\sigma(xy)$ is obtained by applying $\delta(\cdot, y)$ to each block of $\sigma(x)$, splitting the result
if some states gave different outputs on y.

Example. To see how the current state uncertainty works, consider the machine
in Figure 1.4. Initially, we do not know the state, so it may be either s_1, s_2,
or s_3. Thus the current state uncertainty is $\sigma(\varepsilon) = \{\{s_1, s_2, s_3\}\}$. Apply the
string a to the machine. If we receive the output 1, then we were in state s_2
so the current state is s_1. If we receive the output 0, then we were in either
s_1 or s_3 and the current state is either s_1 or s_3. We then describe the current
state uncertainty as $\sigma(a) = \{\{s_1\}_1, \{s_1, s_3\}_0\}$ (the subscripts, included only in
this example for clarity, show which outputs correspond to each block). Now

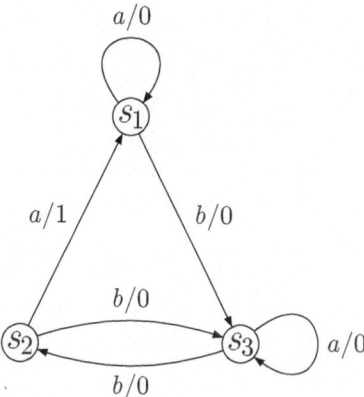

Fig. 1.4. Example illustrating current state uncertainty

we additionally apply the letter b. If we were in s_1 then we end up in s_3 and receive output 0, and if we were in either s_3 or s_1 then we end up in either s_2 or s_3, in both cases receiving output 0. Thus the current state uncertainty after applying ab is $\sigma(ab) = \{\{s_3\}_{10}, \{s_2, s_3\}_{00}\}$. Finally, we apply the letter a at this point. If we were in s_3, then we move to s_3 with output 0, and if we were in s_2, then we move to s_1 and receive output 1. Thus the current state uncertainty becomes $\sigma(aba) = \{\{s_3\}_{100 \text{ or } 000}, \{s_1\}_{001}\}$. We end the example with an important remark: since every set in the current state uncertainty is now a *singleton*, we can determine the current state uniquely, by looking at the output. Thus aba is a homing sequence. (Verify this using Definition 1.3!) □

We conclude this section with two important observations. First, as the sequence is extended, the initial state uncertainty becomes more and more refined. I.e., by applying more input symbols the blocks of the partition may be split but not merged:

Lemma 1.7. *For any sequences $x, y \in I^*$, the following holds.*

$$\forall\, B_i \in \pi(xy) \, \exists\, B_j \in \pi(x) : B_i \subseteq B_j.$$

Proof. All states in a block of $\pi(xy)$ give the same output on xy. In particular they give the same output on x, so they all belong to the same block of $\pi(x)$. □

Second, as a sequence x is extended, the sum $\sum_{B \in \sigma(x)} |B|$ of sizes of all blocks in the current state uncertainty can never increase. This is because if $B \in \sigma(xy)$ then $B = \delta(Q, y)$, where $Q \subseteq B'$ is a subset of some block $B' \in \sigma(x)$: here we must have $|B'| \geq |Q| \geq |B|$. (When is each inequality strict?) Moreover, the number of blocks can only decrease if two blocks are mapped to the same block, in which case the sum of sizes of all blocks also decreases. This (very informally) explains the following lemma, whose proof we delegate to Exercise 1.9.

Lemma 1.8. *If* $x, y \in I^*$ *are any two sequences, the following holds.*

$$\left(\sum_{B \in \sigma(x)} |B| \right) - |\sigma(x)| \geq \left(\sum_{B \in \sigma(xy)} |B| \right) - |\sigma(xy)|. \qquad \square$$

As we will see in the next section, algorithms for computing homing sequences work by concatenating sequences so that in each step the inequality in Lemma 1.8 is *strict*: note that x is homing when $\sum_{B \in \sigma(x)} |B| - |\sigma(x)|$ reaches zero.

Initial and current state uncertainty has been used since the introduction of homing sequences [Moo56, Gil61] although we use a slightly different definition of current state uncertainty [LY96].

Exercise 1.9. Prove Lemma 1.8.

Exercise 1.10. Recall from the discussion before Lemma 1.8 that if $B \in \sigma(xy)$ then $B = \delta(Q, y)$ where $Q \subseteq B'$ for some $B' \in \sigma(x)$. When is $|B'| > |Q|$, and when is $|Q| > |B|$?

1.3   Algorithms for Computing Homing and Synchronizing Sequences

1.3.1   Computing Homing Sequences for Minimized Machines

This section presents an algorithm to compute homing sequences, assuming the machine is *minimized* (for definitions and algorithms for minimization, refer to Chapter 21). This is an important special case that occurs in many practical applications, cf. Section 4.5 and the article by Rivest and Schapire [RS93]. The algorithm for minimized machines is a simpler special case of the general Algorithm 3 in Section 1.3.3: they can be implemented to act identically on minimized machines. Both algorithms run in time $O(n^3 + n^2 \cdot |I|)$, but the one for minimized machines requires less space ($O(n)$ instead of $O(n^2 + n \cdot |I|)$) and produces shorter sequences (bounded by $(n^2 - n)/2$ instead of $(n^3 - n)/6$). The general algorithm, on the other hand, gives additional insight into the relation between homing and synchronizing sequences, and is of course applicable to more problem instances.

The algorithm of this section builds a homing sequence by concatenating many *separating sequences*. A separating sequence for two states gives different output for the states:

Definition 1.11. A **separating sequence** for two states $s, t \in S$ is a sequence $x \in I^*$ such that $\lambda(s, x) \neq \lambda(t, x)$. $\qquad \square$

The Algorithm. Algorithm 1 computes a homing sequence for a minimized machine as follows. It first finds a separating sequence for some two states of the machine. By the definition of separating sequence, the two states give different outputs, hence they now belong to different blocks of the resulting current state uncertainty. Next iteration finds two new states that belong to the same block of the current state uncertainty and applies a separating sequence for them. Again, the two states end up in different blocks of the new current state uncertainty. This process is repeated until the current state uncertainty contains only singleton blocks, at which point we have a homing sequence.

Algorithm 1 Computing a homing sequence for a minimized machine.

```
1    function HOMING-FOR-MINIMIZED(Minimized Mealy machine M)
2        x ← ε
3        while there is a block B ∈ σ(x) with |B| > 1
4            find two different states s, t ∈ B
5            let y be a separating sequence for s and t
6            x ← xy
7        return x
```

Step 5 of the algorithm can always be performed because the machine is minimized. Since y is separating, the block B splits into at least two new blocks (one containing s and one containing t). Thus, Lemma 1.8 holds with strict inequality between any two iterations, i.e., the quantity $\sum_{B \in \sigma(x)} |B| - |\sigma(x)|$ strictly decreases in each iteration. When the algorithm starts, it is $n - 1$ and when it terminates it is 0. Hence the algorithm terminates after concatenating at most $n - 1$ separating sequences.

The algorithm is due to Ginsburg [Gin58] who relies on the adaptive version of Moore [Moo56] which we will see more of in Section 1.3.4.

Length of Separating Sequences. We now show that any two states in a minimized machine have a separating sequence of length at most $n - 1$. Since we only need to concatenate $n - 1$ separating sequences, this shows that the computed homing sequence has length at most $(n - 1)^2$. The argument will also help understanding how to compute separating sequences.

Define a sequence $\rho_0, \rho_1, \ldots$ of partitions, so that two states are in the same class of ρ_i if and only if they do not have any separating sequence of length i. Thus, ρ_i is the partition induced by the relation $s \equiv_i t \stackrel{\text{def}}{\Leftrightarrow}$ "$\lambda(s, x) = \lambda(t, x)$ for all $x \in I^*$ of length at most i". In particular, $\rho_0 = \{S\}$, and ρ_{i+1} is a refinement of ρ_i. These partitions are also used in algorithms for machine minimization; cf. Section 21. The following lemma is important.

Lemma 1.12 ([Moo56]). *If $\rho_{i+1} = \rho_i$ for some i, then the rest of the sequence of partitions is constant, i.e., $\rho_j = \rho_i$ for all $j > i$.*

Proof. We prove the equivalent, contrapositive form: $\rho_{i+1} \neq \rho_i \Rightarrow \rho_i \neq \rho_{i-1}$ for all $i \geq 1$. If $\rho_{i+1} \neq \rho_i$ then there are two states $s, t \in S$ with a shortest separating sequence of length $i + 1$, say $ax \in I^{i+1}$ (i.e., a is the first letter and x the tail of the sequence). Since ax is separating for s and t but a is not, x must be separating for $\delta(s, a)$ and $\delta(t, a)$. It is also a shortest separating sequence, because if $y \in I^*$ was shorter than x, then ay would be a separating sequence for s and t, and shorter than ax. This proves that there are two states $\delta(s, a), \delta(t, a)$ with a shortest separating sequence of length i, so $\rho_i \neq \rho_{i-1}$. $\square$

Since a partition of n elements can only be refined n times, the sequence $\rho_0, \rho_1, \ldots$ of partitions becomes constant after at most n steps. And since the machine is minimized, after this point the partitions contain only singletons. So any two states have a separating sequence of length at most $n - 1$, and the homing sequence has length at most $(n - 1)^2$.

Hibbard [Hib61] improved this bound, showing that the homing sequence computed by Algorithm 1 has length at most $n(n-1)/2$, provided we choose two states with the shortest possible separating sequence in each iteration. Moreover, for every n there is an n-state machine whose shortest homing sequence has length $n(n - 1)/2$, so the algorithm has the optimal worst case behavior in terms of output length.

Computing Separating Sequences. We are now ready to fill in the last detail of the algorithm. To compute separating sequences, we first construct the partitions $\rho_1, \rho_2, \ldots, \rho_r$ described above, where r is the smallest index such that ρ_r contains only singletons. Two states $s, t \in S$ belong to different blocks of ρ_1 if and only if there is an input $a \in I$ so that $\lambda(s, a) \neq \lambda(t, a)$, and thus ρ_1 can be computed. Two states $s, t \in S$ belong to different blocks of ρ_i for $i > 1$ if and only if there is an input a such that $\delta(s, a)$ and $\delta(t, a)$ belong to different blocks of ρ_{i-1}, and thus all ρ_i with $i > 1$ can be computed.

To find a separating sequence for two states $s, t \in S$, find the smallest index i such that s and t belong to different blocks of ρ_i. As argued in the proof of Lemma 1.12, the separating sequence has the form ax, where x is a shortest separating sequence for $\delta(s, a)$ and $\delta(t, a)$. Thus, we find the a that takes s and t to different blocks of ρ_{i-1} and repeat the process until we reach ρ_0. The concatenation of all such a is our separating sequence.

This algorithm can be modified to use only $O(n)$ memory, not counting the space required by the output. Typically, the size of the output does not contribute to the memory requirements, since the sequence is applied to some machine on the fly rather than stored explicitly.

Exercise 1.13. Give an example of a Mealy machine that is not minimized but has a homing sequence. Is there a Mealy machine that is not minimized and has a homing but no synchronizing sequence?

1.3.2   Computing Synchronizing Sequences

Synchronizing sequences are computed in a way similar to homing sequences. The algorithm also concatenates many short sequences into one long, but this time the sequences take two states to the same final state. Analogously to separating sequences, we define merging sequences:

Definition 1.14. A **merging sequence** for two states $s, t \in S$ is a sequence $x \in I^*$ such that $\delta(s, x) = \delta(t, x)$. $\qquad\qquad\square$

The Algorithm. Algorithm 2 first finds a merging sequence y for two states. This ensures that $|\delta(S, y)| < |S|$, because each state in S gives rise to at most one state in $\delta(S, y)$, but the two states for which the sequence is merging give rise to the same state. This process is repeated, in each step appending a new merging sequence for two states in $\delta(S, x)$ to the result x, thus decreasing $|\delta(S, x)|$.

If at some point the algorithm finds two states that do not have a merging sequence, then there is no synchronizing sequence: if there was, it would merge them. And if the algorithm terminates by finishing the loop, the sequence x is clearly synchronizing. This shows correctness. Since $|\delta(S, x)|$ is n initially and 1 on successful termination, the algorithm needs at most $n - 1$ iterations.

Algorithm 2 Computing a synchronizing sequence.

---

1   **function** SYNCHRONIZING(Mealy machine $\mathcal{M}$)
2       $x \leftarrow \varepsilon$
3   **while** $|\delta(S, x)| > 1$
4   find two different states $s_0, t_0 \in \delta(S, x)$
5   let y be a merging sequence for s_0 and t_0
                (if none exists, **return** FAILURE)
6           $x \leftarrow xy$
7   **return** x

As a consequence of this algorithm, we have (see, e.g., Starke [Sta72]):

Theorem 1.15. *A machine has a synchronizing sequence if and only if every pair of states has a merging sequence.*

Proof. If the machine has a synchronizing sequence, then it is merging for every pair of states. If every pair of states has a merging sequence, then Algorithm 2 computes a synchronizing sequence. $\qquad\qquad\square$

To convince yourself, it may be instructive to go back and see how this algorithm works on Exercise 1.4.

Computing Merging Sequences. It remains to show how to compute merging sequences. This can be done by constructing a product machine $\mathcal{M}' = \langle I', S', \delta' \rangle$, with the same input alphabet $I' = I$ and no outputs (so we omit O' and λ'). Every state in $\mathcal{M}'$ is a set of one or two states in $\mathcal{M}$, i.e., $S' = \{\{s\}, \{s, t\} : s, t \in S\}$. Intuitively, these sets correspond to possible final states in $\mathcal{M}$ after applying a sequence to the s_0, t_0 chosen on line 4 of Algorithm 2. Thus we define δ' by setting $\{s, t\} \xrightarrow{a} \{s', t'\}$ in $\mathcal{M}'$ if and only if $s \xrightarrow{a} s'$ and $t \xrightarrow{a} t'$ in $\mathcal{M}$, where we may have $s = t$ or $s' = t'$. In other words, δ' is the restriction of δ to sets of size one or two. Clearly, $\delta'(\{s, t\}, x) = \{s', t'\}$ if and only if $\delta(\{s, t\}, x) = \{s', t'\}$ (where in the first case $\{s, t\}$ and $\{s', t'\}$ are interpreted as states of $\mathcal{M}'$ and in the second case as sets of states in $\mathcal{M}$). See Figure 1.5 for an example of the product machine. Thus, to find a merging sequence for s and t we only need to check if it is possible to reach a singleton set from $\{s, t\}$ in $\mathcal{M}'$. This can be done, e.g., using breadth-first search [CLRS01].

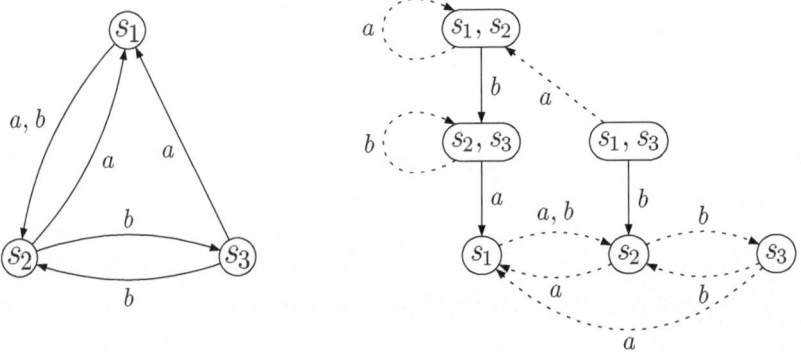

Fig. 1.5. A Mealy machine $\mathcal{M}$ and the corresponding product machine $\mathcal{M}'$. Outputs are omitted here. In the product machine, edges in the shortest path forest are solid and other edges are dashed.

Efficient Implementation. The resulting algorithm is easily seen to run in time $O(n^4 + n^3 \cdot |I|)$. In each of the $O(n)$ iterations, we compute $\delta(S, xy)$ by applying y to every element of $\delta(S, x)$. Since $|y| = O(n^2)$ and $|\delta(S, x)| = O(n)$, this needs $O(n^3)$ time per iteration. The breadth first search needs linear time in the size of $\mathcal{M}'$, i.e., $O(n^2 \cdot |I|)$. We now show how to save a factor n, using several clever tricks due to Eppstein [Epp90].

Theorem 1.16 ([Epp90]). *Algorithm 2 can be implemented to consume time in $O(n^3 + n^2 \cdot |I|)$ and working space $O(n^2 + n \cdot |I|)$ (not counting the space for the output).*

The extra condition "not counting the space for the output" is necessary because the only known upper bound on the length of synchronizing sequences is

$O(n^3)$ (cf. Theorem 1.17). The output may not contribute to the space requirement, in case the sequence is not stored explicitly but applied to some machine
one letter at a time as it is being constructed.

Proof.

Overview. The proof is in several steps. First, we show how to implement the
algorithm to use only the required time, not bothering about how much space is
used. The real bottleneck is computing $\delta(S, x)$. For this to be fast, we precompute
one lookup table per node of the shortest path forest of $\mathcal{M}'$. Each table has size
$O(n)$, and since there are $O(n^2)$ nodes, the total space is $O(n^3)$, which is too
big. To overcome this, we then show how to leave out all but every n'th table,
without destroying the time requirement.

The Shortest Path Forest. We first show how to satisfy the time requirements.
Run breadth-first search in advance, starting simultaneously from all singletons
in the product machine $\mathcal{M}'$ and taking transitions backward. Let it produce a
shortest path forest, i.e., a set of trees where the roots are the singletons and
the path from any node to the root is of shortest length. This needs $O(n^2 \cdot |I|)$
time. For any $\{s, t\} \in S'$, denote by $\tau_{s,t}$ the path from $\{s, t\}$ to the root in this
forest. The algorithm will always select $y = \tau_{s_0, t_0}$ on line 5.

Tables. Recall that we obtain $\delta(S, xy)$ by iterating through all elements u of
the already known set $\delta(S, x)$ and computing $\delta(u, y)$. In the worst case, y is
quadratically long and thus the total work for all $O(n)$ choices of u in all $O(n)$
iterations becomes $O(n^4)$. We now improve this bound to $O(n^2)$. Since $y = \tau_{s_0, t_0}$,
we precompute $\delta(u, \tau_{s,t})$ for every $s, t, u \in S$. Thus, computing $\delta(u, y)$ is done in
$O(1)$ time by a table lookup and we obtain $\delta(S, xy)$ from $\delta(S, x)$ in $O(n)$ time.
The tables need $O(n^3)$ space, but we will improve that later.

Computing Tables. We now show how to compute the tables. For every $\{s, t\} \in$
S' we compute an n element table, with the entries $\delta(u, \tau_{s,t})$ for each $u \in S$, using
totally $O(n^3)$ time and space, as follows. Traverse the shortest path forest in preorder, again following transitions backward. When visiting node $\{s, t\} \in S'$, let
$\{s', t'\}$ be its parent in the forest. Thus, there is some a such that $\tau_{s,t} = a\tau_{s',t'}$.
Note that $\delta(u', \tau_{s',t'})$ has already been computed for all $u' \in S$, since we traverse
in pre-order. To compute $\delta(u, \tau_{s,t})$ we only need to compute $\delta(u, a)$ and plug
it into the table in the parent node: $\delta(u, \tau_{s,t}) = \delta(\delta(u, a), \tau_{s',t'})$. This takes
constant time, so doing it for every $u \in S$ and every node in the tree requires
only $O(n^3)$ time.

We thus achieved the time bound, but the algorithm now needs $O(n^2 \cdot |I|)$
space to store $\mathcal{M}'$ and $O(n^3)$ to store the tables of all $\delta(u, \tau_{s,t})$. We will reduce
the first to $O(n \cdot |I| + n^2)$ and the second to $O(n^2)$.

Compact Representation of $\mathcal{M}'$. The graph $\mathcal{M}'$ has $O(n^2)$ nodes and $O(n^2 \cdot |I|)$
edges. The breadth-first search needs one flag per node to indicate if it has
been visited, so we cannot get below $O(n^2)$ space. But we do not have to store
edges explicitly. The forward transitions δ' can be computed on the fly using
δ. The breadth-first search takes transitions backward. To avoid representing
backwards transitions explicitly, we precompute for every $s' \in S$ and $a \in I$,
the set $\delta^{-1}(s', a) \stackrel{\text{def}}{=} \{s \in S : \delta(s, a) = s'\}$ (requiring totally $O(n \cdot |I|)$ space).

By definition, the backward transitions on input a from some state $\{s', t'\} \in S'$ are all $\{s, t\}$ so that $s \in \delta^{-1}(s', a)$ and $t \in \delta^{-1}(t', a)$. For a single state and a single input, these can be found in time $O(r)$, where r is the number of resulting backward transitions. Consequently, the breadth-first search can still be done in $O(n^2 \cdot |I|)$ time even if edges are not represented explicitly.

Leaving out Tables. To reduce the space needed by tables, we will leave out the tables for all but at most every n'th node of the forest, so the distribution of tables in the forest becomes "sparse". At the same time we will guarantee that following the shortest path from any node toward a root, a node with a table will be found after at most n steps. Thus, when the main algorithm computes $\delta(\delta(S, x), y)$ it has to follow the shortest path in the forest for at most n steps per state in $\delta(S, x)$ before it can look up the answer. As a result, the total time over all iterations to update $\delta(S, xy)$ grows to $O(n^3)$, but that is within the time limit.

Which Tables to Leave out. To determine which nodes in the shortest path forest that should have a table, we first take a copy of the forest. Take a leaf of maximal depth, follow the path from this leaf toward the root for n steps and let $\{s, t\}$ be the node we arrive at. Mark $\{s, t\}$ as a node for which the table should be computed, and remove the entire subtree rooted at $\{s, t\}$. Repeat this process as long as possible, i.e., until the resulting forest has depth less than n. Since every removed subtree has depth n, the path from any node to a marked node has length at most n, thus guaranteeing that updating $\delta(u, xy)$ needs at most n steps. Moreover, every removed subtree has at least n nodes, so tables will be stored in at most every n'th node.

Computing Tables When They Are Few. Finally, computing the tables when they are more sparsely occurring is done almost as before, but instead of using the table value from a parent, we find the nearest ancestor that has a table, requiring $O(n)$ time for every element of every table, summing up to $O(n^3)$ because there are $O(n)$ tables with n entries each.

We conclude the proof with a summary of the requirements of the algorithm.

- The graph $\mathcal{M}'$ needs $O(n^2)$ space for nodes and $O(n \cdot |I|)$ for edges.
- There are $O(n)$ tables, each one taking $O(n)$ space, so totally $O(n^2)$.
- The breadth-first search needs $O(n^2 \cdot |I|)$ time.
- Computing the tables needs $O(n^3)$ time.
- In each of the $O(n)$ iterations, computing $\delta(S, xy)$ needs $O(n^2)$ time.
- In each iteration, writing the merging sequence to the output is linear in its length, which is bounded by $O(n^2)$. $\qquad\qquad\square$

Length of Synchronizing Sequences. The merging sequences computed are of minimal length, because breadth-first search computes shortest paths. Unfortunately, this does not guarantee that Algorithm 2 finds a shortest possible synchronizing sequence, since the order in which states to merge are picked may not be optimal. It is possible to pick the states that provide for the shortest merging sequence without increasing the asymptotic running time, but there are machines where this strategy is not the best. In fact, we will see in Section 1.4.1

that finding shortest possible sequences is NP-hard, meaning that it is extremely unlikely that a polynomial time algorithm exists.

Note that each merging sequence has length at most $n(n-1)/2$ because it is a simple path in $\mathcal{M}'$; thus the length of the synchronizing sequence is at most $n(n-1)^2/2$. We now derive a slightly sharper bound.

Theorem 1.17. *If a machine has a synchronizing sequence, then it has one of length at most $n^3/3$.*

Proof. At any iteration of Algorithm 2, among all states in $Q \stackrel{\text{def}}{=} \delta(S, x)$, find two that provide for a shortest merging sequence. We first show that when $|Q| = k$, there is a pair of states in Q with a merging sequence of length at most $n(n-1)/2 - k(k-1)/2 + 1$. Every shortest sequence passes through each node in the shortest path forest at most once: otherwise we could cut away the sub-sequence between the repeated nodes to get a shorter sequence. Also, it cannot visit any node in the forest that has both states in Q, because those two states would then have a shorter merging sequence. There are $n(n-1)/2$ nodes in the shortest path forest (not counting singletons)[4], and $k(k-1)/2$ of them correspond to pairs with both nodes in $\delta(S, x)$. Thus, there is a merging sequence of length at most $n(n-1)/2 - k(k-1)/2 + 1$.

The number $|\delta(S, x)|$ of possible states is n initially, and in the worst case it decreases by only one in each iteration until it reaches 2 just before the last iteration. Thus, summing the length of all merging sequences, starting from the end, we get

$$\sum_{i=2}^{n} \left(\frac{n(n-1)}{2} - \frac{i(i-1)}{2} + 1 \right),$$

which evaluates to $n^3/3 - n^2 + \frac{5}{3}n - 1 < n^3/3$. □

This is not the best known bound: Klyachko, Rystsov, and Spivak [KRS87] improved it to $(n^3 - n)/6$. Similarly to the proof above, they bound the length of each merging sequence, but with a much more sophisticated analysis they achieve the bound $(n-k+2) \cdot (n-k+1)/2$ instead of $n(n-1)/2 - k(k-1)/2 + 1$. The best known lower bound is $(n-1)^2$, and it is an open problem to close the gap between the lower quadratic and upper cubic bounds. Černý [Čer64] conjectured that the upper bound is also $(n-1)^2$.

Exercise 1.18. Consider the problem of finding a synchronizing sequence that ends in a specified final state. When does such a sequence exist? Extend Algorithm 2 to compute such a sequence.

Exercise 1.19. Show how to modify the algorithm of this section, so that it tests whether a machine has a synchronizing sequence without computing it, in time $O(n^2 \cdot |I|)$.

A similar algorithm for the problem in Exercise 1.19 was suggested by Imreh and Steinby [IS95].

---
[4] Recall that $|S' \setminus \{\text{singletons}\}| =$ the number of two-element subsets of $S = \binom{n}{2} = n(n-1)/2$.

1.3.3   Computing Homing Sequences for General Machines

In this section we remove the restriction from Section 1.3.1 that the machine has to be minimized. Note that for general machines, an algorithm to compute homing sequences can be used also to compute synchronizing sequences: just remove all outputs from the machine and ask for a homing sequence. Since there are no outputs, homing and synchronizing sequences are the same thing. It is therefore natural that the algorithm unifies Algorithm 1 of Section 1.3.1 and Algorithm 2 of Section 1.3.2 by computing separating *or* merging sequences in each step.

Recall Lemma 1.8, saying that the quantity $\sum_{B \in \sigma(x)} |B| - |\sigma(x)|$ does not increase as the sequence x is extended. Algorithm 3 repeatedly applies a sequence that strictly decreases this quantity: it takes two states from the same block of the current state uncertainty and applies either a merging or a separating sequence for them. If the sequence is merging, then the sum of sizes of all blocks diminishes. If it is separating, then the block containing the two states is split. Since the quantity is $n-1$ initially and 0 when the algorithm finishes, it finishes in at most $n-1$ steps.

If the algorithm does not find either a merging or a separating sequence on line 5, then the machine has no homing sequence. Indeed, any homing sequence that does not take s and t to the same state must give different outputs for them, so it is either merging or separating. This shows correctness of the algorithm.

Algorithm 3 Computing a homing sequence for a general machine.

```
1       function HOMING(Mealy machine M)
2           x ← ε
3           while there is a block B ∈ σ(x) with |B| > 1
4               find two different states s, t ∈ B
5               let y be a separating or merging sequence for s and t
                    (if none exists, return FAILURE)
6               x ← xy
7           return x
```

Similar to Theorem 1.15, we have the following for homing sequences.

Theorem 1.20 ([Rys83]). *A Mealy machine has a homing sequence if and only if every pair of states either has a merging sequence or a separating sequence.*

Note that, as we saw already in Section 1.3.1, every minimized machine has a homing sequence.

Proof. Assume there is a homing sequence and let $s, t \in S$ be any pair of states. If the homing sequence takes s and t to the same final state, then it is a merging sequence. Otherwise, by the definition of homing sequence, it must be possible to tell the two final states apart by looking at the output. Thus the homing sequence is a separating sequence.

Conversely, if every pair of states has either a merging or a separating sequence, then Algorithm 3 computes a homing sequence.   □

We cannot hope for this algorithm to be any faster than the one to compute synchronizing sequences, because they have to do the same job if there is no separating sequence. But it is easy to see that it can be implemented not to be worse either. By definition, two states have a separating sequence if and only if they are not equivalent (two states are equivalent if they give the same output for all input sequences: see Section 21). Hence, we first minimize the machine to find out which states have separating sequences. As long as possible, the algorithm chooses non-equivalent states on line 4 and only looks for a separating sequence. Thus, the first half of the homing sequence is actually a homing sequence for the minimized machine, and can be computed by applying Algorithm 1 to the minimized machine. The second half of the sequence is computed as described in Section 1.3.2, but only selecting states from the same block of the current state uncertainty.

1.3.4 Computing Adaptive Homing Sequences

Recall that an **adaptive homing sequence** is applied to a machine as it is being computed, and that each input symbol depends on the previous outputs. An adaptive homing sequence is formally defined as a decision tree, where each node is labeled with an input symbol and each edge is labeled with an output symbol. The experiment consists in first applying the input symbol in the root, then following the edge corresponding to the observed output, applying the input symbol in the reached node and so on. When a leaf is reached, the final state can be uniquely determined. The **length** of an adaptive homing sequence is defined as the depth of this tree.

Using adaptive sequences can be an advantage because they are often shorter than preset sequences. However, it has been shown that machines possessing the longest possible preset homing sequences (of length $n(n-1)/2$) require equally long adaptive homing sequences [Hib61].

It is easy to see that a machine has an adaptive homing sequence if and only if it has a preset one. One direction is immediate: any preset homing sequence corresponds to an adaptive one. For the other direction, note that by Theorem 1.20 it is sufficient to show that if a machine has an adaptive homing sequence, then every pair of states has a merging or a separating sequence. Assume toward a contradiction that a machine has an adaptive homing sequence but there are two states $s, t \in S$ that have neither a merging nor a separating sequence. Consider the leaf of the adaptive homing sequence tree that results when the initial state is s. Since s and t have no separating sequence, the same leaf would be reached also if t was the initial state. But since s and t have no merging sequence, there are at least two possible final states, contradicting that there must be only one possible final state in a leaf.

Algorithms 1 and 3 for computing preset homing sequences can both be modified so that they compute adaptive homing sequences. To make the sequence adaptive (and possibly shorter), note that it can always be determined from the output which block of the current state uncertainty that the current state belongs to. Only separating or merging sequences for states in this block need to be considered. Algorithm 4 is similar to Algorithm 3, except we only consider the relevant block of the current state uncertainty (called B in the algorithm). For simplicity, we stretch the notation a bit and describe the algorithm in terms of the intuitive definition of adaptive homing sequence, i.e., it applies the sequence as it is constructed, rather than computes an explicit decision tree.

Algorithm 4 Computing an adaptive homing sequence.

1	**function** ADAPTIVE-HOMING(Mealy machine $\mathcal{M}$)
2	$B \leftarrow S$
3	**while** $|B| > 1$
4	find two different states $s, t \in B$
5	let y be a separating or merging sequence for s and t
	(if none exists, **return** FAILURE)
6	apply y to $\mathcal{M}$ and let z be the observed output sequence
7	$B \leftarrow \{u \in \delta(B, y) : \lambda(B, y) = z\}$

The same arguments as before show correctness and cubic running time. Algorithm 1 for minimized machines can similarly be made adaptive, resulting in the same algorithm except with the words "or merging" on line 5 left out. Although the computed sequences are never longer than the non-adaptive ones computed by Algorithms 1 and 3, we stress once more that they do not have to be the shortest possible.

Algorithm 4 occurred already in the paper by Moore [Moo56], even before the algorithm of Section 1.3.1 for preset sequences.

Adaptive *synchronizing* sequences were suggested by Pomeranz and Reddy [PR94]. They can be computed, e.g., by first applying a homing sequence (possibly adaptive), and then from the final known state find a sequence that takes the machine to one particular final state.

1.3.5 Computing Minimal Homing and Synchronizing Sequences

The algorithms we saw so far do not necessarily compute the shortest possible sequences. It is of practical interest to minimize the length of sequences: the Mealy machine may be a model of some system where each transition is very expensive, such as a remote machine or the object pushing in Example 1.1.2 where making a transition means moving a physical object, which can take several seconds. An extreme example is the subway map in Exercise 1.4, where, for each transition, a human has to buy a ticket and travel several kilometers. Moreover, the sequence may be computed once and then applied a large number of times. We will see in Section 1.4.1 that finding a minimal length sequence is an NP-complete problem, hence unlikely to have a polynomial time algorithm. The algorithms in this section compute minimal length sequences but need exponential time and space in the worst case.

To compute a shortest synchronizing sequence, we define the *synchronizing tree*. This is a tree describing the behavior of the machine for each possible input string, but pruning off branches that are redundant when computing synchronizing sequences:

Definition 1.21. The **synchronizing tree** (for a Mealy machine) is a rooted tree where edges are labeled with input symbols and nodes with sets of states, satisfying the following conditions.

(1) Each non-leaf has exactly $|I|$ children, and the edges leading to them are labeled with different input symbols.
(2) Each node is labeled with $\delta(S, x)$, where x is the sequence of input symbols occurring as edge labels on the path from the root to the node.
(3) A node is a leaf iff:
   (a) either its label is a singleton set,
   (b) or it has the same label as a node of smaller depth in the tree.   □

By (2), the root node is labeled with S. To find the shortest synchronizing sequence, compute the synchronizing tree top-down. When the first leaf satisfying condition (3a) is found, the labels on the path from the root to the leaf form a synchronizing sequence. Since no such leaf was found on a previous level, this is the shortest sequence and the algorithm stops and outputs it. To prove correctness, it is enough to see that without condition (3b) the algorithm would compute every possible string of length 1, then of length 2, and so on until it finds one that is synchronizing. No subtree pruned away by (3b) contains any *shortest* synchronizing sequence, because it is identical to the subtree rooted in the node with the same label, except every node has a bigger depth.

The term "smaller depth" in (3b) is deliberately a bit ambiguous: it is not incorrect to interpret it as "strictly smaller depth". However, an algorithm that generates the tree in a breadth-first manner would clearly benefit from making a node terminal also if it occurs on the same level and has already been generated.

Example. Figure 1.6 depicts a Mealy machine and its synchronizing tree. The root note is labeled with the set of all states. It has two children, one per input symbol. The leftmost child is labeled with $\delta(\{s_1, s_2, s_3\}, a) = \{s_1, s_2\}$ and the rightmost with $\delta(\{s_1, s_2, s_3\}, b) = \{s_1, s_2, s_3\}$. Thus, it is pointless for the sequence to start with a b, and the right child is made a leaf by rule (3b) of the definition. The next node to expand is the one labeled by $\{s_1, s_2\}$. Applying a gives again $\delta(\{s_1, s_2\}, a) = \{s_2, s_2\}$, so we make the left child a leaf. Applying b gives the child $\delta(\{s_1, s_2\}, b) = \{s_1, s_3\}$. Finally, we expand the node labeled $\{s_1, s_3\}$, and arrive at the singleton $\delta(\{s_1, s_3\}, a) = s_3$. It is not necessary to expand any further, as the labels from the root to the singleton leaf form a shortest synchronizing sequence, *aba*.

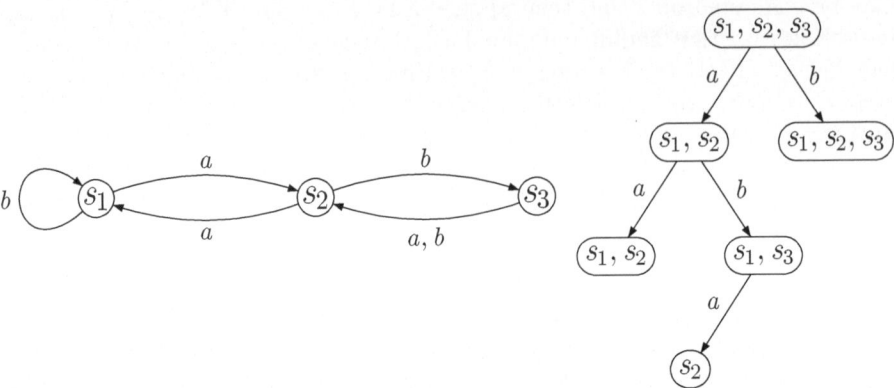

Fig. 1.6. A machine and its corresponding synchronizing tree. Note that the rightmost and leftmost nodes of the tree have been made leaves due to rule (3b) of Definition 1.21. Since the lowest leaf is labeled with a singleton s_2, the path leading to it from the root indicates a shortest synchronizing sequence, aba.

It is possible to replace condition (3b) of Definition 1.21 with a stronger one, allowing to prune the tree more: stipulate that a node becomes a leaf also if its label is a *superset* of some node of smaller depth. This clearly works, because if $P \subseteq Q \subseteq S$ are the node labels, then $\delta(P, x) \subseteq \delta(Q, x)$ for all sequences x. The drawback is that it can be more costly to test this condition.

The homing tree is used analogously to compute shortest *homing* sequences.

Definition 1.22. The **homing tree** (for a Mealy machine) is a rooted tree where edges are labeled with input symbols and nodes with current state uncertainties (i.e., sets of sets of states), satisfying the following conditions.

(1) Each non-leaf has exactly $|I|$ outgoing edges, labeled with different input symbols.
(2) Each node is labeled with $\sigma(x)$, where x is the sequence of input symbols occurring as edge labels on the path from the root to the node.
(3) A node is a leaf iff:
    (a) either each block of its label is a singleton set,
    (b) or it has the same label as a node of smaller depth.   □

Condition (3b) can be strengthened in a similar way for the homing tree as for the synchronizing tree. Here we turn a node into a leaf also if each block of its label is a superset of some block in the label of another node at a smaller depth.

The homing tree method was introduced by Gill [Gil61] and the synchronizing tree method has been described by Hennie [Hen64]. Synchronizing sequences are sometimes used in test generation for circuits without a reset (a reset, here, would be an input symbol that takes every state to one and the same state, i.e., a trivial synchronizing sequence). In this application, the state space is $\{0,1\}^k$ and typically very big. Rho, Somenzi and Pixley [RSP93] suggested a more practical algorithm for this special case based on binary decision diagrams (BDDs).

1.4 Complexity

This section shows two hardness results for related problems. First, Section 1.4.1 shows that it is NP-hard to find a shortest homing or synchronizing sequence. Second, Section 1.4.2 shows that it is PSPACE-complete to determine if there is a homing or synchronizing sequence when the initial state is known to be in a specified subset $Q \subseteq S$ of the states.

1.4.1 Computing Shortest Homing and Synchronizing Sequences Is NP-hard

If a homing or synchronizing sequence is going to be used in practice, it is natural to ask for it to be as short as possible. We saw in Section 1.3.1 that we can always find a homing sequence of length at most $n(n-1)/2$ if one exists and the machine is minimized, and Sections 1.3.2 and 1.3.3 explain how to find synchronizing or homing sequences of length $O(n^3)$, for general machines. The algorithms for computing these sequences run in polynomial time. But the algorithms of Section 1.3.5 that compute minimal-length homing and synchronizing sequences are exponential. In this section, we explain this exponential running time by proving that the problems of finding homing and synchronizing sequences *of minimal length* are significantly harder than those of finding just any sequence: the problems are NP-hard, meaning they are unlikely to have polynomial-time algorithms.

The Reduction Since only decision problems can be NP-complete, formally it does not make sense to talk about NP-completeness of *computing* homing or sequences. Instead, we look at the decision version of the problems: is there a sequence of length at most k?

Theorem 1.23 ([Epp90])**.** *The following problems, taking as input a Mealy machine $\mathcal{M}$ and a positive integer k, are NP-complete:*

(1) *Does $\mathcal{M}$ have a homing sequence of length $\leq k$?*
(2) *Does $\mathcal{M}$ have a synchronizing sequence of length $\leq k$?*

Proof. To show that the problems belong to NP, note that a nondeterministic algorithm easily guesses a sequence of length $\leq k$ (where k is polynomial in the size of the machine) and verifies that it is homing or synchronizing in polynomial time.

   To show that the problems are NP-hard, we reduce from the NP-complete problem 3SAT [GJ79]. Recall that in a boolean formula, a **literal** is either a variable or a negated variable, a **clause** is the "or" of several literals, and a formula is in **conjunctive normal form (CNF)** if it is the "and" of several clauses. In **3SAT** we are given a boolean formula φ over n variables $v_1, \ldots, v_n$ in CNF with exactly three literals per clause, so it is on the form $\varphi = \bigwedge_{i=1}^{m} (l_1^i \vee l_2^i \vee l_3^i)$, where each l_j^i is a literal. The question is whether φ is satisfiable, i.e., whether there is an assignment that sets each variable to either T or F and makes the formula true.

Given any such formula φ with n variables and m clauses, we create a machine with $m(n+1)+1$ states. The machine gives no output (or one and the same output on all transitions, to formally fit the definition of Mealy machines), so synchronizing and homing sequences are the same thing and we can restrict the discussion to synchronizing sequences. There will always be a synchronizing sequence of length $n+1$, but there will be one of length n if and only if the formula is satisfiable. The input alphabet is $\{T, F\}$, and the i'th symbol in the sequence roughly corresponds to assigning T or F to variable i.

The machine has one special state s, and for each clause $(l_1^i \vee l_2^i \vee l_3^i)$ a sequence of $n+1$ states $s_1^i, \ldots, s_{n+1}^i$. Intuitively, s_j^i leads to s_{j+1}^i, except if variable v_j is in the clause and satisfied by the input letter, in which case a shortcut to s is taken. The last state s_{n+1}^i leads to s and s has a self-loop. See Figure 1.7 for an example.

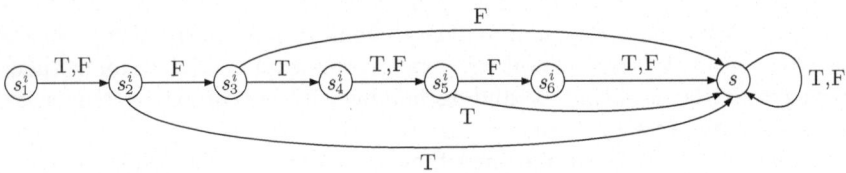

Fig. 1.7. Example of the construction for the clause $(v_2 \vee \neg v_3 \vee v_5)$, where the formula has five variables $v_1, \ldots, v_5$. States s_1^i and s_4^i only have transitions to the next state, because they do not occur in the clause. States s_2^i, and s_5^i have shortcuts to s on input T because v_2 and v_5 occur without negation, and s_3^i has a shortcut to s on input F because it occurs negated. Note that such a chain is constructed for each clause, and they are all different except for the last state s.

Formally, we have the following transitions, for all $1 \le i \le m$:

- The last state goes to s, $s_{n+1}^i \xrightarrow{T,F} s$, and s has a self-loop, $s \xrightarrow{T,F} s$.
- If v_j does not occur in the clause, then $s_j^i \xrightarrow{T,F} s_{j+1}^i$.
- If v_j occurs positively in the clause, i.e., one of l_1^i, l_2^i, or l_3^i is v_j, then $s_j^i \xrightarrow{T} s$ and $s_j^i \xrightarrow{F} s_{j+1}^i$.
- If v_j occurs negatively in the clause, i.e., one of l_1^i, l_2^i, or l_3^i is $\neg v_j$, then $s_j^i \xrightarrow{F} s$ and $s_j^i \xrightarrow{T} s_{j+1}^i$.

To finish the proof, we have to show that the machine thus constructed has a synchronizing sequence of length n if and only if φ is satisfiable. First, assume

φ is satisfiable and let ν be the satisfying assignment, so $\nu(v_i) \in \{T, F\}$. Then the corresponding sequence $\nu(v_1)\nu(v_2) \ldots \nu(v_n) \in I^*$ is synchronizing: starting from any state s_j^i with $j \geq 2$ or from s, we reach s in $\leq n$ steps. Consider state s_1^i and recall that at least one of the literals in the i'th clause is satisfied. Thus, if this literal contains variable v_j, the shortcut from s_j^i to s will be taken, so also from s_1^i will s be reached in $\leq n$ steps.

Conversely, assume there is a synchronizing sequence $b = b_1 b_2 \ldots b_k$ of length $k \leq n$. Hence $\delta(t, b) = s$ for every state t. In particular, starting from s_1^i one of the shortcuts must be taken, say from s_j^i to s. Thus v_j occurs in the i:th clause and setting it to b_j makes the clause true. It follows that the assignment that sets v_j to b_j, for $1 \leq j \leq n$, makes all clauses true. This completes the proof. □

Rivest and Schapire [RS93] mention without proof that it is also possible to reduce from the problem *exact 3-set cover*.

Exercise 1.24. Show that the problem of computing the shortest homing sequence is NP-complete, even if the machine is minimized and the output alphabet has size at most two.

1.4.2 PSPACE-Completeness of a More General Problem

So far we assumed the biggest possible amount of ignorance – the machine can initially be in any state. However, it is sometimes known that the initial state belongs to a particular subset Q of S. If a sequence takes every state in Q to the same final state, call it an Q-*synchronizing sequence*. Similarly, say that an Q-*homing sequence* is one for which the output reveals the final state if the initial state is in Q. In particular, homing and synchronizing are the same as S-homing and S-synchronizing. Even if no homing or synchronizing sequence exists, a machine can have Q-homing or Q-synchronizing sequences (try to construct such a machine, using Theorem 1.15). However, it turns out that even determining if such sequences exist is far more difficult: as we will show soon, this problem is PSPACE-complete. PSPACE-completeness is an ever stronger hardness result than NP-completeness, meaning that the problem is "hardest" among all problems that can be solved using polynomial space. It is widely believed that such problems do not have polynomial time algorithms, not even if nondeterminism is allowed. It is interesting to note that Q-homing and Q-synchronizing sequences are not polynomially bounded: as we will see later in this section, there are machines that have synchronizing sequences but only of exponential length. The following theorem was proved by Rystsov [Rys83]. It is similar to Theorem 3.2 in Section 3.

Theorem 1.25 ([Rys83]). *The following problems, taking as input a Mealy machine $\mathcal{M}$ and a subset $Q \subseteq S$ of its states, are PSPACE-complete:*

(1) *Does $\mathcal{M}$ have an Q-homing sequence?*
(2) *Does $\mathcal{M}$ have an Q-synchronizing sequence?*

Proof. We first prove that the problems belong to NPSPACE, by giving polynomial space nondeterministic algorithms for both problems. It then follows from the general result PSPACE = NPSPACE (in turn a consequence of Savitch's theorem [Sav70, Pap94]) that they belong to PSPACE. The algorithm for synchronizing sequences works as follows. Let $Q_0 = Q$, nondeterministically select one input symbol a_0, apply it to the machine and compute $Q_1 = \delta(Q_0, a_0)$. Iterate this process, in turn guessing a_1 to compute $Q_2 = \delta(Q_1, a_1)$, a_2 to compute $Q_3 = \delta(Q_2, a_2)$, and so on until $|Q_i| = 1$, at which point we verified that $a_0 a_1 \ldots a_{i-1}$ is synchronizing (because $Q_i = \delta(Q, a_0 a_1 \ldots a_i)$). This needs at most polynomial space, because the previously guessed symbols are forgotten, so only the current Q_i needs to be stored. The algorithm for homing sequences is similar, but instead of keeping track of the current $\delta(Q, a_1 a_2 \ldots a_i)$, the algorithm keeps track of the current state uncertainty $\sigma(a_0 a_1 \ldots a_i)$ and terminates when it contains only singletons.

To show PSPACE-hardness, we reduce from the PSPACE-complete problem **Finite Automata Intersection** [Koz77, GJ79]. In this problem, we are given k finite, total, deterministic automata $\mathcal{A}_1, \mathcal{A}_2, \ldots, \mathcal{A}_k$ (all with the same input alphabet) and asked whether there is a string accepted by all $\mathcal{A}_i$, i.e., whether the intersection of their languages is nonempty. Recall that finite automata are like Mealy machines, except they do not produce outputs, they have one distinguished initial state and a set of distinguished final states. We construct a Mealy machine $\mathcal{M}$ with the same input alphabet as the automata, and specify a subset Q of its states, such that a sequence is Q-synchronizing for $\mathcal{M}$ if and only if it is accepted by all $\mathcal{A}_i$. As in Theorem 1.23, $\mathcal{M}$ does not give output, so a sequence is homing if and only if it is synchronizing, and the rest of the discussion will be restricted to synchronizing sequences. To construct $\mathcal{M}$, first take a copy of all $\mathcal{A}_i$. Add one new input symbol z, and two new states, GOOD and BAD. Make z-transitions from each accepting state of the automata to GOOD and from each non-accepting state to BAD, and finally make self-loops on GOOD and BAD: GOOD$\xrightarrow{I \cup \{z\}}$GOOD and BAD$\xrightarrow{I \cup \{z\}}$BAD. See Figure 1.8 for an example.

Let Q be the set of all initial states of the automata, together with GOOD. We will show that all the automata accept a common word x if and only if $\mathcal{M}$ has an Q-synchronizing sequence (and that sequence will be xz). First assume all automata accept x. Then xz is an Q-synchronizing sequence of $\mathcal{M}$: starting from the initial state of any automaton, the sequence x will take us to a final state. If in addition we apply the letter z, we arrive at GOOD. Also, any sequence applied to GOOD arrives at GOOD. Thus $\delta(Q, xz) =$ GOOD so xz is an Q-synchronizing sequence.

Conversely, assume $\mathcal{M}$ has an Q-synchronizing sequence. Since we can only reach GOOD from GOOD, the final state must be GOOD. In order to reach GOOD from any state in $Q \setminus \{$GOOD$\}$, the sequence must contain z. In the situation just before the first z was applied, there was one possible current state in each of the automata. If any of these states was non-accepting, applying z would take us to BAD, and afterward we would be trapped in BAD and never reach GOOD. Thus

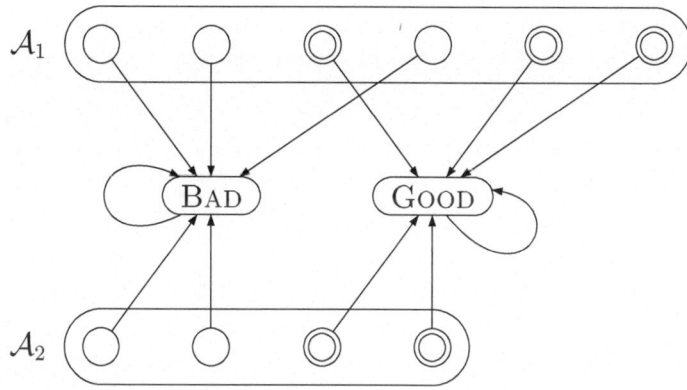

Fig. 1.8. Example of the reduction in Theorem 1.25. We are given two (in general many) automata, $\mathcal{A}_1$ and $\mathcal{A}_2$, and asked if there is a string accepted by all of them. Add a new input symbol z and make z-transitions from accepting and nonaccepting states to the new states GOOD and BAD, respectively, as in the picture. The new states only have self-loops. Let Q be the set of all initial states, together with GOOD; thus a sequence is Q-synchronizing iff it takes every initial state to a final state of the same automaton and then applies z. Thus it corresponds to a word accepted by all automata.

all the automata were in a final state, so the word applied so far is accepted by all automata. This finishes the proof.   □

This result also implies that Q-homing and Q-synchronizing sequences may be exponentially long, another indication that they are fundamentally different from the cubically bounded homing and synchronizing sequences. First, a polynomial upper bound would imply that the sequence can be guessed and checked by an NP-algorithm. So the length is superpolynomial unless PSPACE equals NP. Second, Lee and Yannakakis [LY94] gave a stronger result, providing an explicit family of sets of automata, such that the shortest sequence accepted by all automata in one set is exponentially long. Since, in the reduction above, every Q-synchronizing or Q-homing sequence corresponds to a sequence in the intersection language, it follows that these are also of exponential length.

Theorem 1.26 ([LY94])**.** *The shortest sequence accepted simultaneously by n automata is exponentially long in the total size of all automata, in the worst case (even with a unary input alphabet).*

Proof. Denote by p_i the i'th prime. We will construct n automata, the i'th of which accepts sequences of positive length divisible by p_i. Thus, the shortest word accepted by all automata must be positive, and divisible by $p_1 p_2 \cdots p_n > 2^n$. The input alphabet has only one symbol. The i'th automaton consists of a loop of length p_i, one state of which is accepting. To assure that the empty word is not accepted, the initial state is an extra state outside the loop, that points to the successor of the accepting state: see Figure 1.9. By Gauss' prime number theorem, each automaton has size $O(n \log n)$, so the total size is polynomial in n but the shortest sequence accepted by all automata is exponential. $\square$

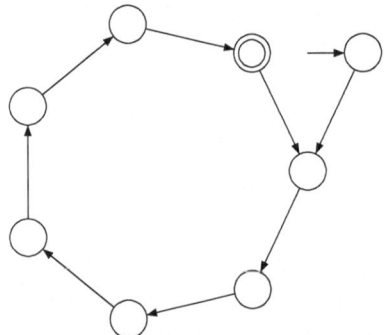

Fig. 1.9. An automaton that accepts exactly the words of positive length divisible by 7. A similar automaton is created for all primes $p_1, \ldots, p_n$.

Consider another generalization of synchronizing sequences, where we are again given a subset $Q \subseteq S$ but now the sequence has to *end* in Q, that is, we want to find a sequence x such that $\delta(S, x) \subseteq Q$. It is not more difficult to show that this problem also is PSPACE-complete; however, it can be solved in time $n^{O(|Q|)}$, so it is polynomial if the size of Q is bounded by a constant [Rys83]. Rystsov shows in the same article that several related problems are PSPACE-complete, and concludes the following result in another paper [Rys92].

Exercise 1.27. A *nondeterministic* Mealy machine is like a Mealy machine except $\delta(s, a)$ is a *set* of states. The transition function δ is extended similarly, so $\delta(Q, a) = \bigcup \{\delta(s, a) : s \in Q\}$ and $\delta(Q, a_1 \ldots a_n) = \delta(\delta(Q, a_1, \ldots, a_{n-1}), a_n)$. Show that the synchronizing sequence problem for nondeterministic Mealy machines is PSPACE-complete. Here, a sequence x is synchronizing for a nondeterministic machine if $|\delta(S, x)| = 1$.

Hint: Use Theorem 1.25

1.5   Related Topics and Bibliography

The experimental approach to automata theory was initiated by the classical article by Moore [Moo56], who introduces several testing problems, including homing sequences and the adaptive version of Algorithm 1. He also shows the upper bound of $n(n-1)/2$ for the length of adaptive homing sequences. The worst-case length of homing sequences for minimized automata was studied by Ginsburg [Gin58] and finally resolved by Hibbard [Hib61]. The book by Kohavi [Koh78] and the article by Gill [Gil61] contain good overviews of the problem.

Length of Synchronizing Sequences and Černý's Conjecture. Synchronizing sequences were introduced a bit later by Černý [Čer64] and studied mostly independently from homing sequences, with some exceptions [Koh78, Rys83, LY96]. The focus has largely been on the worst-case length of sequences, except an article by Rystsov that classifies the complexity of several related problems [Rys83], the article by Eppstein, which introduces the algorithm in Section 1.3.2 [Epp90], and the survey by Lee and Yannakakis [LY96]. Černý [Čer64] showed an upper bound of $2^n - n - 1$ for the length of synchronizing sequences and conjectured that it can be improved to $(n-1)^2$, a conjecture that inspired much of the research in the area. The first polynomial bound was $\frac{1}{2}n^3 - \frac{3}{2}n^2 + n + 1$ due to Starke [Sta66], and as mentioned in Section 1.3.2 the best known bound is $\frac{1}{6}(n^3 - n)$ due to Klyachko, Rystsov and Spivak [KRS87]. Already Černý [Čer64] proved that there are automata that require synchronizing sequences of length at least $(n-1)^2$, so if the conjecture is true then it is optimal.

Proving or disproving Černý's conjecture is still an open problem, but it has been settled for several special cases: Eppstein [Epp90] proved it for *monotonic* automata, which arise in the orientation of parts that we saw in Example 1.1.2; Kari [Kar03] showed it for *Eulerian* machines (i.e., where each state has the same in- and out-degrees); Pin [Pin78b] showed it when n is prime and the machine is *cyclic* (meaning that there is an input letter $a \in I$ such that the a-transitions form a cycle through all states); Černý, Pirická and Rosenauerová [ČPR71] showed it when there are at most 5 states. Other classes of machines were studied by Pin [Pin78a], Imreh and Steinby [IS95], Rystsov [Rys97], Bogdanović et al. [BIĆP99], Trakhtman [Tra02], Göhring [Göh98] and others. See also Trakhtman's [Tra02] and Göhring's [Göh98] articles for more references.

Parallel Algorithms. In a series of articles, Ravikumar and Xiong study the problem of computing homing sequences on parallel computers. Ravikumar gives a deterministic $O(\sqrt{n}\log^2 n)$ time algorithm [Rav96], but it is reported not to be practical due to large communication costs. There is also a randomized algorithm requiring only $O(\log^2 n)$ time but $O(n^7)$ processors [RX96]. Although not practical, this is important as it implies that the problem belongs to the complexity class RNC. The same authors also introduced and implemented a practical randomized parallel algorithm requiring time essentially $O(n^3/k)$, where the number k of processors can be specified [RX97]. It is an open problem whether there are parallel algorithms for the synchronizing sequence problem, but in the special case of monotonic automata, Eppstein [Epp90] gives a randomized parallel algorithm. See also Ravikumar's survey of parallel algorithms for automata problems [Rav98].

Nondeterministic and Probabilistic Automata. The homing and synchronizing sequence problems become much harder for some generalizations of Mealy machines. As shown in Exercise 1.27, they are PSPACE-complete for nondeterministic automata, where $\delta(s, a)$ is a subset of S. This was noted by Rystsov [Rys92] as a consequence of the PSPACE-completeness theorem in another of his papers [Rys83] (our Theorem 1.25). The generalization to nondeterministic automata can be made in several ways; Imreh and Steinby [IS99] study algebraic properties of three different formulations. For probabilistic automata, where $\delta(s, a)$ is a random distribution over S, Kfoury [Kfo70] showed that the problems are algorithmically unsolvable, by a reduction from the problem in a related article by Paterson [Pat70].

Related Problems. As a generalization of synchronizing sequences, many authors study the *rank* of a sequence [Rys92, Kar03, Pin78b]. The rank of a synchronizing sequence is 1, and for a general sequence x it is $|\delta(S, x)|$. Thus, Algorithm 2 decreases the rank by one every time it appends a merging sequence.

A problem related to synchronizing sequences is the *road coloring problem*. Here we are given a machine where the edges have not yet been labeled with input symbols, and asked whether there is a way of labeling so that the machine has a synchronizing sequence. This problem was introduced by Adler [AGW77] and studied in relation to synchronizing sequences, e.g., by Culik, Karhumäki and Kari [CKK02], and by Mateescu and Salomaa [MS99].

The parts orienting problem of Example 1.1.2 was studied in relation to automata by Natarajan [Nat86] and Eppstein [Epp90]. They have a slightly different setup, but the setup of our example was considered by Rao and Goldberg [RG95]. The field has been extensively studied for a long time, and many other approaches have been investigated.

Synchronizing sequences have been used to generate test cases for sequential circuits [RSP93, PJH92, CJSP93]. Here, the states of the machine is the set of all length k bitstrings. This set is too big to be explicitly enumerated, so both the state space and the transition function are specified implicitly. The algorithm of Section 1.3.2 becomes impractical in this setting as it uses too much memory. Instead, several authors considered algorithms that work directly with this symbolic representation of the state space and transition functions [RSP93, PJH92]. Pomeranz and Reddy [PR94] compute both preset and adaptive *homing* sequences for the same purpose, the advantage being that homing sequences exist more often than synchronizing do, and can be shorter since there is more information available to determine the final state.

1.6   Summary

We considered two fundamental and closely related testing problems for Mealy machines. In both cases, we look for a sequence of input symbols to apply to the machine so that the *final* state becomes known. A *synchronizing sequence* takes the machine to one and the same state no matter what the initial state was. A *homing sequence* produces output, so that one can learn the final state by looking at this output. These problems can be completely solved in polynomial time.

Homing sequences always exist if the machine is minimized. They have at most quadratic length and can be computed in cubic time, using the algorithm in Section 1.3.1, which works by concatenating many separating sequences. Synchronizing sequences do not always exist, but the cubic time algorithm of Section 1.3.2 computes one if it exists, or reports that none exists, by concatenating many merging sequences. Synchronizing sequences have at most cubic length, but it is an open problem to determine if this can be improved to quadratic. Combining the methods of these two algorithms, we get the algorithm of Section 1.3.3 for computing homing sequences for general (non-minimized) machines.

It is practically important to compute as short sequences as possible. Unfortunately, the problems of finding the shortest possible homing or synchronizing sequences are NP-complete, so it is unlikely that no polynomial algorithm exists. This was proved in Section 1.4.1, and Section 1.3.5 gave exponential algorithms for both problems. Section 1.4.2 shows that only a small relaxation of the problem statement gives a PSPACE-complete problem.

2 State Identification

Moez Krichen

VERIMAG
moez.krichen@imag.fr

2.1 Introduction

In this chapter, we deal with the problem of state identification of finite-state Mealy machines. Before defining the problem formally, let us illustrate it with a few examples and point out its differences with the similar problem of finding a homing sequence.

Informally, the state identification problem is the following. We are given a (deterministic) Mealy machine for which we know its behavior but not its current state. We want to find an input/output experiment (i.e., an experiment during which we apply inputs on the considered machine and observe the corresponding outputs it produces) such that at the end of the experiment we know which state the machine occupied at the beginning of the experiment. In other words, we know the transition and output functions of the given machine, but we do not know its current state and we want to find the latter by performing the experiment.

Notice the difference with the problem of finding a homing sequence, presented in the previous chapter. There, we want to know the state occupied by the machine *after* the experiment, whereas in state identification we are interested in the state *before* the experiment.

A solution to the state identification problem is also a solution to the homing problem: since the machine is deterministic, if we are able to determine its state before the experiment then we also know its state after the experiment. However, as we shall see later, a solution to the homing problem is not necessarily a solution to the identification problem.

Let us consider a simple example. Consider the machine M_1 shown in Fig. 2.1. According to this figure, M_1 has two states s_1 and s_2. M_1 has two inputs, a and b, and two outputs, 0 and 1. The transition and output functions of the machine are illustrated by directed arrows labeled with corresponding input and output symbols. For instance, applying input b on M_1 when it is at state s_1 will cause the machine to output 1 and move to state s_2.

Now, suppose we do not know which state M_1 is currently occupying. We can determine this by applying input a and observing the response. If the observed output symbol is 0 then we can deduce that the machine was initially at state s_1 otherwise the initial state has been s_2. The input sequence a (consisting of a single symbol, in this case) has allowed us to distinguish between the two states s_1 and s_2 of M_1. It is a distinguishing sequence for this machine.

Of course, the situation is not always as easy, and more complicated experiments may be necessary. Indeed, the state identification problem comes in

M. Broy et al. (Eds.): Model-Based Testing of Reactive Systems, LNCS 3472, pp. 35-67, 2005.
© Springer-Verlag Berlin Heidelberg 2005

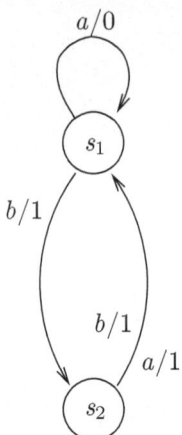

Fig. 2.1. Machine M_1.

many versions, depending on which types of experiments are allowed. A first classification can be made between *simple* experiments and *multiple* experiments [Moo56, Gil61]. In a simple experiment we dispose of a single copy of the machine whereas in a multiple experiment we dispose of multiple *identical* copies of the machine which occupy the same initial (unknown) state. We will only consider simple experiments in this chapter called *distinguishing sequences*.

Another classification can be made between *preset* and *adaptive* distinguishing sequences. A preset distinguishing sequence (PDS) is a sequence of inputs whereas an adaptive distinguishing sequence (ADS) is really a tree where inputs may be different depending on the outputs (thus, the term "sequence" can be considered a misnomer, but it is kept for reasons of tradition). Thus, a PDS models an experiment where the sequence of inputs is determined in advance, independently of the responses of the machine. On the other hand, an ADS models an experiment where at each step the experimenter decides which input to apply next based on the observed output. Clearly, an ADS is a more powerful experiment than a PDS. Indeed, as we will see, there are cases where a machine has an ADS but has no PDS. Thus, it makes sense to make a distinction between the two.

This brings us to another difference between the problem of finding a homing sequence and the state identification problem. We know that for minimal machines a homing sequence always exists. Such a sequence is, by definition, a "preset homing sequence". Indeed, there is no need to consider adaptive sequences since they do not add to the power of the experimenter. On the other hand, a minimal machine may not have a PDS; in fact, it may not have an ADS either. Thus, contrary to the homing problem, there are machines for which the state identification problem cannot be solved, even though these machines are minimal.

As a last difference between the two problems, notice the following. When a machine is not minimal, we are not sure whether it has a homing sequence or not. However, we can be sure that it has no distinguishing sequence: there is no way to distinguish equivalent states because such states produce the same output sequence for any applied input sequence.

Let us illustrate the above differences with a few examples.

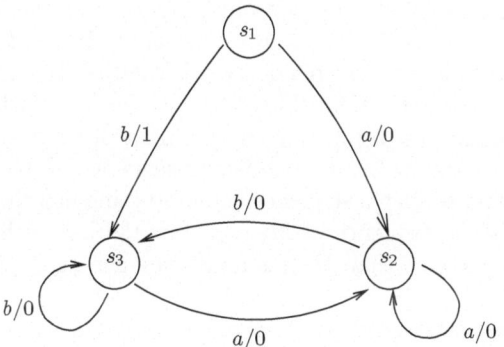

Fig. 2.2. Machine M_2.

Consider, first, machine M_2 shown in Fig. 2.2. This machine is not minimal: its two states s_2 and s_3 are equivalent. As explained above, M_2 cannot have a distinguishing sequence (neither a PDS nor an ADS) because for any input sequence, s_1 and s_2 produce the same output. Thus, the problem of state identification is to be studied only for minimal machines. When a machine is not minimal, we can start by reducing it and then consider the problem of state identification for the obtained reduced machine.

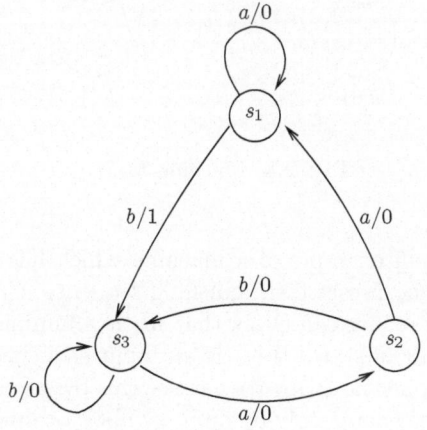

Fig. 2.3. Machine M_3.

Now, even for minimal machines, the existence of a distinguishing sequence (PDS or ADS) is not guaranteed. For instance, consider machine M_3 shown in Fig. 2.3. M_3 is a minimal machine. Indeed, state s_1 can be distinguished from states s_2 and s_3 by input b, and states s_2 and s_3 can be distinguished by input sequence ab. However, machine M_3 has no distinguishing sequence. We can see this by arguing as follows. If we start by applying input symbol a on M_3 and then observe output symbol 0 we can only deduce that the initial state of the machine is either s_1 or s_2. Next, whatever we apply in the future the machine will have the same behavior independently of whether its initial state has been s_1 or s_2. Thus, there is no distinguishing sequence for M_3 which starts with input symbol a, because all these input sequences cannot distinguish the two states s_1 and s_2. In the same manner, a distinguishing sequence of M_3 cannot start with input symbol b because such a sequence cannot distinguish the two states s_2 and s_3. So a distinguishing sequence of M_3 can start neither with input a nor with input b. The conclusion is that M_3 has no distinguishing sequence.

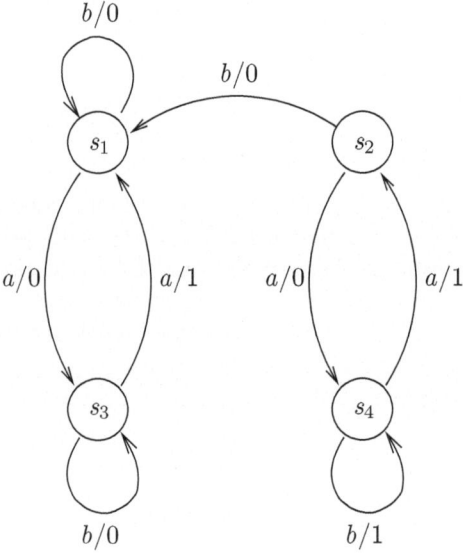

Fig. 2.4. Machine M_4.

Let us finally give an example of a machine which has an adaptive distinguishing sequence but no preset distinguishing sequence. Consider machine M_4 shown in Fig. 2.4. The reader can check that M_4 is a minimal machine, by verifying that for every pair of states there is an input sequence that distinguishes them. The machine M_4 has no PDS. We can see this by arguing as follows. First, it is clear that a sequence made only by input symbol a cannot be a PDS for M_4, since such a sequence cannot distinguish neither between s_1 and s_2 nor between s_3 and s_4. On the other hand, a sequence which contains symbol b cannot be a

PDS either, because it "merges" s_1 and s_2. Indeed, let k be the number of a's applied before the first b. If k is even and the automaton was initially in s_1 or s_2, it will still be in s_1 or s_2 after applying a^k, and no information is gained (notice that, since the sequence is preset, we are not allowed to look at the output at that point). Then, when b is applied, 0 will be output and M_4 will move to s_1. At this point, there is no longer hope of knowing whether the machine was initially in s_1 or s_2. If k is odd and the automaton was initially in s_3 or s_4 then, after applying a^k, we still end up at s_1 or s_2 and the previous argument again applies. Thus, we can conclude that M_4 has no PDS.

However, M_4 has an ADS. One such ADS is shown in Fig. 2.5. It tells us to proceed as follows, when executing the test. Initially, apply a. If the machine outputs 0 then apply b, otherwise, apply a second a, followed by b. The rationale is as follows. If the machine outputs 0 after the initial a, then we can deduce that it was initially at state s_1 or s_2 and it has moved to s_3 or s_4, respectively. We can then distinguish s_3 and s_4 simply by applying b. If, on the other hand, the machine output 1 after the initial a, then we can deduce that it was initially at s_3 or s_4 and has now moved to s_1 or s_2. In this case, we apply sequence ab to distinguish the two latter states.

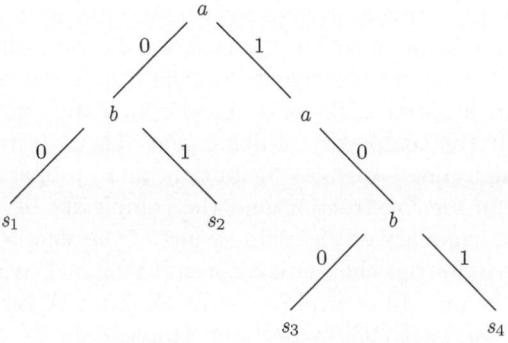

Fig. 2.5. One possible ADS for machine M_4.

History and results There is a lot of literature on the state identification problem and the related homing sequence and state verification problems (Chapters 1 and 3). The earliest work in this field is the seminal 1956 paper by Edward F. Moore [Moo56]. Then in the 60's, many papers on these problems followed this work. These papers were mainly motivated by automata theory and switching circuits. An overview of the major results of these earlier works is in [Koh78] by Zvi Kohavi. Later on, works were also motivated by communication protocol design. Before the work of Lee and Yannakakis [LY94], the proposed algorithms for solving these problems take exponential time and there was no algorithm for computing adaptive distinguishing sequences with polynomial length. The algorithms proposed in these works had exponential time worst-case complexity and the algorithms for computing adaptive distinguishing sequences were not guaranteed to yield sequences of polynomial length. According to [LY94], in [Sok71] Sokolovskii proved a quadratic upper bound for ADSs in a non-constructive way.

The complexity issues were settled by Lee and Yannakakis in [LY94]. There it is shown that solving the preset distinguishing sequence problem is PSPACE-complete. The authors also give examples of machines that have such sequences but only of exponential length. Besides, they present positive results for the adaptive distinguishing sequence problem. They propose deterministic polynomial time algorithms for checking the existence and computing such sequences. The resulting sequences are of length at most polynomial in the size of the machine (i.e., number of states). In this chapter, we report mostly on the results of Lee and Yannakakis.

Chapter Structure: the main goals of this chapter are the following:

- To define preset and adaptive distinguishing sequences.
- To give algorithms for checking existence and constructing such sequences.
- To discuss the complexity of these algorithms.
- To illustrate the algorithms on some simple examples.

The remaining part of this chapter is structured as follows. Section 2.2 recalls the definition of Mealy machine and notation. Section 2.3 deals with preset distinguishing sequences: the mathematical definition of a preset distinguishing sequence, its main properties, the way for checking the existence of such sequences and finally the complexity of doing that. Then, Section 2.4 is devoted to adaptive distinguishing sequences: definition, main properties, algorithm for existence, algorithm for construction and the complexity of each. And finally, Section 2.5 gives a summary of the main results of this chapter.

The main sources for this chapter have been [LY94] by David Lee and Mihalis Yannakakis and Chapter 13 of [Koh78] by Zvi Kohavi. A very valuable source has also been the survey [LY96] by Lee and Yannakakis.

2.2   Brief Recall on Mealy Machines and Used Notation

A Mealy machine M is a quintuple

$$M = (I, O, S, \delta, \lambda)$$

where:

- I, O and S are finite and non-empty sets of input symbols, output symbols and states, respectively;
- $\delta : S \times I \to S$ is the state transition function; $\lambda : S \times I \to O$ is the output function.

The fact that both δ and λ are total functions from $S \times I$ to S and O, respectively, follows from the fact that we only consider deterministic and completely specified

FSMs (finite-state machines). These are machines, the response of which for any initial state and for any applied input is known and unique.

An input sequence of the machine M is a finite sequence of input symbols. Similarly, an output sequence is a finite sequence of output symbols. An input or output sequence may be empty. The (input or output) empty sequence is denoted by ϵ.

We introduce the following extensions of the transition and output functions of a Mealy machine $M = (I, O, S, \delta, \lambda)$. First, we extend the functions λ and δ from input symbols to input sequences. For an initial state s_0 and an input sequence $x = a_1 a_2 \cdots a_l$, we have:

$$\lambda(s_0, x) = b_1 b_2 \cdots b_l \text{ and } \delta(s_0, x) = s_l;$$

where:

$$b_i = \lambda(s_{i-1}, a_i) \text{ and } \delta(s_{i-1}, a_i) = s_i \text{ for } i = 1, \cdots, l.$$

The transition function is also extended from single states to sets of blocks of states. By definition, a **block** of states is a nonempty subset of states. For the block of states B we have:

$$\delta(B, x) = \{\delta(s, x) \mid s \in B\}.$$

Furthermore, we introduce the following notations. For some given input sequence x, $\delta(\cdot, x)$ denotes the mapping defined from S to S such that:

$$\forall s \in S : \delta(\cdot, x)(s) = \delta(s, x).$$

Similarly, $\lambda(\cdot, x)$ denotes the mapping from S to O^* such that:

$$\forall s \in S : \lambda(\cdot, x)(s) = \lambda(s, x).$$

For some input or output sequence x, $|x|$ denotes the length of the considered sequence. In the same manner, $|B|$ denotes the cardinality of B a given subset of S.

More details on Mealy machines are given in Appendix 21.

2.3   Preset Distinguishing Sequences

Here, we deal with **preset distinguishing sequences** (PDS). We first give the mathematical definition of a PDS. Then, we list the main properties it matches. Finally, we deduce the way for checking the existence and constructing a PDS.

2.3.1   What Is a PDS?

Here is the formal definition of a PDS.

Definition 2.1. An input sequence x is a PDS for a Mealy machine $M = (I, O, S, \delta, \lambda)$ if:

$$\forall\, s, s' \in S : s \neq s' \Rightarrow \lambda(s, x) \neq \lambda(s', x).$$

i.e., for any two distinct initial states in S, M produces distinct output sequences after executing x.   □

So, in practice, if we want to check if x is a PDS of M then we need to compute the list of responses (output sequences) M may produce on x for all its possible initial states. If an output sequence is observed more than once (the same output sequence for distinct initial states) then x is not an PDS of M. Equivalently, we deduce that x is a PDS of M if and only if all the responses are distinct from each other.

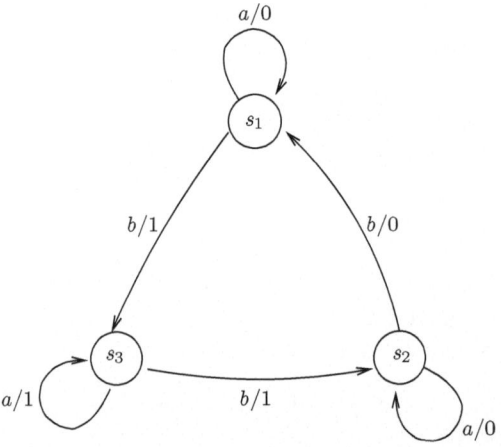

Fig. 2.6. Machine M_5.

Example. Table 2.1 gives the responses of the machine M_5 (Fig. 2.6) on ab. The obtained responses ($\{01, 00, 11\}$) are distinct from each other, so ab is a PDS of M_5.

s	$\lambda(s, ab)$
s_1	01
s_2	00
s_3	11

Table 2.1. Possible responses of machine M_5 for the input sequence ab.

Remark 2.2 (A PDS is a homing sequence). Since we are dealing with deterministic machines, when the initial state of the machine is known, it is easy to determine its final state (i.e., the state after the experiment): if the initial state is s and the PDS is x then final state will be $\delta(s, x)$. Thus, every PDS is also a homing sequence.

What about the converse? Is any homing sequence a PDS? That is not generally true, since (in the general case) the backward exploration of Mealy machines is not deterministic. In Section 2.1, we explain why M_2 (Fig. 2.6) has no distinguishing sequence. However, it has a homing sequence (a for example).

2.3.2   Properties of a PDS

In this subsection, we introduce some definitions and main properties of preset distinguishing sequences. First, we give the definition of the initial and current uncertainties.

Definition 2.3. For some given machine $M = (I, O, S, \delta, \lambda)$ and x an input sequence of it, the initial and current uncertainties of M with respect to x are defined as follows:

(1) **Initial uncertainty**: $\pi(x)$ is the partition $\{C_1, C_2, \cdots, C_r\}$ of S such that s and $s' \in S$ are in the same block C_i if and only if $\lambda(s, x) = \lambda(s', x)$.
(2) **Current uncertainty**: $\sigma(x) = \{\delta(C, x) \mid C \in \pi(x)\}$.

□

According to the definition above, the initial uncertainty $\pi(x)$ is the partition of the set of states S induced by the function $\lambda(\cdot, x)$. This means that $\pi(x)$ groups states which produce the same output sequence on input x.

In terms of distinguishing sequences, this means that two distinct states s and s' in the same block of states C in $\pi(x)$ cannot be distinguished by x. Thus, by applying x and observing the corresponding output sequence we can identify only the block of $\pi(x)$ to which the initial state of the machine belongs and not the initial state itself. So, we say that our uncertainty about the initial state of the machine has been reduced to a block of states. However, if this block is a singleton then our uncertainty is totally reduced.

For example, for machine M_5 (Fig. 2.6) and for the input sequence a we have

$$\pi(a) = \{\{s_1, s_2\}_0, \{s_3\}_1\}.$$

This means that if, on input a, M_5 outputs 0 then our uncertainty about its initial state is reduced to $\{s_1, s_2\}$. Otherwise, if it outputs 1 then its initial state is completely identified and it is s_3.

Note that the subscripts 0 and 1 in $\{s_1, s_2\}_0$ and $\{s_3\}_1$ are used to indicate the corresponding output sequence of each block. However, this piece of information is not actually included in $\pi(x)$.

From the preceding, it is easy to see why the following proposition holds.

Proposition 2.4. *For a given input sequence x of a machine $M = (I, O, S, \delta, \lambda)$:*

x is a PDS of M if and only if $\pi(x)$ is the discrete partition of S.

In this proposition, the **discrete partition** of S means the partition in which all blocks are singletons. The proof of the proposition follows immediately from the definitions of a PDS and the initial uncertainty of x.

Now let us explain a bit about the current uncertainty. First, it provides us with the possible final states of the machine at the end of the distinguishing experiment. For example for machine M_5 (Fig. 2.6), we have:

$$\sigma(ab) = \{\{s_3\}_{01}, \{s_1\}_{00}, \{s_2\}_{11}\}$$

But, that is not very important since, here, our goal is to identify the initial state of the machine and not its final state.

However, our knowledge about the current uncertainty of the intermediary steps of the experiment may help in computing a PDS. Let us consider machine M_5 again for better explaining this. After executing the input symbol a, we have:

$$\sigma(a) = \{\{s_1, s_2\}_0, \{s_3\}_1\}$$

That tells us that if on a M_5 outputs 0 then we deduce that the machine is currently occupying either s_1 or s_2. Similarly, if it outputs 1 we deduce that M_5 is currently occupying s_3. Thus, computing a PDS for M_5 becomes a bit easier. All what remains to do is to find a sequence (b for example) which distinguishes s_1 and s_2. If such a sequence is found then a possible PDS of the machine will be the input sequence obtained by appending this sequence to a.

From the preceding, we deduce that computing a PDS for a given machine can be done recursively by consecutive refinements of the current uncertainty: at each step, we choose an input symbol which refines at least one block of the current uncertainty. We keep on doing that till reaching an uncertainty made only by singletons. In that case, a PDS for the machine is the one obtained by appending the consecutive used input symbols.

Now, the difficulty is with how to choose the suitable input symbol at each step. The idea is that there are some "bad" inputs that must not be used. Let us consider machine M_3 (Fig. 2.3) for explaining this. M_3 is a minimal machine, however, it has no PDS. The problem is that both a and b cause irrevocable loss of information about its initial state. For example, s_1 and s_2 are merged when applying input symbol a. This means that independently on whether the initial state is s_1 or s_2, on input a M_3 outputs 0 and moves to the same final state s_1. Consequently, whatever we will apply next, we will be unable to determine whether M_3 was initially at s_1 or s_2. The input a is said to be **invalid** for the block $\{s_1, s_2\}$. The following gives the mathematical definition of valid inputs.

Definition 2.5. For a given Mealy machine $M = (I, O, S, \delta, \lambda)$:

- An input $a \in I$ is a **valid input** for a set of states $C \subseteq S$ if:

$$\forall s, s' \in C : s \neq s' \Rightarrow \lambda(s, a) \neq \lambda(s', a) \text{ or } \delta(s, a) \neq \delta(s', a).$$

  i.e., on input a, the states s and s' either produce distinct output symbols or move to distinct states.

- An input sequence x is a **valid input sequence** for C if:

$$\forall s, s' \in C: s \neq s' \Rightarrow \lambda(s, x) \neq \lambda(s', x) \text{ or } \delta(s, x) \neq \delta(s', x).$$

- a (resp., x) is a valid input (resp., valid input sequence) for a collection of sets of states τ if a (resp., x) is valid for each member of τ.

□

Let us illustrate this notion of validity on machine M_5 (Fig. 2.6). It has been already shown that ab is a PDS of this machine. When executing this input sequence on M_5, the current uncertainty evolves as follows

$$\{\{s_1, s_2, s_3\}\} \xrightarrow{a} \{\{s_1, s_2\}_0, \{s_3\}_1\} \xrightarrow{b} \{\{s_3\}_{01}, \{s_1\}_{00}, \{s_2\}_{11}\}.$$

First, it is easy to check that both a and ab are valid for $\{s_1, s_2, s_3\}$ and that b is valid for $\{s_1, s_2\}$. More precisely, b is valid for $\{\{s_1, s_2\}, \{s_3\}\}$, but since $\{s_3\}$ is singleton then that it is equivalent to say that it is valid for $\{s_1, s_2\}$.

The second thing to notice is that the total number of states contained in each of the three uncertainties of the example above equals 3 the number of states of the machine. In particular, the last uncertainty is made of as many singletons as the number of states of the machine.

Proposition 2.6, below, argues that these observations remain true in the general case. The proposition uses the following notation:

- $Super(M)$ is the set of multisets of non-empty blocks of states such that $W = \{B_1, B_2, \cdots, B_l\}$ is in $Super(M)$ if and only if $\sum_{B_i \in W} |B_i| = |S|$.
- $Singleton(M)$ is the subset of $Super(M)$ the members of which are sets of singletons.
- For a given multiset of blocks τ and a given input symbol a, $\mu(\tau, a)$ is obtained by partitioning each member C of τ w.r.t $\lambda(\cdot, a)$, then applying $\delta(\cdot, a)$ on each block of the obtained partition.

For instance, if $S = \{s_1, s_2\}$ then:

$$Super(M) = [\{\{s_1\}, \{s_2\}\}; \ \{\{s_1\}, \{s_1\}\}; \ \{\{s_2\}, \{s_2\}\}; \ \{\{s_1, s_2\}\}].$$

and

$$Singleton(M) = [\{\{s_1\}, \{s_2\}\}; \ \{\{s_1\}, \{s_1\}\}; \ \{\{s_2\}, \{s_2\}\}] \ ^1 \ .$$

Moreover, for machine M_5 we have:

$$\mu(\{\{s_1, s_2, s_3\}\}, a) = \{\{s_1, s_2\}_0, \{s_3\}_1\}$$

and

$$\mu(\{\{s_1, s_2\}_0, \{s_3\}_1\}, b) = \{\{s_3\}_{01}, \{s_1\}_{00}, \{s_2\}_{11}\}.$$

---

[1] Here, we use the notation $[C_1; \ C_2]$ instead of the classical notation $\{C_1, C_2\}$ for making things more readable.

Proposition 2.6. *If x is a PDS of $M = (I, O, S, \delta, \lambda)$ then*

(1) *Each prefix x' of x is a valid input sequence for S.*
(2) *For each prefix $x''a$ of x, a is a valid input symbol for $\sigma(x'')$ and $\sigma(x''a) = \mu(\sigma(x''), a)$.*
(3) *For each prefix x' of x, $\sigma(x') \in Super(M)$.*
(4) $\sigma(x) \in Singleton(M)$.

We give only indications for making the proof of the proposition.

Proof. (1) We make it by contradiction: we assume that x' is invalid for S and we deduce that x cannot be a PDS of M.
(2) For proving validity, we proceed just as previously. The second point follows directly from the definitions of function μ and of the current uncertainties.
(3) Can easily be proved by induction.
(4) Follows from Proposition 2.4.   □

2.3.3   Checking the Existence of a PDS

The classical approach ([Koh78]) for checking the existence of a PDS for a given machine is based on the construction of the so-called **successor tree**. The latter is an infinite tree, the root of which is labeled with the set of states of the considered machine. Each node of the successor tree has exactly as many outgoing edges as the number of inputs of the machine. An internal node is labeled with the current uncertainty corresponding to the input sequence spelt by the path from the node of the tree to the considered node.

Fig. 2.7 shows (a portion of) the successor tree of machine M_5 (Fig. 2.6). Clearly, according to this successor tree, both ab, ba and bb are PDSs of M_5 (since the corresponding current uncertainties are made only by singletons).

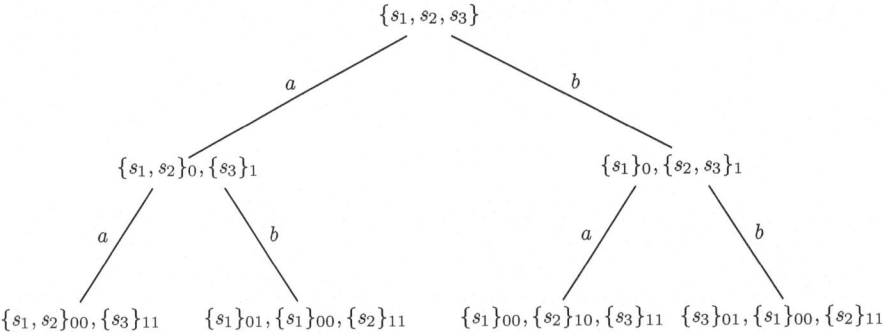

Fig. 2.7. A portion of the successor tree of machine M_5 (Fig. 2.6).

Here, we use a similar structure which is the super graph of a Mealy machine and which is inspired from [LY94].

Definition 2.7. The **super graph** of a Mealy machine M is a directed graph S which is denoted $Super\text{-}G(M)$:

- The set of vertices of $Super\text{-}G(M)$ is $Super(M)$,
- The initial vertex of $Super\text{-}G(M)$ is $V_0 = \{S\}$,
- The edges of $Super\text{-}G(M)$ are labeled by the input symbols of M,
- For an input symbol a and $V, V' \in Super(M) : V \xrightarrow{a} V'$ if and only if a is valid for V and $V' = \mu(V, a)$.

□

A portion of the super graph of machine M_6 (Fig. 2.8) is shown in Fig. 2.11. The main differences between the successor tree and the super graph are the following. First contrary to the successor tree, the super graph is a finite structure. Besides for a given node, the super graph considers only valid inputs for the label of the considered node while the successor tree considers all inputs.

The super graph informs about the existence of a PDS as follows.

Theorem 2.8. *Let x be an input sequence of a Mealy Machine M. One sequence x is a PDS of M if and only if x traces a path in $Super\text{-}G(M)$ from $V_0 = \{S\}$ (the initial vertex of $Super\text{-}G(M)$) to V' in $Singleton(M)$.*

The sequence x traces a path in $Super\text{-}G(M)$ means that if we have $x = a_{i_1} a_{i_2} \cdots a_{i_l}$ then there exist vertices $V_{i_0}, V_{i_1}, \cdots, V_{i_l}$ of $Super\text{-}G(M)$ such that $V_{i_0} \xrightarrow{a_{i_1}} V_{i_1} \xrightarrow{a_{i_2}} \cdots \xrightarrow{a_{i_{l-1}}} V_{i_{l-1}} \xrightarrow{a_{i_l}} V_{i_l}$ is an accepted path by $Super\text{-}G(M)$.

Proof. It is not difficult to see that both directions of the theorem follow immediately from Propositions 2.4 and 2.6. □

Obviously for checking whether a machine has a PDS or not, we do not need to compute its whole super graph. An on-the-fly exploration of the later suffices to inform about the existence or the non-existence of a PDS for the considered machine. The way for doing this is given by Algorithm 5. As just mentioned it consists of a reachability analysis on the super graph of the considered machine.

More precisely, the algorithm maintains a set E of pairs of the form $\sigma = (\{B_1, B_2, \cdots, B_l\}, x)$, where $\{B_1, B_2, \cdots, B_l\}$ is the current uncertainty corresponding to the input sequence x. For some pair $\sigma = (\{B_1, B_2, \cdots, B_l\}, x) \in E$, σunc and σseq denote $\{B_1, B_2, \cdots, B_l\}$ and x, respectively. Furthermore for some input sequence x and input symbol a, $concat(x, a)$ denotes the input sequence xa obtained by appending a to x. At each iteration, Algorithm 5 computes the successors of the elements of E with respect to valid inputs. If one of the computed successors is in $Singleton(M)$ then a PDS for the machine M is found. Otherwise, we shall wait until no new element may be added to E (i.e., when $E' = E$) for announcing that the machine has no PDS.

Remark 2.9 *(How to compute the shortest PDSs?).* It is possible to compute a shortest PDS for the considered machine by a breadth-first search throughout its super graph.

Algorithm 5 Checking the existence of a PDS

- Initialization:

  (1) $\sigma_0 := (\{S\}, \epsilon)$ (S the set of states and ϵ the empty sequence)
  (2) $E := \{\sigma_0\}$
  (3) Mark σ_0 as non-treated

- Iterations: **repeat until** $E = E'$

  (1) $E' := E$
  (2) $\forall \sigma \in E$ marked as non-treated, $\forall a$ valid input for $\sigma \cdot unc$
    − mark σ as treated
    − $\sigma' := (\mu(\sigma \cdot unc, a), concat(\sigma \cdot seq, a))$
    − **if** $\sigma' \cdot unc \in Singleton(M)$ **then** declare "$\sigma' \cdot seq$ is a PDS" and STOP
    − **otherwise, if** $\forall \sigma'' \in E' : \sigma' \cdot unc \neq \sigma'' \cdot unc$ **then** $E' := E' \cup \{\sigma'\}$
                              (and mark σ' as non-treated)
  (3) **if** $E' \neq E$ then $E := E'$, **otherwise** declare "no PDS" and STOP

2.3.4   Complexity

Here, we give an estimation of how difficult checking the existence of a PDS for some given machine is.

Theorem 2.10. *([LY94]) Testing whether a given Mealy machine has a PDS is PSPACE-complete.*

Proof. First, we show that this problem belongs to PSPACE. By Theorem 2.8, we know that the problem of checking whether a machine M has a PDS can be reduced to a reachability problem in the super graph $Super\text{-}G(M)$ of this machine. Moreover, it is clear that every vertex is polynomially bounded in size. Thus, it can be tested whether V_0 (the initial vertex of $Super\text{-}G(M)$) can reach some vertex of $Singleton(M)$ using a nondeterministic polynomial space machine by guessing the path from V_0 to $Singleton(M)$ vertex by vertex. Thus the problem is in NPSPACE, and therefore, also in PSPACE (since PSPACE = NPSPACE).

In [LY94] for proving the PSPACE-hardness of the problem, Lee and Yannakakis reduce from the following problem (**Finite Automata Intersection**): given m deterministic finite automata (language acceptors) over the same input alphabet Σ, determine whether they accept a common word. This problem is known to be PSPACE-complete [Koz77]. □

In [LY94], Lee and Yannakakis show that the result given by theorem above remains true for Mealy machines with binary input and output alphabets. Moreover, about bounds on the length of the shortest PDS of a machine, the two authors give the following result.

Theorem 2.11. *([LY94]) There are machines for which the shortest PDS has exponential length.*

Proof. It suffices to apply the reduction used in the proof of Theorem 2.10 on the following n automata on the unary input alphabet $\Sigma = \{0\}$. The transitions of the ith automaton form a cycle of length p_i, the ith prime, and the only accepting state is the predecessor of the initial state. Then the shortest word accepted by all the automata has length $(\Pi_{i=1}^{n} p_i) - 1$. Thus the length of this common word is exponential in the size of the considered automata.   □

2.4   Adaptive Distinguishing Sequences

In this section, we deal with the second kind of distinguishing sequences: the **adaptive distinguishing sequences**. The acronym **ADS** is used as a shorthand for adaptive distinguishing sequence. As with PDS, we first give the mathematical definition of an ADS. Then, we list the main properties of ADS. We deduce the way for checking the existence (and computing) an ADS. Finally, we estimate the complexity of doing that.

Next, we refer more than once to machine M_6 shown in Fig. 2.8. It is taken from [LY94].

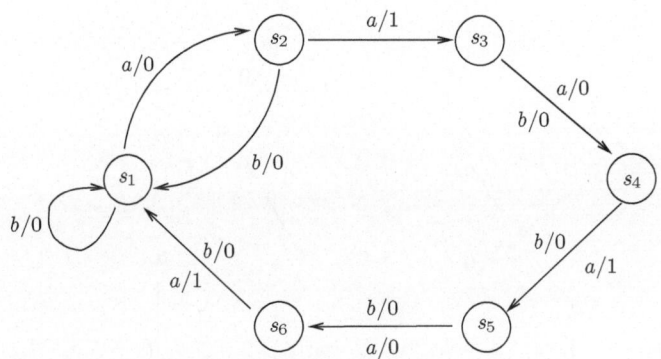

Fig. 2.8. Machine M_6 ([LY94]).

2.4.1   What Is an ADS?

Formally, the definition of an ADS is given by the following.

Definition 2.12. An ADS of a Mealy machine $M = (I, O, S, \delta, \lambda)$ is a rooted tree T such that:

(1) The number of leaves of T equals the cardinality of S,
(2) The leaves of T are labeled with states of M,
(3) The internal nodes of T are labeled with input symbols (from I),
(4) The edges of T are labeled with output symbols (from O),

(5) Edges emanating from a common node are labeled with distinct output symbols,

(6) For each leaf u of T, if s_u is the label of u, x_u and y_u are respectively the input and output sequences formed by the concatenation of the node and edge labels on the path from the root to the leaf u, then $\lambda(s_u, x_u) = y_u$.

The *length* of an ADS is the depth of its corresponding tree T.   □

The execution of an ADS given as mentioned in the definition above is done as follows: first, we execute the input symbol label of the root of the tree. Then, we observe the response of the machine. Among the outgoing edges of the current node of the tree we choose the one labeled by the observed output. Then, we execute the label of the node to which this edge leads. We keep on repeating this until we meet a node (leaf) labeled by a state of the machine. In that case, we terminate the experiment by declaring that the initial state of the machine was the label of that node.

Let us consider an example of an ADS for better understanding this.

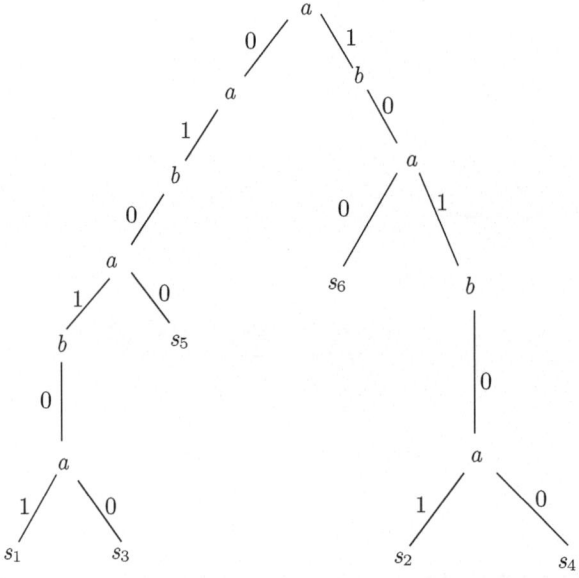

Fig. 2.9. An ADS for machine M_6 ([LY94]).

Example. Consider machine M_6 shown in Fig. 2.8. A possible ADS for this machine is given in Fig. 2.9. Suppose that the initial state of M_6 is s_6. Then, the execution of this ADS will be as follows. We first apply a which is the label of the root of the ADS. The machine returns 1 and moves to s_1. Since 1 is observed, the tester follows the right branch and applies b. The machine returns 0 and remains at s_1. Notice that here the ADS has only one branch, that is, we know that no matter what the initial state was, after the input sequence ab the second output will certainly be 0. The next input given by the tester is a, which causes the machine to move to state s_2 and to output 0. Observing the latter, the tester moves to the leaf node labeled by s_6, which indicates that the initial state was s_6 and we are done.

It can be said that s_6 corresponds to the branch (i.e., path from the root to a leaf of the tree) of the ADS labeled by the input sequence aba and the output sequence 101. Then in the same manner, each other state of the machine corresponds to a different branch of the ADS. The input and output sequences corresponding to the other states of the machine are given in Table. 2.2.

Input sequence	Output sequence	Initial state
$aababa$	010101	s_1
$aababa$	010100	s_3
$aaba$	0100	s_5
aba	100	s_6
$ababa$	10101	s_2
$ababa$	10100	s_4

Table 2.2. The different branches of the ADS shown in Fig. 2.9.

The length of this ADS is 6 which is the length of the input sequence $aababa$.

Remark 2.13 *(From a PDS to an ADS)*. It is easy to see that when a machine has a PDS, then this PDS can be considered as an ADS of this machine too. For example from the PDS ab of machine M_5 (Fig. 2.6), we can deduce the ADS shown by Fig. 2.10. The PDS and the obtained ADS have the same length. Moreover, the internal nodes at the same depth are labeled with the same input symbol.

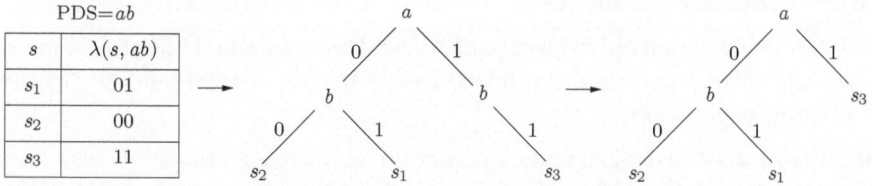

Fig. 2.10. From a PDS to an ADS.

Now about the converse. When a machine has an ADS, we cannot deduce whether it has a PDS or not. For instance, machine M_6 (Fig. 2.8) has an ADS (the one shown in Fig. 2.9). However, by computing *Super-G(M_6)* the super graph of this machine, we deduce that it has no PDS. The super graph *Super-G(M_6)* is shown in Fig. 2.11. The only reachable vertices from the initial node $V_0 = \{\{s_1, s_2, s_3, s_4, s_5, s_6\}\}$ in *Super-G(M_6)* are V_0 itself and $V_1 = \mu(V_0, a) = \{\{s_1, s_3, s_5\}, \{s_2, s_4, s_6\}\}$. Input b is invalid for both V_0 and V_1 since it merges s_2 and s_6. In addition, there is no other reachable vertex since a makes a loop on V_1. That is because we have

$$\{s_1, s_3, s_5\} \xrightarrow{a/0} \{s_2, s_4, s_6\} \text{ and } \{s_2, s_4, s_6\} \xrightarrow{a/1} \{s_1, s_3, s_5\}.$$

Consequently from V_0, there is no reachable vertex in *Singleton(M_6)*. Thus, although M_6 admits an ADS it has no PDS.

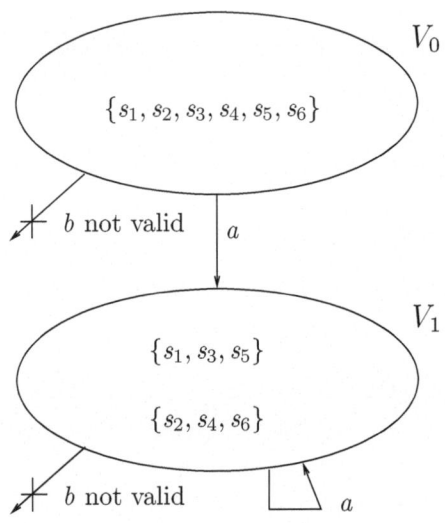

Fig. 2.11. *Super-G(M_6)*.

2.4.2 Properties of an ADS

Here, we study the main properties of ADSs. First, we adapt the definitions of initial and current uncertainties (introduced in the previous section) for the case of adaptive experiments [2].

Definition 2.14. For each node u of a given adaptive experiment T associated with a Mealy machine $M = (I, O, S, \delta, \lambda)$, we associate two sets of states $I(u)$ **the initial set** and $C(u)$ **the current set** which are defined as follows:

- $I(u) = \{s \in S \mid y_u = \lambda(s, x_u)\}$,
- $C(u) = \{\delta(s, x_u) \mid s \in I(u)\} = \delta(I(u), x_u)$,

---

[2] An adaptive experiment is a decision tree which is not necessarily a complete ADS (The mathematical definition is given in Appendix 21).

where x_u and y_u are respectively the input and output sequences formed by the concatenation of the node and edge labels on the path from the root to the node u (excluding u itself).   □

According to the definition, for some node u of an adaptive experiment, the initial set $I(u)$ informs about the set that may contain the initial state of the machine and the current set $C(u)$ about the set containing the state the machine is currently occupying after applying x_u and observing y_u. Thus, the initial state of the machine is identified if and only if $I(u)$ is a singleton. Otherwise, the goal of the subsequent steps shall be the reduction of this uncertainty about the initial state.

It is not difficult to see that the current sets of the leaves of an adaptive experiment form a partition of the set of states. For some adaptive experiment T, let $\pi(T)$ denotes this partition. It is easy to see that the following proposition holds.

Proposition 2.15. *For a given adaptive experiment T of a machine $M = (I, O, S, \delta, \lambda)$: T is an ADS of M if and only if $\pi(T)$ is the discrete partition of S.*

Proposition 2.16. *Let T be an ADS of a Mealy machine M and u an internal node of T*

(1) *The input symbol label of u is valid for $C(u)$,*
(2) *$|I(u)| = |C(u)|$,*
(3) *The initial sets of the nodes children of u form a partition of $I(u)$ the initial set of u,*
(4) *$I(u)$ contains exactly the labels of the leaves of the subtree of T starting from node u.*

Proof. Similar to the proof of Proposition 2.6   □

From this proposition, we can deduce that there exist machines which have no ADS. In fact, if there exists no valid input symbol for the set of states then the considered machine has no ADS. For example, consider machine M_3 (Fig. 2.3), it has no ADS since both a and b are invalid inputs for its set of states.

Example. The Initial and Current sets of the proposed ADS of machine M_6 are shown in Fig. 2.12. For each node of this ADS the initial and current sets are put within a box. The corresponding initial set is I and the corresponding current set is C. For internal nodes, we also indicate the input symbol label of the corresponding node. Clearly, Propositions 2.15 and 2.16 hold for this example.

2.4.3   Checking the Existence of an ADS

In Section 2.3, we have seen that checking the existence of a PDS can be reduced to finding each time a valid input sequence which refines the current uncertainty

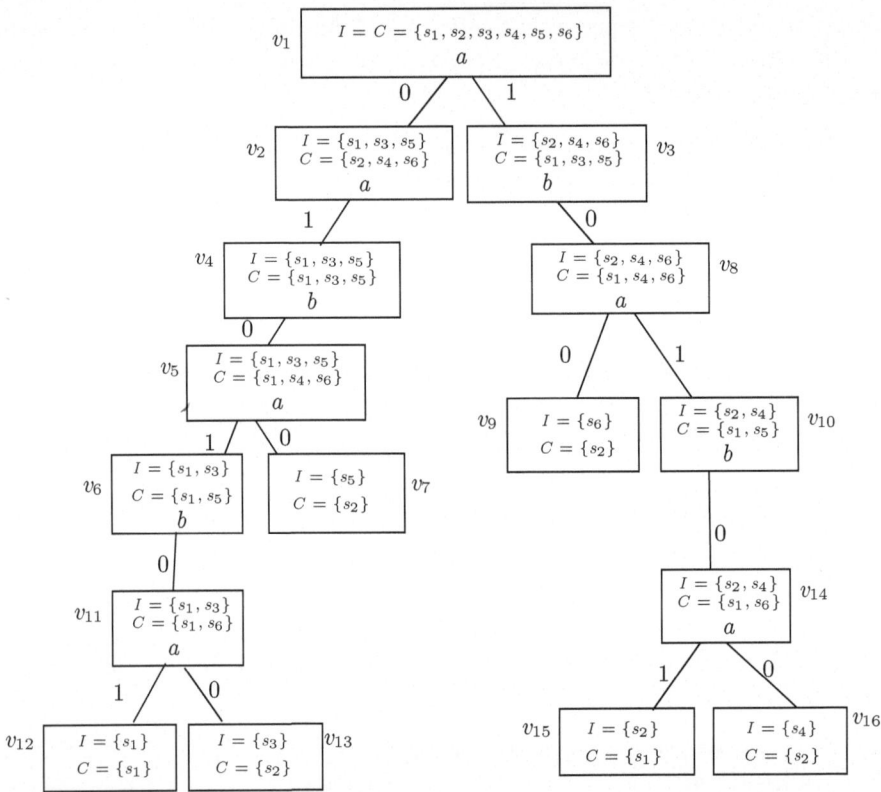

Fig. 2.12. An ADS of machine M_6 with its associated Initial and Current sets.

(with no loss of information). In that case, if the uncertainty is reduced to singletons then we are done. Now for ADS, things are a bit similar. First as for PDS, only valid input symbols are to be considered too, otherwise there will be an irrevocable loss of information. Also at each step, our goal is still to reduce the uncertainty about the initial state. However by difference with PDS, for ADS this is to be done locally. That is, we no longer need to look for a valid refining input sequence for the whole current uncertainty but rather only to the current set of some node of the adaptive experiment.

Consequently, checking the existence of an ADS is equivalent to checking whether for any given block of states a valid input symbol for this block and which distinguishes some of its states exists. This is what Algorithm 6 aims to do.

The algorithm moves from a partition of the set of states to another. It starts with the one block partition. Then at each step, it refines the current partition by executing an input symbol which is valid for one of the blocks of the partition. The considered block is split with respect to both the observed output symbols and the blocks of the partition containing the arrival states due to the execution of the considered input symbol: two states of this block will be in the same subblock if they produce the same output symbol and move to states which are in the same block of this partition. When no more refinement is possible, the algorithm terminates.

In this algorithm, $Partition(B, \pi')$ denotes the partition of B grouping states which produce the same output and move to the same block of π' under all possible inputs.

Algorithm 6 Checking whether an machine M has an ADS([LY94]).

- Initialization: $\pi := \{S\}$

- Iterations: **while** $\exists B \in \pi$, $a \in I$ valid input for B and $s_1, s_2 \in B$ such that $\lambda(s_1, a) \neq \lambda(s_2, a)$ or $\delta(s_1, a)$ and $\delta(s_2, a)$ not in the same block from π

  (1) $\pi' := \pi$
  (2) $\pi := \pi / B$ (we omit B from π)
  (3) $\pi := \pi \cup Partition(B, \pi')$

Depending on whether the last obtained partition is the discrete one or not, the conclusion about the existence of an ADS for the considered machine is given by Theorem 2.17.

Theorem 2.17. *([LY94]) A given machine M has an ADS if and only if Algorithm 6 applied on it ends with the discrete partition of the set of states of M.*

We sketch a proof for this theorem. The proof is split into two parts. We start with the "only if" direction.

Proof. ("only if" direction) We do it by contradiction: we assume that M has an ADS T and that the partition π with which Algorithm 6 terminates is not the discrete one. We consider a block B in π with maximal cardinality (i.e., $|B| \geqslant 2$). We assume that the initial state of the machine is in B and we try to identify it by executing T. By induction on the length of the experiment, it is easy to prove that for the current node u of T there exists a block of states B_u such that

$$|B_u| = |B| \text{ and } B_u \subseteq C(u).$$

In particular, this remains true when the distinguishing experiment T terminates. Thus, there exists a leaf of T the current set of which contains more than one state. So, we come to a contradiction with the fact that T is an ADS (by Proposition 2.15). □

For proving the "if" direction, we need to introduce some extra definitions. Given a partition π of the set of states of the considered machine, we distinguish between three types of valid inputs: a-valid, b-valid and c-valid. For some block

B of π, a is **a-valid** for B if it is valid for B and there are two states of B which produce different outputs on a. The input a is **b-valid** for B with respect to π if it is valid for B and all the states of B produce the same output on a and move to the same block of π. Finally, a is **c-valid** for B w.r.t π if it is valid for B and it is neither a-valid nor b-valid for B.

Moreover, we define the **implication graph** of a given machine corresponding to a partition π of the set of states of this machine as the directed graph G_π the nodes of which are the blocks of π and such that $B \xrightarrow{a/b} B'$ is an arc of G_π if a is c-valid for B and each state in B produces b and moves to a state in B' on a.

Finally, we introduce the notion of closed experiments. An experiment T is said to be **closed** if the current set of each of its leaves is contained in the initial set of some (possibly different) leaf.

Proof. ("if" direction) We assume that Algorithm 6 terminates with the discrete partition and we construct an ADS T for M. First, T is initialized to the one node tree. At each step, every node of T is assigned some initial and current sets. Due to the initialization step, the root of T is assigned S the whole set of states as both initial and current sets.

- If T is not closed then we choose a leaf u of T the current set of which intersects the initial sets of more than one leaf. We identify v the lowest common ancestor (in T) of all such leaves. The tree T is then updated by applying on the current set of u the input sequence spelt by the path from the root of T to v.

- It is when T is closed that the partitioning resulted in by Algorithm 6 is going to be helpful. In that case, we choose a leaf u of T such that $I(u)$ is of maximal cardinality in $\pi(T)$.

  It is not difficult to see that there exists a block B in $\pi(T)$ such that $C(u) = B$ (since T is closed and $I(u)$ is of maximal cardinality). On the implication graph $G_{\pi(T)}$, we identify the blocks $B_1, B_2, \cdots, B_k$ of $\pi(T)$ which are reachable from B. It is not difficult to see that $B_1, B_2, \cdots, B_k$ are of the same cardinality as B.

  Now, since Algorithm 6 terminates with the discrete partition we deduce that there exists a step of the execution of the algorithm which splits for the first time some block B_i. Let a be the valid input symbol used during this step and τ a possible path in G_π which is from B to B_i. The string τa is the input sequence we are going to apply on B the current set of u and update correspondingly the tree T.

  The input a can only be either a-valid or b-valid for B_i and not c-valid (w.r.t $\pi(T)$). It can not be so because all the other blocks $B_j \neq B_i$ (the only possible successors of B_i on c-valid inputs) are not split yet at that step. If a is a-valid for B_i then the new obtained tree T has necessarily more leaves than the old one (i.e., $\pi(T)$ has been refined). Otherwise, if a is b-valid for B_i then it is easy to see that the updated tree T is not closed.

Thus, after a finite number of iterations an ADS for the considered machine is obtained. $\square$

The following example allows to better understand the preceding proof.

Example. We apply Algorithm 6 on machine M_6 (Fig. 2.9). Initially, we start with the one block partition

$$\pi = \{\{s_1, s_2, s_3, s_4, s_5, s_6\}\}.$$

Only a is valid for $\{s_1, s_2, s_3, s_4, s_5, s_6\}$ (b merges s_2 and s_6). It refines π to

$$\pi = \{\{s_1, s_3, s_5\}, \{s_2, s_4, s_6\}\},$$

where $\{s_1, s_3, s_5\}$ corresponds to output 0 and $\{s_2, s_4, s_6\}$ to 1. Now, $\{s_1, s_3, s_5\}$ can be refined to $\{s_1\}$ and $\{s_3, s_5\}$ by use of input symbol b since under b which is valid for $\{s_1, s_3, s_5\}$ s_1 stays at the same block whereas s_3 and s_5 move to the block $\{s_2, s_4, s_6\}$ of the old partition. Thus, due to the execution of b the partition π is refined to

$$\pi = \{\{s_1\}, \{s_3, s_5\}, \{s_2, s_4, s_6\}\}.$$

In a similar way, a refines $\{s_2, s_4, s_6\}$ to $\{s_2\}$ and $\{s_4, s_6\}$ since a is valid for $\{s_2, s_4, s_6\}$ and under a s_2 moves to the block $\{s_1\}$ whereas the states s_4 and s_6 move to the block $\{s_3, s_5\}$ of the old partition. Thus, π is refined to

$$\pi = \{\{s_1\}, \{s_3, s_5\}, \{s_2\}, \{s_4, s_6\}\}.$$

Now, b becomes valid for $\{s_3, s_5\}$ and it can refine it into $\{s_3\}$ and $\{s_5\}$. Partition π becomes

$$\pi = \{\{s_1\}, \{s_3\}, \{s_5\}, \{s_2\}, \{s_4, s_6\}\}.$$

Finally, $\{s_4, s_6\}$ can be refined either by a or by b into $\{s_4\}$ and $\{s_6\}$. Thus, we end with the discrete partition of the set of states of machine M_6 and consequently we verify that it has an ADS.

A summary of the different steps of the execution of Algorithm 6 on machine M_6 is given in Table 2.3.

i	B	valid input	partition of B	π
0	$\{s_1, s_2, s_3, s_4, s_5, s_6\}$	a	$\{s_1, s_3, s_5\}, \{s_2, s_4, s_6\}$	$\{s_1, s_3, s_5\}, \{s_2, s_4, s_6\}$
1	$\{s_1, s_3, s_5\}$	b	$\{s_1\}, \{s_3, s_5\}$	$\{s_1\}, \{s_3, s_5\}, \{s_2, s_4, s_6\}$
2	$\{s_2, s_4, s_6\}$	a	$\{s_2, s_4\}, \{s_6\}$	$\{s_1\}, \{s_3, s_5\}, \{s_2, s_4\}, \{s_6\}$
3	$\{s_3, s_5\}$	a	$\{s_3\}, \{s_5\}$	$\{s_1\}, \{s_3\}, \{s_5\}, \{s_2, s_4\}, \{s_6\}$
4	$\{s_2, s_4\}$	a	$\{s_2\}, \{s_4\}$	$\{s_1\}, \{s_3\}, \{s_5\}, \{s_2\}, \{s_4\}, \{s_6\}$

Table 2.3. Different steps of the execution of Algorithm 6 on machine M_6.

Now from the preceding calculations, we show how a new ADS (Fig. 2.13) for machine M_6 can be constructed. The nodes of this new ADS are numbered in order to explain how it is computed.

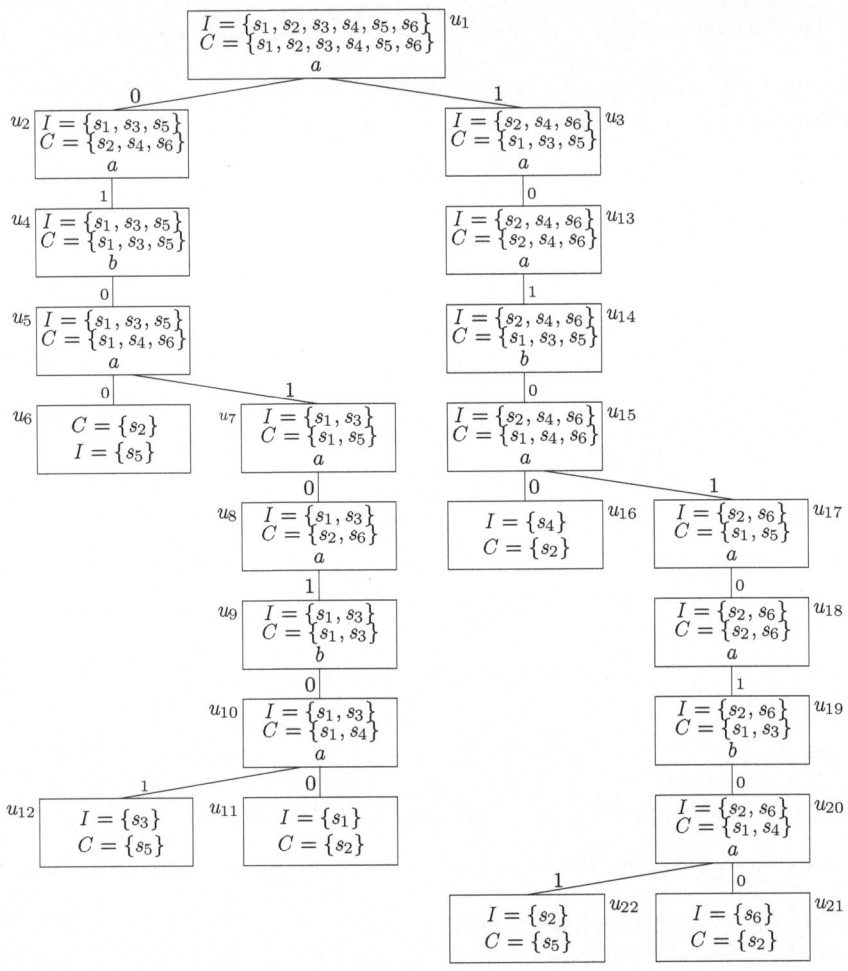

Fig. 2.13. Another ADS for machine M_6.

It is constructed as follows:

- Step 0: T is initialized to the one node tree. The initial and current sets of the root of T are assigned $\{s_1, s_2, s_3, s_4, s_5, s_6\}$. At this step, T contains only node u_1 of the tree shown in Fig. 2.13.
- Step 1: T due to step 0 is not closed. According to the execution of Algorithm 6, the current set $\{s_1, s_2, s_3, s_4, s_5, s_6\}$ of node u_1 can be refined by applying a. Thus, node u_1 is labeled by a and nodes u_2 and u_3 are added to T (with their corresponding current and initial sets).
- Step 2: T due to step 1 is closed since the current set of u_2 equals the initial set of u_3 and vice versa. At this step, we have

$$\pi(T) = \{\{s_1, s_3, s_5\}, \{s_2, s_4, s_6\}\},$$

and

$$\{s_2, s_4, s_6\} \xrightarrow{a/1} \{s_1, s_3, s_5\}.$$

According to the execution of Algorithm 6, b allows to refine $\{s_1, s_3, s_5\}$ since it makes its states move to distinct blocks of $\pi(T)$. Thus, T can be extended by executing the input sequence ab from u_2. As a result, nodes u_4 and u_5 are added to T and node u_2 is labeled by a and node u_4 by b. The suitable current and initial sets are assigned to each new node.

- Step 3: the so far obtained T is not closed since the current set $\{s_1, s_4, s_6\}$ of u_5 intersects both the initial set of u_3 and u_5 (the current leaves of T). The lowest common ancestor of these two nodes is u_1. So, the input sequence to be used is a. Thus at this step, we add to T u_6 and u_7 and to each of them we assign the corresponding current and initial sets.
- Step 4: T is not closed since the current set $\{s_1, s_5\}$ of node u_7 intersects both the initial set of nodes u_7 and u_9. The lowest common ancestor of u_7 and u_9 is u_5. So, the input sequence to be used is $aaba$ (spelt by the path from u_1 to u_5). T is consequently formed by nodes u_1 to u_{12}. Due to this step the two extra states s_1 (node u_{11}) and s_3 (node u_{12}) have become identifiable.
- Step 5: T is not closed since the current set $\{s_1, s_3, s_5\}$ of node u_3 is the union of the initial sets of the nodes u_6, u_{11} and u_{12}. The lowest common ancestor of these node is u_5. So as in step 4, we apply $aaba$ on the current set of u_3. Consequently, we append to T nodes from u_{13} to u_{17}.
- Step 6: T is not closed since the current set $\{s_1, s_5\}$ of node u_{17} is the union of the initial sets of the nodes u_6 and u_{11}. The lowest common ancestor of these node is still u_5. So as in step 4, we apply $aaba$ on the current set of u_3. At this step, nodes from u_{18} to u_{22} are appended to T.

It is easy to see that the obtained T due to step 6 is an ADS for machine M_6.

Remark 2.18. There is a similarity between Algorithm 6 and the classical algorithm for FSM minimization. The only difference between them is that Algorithm 6 uses only valid inputs, whereas the minimization algorithm uses all input symbols.

2.4.4   Computing a Polynomial ADS

In the proof of Theorem 2.17, we gave a first method for constructing an ADS (when Algorithm 6 terminates with the discrete partition of some given machine). This method may give exponential ADSs. For example, the ADS of machine M_6 resulted in by this method (Fig. 2.13) is not optimal (it is longer than the one shown in Fig. 2.9).

In [LY94], Lee and Yannakakis propose methods for computing ADSs with polynomial size and in polynomial time. For computing "optimal" ADSs, they introduce an intermediary structure: the splitting tree. The latter is defined as follows.

Definition 2.19. A **splitting tree** associated with a Mealy machine $M = (I, O, S, \delta, \lambda)$ is a rooted tree T such that:

- Each node of T is labeled by a subset of S and the root of T is labeled with S,
- The children's labels of an internal node of T are disjoint and the label of an internal node of T is the union of its children's labels,
- With each internal node of T is associated an input sequence,
- With each internal node u of T, with associated set-label S_u and input string-label x_u, is associated a mapping $f_u : S_u \rightarrow S$ such that $f_u(s) = \delta(s, x_u)$ for each s in S_u,
- Each edge of T is labeled with an output symbol from O.

Let $\pi(T)$ denotes the collection of sets of states formed by the labels of the leaves of the splitting tree T (it is easy to see that $\pi(T)$ is a partition of S). T is a **complete splitting tree** if $\pi(T)$ is the discrete partition of S.   □

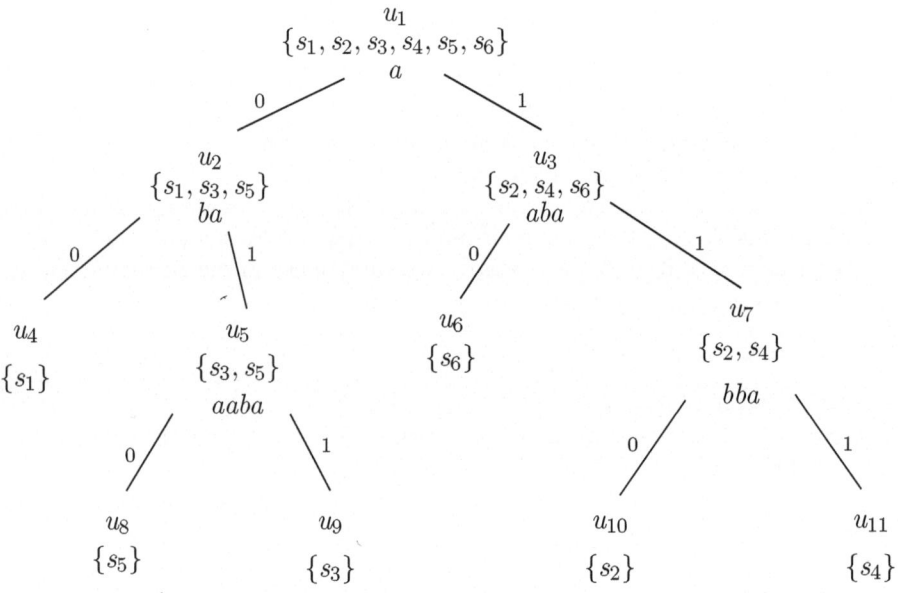

Fig. 2.14. A complete splitting tree of machine M_6.

Example. A complete splitting tree for machine M_6 (Fig. 2.8) is shown in Fig. 2.14. The mappings f_u associated with this splitting tree are given in Table 2.4.

The way for computing such a complete splitting tree is given by Algorithm 7. The Algorithm uses the following notation:

- ST_0 is the tree with a single node whose root is labeled with S.
- π_d is the discrete partition of S.

$f_{u_1} = (s_1, s_2), (s_3, s_5), (s_4, s_5), (s_5, s_6), (s_6, s_1)$
$f_{u_2} = \qquad\qquad (s_1, s_2), (s_2, s_3), (s_5, s_1)$
$f_{u_3} = \qquad\qquad (s_2, s_5), (s_4, s_1), (s_6, s_2)$
$f_{u_5} = \qquad\qquad\quad (s_3, s_1), (s_5, s_2)$
$f_{u_7} = \qquad\qquad\quad (s_2, s_2), (s_4, s_1)$

Table 2.4. The mappings f_u of the splitting tree of machine M_6 (Fig. 2.14).

- $u(B)$ is the leaf of ST with set-label B.
- $u \cdot set$ and $u \cdot string$ are the set and string-labels of the node u, respectively.
- $append(ST, u, B', a)$ is ST to which we append a new node v from u such that the set-label of v is B' and the edge from u to v is labeled by input symbol a.
- $\lambda(s \in B', a) = \lambda(s, a)$ for any arbitrary s in B'.
- $label(v, w)$ is the label of the edge of ST which is from v to w.

The algorithm proceeds as follows. It starts with the one node splitting tree. At each iteration, it considers a block B from R the set of blocks of π with largest cardinality. B is the set-label of one of the leaves of the current splitting tree. Then, it looks for the shortest input sequence that may refine B. Three ways are then possible for finding such an input sequence. If B has an a-valid input symbol ("case 1") then the searched input sequence is the found a-valid input symbol. If no such leaf exists then we look for a leaf which has a b-valid input symbol (w.r.t to π the partition of states induced by the current splitting tree). If such a leaf is found ("case 2"), then we identify the node of the current splitting tree whose set-label contains $\delta(B, a)$, where a is the b-valid input symbol. If σ is the input string-label associated with this node then it is clear that B can be refined by executing $a\sigma$. Now, if the set-label of the considered leaf has neither an a-valid nor a b-valid input symbol then we check whether there exists a sequence of c-valid inputs for B (w.r.t π) which makes the states of B (the set-label to be refined) move to another set-label C which has just been refined by the execution of an input sequence τ. If such a path σ exists ("case 3") then it is clear that $\sigma\tau$ can refine the set-label B.

If none of the three ways works, we conclude that the considered machine has no ADS. In the third case, for obtaining the shortest input sequence which refines B we shall look for the shortest path σ which goes from B to some other possible set-label C. This can be done by performing a reachability analysis on $G_\pi[R]$ the subgraph of G_π (the implication graph corresponding to the partition π) induced by R to find a path from B to some possible block C.

For each of the three cases, the splitting tree is updated as follows: we assign the found input sequence to the input string-label of the considered leaf then new leaves are attached to this (old) leaf. The number of attached leaves equals the number of subsets to which B is refined.

Example. We apply Algorithm 7 to M_6 to obtain the complete splitting tree shown in Fig. 2.14.

Algorithm 7 Computing a complete splitting tree ST ([LY94]).

- Initialization:

  (1) $ST := ST_0$
  (2) $\pi := \{S\}$

- Iterations: **while** $\pi \neq \pi_d$, $\forall B \in R$

  - case 1: **If** $\exists\, a \in I$ a-valid input for B **then**
    (1) $u(B) \cdot string := a$
    (2) $\forall\, B' \in \pi(B) :$
    $$ST := append(ST, u(B), B', \lambda(s \in B', a))$$

    (3) $\forall\, s \in B : f_{u(B)}(s) := \delta(s, a)$

  - case 2: **Otherwise, if** $\exists\, a \in I$ b-valid for B w.r.t π **then**
    (1) $v :=$ the lowest node of ST such that $\delta(B, a) \subseteq v \cdot set$
    (2) $\sigma := v \cdot string$
    (3) $u(B) \cdot string := a\sigma$
    (4) $\forall\, w$ child of v such that $\delta(B, a) \cap w \cdot set \neq \emptyset :$
    $$ST := append(ST, u(B), B \cap \delta^{-1}(\cdot, a)(w \cdot set), label(u, w))$$

    (5) $\forall\, s \in B : f_{u(B)}(s) := f_v(\delta(s, a))$

  - case 3: **Otherwise, if** $\exists\, C \in \pi$ that has fallen under "case 1" or "case 2" and such that $B \xrightarrow{\sigma/\beta} C$ is a path in $G_\pi[R]$ **then**
    (1) $\tau := u(C) \cdot string$
    (2) $u(B) \cdot string := \sigma\tau$
    (3) $\forall\, w$ child of v such that $\delta(B, \sigma) \cap w \cdot set \neq \emptyset :$
    $$ST := append(ST, u(B), B \cap \delta^{-1}(\cdot, \sigma)(w \cdot set), label(u, w))$$

    (4) $\forall\, s \in B : f_{u(B)}(s) := f_{u(C)}(\delta(s, \sigma))$

  - **Otherwise**, no ADS

- Step 0: ST is initialized to ST_0, it contains only u_1. The set-label of this node is assigned $S_1 = S$ the whole set of states.

- Step 1: we are in "case 1" since a is a-valid for S the set-label of u_1. The input symbol a refines S_1 into $S_2 = \{s_1, s_3, s_5\}$ and $S_3 = \{s_2, s_4, s_6\}$. Thus, we assign a to the string-label u_1, we attach the two new leaves u_2 and u_3 to this node and assign S_2 to the set-label of u_2 and S_3 to the set-label of u_3.

- Step 2: we are not in "case 1" since neither S_2 nor S_3 has an a-valid input symbol. The input b is b-valid for S_2 since $\delta(S_2, b) = \{s_1, s_4, s_6\}$ intersects both S_2 and S_3. Thus, we are in "case 2". In ST, we look for the lowest node whose set-label contains $\delta(S_2, b)$. This node is u_1. Since the string-label of this node is a and b is the b-valid input symbol for S_1, S_2 can be refined by applying ba. The latter refines S_2 into $S_4 = \{s_1\}$ and $S_5 = \{s_3, s_5\}$. Thus, we update ST by assigning ba the string-label of u_2, attaching u_4 and u_5 to u_2 and assigning S_4 and S_5 to the set-labels of u_4 and u_5, respectively.

- Step 3: at this step, we refine S_3 the set-label of u_3. The block S_3 has neither a-valid nor b-valid inputs. However, a is c-valid for S_3 and $\delta(S_3, a) = S_2$. Thus, we are in "case 3" and S_3 can be refined by the input sequence obtained by the concatenation of a with the input string-label of u_3 (ba). Consequently, we deduce that S_3 can be refined by the input sequence aba into $S_6 = \{s_6\}$ and $S_7 = \{s_2, s_4\}$. These two blocks are the set-labels of u_6 and u_7 the so far attached nodes to u_2. We also assign aba to the input string-label of u_2.

- Step 4: at this step, the set-labels with maximal cardinality are S_5 and S_7. First, we refine S_5, the latter has no a-valid input symbol. We are in "case 2" since a is b-valid for S_5. The block $\{s_2, s_6\} = \delta(S_5, a)$ intersects the set-labels of both u_6 and u_7. The input string-label by which S_5 is refined is $aaba$. It is the concatenation of a the b-valid input of S_5 and aba the input string-label of u_3 the lowest common ancestor of u_6 and u_7. The input sequence $aaba$ refines S_5 into $S_8 = \{s_5\}$ and $S_9 = \{s_3\}$. Thus, we update ST by assigning $aaba$ to the input string-label of u_5 and attaching u_8 and u_9 to u_5. The set-labels of u_8 and u_9 are respectively S_8 and S_9.

- Step 5: now, it only remains to refine S_7 for obtaining a complete splitting tree. We are in "case 2" again since S_7 has no a-valid input symbol, b is b-valid for S_7 and $\{s_1, s_5\} = \delta(S_7, b)$ intersects the set-labels of both u_4 and u_5. The lowest common ancestor node of u_4 and u_5 is u_1 with input string-label ba. Thus, S_7 can be refined by bba into $S_{10} = \{s_2\}$ and $S_{11} = \{s_4\}$. Finally, we assign bba to the input string-label of u_7 and we attach u_{10} and u_{11} to this node.

All the set-labels of the leaves of the obtained splitting tree ST are singletons. Consequently, ST is a complete splitting tree.

Theorem 2.20. *([LY94]) Algorithm 7 results in a complete splitting tree of some machine M if and only if M has an ADS.*

Proof. Similar to the proof of Theorem 2.17. In particular for the second direction ("only if"), the way for computing an ADS from a complete splitting tree is given by Algorithm 8. □

In Algorithm 8, we use the following notation (in addition to the ones used in Algorithm 7):

- T_0 is the one node tree whose root has its initial and current sets equal to the whole set of states.
- τ_{-1} is the prefix of τ with length $|\tau| - 1$ (λ_{-1} is defined similarly).
- $hang \cdot sequence(T, w, \tau_{-1}, \lambda_{-1})$ is T to which we hang $|\tau_{-1}|$ new degree-two nodes from w, we label w and the new added nodes in a way such that the labels read from w to the new leaf spell τ_{-1} and we finally label the new added edges in a way such that the labels read from the outgoing edge from w to the end of the path spell λ_{-1}.

Algorithm 8 Computing an ADS T given a complete splitting tree ST ([LY94]).

- Initialization: $T := T_0$

- Iterations: **while** $\exists\, w$ a leaf of T such that $|C(w)| \geqslant 2$

  (1) $u :=$ the lowest node of ST such that $C(w) \subseteq u \cdot set$
  (2) $\tau := u \cdot label$
  (3) $\lambda_{-1} := \lambda(s \in C(w), \tau - 1)$
  (4) $T := hang \cdot sequence(T, w, \tau_{-1}, \lambda_{-1})$
  (5) $v :=$ the new obtained leaf of T
  (6) $\forall\, u_i$ child of u such that $C(w) \cap u_i \cdot set \neq \emptyset$
     (a) $T := hang \cdot node(T, v, v_i, label(u, u_i))$
     (b) $C(v_i) := f_u(C(w) \cap u_i \cdot set)$
     (c) $I(v_i) :=$ the initial states associated with the states of $C(w) \cap u_i \cdot set$ at node w

---

- $hang \cdot node(T, v, v_i, a)$ is T to which we hang the node v_i from v and label the new outgoing edge from v with a.

Example. We explain how the ADS of M_6 shown in Fig. 2.12 (and Fig. 2.9 too) can be deduced from the complete splitting tree ST shown in Fig. 2.14.

- Step 0: we initialize T to T_0. The experiment T contains only v_1 with S as initial and current sets for this node (i.e., $I_1 = C_1 = S$).
- Step 1: for reducing the uncertainty about C_1, we apply a the string-label of node u_1 of ST since $C_1 \subseteq S_1$. The nodes v_2 and v_3 are added due to this step. We also calculate the initial and current sets (I_2, I_3, C_2 and C_3) of these two nodes and the labels of the added edges.
- Step 2: we reduce the uncertainty about $C_2 = \{s_2, s_4, s_6\}$ the current set of v_2. The node u_3 is the lowest node of ST whose set-label contains C_2. So, from v_2 we apply the input sequence aba (string-label of u_3). Consequently, we add nodes v_4 to v_7. The node v_2 is labeled by a, v_4 by b and v_5 by a, so that together they spell aba. The corresponding initial and current sets are assigned to the added nodes.
- Step 3: we reduce the uncertainty about $C_3 = \{s_1, s_3, s_5\}$. The lowest node of ST whose set-label contains C_3 is u_2. Thus, we use ba at this step. Nodes v_8, v_9 and v_{10} are added and are assigned the corresponding initial and current sets.
- Step 4: similarly, we reduce the uncertainty about $C_6 = \{s_1, s_5\}$ by applying ba the string-label of u_2. Nodes v_{11}, v_{12} and v_{13} are added due to this step.
- Step 5: finally as in step 4, ba is used again for reducing the uncertainty about $C_{10} = \{s_1, s_5\}$. At this step, nodes v_{14}, v_{15} and v_{16} are attached to T.

The obtained adaptive experiment T is clearly an ADS.

2.4.5   Complexity

In this section, for a machine $M = (I, O, S, \delta, \lambda)$, we let n stand for the number of states of M and p the number of its input symbols (i.e., $n = |S|$ and $p = |I|$).

Theorem 2.21 below summarizes the main complexity results of Lee and Yannakakis [LY94] about ADSs.

Theorem 2.21. *([LY94]) For the considered machine M*

(1) *A straightforward implementation of Algorithm 6 takes time $O(pn^2)$.*
(2) *If Algorithm 7 succeeds in constructing a complete splitting tree ST then its time complexity is $O(pn^2)$ and the size of ST is $O(n^2)$.*
(3) *If Algorithm 7 succeeds in constructing a complete splitting tree ST then the decision tree T of the ADS derived by Algorithm 8 has length at most $n(n-1)/2$ and $O(n^2)$ nodes. Moreover, T can be constructed in time $O(n^2)$ from ST.*

The proof of this theorem given in [LY94] is mainly based on the following lemmas.

Lemma 2.22. *([LY94]) Suppose that $f(\cdot)$ is a function from the set of states to a finite set Y that can be evaluated in constant time. If R is a subset of states stored in a list then we can partition the elements of R according to their value under f in time $O(|R|)$ using workspace $O(n + |Y|)$.*

Lemma 2.23. *([LY94]) Suppose that Algorithm 7 succeeds in constructing a complete splitting tree ST, then:*

- *Each internal node u of ST has at least two children,*
- *The label $L(u)$ of u is the union of the labels of its children,*
- *All states of $L(u)$ produce the same output except for the last symbol,*
- *Two states of $L(u)$ agree in the last output symbol if and only if they belong to the label of the same child of u, furthermore, this output symbol is the label of the edge connecting u to its child.*

Lemma 2.24. *([LY94]) If u is the internal node of a splitting tree whose label $L(u)$ has cardinality i, then its associated input sequence $\rho(u)$ has length at most $n + 1 - i$.*

In order not to overload the chapter, we give neither the proof of the theorem nor of the three lemmas. Interested readers are referred to [LY94].

About the time complexity of checking the existence of an ADS for a given machine, Lee and Yannakakis [LY94] propose an implementation of Algorithm 6 which takes $O(pn\log n)$ time inspired by Hopcroft's algorithm [Hop71] allowing to minimize FSMs in $O(pn\log n)$ time. The main idea behind this implementation consists on splitting blocks by examining transitions in the reverse direction instead of forward.

The two authors also argue a more general problem, similar to the problem of checking the existence of an ADS for some given machine. It consists of identifying the initial state of a given machine with the extra assumption that this initial state belongs to a subset of the set of states. It is shown that this problem is harder than the initial problem of checking the existence of an ADS as stated by the following.

Theorem 2.25. *([LY94]) Given an FSM M and a set of possible initial states Q, It is PSPACE-complete to tell whether there is an (adaptive) experiment that identifies the initial state of M.*

2.5   Summary

In this chapter, we addressed the state identification problem for Mealy machines. It consists in checking whether it is possible to determine the initial state of a given Mealy machine by applying inputs on it and observing the corresponding outputs. A solution of this problem is called a distinguishing sequence.

Not all Mealy machines have distinguishing sequences. In particular, non-minimal machines have no distinguishing sequences, since there is no way for distinguishing their equivalent states. In this chapter, we have only considered Mealy machines which are minimal, deterministic and fully specified.

Distinguishing sequences can be either preset or adaptive. A PDS is a sequence of inputs whereas an ADS is a decision tree where inputs may be different depending on the observed outputs during the experiment. If a machine has a PDS then it has an ADS (because a PDS is an ADS), however, the converse is not true.

Main results about PDSs: it is PSPACE-complete to test whether a given FSM has a PDS. In [LY94], Lee and Yannakakis show that this remains true even for Mealy machines with binary input and output alphabets. Checking the existence of a PDS can be reduced to a reachability analysis in the super graph of the considered machine. The size of this graph is exponential with respect to the number of states of the corresponding machine. It is possible to compute a shortest PDS of a given machine by performing a breadth-first search throughout the super graph of the machine. In [LY94], Lee and Yannakakis also show that there are machines for which the shortest PDS has exponential length.

Main results about ADSs: it can be checked whether a given Mealy machine has an ADS in time $O(pn^2)$, where n and p are the number of states and inputs of the considered machine, respectively. This can be done by executing an algorithm similar to the classical minimization algorithm. $O(pn^2)$ can be reduced to $O(pnlogn)$ by executing an algorithm inspired by Hopcroft's minimization algorithm [Hop71]. For computing "optimal" ADSs, in [LY94], Lee and Yannakakis define the so-called splitting tree. The latter provides for some subset of states an input sequence which allows to reduce the uncertainty about this subset. A given machine has an ADS if and only if it has a complete splitting tree. The algorithm (Algorithm 7) for checking the existence and computing a splitting tree takes time $O(pn^2)$. The size of the splitting tree it results in is $O(n^2)$. Finally, if a complete splitting tree is found, then an ADS for the corresponding machine can be deduced from it in time $O(n^2)$. Moreover, the obtained ADS has $O(n^2)$ nodes and length at most $n(n-1)/2$.

Sources: the main sources for this chapter have been [LY94, LY96] by David Lee and Mihalis Yannakakis and Chapter 13 of [Koh78] by Zvi Kohavi.

3 State Verification

Henrik Björklund

Computer Science Department
Uppsala University
henrikbj@it.uu.se

3.1 Introduction

State verification is a more restricted problem than state identification, discussed in Chapter 2. As in state verification, we know the state diagram of the system under test. The difference is that we have an assumption about which state the system is currently in, and the objective is to check that this assumption is correct. The basic idea is that when testing a machine, we can give it an input sequence, and then use state verification to verify that the sequence took the machine under test to the expected state.

Definitions of many of the concepts used in this chapter can be found in Appendix 21.

In a state verification experiment, we want to find out whether a Mealy machine $M = (I, O, S, \delta, \lambda)$ is in a particular state $s \in S$. An input sequence is applied to the machine, and we observe the output.

Given a Mealy machine $\mathcal{M} = (I, O, S, \delta, \lambda)$ and a state $s \in S$, it is possible to verify that $\mathcal{M}$ is in state s by only observing the input-output behavior of $\mathcal{M}$ if and only if there is an input sequence $x = (a_1, \dots, a_k)$ such that $\lambda(s, x) \neq \lambda(s', x)$ for all $s' \neq s$.[1] Since only the input-output behavior of the machine is observable, state verification for state s is possible if and only if s has a *unique input-output sequence*, or UIO sequence for short.

Definition 3.1 (UIO sequence). Given a Mealy machine $\mathcal{M} = (I, O, S, \delta, \lambda)$ and a state $s \in S$, a *UIO sequence* for s is an input sequence x such that $\lambda(s, x) \neq \lambda(s', x)$ for every state $s' \neq s$.

These sequences were introduced by Hsieh [Hsi71],[2] and algorithms for finding them have been studied by, e.g., Kohavi [Koh78], Sabnani and Dahbura [SD88], Lee and Yannakakis [LY94], and Naik [Nai97]. The presentation in this chapter builds mainly on the results from these papers.

Not all states of all machines have UIO sequences. Consider for example the machine in Figure 3.1, with input alphabet $I = \{a, b\}$ and output alphabet $O = \{0, 1\}$. For state s_1 the singleton sequence b is a UIO sequence, since s_1 is the only state that produces output 1 on input b. Similarly, a is a UIO sequence for s_2 since it is the only state that produces output 1 on input a. State s_3, however, does not have a UIO sequence. On input a, states s_1 and s_3 will both

---

[1] For extensions of λ and δ to sequences of input symbols, see Appendix 21.
[2] Hsieh uses the term *simple I/O sequence* rather than UIO sequence [Hsi71].

M. Broy et al. (Eds.): Model-Based Testing of Reactive Systems, LNCS 3472, pp. 69-86, 2005.
© Springer-Verlag Berlin Heidelberg 2005

give output 0, and in both cases the machine will be taken to the same state, s_2. Thus for any input sequence starting with an a, states s_1 and s_3 will give the same output. Similarly, both s_2 and s_3 give output 0 on input b, and the machine is in both cases taken to s_3. Thus s_2 and s_3 give the same output on all input sequences starting with a b. Since all input sequences start either with an a or a b, state s_3 cannot have a UIO sequence. Notice that for any one of s_1 and s_2, there is a sequence that *separates* it from s_3. There is, however, no one sequence that separates s_3 from both s_1 and s_2.

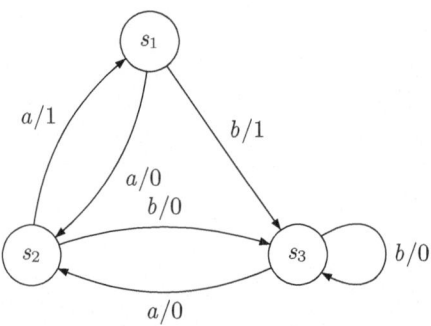

Fig. 3.1. A Mealy machine in which states s_1 and s_2 have UIO sequences, but s_3 does not.

There are machines such that all, some, or no states have UIO sequences. In any machine with only one state, all states have UIO sequences. As we saw above, the machine in Figure 3.1 has UIO sequences for some, but not all states. In contrast, there is no state that has a UIO sequence in the machine in Figure 3.2.

A **distinguishing sequence** for a machine is a more powerful sequence, that can be used for **state identification**. A preset distinguishing sequence for a machine $\mathcal{M}$ is an input sequence x such that for all states s, s' of $\mathcal{M}$, if $s \neq s'$ then $\lambda(s, x) \neq \lambda(s', x)$; see Chapter 2 for an extensive treatment. If a machine has a distinguishing sequence, then all its states have UIO sequences. In fact, if x is a preset distinguishing sequence for $\mathcal{M}$, then x is also a UIO sequence for every state s of $\mathcal{M}$.

Even though UIO sequences do not always exist, there are cases when there are no distinguishing sequences, but all states have UIO sequences [Koh78, Lal85, ADLU91]. This is one of the main reasons for studying state verification. Ideally, we would like to have distinguishing sequences, preferably short, for all machines, but since this is not possible, we often have to settle for something less ambitious, namely trying to find UIO sequences. Consider the machine in Figure 3.3. It has no preset distinguishing sequence,[3] since states s_2 and s_3 give the same output

---

[3] In fact, the machine has no preset *or* adaptive distinguishing sequence. For more about adaptive distinguishing sequences, see Chapter 2.

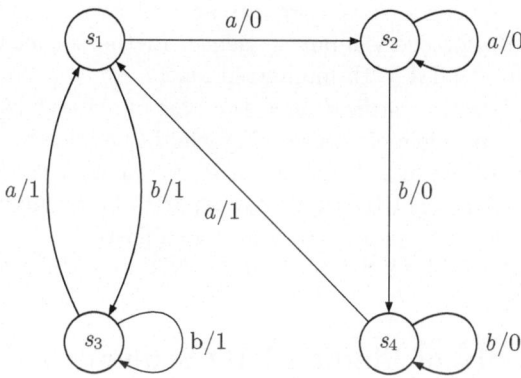

Fig. 3.2. A Mealy machine in which no state has a UIO sequence.

for any input starting with an a, and s_1 and s_4 give the same output when the input starts with a b. All states do, however, have UIO sequences:

- UIO sequence for s_1: ab
- UIO sequence for s_2: ba
- UIO sequence for s_3: b
- UIO sequence for s_4: a

We will return to the machine in Figure 3.3 as an example later in the chapter.

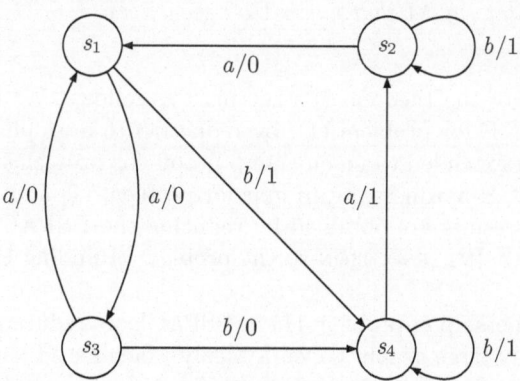

Fig. 3.3. A Mealy machine in which all states have UIO sequences. There is no preset distinguishing sequence for the machine.

A Mealy machine $\mathcal{M}$ is *minimized* if it has no equivalent states; see Appendix 21. If a Mealy machine is not minimized, there are always states that do not have UIO sequences, since there are at least two states that produce the exact same outputs for every input sequence. In the sequel we will therefore assume that we are dealing with minimized machines.

The main use for state verification is as a part of algorithms for *conformance testing*, that is, the problem of determining whether a machine in a black box is a correct implementation of a given specification machine. Many suggested algorithms for this problem use UIO sequences as parts of sequences for conformance testing; see Chapter 4 and papers by, e. g., Hsieh [Hsi71], Aho et. al. [ADLU91], Sabnani and Dahbura [SD85, SD88], Naik [Nai97], and Miller and Paul [MP93].

3.2   Complexity of Finding UIO Sequences

Finding UIO sequences for states in large Mealy machines is no trivial task. The problem was studied in the 1970s, but no efficient algorithms were found [Hsi71, Koh78].

It is not only difficult to find UIO sequences, even determining whether they exist has proved to be challenging. In 1994, Lee and Yannakakis proved that this decision problem is PSPACE-complete. We here reproduce and flesh out their proof.

Theorem 3.2 (Lee and Yannakakis [LY94]). *For Mealy machines $\mathcal{M}$, the following three problems are PSPACE-complete.*

(1) *Does a specific state s of $\mathcal{M}$ have a UIO sequence?*
(2) *Do all states of $\mathcal{M}$ have UIO sequences?*
(3) *Is there any state of $\mathcal{M}$ that has a UIO sequence?*

Proof. The proof of the theorem is structured as follows. We first show membership in PSPACE for problem (1), by reduction to a graph search problem. The result is then extended to membership proofs for problems (2) and (3). We then show PSPACE-hardness, again first for problem (1) and then for (2) and (3). All hardness results are obtained by reducing the PSPACE-hard problem FINITE AUTOMATA INTERSECTION to the problem of finding UIO sequences in Mealy machines.

To show membership of problem (1) in PSPACE we reduce it to reachability in an exponentially large graph. Given a Mealy Machine $\mathcal{M} = (I, O, S, \delta, \lambda)$ we construct a directed graph $G = (V, E)$ with labeled edges in the following way. The vertex set V is $S \times \mathcal{P}(S)$, where $\mathcal{P}(S)$ is the powerset of S. Thus, all pairs of a state s and a subset $Q \subseteq S$ are vertices of G. This means that G has $|S| \cdot 2^{|S|}$ vertices, and is exponentially larger than $\mathcal{M}$. There is an edge from $(s, Q) \in V$ to $(t, P) \in V$ labeled with $a \in I$ if and only if

$$t = \delta(s, a), \text{ and} \tag{3.1}$$
$$P = \{\delta(r, a) \mid r \in Q \text{ and } \lambda(r, a) = \lambda(s, a)\}. \tag{3.2}$$

Thus $(s, Q) \xrightarrow{a} (t, P)$ if and only if t is reachable from s with an a-transition in $\mathcal{M}$, and P is the subset of $\delta(Q, a)$ that can be reached by an a-transition from Q *with the same output* as the a-transition from s to t.

Consider a vertex (s, Q) of G, and an input sequence $x \in I^*$. It is straight-forward to prove by induction on the length of x that if Q' is the subset of Q that produces the same output as s on input x, then the unique path in G that starts in (s, Q) and is labeled with x ends in $(\delta(s, x), \delta(Q', x))$.

If a vertex $(s, S \setminus \{s\})$ in G can reach a vertex $(t, \emptyset)$, for some state t, via a directed path labeled x, then it follows from the above that it has a UIO sequence. Indeed, the subset of $S \setminus \{s\}$ that gives the same output as s on input x is empty. Thus s can be uniquely identified by its output on x. On the other hand, if there is no such path, then there is no input sequence x such that s gives a different output than all other states on x. Thus s does not have a UIO sequence.

In problem (1) we are given a state s and want to know if it has a UIO sequence. Thus what we need to do is to determine whether some vertex $(t, \emptyset)$ is reachable from the vertex $(s, S \setminus \{s\})$ in G. This can be done in nondeterministic polynomial space. There is no need to explicitly compute the whole graph G, which would require exponential space. Instead, the search procedure keeps track only of the current vertex, and for each step computes all its successors and nondeterministically chooses to proceed to one of them. Representing a vertex only requires polynomial space, and each vertex has at most one successor for each symbol in the input alphabet. As Chapter 1.4.2 explains, a consequence of Savitch's theorem is that PSPACE=NPSPACE, and the membership of problem (1) in PSPACE follows. The result for problem (1) extends to problems (2) and (3), since they can be solved by applying the nondeterministic polynomial space procedure for problem (1) once for each state.

(1) We now proceed to showing that the problem of determining whether a specific state s of a given machine $\mathcal{M}$ has a UIO sequence is PSPACE-hard. This is achieved by reduction from the following problem. In Finite Automata Intersection we are given k deterministic total finite automata, $A_1, \dots A_k$, all defined over the same alphabet Σ. The question is whether the intersection of the languages accepted by the automata is nonempty, i.e., if there is some string in Σ^* that is accepted by all k automata. As seen in Chapter 1.4.2, this problem is PSPACE-complete.

The reduction composes the automata to a Mealy machine $\mathcal{M}$ in the following way. The machine has the same input alphabet as the automata, plus two letters, r (reset) and f (finish). Its output alphabet is $\{0, 1\}$. The states of the machine are the states of the automata plus one additional state s. Every transition in one of the automata is a transition of $\mathcal{M}$, with the same input as in the automaton, and output 0. Also, every state t of an automaton A_i gets a transition to the initial state of A_i with input r and output 0, and a transition to s with input f. This transition has output 1 if t is accepting in A_i and 0 if it is non-accepting. Finally, s has a transition to itself for every input, including r and f, with output 0. An example of the construction for two small automata, accepting the common string a is shown in Figure 3.4.

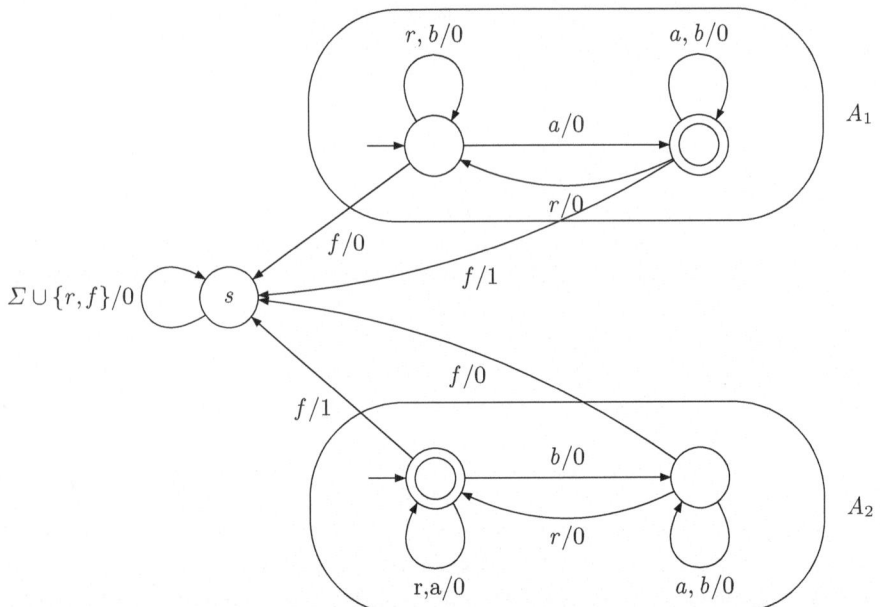

Fig. 3.4. An example of the reduction. The automata A_1 and A_2 over the alphabet $\Sigma = \{a, b\}$ are combined into a Mealy machine with input alphabet $I = \{a, b, r, f\}$ and output alphabet $O = \{0, 1\}$. The automata both accept the string a from their initial states (the leftmost state of each automaton), and the input-output sequence raf is a UIO sequence for state s of the machine.

The state s in the constructed Mealy machine has a UIO sequence if and only if the automata accept a common string x. We first show the if direction. Suppose all the automata accept $x = a_1 \ldots a_k$. Then $ra_1 \ldots a_k f$ is a UIO sequence for s. From state s, input rxf will obviously give a sequence of only zeroes as output. If the machine is initially in some state $t \neq s$, then the first symbol, r, will take it to the initial state of the automaton A_i that t belongs to. The sequence x will then lead to an accepting state of A_i. Finally, the symbol f will give a transition to s *with output 1.* Thus no other state can have an output of only zeroes on input rxf.

For the other direction, assume that there is a UIO sequence x for s. Then x must contain an f, because input f is the only symbol that can produce an output different from 0. Assume that no r appears before the first occurrence of f in x. Consider the prefix $x' = a_1 a_2 \ldots a_k f$ of x that cuts x after the first f. We claim that $\lambda(q, x') = 0^k 1$ for all $q \neq s$. This is because $\delta(q, f) = s$ for all states, so if the f produces output 0, then all subsequent outputs will be

0, and x cannot be a UIO sequence for s. This means that from every state except s, input sequence $a_1 a_2 \ldots a_k$ leads to an accepting state. This includes the initial states of the automata, and we conclude that $a_1 a_2 \ldots a_k$ is accepted by all automata. If x contains an r before the first occurrence of f, a similar argument shows that the part of x between the last occurrence of r before the first f and the first f is a string accepted by all automata.

(2) To show that it is PSPACE-hard to find out whether all states of a given machine $\mathcal{M}$ have UIO sequences, we again use the Finite Automata Intersection problem, with a very similar reduction. The same transitions as above are used, plus some more, as described below. Add a new symbol a_t to the input alphabet for every state t of every automaton. State t gets a transition on input a_t to s with output 0. Every state $u \neq t$, belonging to automaton A_i gets a transition to the initial state of A_i on input a_t, with output 0. State s gets a transition with input a_t to the initial state of the automaton which t belongs to, also with output 0.

If the automata do not accept a common string, state s does not have a UIO sequence, by the same argument as for problem (1) above. On the other hand, if all automata accept the string $x = a_1 \ldots a_k$, then $ra_1 \ldots a_k f$ is a UIO sequence for s, and for every other state t, the sequence $a_t a_1 \ldots a_k f$ is a UIO sequence.

(3) Finally, we show that it is PSPACE-hard to determine whether any state of a given machine has a UIO sequence. The same construction as in the proof of claim (1) is used, except that *two identical copies* of each automaton A_i are used. This means that only state s can have a UIO sequence, and as above, if all automata accept string $x = a_1 \ldots a_k$ then $ra_1 \ldots a_k f$ is a UIO sequence for s, and otherwise there is none. This finishes the proof of Theorem 3.2.

In fact, Theorem 3.2 holds even if we consider only Mealy machines with binary input and output alphabets [LY94].

The proof of Theorem 3.2 also yields an upper bound on the length of the shortest UIO sequence for a given state. Since paths in the exponentially large graph constructed in the PSPACE membership proof correspond directly to input-output sequences with attached output sequences, it follows that if there is a path of length m in the constructed graph from vertex $(s, S \setminus \{s\})$ to some vertex $(s', \emptyset)$, for some states s, s', then s has a UIO sequence of length m. Since no simple path in the graph can be longer than the number of vertices in the graph, this shows that if s has a UIO sequence, then it has a UIO sequence of length at most $|S| \cdot 2^{|S|}$.

Lee and Yannakakis proved a lower bound on the length of UIO-sequences as well, showing that even if a state has a UIO sequence, it does not always have one of polynomial length.

Theorem 3.3 (Lee and Yannakakis [LY94]). *There are machines with states that have UIO sequences, but only of exponential length.*

Proof. Consider n deterministic finite automata $A_1, \ldots, A_n$ over the alphabet $\{0\}$, such that the transitions of A_i form a cycle of length p_i, where p_i is the ith prime number. The only accepting state of A_i is the predecessor of the initial state. Thus A_i accepts 0^k if and only if $p_i \mid (k+1)$. This means that the shortest string accepted by all automata has length $m = \prod_{i=1}^{n} p_i - 1$. If there was a string of length $m' < m$, accepted by all automata, then for all $i \in \{1, \ldots, n\}$, we have $p_i \mid (m' + 1)$. Thus, by unique prime factorization, $m' + 1 = \prod_{i=1}^{n} p_i$, a contradiction.

Now note that $\prod_{i=1}^{n} p_i - 1 \geq 2^n$ is exponential in the total representation size of the automata, which is polynomial in n by Gauss' prime number theorem, and apply the reduction used in the proof of Theorem 3.2.1. The sequence $r0^m f$ will be the shortest UIO sequence for state s, since for any shorter string, the states of at least one automaton will produce an output of all zeroes.

3.3   Convergence and Inference Graphs

Since we saw in Section 3.2 that it is in general PSPACE-hard to determine whether a state has a UIO sequence, it is interesting to identify subclasses of machines and states, for which the question can be answered efficiently. Using the concept of *convergence*, first made explicit by Miller and Paul [MP93], Naik presents a number of results of this kind [Nai97], which are surveyed in this section.

Definition 3.4 (Convergence [MP93]). Let Mealy machine $\mathcal{M}$ have states $t_1, t_2, \ldots, t_k$ that all have edges to the state s with the same edge label a/b. Say that

- states $t_1, \ldots, t_k$ are *converging states*,
- state s is a *convergent state*,
- edges $(t_1, s), \ldots, (t_k, s)$ with label a/b are *converging edges*.

If a machine has some converging states it is a *converging machine*. Otherwise, the machine is *nonconverging*.

Using these concepts, Naik invented a way of using a UIO sequence for one state to infer sequences for other states. The basic construction used is the following.

Definition 3.5 (Inference Graph [Nai97]). Let G be the transition graph of a Mealy machine $\mathcal{M}$. The *inference graph* of $\mathcal{M}$ is the graph G_I, obtained from G by removing all converging edges.

Given graph G for machine $\mathcal{M}$, the inference graph G_I is computable in time $O(|E|^2)$, where E is the set of edges of G.

Figure 3.5 shows the inference graph for the machine in Figure 3.3. We see that the two edges (s_3, s_1) and (s_2, s_1) have been taken away. Since they both end in the same state and have the same label they are converging. The same is true for the edges (s_1, s_4) and (s_4, s_4).

The inference graph is used as follows.

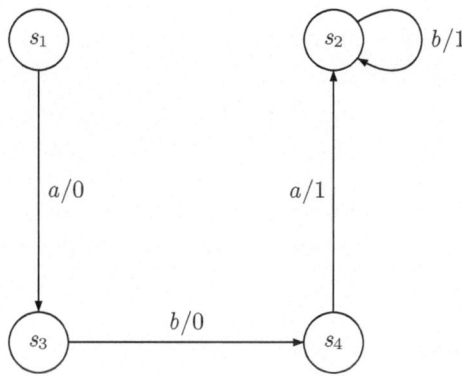

Fig. 3.5. The inference graph of the machine in Figure 3.3.

Proposition 3.6 (Inference [Nai97]). *Let G be the transition graph of a Mealy machine $\mathcal{M}$. If state s_i is reachable from state s_j in the inference graph G_I, and s_i has a UIO sequence, then s_j has a UIO sequence.*

Proof. Let x be a UIO sequence for state s_i, and x' the sequence of inputs along a path from s_j to s_i in G_I. The claim is that $x' \cdot x$ is a UIO sequence for s_j.[4] Suppose this is not the case, i.e., $\lambda(s_k, x' \cdot x) = \lambda(s_j, x' \cdot x)$ for some state $s_k \neq s_j$. We first show that the unique path with label x' from s_k must end in s_i. If it ended in some other state $s_l \neq s_i$, then $\lambda(s_l, x) = \lambda(s_i, x)$, since $\lambda(s_k, x' \cdot x) = \lambda(s_j, x' \cdot x)$, but this is impossible, since x is a UIO sequence for s_i.

Next, we show that in fact there can be no state $s_k \neq s_j$ such that $\lambda(s_k, x' \cdot x) = \lambda(s_j, x' \cdot x)$. Again assume that there is. Let $s_j = s_{j_1}, s_{j_2}, \ldots, s_{j_m} = s_i$ and $s_k = s_{k_1}, s_{k_2}, \ldots, s_{k_m} = s_i$ be the two paths with input label x' from s_j and s_k, respectively. Consider the smallest i such that s_{j_i} and s_{k_i} are identical. The edges from $s_{j_{i-1}}$ to s_{j_i} and from $s_{k_{i-1}}$ to s_{j_i} in G must have the same label and end up in the same state. Therefore, they are converging, and none of them belongs in the inference graph G_I. This means that s_i cannot be reachable from s_j along a path with input label x' and output label $\lambda(s_j, x')$ in G_I. This is a contradiction, and we conclude that $\lambda(s_j, x' \cdot x) \neq \lambda(s_k, x' \cdot x)$ for all $s_k \neq s_j$. Thus $x' \cdot x$ is a UIO sequence for s_j.

As an example, once we know that b is a UIO sequence for s_3 in the machine from Figure 3.3, we can use the inference graph in Figure 3.5 to conclude that ab must be a UIO sequence for state s_1.

The inference graph can also be used to obtain negative answers to the question whether a state has a UIO sequence.

---

[4] The dot operator for sequences $(X \cdot Y)$ denotes concatenation.

Proposition 3.7 ([Nai97]). *If G_I is the inference graph of Mealy machine $\mathcal{M}$, and state s does not have any outgoing edges in G_I, then s does not have a UIO sequence.*

Proof. In the transition graph G of $\mathcal{M}$, all outgoing edges from s must be converging, since none of them appear in G_I. This means that for every transition from s to some state t, there is another state $s' \neq s$ such that s' has a transition with the same label that also leads to t. Thus for any input sequence, there is some state other than s that produces the same output as s, so s cannot have a UIO sequence.

3.4   Algorithms

In Section 3.2 it was shown that the problem of determining whether a given state of a Mealy machine has a UIO sequence is PSPACE-complete. Thus there is presumably no efficient, polynomial time, algorithm for the general state verification problem. However, it turns out that in practice, it is solvable for many machines, and UIO sequences are used as parts of many conformance testing algorithms. In this section, algorithms for finding UIO sequences are discussed. The first two have exponential worst-case complexity, but work better in many practical applications. The third is a genetic algorithm, that is not always guaranteed to find all UIO sequences.

3.4.1   The Sabnani-Dahbura Algorithm

In 1988 Sabnani and Dahbura presented a test generation procedure for conformance testing [SD88]. It uses state verification, and includes a procedure for computing UIO sequences. For their purposes, it is enough to compute sequences of length at most $2n^2$, where n is the number of states, if they exist, but the procedure can be extended to compute longer sequences.

The basic idea when trying to find a UIO sequence for a given state s is to naively generate all input sequences, in order of ascending length. For each sequence x, the algorithm then computes $\lambda(s,x)$ and tests it for uniqueness, until a UIO sequence for s is found. The search space of all possible input-output sequences is thus examined in a breadth-first manner. Since the test generation procedure of Sabnani and Dahbura [SD88] is only interested in sequences of length at most $2n^2$, the search is terminated at this depth, even if a UIO sequence has not been found. If we are also interested in longer sequences, another upper bound, e.g., the $n \cdot 2^n$ from Section 3.2, must be supplied to ensure termination.

The algorithm searches the tree of all possible input-output sequences breadth first, without trying to take advantage of any structural properties of the machine under test.

Since the problem is PSPACE-complete, we cannot hope to solve the problem quickly in the general case. The algorithms are, however, intended for practical use, and therefore it seems like a good idea to analyze the input machine in order to take advantage of any particularities that can help us. The next algorithm we consider tries to do this.

3.4.2   Naik's Algorithm

Naik's algorithm for computing UIO sequences was presented in 1997 [Nai97], when the problem was already known to be PSPACE-complete [LY94]. The algorithm is complete, in the sense that it computes a UIO sequence for every vertex that has one, and always terminates. The basic idea is still to examine all possible input sequences, but it is augmented by a number of other ideas, including:

(1) Techniques for ensuring termination.
(2) Inference rules to extend a sequence for one state to sequences for other states.
(3) Heuristics that under some circumstances provide UIO sequences for some states in polynomial time.
(4) A modified depth-first search to find UIO sequences for some states.
(5) Techniques for shortening found sequences.

We will examine the first four items in this list.

Naik uses **UIO trees**, which are trees with edges labeled by input-output pairs, and nodes labeled by vectors that represent paths in the machine that exhibit the input-output behavior indicated by the edges from the root to the node.

Definition 3.8 (Path Vectors). Given a Mealy machine $\mathcal{M}$, a *path vector* is a vector of state pairs $PV = <s_1/s_1', \ldots, s_k/s_k'>$ satisfying the following. There is an input sequence x and an output sequence y such that $\lambda(s_i, x) = y$ and $\delta(s_i, x) = s_i'$ for every pair s_i/s_i' in PV. The vector $IV(PV) = <s_1, \ldots, s_k>$ consisting of the first components of the pairs in PV is called the *initial vector* of PV. The vector $CV(PV) = <s_1', \ldots, s_k'>$ consisting of the second components is called the *current vector*.

Given a Mealy machine $\mathcal{M} = (I, O, S, \delta, \lambda)$, its *IO tree* is an infinite tree in which every node has $|I| \cdot |O|$ children, one for each possible input-output pair in $\mathcal{M}$. The edges to the children are labeled by distinct input-output pairs. Thus the nodes of the tree correspond to every possible input-output sequence.

Definition 3.9 (Full UIO Tree). Let $\mathcal{M} = (I, O, S, \delta, \lambda)$ be a Mealy machine. The *full UIO tree* of $\mathcal{M}$ is a labeling of the IO tree by path vectors. The root of the tree is labeled by $<s_1/s_1, \ldots, s_n/s_n>$, where n is the number of states of $\mathcal{M}$. If a node in the tree is reachable from the root by a path labeled by input sequence x and output sequence y, and has label $PV = <s_1/s_1', \ldots, s_k/s_k'>$, then for every s_i/s_i' in PV, it must hold that $\lambda(s_i, x) = y$ and $\delta(s_i, x) = s_i'$. Furthermore, PV contains *all* pairs s_i/s_i' such that $\lambda(s_i, x) = y$ and $\delta(s_i, x) = s_i'$. Notice that some nodes may be labeled by empty path vectors.

It immediately follows that if a node, labeled by a singleton $<s/s'>$, is reachable from the root by a path labeled with input sequence x and output sequence y, then x is a UIO sequence for s. This is because s must be the only state that produces output y on input x. If we search the full UIO tree, looking for nodes labeled by singletons, we will eventually find a UIO sequences for every state that has one, but unless all states have UIO sequences, the search will never terminate.

Ensuring Termination. A vector $< s_1/s', s_2/s', \ldots, s_k/s' >$, where all the second components of the pairs are identical, is called *homogeneous*. In particular, any singleton path vector is homogeneous. If a node v in the UIO tree, reachable by a path labeled with input sequence x and output sequence y from the root, is labeled by a homogeneous vector PV, then there is no need to search the subtree rooted at v. If PV is a singleton, then a UIO sequence for the only vertex s such that $\lambda(s, x) = y$ has already been found. If, on the other hand, PV is not a singleton, then no extension of x can be a UIO sequence for any state of $\mathcal{M}$, since for all s such that $\lambda(s, x) = y$, the machine ends up in the same state after this sequence.

Also, if node v in the UIO tree is labeled by PV and on the path from the root to v, there is a node v' labeled by PV' such that $PV \subseteq PV'$, there is no need to search the subtree rooted at v. Suppose the path from the root to v' is labeled by the input sequence x', and the path from v' to v by x. Let s_1/s_1' and s_2/s_2' be two pairs that appear in PV, and suppose that $\lambda(s_1, x' \cdot x \cdot x'') \neq \lambda(s_2, x' \cdot x \cdot x'')$. Then $\lambda(s_1, x' \cdot x'') \neq \lambda(s_2, x' \cdot x'')$. In particular, if $x' \cdot x \cdot x''$ is a UIO sequence for s_1, then so is $x' \cdot x''$. Thus if s_1 has a UIO sequence with x' as a prefix, such a sequence can be found by searching the subtree rooted at v', without descending into the subtree rooted at v.

Call the label of node v in the full UIO tree a *repeated label* if a superset of the label appears in a node on the path from the root to v.

Any node in the full UIO tree with a homogeneous or repeated label is called *terminal*. Since it is now clear that there is no point in searching the subtrees rooted at terminal nodes, we may cut away all children of terminal nodes. We also remove all subtrees rooted at nodes with empty path vectors as labels. All vertices in such subtrees have empty labels. The result is called the *pruned UIO tree* of the machine. Note that the pruned UIO tree is finite, since there are only finitely many possible path vectors, and no path vector appears more than once on any path from the root. Figure 3.6 shows the pruned UIO tree for the machine in Figure 3.3.

If we search the pruned UIO tree for nodes labeled by singletons, we are still guaranteed to find a UIO sequence for every state that has one, and can also be sure that the search terminates.

To further improve efficiency, we can also define vertices labeled with path vectors such that *no state appears exactly once in the current vector* as terminal. It is clear that the input sequence labeling the path to such a vertex cannot be a prefix of a UIO sequence for any state.

The pruned UIO trees described here bear some resemblance to the splitting trees used to compute distinguishing sequences; see [LY96] and Chapter 2. The details of the two data structures are quite different, however. The UIO tree is labeled by a set of *pairs* of states, rather than a set of states. Thus it does

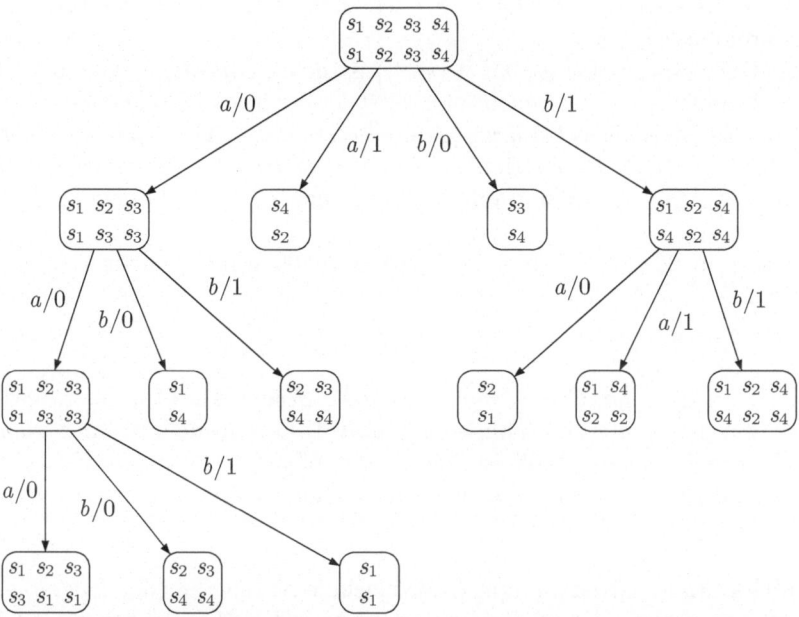

Fig. 3.6. The pruned UIO tree for the machine in Figure 3.3. Each node in the tree is labeled by the corresponding path vector. Path vectors are depicted with two lines, where the first is the initial vector, and the second is the current vector. For instance, it can be read from the figure that the input sequence ab gives output 01 for initial states s_2 and s_3. In both cases, it takes the machine to state s_4. The node that is reached from the root by following the path labeled $(a/0)(b/1)$ has a homogeneous path vector and is thus terminal. Therefore, it is a leaf in the tree.

not only keep track of the states for which a certain input-output sequence is consistent, but also the states the machine is taken to by the sequence. In each internal node, the UIO tree branches for *every input-output label* such that there is a state in the current vector of the node that has the label on one of its outgoing edges. The splitting tree, on the other hand, branches only on one input symbol per interior node, and splits the states in the node label according to their behavior on this input. This means that there are many different possible splitting trees, while the UIO tree is unique for each machine. The splitting tree is used to find adaptive distinguishing sequences. If such a sequence exists, there is always one of at most quadratic depth. Thus we never have to build very deep splitting trees. In fact it is enough to construct trees of total size $O(n^2)$; see Chapter 2. Since UIO trees are used to find UIO sequences, which may have superpolynomial length, we might have to build exponentially large trees.

Inference Rules. In many cases, it is possible to infer UIO sequences for one state, given a UIO sequence for some other state, as discussed in Section 3.3.

This sometimes makes it unnecessary to search the whole pruned UIO tree, which is still prohibitively big.

The basic observation is that if (s_i, s_j) is the only incoming edge to s_j with label a/b, and x is a UIO sequence for s_j, then $a \cdot x$ is a UIO sequence for s_i. An edge such as (s_i, s_j) is called a *unique predecessor edge*. The *inference graph* G_I of machine $\mathcal{M}$, defined in Section 3.3, can also be described as the edge-induced subgraph of $\mathcal{M}$'s transition graph G that is induced by all unique predecessor edges.

As seen in Section 3.3, if s_j is reachable in G_I from s_i, along a path with input labels x', and x is a UIO sequence for s_j, then $x' \cdot x$ is a UIO sequence for s_i.

Projection Graphs for Computing Initial UIO Sequences. In order to get any profits from the inference graph, some initial UIO sequences to infer from are needed. For this purpose, Naik uses the concept of *projection graphs*. If successful, this method produces some sequences in polynomial time. Otherwise, we must resort to searching the pruned UIO tree.

Definition 3.10. Given a graph G for machine $\mathcal{M}$, and an edge label a/b, the projection graph $G(a/b)$ of G with respect to a/b is the graph obtained from G by removing all edges that are not labeled by a/b.

Figure 3.7 shows the projection graph with respect to $a/0$ for the machine in Figure 3.3.

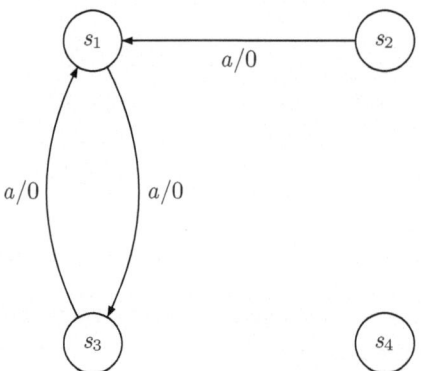

Fig. 3.7. The projection graph with respect to label $a/0$ for the machine from Figure 3.3.

Thus all edges in the projection graph $G(a/b)$ have the same label. If for some label a/b, the projection graph has only one edge (s_i, s_j), then trivially a is a UIO sequence for s_i.

Since the machine $\mathcal{M}$ is assumed to be deterministic, there is only one possible path from each state in $G(a/b)$. If this path ends in a sink it is called linear, otherwise it is cyclic.

Proposition 3.11 (Naik [Nai97]). *If the path from state s in $G(a/b)$ is linear and of length k, and no other state has a linear path of length $\geq k$, then s has a UIO sequence of length k or $k + 1$.*

Proof. Suppose that $G(a/b)$ has no cycles. If we apply input a^k to s, then the output produced will be b^k. This is not true for any other state, since all other paths in $G(a/b)$ have length smaller than k. Thus a^k is a UIO sequence of length k for s.

If, on the other hand, $G(a/b)$ has cycles, consider the input sequence a^{k+1}. Applied to states with cyclic paths in $G(a/b)$, it will produce output b^{k+1}. For s, the output produced will be $b^k b'$, for some output symbol b' different from b. For all other states, the output produced will have fewer than k initial copies of b. Thus a^{k+1} is a UIO sequence for s.

It is also easy to see from the first part of the above proof that if all paths in $G(a/b)$ are linear, then every vertex with a unique path length different from 0 has a UIO sequence.

Depth-First Search in the Pruned UIO Tree. Analysis of the projection graphs may not produce any UIO sequences at all, or it may, even when combined with the inference rules, not produce conclusive results for all states of the machine. In these cases, the pruned UIO tree must be searched. The search can be aborted as soon as UIO sequences have been found for all vertices except those that were found to have none during the analysis of the inference graph.

Every time a UIO sequence is found, the inference rules are applied to generate sequences for other states, and a check is made to determine whether the search must be continued.

In order to make maximal use of the inference rules, it is desirable to find at least some sequences as soon as possible. To achieve this, Naik suggests that the tree be searched depth first, rather than breadth first. This is because if all states have UIO sequences of approximately the same length, then the breadth-first search would go through more or less the whole pruned tree before finding even one sequence.

The problem with the depth first approach is that longer sequences may be found before shorter ones for the same state, and when using UIO sequences for conformance testing (see Chapter 4), it is desirable to find sequences that are as short as possible.

In order to at least partially get around this drawback, Naik suggests what he calls a hybrid search, which runs in the following way:

(1) Let ϕ be the root node of the pruned UIO tree.
(2) Visit every child of ϕ. If a child is terminal, mark it as such. If it represents a UIO sequence for some state, use the inference rules and determine whether the search can be terminated.

(3) If ϕ has at least one nonterminal child ϕ', let $\phi \leftarrow \phi'$ and restart from step 2. If ϕ has no nonterminal children that have not been searched, and ϕ is the root of the tree, then terminate. If ϕ has no nonterminal children that have not been searched but ϕ is not the root, then set $\phi \leftarrow parent(\phi)$ and restart from step 3.

In other words, the procedure looks one step ahead before deepening the search. Naik [Nai97] claims that this approach mostly solves the major problem with pure depth first search, that longer sequences are found before shorter sequences for the same state. While this is true in some cases, it somewhat overstates the merit of the method. For some machines, the procedure will still be likely to find long sequences before much shorter ones.

If we are only interested in relatively short sequences, like in the conformance testing algorithm by Sabnani and Dahbura discussed in Section 3.4.1 [SD88], the search depth of Naik's algorithm can of course be limited.

3.4.3   Genetic Algorithms

Guo, Hierons, Harman, and Derderian recently suggested the use of **genetic algorithms** to find UIO sequences [GHHD04]. The basic idea of genetic algorithms is to mimic the process of natural selection in nature. An algorithm keeps a collection of possible solutions to the problem at hand, called the *population*, and measures the quality of its members using a *fitness function*. The best individuals in the population are paired together using *recombination* to form the next generation. Random changes of individuals, called *mutations*, can also be applied to individuals. For a survey on the theory of genetic algorithms, see [Müh97].

In more detail, an individual is assumed to be a sequence of some kind, and all individuals are generally assumed to have the same length. To start computation, an initial population is generated randomly, and the fitness of each individual is computed using the fitness function. To form the next generation, two individuals are selected in some way that gives preference to high fitness values. The algorithm has a set value for crossover probability p. With this probability, the two parents are mixed to form an offspring. With probability $1 - p$, a copy of one of the parents are instead added to the next generation. This is repeated until the new population is full. According to some other probability distribution, each individual in the new generation is mutated, i.e., randomly changed. This is intended to prevent the process from getting stuck in local minima. The algorithm proceeds to create a preset number of further generation, and then returns the final population. Ideally, all individuals are then identical and represent an optimal solution to the problem.

In the approach of Guo et al. [GHHD04], the population is a set of input sequences, all of the same length. The idea is to use a fitness function that rewards sequences whose prefixes are the input components of UIO sequences for many states, while punishing unnecessarily long sequences. All sequences in the population are assumed to have the same length k. Given a sequence

$x = a_1 a_2 \ldots a_k \in I^*$, let u_i be the number of states for which $a_1 a_2 \ldots a_i$ is a UIO sequence ($u_0 = 0$). For $i \geq 1$, let $\Delta u_i = u_i - u_{i-1}$. Also, let v_i be the number of sets in the initial state uncertainty[5] for $a_1 a_2 \ldots a_i$ and $\Delta v_i = v_i - v_{i-1}$. Now, for each $i \in \{1, \ldots, k\}$ we define

$$f_i(a_1 \ldots a_i) = \alpha \frac{u_i e^{u_i + \Delta u_i}}{i^\gamma} + \beta \frac{v_i + \Delta v_i}{i}, \qquad (3.3)$$

where α, β, and γ are constants. It is clear that when the number of states a prefix uniquely identifies grows, the value of the prefix grows exponentially. On the other hand, an increase in length gives a polynomial reduction in value. The second term in the function definition rewards having many sets in the initial state uncertainty, even when not so many UIO sequences have been found yet. We can now define the fitness of a sequence as the average of the f_i-values of its prefixes:

$$f(a_1 \ldots a_k) = \frac{1}{k} \sum_{i=1}^{k} f_i(a_1 \ldots a_i). \qquad (3.4)$$

After creating an initial population randomly, Guo et al. suggest using roulette wheel selection to find the parents that are recombined. This means that each individual has a probability of being selected that is proportional to its fitness value. Further, uniform crossover is used, which means that in each position, the value for the offspring is selected with uniform probability from the values of the parents at the corresponding positions. In order for the population not to stagnate too quickly, Guo et al. suggest using wild-card characters in the strings representing sequences.

One drawback of the approach is that the length k of the sequences used must be set in advance, and the algorithm will not find UIO sequences of length $> k$.

Guo et al. only present tests of the algorithm on two small machines, with reportedly good results. It remains to be be seen in larger scale tests whether the method is practical.

3.5 Summary

State verification is the problem of verifying that a Mealy machine, placed in a black box, is in a specified state s. The state diagram of the machine is assumed to be known. The only way of doing this, short of opening the box, is to feed input to the machine, and study the output. Therefore, state verification for state s is only possible if there is an input sequence x such that the output produced by the machine when it is in state s and is given input x is unique, i.e., there is no other state that would produce the same output on input x. Such an input

---

[5] The initial state uncertainty of sequence x is a partitioning of the states in the machine such that if s and t belong to the same set, then $\lambda(s, x) = \lambda(t, x)$; see Chapter 1.

sequence is called a *unique input-output*, or UIO sequence. Thus the problem of state verification reduces to that of computing UIO sequences for the states to be verified.

Unfortunately, not all states of all Mealy machines have UIO sequences. However, they are frequent enough in many practical test settings to be a valuable tool in conformance testing of Mealy machines; see Chapter 4. Specifically, UIO sequences are more common than distinguishing sequences, either adaptive or preset; see Chapter 2.

Computing UIO sequences is a hard problem. In fact, even determining whether a given state has a UIO sequence is PSPACE-complete [LY94]. Thus there is most probably no polynomial time algorithm for computing the sequences. Also, some states have UIO sequences, but none of polynomial length [LY94], which is a problem in testing applications.

Still, some algorithms have been proposed and tried in practice. They have exponential worst case complexity, but use heuristics that allow efficient computations for many relevant problem instances. The most elaborate algorithm is that of Naik [Nai97]. It tries to compute sequences for some states quickly, and then use them to infer sequences for other states. Guo et al. suggest a genetic algorithm, where a fitness function is used to evaluate candidate sequences, which are then paired using crossover and mutated, for a certain number of generations [GHHD04].

The research field is still open for new algorithmic ideas and better analysis of performance on interesting subclasses of Mealy machines.

4 Conformance Testing

Angelo Gargantini

Dipartimento di Matematica e Informatica
University of Catania
gargantini@dmi.unict.it

4.1 Introduction

In this chapter we tackle the problem of **conformance testing** between finite
state machines. The problem can be briefly described as follows [LY96]. Given
a finite state machine M_S which acts as specification and for which we know
its transition diagram, and another finite state machine M_I which is the alleged implementation and for which we can only observe its behavior, we want
to test whether M_I correctly implements or *conforms* to M_S. The problem of
conformance testing is also called **fault detection**, because we are interested in
uncovering where M_I fails to implement M_S, or **machine verification** in the
circuits and switching systems literature.

We assume that the reader is familiar with the definitions given in Chapter
21, that we briefly report here. A finite state Mealy machine (FSM) is a quintuple
$M = \langle I, O, S, \delta, \lambda \rangle$ where I, O, and S are finite nonempty sets of *input symbols*,
output symbols, and *states*, respectively, $\delta : S \times I \rightarrow S$ is the *state transition
function*, $\lambda : S \times I \rightarrow O$ is the *output function*. When the machine M is a
current state s in S and receives an input a in I, it moves to the next state
$\delta(s, a)$ producing the output $\lambda(s, a)$. An FSM can be represented by a state
transition diagram as shown in Figure 4.1. $n = |S|$ denotes the number of states
and $p = |I|$ the number of inputs. An input sequence x is a sequence $a_1, a_2, \ldots, a_k$
of input symbols, that takes the machine successively to states $s_{i+1} = \delta(s_i, a_i)$,
$i = 1, \ldots, k$, with the final state s_{k+1} that we denote by $\delta(s_1, x)$. The input
sequence x produces the output sequence $\lambda(s_1, x) = b_1, \ldots, b_k$, where $b_k = \lambda(s_i, a_i)$, $i = 1, \ldots, k$. Given two input sequences x and y, $x.y$ is the input
sequence obtained by concatenating x with y.

The detection of faults in the implementation M_I can be performed by the
following experiment. Generate a set of input sequences from the machine M_S.
By applying each input sequence to M_S, generate the expected output sequences.
Each pair of input sequence and expected output sequence is a test and the set
of tests is a test suite (according to the definitions given in Chapter 20). Apply
each input sequence to M_I and observe the output sequence. Compare this actual
output sequence with the expected output sequence and if they differ, then a
fault has been detected. As well known, this procedure of testing, as it has been
presented so far, can only *be used to show the presence of bugs, but never to
show their absence*[1]. The goal of this chapter is to present some techniques and

---

[1] Dijkstra, of course

M. Broy et al. (Eds.): Model-Based Testing of Reactive Systems, LNCS 3472, pp. 87-111, 2005.
© Springer-Verlag Berlin Heidelberg 2005

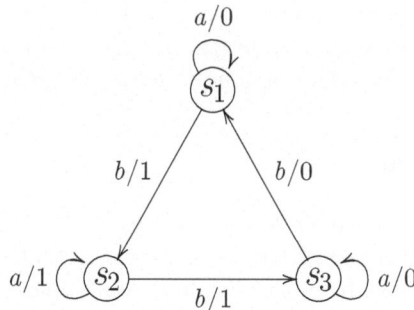

Fig. 4.1. Machine M_S [LY96]

algorithms able to detect faults of a well defined class, and to eventually prove, under some assumptions, that an implementation conforms to its specification. This chapter presents methods leaning toward the definition of ideal testing criteria as advocated in [GG75], i.e. test criteria that can discover any fault in the implementation (under suitable assumptions). Although this approach is rather theoretical, Section 4.8 presents the justifications for theoretical assumptions and the practical implications of the presented results.

Conformance is formally defined as equivalence or isomorphism (as defined in Chapter 21): M_I conforms to its specification M_S if and only if their initial states are equivalent, i.e. they will produce the same output for every input sequence. To prove this equivalence we look for a set of input sequences that we can apply to M_I to prove that it is equivalent to its specification. Note that successively applying each input sequence in the test set is equivalent to applying one input sequence that is obtained concatenating each input sequence in the set. Such an input sequence is called checking sequence.

Definition 4.1. (Checking sequence) A checking sequence for M_S is an input sequence that distinguishes the class of machines equivalent to M_S from all other machines.

Although all the presented methods share the unique goal to verify that M_I correctly implements M_S, generating a checking sequence (or a set of sequences, that concatenated act as a unique checking sequence), they differ for their cost to produce test sequences, for the total size of the test suite (i.e. the total length of the checking sequence), and for their fault detection capability. In fact, test suites should be rather short to be applicable in practice. On the other hand a test suite should cover the implementation as much as possible and detect as many faults as possible. The methods we present in this chapter differ with respect to the means and techniques they use to achieve these two opposite goals. However, the main difference among the methods we present regards the assumptions they make about the machines M_S and M_I. Some methods are very efficient to produce a checking sequence but usable only under very strong assumptions. Others produce exponentially long checking sequences, but perform the test under more general assumptions. Therefore, the choice of one method instead of another is driven more by the facts we know or assume about the machines M_S and M_I, and these assumptions are of great importance.

4.2   Assumptions

Developing a technique for conformance testing without any assumption is impossible, because for every conformance test one can build a faulty machine that would pass such test. We have to introduce some assumptions about the machines we want to verify. These first four assumptions are necessary for every method we present in this chapter.

(1) M_S is *reduced* or *minimal*: we have to assume that machines are reduced, because equivalent machines have the same I/O behavior, and it is impossible to distinguish them by observing the outputs, regardless the method we use to generate the checking sequence. If M_S it is not minimal, we can minimize it and obtain an equivalent reduced machine (algorithms can be found in literature [Moo56, LY96] as well as in Chapter 21). In a minimal machine there are no equivalent states. For every pair of states s and t, there exists an input sequence x, called *separating sequence*, that can distinguish s from t because the outputs produced by applying x to s and t, $\lambda(s, x)$ and $\lambda(t, x)$ differ (see Section 1.3).

(2) M_S is *completely specified*: the state transition function δ and the output function λ are total: they are defined for every state in S and every input in I.

(3) M_S is *strongly connected*: every state in the graph is reachable from every other state in the machine via one or more state transitions. Note that some methods require only that all states are reachable from the initial one, allowing machines with deadlocks or states without any exiting transition. However these methods must require a reset message (Assumption 7) that can take the machine back to its initial state, otherwise a deadlock may stop the test experiment. The reset message makes de facto the machine strongly connected.

(4) M_I does not change during testing. Moreover it has the same sets of inputs and outputs as M_S. This implies that M_I can accept and respond to all input symbols in I (if the input set of M_I is a subset of the input set of M_S, we could redefine conformance).

The four properties listed above are requirements. Without them a conformance test of the type to be discussed is not possible. Unlike the first four requirements, the following assumptions are convenient but not essential. Throughout this chapter we present methods that can successfully perform conformance testing even when these assumptions do not hold.

(5) *Initial state*: machines M_I and M_S have an initial state, and M_I is in its initial state before we conduct a conformance test experiment. If M_I is not

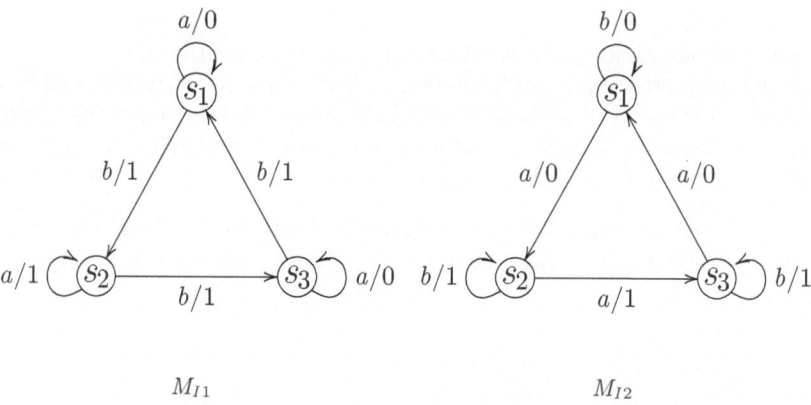

Fig. 4.2. Two faulty implementations of M_S

in its initial state we can apply a homing sequence (presented in Section 1.1.3) and then start the conformance test. If the machine M_I does not conform to its specification and the homing sequence fails to bring M_I to its initial state, this will be discovered during the conformance test. We denote the initial state by s_1.

(6) *Same number of states*: M_I has the same number of states as M_S, hence faults do not increase the number of states. Due to this assumption, the possible faults in M_I are of two kinds: *output faults*, i.e. a transition in the implementation produces the wrong output, and *transfer faults*, i.e. the implementation goes to a wrong state. Figure 4.2 shows two faulty implementations of the specification machine M_S given in Figure 4.1. Machine M_{I1} contains only one output fault for the transition from s_3 to s_1 with the input b: the output produced by M_{I1} is 1 instead of 0. Machine M_{I2} has several transfer faults: every transition moves the machine to a wrong final state. Moreover the transitions in M_{I2} from state s_3 and s_1 with input b produce wrong outputs.

Although this assumption is very strong, we show in Section 4.7 that many methods we present work well with modifications under the more general assumption that the number of states of M_I is bounded by an integer m, which may be larger than the number of states n in M_S.

(7) *reset* message: M_I and M_S have a particular input *reset* (or briefly r) that from any state of the machine causes a transition which ends in the initial state s_1 and produces no output. Formally, for all $s \in S$, $\delta(s, reset) = s_1$ and $\lambda(s, reset) = -$. Starting from Section 4.5 we present some methods that do not need a *reset* message.

(8) *status* message: M_I and M_S have a particular input *status* and they respond to a *status* message with an output message that uniquely identifies their current state. Since we label the states $s_1, s_2, ..., s_n$, we assume that *status* outputs the index i when applied to state s_i. The machines do not change

state. Formally for all $s_i \in S$, $\lambda(s_i, status) = i$ and $\delta(s_i, status) = s_i$. This rather strong assumption is relaxed starting from Section 4.4.

(9) *set* message: the input set I contains a particular set of inputs $set(s_j)$ and when a $set(s_j)$ message is received in the initial system state, the machines move to state s_j without producing any output. Formally for all $t \in S$, $\delta(reset, set(t)) = t$ and $\lambda(s, set(t)) = -$.

Given a machine with all the properties listed above, a simple conformance test can be performed as described by the simple Algorithm 9 (Chapter 9 of [Hol91]).

Algorithm 9 Conformance testing with a *set* message

For all $s \in S$, $a \in I$:

(1) Apply a *reset* message to bring the M_I to the initial state.
(2) Apply a *set(s)* message to transfer M_I to state s.
(3) Apply the input message a.
(4) Verify that the output received conforms to the specification M_S, i.e. is equal to $\lambda_S(s, a)$
(5) Apply the *status* message and verify that the final state conforms to the specification, i.e. it is equal to $\delta_S(s, a)$

This algorithm verifies that M_I correctly implements M_S and it is capable to uncover any output or transfer fault. An output fault would be detected by step 4 while a transfer fault would be uncovered by step 5. Note that should the set of input signals I to be tested include the *set*, *reset*, and *status* messages, the algorithm must test also these messages. To test the *status* message we should apply it twice in every state s_i after the application of $set(s_i)$. The first application, given in step 3, is to check that in s_i the *status* message correctly outputs i (if also *set* is faulty and sets the current state to s_j instead of s_i and the *status* message in s_j has the wrong output i, we would discover this fault when testing s_j). The second application of *status*, given by step 5, is to check that the first application of *status* did not change the state. Indeed, if the first application of *status* in s_i did change the state to s_j and in s_j *status* is wrongly implemented and outputs i instead of j, we would discover this fault when testing s_j. Once that we are sure that *status* is correctly implemented, we can test *set* and *reset* applying them in every state and then applying *status* to check that they take the machine to the correct state.

Note that the resulting checking sequence obtained by Algorithm 9 is equal to the concatenation of the sequence *reset*, *set(s)*, *a*, and *status*, repeated for every s in S and every a in I. The length of the resulting checking sequence is exactly $4 \cdot p \cdot n$ where $p = |I|$ is the number of inputs and $n = |S|$ is the number of states.

The main weakness of Algorithm 9 is that it needs the *set* message, which may be not available. To avoid the use of *set* and to possibly shorten the test suite, we can build a sequence that traverses the machine and visits every state and every transition at least once without restarting from the initial state after every test and without using a *set* message. Such sequence is called *transition tour*. Formally

Definition 4.2. An input sequence $x = a_1 a_2 \ldots a_n$ that takes the machine to the states $s_1, s_2, \ldots, s_n$ such that for all $s \in S$ there exists j such that $s_j = s$ (x visits every state) and such that for all $b \in I$ and for all $s \in S$ there exists j such that $a_j = b$ and $s_j = s$ (every input b is applied to each s), is a **transition tour**.

In the next section we present some basic techniques for the generation and use of transition tours for conformance testing that does not assume anymore the existence of a *set* message, i.e. relaxing Assumption 9.

4.3   State and Transition Coverage

By applying the *transition tour* (TT) *method*, the checking sequence is obtained from a transition tour, by adding a *status* message, that we assume reliable, after every input. Formally if $x = a_1 a_2 \ldots a_n$ is a transition tour, the input sequence is equal to $a_1 \, status \, a_2 status \ldots a_n \, status$. This is a checking sequence. Indeed, since every state is checked with its *status* message after every transition, this input sequence can discover any transfer fault. Furthermore, every output fault is uncovered because every transition is tested (by applying the input a_j) and its output observed explicitly.

At best this checking sequence starts with a reset and exercises every transition exactly once followed by a *status* message. The length of such sequence is always greater than $2 \cdot p \cdot n$. The shortest transition tour that visits each transition exactly once is called **Euler tour**. Since we assume that the machine is strongly connected (Assumption 3), a sufficient condition for the existence of an Euler tour is that the FSM is *symmetric*, i.e. every state is the start state and end state of the same number of transitions. In this case, an Euler tour can be found in a time that is linear in the number of transitions, pn [EJ73]. This is a classical result of the graph theory and algorithms for generating an Euler tour can be found in an introductory book about graphs [LP81] and in the Chapter 9 of [Hol91]. In non symmetric FSMs searching the shortest tour is another classical direct graph problem, known as the *Chinese Postman Problem*, that can be solved in polynomial time. It was originally introduced by a Chinese mathematician [Kwa62] and there exist several classical solutions [EJ73] for it.

Example. For the machine in Fig. 4.1 the following checking sequence is obtained from the transition tour *bababa* (that is, more precisely, an Euler tour).

checking sequence	b	status	a	status	b	status	a	status	b	status	a	status
start state	1	2	2	2	2	3	3	3	3	1	1	1
output	1	*2*	1	*2*	1	*3*	0	*3*	0	*1*	0	*1*
end state	2	2	2	2	3	3	3	3	1	1	1	1

This checking sequence is able to detect the faults in the machines shown in Figure 4.2. The fault in M_{I1} is detected by the application of a b message in state s_3, while the faults in M_{I2} are immediately detected by the first *status* message.

If the *status* message is unreliable, we have to test it too. Assume that the *status* message may produce a wrong output or it may erroneously change the machine state. Both faults are detected by applying a *status* message twice in every state, the first one to test that the previous message has taken the machine to the correct state and to check that *status* message produces the correct output and the second one to verify that the first *status* message did not change the state of the machine.

Note the TT method was originally proposed without using a *status* message [NT81]. In this case the TT methods achieves only *transition coverage*. A test that visits only all the states, but not necessarily all the transitions, is often called *state tour* (ST) *method* [SMIM89] and achieves only *state coverage*. The coverage of every transition and the use of a *status* message are needed to discover every fault. Indeed, simply generating input sequences covering all the edges of M_S and test whether M_I produces the same outputs is not enough, as demonstrated by the following example.

Example. Consider the machines in Figure 4.2 as alleged equivalent machines to M_S in Figure 4.1. The sequence *ababab* is an Euler tour. Applying this tour to M_{I1} without using the *status* message, we would discover the output fault of the transition from s_3 to s_1: M_{I1} produces the output sequence 011101 instead of 011100. However, if we apply this Euler tour to M_{I2}, we do not discover the faults: M_{I2} produces the output sequence 011100, identical to the expected output sequence produced by M_S. However M_{I2} is a faulty implementation of M_S as demonstrated by another tour, namely *bababa*. This demonstrates that transition coverage is not capable to detect all the faults, in particular, to detect transfer faults.

Unfortunately, a *status* message is seldom available. In the next section we learn how not to rely on a *status* message to determine the current state during a test.

4.4 Using Separating Sequences Instead of Status Messages

We assume now that the machines have no *status* message (but they still have a *reset* message), and we wish to test whether M_S is equivalent to M_I only observing the external behavior. In the following we present some methods that can be unified as proposed by Lee and Yannakakis [LY96]. All these methods share the same technique to identify a state: they replace the use of the *status* message with several kinds of sequences that we can generally call *separating sequences* [LY96] and that are able to identify the state to which they have been applied. Remember that, since M_S is minimal, it does not contain two equivalent states, i.e. for every pair of states s_i, s_j there exists an input sequence x that we call separating sequence and that distinguishes them because produces different outputs, i.e. $\lambda(s_i, x) \neq \lambda(s_j, x)$. Section 1.3 presents a classical algorithm to compute a separating sequence for two states.

4.4.1   W Method

The W method [Cho78] uses a particular set of separating sequences that is called characterizing set and another set to visit each transition in the machine, that is called *transition cover set* or *P set* for short, and is defined as follows.

Definition 4.3. (Transition Cover Set) the transition cover set of M_S is a set P of input sequences such that for each state $s \in S$ and each input $a \in I$ there exists an input sequence $x \in P$ starting from the initial state s_1 and ending with the transition that applies a to state s. Formally for all $s \in S$ and for all $a \in I$ there exist an input sequence $x \in P$ and an input sequence $y \in P$ such that $x = y.a$ and $\delta(s_1, y) = s$.

A P set forces the machine to perform every transition and then stop. A P set can be built by using a normal breadth-first visit of the transition diagram of the machine M_S. Note that a P set is closed under the operation of selecting a prefix: if x belongs to P, then any prefix of x is in P too. One way of constructing P [Cho78] is to build first a testing tree T of M_S as explained in Algorithm 10 and then to take the input sequences obtained from all the *partial paths* of T. A partial path of T is a sequence of consecutive branches, starting from the root of T and ending in a terminal or non terminal node. Since every branch in T is labeled by an input symbol, the input sequence obtained from a partial path q is the sequence of input symbols on q. The empty input sequence ε is considered to be part of any P set. Note that Algorithm 10 terminates because the number of states is finite.

Algorithm 10 Building a test tree

---

(1) Label the root of the tree T with s_1, the initial state of M_S. This is the level 1 of T

(2) Suppose that we have already built the tree T up to the level k. Now we build the $k + 1$st level.

    (a) consider every node t at level k from left to right

    (b) if the node t is equal to another node in T at level j, with $j \leqslant k$, then t is terminated and must be considered a leaf of T

    (c) otherwise, let s_i be the label of the node t. For every input x, if the machine M_S goes from state s_i to state s_j, we attach to t a branch with label x and a successor node with label s_j

---

Example. A test tree for M_S of Fig. 4.1 is shown in Fig. 4.3. From this test tree we obtain $P = \{\varepsilon, a, b, ba, bb, bba, bbb\}$.

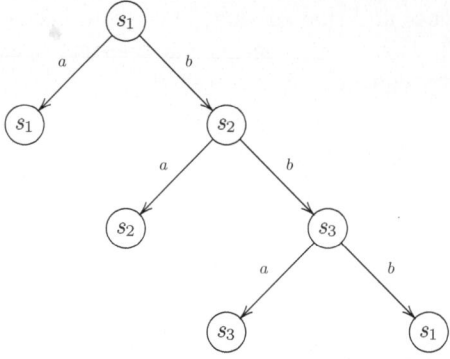

Fig. 4.3. A test tree for M_S of Figure 4.1

The W method uses a P set to test every transition of M_I and uses another set, called *characterizing set* of M_S or W set, instead of the *status* message, to verify that the end state of each transition is the one expected. A characterizing set is defined as follows.

Definition 4.4. (**Characterizing Set**) a characterizing set of M_S is a set W of input sequences such that for every pair of distinct states s and t in S, there exists an input sequence x in W such that $\lambda(s,x) \neq \lambda(t,x)$

The characterizing set is briefly called W set or sometimes *separating set*. The input sequences in the W set are also called *separating sequences*. A W set exists for every machine that is minimal (Assumption 1). The choice of a W set is not unique and the fewer are the elements in the W set the longer are the separating sequences in the W set. An algorithm for building a W set follows.

Partition the set of states S into blocks B_i with $i = 1, \ldots, r$. Initially W is $\emptyset$, $B_1 = S$ and $r = 1$. Until every B_i is a singleton, take two distinct states s and t in a B_i (that contains at least two states) and build their separating sequence x by means of the algorithm presented in Section 1.3. Add x to W and partition the states s_{ik} in every B_j into smaller blocks $B_{j1}, \ldots, B_{jh}$ based on their different output $\lambda(s_{ik}, x)$. Repeat the process until each B_i becomes a singleton and r becomes n. For every pair of states s_i and s_j, the resulting W set contains an input sequence x that separates s_i from s_j. Note that there are no more than $n - 1$ partition and therefore W set has no more than $n - 1$ separating sequences.

The W method consists in using the entire W set instead of the *status* message to test that the end state of each transition is the one expected. Since W may contain several sequences, we have to visit the same end state of every transition several times to apply all the separating sequences in a W set and for this goal we can use a *reset* message and the sequences in a P set. The set of input sequences is simply obtained concatenating every input sequence in a P set with every input sequences in a W set and apply them in order after a reset message to take the machine back to the initial state. In this way each input sequence p_{ij}

is the concatenation of the i-th sequence of a P set (to test the i-th transition) with the j-th sequence of a W set, with an initial *reset* input.

Formally, given two sets of input sequences X and Y, we denote with $X.Y$ the set of input sequences obtained concatenating all the input sequences of X with all the input sequences of Y. The set of input sequences produced by the W method is equal to $\{reset\}.P.W$.

If we do not observe any fault, the implementation is proved to be correct [Cho78]. Indeed, any output fault is detected by the application of a sequence of P, while any transfer fault is detected by the application of W.

Example. For the machine in Fig. 4.1 a characterizing set W is $\{a,b\}$ (equal to the input set I). In fact we have:

For state s_1, transitions $a/0$ $b/1$
For state s_2, transitions $a/1$ $b/1$
For state s_3, transitions $a/0$ $b/0$
a distinguishes s_1 from s_2 and s_3 from s_2. b distinguishes s_1 from s_3.
$P = \{\varepsilon,\ a,\ b,\ ba,\ bb,\ bba,\ bbb\}$

The set of test sequences $P.W$ is reported in the following table, where we indicate with r the *reset* message.

P	ε		a		b		ba		bb		bba		bbb	
r.P.W	ra	rb	raa	rab	rba	rbb	$rbaa$	$rbab$	rbb	$rbbb$	$rbbaa$	$rbbab$	$rbbba$	$rbbbb$
trans. to test	$s_1 \xrightarrow{\varepsilon}$		$s_1 \xrightarrow{a/0} s_1$		$s_1 \xrightarrow{b/1} s_2$		$s_2 \xrightarrow{a/1} s_2$		$s_2 \xrightarrow{b/1} s_3$		$s_3 \xrightarrow{a/0} s_3$		$s_3 \xrightarrow{b/0} s_1$	
output	0	1	00	11	11	11	111	111	110	110	1100	1100	1100	1101

The total length of the checking sequence is 52.

The fault in machine M_{S1} of Figure 4.2 is detected by the input sequence $rbbb$, while the transfer faults in machine M_{S2} are detected by the pair of input sequences that tests the end state of the transition: for example the fact that the transition from s_1 with input a erroneously moves the machine to s_2 is detected by the input sequences raa and rab.

4.4.2   Wp Method

The partial W or Wp method [FvBK$^+$91] has the main advantage of reducing the length of the test suite with respect to the W method. This is the first method we present that splits the conformance test in two phases. During the first phase we test that every state defined in M_S also exists in M_I, while during the second phase we check that all the transitions (not already checked during the first phase) are correctly implemented.

For the first phase, the Wp method uses a *state cover set* instead of a transition cover set. The state cover set or Q *set*, for short, covers only the states, is smaller than the transition cover set, and it is defined as follows.

Definition 4.5. (State Cover Set) the state cover set is a set Q of input sequences such that for each $s \in S$, there exists an input sequence $x \in Q$ that takes the machine to s, i.e. $\delta(s_1, x) = s$

Using a Q set we can take the machine to every state. A Q set can be built using a breadth first visit of the transition graph of M_S. For the second phase, the Wp method uses an *identification set* W_i for state s_i instead of a unique characterizing set W for all the states. W_i is a subset of W and is defined as follows.

Definition 4.6. (Identification Set) an identification set of state s_i is a set W_i of input sequences such that for each state s_j in S (with $i \neq j$) there exists an input sequence x of W_i such that $\lambda(s_i, x) \neq \lambda(s_j, x)$ and no subset of W_i has this property.

Note that the union of all the identification sets W_i is a characterizing set W.

Wp Method Phase 1 The input sequences for phase one consist in the concatenation of a Q set with a characterizing set (W set) after a reset. Formally, the set of input sequences is $\{reset\}.Q.W$. In this way every state is checked in the implementation with a W set.

We say that a state q_i in M_I is *similar* to state s_i if it produces the same outputs on all the sequences in a W set. A state q_i in M_I can be similar to at most one state of M_S, because if we suppose that q_i is similar to states s_i and s_j then s_i and s_j produce the same output for each sequence in a W set, that is against Definition 4.4. We say that the machine M_I is *similar* to M_S if for every state s_i of M_S, the machine M_I has a state similar to s_i. If M_I is similar, since it has n states (Assumption 6), then there exists a one-to-one correspondence between similar states of M_S and M_I.

If the input sequences do not uncover any fault during the first phase, we can conclude that every state in M_S has a similar state in the implementation and we can say that M_I is similar to M_S. Note that is not sufficient to verify that it is also equivalent. The equivalence proof is obtained by the next phase.

Wp Method Phase 2 The second phase tests all the transitions. To this aim, Wp method uses the identification sets. For every transition from state s_j to state s_i on input a, we apply a sequence x (after a *reset* message) that takes the machine to the state s_j along transitions already verified, then we apply the input a, which takes the machine to s_i and we apply one identification sequence of W_i. We repeat this test for every identification sequence in W_i and if these tests do not uncover any fault, we have verified that the transition in the machine M_I from a state that is similar to s_j on input a produces the right output (there is no output fault) and goes to a state that is similar to s_i (there is no transfer fault). By applying these tests to every transition, we can verify that M_I conforms to its specification.

The set of input sequences that covers every transition (and that is closed under the operation of selecting a prefix) is a P set. Therefore, the input sequences of phase 2 consist of the sequences of a P set ending in state s_i that are not contained in the Q set used during phase 1, concatenated with all the sequences contained in the identification set W_i. Formally if $R = P - Q$ and x_i in R ends in s_i, the set of sequences applied during the second phase is $\{reset\}.R.W_i$.

A complete formal proof of correctness for the Wp method is given in the paper that introduced the Wp method [FvBK+91].

Example. The machine in Fig. 4.1 has the following state cover set $Q = \{\varepsilon, b, bb\}$.

During the first phase we generate the following test sequences:

state to test	1		2		3	
Q	ε		b		bb	
r.Q.W	ra	rb	rba	rbb	$rbba$	$rbbb$
output	0	1	11	11	110	110

During the second phase, we first compute the identification sets.
$W_1 = \{a,b\}$ all the sequences in W are needed to identify s_1
$W_2 = \{a\}$ distinguishes the state s_2 from all other states
$W_3 = \{b\}$ distinguishes the state s_3 from all other states
$R = P - Q = \{ a, ba, bba, bbb\}$

R	a	ba	bba	bbb	
start state	1	2	3	1	1
r.R.Wi	raa	rab	$rbaa$	$rbbab$	$rbbba$	$rbbbb$
output	00	01	111	1100	1100	1101
end state	1	2	2	1	1	2

The total length of the checking sequence is 44 (note that Wp method yields a smaller test suite than the W method).

The output fault in machine M_{I1} of Figure 4.2 is detected during the first phase again by the input sequence $rbbb$. Some transfer faults in machine M_{I2} are detected during the first phase, while others, like the transfer fault from state s_3 with input a is detected only by the input sequences $rbbab$ during phase 2.

4.4.3   UIO Methods

If a W_i set contains only one sequence, this sequence is called *state signature* [YL91] or *unique input/output* (UIO) sequence [SD88] , that is unique for the state s_i. UIO sequences are extensively studied in Chapter 3 for state verification. Remember that applying a UIO sequence we can distinguish state s_i from any other state, because the output produced applying a UIO sequence is specific to s_i. In this way a UIO sequence can determine the state of a machine before its application. A UIO sequence has the opposite role of a homing sequence or a synchronizing sequence, presented in Chapter 1: it identifies the first state in the sequence instead of the last one. Note that not every state of a FSM has UIOs and algorithms to check if a state has a UIO sequence and to derive UIOs provided that they exist, can be found in Chapter 3. If an UIO sequence exists for every state s_i, then UIOs can be used to identify each state in the machine; in this case the UIO sequence acts as *status* message, except it moves the machine to another state.

The original UIO method [SD88] builds a set of input sequences that visit every transition from s_i to s_j by applying a transition cover set P and then check the end state s_j by applying its UIO sequence. In this case the UIO sequence is used instead of a *status* message.

Although used in practice, the UIO method does not guarantee to discover every fault in the implementation [VCI90] because the uniqueness of the UIO sequences may not hold in a faulty implementation. A faulty implementation may contain a state s' that has the same UIO as another state s (because of some faults) and a faulty transition ending in s' instead of s may be tested as correct. Note that for this reason the Wp method uses the W_i sets only in the second phase, while in the first phase it applies the complete W instead.

A modified version of the UIO method, called UIOv, generates correct checking sequences [VCI90]. The UIOv method builds the test suite in three phases:

(1) *Uv process*: for every state s in M_S, apply an input sequence x that begins with a *reset* and reaches s and then apply the UIO sequence of s. To reach each state use a Q set. The set of input sequences consist of the concatenation of Q with the UIO sequence of the final state of the sequence in Q with an initial *reset*.

(2) $\neg Uv$ *process*: visit every state s and apply the input part of the UIO sequences of all other states and check that the obtained output differs from the output part of the UIO sequence applied. Skip UIO sequences that have the input part equal to a prefix α of the input part of the UIO sequence of s. Indeed, in this case, we have already applied α during the Uv process and we know that the output differs, because two states cannot have the same input and output part of their UIO sequences. At the end of Uv and $\neg Uv$ process we have verified that M_I is similar to M_S.

(3) *Transition test phase*: check that every transition not already verified in 1 and 2 produces the right output and ends in the right state by applying its UIO sequence.

Note that the UIOv method can be considered as a special case of Wp method, where the W set is the union of all the UIO sequences and phase 1 of the Wp method includes both Uv process and $\neg Uv$ process and phase 2 is the transition test phase.

Example. For the machine in Fig. 4.1 the UIO sequences are:

$UIO_1 = ab/01$ distinguishes the state s_1 from all other states
$UIO_2 = a/1$ distinguishes the state s_2 from all other states
$UIO_3 = b/0$ distinguishes the state s_3 from all other states

1. *Uv* process

Q	ε	b	bb
state to test	1	2	3
r.Q.UIO	*rab*	*rba*	*rbbb*
output	01	11	110

2. $\neg Uv$ process

state to test	1	2		3	
r.Q.¬UIO	rb	$rbab$	rbb	$rbbab$	$rbba$
output	1	111	11	1100	110

3. Transition test phase:

transition to test	$s_1 \xrightarrow{a/0} s_1$	$s_2 \xrightarrow{a/1} s_2$	$s_3 \xrightarrow{b/0} s_1$	$s_3 \xrightarrow{a/0} s_3$
input sequence	$raab$	$rbaa$	$rbbbab$	$rbbab$
output	001	111	11001	1100

The output fault of machine M_{I1} of Figure 4.2 is detected during the Uv process again by the input sequence $rbbb$. Some transfer faults in machine M_{I2} are detected during the first phases, while others, like the transfer fault from state s_3 with input a is detected only by the input sequences $rbbab$ during the transition test phase.

4.4.4   Distinguishing Sequence Method

In case we can find one sequence that can be used as UIO sequence for every state, we call such sequence **distinguishing sequence** (DS) (defined and extensively studied in Chapter 2). In this situation we can apply the DS method using the *reset* message [SL89]. Note that this DS method can be viewed as a particular case of the W method when the characterizing set W contains only a preset distinguishing sequence x. The test sequences are simply obtained combining a P set with x.

Example. For the machine in Fig. 4.1 we can take the sequence $x = ab$ as a preset distinguishing sequence. In fact

$\lambda_{Ms}(s_1, x) = 01$
$\lambda_{Ms}(s_2, x) = 11$
$\lambda_{Ms}(s_3, x) = 00$

P	ε	a	b	ba	bb	bba	bbb
r.P.x	rab	$raab$	$rbab$	$rbaab$	$rbbab$	$rbbaab$	$rbbbab$
trans. to test	$s_1 \xrightarrow{\varepsilon} s_1$	$s_1 \xrightarrow{a/0} s_1$	$s_1 \xrightarrow{b/1} s_2$	$s_2 \xrightarrow{a/1} s_2$	$s_2 \xrightarrow{b/1} s_3$	$s_3 \xrightarrow{a/0} s_3$	$s_3 \xrightarrow{b/0} s_1$
output	01	001	111	1111	1100	11000	11001

4.4.5   Cost and Length

All the methods presented in Section 4.4 share the same considerations about the length of the checking sequence and the cost of producing it. For the W method, the cost to compute a W set is $\mathcal{O}(pn^2)$ and a W set contains no more than $n-1$ sequences of length no more than n. The cost to build the tree T set using the Algorithm 10 is $\mathcal{O}(pn)$ and its maximum level is n. The generation of a P set, by visiting T, takes time $\mathcal{O}(pn^2)$ and produces up to pn sequences with the maximum length n. Since we have to concatenate each transition from in a P set with each transition in a W set, we obtain up to pn^2 sequences of length $n + n$, for a total length of $\mathcal{O}(pn^3)$ and a total cost of $\mathcal{O}(pn^3)$. The Wp method has the same total cost $\mathcal{O}(pn^3)$ and same length $\mathcal{O}(pn^3)$. Experimental results [FvBK$^+$91] show that checking sequences produced by the Wp method are generally shorter than the checking sequences produced by the W method.

The UIO method and the method using a preset distinguishing sequence are more expensive, because determining if a state has UIO sequences or a preset distinguishing sequence was proved to be PSPACE hard (as shown in Sections 3.2 and 2.3). Note that in practice UIO sequences are more common than distinguishing sequences (as explained in Chapter 3). However, as shown in Section 2.4, finding an *adaptive* distinguishing sequences has cost $\mathcal{O}(n^2)$ and adaptive distinguishing sequences have maximum length n^2. We can modify the method of Section 4.4.4 by using adaptive distinguishing sequences instead of preset distinguishing sequences. Because there are pn transitions, the total length for the checking sequence is again pn^3.

There are specification machines with a *reset* message, that require checking sequences of length $\Omega(pn^3)$ [Vas73].

4.5   Using Distinguishing Sequences Without Reset

If the machine M_S has no *reset* message, the reset message can be substituted by a *homing sequence,* already introduced in Section 1.1.3. However this can lead to very long test suites and it is seldom used in practice.

On the other hand, since methods like UIO (Section 4.4.3) and DS (Section 4.4.4) require the application of a single input sequence for each state, instead of a set of separating sequences as in W and Wp methods, they can be easily optimized for the use without *reset,* using instead a unique checking sequence similar to a transition tour. These methods can substitute the transition tour method when a *status* message is not available and they are often used in practice. The optimized version of the UIO method without *reset* is presented by Aho et al. [ADLU91], while the optimized version of the DS method [Hen64] without *reset* is presented in this section. Some tools presented in Chapter 14 are based on these methods.

To visit the next state to be verified we can use transfer sequences, that are defined as follows.

Definition 4.7. (Transfer Sequence) A transfer sequence $\tau(s_i, s_j)$ is a sequence that takes the machine from state s_i to s_j

Such a transfer sequence exists for each pair of states, since M_S is strongly connected (by Assumption 3) and cannot be longer than $n-1$. Moreover, if the machine has a distinguishing sequence x, this sequence can be used as unreliable *status* message because it gives a different output for each state. It is like a *status* message, except that it moves the machine to another state when applied.

The method presented in this section has, as many methods presented in the previous section, two phases. It first builds an input sequence that visits each state using transfer sequences instead of reset and then applies its distinguishing sequence to test whether M_I is similar to M_S. It then builds an input sequence to test each transition to guarantee that M_I conforms to M_S.

Phase 1 Let t_i be the final state when applying the distinguishing sequence x to the machine from state s_i, i.e. $t_i = \delta(s_i, x)$ and $\tau(t_i, s_{i+1})$ the transfer sequence from t_i to s_{i+1}. For the machine in the initial state s_1, the following input sequence checks the response to the distinguishing sequence in each state.

$$x\,\tau(t_1, s_2)\,x\,\tau(t_2, s_3)\,x\,\ldots\,\tau(t_n, s_1)\,x \tag{4.1}$$

This sequence can be depicted as follows.

Starting from s_1 the first application of the distinguishing sequence x tests s_1 and takes the machine to t_1, then the transfer sequence τ_1 takes the machine to s_2 and the second application of x tests this state and so on till the end of of the state tour. At the end, if we observe the expected outputs, we have proved that every state of M_S has a similar state in M_I, since we have tested that every state in M_I correctly responds to its distinguishing sequence.

Phase 2 In the second phase, we want to test every transition. To test a transition from s_i to s_j with input a we can take the machine to s_i, apply a, observe the output, and verify that the machine is in s_j by applying x. Assuming that the machine is in state t, to take the machine to s_i we cannot use $\tau(t, s_i)$ because faults may alter the final state of $\tau(t, s_i)$. Therefore, we cannot go directly from t to s_i. On the other hand, we have already verified by (4.1) that $x\tau(t_{i-1}, s_i)$ takes the machine from s_{i-1} to s_i. We can build an input sequence that takes the machine to s_{i-1}, verifies that the machine is in s_{i-1} applying x and moves to s_i using $\tau(t_{i-1}, s_i)$, then applies a, observes the right output, and verifies that the end state is s_j by applying again the distinguishing sequence x:

$$\tau(t, s_{i-1})x\tau(t_{i-1}, s_i)ax \tag{4.2}$$

$$- - \twoheadrightarrow \boxed{t} \xrightarrow{(t,s_{i-1})} \boxed{s_{i-1}} \xrightarrow{x\tau\tau_{i-1},s} \boxed{s_i} \xrightarrow{a} \boxed{s_j} \xrightarrow{x} \boxed{t_j}$$

Therefore, the sequence (4.2) tests the transition with input a from state s_i to s_j and moves the machine to t_j. We repeat the same process for each transition to obtain a complete checking sequence.

Example. A distinguishing sequence for the machine in Fig. 4.1 is $x = ab$ and the corresponding responses from state s_1, s_2, and s_3 are: 01 11, and 00 respectively. The distinguishing sequence, when applied in states s_1, s_2, and s_3 takes the machine respectively to $t_1 = s_2$, $t_2 = s_3$ and $t_3 = s_1$. the transfer sequences are $\tau(t_1, s_2) = \tau(t_2, s_3) = \tau(t_3, s_1) = \varepsilon$.

The sequence (4.1) becomes

	x	$\tau(t_1, s_2)$	x	$\tau(t_2, s_3)$	x	$\tau(t_3, s_1)$	x
checking sequence	ab		ab		ab		ab
output	01		11		00		01

This input sequence ends in state $t_1 = s_2$

The input sequences (4.2) can be concatenated to obtain:

trans. to test	$s_3 \xrightarrow{b/0} s_1$	$s_2 \xrightarrow{a/1} s_2$	$s_3 \xrightarrow{a/0} s_3$	$s_1 \xrightarrow{a/0} s_1$	$s_2 \xrightarrow{b/1} s_3$	$s_1 \xrightarrow{b/1} s_2$
	$\tau(t_1, s_3)bx$	$\tau(t_1, s_2)ax$	$\tau(t_2, s_3)ax$	$\tau(t_3, s_2)ax$	$\tau(t_1, s_2)bx$	$\tau(t_3, s_1)bx$
input sequence	$bbab$	aab	aab	aab	bab	bab
end state	2	3	1	2	1	3
output	1001	111	000	001	100	111

The total length of the checking sequence is 27.

Note that the first input sequence is not able to find the faults in machine M_{I2} of Fig. 4.2, since M_{I2} when we apply the input sequence $abababab$ produces the expected output 01110001. Only during the second phase the faults are detected.

Adaptive DS Instead of using a unique preset distinguishing sequence for all the states, we can use an adaptive distinguishing sequence as explained in the following. An adaptive distinguishing sequence (ADS) is a decision tree that specifies how to choose the next input adaptively based on the observed output to identify the initial state. Adaptive distinguishing sequences are studied in Section 2.4. In that Chapter, the reader can find the definition (2.12), an algorithm to check the existence of an ADS and to build an ADS if it exists.

Example. An adaptive distinguishing sequence for the machine in Fig. 4.1 is depicted in Figure 4.4. We apply the input a and if we observe the output 1 we know that the machine was in the state s_2. If we observe the output 0, we have to apply b and if we observe the output 1 the machine was in s_1 otherwise we observe 0 and the machine was in s_3.

Using adaptive distinguishing sequence for our example, we obtain $x_1 = ab$, $x_2 = a$, $x_3 = b$, and $\tau = \varepsilon$ and the sequence (4.1) becomes

	x_1	$\tau(t_1, s_2)$	x_2	$\tau(t_2, s_3)$	x_3	$\tau(t_3, s_1)$	x_1
input sequence	ab		a	b	ab		ab

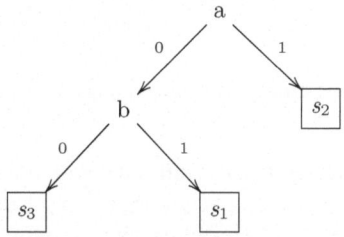

Fig. 4.4. Adaptive distinguishing sequence of machine in Fig. 4.1

Length and Cost An adaptive distinguishing sequence has length $\mathcal{O}(n^2)$, and a transfer sequence cannot be longer than n. The sequence (4.1) is long $\mathcal{O}(n^3)$. Because there are pn transitions, and every sequence (4.2) has length $\mathcal{O}(n^2)$, the cost is again $\mathcal{O}(pn^3)$ to find the complete checking sequence. Therefore, all the methods presented in Section 4.4 and in this section, have the same cost. The advance of the method presented in this section, is that it does not need a *reset* message. A comparison among methods from a practical point of view is presented in Section 4.8.

Minimizing the Sequence Length Note that there exist several techniques to shorten the length of the checking sequence obtained by applying the distinguishing sequence method [UWZ97], but still resulting checking sequences have length $\mathcal{O}(pn^3)$. The problem of finding the shortest transition tour covering all the transitions and then applying an extra sequence, that is a UIO or a DS sequence in this case, to their end state is called the *Rural Chinese Postman Problem* [ADLU91].

4.6 Using Identifying Sequences Instead of Distinguishing Sequences

Not every finite state machine has distinguishing sequences (as shown in Section 2.1). In case the machine has no *reset* message, no *status* message, no UIO sequences, and no distinguishing sequences, we cannot apply the methods proposed so far. We can still use the Assumption 1 and exploit the existence of separating sequences, that can distinguish a state from any other state in M_S. In this case, conformance testing is still possible [Hen64], although the resulting checking sequences may be exponentially long.

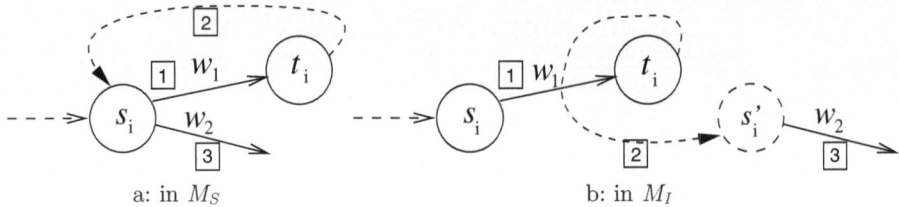

Fig. 4.5. Using two separating sequences to identify the state

As usual, we first check that M_I is similar to M_S. We display for each state s_i the responses to all the separating sequences in a characterizing set W (Definition 4.4). Suppose that W has two separating sequences w_1 and w_2. We want to apply the steps shown (in square boxes) in Figure 4.5 (a) : take M_I to s_i, apply w_1 (step 1), take the machine back again to s_i (step 2) and then apply w_2 (step 3). If we observe the right output, we can say that the machine M_I has a state q_i similar to s_i. We can start from $i = 1$ and proceed to verify all the states without using neither reset nor a distinguishing sequence. The problem is that we do not know how to bring the machine M_I back to s_i in a verifiable way, because in a faulty machine, as shown in Figure 4.5 (b), the transfer sequence $\tau(t_i, s_i)$ (step 2) may take the machine to another state s_i' where we could observe the expected output applying the w_2 sequence, without being able to verify that s_i' is s_i and without able to apply again w_1. We use now the Assumption 6 on page 90, namely that M_I has only n states. Let x be an input sequence and n be an integer, x^n is the concatenation n times of x.

Theorem 4.8. *Let s be a state of M_I, x be an input sequence, o the expected output sequence produced applying x to s, i.e. $o = \lambda(s, x)$, τ a transfer sequence from $t = \delta(s, x)$ back to s, and o' the expected output produced applying τ to t. By applying the input sequence $(x\,\tau)^n$ to state s in M_I, if we observe the output sequence $(o\,o')^n$, then the machine ends in a state where applying again x we observe the same output o.*

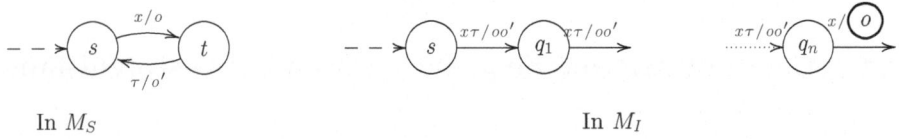

Fig. 4.6. Applying n times x and τ

Proof. The scenario described in theorem is shown in Figure 4.6. Suppose that M_I is initially in state s. Applying $x\,\tau$ the machine should come back to s. However, due to some faults, the machine M_I may go to another state q_1 even if the output we observe is the one expected, i.e. $o\, o'$. Assume that applying n times $x\,\tau$, we observe every time the same output $o\, o'$. Let q_r be the state of M_I after the application of $(x\,\tau)^r$. Note that even if the n applications of $x\,\tau$ produce n times the same correct output $o\, o'$, we are not sure that $s, q_1, \ldots, q_n$ are the same state yet. However the $n+1$ states $s, q_1, \ldots, q_n$ cannot be all distinct, because M_I has n states. Hence q_n is equal to some q_r with $r < n$ and, therefore, it would produce the same output o if we apply x.

Example. Consider the machine in Figure 4.1 and take any alleged implementation M_I. Apply the input a (in this case $\tau = \varepsilon$) to the initial state s_1 of M_I and check that the output is 0. We are not sure that M_I is now in state s_1 as well. We can apply again a and observe the output 0 and so on. When we have applied aaa and observed the output 000, M_I may have traversed states s_1, q_1, q_2, and the final state q_3. Because M_I has only 3 states, q_3 is equal to one of s_1, q_1, or q_2 and we are sure that if we applied again a we would observe 0.

We use Theorem 4.8 as follows. Assume that M_S has the characterizing set $W = \{w_1, w_2\}$ and let s_i be the state we are going to verify. Let τ be the transfer sequence that takes M_S back to s_i from $t_i = \delta(w_1, s_i)$. We first apply $(w_1\tau)^n$ to s_i. If we observe a wrong output we have proved that M_I does not conform to M_S. Otherwise we can apply theorem with $x = w_1$ and we are sure that M_I ends in a state that would produce the same output as if we applied w_1. We apply w_2 instead. If we observe the specified output we can conclude that s_i has a similar state in M_I.

We can generalize this method when the characterizing set W contains m separating sequences. Suppose that the characterizing set is $W = \{w_1, \ldots, w_m\}$. Let τ_j be the transfer sequence that takes the machine back to s after the application of w_j, i.e. $\tau_j = \tau(\delta(s, w_j), s)$. We can define inductively the sequences β_r as follows:

$$
\begin{aligned}
\beta_1 &= w_1 \\
\beta_r &= (\beta_{r-1}\tau_{r-1})^n w_r
\end{aligned}
\tag{4.3}
$$

By induction, one can prove that applying β_{r-1} after applying $(\beta_{r-1}\tau_{r-1})^n$ would produce the same output. Considering how β_i are defined, this means that applying $w_1, \ldots, w_{r-1}$ would produce the same output . For this reason we apply w_r after $(\beta_{r-1}\tau_{r-1})^n$. Therefore, one can prove that β_m is an *identifying sequence* of s_i, in the following sense: if the implementation machine M_I applying β_m produces the same output as that produced by the specification machine starting from s_i, then M_I has a state that is similar to s_i and such state is the state right before the application of the last w_m (regardless of which state M_I started from). We indicate the identifying sequence for state s_i with I_i.

Once we have computed the identifying sequence for every state, we can apply a method similar to that explained in Section 4.5 to visit each state, verify its response to the identifying sequence, and then transfer to the next state. Let I_i be the identifying sequence of state s_i and $\tau(t_i, s_{i+1})$ the transfer sequence from

$t_i = \delta(s_i, I_i)$ to s_{i+1}, by applying the following input sequence we can verify that M_I is similar to M_S.

$$I_1\,\tau(t_1, s_2)\,I_2\tau(t_2, s_3)\ldots I_1 \qquad\qquad (4.4)$$

Once we have proved that M_I is similar to M_S we have to verify the transitions. To do this we can use any I_i as reliable reset. For example, we can take I_1 as reset to the state $t_1 = \delta_I(s_1, w_m)$ and use t_1 as the initial state to test every transition. Indeed, we are sure that if we do not observe any fault, I_1 takes the machine to t_1. If we want to reset the machine from the state s_k to t_1 we apply $\tau(s_k, s_1)I_1$ and even if $\tau(s_k, s_1)$ fails to take the machine to s_1, we are sure that I_1 will take it to t_1. Now we proceed as explained in Section 4.4. To test a transition from s_i to s_j we apply a pseudo reset I_1 to t_1, then a transfer sequence along tested transitions to s_i, then we apply the input, observe the output, and apply the identifying sequence I_j to check that the end state is s_j.

Example. Consider the machine M_S in Fig. 4.1. $W = \{a, b\}$.
   For s_1, $\tau_1 = \varepsilon$, $I_1 = (w_1\tau)^3 w_2 = aaa\,b$
   For s_1, $\tau_1 = \varepsilon$, $I_2 = (w_1\tau)^3 w_2 = aaa\,b$
   For s_1, $\tau_1 = \varepsilon$, $I_3 = (w_1\tau)^3 w_2 = aaa\,b$
   The sequence (4.4) becomes

	I_1	$\tau(t_1, s_2)$	I_2	$\tau(t_2, s_3)$	I_3	$\tau(t_3, s_1)$	I_1
input sequence	$aaab$	ε	$aaab$	ε	$aaab$	ε	$aaab$

Length and Cost The length of an identifying sequence grows exponentially with the number of separating sequences and with n the number of the states. Indeed, by equation 4.3, every β_i is n times longer than β_{i-1}, the identifying sequence I is equal to β_m and m is the number of separating sequences that can be up to n. The resulting checking sequence is exponentially long. The IS method can be optimized using a different separating family Z_i for every state s_i [LY96].

4.7   Additional States

The Assumption 6, that the implementation has the same number of states as the specification, may not hold in general. The problem of testing each edge in a finite state machine with arbitrary extra states, is similar to the classical problem of traversing an unknown graph, that is called the *universal traversal* problem [LY96].

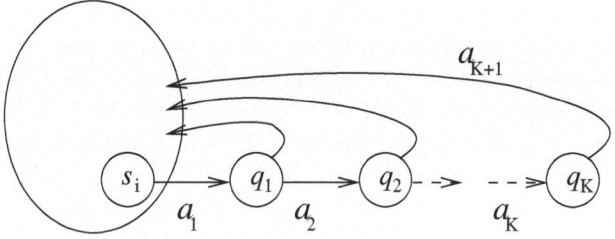

Fig. 4.7. A faulty machine M_I with K extra states

Assume that a faulty machine M_I, depicted in Figure 4.7, is identical to M_S except it has K extra states $q_1, \ldots, q_k$ and except for the transition from state s_i on input a_1 where M_I moves to the extra state q_1. Moreover M_I moves from q_1 to q_2 on input a_2, from q_2 to q_3 on input a_3, and so on. Assume the worst case, that only the transition from state q_k on input a_{K+1} has a wrong output or moves to a wrong next state. To be sure to test such transition, the input sequence applied to state s_i must include all possible input sequences of length K+1, and thus it must have length p^{K+1}. Such input sequence is also called *combination lock* because in order to unlock the machine, it must reach the state q_K and apply the input a_{K+1}. Vasilevski [Vas73] showed that also the lower bound on the input sequence is multiplied by p^K; i.e. it becomes $\Omega(p^{K+1}n^3)$ (discussed also in Section 5 of Chapter 19). Note that such considerations hold for every state machine M_I with K extra state: to test all the transitions we need to try all possible input combinations of length K+1 from all the states of M_I, and thus the input sequence must have length at least $p^{K+1}n$.

Using similar considerations, many methods we have presented can be easily extended to deal with implementations that may add a bounded number of states. This extension, however, causes an exponential growth of the length of the checking sequence.

In this section we present how the W method presented in Section 4.4.1 is extended to test an implementation machine with m states with $m > |S_S| = n$ [Cho78]. Let Q be a set of input sequences and k be an integer, Q^k is the concatenation k times of Q. Let W be a characterizing set (Definition 4.4). The W method in this case uses instead of a W set another set of sequences called the *distinguishing set* $Y = (\varepsilon \cup I \cup I^2 \cup \ldots \cup I^{m-n}).W$. Therefore, we apply up to m-n inputs before applying W. The use of Y instead of W has the goal to discover states that may be added in M_I. Let P be a transition cover set. The resulting set of input sequences is equal to $\{reset\}.P.Y$. Each input sequence starts with a *reset*, then applies a sequence to test each transition, applies up to $m - n$ inputs, then applies a separating sequence of W. The set of input sequences $P.Y$ detects any output or transfer error as long as the implementation has no more than m states. The proof is given in [Cho78]. If $m = n$ then Y=W and we obtain the W method of Section 4.4.1.

Example. Consider the machine in Fig. 4.8 as faulty implementation of the specification machine M_S of Fig. 4.1 with one state more, namely s_4. The original sequences generated with the W method assuming that the machine has the same number of states are not capable to discover the fault. If we use the W method with $m = 4$, we generate for *bbb* in P, *b* in I and *b* in W the sequence *rbbbbb* that is able to expose the fault.

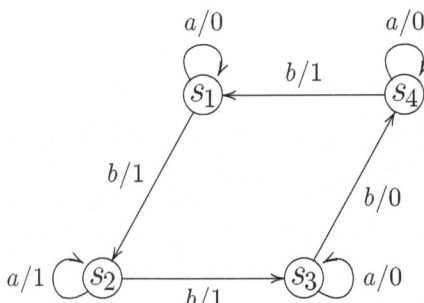

Fig. 4.8. A faulty implementation of machine M_S with 4 states

4.8   Summary

In this chapter we have presented several methods, which can uncover any fault in an implementation under different assumptions and producing checking sequences of different length and with different cost. We have initially supposed that all the assumptions of Section 4.2 hold, mainly that the machines are minimal, that the implementation does not add extra states, and that the machines have *reset*, *status* and *set* messages. Throughout the chapter we have presented the following methods which are capable to discover faults under a successively restricted subset of assumptions.

- The method of Section 4.3, the Transition Tour (TT) method, exploits all the assumptions, except the *set* message. It uses a *status* message to check that the implementation is in the correct state. The checking sequence has length and cost linear with pn. Without a *status* message this method does not guarantee the detection of transfer faults.
- If even a *status* message is not available, but the machine has still a *reset* message, one can use one of the methods proposed in Section 4.4, namely the W method, the Wp method, the unique input output (UIO) sequence method, the UIOv method, and the method using distinguishing sequences (DS) with *reset*. The DS method requires a distinguishing sequence, the UIO methods need UIOs, while W and Wp method are always applicable for minimized machines. The W, Wp, UIOv, and DS methods detect faults

of any kind, while the UIO method may miss some faults. The W, Wp, and DS method with an adaptive distinguishing sequence produce checking sequences of length $\mathcal{O}(pn^3)$ with cost $\mathcal{O}(pn^3)$. The others have greater cost.

- If even a *reset* message is not available, but a machine has a distinguishing sequence, the method presented in Section 4.5 uses transfer sequences instead of *reset*, produces checking sequences of length $\mathcal{O}(pn^3)$ and has cost $\mathcal{O}(pn^3)$ when used in conjunction with adaptive distinguishing sequences.
- If the machine has not even a distinguishing sequence nor UIOs, the identifying sequences (IS) method, presented in Section 4.6, still works. The IS method uses only the assumptions that the implementation does not add states and that the machines are minimized and therefore they have separating sequences. It produces exponentially long checking sequences.
- The problem of testing finite state machines with extra states is discussed more in general in Section 4.7, where the method originally presented by Chow [Cho78] is introduced.

It is of practical interest to compare the fault detection capability of the methods when the assumptions under which they should be applied, do not hold [SL88, ZC93]. Indeed, assumptions like the equal number of states for implementation may be not verifiable in practice. The assumption of the existence of a *reset* message is more meaningful, but empirical studies suggest to avoid the use of the methods using reset messages for the following reason. As shown in Section 4.7, faults in extra states are more likely to be discovered when using long input sequences. The use of a *reset* message may prevent the implementation to reach such extra states where the faults are present. For this reason methods like UIO or DS method without reset are better in practice than the UIOv method or the DS method with reset.

Although the study presented in this chapter is rather theoretical, we can draw some useful guidelines for practice testing for FSMs or for parts of models that behave like finite state machine and the reader should be aware that many ideas presented in this chapter are the basics for tools and case studies presented in Chapters 14 and 15. Such practical suggestions can improve the fault detection capability of the testing activity.

- Visiting each state in a FSM (like a *statement* coverage) using a ST method, should not be considered enough. One should at least visit every transition using a transition tour (TT) method, that can be considered as a *branch* coverage.
- Transition coverage should be used in conjunction of a *status* message to really check that the end state of every transition is the one expected. The presence of a *status* message in digital circuits is often required by the tester because it is of great help to uncover faults. If a *status* message may be not reliable, a double application of it helps to discover when it fails to reveal the correct state.
- If a *status* message is not available (very often in software black box testing), one should use some extra inputs to verify the states. Such inputs should be unique, like in Wp, UIO and DS.

- If one suspects that the implementation has more states than the implementation, he/she should prefer methods that produce long input sequences, like the DS and the IS method. However, only methods like the W method with extra states [Cho78], that add some extra inputs after visiting the transition and before checking the state identity, can guarantee to detect faults in this case.

Part II

Testing of Labeled Transition Systems

This part of the book is concerned with the theory of model-based testing where real systems are assumed to be modeled as *labeled transition systems* (and extensions thereof). Labeled transition systems were proposed by Keller [Kel76] and are widely used as underlying models for data-intensive systems (sequential and concurrent programs) as well as hardware circuits. The starting point of this form of model-based testing is a precise, unambiguous model description of the system under test. Based on this formal specification, test generation algorithms generate provably valid tests, i.e., tests that test what should be tested and no more than that. These algorithms provide automatic, faster and less error-prone test generation facilities. A sketch of the testing approach is given in Figure 9.

By hypothesis, it is assumed that for any implementation a model does exist. This assumption allows for reasoning about implementations as if they were formal objects. Consequently, it allows to express conformance – is the implementation under test a correct implementation of the specification? – as a formal relation, denoted **imp**, between models of implementations and specifications. Such a relation is called an *implementation relation* (sometimes also called conformance relation). An implementation i is said to be correct with respect to specification s if and only if the model of i is related to s by the implementation relation: $model\_of(i)$ **imp** s. Implementation relatiuons are typically preorder relations, i.e., relations that are reflexive and transitive (but not necessarily symmetric).

The behaviour of an implementation under test (IUT, for short) is investigated by performing experiments on the implementation and observing the

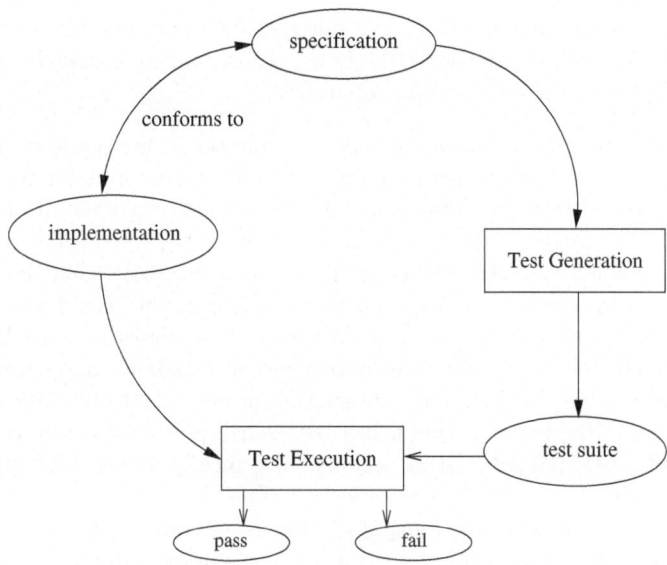

Fig. 9. Schematic view of model-based testing of labeled transition systems

reactions that the implementation produces to these experiments. The specification of such experiment is called a *test case*, and the process of applying a test to an implementation under test is called *test execution*. During test execution a number of observations will be made, e.g., occurring events will be logged, or the respondse of the implementation to a particular stimulus will be recorded. The basic concept of formal testing is now that if the IUT and its model are put into black boxes and we would perform all possible test cases, then it would not be possibel to distinguish between the IUT and its model. This is formally represented by testing equivalences, as originated by De Nicola and Hennessy [HN83].

Based on the observations, it is decided whether the IUT is correct (verdict "pass") or not (verdict "fail"). A set of test cases is *sound* whenever all correct implementations, and possibly some incorrect ones, will pass the test cases. Stated differrently, any detected erroneous implementation is indeed not a correct implementation. Ideally, a set of test cases is *exhaustive* if all non-conforming implementations will be detected. This theoretical notion is typically too strong in practice as exhaustiveness requires infinitely many test cases. An important requirement for test generatiikn algorithms therefore is that they produce sound test cases.

Implementation relations and test generation algorithms are the key concepts of this part of this book. In particular, we focus on:

- *Implementation relations* for labeled transitions systems and their relationship
- *Test generation algorithms* for labeled transition systems

- *Extensions* of implementation relations and their corresponding test generation algorithms for extensions of labeled transitions systems with input and output actions, real-time, and probabilities.

This part is further organised as follows. Chapter 5 surveys several preorder relations that have been proposed as implementation relations for testing of labeled transition systems. It defines and justifies seven implementation relations and studies how these notions are related. Chapter 6 presents test generation methods for labeled transition systems. It details a technique that maps labeled transition systems onto finite state machines allowing the use of algorithms as described in the first part of this book. Whereas these algorithms are focused on using trace inclusion as implementation relation, alternative – and compositional – algorithms are described for more interesting implementation relations such as refusal testing. Chapter 7 distinguishes between inputs and outputs. For testing, this is of particular interest as actions are typically directed: on stimulating the IUT (i.e., input), its output is observed. The chapter describes alternative ways to deal with inputs and outputs, defines several confromance relations, and detail out test generation algorithm for the major techniques. Chapters 5 through 7 focus on the functional aspects of implementations and abstract from non-functional aspects such as the timing of events – is an output produced in time? – or probability. The last two chapters of this part consider extensions of implementation relations and necessary adaptations to test generation algorithms when such aspects are taken into account. Chapter 8 surveys some existing approaches towards the testing of timed automata, an important extension of labeled transition systems with clock variables that are aimed to record the passage of time. Chapter 9 presents the most prominent approaches towards testing of probabilistic systems, in particular discrete-time (and continuous-time) Markov chains and Markov decision processes.

5 Preorder Relations*

Stefan D. Bruda

Department of Computer Science
Bishop's University
Lennoxville, Quebec J1M 1Z7, Canada
bruda@cs.ubishops.ca

5.1 Introduction

The usefulness of formalisms for the description and the analysis of reactive systems is closely related to the underlying notion of *behavioral equivalence*. Such an equivalence should formally identify behaviors that are informally indistinguishable from each other, and at the same time distinguish between behaviors that are informally different.

One way of determining behavioral equivalences is by observing the systems we are interesting in, experimenting on them, and drawing conclusions about the behavior of such systems based on what we see. We refer to this activity as *testing*. We then consider a set of relevant observers (or tests) that interact with our systems; the tests are carried out by human or by machine, in many different ways (i.e., by using various means of interaction with the system being tested).

In this context, we may be interested in finding out whether two systems are equivalent; for indeed two equivalent (sub)systems can then be replaced with each other without affecting the overall functionality, and we may also want to compare the specification of a system with its implementation to determine whether we actually implemented what we wanted to implement. We could then create an equivalence relation between systems, as follows: two systems are equivalent (with respect to the given tests) if they pass exactly the same set of tests. Such an equivalence can be further broken down into **preorder relations** on systems, i.e., relations that are reflexive and transitive (though not necessarily symmetric).

Preorders are in general easier to deal with, and one can reconstruct an equivalence relation by studying the preorder that generates it. Preorders are also more convenient—indeed, more meaningful—than equivalences in comparing specifications and their implementation: If two systems are found to be in a preorder relation with each other, then one is the implementation of the other, in the sense that the implementation is able to perform the same actions upon its computational environment as the other system (by contrast with equivalences the implementation may be now able to perform more actions, but this

---

* This work was supported by the Natural Sciences and Engineering Research Council of Canada, and by the Fond québécois de recherche sur la nature et les technologies.

M. Broy et al. (Eds.): Model-Based Testing of Reactive Systems, LNCS 3472, pp. 117-149, 2005.
© Springer-Verlag Berlin Heidelberg 2005

is immaterial as far as the capacity to implement is concerned). Preorders can thus be practically interpreted as *implementation relations*.

Recall from the first paragraph that we are interested in a formal approach to systems and their preorders. We are thus not interested how this system is built, whether by system we mean a reactive program or a protocol, they are all representable from a behavioral point of view by a common model. We shall refer to the behavior of a system as a *process*, and we start this chapter by offering a formal definition for the notion of process.

Depending on the degree of interaction with processes that we consider allowable, many preorder relations can be defined, and many have been indeed defined. In this chapter we survey the most prominent preorder relations over processes that have been developed over time. We leave the task of actually using these preorders to subsequent chapters.

Preorders are not created equal. Different preorders are given by varying the ability of our tests to examine the processes we are interested in. For example we may restrict our tests and only allow them to observe the processes, but we may also allow our tests to interact with the process being observed in some other ways. By determining the abilities of the tests we establish a *testing scenario*, under the form of a set of tests. By varying the testing scenario—i. e., the capabilities of tests to extract information about the process being tested—we end up with different preorders. We start with a generic testing scenario, and then we vary it and get a whole bunch of preorders in return.

It is evident that one testing scenario could be able to extract more information about processes (and thus to differentiate more between them). It is however not necessarily true that more differentiation between processes is better, simply because for some particular application a higher degree of differentiation may be useless. It is also possible that one testing scenario may be harder to implement[1] than another. In our discussion about various testing scenarios and their associated preorders we shall always keep in mind these practical considerations, and compare the preorders in terms of how much differentiation they make between processes, but also in terms of the practical realization of the associated testing scenario. In other words, we keep wondering how difficult is to convince the process being tested to provide the information or perform the actions required by the testing scenario we have in mind. For instance, it is arguably harder to block possible future action of the process under test (as we need to do in the testing scenario inducing the refusal preorder and presented in Section 5.6 on page 137) than to merely observe the process and write down the actions that have been performed (as is the case with the testing scenario inducing trace preorders presented in Section 5.3 on page 127). The increase in differentiation

---

[1] Implementing a testing scenario means implementing the means of interaction between a process and a test within the scenario. Implementing a preorder then means implementing an algorithm that takes two processes and determines whether they are in the given preorder relation or not by applying tests from the associated testing scenario.

power of refusal preorder over trace preorder comes thus at a cost which may or may not be acceptable in practice.

One reason for which practical considerations are of interest is that preorders are a key element in conformance testing [Tre94]. In such a framework we are given a formal specification and a possible implementation. The implementation is treated as a black box (perhaps somebody else wrote a poorly commented piece of code) exhibiting some external behavior. The goal is then to determine by means of testing whether the implementation implements correctly the specification. Such a goal induces naturally an implementation relation, or a preorder. Informally, the practical use of a preorder relation $\sqsubseteq$ consists then in the algorithmic problem of determining whether $s \sqsubseteq i$ for two processes i (the implementation) and s (the specification) by means of applying on the two processes tests taken from the testing scenario associated with $\sqsubseteq$. If the relation holds then i implements (or conforms to) s (according to the respective testing scenario). The formal introduction of conformance testing is left to the end of this chapter, namely to Section 5.9 on page 145 to which we direct the interested reader for details. For now we get busy with defining preorders and analyzing their properties.

Where we go from here We present in the next section the necessary preliminaries related to process representation and testing (including a first preorder to compare things with). Sections 5.3 to 5.8 are then the main matter of this chapter; we survey here the most prominent preorders and we compare them with each other. We also include a presentation of conformance testing in Section 5.9.

5.1.1   Notations and Conventions

It is often the case that our definitions of various sets (and specifically inductive definitions) should feature a final item containing a statement along the line that "nothing else than the above constructions belong to the set being defined." We consider that the presence of such an item is understood and we shall not repeat it over and over. "Iff" stands for "if and only if." We denote the empty string, and only the empty string by ε.

We present a number of concepts throughout this chapter based on one particular paper [vG01] without citing it all the time, in order to avoid tiresome repetitions.

Many figures show processes that are compared throughout the paper using various preorders. We show parenthetically in the captions of such figures the most relevant relations established between the depicted processes. Parts of these parenthetical remarks do not make sense when the figures are first encountered, but they will reveal themselves as the reader progresses through the chapter.

5.2   Process Representation and Testing

Many formal descriptions for processes have been developed in the past, most notably under the form of process algebraic languages such as CCS [Mil80] and

LOTOS [BB87]. The underlying semantics of all these descriptions can be described by **labeled transition systems**. We will use in what follows the labeled transition system as our semantical model (feeling free to borrow concepts from other formalisms whenever they simplify the presentation).

Our model is a slight variation of the model presented in Appendix 22 in that we need a notion of divergence for processes, and we introduce the concept of derived transition system; in addition, we enrich the terminology in order to blend the semantic model into the bigger picture on an intuitive level. For these reasons we also offer here a short presentation of labeled transition systems [vG01, Abr87]. Our presentation should be considered a complement to, rather than a replacement for Appendix 22.

5.2.1   Processes, States, and Labeled Transition Systems

Processes are capable of performing *actions* from a given, countable set Act. By action we mean any activity that is a conceptual entity at a given, arbitrary level of abstraction; we do not differentiate between, say input actions and output actions. Different activities that are indistinguishable on the chosen level of abstraction are considered occurrences of the same action.

What action is taken by a process depends on the *state* of the process. We denote the countable set of states by $\mathbf{Q}$. A process goes from a state to another by performing an action. The behavior of the process is thus given by the *transition relation* $\rightarrow \subseteq \mathbf{Q} \times \mathsf{Act} \times \mathbf{Q}$.

Sometimes a process may go from a state to another by performing an internal action, independent of the environment. We denote such an action by τ, where $\tau \notin \mathsf{Act}$.

The existence of partially defined states stem from (and facilitate) the semantic of sequential computations (where Ω is often used to denote a partial program whose behavior is totally undefined). The existence of such states is also useful for reactive programs. They are thus introduced by a *divergence predicate* $\uparrow$ ranging over $\mathbf{Q}$ and used henceforth in postfix notation; a state p for which $p \uparrow$ holds is a "partial state," in the sense that its properties are undefined; we say that such a state diverges (is divergent, etc.). The opposite property (that a state converges) is denoted by the postfix operator $\downarrow$.

Note that divergence (and thus convergence) is a property that is inherent to the state; in particular, it does not have any relation whatsoever with the actions that may be performed from the given state. Consider for example state x from Figure 5.4 on page 130 (where states are depicted by nodes, and the relation $\rightarrow$ is represented by arrows between nodes, labeled with actions). It just happens that x features no outgoing actions, but this does not make it divergent (though it may be divergent depending on the definition of the predicate $\uparrow$ for the respective labeled transition system). Divergent states stand intuitively for some form of error condition in the state itself, and encountering a divergent state during testing is a sure sign of failure for that test.

To summarize all of the above, we offer the following definition:

Definition 5.1. A labeled transition system with divergence (simply labeled transition system henceforth in this chapter) is a tuple $(\mathbf{Q}, \mathsf{Act} \cup \{\tau\}, \rightarrow, \uparrow)$, where $\mathbf{Q}$ is a countable set of states, Act is a countable set of (atomic) actions, $\rightarrow$ is the transition relation, $\rightarrow \subseteq \mathbf{Q} \times (\mathsf{Act} \cup \{\tau\}) \times \mathbf{Q}$, and $\uparrow$ is the divergence predicate. By τ we denote an internal action, $\tau \notin \mathsf{Act}$.

For some state $p \in \mathbf{Q}$ we write $p \downarrow$ iff $\neg \, (p \uparrow)$. Whenever $(q, a, p) \in \rightarrow$ we write $p \xrightarrow{a} q$ (to be read "p offers a and after executing a becomes q"). We further extend this notation to the reflexive and transitive closure of $\rightarrow$ as follows: $p \xrightarrow{\varepsilon} p$ for any $p \in \mathbf{Q}$; and $p \xrightarrow{\sigma} q$, with $\sigma \in \mathbf{Q}^*$, iff $\sigma = \sigma_1 \sigma_2$ and there exists $q' \in \mathbf{Q}$ such that $p \xrightarrow{\sigma_1} q' \xrightarrow{\sigma_2} q$. □

We use the notation $p \xrightarrow{\sigma}$ as a shorthand for "there exists $q \in \mathbf{Q}$ such that $p \xrightarrow{\sigma} q$," and the notation $\nrightarrow$ as the negation of $\rightarrow$ ($p \xrightarrow{a}\!\!\!\!\!/ \, q$ iff it is not the case that $p \xrightarrow{a} q$, etc.).

Assume now that we are given a labeled transition system. The internal action τ is unobservable. In order to formalize this unobservability, we define an associated derived transition system in which we hide all the internal actions; the transition relation $\Rightarrow$ of such a system ignores the actions τ performed by the system. Formally, we have:

Definition 5.2. Given a transition system $B = (\mathbf{Q}, \mathsf{Act} \cup \{\tau\}, \rightarrow, \uparrow_B)$, its **derived transition system** is a tuple $D = (\mathbf{Q}, \mathsf{Act} \cup \{\varepsilon\}, \Rightarrow, \uparrow)$, where $\Rightarrow \subseteq \mathbf{Q} \times (\mathsf{Act} \cup \{\varepsilon\}) \times \mathbf{Q}$ and is defined by the following relations:

$$p \xrightarrow{a}{}\!\!\!\!\!\!\Rightarrow q \text{ iff } p \xrightarrow{\tau^* a} q$$
$$p \xrightarrow{\varepsilon}{}\!\!\!\!\!\!\Rightarrow q \text{ iff } p \xrightarrow{\tau^*} q$$

The divergence predicate is defined as follows: $p \uparrow$ iff there exists q such that $q \uparrow_B$ and $p \xrightarrow{\varepsilon}{}\!\!\!\!\!\!\Rightarrow q$, or there exists a sequence $(p_i)_{i \geq 0}$, such that $p_0 = p$ and for any $i > 0$ it holds that $p_i \xrightarrow{\tau} p_{i+1}$. □

In passing, note that we deviate slightly in Definition 5.2 from the usual definition of $\Rightarrow$ ($p \xrightarrow{a}{}\!\!\!\!\!\!\Rightarrow q$ iff $p \xrightarrow{\tau^* a \tau^*} q$, see Appendix 22), as this allows for a clearer presentation.

Also note that a state can diverge in two ways in a derived transition system: it can either perform a number of internal actions and end up in a state that diverges in the associated labeled transition system, or evolve perpetually into new states by performing internal actions. Therefore this definition does not make distinction between *deadlock* (first case) and *livelock* (second variant). We shall discuss in subsequent sections whether such a lack of distinction is a good or a bad thing, and we shall distinguish between these variants using the original labeled transition system (since the derived system is unable to make the distinction).

It is worth emphasizing once more (this time using an example) that the definition of divergence in a derived transition system is different from the correspondent definition in a labeled transition system. Indeed, consider state y

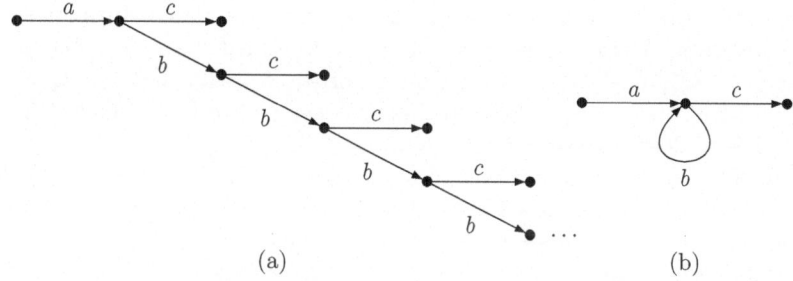

Fig. 5.1. Representation of infinite process trees: an infinite tree (a), and its graph representation (b).

from Figure 5.6 on page 133 (again, states are depicted by nodes, and the relation $\rightarrow$ is represented by arrows between nodes, labeled with actions). It may be the case that y is a nice, convergent state in the respective labeled transition system (i.e., $y \downarrow_B$). Still, it is obviously the case that $y \uparrow$ in the derived transition system (we refer to this as "y may diverge" instead of "y diverges," given that y may decide at some time to perform action b and get out of the loop of internal actions).

Again, we shall use in what follows natural extensions of the relation $\Rightarrow$ such as $p \stackrel{a}{\Rightarrow}$ and $\not\Rightarrow$. We also use by abuse of notation the same operator for the reflexive and transitive closure of $\Rightarrow$ (in the same way as we did for $\rightarrow$).

A transition system gives a description of the actions that can be performed by a process depending on the state that process is in. A process does in addition start from an *initial state*. In other words, a process is fully described by a transition system and an initial state. In most cases we find it convenient to fix a global transition system for all the processes under consideration. In this setting, a process is then uniquely defined by its initial state. We shall then blur the distinction between a process and a state, often referring to "the process $p \in \mathbf{Q}$."

Finally, a process can be represented as a tree in a natural way: Tree nodes represent states. The root node is the initial state. The edges of the tree will be labeled by actions, and there exists an edge between nodes p and q labeled with a iff it holds that $p \stackrel{a}{\rightarrow} q$ in the given transition system (or that $p \stackrel{a}{\Rightarrow} q$ if we talk about a derived transition system). We shall not make use of this representation except when we want to represent a process (or part thereof) graphically for illustration purposes. Sometimes we find convenient to "abbreviate" tree representation by drawing a graph rather than a tree when we want to represent infinite trees with states whose behavior repeats over and over (in which case we join those states in a loop). The reader should keep in mind that this is just a convenient representation, and that in fact she is in front of a finite representation of an infinite tree. As an example, Figure 5.1 shows such a graph together with a portion of the unfolded tree represented by the graph.

Two important properties of transition systems are **image-finiteness** and **sort-finiteness**. A transition system is image-finite if for any $a \in \mathsf{Act}$, $p \in \mathbf{Q}$ the set $\{q \in \mathbf{Q} \mid p \xrightarrow{a} q\}$ is finite, and is sort-finite if for any $p \in \mathbf{Q}$ the set $\{a \in \mathsf{Act} \mid \exists \sigma \in \mathsf{Act}^*, \exists q \in \mathbf{Q}$ such that $p \xrightarrow{\sigma} q \xrightarrow{a}\}$ is finite. This definition also applies to derived transition systems.

In all of the subsequent sections we shall assume a transition system $(\mathbf{Q}, \mathsf{Act} \cup \{\tau\}, \rightarrow, \uparrow_B)$ with its associated derived transition system $(\mathbf{Q}, \mathsf{Act} \cup \{\tau\}, \Rightarrow, \uparrow)$, applicable to all the processes under scrutiny; thus a process shall be identified only by its initial state.

5.2.2 Processes and Observations

As should be evident from the need of defining derived transition systems, we can determine the characteristics of a system by performing observations on it. Some observations may reveal the whole internal behavior of the system being inspected, some may be more restricted.

In general, we may think of a set of processes and a set of relevant observers (or *tests*). Observers may be thought of as agents performing observations. Observers can be viewed themselves as processes, running in parallel with the process being observed and synchronizing with it over visible actions. We can thus represent the observers as labeled transition systems, just as we represent processes; we prefer however to use a different, "denotational" syntax for observers in our presentation.

Assume now that we have a predefined set $\mathcal{O}$ of observers. The effect of observers performing tests is formalized by considering that for every observer o and process p there exists a set of runs $\mathrm{RUNS}(o, p)$. If we have $r \in \mathrm{RUNS}(o, p)$ then the result of o testing p may be the run r.

We take the outcomes of particular runs of a test as being success or failure [Abr87, dNH84] (though we shall differentiate between two kinds of failure later). We then represent outcomes as elements in the two-point lattice

$$\mathbb{O} \overset{\text{def}}{=} \begin{array}{c} \top \\ | \\ \bot \end{array}$$

The notion of failure incorporates divergence, so for some observer o and some process p, the elements of $\mathbb{O}$ have the following meaning:

- the outcome of o testing p is $\top$ if there exists $r \in \mathrm{RUNS}(o, p)$ such that r is successful;
- the outcome of o testing p is $\bot$ if there exists $r \in \mathrm{RUNS}(o, p)$ such that either r is unsuccessful, or r contains a state q such that $q \uparrow$ and q is not preceded by a successful state.

Note that for the time being we do not differentiate between runs with a deadlock (i.e., in which a computation terminates without reaching a successful state) and runs that diverge; the outcome is $\bot$ in both cases.

Processes may be nondeterministic, so there may be different runs of a given test on a process, with different outcomes. In effect, the (overall) outcome of an observer testing a process is a *set*, and therefore we are led to use powerdomains of $\mathbb{O}$. In fact, we have three possible powerdomains:

$$\mathbb{P}_{\text{may}} \overset{\text{def}}{=} \begin{matrix} \{\top\} = \{\bot, \top\} \\ | \\ \{\bot\} \end{matrix} \qquad \mathbb{P}_{\text{conv}} \overset{\text{def}}{=} \begin{matrix} \{\top\} \\ | \\ \{\bot, \top\} \\ | \\ \{\bot\} \end{matrix} \qquad \mathbb{P}_{\text{must}} \overset{\text{def}}{=} \begin{matrix} \{\top\} \\ | \\ \{\bot\} = \{\bot, \top\} \end{matrix}$$

The names of the three powerdomains are not chosen haphazardly. By considering $\mathbb{P}_{\text{may}}$ as possible outcomes we identify processes that *may* pass a test in order to be considered successful. Similarly, $\mathbb{P}_{\text{must}}$ identifies tests that *must* be successful, and by using $\mathbb{P}_{\text{conv}}$ we combine the may and must properties. The partial order relations induced by the lattices $\mathbb{P}_{\text{may}}$, $\mathbb{P}_{\text{must}}$, and $\mathbb{P}_{\text{conv}}$ shall be denoted by $\sqsubseteq_{\text{may}}$, $\sqsubseteq_{\text{must}}$, and $\sqsubseteq_{\text{conv}}$, respectively.

We also need to introduce the notion of **refusal**. A process refuses an action if the respective action is not applicable in the current state of the process, and there is no internal transition to change the state (so that we are sure that the action will not be applicable unless some other visible action is taken first).

Definition 5.3. Process $p \in \mathbf{Q}$ refuses action $a \in \mathsf{Act}$, written p **ref** a, iff $p \downarrow_B$, $p \overset{\tau}{\not\rightarrow}$, and $p \overset{a}{\not\rightarrow}$. □

We thus described the notions of test and test outcomes. We also introduce at this point a syntax for tests. In fact tests are as we mentioned just processes that interact with the process under test, so we can represent tests in the same way as we represent processes. Still, we find convenient to use a "denotational" representation for tests since we shall refer quite often to such objects. We do this by defining a set $\mathcal{O}$ of test expressions.

While we are at it, we also define the "semantics" of tests, i.e., the way tests are allowed to interact with the processes being tested. Such a semantics for tests is defined using a function obs : $\mathcal{O} \times \mathbf{Q} \rightarrow \mathcal{P}$, where $\mathcal{P} \in \{\mathbb{P}_{\text{may}}, \mathbb{P}_{\text{conv}}, \mathbb{P}_{\text{must}}\}$ such that $\text{obs}(o, p)$ is the set of all the possible outcomes.

To concretize the concepts of syntax and semantics, we introduce now our first *testing scenario* (i.e., set of test expressions and their semantics), of *observable testing equivalence*[2] [Abr87]. This is a rather comprehensive testing model, which we will mostly restrict in order to introduce other models—indeed, we shall restrict this scenario in all but one of our subsequent presentations. A concrete model for tests also allows us to introduce our first preorder.

For the remainder of this section, we fix a transition system $(\mathbf{Q}, \mathsf{Act} \cup \{\tau\}, \rightarrow, \uparrow_B)$ together with its derived transition system $(\mathbf{Q}, \mathsf{Act} \cup \{\varepsilon\}, \Rightarrow, \uparrow)$.

---

[2] Just *testing equivalence* originally [Abr87]; we introduce the new, awkward terminology because the original name clashes with the names of preorders introduced subsequently.

$\wedge$	$\bot$	T
$\bot$	$\bot$	$\bot$
T	$\bot$	T

$\wedge$	$\{\bot\}$	$\{\bot,T\}$	$\{T\}$
$\{\bot\}$	$\{\bot\}$	$\{\bot\}$	$\{\bot\}$
$\{\bot,T\}$	$\{\bot\}$	$\{\bot,T\}$	$\{\bot,T\}$
$\{T\}$	$\{\bot\}$	$\{\bot,T\}$	$\{T\}$

$\forall$	
$\{\bot\}$	$\{\bot\}$
$\{\bot,T\}$	$\{\bot\}$
$\{T\}$	$\{T\}$

$\vee$	$\bot$	T
$\bot$	$\bot$	T
T	T	T

$\vee$	$\{\bot\}$	$\{\bot,T\}$	$\{T\}$
$\{\bot\}$	$\{\bot\}$	$\{\bot,T\}$	$\{T\}$
$\{\bot,T\}$	$\{\bot,T\}$	$\{\bot,T\}$	$\{T\}$
$\{T\}$	$\{T\}$	$\{T\}$	$\{T\}$

$\exists$	
$\{\bot\}$	$\{\bot\}$
$\{\bot,T\}$	$\{T\}$
$\{T\}$	$\{T\}$

Fig. 5.2. Semantics of logical operators on test outcomes.

Definition 5.4. The set $\mathcal{O}$ of test expressions inducing the observable testing equivalence contains exactly all of the following constructs, with o, o_1, and o_2 ranging over $\mathcal{O}$:

$$o \stackrel{\text{def}}{=} \text{SUCC} \tag{5.1}$$
$$\mid \text{FAIL} \tag{5.2}$$
$$\mid ao \qquad \text{for } a \in \text{Act} \tag{5.3}$$
$$\mid \tilde{a}o \qquad \text{for } a \in \text{Act} \tag{5.4}$$
$$\mid \varepsilon o \tag{5.5}$$
$$\mid o_1 \wedge o_2 \tag{5.6}$$
$$\mid o_1 \vee o_2 \tag{5.7}$$
$$\mid \forall\, o \tag{5.8}$$
$$\mid \exists\, o \tag{5.9}$$

$\square$

Intuitively, Expressions (5.1) and (5.2) state that a test can succeed or fail by reaching two designated states SUCC and FAIL, respectively. A test may check whether an action can be taken when into a given state, or whether an action is not possible at all; these are expressed by (5.3) and (5.4). We can combine tests by means of boolean operators using expressions of form (5.6) and (5.7). By introducing tests of form (5.5) we allow a process to "stabilize" itself through internal actions. Finally, we have universal and existential quantifiers for tests given by (5.8) and (5.9). Nondeterminism is introduced in the tests themselves by the Expressions (5.7) and (5.9), the latter being a generalization of the former.

Definition 5.5. With the semantics of logical operators as defined in Figure 5.2, the function obs inducing the observable testing equivalence, obs : $\mathcal{O} \times \mathbf{Q} \to \mathbb{P}_{\text{conv}}$, is defined as follows:

$$\mathrm{obs}(\textsc{Succ}, p) = \{\top\}$$

$$\mathrm{obs}(\textsc{Fail}, p) = \{\bot\}$$

$$\mathrm{obs}(ao, p) = \bigcup \{\mathrm{obs}(o, p') \mid p \overset{a}{\Longrightarrow} p'\} \cup \{\bot \mid p \uparrow\} \cup \{\bot \mid p \overset{\varepsilon}{\Longrightarrow} p', p' \textbf{ ref } a\}$$

$$\mathrm{obs}(\tilde{a}o, p) = \bigcup \{\mathrm{obs}(o, p') \mid p \overset{a}{\Longrightarrow} p'\} \cup \{\bot \mid p \uparrow\} \cup \{\top \mid p \overset{\varepsilon}{\Longrightarrow} p', p' \textbf{ ref } a\}$$

$$\mathrm{obs}(\varepsilon o, p) = \bigcup \{\mathrm{obs}(o, p') \mid p \overset{\varepsilon}{\Longrightarrow} p'\} \cup \{\bot \mid p \uparrow\}$$

$$\mathrm{obs}(o_1 \wedge o_2, p) = \mathrm{obs}(o_1, p) \wedge \mathrm{obs}(o_2, p)$$

$$\mathrm{obs}(o_1 \vee o_2, p) = \mathrm{obs}(o_1, p) \vee \mathrm{obs}(o_2, p)$$

$$\mathrm{obs}(\forall o, p) = \forall \mathrm{obs}(o, p)$$

$$\mathrm{obs}(\exists o, p) = \exists \mathrm{obs}(o, p)$$

□

The function from Definition 5.5 follows the syntax of test expressions faithfully, so most cases should need no further explanation. We note that tests of form (5.3) are allowed to continue only if the action a is available to, and is performed by the process under test; if the respective action is not available, the test fails. In contrast, when a test of form (5.4) is applied to some process, we record a success whenever the process refuses the action (the primary purpose of such a test), but then we go ahead and allow the action to be performed anyway, to see what happens next (i.e., we remove the block on the action; maybe in addition to the noted success we get a failure later). As we shall see in Section 5.7 such a behavior of allowing the action to be performed after a refusal is of great help in identifying crooked coffee machines (and also in differentiating between processes that would otherwise appear equivalent).

As a final thought, we note again that tests can be in fact expressed in the same syntax as the one used for processes. A test then moves forward synchronized with the process under investigation, in the sense that the visible action performed by the process should always be the same as the action performed by the test. This synchronized run is typically denoted by the operator |, and the result is itself a process. We thus obtain an operational formulation of tests, which is used as well [Abr87, Phi87] and is quite intuitive. Since we find the previous version more convenient for this presentation, we do not insist on it and direct instead the reader elsewhere [Abr87] for details.

5.2.3   Equivalence and Preorder Relations

The semantics of tests presented in the previous section associates a set of outcomes for each pair test–process. By comparing these outcomes (i.e., the set of possible observations one can make while interacting with two processes, or the observable behavior of the processes) we can define the *observable testing preorder*[3] $\sqsubseteq$. Given the preorder one can easily define the *observable testing equivalence* $\simeq$.

---

[3] Recall that this was originally named testing preorder [Abr87], but we introduce the new name because of name clashes that developed over time.

Definition 5.6. The **observable testing preorder** is a relation $\sqsubseteq \subseteq \mathbf{Q} \times \mathbf{Q}$, where $p \sqsubseteq q$ iff $\mathrm{obs}(o, p) \subseteq \mathrm{obs}(o, q)$ for any test $o \in \mathcal{O}$. The observable testing equivalence is a relation $\simeq \subseteq \mathbf{Q} \times \mathbf{Q}$, with $p \simeq q$ iff $p \sqsubseteq q$ and $q \sqsubseteq p$.   □

If we restrict the definition of $\mathcal{O}$ (and thus the definition of the function obs), we obtain a different preorder, and thus a different equivalence. In other words, if we change the set of possible tests that can be applied to processes (the **testing scenario**), then we obtain a different classification of processes.

We will present in what follows various preorder relations under various testing scenarios. These preorders correspond to sets of changes imposed on $\mathcal{O}$ and obs, and we shall keep comparing various scenarios with the testing scenario presented in Section 5.2.2. As it turns out, the changes we impose on $\mathcal{O}$ are in all but one case restrictions (i.e., simplification of the possible tests).

We will in most cases present an equivalent modal characterization corresponding to these restrictions. Such a modal characterization (containing a set of testing formulae and a satisfaction operator) will in essence model exactly the same thing, but we are able to offer some results that are best shown using the modal characterization rather than other techniques.

When we say that a preorder $\sqsubseteq_\alpha$ makes more distinction than another preorder $\sqsubseteq_\beta$ we mean that there exist processes that are distinguishable under $\sqsubseteq_\alpha$ but not under $\sqsubseteq_\beta$. This does not imply that $\sqsubseteq_\alpha$ and $\sqsubseteq_\beta$ are comparable, i.e., it could be possible that $\sqsubseteq_\alpha$ makes more distinction than $\sqsubseteq_\beta$ *and* that $\sqsubseteq_\beta$ makes more distinction than $\sqsubseteq_\alpha$. Whenever $\sqsubseteq_\alpha$ makes more distinction than $\sqsubseteq_\beta$ but not the other way around we say that $\sqsubseteq_\alpha$ is *coarser* than $\sqsubseteq_\beta$, or that $\sqsubseteq_\beta$ is *finer* than $\sqsubseteq_\alpha$.

5.3   Trace Preorders

We thus begin our discussion on preorder and equivalence relations with what we believe to be the simplest assumption: we compare two processes by their *trace*, i.e., by the sequence of actions they perform. In this section we follow roughly [vG01, dN87].

We consider that the divergence predicate $\uparrow_B$ of the underlying transition system is empty (no process diverges). The need for such a strong assumption will become clear later, when we discover that trace preorders do not cope well with divergence.

The trace preorder is based on the following *testing scenario*: We view a process as a black box that contains only one interface to the real world. This interface is a window displaying at any given moment the action that is currently carried out by the process. The process chooses its execution path autonomously, according to the given transition system. As soon as no action is carried out, the display becomes empty. The observer records a sequence of actions (a trace), or a sequence of actions followed by an empty window (a complete trace). Internal moves are ignored (indeed, by their definition they are not observable). We regard two processes as equivalent if we observe the same complete trace using our construction for both processes.

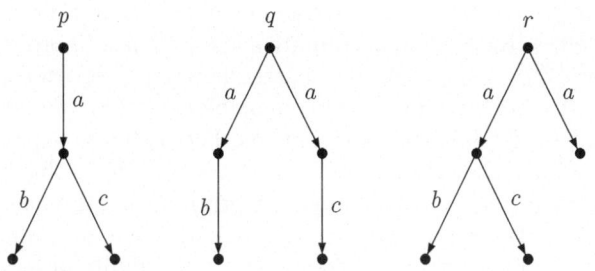

Fig. 5.3. Three sample processes ($p \simeq_{CT} q \simeq_{CT} r$; $q \not\sqsubseteq_B p$).

Specifically, $\sigma \in \mathsf{Act}^*$ is a **trace** of a process p iff there exists a process q such that $p \overset{\sigma}{\Longrightarrow} q$. A **complete trace** $\sigma \in \mathsf{Act}^*$ is a trace such that $p \overset{\sigma}{\Longrightarrow} q$ and $q \not\Rightarrow$.

The set $\mathcal{L}_{CT}$ of **complete trace formulae** is inductively defined as follows:

- $\top \in \mathcal{L}_{CT}$ ($\top$ marks the end of a trace);
- $0 \in \mathcal{L}_{CT}$ (0 marks the end of a complete trace);
- if $\psi \in \mathcal{L}_{CT}$ and $a \in \mathsf{Act}$ then $a\psi \in \mathcal{L}_{CT}$.

A modal characterization for trace formulae is given by the **satisfaction operator** $\vDash \subseteq \mathbf{Q} \times \mathcal{L}_{CT}$ inductively defined by:

- $p \vDash \top$ for all $p \in \mathbf{Q}$;
- $p \vDash 0$ if $p \not\Rightarrow$;
- $p \vDash a\psi$ if $p \overset{a}{\Longrightarrow} q$ and $q \vDash \psi$ for some $q \in \mathbf{Q}$.

We can now define the **complete trace preorder** $\sqsubseteq_{CT}$ and implicitly the complete trace equivalence $\simeq_{CT}$:

Definition 5.7. $p \sqsubseteq_{CT} q$ iff $p \vDash \psi$ implies $q \vDash \psi$ for any $\psi \in \mathcal{L}_{CT}$. □

The complete trace preorder induces the equivalence used in the theory of automata and languages. Indeed, consider the processes as language generators and then the trace preorder is given by the inclusion of the language of complete traces generated by one process into the language of complete traces generated by the other process. Take for instance the processes shown in Figure 5.3. We notice that $p \simeq_{CT} q$ since they both generate the language $\{\top, a\top, ab0, ac0\}$, and that $q \sqsubseteq_{CT} r$ (since r generates the larger language $\{\top, a\top, ab0, ac0, a0\}$).

We note in passing that an even weaker (in the sense of making less distinction) preorder relation can be defined [vG01] by eliminating the distinction between traces and complete traces (by putting $\top$ whenever we put 0). Under such a preorder (called **trace preorder**), the three processes in Figure 5.3 are all equivalent, generating the language $\{\top, a\top, ab\top, ac\top\}$. (We note however that the complete trace preorder is quite limited so we do not find necessary to further elaborate on an even weaker preorder.)

For one thing, trace preorder (complete or not) does not deal very well with diverging processes. Indeed, we need quite some patience in order to determine whether a state diverges or not; no matter how long we wait for the action to change in our display window, we cannot be sure that we have a diverging process or that we did not reach the end of an otherwise finite sequence of internal moves. We also have the problem of infinite traces. This is easily fixed in the same language theoretic spirit that does not preclude an automaton to generate infinite words, but then we should arm ourselves with the same immense amount of patience. Trace preorders imply the necessity of infinite observations, which are obviously impractical.

Despite all these inconveniences, trace preorders are the most elementary preorders, and perhaps the most intuitive (that's why we chose to start our presentation with them). In addition, such preorders seem to capture the finest differences in behavior one would probably like to distinguish (namely, the difference between observable sequences of actions). Surprisingly, it turns out that other preorders make an even greater distinction. Such a preorder is the subject of the next section.

5.4   Observation Preorders and Bisimulation

As opposed to the complete trace preorder that *seems* to capture the finest observable differences in behavior, the **observation preorder** [Mil80, HM80], the subject of this section, *is* the finest behavioral preorder one would want to impose; i.e., it incorporates all distinctions that could reasonably be made by external observation. The additional discriminating power is the ability to take into account not only the sequences of actions, but also some of the intermediate states the system goes through while performing the respective sequence of actions. Indeed, differences between intermediate states can be exploited to produce different behaviors.

It has also been argued that observation equivalence makes too fine a distinction, even between behaviors that cannot be really differentiated by an observer. Such an argument turns out to be pertinent, but we shall postpone such a discussion until we introduce other preorder relations and have thus something to compare.

The **observation preorder** $\sqsubseteq_B$ is defined using a family of preorder relations $\sqsubseteq_n$, $n \geq 0$ [Abr87]:

(1) it is always the case that $p \sqsubseteq_0 q$;
(2) $p \sqsubseteq_{n+1} q$ iff, for any $a \in \mathsf{Act}$ it holds that
   - for any p' such that $p \stackrel{a}{\Longrightarrow} p'$ there exists q' such that $q \stackrel{a}{\Longrightarrow} q'$ and $p' \sqsubseteq_n q'$, and
   - if $p \downarrow$ then (i) $q \downarrow$ and (ii) for any q' such that $q \stackrel{a}{\Longrightarrow} q'$ there exists p' such that $p \stackrel{a}{\Longrightarrow} p'$ and $p' \sqsubseteq_n q'$;
(3) $p \sqsubseteq_B q$ iff for any $n \geq 0$ it holds that $p \sqsubseteq_n q$.

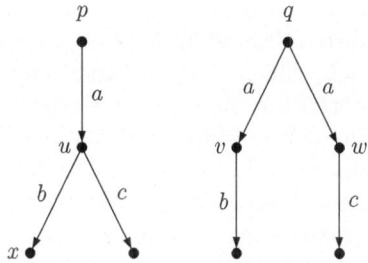

Fig. 5.4. Processes not equivalent under observation preorder ($p \not\simeq_B q$; $p \simeq_{CT} q$; $p \simeq_R q$).

The equivalence $\simeq_B$ induced by $\sqsubseteq_B$ ($p \simeq_B q$ iff $p \sqsubseteq_B q$ and $q \sqsubseteq_B p$) is called *observation equivalence*.

The observation equivalence is often called **(weak) bisimulation** equivalence, hence the B subscript (the other logical–and often used–subscript O having the inconvenience of being easily confused with a zero).

It is clear that the observation preorder makes more distinction than trace preorders. Consider the processes p and q from Figure 5.3, shown again in Figure 5.4 this time with names for some of the extra states. It is immediate that $v \sqsubseteq_1 u$, and that $w \sqsubseteq_1 u$. It follows that $q \sqsubseteq_2 p$. However, it is *not* the case that $u \sqsubseteq_1 v$, and thus $q \not\sqsubseteq_2 p$. We have a strict implementation relation between q and p. Recall however that these two processes are equivalent under trace preorders.

Observation preorder corresponds to a *testing scenario* identical with the general scenario presented in Definitions 5.4 and 5.5 (in Section 5.2.2). As is the case with trace preorder we can *inspect* the sequence of *actions* performed by the process under scrutiny. This is given by expressions of form (5.1), (5.2), and (5.3).

As a side note, we mentioned at the beginning of this section that observation preorder makes more distinction than trace preorder. The expressions we allow up to this point are enough to show this: Then the tests only have the form $a_1 a_2 \ldots a_n \text{SUCC}$ or $a_1 a_2 \ldots a_n \text{FAIL}$ for some $n \geq 0$. This way we can actually distinguish between processes such as p and q from Figure 5.4. Indeed, we notice that

$$\text{obs}(ab\text{SUCC}, p) = \{\top\}$$

whereas

$$\text{obs}(ab\text{SUCC}, q) = \{\top, \bot\}$$

(we can start on the ac branch of q, which will produce $\bot$). In other words, we are able to distinguish between distinct paths in the run of a process, not only between different sequences of actions.

We close the side remark and go on with the description of the testing scenario for observation preorder. The addition of expressions of form (5.4) introduces the concept of *refusals*, which allow one to obtain information about the failure of the process to perform some action (as opposed to its ability to perform something). The expressions of form (5.6) and (5.7) allows us to *copy* the process being tested at any time during its execution, and to further test the copies by performing separate tests. *Global testing* is possible given expressions of form (5.8) and (5.9). This is a generalization of the two copy operations, in the sense that information is gathered independently for each possible test, and the results are then combined together. Finally, *nondeterminism* is introduced in the tests themselves by Expression (5.5). Such a nondeterminism is however controlled by the process being tested; indeed, if the process is convergent then we will eventually perform test o from an εo construction. By this mechanism we allow the process to "stabilize" before doing more testing on it.

Proposition 5.8. *With the set $\mathcal{O}$ of tests as defined in the above testing scenario, $p \sqsubseteq_B q$ iff $\mathrm{obs}(o, p) \subseteq \mathrm{obs}(o, q)$ for any test $o \in \mathcal{O}$.*

In other words, observation preorder and observable testing preorder are the same, i.e., observation equivalence corresponds exactly to indistinguishability under testing.

A modal characterization of observation equivalence can be given in terms of the set $\mathcal{L}_{HM}$ of *Hennessy-Milner formulae*:

- $\top, \bot \in \mathcal{L}_{HM}$;
- if $\phi, \psi \in \mathcal{L}_{HM}$ then $\phi \wedge \psi, \phi \vee \psi, [a]\psi, \langle a \rangle \phi \in \mathcal{L}_{HM}$ for some $a \in \mathsf{Act}$.

The satisfaction operator $\vDash \in \mathbf{Q} \times \mathcal{L}_{HM}$ is defined in the following manner:

- $p \vDash \top$ is true;
- $p \vDash \bot$ is false;
- $p \vDash \phi \wedge \psi$ iff $p \vDash \phi$ and $p \vDash \psi$;
- $p \vDash \phi \vee \psi$ iff $p \vDash \phi$ or $p \vDash \psi$;
- $p \vDash [a]\phi$ iff $p \downarrow$ and for any p' such that $p \stackrel{a}{\Longrightarrow} p'$ it holds that $p' \vDash \phi$;
- $p \vDash \langle a \rangle \phi$ iff there exists p' such that $p \stackrel{a}{\Longrightarrow} p'$ and $p' \vDash \phi$.

The following is then the modal characterization of the observation equivalence [Abr87]:

Proposition 5.9. *In an underlying sort-finite derived transition system, $p \sqsubseteq_B q$ iff $p \vDash \psi$ implies $q \vDash \psi$ for any $\psi \in \mathcal{L}_{HM}$.*

The translation between expressions in $\mathcal{L}_{HM}$ and tests is performed by the function $(\cdot)^* : \mathcal{L}_{HM} \to \mathcal{O}$ defined as follows [Abr87]:

$$
\begin{aligned}
&(\top)^* = \textsc{Succ} && (\bot)^* = \textsc{Fail} \\
&(\psi \wedge \phi)^* = (\psi)^* \wedge (\phi)^* && (\psi \vee \phi)^* = (\psi)^* \vee (\phi)^* \\
&([a]\psi)^* = \forall\, \tilde{a}(\psi)^* && (\langle a \rangle \psi)^* = \exists\, a(\psi)^* \\
&([\varepsilon]\psi)^* = \forall\, \varepsilon(\psi)^* && (\langle \varepsilon \rangle \psi)^* = \exists\, \varepsilon(\psi)^*
\end{aligned}
\tag{5.10}
$$

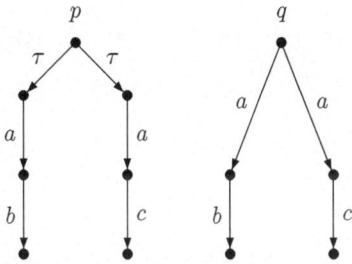

Fig. 5.5. More processes not equivalent under observation preorder ($p \not\simeq_B q$; $p \simeq_{CT} q$; $p \simeq_{\text{must}} q$; $p \simeq_R q$).

Essentially all the testing techniques from the general testing scenario are combined together in a rather comprehensive set of testing techniques to create observation preorder. The comprehensiveness of the testing scenario itself is a problem. While it has an elegant proof theory (which is not presented here, the interested reader is directed elsewhere [Abr87]), observation preorder induces a too complex testing scenario. We have constructed indeed a very strong notion of observability; most evidently, according to Expressions (5.8) and (5.9) we assume the ability to enumerate all possible operating environments, so as to guarantee that all the nondeterministic branches of the process are inspected. The number of such branches is potentially infinite. It is not believed that global testing is really acceptable from a practical point of view. Preorder relations that will be presented in what follows place restrictions in what we can observe, and thus have a greater practical potential.

It is also the case that observation preorder makes too much of a distinction between processes. One example of distinction not made in trace preorder has been given in Figure 5.4. One can argue that such a distinction may make sense in some cases, but such an argument is more difficult in the case of processes shown in Figure 5.5, which are slight modifications of the processes from Figure 5.4. Under (any) trace preorder the two processes p and q are equivalent, and we argue that this makes sense; for indeed by the very definition of internal moves they are not manifest to the outside world, and besides internal moves the two processes behave similarly. However, it is not the case that $q \simeq_B p$. Indeed, notice that q **ref** b, whereas it is not the case that p **ref** b (since p can move ahead by means of internal actions, and thus the refusal does not take place according to Definition 5.3). Then the test $\tilde{b}\text{SUCC}$ introduces a $\top$ outcome in q but not in p according to Definition 5.5; the non-equivalence follows. This certainly looks like nitpicking; we shall introduce below preorders that are not that sensitive to internal moves.

We observe on the other hand that the processes s and t from Figure 5.6 are equivalent under observation preorder. We saw observation preorder giving too much weight to internal moves; now we see the same preorder ignoring this kind of moves altogether. The reason for this is that the internal move never changes

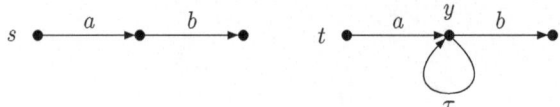

Fig. 5.6. Processes equivalent under observation preorder ($s \simeq_B t$; $s \simeq_R t$; $s \not\simeq_{\text{must}} t$; $s \simeq_{\text{fmust}} t$).

the state, so no matter how many times we go through it we end where we left from. Still, the τ-loop is not without significance in practice since such a loop may produce divergence (if the process keeps iterating through it). However, it can also be argued that the τ-loop is executed an arbitrary but finite number of times and so the process executes b eventually (under some notion of fairness). We shall actually argue back and forth about these two processes as we go along with the description of other preorder relations, so you do not have to make up your mind just yet.

5.5   Testing Preorders

Testing preorders [dNH84] are coarser than observation preorder. Essentially, testing preorders differentiate between processes based on differences in deadlock behavior. We may differentiate by the ability to respond positively to a test, or the ability to respond negatively to a test, or both. In practical cases this is often sufficient.

Recall the concept of outcome of a test presented in Section 5.2.2. For a test o and a process p the result of applying o to p is the set of runs $\text{RUNS}(o, p)$ with outcomes from the set $\{\bot, \top\}$. Also recall the lattices $\mathbb{P}_{\text{may}}$, $\mathbb{P}_{\text{must}}$, and $\mathbb{P}_{\text{conv}}$ over the powerset of $\{\bot, \top\}$, together with the corresponding partial order relations.

We then have the following *testing scenario* for testing preorders: We run a test in parallel to the process being tested, such that they perform the same actions. If the test reaches a success state, then the test succeeds; if on the other hand the process reaches a deadlock state (i.e., a state with no way out), or if the process diverges before the test has reached a success state, the test fails. Sometimes we are interested in running the same test repeatedly and collect all of the possible outcomes; we need this when we want to make sure that a test succeeds no matter what.

Formally, we change in what follows (simplify in fact) the semantics of Expression (5.3) from Definition 5.4 on page 125 to

$$\text{obs}(ao, p) = \bigcup \{\text{obs}(o, p') \mid p \overset{a}{\Longrightarrow} p'\} \cup \{\bot \mid p \uparrow\} \cup \{\bot \mid p \not\Rightarrow\} \qquad (5.11)$$

Then we look at two alternative ways to restrict the set of tests $\mathcal{O}$:

(1) Let $\mathcal{O}_{\text{may}}$ be defined only by expressions of form (5.1), (5.3), and (5.5). We do not need any test that signifies failure; instead, failure under test happens

whenever we reach a deadlock, according to Expression (5.11). Indeed, we are not allowed to combine different testing outcomes at all (there are no boolean operators such as $\wedge$, $\vee$ on outcomes), so a test that fails does not differentiate between anything (it fails no matter what); therefore these tests are excluded as useless. According to the same Expression (5.11) we do not differentiate between deadlock and divergence—both constitute failure under test.

Incidentally, the inability to combine test outcomes makes sense in practice; for indeed recall our criticism with respect to the "global testing" allowed in the observation preorder and that we considered impractical. As it turns out it may also be a too strong restriction, so we end up introducing it again in our next set of tests.

(2) We are now interested in all the possible outcomes of a test. First, let $\mathcal{O}_{\mathrm{must}}$ be defined only by expressions of form (5.1), (5.2), (5.3), and (5.5). This time we do like to combine tests, but only by taking the union of the outcomes without combining them in any smarter way. This is the place where we deviate from (i.e., enhance) our generic testing scenario, and we add the following expression to our initial set of tests $\mathcal{O}$:

$$o = o_1 + o_2 \qquad\qquad\qquad (5.12)$$

with the semantics

$$\mathrm{obs}(o_1 + o_2, p) = \mathrm{obs}(o_1, p) \cup \mathrm{obs}(o_2, p)$$

(3) A combination between these two testing scenarios is certainly possible, so put $\mathcal{O} = \mathcal{O}_{\mathrm{may}} \cup \mathcal{O}_{\mathrm{must}}$.

In order to complete the test scenario, we define the following relations between processes and tests:

Definition 5.10. Process p may satisfy test o, written p **may** o iff $\top \in \mathrm{obs}(o, p)$. Process p must satisfy test o, written p **must** o iff $\{\top\} = \mathrm{obs}(o, p)$. $\qquad\square$

The two relations introduced in Definition 5.10 correspond to the lattices $\mathbb{P}_{\mathrm{may}}$ and $\mathbb{P}_{\mathrm{must}}$, respectively. When we use the **may** relation we are happy with our process if it does not fail every time; if we have a successful run of the test, then the test overall is considered successful. Relation **must** on the other hand considers failure catastrophic; here we accept no failure, all the runs of the test have to be successful for a test to be considered a success. An intuitive comparison with the area of sequential programs is that the **may** relation corresponds to partial correctness, and the **must** relation to total correctness. We have one lattice left, namely $\mathbb{P}_{\mathrm{conv}}$; this obviously corresponds to the conjunction of the two relations.

Based on this testing scenario, and according to our discussion on the relations **may** and **must** we can now introduce three testing preorders[4] $\sqsubseteq_{\mathrm{may}}, \sqsubseteq_{\mathrm{must}}$, $\sqsubseteq_{\mathrm{conv}} \subseteq \mathbf{Q} \times \mathbf{Q}$:

---

[4] These preorders were given numerical names originally [dNH84]. We choose here to give names similar to the lattices they come from in order to help the intuition.

(1) $p \sqsubseteq_{\text{may}} q$ if for any $o \in \mathcal{O}_{\text{may}}$, p **may** o implies that q **may** o.
(2) $p \sqsubseteq_{\text{must}} q$ if for any $o \in \mathcal{O}_{\text{must}}$, p **must** o implies that q **must** o.
(3) $p \sqsubseteq_{\text{conv}} q$ if $p \sqsubseteq_{\text{may}} q$ and $p \sqsubseteq_{\text{must}} q$.

The equivalence relations corresponding to the three preorders are denoted by $\simeq_{\text{may}}$, $\simeq_{\text{must}}$, and $\simeq_{\text{conv}}$, respectively. We shall use $\sqsubseteq_T$ (for "testing preorder") instead of $\sqsubseteq_{\text{conv}}$ in subsequent sections.

Note that the relation $\sqsubseteq_{\text{conv}}$ is implicitly defined in terms of observers from the set $\mathcal{O} = \mathcal{O}_{\text{may}} \cup \mathcal{O}_{\text{must}}$. Also note that actually we do not need three sets of observers, since all the three preorders make sense under $\mathcal{O}$. The reason for introducing these three distinct sets is solely for the benefit of having different testing scenarios for the three testing preorders (that are also tight, i.e., they contain the smallest set of observers possible), according to our ways of presenting things (in which the testing scenario defines the preorder).

The most discerning relation is of course $\sqsubseteq_{\text{conv}}$. It is also the case that in order to see whether two processes are in the relation $\sqsubseteq_{\text{conv}}$ we have to check both the other relations, so our subsequent discussion will deal mostly the other two preorders (since the properties of $\sqsubseteq_{\text{conv}}$ will follow immediately).

One may wonder what we get out of testing preorders in terms of practical considerations. First, as opposed to trace preorders, we no longer need to record the whole trace of a process; instead we only distinguish between success and failure of tests. It is also the case that we do not need to combine all the outcomes of test runs as in observation preorder. We still have a notion of "global testing," but the combination of the outcomes is either forbidden (in $\sqsubseteq_{\text{may}}$) or simplified. In all, we arguably get a preorder that is more practical. We also note that, by contrast to trace preorders *we can have finite tests (or observers) even if the processes themselves consist in infinite runs*. Indeed, in trace preorders a test succeeds only when the end of the trace is reached, whereas we can now stop our test whenever we are satisfied with the behavior observed so far (at which time we simply insert a SUCC or FAIL in our test).

In terms of discerning power, recall first the example shown in Figure 5.5 on page 132, where the two processes p and q are not equivalent under observation preorder. We argued that this is not necessarily a meaningful distinction. According to this argument testing preorders are better, since they do not differentiate between these two processes. Indeed, p and q always perform an action a followed by either an action b or an action c, depending on which branch of the process tree is taken (recall that the distinction between p and q under observation preorder was made in terms of nitpicking refusals, that are no longer present in testing preorders). We thus revert to the "good" properties of trace preorders.

Recall now our argument that the processes from Figure 5.6 on page 133 should be considered the same. We also argued the other way around, but for now we stick with the first argument because we also have $s \simeq_{\text{may}} t$. Indeed, it is always the case that processes such as the ones depicted in Figure 5.7 are equivalent under $\simeq_{\text{may}}$, and the equivalence of s and t follows. In other words, we keep the "good" properties of observation preorder.

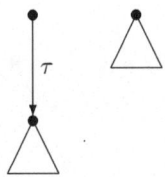

Fig. 5.7. Processes equivalent under $\simeq_{\text{may}}$.

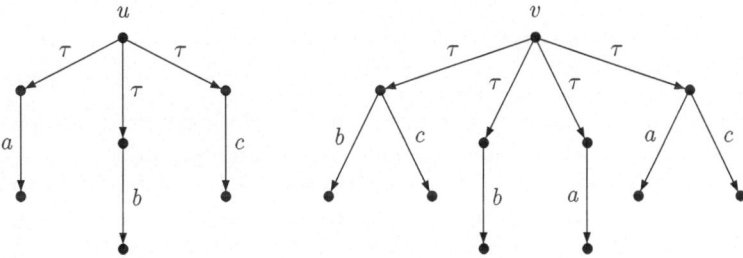

Fig. 5.8. Two processes not equivalent under testing preorder ($u \not\simeq_{\text{must}} v$; $u \simeq_{CT} v$).

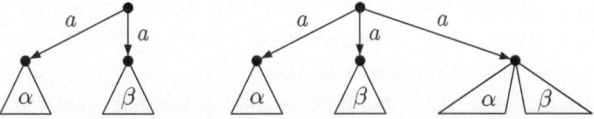

Fig. 5.9. Processes equivalent under any testing preorder.

In general, $\simeq_{\text{may}}$ ignores the tree structure of processes, which shows that this preorder is a very weak relation. This is not the case with $\simeq_{\text{must}}$. It is now the time to argue that the two processes depicted in Figure 5.6 should be considered different. They are so under $\simeq_{\text{must}}$, for indeed one branch of t diverges while no divergent computations are present in s. A suitable test such as $ab\text{SUCC}$ will exploit this property under the **must** operator. In general, the presence of divergence in the form of an infinite path of internal moves will ruin a test under $\simeq_{\text{must}}$. Whether this is desired or not depends on one's interpretation of such an infinite path of internal moves.

Continuing with examples for $\simeq_{\text{must}}$, consider the processes shown in Figure 5.8. No matter what internal move is chosen by v, it can always perform either a or b. It follows that v **must** ($a\text{SUCC} + b\text{SUCC}$). On the other hand, at its point of choosing which way to go, u has the choice of performing c. It thus follow that u **may** ($a\text{SUCC} + b\text{SUCC}$), but it is not the case that u **must** ($a\text{SUCC} + b\text{SUCC}$). In general, it is easy to see that $u \simeq_{\text{may}} v$, but that $u \not\simeq_{\text{must}} v$. Incidentally, these processes are equivalent in trace preorders.

We should emphasize that, though $\simeq_{\text{must}}$ takes into consideration the tree structure of the process under scrutiny, it does so in a more limited way. This

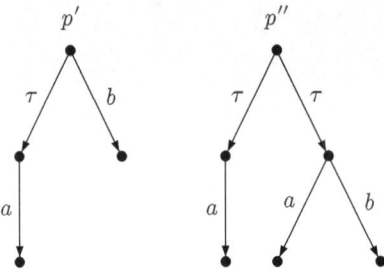

Fig. 5.10. More processes equivalent under testing preorders ($p' \simeq_T p''$; $p' \not\simeq_R p''$).

was shown in our discussion based on Figure 5.5. More generally, the processes depicted in Figure 5.9 are equivalent under any testing preorder.

Finally, an example that will come in handy when we compare testing preorders with refusal preorders (that is the subject of the next section) is given by the two processes shown in Figure 5.10, which are equivalent under $\sqsubseteq_{\text{conv}}$.

All of the examples presented here allow us to conclude the following: The preorder $\sqsubseteq_{\text{may}}$ is a very weak relation, but has the advantage of needing no global testing. The other testing preorders do make use of global testing, but in a restricted way compared with observation preorder. The distinctions they make are not as rich as in the case of observation preorder, but they are nonetheless quite rich. On the principle that the most distinction we can make between processes the better we are, one now wonders whether we can do better in distinctions without the complexity of observation preorder.

Since $\sqsubseteq_{\text{conv}}$ is clearly the testing preorder that makes the most distinctions, we shall henceforth understand this preorder when we refer simply to testing preorder. Recall that we also decided to denote it by $\sqsubseteq_T$ in subsequent sections (with $\simeq_T$ as the name of the induced equivalence).

5.6   Refusal Testing

The only reasonable way in which one can obtain information about a process is by communicating with it by means of actions. This is precisely what we modeled in all this chapter. For example, we just inspect the actions performed by a process in trace preorders; we then take it one step further in the testing preorder, where we request sequences of actions that depend on the information gained about the process as the test progresses. In our generic testing scenario presented in Section 5.2.2 we go even further by adding to tests the ability of *refusing* actions. This is an interesting feature, that looks powerful and arguably practically feasible. Recall on the other hand that we definitely did not see observation preorder (the only preorder involving the concept of refusals) as practical, at least not as practical as testing preorders.

So on one hand we have refusals, that look promising (and practical enough), and on the other hand we have testing preorders, that look practical. We now combine them. While we are at it, we also differentiate between failure by dead-lock (no outgoing actions) and divergence. We thus obtain the **refusal pre-orders** [Phi87].

Refusal preorders rely on the following *testing scenario*: We start from the scenario of complete trace semantics, i.e., we view a process as a black box with a window that displays the current action and becomes empty when a deadlock occurs. We now equip our box with one switch for each possible action $a \in$ Act. By flipping the switch for some action a to "on" we *block* a; the process continues to choose its execution path autonomously, but it may only start by executing actions that are not blocked by our manipulation of switches. The configuration of switches can be changed at any time during the execution of the process.

Formally, we restrict our set of tests $\mathcal{O}$ introduced in Definition 5.4 on page 125 by allowing only expressions of form (5.1)–(5.5), and a restricted variant of (5.12 on page 134) as follows:

$$o = ao_1 + \tilde{a} o_2 \tag{5.13}$$

The semantics of this kind of expressions is immediately obtained by the seman-tics of Expressions (5.12) and (5.4) (since we are starting here from the scenario of the testing preorder, the semantics of tests of form (5.4) is given by Expres-sion (5.11)). This is our "switch" that we flip to blocks a (and then we follow with o_2) or not.

We also differentiate between deadlock and divergence. We did not make such a differentiation in the development of previous preorders, because we could not do this readily (and in those cases when we could, we would simply express this in terms of the divergence predicate). However, now that we talk about refusals we will need to distinguish between tests that fail because of divergent processes, and tests that fail because all the actions are blocked. We find it convenient to do this explicitly, so we enrich our set of test outcomes to $\{\top, 0, \bot\}$, with $\bot$ now signifying only divergence, while 0 stands for deadlock. In order to do this, we alter the semantics of expressions of form (5.2), (5.3), and (5.4) to

$$\mathrm{obs}(\mathrm{FAIL}, p) = \{0\}$$

$$\mathrm{obs}(ao, p) = \bigcup \{\mathrm{obs}(o, p') \mid p \xrightarrow{a} p'\} \cup \{\bot \mid p \uparrow\} \cup \{0 \mid p \xrightarrow{a} \!\!\!\!/ \; \}$$

$$\mathrm{obs}(\tilde{a} o, p) = \bigcup \{\mathrm{obs}(o, p) \mid p \xrightarrow{a} \!\!\!\!/ , p \xrightarrow{\tau} \!\!\!\!/ \; \} \cup \{\bot \mid p \uparrow\} \cup \{0 \mid p \xrightarrow{a} \text{ or } p \xrightarrow{\tau} \}$$

Note that in the general testing scenario we count a failure whenever we learn about a refusal. In this scenario, a refusal generates a failure only when no other action can be performed. Also note that this scenario imposes further restric-tions on the applicable tests by restricting the semantics of the allowable test expressions. As a further restriction, we have the convention that test expres-sions of form (5.5) shall be applied with the highest priority of all the expressions (i.e., internal actions are performed before anything else, such that the system is allowed to fully stabilize itself before further testing is attempted—this is also the reason for replacing relation $\Rightarrow$ with the stronger $\rightarrow$ in the semantics of the tests ao and $\tilde{a} o$).

It should be mentioned that the original presentation of refusal testing [Phi87] allows initially to refuse sets of actions, not only individual actions. In this setting we can flip sets of switches as opposed to one switch at a time as we allow by the above definition of $\mathcal{O}$. However, it is shown later in the same paper [Phi87] that refusing sets of actions is not necessary, hence our construction. Now that the purpose of our test scenario is clear, we shall further restrict the scenario. Apparently this restriction is less expressive, but the discussion we mentioned above [Phi87] shows that—against intuition—we do not lose anything; although the language is smaller, it is equally expressive. In the same spirit as for testing preorders, we restrict our set of tests in two ways, and then we introduce a new version of the operators **may** and **must**.

(1) Let the set $\mathcal{O}_1$ contain exactly all the expressions of form (5.1) and a re-
     stricted version of form (5.13) where either $o_1 = \text{FAIL}$ or $o_2 = \text{FAIL}$.
     Let then p **may** o iff $\top \in \text{obs}(p, o)$.
(2) Let the set $\mathcal{O}_2$ contain exactly all the expressions of form (5.2) and a re-
     stricted version of form (5.13) where either $o_1 = \text{SUCC}$ or $o_2 = \text{SUCC}$.
     Let then p **must** o iff $\{\top\} = \text{obs}(p, o)$.
(3) As usual, put $\mathcal{O} = \mathcal{O}_1 \cup \mathcal{O}_2$.

In other words, at any given time we either block an action and succeed or fail (as the case may be), or we follow the action we would have blocked otherwise and move forward; no other test involving blocked actions is possible. One may wonder about the cause of the disappearance of form (5.5). Well, this expression was not that "real" to begin with (we never wrote ε down in our test expressions, we provided it instead to allow the process to "stabilize" itself), and we can now replace the expression εo by $e\text{FAIL} + \tilde{e}o$, where e is a new action we invent outside Act (thus knowing that the process will never perform it).

With these helper operators and sets of tests we now define the **refusal preorder** $\sqsubseteq_R$ as follows: $p \sqsubseteq_R q$ iff (a) p **may** o implies q **may** o for any $o \in \mathcal{O}_1$, and (b) p **must** o implies q **must** o for any $o \in \mathcal{O}_2$. The induced refusal equivalence $\simeq_R$ is defined in the usual way.

The alert reader has noticed that the refusal preorder is by far the most restricted preorder we have seen. Let us now take a look at its power of discrimination. Since it has been shown that the generic refusal testing scenario (that we started with) and our restricted variant are in fact equally expressive, we shall feel free to use either of them as it suits our needs.

We now compare refusal preorder with the testing preorder. First, it is immediate that processes depicted in Figures 5.4 on page 130, 5.5 on page 132, and 5.9 on page 136 continue to be equivalent under refusal preorders.

On the other hand, consider the processes shown in Figure 5.10 on page 137 which are equivalent under testing preorder. We then notice that under refusal preorder we have $\text{obs}(b\text{SUCC}, p') = \{0\}$, for indeed the internal action is performed first to stabilize the process, and after this no b action is possible. However, it is immediate that $\text{obs}(b\text{SUCC}, p'') = \{\top, 0\}$. We do not even use refusals here, the two processes become non-equivalent because our convention that test expressions of form (5.5) shall always be performed first.

140   Stefan D. Bruda

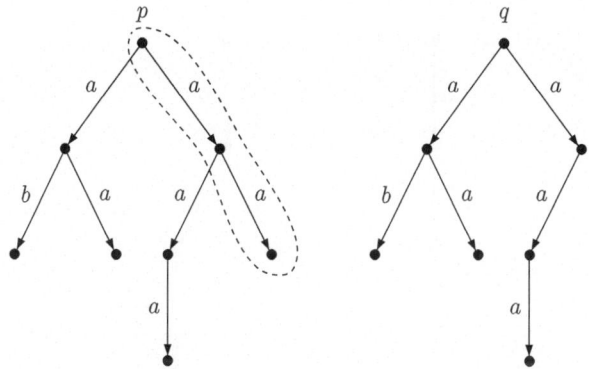

Fig. 5.11. Processes not equivalent under refusal preorder ($p \not\simeq_R q$; $p \simeq_T q$).

Even in the absence of such a convention we have a more precise preorder. Consider for instance the processes from Figure 5.11. They are immediately equivalent under testing preorder, but not so under refusal preorder. Indeed, it holds that $obs(\overline{ab}a\widetilde{a}\textsc{Succ}, p) = \{\top, 0\}$ and $obs(\overline{ab}a\widetilde{a}\textsc{Succ}, q) = \{0\}$ (the path circled in the figure is the only successful path under this test).

It is then apparent that refusal preorder makes more distinction than the testing preorder. We shall tackle the reverse comparison by giving a precise comparison of refusal preorder with the observation preorder. Such a comparison is possible by developing a modal characterization for the refusal preorder. As it turns out, this characterization can also be given in terms of a subset of $\mathcal{L}_{HM}$ (which is the set of formulae corresponding to observation preorder). This subset (denote it by $\mathcal{L}_R$) is the domain of the following partial function $(\cdot)^* : \mathcal{L}_{HM} \to \mathcal{O}$ translating between expressions in $\mathcal{L}_{HM}$ and tests and given by:

$$
\begin{array}{ll}
(\top)^* = \textsc{Succ} & (\bot)^* = \textsc{Fail} \\
([a]\psi)^* = a(\psi)^* & ([a]\psi)^* = \widetilde{a}(\psi)^* \\
(\langle\varepsilon\rangle([a]\bot \wedge [\varepsilon]\psi))^* = \widetilde{a}(\psi)^* & ([\varepsilon](\langle a\rangle\top \vee \langle\varepsilon\rangle\psi))^* = \underline{a}(\psi)^*
\end{array}
\tag{5.14}
$$

For succinctness we abbreviated $ao + \widetilde{a}\textsc{Fail}$ by ao, $a\textsc{Fail} + \widetilde{a}o$ by $\widetilde{a}o$, $ao + \widetilde{a}\textsc{Succ}$ by $\underline{a}o$, and $a\textsc{Succ} + \widetilde{a}o$ by $\widetilde{\underline{a}}o$. We have [Phi87]:

Proposition 5.11. *For any process $p \in \mathbf{Q}$ and for any expression $\psi \in \mathcal{L}_R$, it holds that $p \models \psi$ iff p **may** $(\psi)^*$, and that $p \models \psi$ iff p **must** $(\psi)^*$. It then follows that $p \sqsubseteq_R q$ iff $p \models \psi$ implies $q \models \psi$ for any expression $\psi \in \mathcal{L}_R$.*

It then follows that:

Theorem 5.12. *For any two processes p and q, $p \sqsubseteq_B q$ implies $p \sqsubseteq_R q$, but not the other way around.*

Proof. The implication is immediate from Proposition 5.11 given that $\mathcal{L}_R$ is a strict subset of $\mathcal{L}_{HM}$. That observation preorder is strictly finer than refusal preorder is shown by the example depicted in Figure 5.5 on page 132.   □

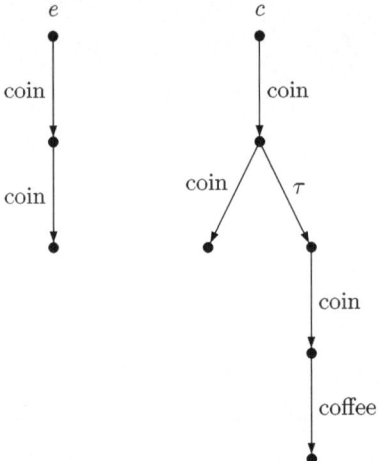

Fig. 5.12. Two vending machines ($e \sqsubseteq_R c$; $e \not\sqsubseteq_{FT} c$).

So we find that refusal preorder is coarser than observation preorder. This also allows us to compare refusal and testing preorders. Indeed, recall that the infinite processes shown in Figure 5.6 on page 133 are equivalent under observation preorder (and then according to Proposition 5.12 under refusal preorder). We have shown in the previous section that these processes are not equivalent under testing preorder. Given that on the other hand refusal preorder distinguishes between processes indistinguishable in testing preorder, we have

Corollary 5.13. *The preorders $\sqsubseteq_T$ and $\sqsubseteq_R$ are not comparable.*

We note here an apparent contradiction with results given elsewhere [Phi87] that the two preorders are comparable. This contradiction turns out to be caused by the unfortunate (and incorrect) terminology used in [Phi87].

In practical terms, refusal preorder is clearly more appealing than observation preorder. Arguably, it is also more appealing than testing preorder, because of the simplicity of tests; indeed, we eliminated all nondeterminism from the tests in $\mathcal{O}_1$ and $\mathcal{O}_2$ (and thus in $\mathcal{O}$). The only possible practical downside (of refusal preorder compared with testing preorder) is that we need the ability to block actions.

5.7   Failure Trace Testing

In refusal testing, whenever we observe a process that cannot continue because we blocked all of its possible actions we have a failed test. This seems a reasonable testing strategy, but we end up with surprising preorder relations because of it. Consider for example the rather instructive example [Lan90] of the two vending machines c and e depicted in Figure 5.12. Machine c may give us coffee if we insert two coins, while machine e eats up our money, period. In terms of refusal preorder, it is immediate that c passes strictly more tests than e, so $e \sqsubseteq_R c$. In other words, e is an implementation of c! Clearly, this contradicts most people's idea of a working coffee machine.

Such a strange concept of correct implementation is corrected by the **failure trace preorder** [Lan90]. This preorder is based on the following *testing scenario*: We have the same black box we did in the testing scenario for refusal preorder. The only difference is in our actions; when we observe the deadlock (by the empty window) we record such an occurrence (as a failure) and then we are allowed to flip switches off to allow the process to continue.

Formally, we allow exactly the same test expressions for the set $\mathcal{O}$ as we did initially in the previous section, but we revert the semantics of expressions of form (5.4) to its original form (continuing to make the distinction between failure as deadlock versus failure as divergence), i.e.,

$$\mathrm{obs}(\tilde{a}o, p) = \bigcup \{\mathrm{obs}(o, p') \mid p \overset{a}{\Longrightarrow} p'\} \cup \{\bot \mid p \uparrow\} \cup \{0 \mid p \overset{\varepsilon}{\Longrightarrow} p', p' \text{ ref } a\}$$

We then define the operators **may** and **must** exactly as we did in the previous section, i.e., p **may** o iff $\top \in \mathrm{obs}(p, o)$, and p **must** o iff $\{\top\} = \mathrm{obs}(p, o)$. Finally, the **failure trace preorder** $\sqsubseteq_{FT}$ is defined as $p \sqsubseteq_{FT} q$ iff for all $o \in \mathcal{O}$ it holds that p **may** o implies q **may** o and p **must** o implies q **must** o. As usual, the failure trace preorder induces the failure trace equivalence $\simeq_{FT}$.

Let us go back to our vending machines from Figure 5.12, and consider the test

$$o = \text{coin } \widetilde{\text{coin}} \text{ coin coffee } \textsc{Succ}$$

As opposed to refusal testing, we now have $\mathrm{obs}(o, e) = \{0\}$ (the action "coffee" is not available for the test), whereas $\mathrm{obs}(o, c) = \{\top, 0\}$ (we record a failure when we block action "coin" and then we move on to obtain a successful test on the right side branch). We thus notice that c **may** o but that it is not the case that e **may** o; a machine that does not give us coffee does not pass this test. Our two vending machines become thus incomparable (and justly so).

Failure trace preorder thus makes more distinction than refusal preorder. It is also easy to see that refusal preorder does not distinguish between processes that are not distinguishable under failure trace. Indeed, it is enough to place a FAIL test after each action that is blocked in the tests and those tests become tests for the refusal preorder.

It is immediate to see that observation preorder is strictly finer than failure trace preorder. Indeed, we introduced on top of refusal order a semantics that is otherwise included in the semantics of observation preorder. So we have:

Proposition 5.14. *For any two processes p and q, $p \sqsubseteq_B q$ implies $p \sqsubseteq_{FT} q$ (but not the other way around), and $p \sqsubseteq_{FT} q$ implies $p \sqsubseteq_R q$ (but not the other way around).*

Using the failure trace preorder we can make distinctions that cannot be made using refusal preorder. However, this increase does not necessarily come for free. Indeed, the tests in the sets $\mathcal{O}_1$ and $\mathcal{O}_2$ described in the previous sections are *sequential*, in the sense that unions always occur between a test whose result that is immediately available (SUCC or FAIL) and some other, possibly longer test. In testing preorders as well as in failure trace preorder we need to copy the process while it runs; indeed, we may need to combine the outcomes of two (or more) different runs of the process, which means that we need to run two copies of the process to obtain these outcomes independently from each other. Because of the sequential tests used by refusal preorder copying is no longer necessary (but it becomes necessary once more in failure trace preorder). This being said, the definition of the **must** operator from refusal preorder implies that processes need to be copied anyway (since we have to apply many tests on them), so the failure trace testing scenario is not that bad after all.

5.8   Fair Testing

Recall the processes depicted in Figure 5.6 on page 133 and our back and forth argument that they should be considered equivalent (or not). When we considered them under the testing preorder, s and t were not equivalent, whereas they are so under the other preorders. Testing preorder, with its habit that the presence of divergence may ruin a test, will differentiate between these two processes as opposed to all the other preorders we have seen so far. As we mentioned, whether such a behavior is a good or bad thing depends on one's opinion about divergences.

For those who prefer to ignore divergences as long as there is a hope that the process will continue with its visible operation, i.e., for those who prefer to consider the processes shown in Figure 5.6 equivalent, **fair testing** is available [BRV95].

We have the same *testing scenario* for fair testing as the one used in Section 5.5, except that the operator **must** is enhanced, such that it chooses a visible action whenever such an action is available. With the same set $\mathcal{O}$ of observers as the one used to define the testing preorder, the new operator **fmust** is defined as follows:

> p **fmust** o iff for any $\sigma \in \mathsf{Act}^*$ and $o' \in \mathcal{O}$ with $o = \sigma o'$, it holds that: $\mathrm{obs}(o', p') = \mathrm{obs}(o, p)$ for some $p' \in \mathbf{Q}$, $p \overset{\sigma}{\Longrightarrow} p'$, implies that there exists $a \in \mathsf{Act} \cup \{\text{SUCC}\}$ such that $o' = a o''$, $o'' \in \mathcal{O} \cup \{\varepsilon\}$.

The preorder $\sqsubseteq_{\mathrm{fmust}}$, as well as the equivalence $\simeq_{\mathrm{fmust}}$ induced by the operator **fmust** are defined in the usual manner.

The operator **fmust** is the "fair" variant of the operator **must** of testing preorder lineage. It ignores the divergences as long as there is a visible action (a in the above definition) accessible to the observer. The following characterization of $\sqsubseteq_{\mathrm{fmust}}$ in terms of other preorders is easily obtained from the results presented elsewhere [BRV95]:

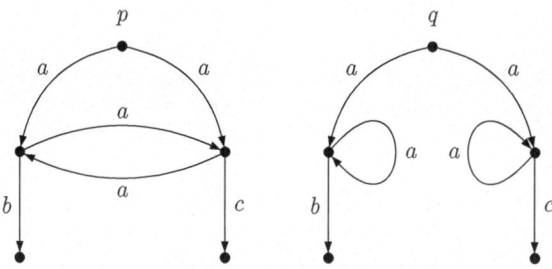

Fig. 5.13. Processes different after hiding $\{a\}$.

Proposition 5.15. *For any two processes p and q, $p \sqsubseteq_R q$ implies $p \sqsubseteq_{\text{fmust}} q$ (but not the other way around), and $p \sqsubseteq_{\text{must}} q$ implies $p \sqsubseteq_{\text{fmust}} q$ (but not the other way around).*

The modification of the testing preorder introduced by the preorder $\sqsubseteq_{\text{fmust}}$ brings us back into the generic testing scenario. In the following we go even further and tackle a problem that we did not encounter up to this point, but that is common to many preorders. This problem refers to the process of *hiding* a set of actions.

Given a transition system $B = (\mathbf{Q}, \text{Act} \cup \{\tau\}, \rightarrow, \uparrow_B)$ and some set $A \subseteq \text{Act}$, the result of *hiding* A is a transition system $B/A = (\mathbf{Q}, \text{Act} \setminus A \cup \{\tau\}, \rightarrow_h, \uparrow_B)$, where $\rightarrow_h$ is identical to $\rightarrow$ except that all the transitions of form $p \xrightarrow{a} q$ for some $a \in A$ are replaced by $p \xrightarrow{\tau}_h q$.

Under a suitable transition system B, consider now the processes depicted in Figure 5.13, and the equivalent processes in $B/\{a\}$; the processes become non-equivalent under $\sqsubseteq_R$. Similar examples can be found for the other preorders presented in this chapter. These preorders are not pre-congruence relations under hiding.

A preorder based on the testing preorder and that is pre-congruent can also be introduced [BRV95]. Call such a preorder **should-testing**. The *testing scenario* is again the same as the one presented in Section 5.5, with the exception that the operators **must** and **may** are replaced by the operator **should** defined as follows (again, we have the same set $\mathcal{O}$ of observers as the one used to define the testing preorder):

> p **should** o iff for any $\sigma \in \text{Act}^*$ and $o' \in \mathcal{O}$ with $o = \sigma o'$, it holds that: $\text{obs}(o, p) = \text{obs}(o', p')$ for some $p' \in \mathbf{Q}$, $p \overset{\sigma}{\Longrightarrow} p'$, implies that there exists $\sigma' \in \text{Act}^*$ such that $o' = \sigma' \text{SUCC}$ and $\top \in \text{obs}(o', p')$.

The preorder and the equivalence induced by the **should** operator are denoted by $\sqsubseteq_{\text{should}}$ and $\simeq_{\text{should}}$, respectively.

The idea of should-testing is that in a successful test there is always a reachable successful state, so if the choices are made fairly that state will eventually be reached. Fair testing states that a system passing the test may not deadlock unless success has been reported before; should-testing requires a stronger condition in that a successful state must be reached from every state in the system.

It is immediate that $\sqsubseteq_{should}$ is coarser than $\sqsubseteq_{fmust}$ (since the success condition is stronger). This relationship is even stronger for processes with only finite visible runs:

Proposition 5.16. *For any two processes p and q, $p \sqsubseteq_{should} q$ implies $p \sqsubseteq_{fmust} q$ (but not the other way around); for any two processes p and q for which all the visible runs are finite $p \sqsubseteq_{should} q$ iff $p \sqsubseteq_{fmust} q$.*

In addition $\sqsubseteq_{should}$ is a pre-congruence under hiding—as well as under prefixing and synchronization [BRV95]; in fact we have:

Proposition 5.17. *The relation $\sqsubseteq_{should}$ is the largest relation contained in $\sqsubseteq_{fmust}$ that is a pre-congruence under synchronization and hiding.*

5.9   Conformance Testing, or Preorders at Work

This section is different from the previous ones, because it does not introduce new testing scenarios and new preorders. Instead, it puts the existing scenarios in a formalization of the concept of conformance testing [Tre94]. The description of such an environment in which preorders are put to good use is indeed a nice wrap up of our presentation.

We mentioned at least two times that preorders can be interpreted as implementation relations. In this sections we elaborate on this idea. We thus present here the *application* of everything we talked about before.

Conformance testing consists in testing the implementation of a system against that system's specification. Formally, we are given a formal specification language $\mathcal{L}_{FDT}$ (such as CCS [Mil80] or even labeled transition systems), and we have to determine for some specification $s \in \mathcal{L}_{FDT}$ what are the implementations that conform to s (i.e., are a correct implementation of s). Of course, implementations are physical objects, so we analyze their properties by means of formal models of such implementations, that are also members of $\mathcal{L}_{FDT}$. We assume that any concrete implementation can be modeled in $\mathcal{L}_{FDT}$.

There usually are more than one correct implementation of some specification, so we actually work with a set CONFORM$_s$ of implementations conforming to a specification s. This set can be defined using either a *behavior* (or model-based) *specification*, or a *requirement* (or logical) *specification*.

In the behavior specification approach the set CONFORM$_s$ is defined by means of an *implementation relation* **imp**, such that i **imp** s iff i conforms to s:

$$\text{CONFORM}_s = \{i \in \mathcal{L}_{FDT} \mid i \text{ imp } s\}.$$

In the requirement specification approach we define the set CONFORM$_s$ by giving all the properties that should hold for all of its elements. Such properties, or *requirements* are specified in a formal language $\mathcal{L}_{RQ}$, and if an implementation i has property r we say that i satisfies r and we write i **sat** r. A conforming implementation will have to satisfy all the properties from a set $R \subseteq \mathcal{L}_{RQ}$, so we have:

$$\text{CONFORM}_s = \{i \in \mathcal{L}_{FDT} \mid \text{for all } r \in R, i \text{ \textbf{sat} } r\}.$$

If a suitable specification language has been chosen, we can define a *specification relation* **spec** $\subseteq \mathcal{L}_{FDT} \times \mathcal{L}_{RQ}$ which expresses the requirements that are implicitly specified by a behavior specification. Our definition for CONFORM_s then becomes:

$$\text{CONFORM}_s = \{i \in \mathcal{L}_{FDT} \mid \text{for all } r \in \mathcal{L}_{RQ}, s \text{ \textbf{spec} } r \text{ implies } i \text{ \textbf{sat} } r\}.$$

Both these approaches to the definition of CONFORM_s are valid and they can be used independently from each other. They are both useful too: if we want to check an implementation against a specification the behavioral specification is appropriate; if on the other hand we want to determine conformance by testing the implementation, it is typically more convenient to derive requirements from the specification and then test them.

Of course, the two descriptions of CONFORM_s should be *compatible* to each other, i.e., they should define the same set. We then have the following restriction on the relations **imp**, **sat**, and **spec**:

$$\text{for all } i \in \mathcal{L}_{FDT}, i \text{ \textbf{imp} } s \text{ iff (for all } r \in \mathcal{L}_{RQ}, s \text{ \textbf{spec} } r \text{ implies } i \text{ \textbf{sat} } r).$$

We note that the formal specification s is in itself not enough to allow for conformance testing. We need instead either a pair s and **imp**, or the combination of s, $\mathcal{L}_{RQ}$, **sat**, and **spec**.

Consider now our definition of processes, tests, and preorders, and pick one particular preorder $\sqsubseteq_\alpha$. We clearly have a specification language $\mathcal{L}_{FDT}$ given by the set of processes and the underlying transition system. We then model s using our language and we obtain a specification. Then the relation **imp** is precisely given by the preorder $\sqsubseteq_\alpha$. The preorder gives us the tools for conformance testing using the behavior specification. If we provide a modal characterization for the preorder we can do testing using requirement specification too. Indeed, the set $\mathcal{L}_{RQ}$ is the set of formulae that constitute the modal characterization, the relation **sat** is our satisfaction predicate $\vDash$, and the function $(\cdot)^*$ defines the relation **spec**.

It turns out that our theory of preorders has an immediate application in conformance testing. Indeed, all we did in this section was to translate the notation used elsewhere [Tre94] into the notation that we used in this chapter, and presto, we have a framework for formal conformance testing.

However, our framework is not fully practical because of the number of tests one needs to apply in order to check for conformance, which is often countably infinite. Elegant proof systems are not enough from a practical point of view, we also need to test implementations in a reasonable amount of time. We come

$$\sqsubseteq \longleftrightarrow \sqsubseteq_B \longrightarrow \sqsubseteq_{FT} \longrightarrow \sqsubseteq_R \longrightarrow \sqsubseteq_{fmust} \longrightarrow \sqsubseteq_{should}$$

$$\nearrow$$

$$\sqsubseteq_T$$

Fig. 5.14. Relations between preorders. The arrows $\sqsubseteq_\alpha \longrightarrow \sqsubseteq_\beta$ stand for "$p \sqsubseteq_\alpha q$ implies $p \sqsubseteq_\beta q$, but not the other way around."

back to our discussion on practical considerations. The observation preorder for instance, with its strong notion of observability, is unlikely in our opinion to create a realistic framework for conformance testing.

In any case, testing and test case generation in particular are also the subject of subsequent chapters, so our discussion about applications ends here.

5.10 Summary

We now conclude our presentation of preorder relations. We have surveyed quite a number of preorders, so before going any further a summary is in order. We have talked throughout this chapter about the following preorders:

$\sqsubseteq$	the observational testing preorder, as a general framework presented in Section 5.2.3
$\sqsubseteq_{CT}$	the complete trace preorder, presented in Section 5.3;
$\sqsubseteq_B$	observation preorder, the subject of Section 5.4;
$\sqsubseteq_T$	(aka $\sqsubseteq_{conv}$, together with $\sqsubseteq_{may}$ and $\sqsubseteq_{must}$), surveyed in Section 5.5;
$\sqsubseteq_R$	refusal preorder, presented in Section 5.6;
$\sqsubseteq_{FT}$	failure trace preorder, in Section 5.7;
$\sqsubseteq_{fmust}$	fair testing preorder, the subject of Section 5.8;
$\sqsubseteq_{should}$	should-testing preorder, a variant of $\sqsubseteq_{fmust}$, also a precongruence.

In addition, we have defined a generic testing scenario and the associated observable testing preorder $\sqsubseteq$. There exist preorders we did not consider specifically, such as Darondeau's preorder, because they were shown to coincide with preorders presented here [dN87]. We introduced trace preorders only because we had to start with something (and we decided to start with something simple), and because sometimes they make for useful comparison tools. However, trace preorders are awkward to work with, so we do not give too much thought to them henceforth.

One of the comparison criteria between preorders is their power of discrimination. In this respect, the observation preorder has been shown to coincide with the generic preorder $\sqsubseteq$. The remaining preorders are strictly less discriminating and arrange themselves in a nice hierarchy. The only exception is the testing preorder, which is not comparable with the observation, failure trace, and refusal preorders. This is one reason for the introduction of $\sqsubseteq_{fmust}$, which has its place in the hierarchy alright. This comparison has been shown throughout the chapter by examples and propositions, and is summarized in Figure 5.14.

The relation $\sqsubseteq_{fmust}$ was also introduced because of fairness considerations (hence the name fair testing preorder). Specifically, the testing preorder deals unfairly with divergence, in the sense that divergence is reported as failure. In contrast, the fair interpretation of divergence implies that the tests succeed in presence of divergences as long as the system has a chance to eventually perform a visible action despite divergences. Since $\sqsubseteq_{fmust}$ is not a pre-congruence relation, the variant $\sqsubseteq_{should}$ (which is the largest pre-congruence included in $\sqsubseteq_{fmust}$) has also been defined.

Of course, the presence of fairness, or the greater power of discrimination are not an a priori good thing; it all depends on the desired properties one is interested in. The unfair interpretations of divergence in particular are useful in differentiating between livelock and deadlock, i.e., in detecting whether the system under test features busy-waiting loops and other such behaviors that are not deadlocked but are nonetheless unproductive (and undetectable under the fair testing scenario).

In terms of power of discrimination, we have noticed in Section 5.4 that the most discriminating preorder differentiates between processes that are for all practical purposes identical (see for example the processes shown in Figures 5.4 on page 130 and 5.5 on page 132). This is not to say that more differentiation is bad either, just look at the coffee machine examples from Figure 5.12 on page 141, which are in a strange implementation relation under refusal testing (only a crooked merchant would accept this) but are not comparable under failure trace preorder.

Another comparison of preorders can be made in terms of the complexity of the tests and their practical feasibility. It is no surprise that the most discriminating preorder, namely the observation preorder, appears to be the least practical of them all. In this respect the award of the most practically realizable preorder seems to go to refusal preorder. This is the only preorder based exclusively on sequential tests. This being said, we are not necessarily better off since in the general case we need a number of tests to figure out the properties of the system, so that the advantage of the tests being sequential pales somehow.

Another practical issue in refusal preorder is the concept of refusal itself. One can wonder how practical such a concept is. Recall that actions are an abstraction; in particular, they do not necessarily represent the acceptance of input. So how does one refuse an action without modifying the process under scrutiny itself? This does not seem realizable in the general case (whenever we cannot access the internals of the process under test). Do we take away the award from refusal preorder?

In all, practical considerations do differentiate between the preorders we talked about, especially for the observation preorder which combines results in a more complex way than other preorders (that simply take the union of the results of various runs and tests) and requires a rather unrealistic concept of global testing. However, when testing systems we are in the realm of the halting problem, so practical considerations cannot ever make an a priori distinction.

The utility of various preorders should thus be estimated by taking all of their features into consideration.

In the same line of thought, namely practical applications, we have presented a practical framework for conformance testing based on the theory of preorders.

Finally, it is worth pointing out that our presentation has been made in terms of labeled transition systems, as opposed to most of the literature, in which process algebraic languages such as CCS, LOTOS, and variants thereof are generally used. Labeled transition systems define however the semantics of all these languages, so the translation of the results surveyed here into various other formalisms should not be a problem. The upside of our approach is the uniform and concise characterization of the preorders, although we lose some expressiveness in doing so (however the literature cited therein always offers a second, most of the time process algebraic view of the domain).

As well, we did not pay attention to contexts. Contexts admit however a relatively straightforward approach once the rest of the apparatus is in place.

6 Test Generation Algorithms Based on Preorder Relations

Valéry Tschaen

IRISA / Université Rennes I
Valery.Tschaen@irisa.fr

6.1 Introduction

Testing theory has been studied for a long time. Based on finite state machines at the beginning, it has been extended to conformance testing of transition systems. Test generation methods have been developed for both of these models.

In this section, we are interested in test generation for transition systems. The goal of test generation is to produce a test suite. A test suite is a set of test cases that a tester process will run to exercise an implementation (the system under test) in order to check its conformance to a specification (the expected behavior). The conformance criterion is a relation that must hold between an implementation and its specification.

First, the models and notations used to describe the algorithms are introduced in Section 6.2. Then, in Section 6.3, we present generation algorithms inspired by finite state machine testing. Next, methods based on the notion of canonical tester are explained in Section 6.4. Finally, Section 6.5 is a brief summary of this chapter.

6.2 Models and Their Relations

This section introduces the two models used in the test generation methods presented in the sequel: labeled transition systems and finite state machines. For each of these models we also define some practical notations and relations. The intentional goal of this section is to be a reference for definitions while reading the description of the test generation methods.

6.2.1 Labeled Transition Systems

The main model of this chapter is Labeled Transition Systems.

Definition 6.2.1 (Labeled Transition Systems) *A labeled transition system (LTS for short) is a 4-tuple $M = (Q, L, \rightarrow, q_0)$ where:*

- *Q is a countable, non-empty set of states;*
- *$q_0 \in Q$ is the initial state;*
- *L is a countable set of labels;*
- *$\rightarrow \subseteq Q \times (L \cup \{\tau\}) \times Q$ is the transition relation.*

M. Broy et al. (Eds.): Model-Based Testing of Reactive Systems, LNCS 3472, pp. 151-171, 2005.
© Springer-Verlag Berlin Heidelberg 2005

The labels represent the observable events (or actions) of the system, whereas τ represents an internal event. The LTSs considered in this chapter correspond to rooted LTSs defined in Appendix 22 (as all LTSs of this chapter are rooted LTSs, they are simply called LTSs).

We recall standard notations concerning LTS. Let $a, a_i \in L$; $\mu, \mu_i \in L \cup \{\tau\}$; $\sigma \in L^*$; $q, q', q_i \in Q$; $Q', Q'' \subseteq Q$:

- general transitions:

$$q \xrightarrow{\mu} q' \quad =_{def} (q, \mu, q') \in \rightarrow$$
$$q \xrightarrow{\mu_1 \cdots \mu_n} q' =_{def} \exists q_0, \ldots, q_n : q = q_0 \xrightarrow{\mu_1} q_1 \xrightarrow{\mu_2} \ldots \xrightarrow{\mu_n} q_n = q'$$
$$q \xrightarrow{\mu_1 \cdots \mu_n} \quad =_{def} \exists q' : q \xrightarrow{\mu_1 \cdots \mu_n} q'$$
$$q \xnrightarrow{\mu_1 \cdots \mu_n} \quad =_{def} \nexists q' : q \xrightarrow{\mu_1 \cdots \mu_n} q'$$

- observable transitions:

$$q \xRightarrow{\epsilon} q' \quad =_{def} q = q' \, or \, q \xrightarrow{\tau \ldots \tau} q'$$
$$q \xRightarrow{a} q' \quad =_{def} \exists q_1, q_2 : q \xRightarrow{\epsilon} q_1 \xrightarrow{a} q_2 \xRightarrow{\epsilon} q'$$
$$q \xRightarrow{a_1 \cdots a_n} q' =_{def} \exists q_0, \ldots, q_n : q = q_0 \xRightarrow{a_1} q_1 \xRightarrow{a_2} \ldots \xRightarrow{a_n} q_n = q'$$
$$q \xRightarrow{\sigma} \quad =_{def} \exists q' : q \xRightarrow{\sigma} q'$$
$$q \xnRightarrow{\sigma} \quad =_{def} \nexists q' : q \xRightarrow{\sigma} q'$$
$$Q' \xRightarrow{\sigma} Q'' =_{def} \forall q'' \in Q'', \exists q' \in Q' : q' \xRightarrow{\sigma} q''$$

- traces:

$$Traces(q) \;\; =_{def} \{\sigma \in L^* \mid q \xRightarrow{\sigma}\}$$
$$Traces(M) =_{def} Traces(q_0)$$

- event sets:

$$Act(q) \;\; =_{def} \{\mu \in L \cup \{\tau\} \mid q \xrightarrow{\mu}\}$$
$$Out(q) \;\; =_{def} Act(q) \setminus \{\tau\}$$
$$init(q) \;\; =_{def} \{a \in L \mid q \xRightarrow{a}\}$$
$$init(Q') =_{def} \bigcup_{q \in Q'} init(q)$$

- state sets:

$$q \text{ after } \sigma \;\; =_{def} \{q' \in Q \mid q \xRightarrow{\sigma} q'\}$$
$$Q' \text{ after } \sigma =_{def} \bigcup_{q \in Q'} q \text{ after } \sigma$$

- refusal sets:

$$Ref(q) \;\;\;\; =_{def} L \setminus init(q)$$
$$Ref(q, \sigma) \;\; =_{def} \{Ref(q') \mid q' \in (q \text{ after } \sigma)\}$$
$$Ref(M, \sigma) =_{def} Ref(q_0, \sigma)$$

Most of the notations are illustrated by the example given in Fig. 6.1.

A state of an LTS is *stable* if it cannot perform an internal action. Roughly speaking, leaving a stable state is observable as it can only be done by means of an observable event. Concerning the LTS given in Fig. 6.1, q_0 is *unstable*, whereas q_2 is *stable*.

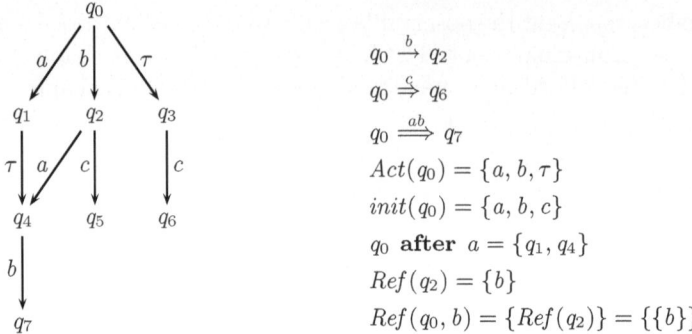

Fig. 6.1. An LTS and some corresponding notations

Definition 6.2.2 (Stable state and stable LTS) *A state q is* unstable *if* $q \xrightarrow{\tau}$, *otherwise it is* stable. *An LTS is* stable *if it has no unstable state, otherwise it is* unstable.

LTSs can be compared with respect to several relations. Relations used to compare the behavior of an implementation (assumed to be an LTS) to its specification are called *conformance relations*. The relations used in the sequel are defined below. See Chapter 5 for further details.

Definition 6.2.3 (Trace equivalence) *The trace equivalence relation between two LTSs* I *and* S, *written* I $=_{tr}$ S, *holds iff* $Traces(I) = Traces(S)$.

The trace equivalence relation only requires that I and S have the same traces.

Definition 6.2.4 (Failure reduction) *The failure reduction relation between two LTSs* I *and* S, *written* I **red** S, *holds iff* $\forall \sigma \in L^*, Ref(I, \sigma) \subseteq Ref(S, \sigma)$.

Intuitively, the failure reduction relation requires, for every trace σ of I, that σ is also a trace of S and that, after σ, an event set may be refused by I only if it may also be refused by S. The failure reduction relation is a preorder. Brinksma uses this relation to define an equivalence [Bri89]:

Definition 6.2.5 (Testing equivalence) *The testing equivalence relation (also known as* failure equivalence*) between two LTSs* I *and* S, *written* I $=_{te}$ S, *holds iff* $\forall \sigma \in L^*, Ref(I, \sigma) = Ref(S, \sigma)$.

The testing equivalence relation requires that I and S have the same refusal sets after each trace. This implies that I and S have the same traces and thus I $=_{te}$ S $\Rightarrow$ I $=_{tr}$ S.

Finally, we will consider the **conf** relation defined by Brinksma [Bri89]:

Definition 6.2.6 (conf) *Let* I *and* S *be LTSs. Then:*

$$I \textbf{ conf } S =_{def} \forall \sigma \in Traces(S), Ref(I, \sigma) \subseteq Ref(S, \sigma)$$

Intuitively, the **conf** relation holds between an implementation I and a specification S if, for every trace in the specification, the implementation does not contain unexpected deadlocks. That means that if the implementation refuses an event after such a trace, the specification also refuses this event. Note that the implementation is allowed to accept traces not accepted by the specification (contrary to the failure reduction relation). For instance, considering the LTS given in Fig. 6.1 as the implementation I and the LTS given in Fig. 6.2 as the specification S, the **conf** relation does not hold because $\{a, b\} \in Ref(q_0, \epsilon)$ for I but $\{a, b\} \notin Ref(q_0, \epsilon)$ for S.

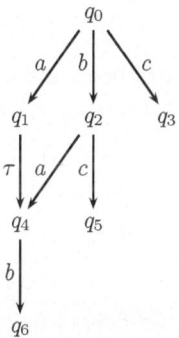

Fig. 6.2. A specification given by an LTS

To test whether an implementation conforms to its specification or not, Brinksma introduces the notion of canonical tester [Bri89]. A canonical tester for **conf** is an LTS with the same traces as the traces of the specification. Moreover, every deadlock of the concurrent execution of a conformant implementation and the canonical tester has to be a deadlock of the canonical tester.

Definition 6.2.7 (Canonical tester) *Given an LTS* $S = (Q, L, \rightarrow, q_0)$, *the canonical tester* $T(S)$ *is defined as the solution satisfying the following equations :*

- $Traces(T(S)) = Traces(S)$
- $\forall I, I \textbf{ conf } S \textit{ iff } \forall \sigma \in L^*,$
  $L \in Ref(I \parallel T(S), \sigma) \Rightarrow L \in Ref(T(S), \sigma)$

The $\parallel$ operator denotes the synchronous (w.r.t. observable events) composition of the LTSs.

Definition 6.2.8 (LTSs synchronous composition) *Let* $M_1 = (Q_1, L, \rightarrow_1, q_0^1)$ *and* $M_2 = (Q_2, L, \rightarrow_2, q_0^2)$ *be two LTSs. The* synchronous composition *of* M_1 *and* M_2, *denoted* $M_1 \parallel M_2$, *is the LTS* $M = (Q, L, \rightarrow, q_0)$ *where:*

- $Q = Q_1 \times Q_2;$
- $q_0 = (q_0^1, q_0^2);$

- $\rightarrow$ *is the minimal relation verifying:*
  - $(q_1, q_2) \xrightarrow{a} (q'_1, q'_2)$ *if* $q_1 \xrightarrow{a}_1 q'_1 \wedge q_2 \xrightarrow{a}_2 q'_2 \wedge a \in L$;
  - $(q_1, q_2) \xrightarrow{\tau} (q'_1, q_2)$ *if* $q_1 \xrightarrow{\tau}_1 q'_1$;
  - $(q_1, q_2) \xrightarrow{\tau} (q_1, q'_2)$ *if* $q_2 \xrightarrow{\tau}_2 q'_2$.

A trace of $I \parallel T(S)$ corresponds an execution of the tester $T(S)$ concurrently with an implementation I. One execution of the tester concurrently with an implementation only exercises one trace of the specification. The tester has to be rerun until all the traces of the specification have been tested in order to test conformance.

6.2.2   Finite State Machines

The *finite state machines* model has been already introduced in previous chapters. We briefly recall important definitions in this section.

Definition 6.2.9 (Finite State Machine) *A finite state machine (FSM for short) is a 5-tuple* $M = (S, X, Y, h, s_0)$ *where:*

- S *is a finite non-empty set of states;*
- $s_0 \in S$ *is the initial state;*
- X *is a finite set of inputs;*
- Y *is a finite set of outputs, and it may include* Θ *which represents the null output;*
- h *is a behavior function* $h : (S \times X) \rightarrow \mathcal{P}(S \times Y) \setminus \{\emptyset\}$.

We recall some notations. Let $a \in X, b \in Y, v_i \in X \times Y$ and $\gamma \in (X \times Y)^*$:

$$
\begin{aligned}
s \xrightarrow{a/b} s' &=_{def} (s', b) \in h(s, a) \\
s \xRightarrow{\epsilon} s' &=_{def} s = s' \text{ (i.e. } \epsilon \text{ is the empty sequence)} \\
s \xRightarrow{v_0 \ldots v_n} s' &=_{def} \exists s_0, \ldots, s_n : s = s_0 \xrightarrow{v_0} s_1 \ldots \xrightarrow{v_n} s_n = s' \\
s \xRightarrow{\gamma} &=_{def} \exists s' : s \xRightarrow{\gamma} s' \\
Traces(s) &=_{def} \{\gamma \mid s \xRightarrow{\gamma}\} \\
\gamma^{in} &=_{def} \text{input sequences obtained by deleting all outputs in } \gamma \\
Traces^{in}(s) &=_{def} \{\gamma^{in} \mid s \xRightarrow{\gamma}\} : \text{input sequences of } s
\end{aligned}
$$

Now we can define two useful relations for test generation.

Definition 6.2.10 (Reduction relation) *An FSM I (with initial state* i_0*) is a reduction of an FSM S, (with initial state* s_0*), written* $I \leq S$*, iff* i_0 *is a reduction of* s_0*. Given two FSM states,* i *and* s*,* i *is a reduction of* s*, written* $i \leq s$*, iff* $Traces^{in}(s) \subseteq Traces^{in}(i)$ *and for all* $\gamma \in Traces(i) : \gamma^{in} \in Traces^{in}(s) \Rightarrow \gamma \in Traces(s)$.

That is, if $I \leq S$, every input sequence of S is an input sequence of I and a trace γ of I is also a trace of S if γ^{in} is an input sequence of S. Roughly speaking, an implementation I and a specification S must have the same behavior for the input sequences of S, but I may have more input sequences than S.

The reduction relation is a preorder and can be used to define an equivalence:

Definition 6.2.11 (Equivalence) *Two FSMs* I *and* S *are equivalent, written* I $\sim$ S, *iff* I $\leq$ S *and* S $\leq$ I. *Two FSM states* i *and* s *are equivalent, written* i $\sim$ s, *iff* i $\leq$ s *and* s $\leq$ i.

In other words, two equivalent FSMs have the same traces (and thus the same input sequences).

We can differentiate between two kinds of test generation algorithms. The first one is directly inspired from former research on test generation for FSMs. The second one is based on the **conf** relation and on the notion of canonical tester (Definition 6.2.7).

6.3   FSM-like Methods

We present two test generation methods based on FSM testing. These methods try to take advantage of years of research in FSM testing. The first method is a transformation of the LTS model into the FSM model. The second one is an adaptation of the FSM test generation techniques to LTS.

6.3.1   Transforming the Model into FSM

Tan, Petrenko and Bochmann present a method that is mainly an LTS to FSM, and vice versa, transformation method [TPvB96]. Using the presented transformations, the test generation method for LTSs is quite simple. The main steps of this method are:

- transformation of the model of the specification into an FSM;
- classical generation of tests on the obtained FSM;
- transformation of the test cases back to the LTS world.

Testing of FSMs has already been explained in previous chapters. We will focus on the transformation of the LTS of the specification into an FSM and on the transformation of test cases into LTSs.

From LTS to FSM The transformation depends on the LTS equivalence considered, but the principle is identical. The goal is to derive an FSM such that the FSM equivalence (Definition 6.2.11) corresponds exactly to the LTS equivalence considered, either the trace equivalence (Definition 6.2.3) or the testing equivalence (Definition 6.2.5): two LTSs I and S are equivalent iff the two FSMs obtained by transformation of I and S are equivalent.

Trace equivalence For the trace equivalence (Definition 6.2.3), the idea is to construct an FSM that produces, as output sequences, all the traces of the LTS. For input actions that do not belong to traces of the LTS, the FSM produces the null output Θ. In each state of the FSM, for each action a of the LTS, there is either a transition $\xrightarrow{a/a}$ or a transition $\xrightarrow{a/\Theta}$. The former means that a is a valid continuation of the output sequences leading to that state while the latter means that a is an invalid continuation. Moreover, transitions labeled with a null output go into a sink state, s_Θ, that produces a null output for every input. The FSM corresponding to an LTS is called a *Trace Finite State Machine* (TFSM).

Definition 6.3.1 (TFSM: Trace Finite State Machine) *For an LTS* $M = (Q, L, \rightarrow, q_0)$, *let* $\Pi = \{q_0 \text{ after } \sigma \mid \sigma \in Traces(q_0)\}$, *its corresponding TFSM is an FSM* $TraceFSM(M) = (S, L, L \cup \{\Theta\}, h, s_0)$ *such that:*

- *S is a finite set of states, containing the sink state s_Θ.*
- *There exists a one-to-one mapping $\psi : \Pi \rightarrow S \setminus \{s_\Theta\}$ and for all $Q_i \in \Pi$ and all $a \in L$:*
  $(\psi(Q_j), a) \in h(\psi(Q_i), a)$ *iff* $Q_i \overset{a}{\Rightarrow} Q_j$ (α)
  $(s_\Theta, \Theta) \in h(\psi(Q_i), a)$ *iff* $a \in L \setminus Out(Q_i)$ (β)
  $\{(s_\Theta, \Theta)\} = h(s_\Theta, a)$ (γ)

More intuitively, an element of Π is a set of states reachable after a trace of M, (α) means that there is a transition $\psi(Q_i) \overset{a/a}{\longrightarrow} \psi(Q_j)$ in $TraceFSM(M)$ iff $Q_i \overset{a}{\Rightarrow} Q_j$ in M. (β) means that $\psi(Q_i) \overset{a/\Theta}{\longrightarrow} s_\Theta$ in $TraceFSM(M)$ iff $Q_i \overset{a}{\nRightarrow}$ in M. Finally, (γ) states that s_Θ is a sink state. This definition can be seen as an algorithm for the construction of a corresponding TFSM of an LTS. An example of TFSM is given in Fig. 6.3.

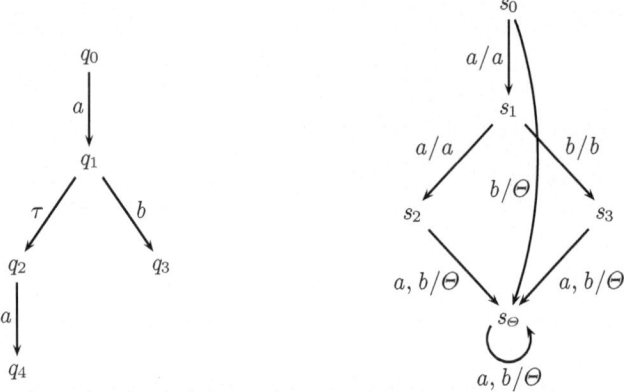

Fig. 6.3. An LTS and its corresponding TFSM [TPvB96]

It was shown that the trace equivalence for LTSs corresponds to the FSM equivalence for the corresponding TFSMs [TPvB96].

Theorem 6.3.1 ([TPvB96]) *For any given two LTSs* I, S, *and their corresponding TFSMs* I′, S′ : I $=_{tr}$ S *iff* I′ $\sim$ S′

By this theorem, tests derived from a corresponding TFSM $TraceFSM(M)$ are also relevant to check the trace equivalence of the LTS M (provided that they are transformed into LTSs).

Testing equivalence The transformation for testing equivalence (Definition 6.2.5) is based on the same idea as the one for trace equivalence. The difference is that input of the FSM are sets of actions, not only single actions. In a state, the null output, Θ, indicates that a set of actions belongs to the refusal set of the LTS after traces leading to this state. The FSM corresponding to an LTS is called a *Failure Finite State Machine* (FFSM).

Definition 6.3.2 (FFSM: Failure Finite State Machine) *For an LTS $M = (Q, L, \to, q_0)$, let $\Pi = \{q_0 \text{ after } \sigma \mid \sigma \in Traces(q_0)\}$, its corresponding FFSM is an FSM $FailFSM(M) = (S, X, Y, h, s_0)$ such that:*

- $X = \mathcal{P}(L) \setminus \{\emptyset\}$.
- $Y = L \cup \{\Theta\}$, Θ *represents the null output.*
- S *is a finite set of states, containing the sink state s_Θ.*
- *There exists a one-to-one mapping $\psi : \Pi \to S \setminus \{s_\Theta\}$ and for all $Q_i \in \Pi$ and all $X' \in X$:*
  $(\psi(Q_j), a) \in h(\psi(Q_i), X')$ *iff* $a \in X'$ *and* $Q_i \overset{a}{\Rightarrow} Q_j$ (α)
  $(s_\Theta, \Theta) \in h(\psi(Q_i), X')$ *iff* $X' \in Ref(Q_i)$ (β)
  $\{(s_\Theta, \Theta)\} = h(s_\Theta, X')$ (γ)

Given an LTS, the above definition directly gives an algorithm for the construction of its corresponding FFSM. That is, for any state $\psi(Q_i)$ of the FFSM, its transition relation is computed from its corresponding states Q_i in the LTS, according to the α, β and γ rules. For any $X' \in X$:

- (α) for every $a \in X'$ such that there is a transition $Q_i \overset{a}{\Rightarrow} Q_j$ in the LTS, add a transition $\psi(Q_i) \overset{X'/a}{\longrightarrow} \psi(Q_j)$ in the FFSM.
- (β) if $X' \in Ref(Q_i)$, add a transition $\psi(Q_i) \overset{X'/\Theta}{\longrightarrow} s_\Theta$ in the FFSM.
- (γ) s_Θ is a sink state, add a transition $s_\Theta \overset{X'/\Theta}{\longrightarrow} s_\Theta$ in the FFSM.

An example of FFSM is given in Fig. 6.4.

It was shown that the testing equivalence and the failure reduction relation for LTS correspond to the FSM equivalence and reduction relation for corresponding FFSM [TPvB96].

Theorem 6.3.2 ([TPvB96]) *For any given two LTSs I, S, and their corresponding FFSMs I', S': I **red** S iff I' $\leq$ S' and I $=_{te}$ S iff I' $\sim$ S'.*

As for trace equivalence, tests derived from a corresponding FFSM $FailFSM(M)$ are also relevant to check the testing equivalence of the LTS M (provided that they are transformed into LTSs).

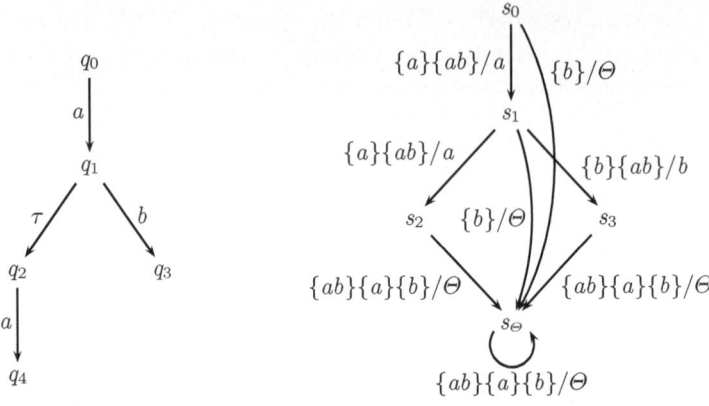

Fig. 6.4. An LTS and its corresponding FFSM [TPvB96]

Test Generation Once the LTS model of a specification has been transformed into an FSM, classical test generation algorithms for FSM can be used. For instance ([TPvB96]) a TFSM is minimized and a complete test suite, w.r.t. a certain class of FSMs, is generated using the W-method [Cho78]. Using the fact that a null output represents a deadlock, the test suite is then simplified. It is shown that removing suffixes of each test case after the first null output preserves the completeness of the test suite (a test suite is complete w.r.t. a class of FSMs if it allows to detect any non conformant implementation of this class). See Chapter 4 for more details.

From FSM to LTS Now, consider a test suite that has been generated from a TFSM (the method is analogous for FFSMs). The test suite produced is a set of test cases. A test case is a sequence of actions. The test cases have to be transformed into LTSs with state verdicts. The transformation of a sequence into an LTS is straightforward. $q_0 \xrightarrow{a_1} q_1 \ldots q_{n-1} \xrightarrow{a_n} q_n$ is the LTS corresponding to a test case whose input sequence is $a_1.a_2 \ldots a_n$. Let k be the minimal index such that $q_{k-1} \xrightarrow{a_k/\Theta} q_k$ (i.e. the first null output), the state verdicts are assigned as follows :

$$verdict(q_i) = \begin{cases} \textbf{inconc} & 0 \leq i < k-1 \\ \textbf{pass} & i = k-1 \\ \textbf{fail} & i \geq k \end{cases}$$

Intuitively:

- if the test execution stops in q_{k-1}, this is OK because a_k is not fireable.
- if a_k is executed, the **fail** verdict indicates that the implementation is not trace-equivalent to the specification.
- if the test execution stops before q_{k-1}, **inconc** means that this test case cannot determine whether this is OK or not.

160   Valéry Tschaen

The test suite obtained can be used to check if implementations are trace-equivalent to the LTS of the specification.

We explained here test generation and transformation of the test suite only for TFSM. The same method can be applied to FFSM to generate a test suite for the testing equivalence.

6.3.2   Adapting FSM Methods to LTS

In order to re-use FSM testing knowledge, the method presented above is based on the transformation of LTSs into FSMs. This section presents a method that takes a different approach: well-known techniques in FSM testing are adapted to LTS testing. To achieve this goal, the notion of *state identification* (see Chapter 2) is defined for LTSs. Then, Tan, Petrenko and Bochmann show how test generation methods based on state identification can be adapted to LTSs [TPvB97]. This method is briefly described in the following.

State Identification State identification is based on the notion of *distinguishable states*. Two states are distinguishable (w.r.t. trace equivalence) if they are not trace equivalent. In this case, there is a sequence of observable actions that is a valid trace for one of the two states, and not for the other one. We say that such a sequence distinguishes the two states. An LTS is said to be *reduced* if its states are distinguishable.

Specification To be able to use state identification, the states of a specification have to be distinguishable. If not, the specification must be transformed.

Definition 6.3.3 (TOS: Trace Observable System) *Given an LTS M, a deterministic (see Appendix 22) LTS $\overline{M}$ is said to be the trace observable system corresponding to M, if $M =_{tr} \overline{M}$ and $\overline{M}$ is reduced.*

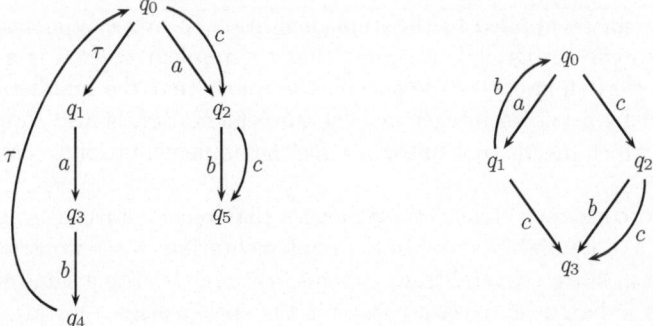

Fig. 6.5. An LTS (on the left) and its corresponding TOS (on the right)[TPvB97]

An example of TOS is given in Fig. 6.5. From any given LTS specification, there exists algorithms (see e.g. [Koh78]) to compute its corresponding TOS (which is unique). Thus, we can assume that specifications are in their TOS form. Based on this hypothesis, Tan, Petrenko and Bochmann present a set of concepts for state identification:

- A *distinguishable sequence*, for a specification M, is a sequence that distinguishes any two different states of M. A sequence distinguishes two states of an LTS M if the sequence has a prefix that is a trace for one of the two states and not for the other one. A distinguishable sequence does not always exist.
- A *unique sequence* for a state is a sequence that distinguishes this state from all the others. A set of unique sequences for M, is a set containing a unique sequence for each state of M. As for distinguishable sequences, a set of unique sequences does not always exist.
- A *characterization set* for M is a set of observable sequences containing, for any two different states, a sequence that distinguishes them. A characterization set exists for any LTS in TOS form.
- A *partial characterization set* is a tuple of n sets of observable sequences, where n is the number of states of the specification. For the nth state and a different one, the nth set contains a sequence that distinguishes them. Partial characterization sets always exist.
- A set of *harmonized state identifiers* is a partial characterization set such that any two different sets have at least one sequence prefix in common. They always exist.

Given a specification, the choice of one of the state identification means listed above and its construction constitutes the first step of the test generation method.

For instance, harmonized state identifiers can be constructed for the example of Fig. 6.5 : $H_0 = \{a, b\}, H_1 = \{b.a\}, H_2 = \{b.a\}, H_3 = \{a, b\}$ (where $b.a$ denotes the the the sequence formed by the concatenation of b and a) [TPvB97].

Implementation The second step consists in checking whether the state identification facility can be applied to the implementation to properly identify its states. In order to check this, it is assumed that the implementation is a TOS with the same action alphabet as the specification, and that the number of its states is bounded by a known integer m. The implementation is also supposed to be resettable, which means that one can force the implementation to enter its initial state.

The idea is to construct "transfer" sequences that reach, starting from the initial state, all the potential m states of the implementation (if the implementation has less than m states, several transfer sequences may lead to a same state). The construction is based on a *state cover* for the specification. A state cover for M is a set of sequences such that for each state of M, there is exactly one sequence (in the state cover) leading to this state. To be able to reach the possible additional states of the implementation, the sequences of the state cover of the specification have to be completed in order to be of length m. The completion consists in considering every possible continuation for each sequence. That is, each sequence (in the state cover) σ of length n ($n < m$) is concatenated with each possible sequence σ' of length $m - n$ (thus, each sequence $\sigma.\sigma'$ is of length m). These transfer sequences are used to bring the implementation in each of its possible states. Then, the state identification facility is used to identify all the states of the implementation. Each transfer sequence is concatenated with each sequence used for state identification in order to identify the states reached after the transfer sequences. This form a set of test sequences. This identification phase is the first testing phase.

As we are interested in testing the trace equivalence, the second testing phase consists in checking all the possible transitions. For each state q_i^s of the specification M, let $f(q_i^s)$ be the set of states of the implementation I that have been identified to q_i^s in the previous testing phase (thanks to the state identification facility). In order to test trace equivalence, test cases have to check if:

- each transition $q_i^s \xrightarrow{a} q_j^s$ is fireable from $f(q_i^s)$ and the state reached after performing a is in $f(q_j^s)$;
- each action not fireable in M from q_i^s, i.e. $q_i^s \xnrightarrow{a}$, is not fireable in I from $f(q_i^s)$, i.e. $q \xnRightarrow{a}$ for each q in $f(q_i^s)$.

Due to nondeterminism, $f(q^s)$ may be a set of states, not a single state. In this case, test cases will have to be executed several times to exercise the different possible behaviors. Using the transfer sequences constructed in the first phase, the computation of test sequences for the second phase consists in firing all the possible actions a after these sequences. If the action a is fireable in the specification, it is also necessary to identify the state reached in the implementation after a.

The global test suite is the union of the test cases of the two phases. These test cases are obtained from the test sequences computed, by transforming these sequences into LTSs. The LTS corresponding to a sequence $a_1.a_2 \ldots a_k$ is $q_0^t \xrightarrow{a_1} q_1^t \xrightarrow{a_2} \ldots \xrightarrow{a_k} q_k^t$. Let $(q_i^s)_{0 \leqslant i < n}$ be the states of the specification and for all $\sigma \in Traces(q_0^t)$, $\{q_i^t\} = q_0^t$ after σ. The verdicts are assigned as follows:

$$verdict(q_i^t) = \begin{cases} \textbf{pass} & \text{if } \sigma \in Traces(q_0^s) \wedge init(q_i^t) \cap Out(q_0^s \text{ after } \sigma) = \emptyset \\ \textbf{fail} & \text{if } \sigma \notin Traces(q_0^s) \\ \textbf{inconc} & \text{otherwise} \end{cases}$$

Under the assumption that the number of states of the implementation is bounded by m, the test suite computed is complete w.r.t. the trace equivalence [TPvB97].

Consider the LTS in Fig. 6.5 as the specification and assume that the number of states of the implementation is bounded by 4. Using harmonized state identifiers, a complete test suite can be constructed [TPvB97]:

$$TS = \{b, a.a, c.a, a.b.b, a.b.a, a.c.a, a.c.b, a.c.c, c.b.a, c.b.b, c.c.a, c.c.b\}$$

Fig. 6.6 shows the corresponding test cases.

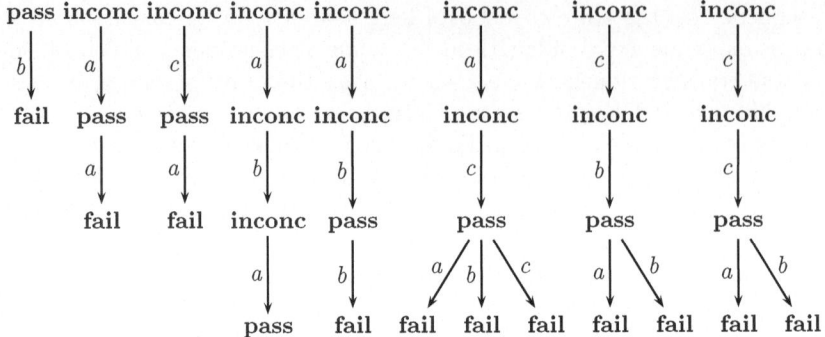

Fig. 6.6. Test cases for the LTS specification of Fig. 6.5 [TPvB97]

6.4   Test Generation for conf

The next three methods presented in this chapter are based on the notion of canonical tester [Bri89]. They represent three different ways to generate tests for the **conf** relation (roughly speaking, a canonical tester has no explicit verdicts but is equivalent to a complete test suite). These methods are more or less connected to the basic LOTOS language. Basic LOTOS is a restriction of the LOTOS language ([ISO88]) where value passing is not considered. LTSs are the basic semantics for LOTOS. In the sequel, only two LOTOS operators are used: *action prefix* and *choice*. Below are the syntax of these operators and the inference rules for the construction of the underlying LTSs. Let $B, B1, B1', B2$ and $B2'$ be LOTOS processes, let τ be an internal event, let a be an observable event ($a \in L$ from the LTS point of view) and let $b1$ and $b2$ be internal or observable events:

- the *action prefix* operator is denoted $\tau; B$ for an internal event and $a; B$ for an observable event. In terms of LTSs, it corresponds respectively to an internal transition $\tau; B \xrightarrow{\tau} B$ and to an observable transition $a; B \xrightarrow{a} B$
- the *choice* operator is denoted $B1[]B2$. In terms of LTSs, it corresponds to the union of the behaviors of $B1$ and $B2$. That is, $B1 \xrightarrow{b1} B1'$ implies $B1[]B2 \xrightarrow{b1} B1'$ and $B2 \xrightarrow{b2} B2'$ implies $B1[]B2 \xrightarrow{b2} B2'$.

A more detailed presentation can be found in the introduction article to the LOTOS language written by Bolognesi and Brinksma [BB87].

6.4.1   Derivation of Conformance Tests from LOTOS Specifications

The method presented by Pitt and Freestone [PF90] is a test generation method directly based on the structure of LOTOS specifications. It consists in the compositional construction of a tester. The construction is compositional in the sense that the construction of a tester for $B1 * B2$, called $Test(B1 * B2)$, where $B1$

and $B2$ are LOTOS processes and $*$ is a LOTOS operator, is syntactically derived from $Test(B1)$ and $Test(B2)$. Arguing that any LOTOS specification is semantically equivalent to one involving only *choice, guards, action prefix* and *recursion*, the authors do not consider other operators. Furthermore, they argue that guards and recursion can be neglected without loss of generality. So, we only have to deal with the *choice* and *action prefix* operators.

Tests Construction For each of these operators, the authors define a law for the construction of a tester.

Action prefix This law is simple: $Test(b;\ B) = b;\ Test(B)$. It means that to test an implementation that accepts b and then behaves like B consists in offering b and then testing that the implementation behaves like B.

Choice The test construction for the choice operator (denoted $[]$) is more complicated. Several cases have to be considered. The law to define $Test(B1[]B2)$ depends on the internal structure of $B1$ and $B2$. For instance, if the first actions of $B1$ and $B2$ are different, the tester can exactly determine what the subsequent behavior of the implementation should be. Moreover, as the implementation must be able to perform the two actions, the choice is internal to the tester. Thus, if $b1 \neq b2$,

$$Test(b1;\ B1'[]b2;\ B2') = (\tau;\ b1;\ Test(B1')[]\tau;\ b2;\ Test(B2'))$$

But if the first action of each process is internal, the choice between the two processes is no longer made by the tester. In this case, it is an internal choice of the implementation and the tester has to take the two possibilities into account. Thus, if $b1 \neq b2$,

$$Test(\tau;\ b1;\ B1'[]\tau;\ b2;\ B2') = b1;\ Test(B1')[]b2;\ Test(B2')$$

Finally, if the first action of $B1$ is the same as the one of $B2$, the tester has to consider that after this action, the implementation can behave either like $B1$ or like $B2$. That is:

$$Test(b;\ B1'[]b;\ B2') = b;\ Test(\tau;\ B1'[]\tau;\ B2')$$

Note that the computation of the right hand side still depends on the structure of $B1'$ and $B2'$ (see the article for further details [PF90]). All these cases can be grouped in one general case considering processes of the form:

$$B = \underset{U \in W}{[]}\ \tau;\ \left(\underset{a \in U}{[]}\ a;\ B/{<}a{>} \right) \qquad (6.1)$$

where $B/{<}a{>}$ denotes the behavior of process B after event a. Processes matching (6.1) present an internal choice between sets of events. W is the set of the sets of events available after a τ.

For such processes :

$$Test\left(\underset{U \in W}{[]}\ \tau;\ \underset{a \in U}{[]}\ a;\ B/{<}a{>} \right) = \underset{V \in orth(W)}{[]}\ \tau;\ \underset{a \in V}{[]}\ a;\ Test(B/{<}a{>}) \qquad (6.2)$$

where for a set of sets $W \neq \{\}$, $orth(W)$ is defined as the set of all sets which can be formed by choosing exactly one member from each element of W.

Pitt and Freestone have shown that testers constructed in this way are canonical testers (cf. Def. 6.2.7) [PF90]. As the considered processes may have infinite behaviors, the authors present also a notion of *n-testers* which are testers considering traces of bounded length. An implementation passes a n-test if its traces of length at most n conform to the specification. The implementations that pass all n-tests are called *n-implementations*. As it is not possible to test infinite behaviors in practice, the notion of n-tester is a way to ensure finite testing. Thus, n-testers can be seen as pragmatic approximations of canonical testers.

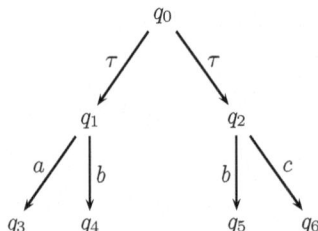

Fig. 6.7. LTS of process B

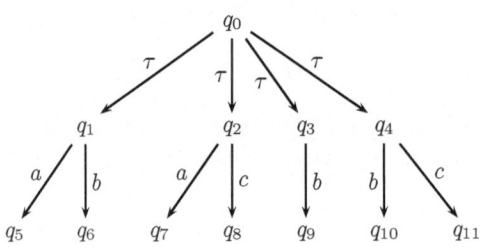

Fig. 6.8. LTS of $Test(B)$

Example Consider the process:

$$B = \tau;\ (a[]b)\ []\ \tau;\ (b[]c)$$

Its LTS is given in Fig. 6.7. B is obviously of the form (6.1) with $W = \{\{a, b\},$ $\{b, c\}\}$ and thus $orth(W) = \{\{a, b\}, \{a, c\}, \{b\}, \{b, c\}\}$. From (6.2), we get:

$$Test(B) = (\tau;\ (a[]b))\ []\ (\tau;\ (a[]c))\ []\ (\tau;\ b)\ []\ (\tau;\ (b[]c))$$

The LTS corresponding to $Test(B)$ (i.e. the canonical tester for B) is shown in Fig. 6.8.

6.4.2   The CO-OP Method

As the method of Pitt and Freestone [PF90], the CO-OP method, presented by Wezeman [Wez90], is a compositional method for the derivation of testers. This method is defined on the general LTS model but is also applied to the basic LOTOS language. This method produces a canonical tester for the **conf** relation. It consists mainly in the construction of two sets : Compulsory and Options. This is where the name of the method comes from. In the sequel, we first explain the CO-OP method on LTS and then briefly see how it can be adapted to the structure of the basic LOTOS language.

Compulsory Set Given an LTS state q, $Compulsory(q)$ is a set of sets of events. A set in $Compulsory(q)$ is a set of events enabled in state q', internally reachable from q, and such that q' is a stable state (Def. 6.2.2). A tester cannot prevent a system to reach the state q' from q, and there is no internal action enabled in q'. Thus, to avoid deadlock, in the derivation of a test case for q, at least one event from each set in $Compulsory(q)$ must be kept.

Definition 6.4.1 (Compulsory) *Let* $M = (Q, L, \rightarrow, q_0)$ *be a labeled transition system,*

$$Compulsory(M) = Compulsory(q_0) = \{Out(q) \mid q_0 \stackrel{\epsilon}{\Rightarrow} q \not\stackrel{\tau}{\rightarrow}\}$$

Options Set Given an LTS state q, $Options(q)$ is a set of events. An event in $Options(q)$ is an event enabled in an unstable state q' that is internally reachable from q. Events in $Options(q)$ may be kept or not when deriving a test case for q.

Definition 6.4.2 (Options) *Let* $M = (Q, L, \rightarrow, q_0)$ *be a labeled transition system,*

$$Options(M) = Options(q_0) = \{a \in Out(q) \mid q_0 \stackrel{\epsilon}{\Rightarrow} q \stackrel{\tau}{\rightarrow}\}$$

With these definitions, test cases for an LTS M can start by following one of these rules (LOTOS notation is used for conciseness):

$$T1 = \underset{a\in V}{[]} a; \ldots$$

$$T2 = \left(\underset{a\in V}{[]} a; \ldots\right) [] option; \ldots$$

where $V \in orth(Compulsory(M))$ and $option \in Options(M)$. Test cases beginning as indicated by these rules are called *basic test cases*. Basic test cases can be combined using the choice operator. The set containing the basic test cases and all their possible combinations is a complete conformance test suite. Note that if a deadlock is internally reachable in M from the initial state q_0,

$\emptyset \in Compulsory(M)$ and thus $orth(Compulsory(M))$ is empty and test cases have to be constructed according to the following rules:

$$T3 = \tau; \ stop$$

$$T4 = \tau; \ stop \ [] \ a; \ \ldots \quad for \ some \ a \in init(q_0)$$

After a first interaction a, the behavior of a tester depends on the behavior of the specification after a. In case of nondeterminism, the behavior of an LTS M after a can be represented by a nondeterministic LTS written $M/\!\!<\!\!a\!\!>$. For each state q reachable after a in M, there is an internal transition in $M/\!\!<\!\!a\!\!>$ leading to a state that have the same behavior as q. This representation of the behavior of an LTS after an interaction has been chosen in order to keep the definition of the Compulsory and Options sets as simple as possible.

The Method   Then, the CO-OP method is inferred from the above notions. Given an LTS M, it consists in constructing recursively its conformance tester $Test(M)$ as follows:

1 Construct $Compulsory(M)$ and $Options(M)$
2 For each $a \in init(q_0)$, construct $M/\!\!<\!\!a\!\!>$
3 If $\emptyset \notin Compulsory(M)$,

$$Test(M) = \underset{V \in orth(Compulsory(M))}{[]} \tau; \left(\underset{a \in V}{[]} a; \ Test(M/\!\!<\!\!a\!\!>) \right)$$

$$[] \left(\underset{b \in Options(M)}{[]} b; \ Test(M/\!\!<\!\!b\!\!>) \right)$$

else,

$$Test(M) = \tau; \ stop \ [] \left(\underset{a \in init(q_0)}{[]} a; \ Test(M/\!\!<\!\!a\!\!>) \right)$$

Wezeman has shown that $Test(M)$ is a canonical tester for M and explained how a minimized set of basic test cases can be derived from $Test(M)$ [Wez90].

Example   Consider again the LTS specification given in Fig. 6.7. Then, the attributes are:

- $Options(B) = \emptyset$
- $Compulsory(B) = \{\{a, b\}, \{b, c\}\}$
- $orth(Compulsory(B)) = \{\{a, b,\}, \{a, c\}, \{b\}, \{b, c\}\}$

Following the CO-OP method, the canonical tester $Test(B)$ is given in as in Fig. 6.9. This is exactly the same LTS as in the method described in Section 6.4.1. In fact, when $\emptyset \notin Compulsory(M)$ and $Options(M) = \emptyset$ (it is the case for this example), the constructions given in these two methods are identical.

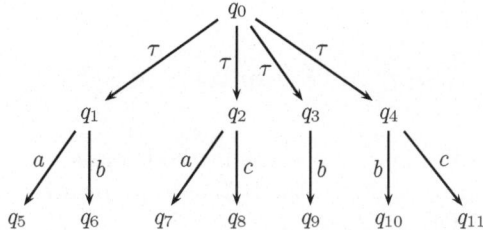

Fig. 6.9. *Test(B)* following the CO-OP method

CO-OP for Basic LOTOS The application of the CO-OP method to basic LOTOS is interesting because it allows a compositional construction of the Compulsory and Options sets. For any basic LOTOS operator $*$, *Compulsory(B)* and *Options(B)*, such as $B = B1 * B2$, can be constructed from the Compulsory and Options sets of $B1$ and $B2$. The construction of *Test(B)* is also based on two other attributes : $B/<a>$ and *unstable(B)*. The construction of these two attributes is also compositional. Thus, the CO-OP method offers a compositional construction of a canonical tester for any basic LOTOS process. Wezeman gives the compositional construction of each attribute for each basic LOTOS operator [Wez90]. Compared to the method described in Section 6.4.1, this method can be applied to all basic LOTOS processes, they do not have to match any particular form.

6.4.3   Refusal Graph

In the two previous methods, a canonical tester is derived from specification syntax. Drira, Azèma and Vernadat present a method with a different approach [DAV93]. It is based on the construction and transformation of a *refusal graph*.

Definition 6.4.3 (RG: Refusal Graph) *A refusal graph, denoted RG, is a deterministic bilabeled graph represented by a 5-tuple* (G, L, Δ, Ref, g_0) *where:*

- *G is a finite set of states;*
- *$g_0 \in G$ is the initial state;*
- *L is a finite set of actions;*
- *$\Delta \subseteq (G \times L \times G)$ is a set of transitions. $(g, a, g') \in \Delta$ is denoted $g \overset{a}{\Rightarrow} g'$;*
- *Ref : $G \rightarrow \mathcal{P}(\mathcal{P}(L))$ defines for each state, the sets of actions that may be refused after the sequence leading to this state.*

Refusal sets must be minimal. R is a minimal refusal set if all elements of R are incomparable w.r.t. set inclusion $\subseteq$. Furthermore, all $E \in Ref(g)$ must either be (*i*) a subset of *init(g)* or be (*ii*) saturated w.r.t. $L \setminus init(g)$ (*i.e.* $L \setminus init(g) \subseteq E$). As for LTSs, $init(g) = \{a \in L \mid \exists g', g \overset{a}{\Rightarrow} g'\}$. A refusal set $Ref(g)$ in the first form can be changed into a refusal set in the second form by the transformation:

$$\lceil Ref(g) \rceil = \{E \cup (L \setminus init(g)) \mid E \in Ref(g)\}$$

The reverse transformation is:

$$\lfloor Ref(g) \rfloor = \{E \cap init(g) \mid E \in Ref(g)\}$$

From LTS to RG The first step of the method consists in the construction of the refusal graph corresponding to the LTS of a specification. As for the CO-OP method, we use LOTOS notation.

Definition 6.4.4 (RG associated with an LTS) *The refusal graph* $rg(M)$ *associated to the LTS* $M = (Q, L, \rightarrow, q_o)$ *is defined by the 5-tuple* (G, L, Δ, Ref, g_0) *where:*

- $g_0 = q_0$ **after** ϵ;
- $(G \subseteq \mathcal{P}(Q), L, \Delta \subseteq G \times L \times G)$ *is the labeled graph* $rg(g_0)$, *where for all* $g \subseteq Q$, $rg(g)$ *is recursively defined by:*

$$rg(g) = \underset{a \in init(g)}{[]} a;\ rg(g\ \textbf{after}\ a)$$

- *for all* $g \in G, \lfloor Ref(g) \rfloor = Min(\{init(g) \setminus init(q) \mid q \in g\})$.

where for $E \in \mathcal{P}(\mathcal{P}(L))$, $Min(E) = E \setminus \{X \mid \exists Y \in L : X \subseteq Y\ and\ X \neq Y\}$ *and for* $R \subseteq \mathcal{P}(\mathcal{P}(L))$, $Min(R) = \{Min(E) \mid E \in R\}$.

Consider again the LTS shown in Fig. 6.7, its associated refusal graph is given in Fig. 6.10. The label of each node g is the value of $\lfloor Ref(g) \rfloor$. Intuitively, the value of $\lfloor Ref(g_0) \rfloor$ means that, in the initial state of he specification, either a or c may be refused, but not both.

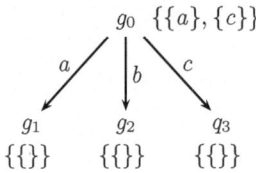

Fig. 6.10. Refusal graph $\mathcal{G}$

Transformation of RG The second step of the method is to transform the refusal graph constructed. The goal is to obtain a refusal graph from which a canonical tester will be constructed. This transformation, denoted T_g, only acts on the refusal sets. The transformation of a refusal graph $\mathcal{G} = (G, L, \Delta, Ref, g_0)$ is a refusal graph $T_g(\mathcal{G}) = (G, L, \Delta, Ref', g_0)$ where:

- $\lceil Ref'(g) \rceil = \{L\}$ if $\lceil Ref(g) \rceil = \{L\}$
- $\lceil Ref'(g) \rceil = Min(\{L \setminus E \mid E \subseteq L, E \notin \lceil Ref(g) \rceil\})$ if $\lceil Ref(g) \rceil \neq \{L\}$

Concerning the refusal graph of Fig. 6.10:

- $\lceil Ref(g_0) \rceil = \lfloor Ref(g_0) \rfloor = \{\{a\}, \{c\}\}$
- $\lceil Ref(g_1) \rceil = \lceil Ref(g_2) \rceil = \lceil Ref(g_3) \rceil = \{\{a, b, c\}\}$

And thus:

- $\lceil Ref'(g_0) \rceil = \{\{b\}, \{a, c\}\}$
- $\lceil Ref'(g_1) \rceil = \lceil Ref'(g_2) \rceil = \lceil Ref'(g_3) \rceil = \{\{a, b, c\}\}$

Then, $T_g(\mathcal{G})$ is given in Fig. 6.11.

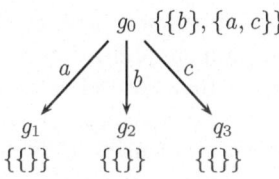

Fig. 6.11. $T_g(\mathcal{G})$

Roughly speaking, the value of $\lfloor Ref'(g_0) \rfloor$ means that a canonical tester has to enable whether the event b or the events a and c to a conformant implementation to avoid blocking.

From RG to LTS Once the refusal graph has been transformed, it remains to construct its corresponding LTS.

Definition 6.4.5 (LTS associated to a RG) *From a refusal graph g_0, the LTS $lts(g_0)$ may be derived according to the following recursive definition :*

$$lts(g) = \left(\underset{E \in \lfloor Ref(g) \rfloor}{[]} \tau; \underset{a \in init(g) \setminus E}{[]} a; \ lts(g \ \textbf{after} \ a) \right)$$

$$[] \left(\underset{b \in \bigcap_{E \in \lfloor Ref(g) \rfloor} E}{[]} b; \ lts(g \ \textbf{after} \ b) \right)$$

For any LTS specification S, it has been shown that $T(S) = lts(T_g(rg(S)))$ is a canonical tester for S [DAV93].

Consider again the specification shown in Fig. 6.7, the canonical tester obtained from the LTS specification given in Fig. 6.7 is shown in Fig. 6.12. This canonical tester has less states and transitions than the canonical testers obtained with the two previous methods.

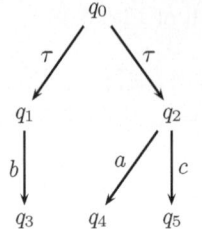

Fig. 6.12. $lts(T_g(rg(B)))$

Simplification of Conformance Tester An interesting point of this method is that it offers a simple and automatic way to generate simplified conformance testers. Drira, Azèma and Vernadat show how to generate such testers [DAV93]. The transformation is based on a simplification of the refusal graph $rg(S)$. The idea of the simplification is to remove useless, w.r.t. **conf**, states and transitions from $rg(S)$. The authors argue that this is an interesting point as such a simplification of a conformance tester using LTS cannot be automated.

6.5   Summary

Five test generation methods for LTSs have been presented in this chapter. This is certainly not an exhaustive presentation. A lot more methods exist.

The first two methods have been chosen because they make an interesting link between FSM testing and LTS testing. These methods take advantage of former works concerning FSM and explain how to apply the FSM recipes to the LTS world. A drawback of this approach is that the conformance relation considered is the FSM (trace or testing) equivalence and not **conf**, the "standard" conformance relation in the LTS world.

The other three methods presented in this chapter are well-known methods. The goal of each of them is the construction of a canonical tester. The method presented in Section 6.4.1 is compositional but limited to processes having a certain form. The CO-OP method removes this limitation. Finally, the method based on refusal graphs takes a different approach and allows us to construct automatically simplified (contrary to other methods) canonical testers.

The main drawback is that, from a practical point of view, none of these methods is very useful. In fact, they can hardly be applied to realistic systems with many states and transitions. At best, they are limited to an academic use in academic tools. For instance, the CO-OP method has been implemented in a tool called Cooper (see 14.2.9 for further details). In order to tackle realistic systems, we need more realistic models (that differentiate inputs and outputs for instance) and methods that allow to handle huge (even infinite) systems. The next chapter will give you a picture of such methods.

7 I/O-automata Based Testing

Machiel van der Bijl[1] and Fabien Peureux[2]

[1] Software Engineering
Department of Computer Science
University of Twente
P.O. Box 217, 7500 AE Enschede, The Netherlands
vdbijl@cs.utwente.nl

[2] Laboratoire d'Informatique (LIFC)
Université de Franche-Comté - CNRS - INRIA
16, route de Gray - 25030 Besançon, France
peureux@lifc.univ-fcomte.fr

7.1 Introduction

The testing theories on labeled transition systems, that we have seen so far, abstract from input and output actions. They only use the general concept "action" without a notion of direction. Although theoretically appealing, this may seem strange from a practical perspective. As a tester, we stimulate the system under test by providing inputs and observe its responses; the outputs of the system under test.

This chapter introduces the concepts from the conformance testing framework, as introduced in Part II (the section introducing "testing of labeled transition systems"), with the notion of inputs and outputs. We start with the introduction of three models for specifications and/or implementations in Section 7.3. After this we continue with several implementation relations in Section 7.4. Next we show how these models and implementation relations can be put to practice in Section 7.5. In this section we treat the derivation and execution of test cases on a system under test. We finish with our conclusions in Section 7.6.

In this chapter we made a deliberate choice to restrict the number of theories presented. We choose these theories, that –in our opinion– are relevant to get a good introduction into the field of testing with inputs and outputs. As a result, the chapter is centered around work from the following people (presented more or less in historical order).

- Lynch and Tuttle, who introduced the Input-Output Automata model and several implementation relations that use this model [LT87],
- Segala, who extended may and must testing with inputs and outputs [Seg92],
- Phalippou, who introduced the Input-Output State Machine and several implementation relations that use this machine [Pha94b],
- Tretmans, who introduced the Input-Output Transition System model and showed that his framework of **ioco** unifies several implementation relations [Tre96b]. Furthermore, Tretmans is one of the few that actually used his input-output testing theory in practice and therefore we use the **ioco** theory as the main example for test derivation and test execution,

M. Broy et al. (Eds.): Model-Based Testing of Reactive Systems, LNCS 3472, pp. 173-200, 2005.
© Springer-Verlag Berlin Heidelberg 2005

- Petrenko, who developed a theory to test Input-Output Automata in a similar way as Finite State Machines [TP98].

Although we do not treat symbolic testing in this chapter, we want to mention that Rusu et al. developed a theory to enable symbolic test generation for Input-Output Automata [RdBJ00].

7.2   Formal Preliminaries

In this section we introduce some standard notation for labeled transition systems. People that are familiar with this notation can skip this section.

Labeled Transition Systems. A labeled transition system (LTS) description is defined in terms of states and labeled transitions between states, where the labels indicate what happens during the transition. Labels are taken from a global set $\mathbf{L}$. We use a special label $\tau \notin \mathbf{L}$ to denote an internal action. For arbitrary $L \subseteq \mathbf{L}$, we use L_τ as a shorthand for $L \cup \{\tau\}$. We deviate from the standard definition of labeled transition systems in that we assume the label set of an LTS to be partitioned in an input and an output set and that the LTS is rooted; see for example definition 22.1.

Definition 7.1. A *labeled transition system* is a 5-tuple $\langle Q, I, U, T, q_0 \rangle$ where Q is a non-empty countable set of *states*; $I \subseteq \mathbf{L}$ is the countable set of *input labels*; $U \subseteq \mathbf{L}$ is the countable set of *output labels*, which is disjoint from I; $T \subseteq Q \times (I \cup U \cup \{\tau\}) \times Q$ is a set of triples, the *transition relation*; $q_0 \in Q$ is the *initial state*.

We use L as shorthand for the entire label set $(L = I \cup U)$; furthermore, we use Q_p, I_p etc. to denote the components of an LTS p. We commonly write $q \xrightarrow{\lambda} q'$ for $(q, \lambda, q') \in T$. Since the distinction between inputs and outputs is important, we sometimes use a question mark before a label to denote input and an exclamation mark to denote output. We denote the class of all labeled transition systems over I and U by $\mathcal{LTS}(I, U)$. We represent a labeled transition system in the standard way, by a directed, edge-labeled graph where nodes represent states and edges represent transitions.

A state that cannot do an internal action is called *stable*. A state that cannot do an output or internal action is called *quiescent*. We use the symbol δ ($\notin \mathbf{L}_\tau$) to represent quiescence: that is, $p \xrightarrow{\delta} p$ stands for the absence of any transition $p \xrightarrow{\lambda} p'$ with $\lambda \in U_\tau$. For an arbitrary $L \subseteq \mathbf{L}$, we use L_δ as a shorthand for $L \cup \{\delta\}$.

An LTS is called *strongly responsive* or *strongly convergent* if it always eventually enters a quiescent state; in other words, if it does not have any infinite U_τ-labeled paths. For technical reasons we restrict $\mathcal{LTS}(I, U)$ to strongly responsive transition systems.

A *trace* is a finite sequence of observable actions. The set of all traces over L ($\subseteq \mathbf{L}$) is denoted by L^*, ranged over by σ, with ϵ denoting the empty sequence. If $\sigma_1, \sigma_2 \in L^*$, then $\sigma_1 \cdot \sigma_2$ is the concatenation of σ_1 and σ_2. We use the standard notation with single and double arrows for traces: $q \xrightarrow{a_1 \cdots a_n} q$ denotes $q \xrightarrow{a_1} \cdots \xrightarrow{a_n} q'$, $q \xRightarrow{\epsilon} q'$ denotes $q \xrightarrow{\tau \cdots \tau} q'$ and $q \xRightarrow{a_1 \cdots a_n} q$ denotes $q \xRightarrow{\epsilon} \xrightarrow{a_1} \xRightarrow{\epsilon} \cdots \xrightarrow{a_n} \xRightarrow{\epsilon} q'$ (where $a_i \in \mathbf{L}_{\tau\delta}$).

We will not always distinguish between a labeled transition system and its initial state. We will identify the process $p = \langle Q, I, U, T, q_0 \rangle$ with its initial state q_0, and we write, for example, $p \xRightarrow{\sigma} q_1$ instead of $q_0 \xRightarrow{\sigma} q_1$.

Below we give some often used definitions for transition systems. $init(p)$ is the set of actions for which there is a transition in p, p **after** σ is the set of states that can be reached by performing the trace σ in p, $out(p)$ is the set of output actions for which there is a transition in p. Finally, the set of *suspension traces* of an LTS p, or $Straces(p)$ for short, is the set of traces over the label set L_δ that are possible in p.

Definition 7.2. Let $p \in \mathcal{LTS}(I, U)$, let $P \subseteq Q_p$ be a set of states in p and let $\sigma \in \mathbf{L}_\delta^*$.

(1) $init(p) =_{\text{def}} \{ \mu \in L_\tau \mid p \xrightarrow{\mu} \}$
(2) p **after** $\sigma =_{\text{def}} \{ p' \mid p \xRightarrow{\sigma} p' \}$
(3) P **after** $\sigma =_{\text{def}} \bigcup \{ p \text{ \textbf{after} } \sigma \mid p \in P \}$
(4) $out(p) =_{\text{def}} \{ x \in U_\delta \mid p \xrightarrow{x} \}$
(5) $out(P) =_{\text{def}} \bigcup \{ out(p) \mid p \in P \}$
(6) $Straces(p) =_{\text{def}} \{ \sigma \in L_\delta^* \mid p \xRightarrow{\sigma} \}$

7.3 Input Output Automata

We start with the introduction of several models for the specification and/or implementation as explained in the conformance testing framework, introduced in Part II. In model-based testing with inputs and outputs, input-output automata are a popular model. Several models with inputs and outputs have been proposed and all of these are quite similar. In this section we introduce the following three models. We will use these models in the rest of this chapter.

- Input Output Automata (IOA) as introduced by Lynch and Tuttle [LT89].
- Input Output State Machines (IOSM) as introduced by Phalippou [Pha94b].
- Input Output Transition Systems (IOTS) as introduced by Tretmans [Tre96c].

The general notion underlying all of these models is the distinction between actions that are locally controlled and actions that are not locally controlled. The output and internal actions of an automaton are locally controlled. This means that these actions are performed autonomously, i.e., independent of the environment. Inputs on the other hand, are not locally controlled; they are under control of the environment. This means that the automaton can never block an input action; this property is called input-enabledness or input completeness.

Input-output automaton. The input-output automaton is the first model with the notion of input completeness. It was introduced by Lynch and Tuttle in 1987 [LT87]. After this paper, they wrote a paper dedicated to input-output automata [LT89]. An automaton's actions are classified as either 'input', 'output' or 'internal'. Communication of an IOA with its environment is performed by synchronization of output actions of the environment with input actions of the IOA and vice versa. Because locally controlled actions are performed autonomously, it requires that input actions can never be blocked. Therefore an IOA is input enabled (it can process all inputs in every state).

Definition 7.3 (I/O automaton).
An input-output automaton $p = \langle sig(p), states(p), start(p), steps(p), part(p)\rangle$ is a five-tuple, where

- $sig(p)$ is the action signature. Formally an action signature $sig(p)$ is a partition of a set $acts(p)$ of actions into three disjoint sets: $in(p)$ input actions, $out(p)$ output actions and $int(p)$ internal actions.
- $states(p)$ is a countable, non-empty set of states.
- $start(p) \subseteq states(p)$ is a non-empty set of start states.
- $steps(p) \subseteq states(p) \times acts(p) \times states(p)$ is the transition relation with the property: $\forall a \in in(A), q \in states(p) : q \xrightarrow{a}$. This means that for every state q, there exists a state q', such that for every input action a, there is a transition $(q, a, q') \in steps(p)$ (input enabledness).
- $part(p)$ is an equivalence relation that partitions the set $local(p) = int(p) \cup out(p)$ of locally controlled actions into at most a countable number of equivalence classes.

The signature partitions the set of actions into input, output and internal actions. The input actions are actions *from* the environment, the output actions are actions *to* the environment and internal actions are actions that are *not observable* by the environment. The transition relation relates the actions to the states; by performing an action the automaton goes from one state to another. A possible problem with the input-output automata model is that an automaton cannot give an output action, because it has to handle a never ending stream of input actions. Since it is input-enabled it will synchronize on an input from the environment. Lynch and Tuttle therefore introduce the notion of fairness for IOA. In short this means that a locally controlled action cannot be blocked by input actions forever. This is the reason that the set $local(p)$ is introduced. The partitioning $part(p)$ of the locally controlled actions is used in the operationalization of fair testing. We will treat fairness in more detail in Section 7.4.1. Note that the problem of fair testing exists for all models that implement the notion of *input enabledness*. IOA implement strong input enabledness. This is formally defined by $\forall a \in in(p), q \in states(p) : q \xrightarrow{a}$. For weak input enabling it is also allowed to perform a number of internal actions before the input action can be performed: $\forall a \in in(p), q \in states(p) : q \xRightarrow{a}$.

Example. In Figure 7.1 we show three transition systems: an IOA (left), an IOSM (middle) and an IOTS (right). We will discuss the IOSM and the IOTS later on, now we focus on the IOA. The IOA represents a coffee machine. We can push two buttons: button1 and button2. After pushing button1 the machine initializes and outputs coffee, and after pushing button2 the machine initializes and outputs tea. button1 and button2 are input actions, coffee and tea are output actions and init is an internal action. To make the picture easier to read, we have abbreviated button1 and button2 to $b1$ and $b2$ respectively. The self-loops with $b1$ and $b2$ in states q_1 till q_6 show that the automaton is input enabled in every state. q_0 does not need these self loops, since button1 and button2 are already enabled in this state.

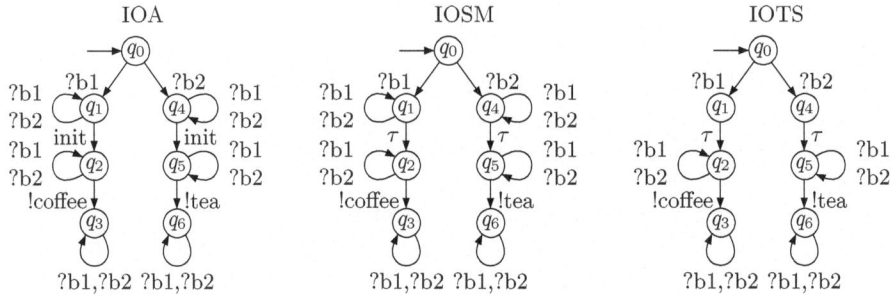

Fig. 7.1. Examples of an IOA, IOSM and IOTS

Input output state machine. This is the model as introduced by Phalippou [Pha94b]. The model is quite similar with the input-output automaton.

Definition 7.4 (input-output state machine (IOSM)).
An input-output state machine is a 4-tuple $M = \langle S, L, T, s_0 \rangle$ where:

- S is a finite, non-empty set of states.
- L is a finite, non-empty set of labels.
- $T \subseteq S \times ((\{?,!\} \times L) \cup \{\tau\}) \times S$ is the transition relation. Every element of T is a transition between a source and a target state. The associated action is either observable (input (?) or output (!)) or internal, denoted by τ. Furthermore, every state is strongly input-enabled.
- $s_0 \in S$ is the start state of the state machine.

These automata model systems whose operation can be interpreted in the following way:

- transition $(s_1, !a, s_2)$: the automaton, which is in the state s_1, performs the interaction a and goes to the state s_2. The decision to start the transition is local to the automaton.
- transition $(s_1, ?a, s_2)$: the automaton, which is in the state s_1, receives the interaction a and goes to the state s_2. The decision to start the transition is external to the automaton, since the transition is started when the interaction is received.
- transition (s_1, τ, s_2): the automaton, which is in the state s_1, goes to the state s_2 after an internal decision, without performing any observable interaction.

The main difference between an IOSM and an IOA is that there is no equivalence relation in the IOSM definition. Furthermore internal actions are abstracted into one action τ. Another difference is that the sets of states, input labels and output labels are restricted to be finite. Phalippou also uses the notion of locally (output and internal) and exteriorly (input) controlled actions and strong input-enabledness.

Example. In Figure 7.1, the transition system in the middle is an IOSM. It is very similar to the IOA on the left. The only difference is that the internal action 'init' is replaced by τ.

Input output transition system. This is the model as introduced by Tretmans [Tre96c].

Definition 7.5. An *input-output transition system* is a 5-tuple $\langle Q, I, U, T, q_0 \rangle$ where

- Q is a countable, non-empty set of *states.*
- I is a countable set of *input labels.*
- U is a countable set of *output labels*, such that $I \cap U = \emptyset$.
- $T \subseteq Q \times (I \cup U \cup \{\tau\}) \times Q$ is the *transition relation*, where $\tau \notin I, \tau \notin U$. Furthermore, every state is weakly input-enabled: $\forall q \in Q, a \in I : q \overset{a}{\Longrightarrow}$.
- $q_0 \in Q$ is the *start state.*

The input-output transition system (IOTS) is a more general version of the IOSM. Like the IOSM it does not have the equivalence relation of the IOA and it also models internal actions with the τ label. However, it does not restrict the set of states and labels to be finite. Furthermore, there is a clean partitioning of the label set in inputs and outputs, where the IOSM hides this in the transition relation. A subtle but important difference with IOA is that an IOTS is weakly input enabled: $\forall a \in I, q \in Q : q \overset{a}{\Longrightarrow}$. We denote the class of input-output transition systems over I and U by $\mathcal{IOTS}(I, U)$.

Example. In Figure 7.1, the transition system on the right is an IOTS. We see that the internal action init is replaced by τ. Notice furthermore that the states q_1 and q_4 do not have the self-loops with button1 and button2. This is allowed because an IOTS is weakly enabled. With an internal action we can go from q_1 to the input enabled state q_2 (note that the same holds for q_4 and q_5).

7.4   Implementation Relations with Inputs and Outputs

In this section, we will introduce a number of implementation relations. As was introduced in the conformance testing framework in Section II, an implementation relation (or conformance relation) is a relation that defines a notion of correctness between an implementation and a specification. When the implementation relation holds we say that the specification is implemented by the implementation or, in other words, that the implementation conforms to the specification. Several implementation relations have been defined for the automata that were introduced in the previous section. In this section, we start with implementation relations defined on IOA and continue with implementation relations on labeled transition systems.

7.4.1 Preorders on IOA

In this section, we treat implementation relations on Input Output Automata. Some of these implementation relations can also be expressed on labeled transition systems as we will explain in the next section. All of the implementation relations that we treat in this section are preorders.

We first recapitulate some concepts that are used with IOA. An *execution fragment* of an IOA p is an alternating, possibly infinite sequence of states and actions $\alpha = q_0 a_1 q_1 a_2 q_2 \cdots$ such that $(q_i, a_{i+1}, q_{i+1}) \in steps(p)$. When q_0 is a start state of p we call the execution fragment an execution of p. An external trace of an IOA p is an execution (fragment) that is restricted to the set of external actions. We use the notation $etraces(p)$ to denote the external traces of IOA p, where $etraces^*(p)$ denotes the set of finite external traces of p. We use the notation $a \in enabled(q)$ to denote that state q enables a transition with action a. This means that there is a state q' for which $(q, a, q') \in steps(p)$. To denote the set of enabled external actions in a state q, we use the notation $wenabled(q)$. An IOA p is finitely branching iff each state of p enables finitely many transitions.

We start with the trace inclusion preorder. This is a very weak relation. It expresses that one system is an implementation of the other if its set of external traces is a subset of the set of external traces of the specification.

Definition 7.6 (External trace inclusion). For IOA i and s:

$$i \leq_{tr} s =_{\text{def}} etraces(i) \subseteq etraces(s)$$

The above definition is defined in a so-called intentional way. Many implementation relations can also be defined in an extensional way in the style of De Nicola and Hennessy [NH84]. The term *extensional* refers to an external observer. The intuition behind this idea is that an implementation conforms to a specification if no external observer can see the difference. We will not use the extensional definition in this section, but we refer to Chapter 5 for more information about extensional definitions of implementation relations and to [Tre96b] for more information on extensional definitions of implementation relations with inputs and outputs.

Example. We give an example of the external trace inclusion preorder in Figure 7.2. On the left hand side we see a specification of a coffee machine. It prescribes that after pressing the button at least twice we expect to observe either coffee or tea as output. We will reuse this coffee machine specification in other examples. On the right hand side we see two implementations. The first implementation does not implement coffee as an output. It is still correct, because the set of traces of the implementation is a subset of the set of traces of the specification, even with the trace $button \cdot button \cdot button^* \cdot coffee \cdot button^*$ missing. External trace inclusion is not a very realistic implementation relation, because it also approves implementations that are intuitively incorrect. For example, the implementation on the right only implements the pushing of the button, without serving any drink. This is correct, because the set of traces $button \cdot button \cdot button^*$ is a subset of the external traces of the specification.

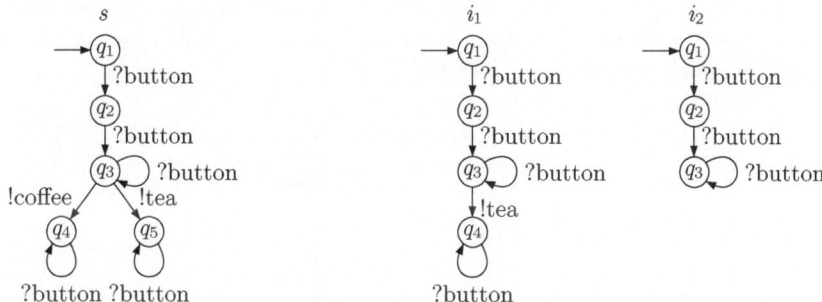

Fig. 7.2. Example of the external trace inclusion preorder

Lynch and Tuttle introduced the notion of fair execution for IOA. Remember that IOA are (strong) input enabled. This means that an infinite stream of input actions can prevent an output or internal action from occurring. Intuitively the idea behind fair execution is that locally controlled actions cannot be blocked by input actions for ever. This is expressed formally in the definition below.

The definition uses the concept of *quiescent* executions. Similar to transition systems, for IOA an execution is quiescent if it ends in a quiescent state, i.e., a state that can only perform input actions (so no locally controlled actions). A quiescent trace, is a trace that leads to a quiescent state. The set of quiescent traces is the set of finite external traces that lead to a quiescent state :
$qtraces(p) = \{\sigma \in etraces^* p^* \mid \exists q \in states(p) : p \xRightarrow{\sigma} q \wedge enabled(q) = in(p)\}$.

An execution α of an IOA p is *fair* if either α is *quiescent* or α is infinite and for each class $c \in part(p)$ either actions from c occur infinitely often in α or states from which no action from c is enabled appear infinitely often in α. A fair trace of an IOA p is the external trace of a fair execution of p. The set of fair traces of an IOA p is denoted by $ftraces(p)$. Given the notion of fair traces we can define a preorder over the sets of fair traces of IOA.

Definition 7.7 (Fair preorder). Given two IOA's i and s with the same external action signature, the fair preorder is defined as:

$i \sqsubseteq_F s \Leftrightarrow ftraces(i) \subseteq ftraces(s)$.

We will give examples of the fair preorder a little later in this section, because we first want to introduce a preorder that is strongly related to the fair preorder, namely the quiescent preorder introduced by Vaandrager [Vaa91]. It uses the concept of quiescent traces, introduced above.

Definition 7.8 (Quiescent preorder). Given two IOA's i and s with the same external action signature, the quiescent preorder is defined as:

$$i \sqsubseteq_Q s \Leftrightarrow etraces^*(i) \subseteq etraces^*(s) \wedge qtraces(i) \subseteq qtraces(s).$$

The fair and quiescent preorders look much alike, but there are some important differences. The quiescent preorder uses finite traces to test for trace inclusion, whereas the fair preorder includes infinite traces. The relation between the two preorders is easiest explained with an example (the examples are reused with kind permission of Segala [Seg97]).

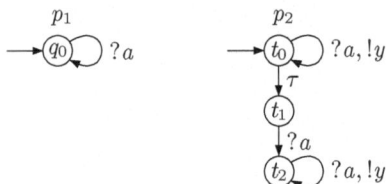

Fig. 7.3. Quiescent versus fair preorder, example 1

Example. Figure 7.3 shows two IOA p_1 and p_2, a is an input action, y is an output action and τ is an internal action. The partition of locally controlled actions for both IOA is a single class $\{y, \tau\}$. Let us first illustrate the set of external and quiescent traces. For p_1 we have $etraces(p_1) = qtraces(p_1) = a^*$, meaning a set of zero or more occurrences of a. For p_2 we have $etraces(p_2) = \{a, y\}^* \cdot a \cdot \{a, y\}^*$, $qtraces(p_2) = \{a, y\}^*$. With $\{a, y\}^*$ we mean an arbitrary number of times, an arbitrary number of a's followed by an arbitrary number of y's (or vice versa), like $aayayya$. Regarding the fair traces, for p_1 it is trivial that each finite sequence a^n is quiescent and therefore a fair trace. Also for p_2, the finite sequence a^n is a quiescent and fair trace. After looping n times in t_0 we move to t_1 by a τ transition. Therefore $p_1 \sqsubseteq_Q p_2$. However, the sequence a^ω (infinite times a) is a fair trace of p_1 but not of p_2. The latter is because, we are either infinitely often in t_0 or t_2 but neither $\{\tau, y\}$ is not enabled, nor $\{\tau, y\}$ is occurring infinitely often. Thus $p_1 \not\sqsubseteq_F p_2$.

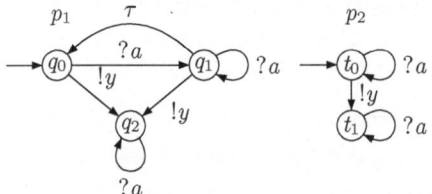

Fig. 7.4. Quiescent versus fair preorder, example 2

Example. Another similar difference is illustrated in Figure 7.4. We have the IOA p_1 and p_2, both can perform an arbitrary number of a input actions followed by one y output action, followed again by an arbitrary amount of a actions. p_1 and p_2 are equivalent according to the quiescent preorder (both $p_1 \sqsubseteq_Q p_2$ and $p_2 \sqsubseteq_Q p_1$), because they have the same external traces and their quiescent traces contain at least a y action. However, p_1 and p_2 are not equivalent according to the fair preorder, when considering the same partitioning as before: $\{y, \tau\}$. This is because a^ω is a fair trace of p_1 but not of p_2. This might not be easy to see at first glance, but remember that the partition of locally controlled actions is $\{y, \tau\}$. In p_1 we can do the fair execution $(q_0 \cdot a \cdot q_1 \cdot \tau q_0)^\omega$ (and thus the fair trace a^ω).

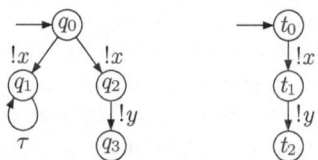

Fig. 7.5. Quiescent versus fair preorder example 3

Divergence (i.e., the possibility for a system of to do an infinite number of internal transitions) shows another difference between the quiescent and fair preorder. Because of divergence, a fair trace is not necessarily a quiescent trace, as is illustrated in the next example.

Example. In Figure 7.5, we have two IOA p_1 and p_2 with output actions x and y. According to the quiescent preorder both automata are equivalent. But they are not equivalent according to the fair preorder, since x is a fair trace of p_1, but not of p_2.

As we can see from these examples, the fair preorder is a stronger relation than the quiescent preorder. Because of the definition of the quiescent preorder, this is not very surprising. As a side step, Segala shows a way to make the quiescent preorder and the fair preorder equivalent by making some restrictions on the IOA's that we allow [Seg97]. Basically, the property we are looking for is that we can approximate an infinite fair trace by a finite trace and can extend a finite fair trace to an infinite fair trace. This is expressed by the properties *fair continuity* and *fair approximability*. An IOA p is fair continuous if the limit of any chain of fair traces of p is also a fair trace. Fair continuity is nicely illustrated in Figure 7.3. The sequence a^n is a fair trace of p_2, but if we take n to infinity this is not the case. In other words the trace a^n is not fair continuous. An IOA p is fair approximable if each infinite trace of p is the limit of a chain of fair traces of p. This is illustrated in Figure 7.4. The trace a^ω is a fair trace of p_1 but it is not fair approximable because the finite trace a^n is not fair.

Under the restrictions of fair approximability and fair continuity we can show that the fair preorder and the quiescent preorder are equivalent for strongly converging IOA (we need strong convergence to rule out divergence).

Theorem 7.9. *Let* i, $s \in IOA$ *be strongly convergent.*

$$i \sqsubseteq_F s \Rightarrow i \sqsubseteq_Q s$$

If p_1 *is fair approximable, and* p_2 *is fair continuous, then* $p_1 \sqsubseteq_Q p_2 \Rightarrow p_1 \sqsubseteq_F p_2$

In the next part of this section we will introduce may and must testing for systems with inputs and outputs. First we quickly recapitulate some of this theory. The method for comparing transition systems that was initiated by De Nicola and Hennessy is based on the observation of the interactions between a transition system and an external experimenter as introduced in Chapter 5. An experimenter e for a transition system p is a transition system that is compatible with p. The input actions of e are the output actions of p $(in(e) = out(p))$ and the output actions of e are the input actions of p, plus an action w called the success action $(out(e) = in(p) \cup \{w\})$. The experimenter e runs in parallel with p and synchronizes its output actions with input actions of p and vice versa (except w). An experiment x is an execution of $p\|e$ which is infinite or ends in a deadlocked state. We say that the experiment is successful if w is enabled in at least one state of the execution x. If there is a successful experiment of $p\|e$ we use the notation p **may** e. If every experiment of $p\|e$ is successful we use the notation p **must** e. On this notion of may and must we can define preorder relations. We will start with the may preorder.

Definition 7.10 (MAY preorder). Let i, $s \in IOA$:

$$s \sqsubseteq_{\text{MAY}} i \Leftrightarrow \forall e : s \text{ may } e \Rightarrow i \text{ may } e$$

Hennessy has shown that the may preorder and external trace inclusion are equivalent [Hen88].

Theorem 7.11. *Let* i, $s \in IOA$: $s \sqsubseteq_{\text{MAY}} i \Leftrightarrow etraces(s) \subseteq etraces(i)$

For the must preorder we need a little more work. Segala uses the following definition of the must relation [Seg97]:

Definition 7.12 (MUST). Given an IOA p, a set of states Q_1 and a set of external actions A.
Q_1 **must** $A \Leftrightarrow$

(1) $A \cap in(p) \neq \emptyset$, or
(2) for each $q \in Q_1$:
    (a) wenabled$(q) \cap out(p) \subseteq A$, and
    (b) wenabled$(q) \cap A \neq \emptyset$

With this definition of the must relation on IOA we define the must preorder in the following way.

Definition 7.13 (MUST preorder). Let i, $s \in IOA$:

$$s \sqsubseteq_{\text{MUST}} i \Leftrightarrow \forall \sigma \in ext(s)^*, A \subseteq ext(s) : s \text{ after } \sigma \text{ must } A \Rightarrow i \text{ after } \sigma \text{ must } A$$

Segala has shown that this definition of the must preorder is equivalent with the quiescent preorder. The only restriction we need is that the IOA are strongly converging and finitely branching.

Theorem 7.14. *Let i and s be finitely branching and strongly convergent IOA.*

$$s \sqsubseteq_{\text{MUST}} i \Leftrightarrow i \sqsubseteq_Q s.$$

7.4.2 IOCO Based Testing

In this section, we introduce input-output variants of several pre-order based testing relations that were introduced in Chapter 5. All the input-output testing relations that we show in this section take an LTS with inputs and outputs as a specification and assume the implementation to be an IOTS. We show that all the implementation relations that we present in this chapter can be unified in the **ioco** implementation relation, hence the name of this chapter. In order to relate the implementation relations we use definitions that deviate from the original definitions. The equivalence of our definitions with the original definitions is proved in [Tre96b]. The way that our definitions differ is that we use an intentional characterization of the implementation relations, i.e., a characterization in terms of properties of the labeled transition systems themselves. This in contrast to an extensional characterization where an implementation relation is defined in terms of observations that an external observer can make. In the intentional characterization observations are expressed in possible outputs of the labeled transitions system after performing a certain trace.

We will introduce the following input output implementation relations:

- The input-output variant of testing preorder, denoted by $\leq_{iot}$.
- The input-output variant of the **conf** relation, denoted by **ioconf**.
- The input-output variant of refusal preorder, denoted by $\leq_{ior}$.
- The **ioco** implementation relation.

Input-output testing relation The first implementation relation that we introduce is the input-output testing relation. This is testing pre-order with a notion of input and output actions. The set of traces with which we test are in L^*. This means that we can use any trace to test with, even if its behavior is not specified by the specification.

Definition 7.15 (Input output testing relation). Let $i \in \mathcal{IOTS}(I, U), s \in \mathcal{LTS}(I, U)$

$$i \leq_{iot} s =_{\text{def}} \forall \sigma \in L^* : out(i \text{ after } \sigma) \subseteq out(s \text{ after } \sigma).$$

We can read this definition in the following way. An implementation i is $\leq_{iot}$-correct with respect to a specification s if for all traces with which we test, the set of outputs of the implementation after such a trace is a subset of the set of outputs of the specification after the same trace. In terms of observations this means that we should not be able to observe different or more behavior from the implementation than from the specification. A possible output is the absence of output or quiescence. We use the meta-label δ to denote quiescence. It is interesting to know that the $\leq_{iot}$ relation is equivalent with the quiescent preorder (and thus with the must preorder) [Tre96b].

Example. We will illustrate the input output testing relation with the example of the trace inclusion preorder in Figure 7.2. The implementation i_1 is $\leq_{iot}$-correct with respect to specification s. We see that it does not implement the coffee output after pressing the button twice, so how can it be correct? Let us take a look at the definition of $\leq_{iot}$. The specification prescribes that the set of outputs after the trace $button \cdot button = \{coffee, tea\}$. When we take a look at i_1 we see that the set of outputs after $button \cdot button = \{tea\}$. Because $\{tea\} \subseteq \{coffee, tea\}$ it is correct behavior. So the intuition behind non deterministic output is that we do not care which branch is implemented as long as at least one is. We can do the same analysis for implementation i_2. Here we find that after pressing the button twice i_2 does not give any output; it is quiescent. This means that $out(i_2 \textbf{ after } button \cdot button) = \{\delta\}$. This is not a subset of $\{coffee, tea\}$ and there fore $i_2 \not\leq_{iot} s$. We see that $\leq_{iot}$ is a stronger implementation relation than external trace inclusion and furthermore one that agrees more with our intuition.

ioconf relation The input-output variant of the **conf** relation is called **ioconf** [Tre96b]. The difference with the input-output testing relation is that it uses a different set of traces to test with, namely the set of all possible traces of the specification: $traces(s)$. This means that we will not test behavior that is not specified. One way to interpret this is as *implementation freedom*: "We do not know or care what the implementation does after an unspecified trace". The advantage of this is that we can test with incomplete specifications. Since $traces(s) \subseteq L^*$, the **ioconf** relation is weaker than the $\leq_{iot}$ relation.

Definition 7.16 (ioconf). Let $i \in \mathcal{IOTS}(I, U), s \in \mathcal{LTS}(I, U)$

$$i \textbf{ ioconf } s =_{\text{def}} \forall \sigma \in traces(s) : out(i \textbf{ after } \sigma) \subseteq out(s \textbf{ after } \sigma).$$

Example. In Figure 7.6 we illustrate the **ioconf** relation. i_1 is the same implementation as in the examples for external trace inclusion and $\leq_{iot}$. This implementation is still correct under **ioconf**. This is easy to see, because the trace $button \cdot button \in traces(s)$; it is a trace of the specification and $out(i_1 \textbf{ after} button \cdot button) = \{tea\} \subseteq out(s \textbf{ after} button \cdot button) = \{coffee, tea\}$. Implementation i_2 introduces new behavior. When we kick the coffee machine it outputs soup. This kind of behavior is nowhere to be found in the specification; the behavior of kicking the machine is underspecified. This kind of behavior would be a problem for $\leq_{iot}$ since it will test on all possible behavior of the label set: L^*. When we test the kicking of the machine with $\leq_{iot}$ we get the following result: $out(i_2 \text{ after } kick) = \{soup\} \not\subseteq out(s \text{ after } kick) = \emptyset$. This is the reason that with $\leq_{iot}$ we need a completely specified specification. Else we know up front that no implementation will conform to the specification. **ioconf** does not have this restriction, because it will only test behavior that is specified. Since $kick \notin traces(s)$, we will not test its behavior. Because all the other behavior of i_2 is identical to i_1 we have i_2 **ioconf** s. In case one does not like this kind of implementation freedom, the specification can be made complete and as a result the same testing power as the $\leq_{iot}$ relation is obtained.

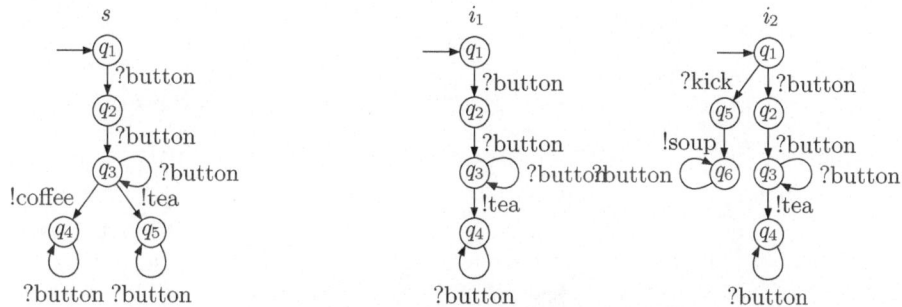

Fig. 7.6. Example of **ioconf**

Input-output refusal relation The next implementation relation, the input-output refusal relation, is the input output version of the refusal preorder (Chapter 5). What we saw with the $\leq_{iot}$ and **ioconf** implementation relations was that they both used traces that did not have δ's in them (no intermediate quiescence). It was only possible to observe quiescence at the end of a trace. The input-output refusal relation can do just that, it uses δ as an expected output in its set of traces to test with; so called repetitive quiescence. Quiescence can be seen as *refusal* to do an output action, hence the name of the implementation relation. We can see this as follows in the definition of the input-output refusal relation $\leq_{ior}$. The set of traces over which we test is: L_δ^*. Or, in other words, all possible combinations of actions from the label set with δ (quiescence). This means that it only makes sense to test with complete specifications as illustrated for $\leq_{iot}$ in Figure 7.6. Again the correctness criterion is that an implementation does not show more behavior than is allowed by the specification.

Definition 7.17 (Input output refusal). Let $i \in \mathcal{IOTS}(I, U), s \in \mathcal{LTS}(I, U)$

$$i \leq_{ior} s =_{\text{def}} \forall \sigma \in L_\delta^* : out(i \text{ after } \sigma) \subseteq out(s \text{ after } \sigma).$$

We give an example of the $\leq_{ior}$ implementation relation together with **ioco**, because these two implementation relations are closely related.

ioco relation The **ioco** testing theory is named after its implementation relation **ioco**. The difference with the implementation relations that we have treated so far lies again in the set of traces over which we test. Just like $\leq_{ior}$, **ioco** also uses the notion of quiescence. But the set of traces with which we test are the so-called *suspension traces* of the specification. These are the traces (with or without quiescence) that are specified in the specification. This set is smaller than the set of traces of $\leq_{ior}$. In other words, **ioco** is a weaker implementation relation than $\leq_{ior}$.

Definition 7.18 (ioco). Let $i \in \mathcal{IOTS}(I, U), s \in \mathcal{LTS}(I, U)$.

i **ioco** $s =_{\text{def}} \forall \sigma \in Straces(s) : out(i \text{ after } \sigma) \subseteq out(s \text{ after } \sigma)$.

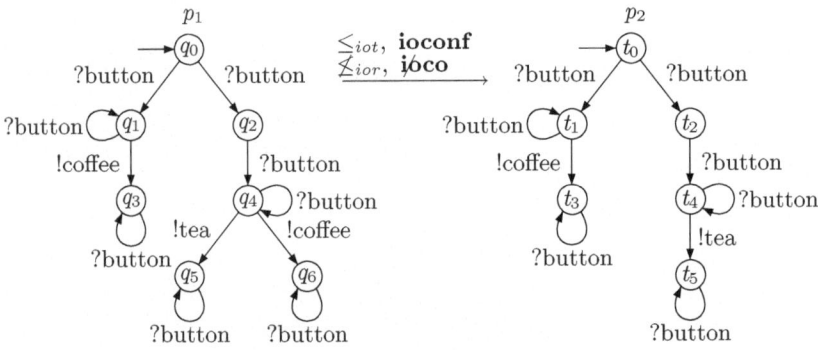

Fig. 7.7. Example of **ioco**

Example. We illustrate the $\leq_{ior}$ and **ioco** implementation relations in Figure 7.7. The example is reused with kind permission of Tretmans [Tre96b]. We see two IOTS's p_1 and p_2 that model a coffee machine with peculiar behavior. p_1 models a machine where after pressing a button once, you get either coffee or nothing (quiescence). If you got nothing and you press the button again you get either tea or coffee. p_2 models an almost identical machine, except after you press the button again after obtaining nothing after the first button press you will only get tea (so no coffee). If p_1 is the implementation and p_2 the specification we can see that $\leq_{iot}$ and **ioconf** hold, whereas $\leq_{ior}$ and **ioco** do not. Let us begin with **ioco**, **ioco** can see the difference between the transition systems because of the following trace. After *button·δ·button* we will observe tea and coffee for p_1, whereas p_2 prescribes that only tea is allowed. The same holds for $\leq_{ior}$ since it is also capable of this same test case. However $\leq_{iot}$ and **ioconf** are not capable of observing quiescence during testing and can therefore not tell the difference between the trace *button·button·coffee* in the left branch of the transition system or in the right branch of the transition system. In other words, they are not powerful enough to see the difference.

When we take p_2 as the implementation and p_1 as the specification we see that all implementation relations identify the implementation as correct. This is logical since the only difference between p_1 and p_2 is that p_2 does not offer the possibility of coffee in the right branch. This is correct, since the specification p_1 gives the choice between implementing either one (or both).

The difference between **ioco** and $\leq_{ior}$ is the same difference as between $\leq_{iot}$ and **ioconf**. **ioco** is capable of dealing with incomplete specifications, whereas $\leq_{ior}$ is not.

The input-output implementation relations that we have introduced so far can be easily related. The only variable is the set of traces over which we test. Based on the relations between the sets of tested traces we can relate the strength of the implementation relations. This is easy to see since $traces(s) \subseteq Straces(s), L^* \subseteq L^*_\delta$. For reasons of completeness we have also added the pre-orders of the previous section. We know that these are defined on IOA and not on LTS's and IOTS's, but these relations can be easily converted to each others realms. The fair testing preorder is not in this comparison. As far as we know, nobody has made a comparison between the fair testing preorder and the other implementation relations in this chapter. It is clear that the fair testing preorder is stronger than the quiescent preorder, but it is not clear to what extent the fair testing preorder is comparable to **ioco**.

Proposition 7.19. *Comparison of expressiveness of the implementation relations.*

$$\left\{ \begin{array}{c} \sqsubseteq_{\text{MAY}} \\ \leq_{tr} \end{array} \right\} \subset \leq_{ior} \subset \left\{ \begin{array}{c} \sqsubseteq_Q \\ \sqsupseteq_{\text{MUST}} \\ \leq_{iot} \\ \textbf{ioco} \end{array} \right\} \subset \textbf{ioconf}$$

7.4.3 Work Introduced by M. Phalippou

We present in this section the implementation relations used in the method introduced by M.Phalippou [Pha94b]. This method is defined on a particular model of automata: input/output state machine (see IOSM definition 7.4).

Moreover, we are only interested in the states which are reachable from the initial state by a finite number of transitions. We can thus remove the set of all the states which do not verify this condition, or we only use the connex graph of the automaton containing the initial state. In a more formal way, this connex component of an automaton is defined as follows.

Definition 7.20 (Connex component of IOSM).
Let $\langle S, L, T, s_0 \rangle$ be an IOSM. The connex component of this IOSM containing the initial state is an IOSM $CC(\langle S, L, T, s_0 \rangle) = \langle S_C, L_C, T_C, s_{0C} \rangle$ defined by:

(1) $L_C = L$
(2) $s_{0C} = s_0$
(3) S_C is recursively defined by the rules:
    (a) $s_{0C} \in S_C$
    (b) if $s \in S_C$ and $(s, \mu, s') \in T$ then $s' \in S_C$
(4) $T_C = \{(s, \mu, s') \in T, s \in S_C\}$

The properties relating to testing only depend on the traces of the handled automata. In order to introduce a formal definition of the traces on IOSM, we firstly need to define IOSM sequence and opposite sequence.

Definition 7.21 (Sequence and opposite sequence).
Given an IOSM $S = \langle S_s, L_s, T_s, s_0 \rangle$ and a sequence $(\sigma = \mu_1...\mu_n) \in (\{!,?\} \times L_s)^*$. The opposite sequence, noted $\overrightarrow{\sigma}$ is defined by the sequence generated from σ by reversing the output (!) and the input (?) in the different actions. The following properties about sequence and opposite sequence can now be introduced:

(1) (s_0, σ, s_n) iff $(\exists (s_i)_{1 \leq i < n} \in S_s^n)(\forall i, 1 \leq i \leq n)((s_{i-1}, \mu_i, s_i) \in T_s)$

(2) (S, σ, s_n) iff (s_0, σ, s_n)

(3) (s_0, ε, s_1) iff $s_0 = s_1$ or $(\exists n \geq 1)(s_0, \tau^n, s_1)$

(4) (s_0, μ, s_1) iff $(\exists s_2, s_3 \in S_s)((s_0, \varepsilon, s_2) \wedge (s_2, \mu, s_3) \wedge (s_3, \varepsilon, s_1))$

(5) $(s_0, \overrightarrow{\sigma}, s_n)$ iff $(\exists (s_i)_{1 \leq i < n} \in S_s^n)(\forall i, 1 \leq i \leq n)((s_{i-1}, \mu_i, s_i) \in T_s)$

Definition 7.22 (Trace).
An observable trace of S is a sequence σ of observable actions such as $(\exists s_n \in S_s)(s_0, \overrightarrow{\sigma}, s_n)$. The set of all the traces of S is denoted by $Tr(S)$.

The concept of trace makes it possible to disregard internal action τ. Thus, a trace is an observable behavior, i.e. visible from the interface of the IOSM. It should be noted that the traces of an IOSM are the same ones as those of its connex component containing the initial state.

Property 7.23. $Tr(S) = Tr(CC(S))$

To illustrate implementation relations on IOSM, we will use the example of coffee machine. Its specification S is presented in figure 7.8.

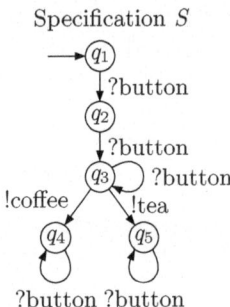

Specification S

Fig. 7.8. IOSM specification of coffee machine

In the approach introduced by M. Phalippou, both the specification and the implementation to be tested are represented by an IOSM. Four possible implementations (I_1, I_2, I_3 and I_4) of the coffee machine are described in figure 7.9.

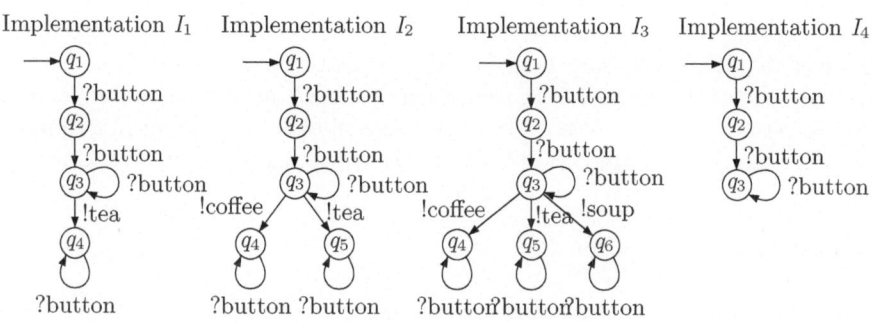

Fig. 7.9. Examples of IOSM implementation of coffee machine

The conformance is then defined as a relation, called implementation relation, between the implementation and its relevant specification. The next definition formally expresses this relation by means of IOSM as introduced by M. Phalippou.

Definition 7.24 (Implementation relation on IOSM).
An implementation relation on IOSM is a relation R on $IOSM \times IOSM$. Given an implementation I and a specification S such as $I, S \in IOSM$, if $R(I, S)$ holds then we say that I conforms to S.

The choice of an implementation relation is generally arbitrary, although some minimal properties have to be respected according to the conformance objectives [PBD93]. To elaborate such relations, we place ourselves in a testing situation where all that we can do is to send interactions towards a black box system to be tested, and to analyze the outputs returned by the black box.

Definition 7.25 (Outputs authorized by the specification).
Given $\sigma \in Tr(S)$ and L a finite non empty set of labels, $O = (\sigma, S) = \{a \in L \mid \sigma!a \in Tr(S)\}$ denotes the set of all the outputs authorized by the specification S after the trace σ.

All the definitions needed to present implementation relations on IOSM are now described. M. Phalippou defines five implementation relations adapted to the IOSM (these examples illustrate the variety of the arbitrary choices) [Pha93].

A first idea, to ensure that an implementation conforms to a specification, consists in verifying that the outputs returned by the implementation never contradict what is envisaged by the specification when something is envisaged. The goal of applying this kind of implementation relation, is not to know what it occurs when interactions, that are not specified by the specification, are send to the implementation. This implementation relation is known as R_1.

Definition 7.26 (Relation R_1).
$R_1(I, S)$ iff $(\forall \sigma \in Tr(S))(\sigma \in Tr(I) \Rightarrow O(\sigma, I) \subseteq O(\sigma, S))$

According to the implementation relation R_1 and among the implementations of the figure 7.9, only I_3 is considered not to be in conformance with the specification of the figure 7.8. Indeed, the relation R_1 authorizes an implementation to return no output even if the specification envisages one or more possible behavior (see for example I_4). To avoid this lack, M. Phalippou thus consider a new implementation relation called R_2.

Definition 7.27 (Relation R_2).
$R_2(I, S)$ iff
$(\forall \sigma \in Tr(S))(\sigma \in Tr(I) \Rightarrow \{O(\sigma, I) \subseteq O(\sigma, S) \wedge (O(\sigma, I) = \emptyset) \Leftrightarrow (O(\sigma, S) = \emptyset)\})$

This new implementation relation does not change the conformance of the implementation I_1 and I_2, and the non-conformance of I_3, but the implementation I_4 does not conform any more to the specification S. Indeed, according to R_2, an implementation conforms to a specification if the implementation gives less possible outputs than the specification does. But, this view could not be strong enough: it could be expected that the implementation must at least have all the capacities envisaged by the specification (but has freedom to make some more). The two following relations R_3 and R_4 express this idea : according to R_3 and R_4, I_1 does not conform to S while I_3 does.

Definition 7.28 (Relation R_3).
$R_3(I, S)$ iff $Tr(S) \subseteq Tr(I)$

Definition 7.29 (Relation R_4).
$R_4(I, S)$ iff $Tr(S) \subseteq Tr(I) \wedge (\forall \sigma \in Tr(S))((O(\sigma, I) = \emptyset) \Leftrightarrow (O(\sigma, S) = \emptyset))$

Finally, we can choose to require that the implementation makes exactly what is envisaged by the specification. The relation R_5 is built on this principle: it is built in fact by the conjunction of the implementation relations R_1 and R_3 (or R_2 and R_4). Using this last implementation relation, only I_2 conforms to the specification S.

Definition 7.30 (Relation R_5).
$R_5(I, S)$ iff $(\forall \sigma \in Tr(S))(\sigma \in Tr(I) \wedge (O(\sigma, S) = O(\sigma, I)))$

It should be noted that the implementation relations R_1, R_2, R_3 and R_4 are expressed as preorder relations (see section 7.4.1). But, the most studied relation about Input Output Automata is the equivalence relation. When input complete specifications are used, the equivalence relation has to be modified, and we naturally obtain the relation R_5 introduced by M. Phalippou. Therefore, this last implementation relation appears to be a major result in the domain of Input Output Automata based testing. For example, G. Luo, A. Petrenko and G. Bochmann used an implementation relation similar to R_5 in order to select test cases from nondeterministic Finite State Machine [LvBP94].

7.5   Testing Transition Systems

In the previous section, we have discussed several implementation relations. In this section, we introduce two more concepts of the conformance testing framework, namely test derivation and test execution. We will show the relation between the conformance relation and test generation and execution. The **ioco** conformance relation is one of the few relations that is used for testing in practice. Apparently the other relations are more used for verification than testing. Therefore we use the **ioco** implementation relation as the example implementation relation for the test derivation and test execution sections. For more information about the practical application of the **ioco** theory we refer to Chapter 14.

Test cases Before we introduce test derivation, we first explain what a test case is; see also Section 20. A test case is a specification of the experiment that an experimenter wants to conduct on an implementation. A test case can be described by an LTS. In order to test according to implementation relations that have the notion of quiescence we introduce a new label in the label set of the tester: θ; θ is the tester's counter part of δ. With the θ label the test case can observe quiescence. So test cases will be in the domain $\mathcal{LTS}(U \cup \theta, I)$. We will add a couple of restrictions to the behavior of a test case. To guarantee that a test case finishes in finite time it should have finite behavior. Furthermore to ensure maximal control over the testing process we do not allow non-deterministic behavior. We also do not allow choice between multiple input actions and between input actions and output actions. This implies that a state in a test case is either a terminal state, or a state that offers exactly one input to the implementation or accepts all outputs of the implementation. To give a verdict over the success of the test case we label terminal states with **pass** and **fail**. These restrictions are formally expressed in the following definition of a test case. Note that a test case could in principle be defined without these restrictions. It could be an arbitrary LTS that synchronizes on the actions of the implementation under test. The definition we introduce here has shown to be both theoretically and practically useful.

Definition 7.31 (Test case).

- An LTS $t = \langle Q, U \cup \{\theta\}, I, T, q_0 \rangle \in \mathcal{LTS}(U \cup \{\theta\}, I)$ is a test case if:
  - t is deterministic and has finite behavior. t is deterministic if $\forall \sigma \in L_\theta^*, p$ **after** σ has at most one element.
  - Q contains terminal states **pass** and **fail**, with $init(\textbf{pass}) = init(\textbf{fail}) = \emptyset$.
  - For any state $q \in Q$ of the test case, if $q \neq \textbf{pass}, \textbf{fail}$ then either $init(q) = \{a\}$ for some $a \in I$, or $init(q) = U \cup \{\theta\}$.
- The class of test cases over U and I is denoted as $\mathcal{TEST}(U, I)$.
- A test suite T is a set of test cases: $T \subseteq \mathcal{TEST}(U, I)$.

In the definition of a test case we can see that the label sets of the specification are reversed: Inputs of the specification are outputs of the implementation and vice versa. This makes it difficult to talk about inputs and outputs, since it is not always clear if it is an input for the test case or for the implementation. Therefore we will use the terms *stimulus* for an output of the test case (i.e., an input of the implementation) and *response* for an input of the test case (i.e., an output of the implementation).

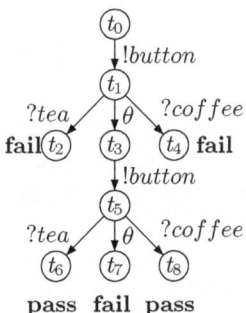

Fig. 7.10. Example test case

Example. In Figure 7.10 we show an example test case. With this test case we can test our coffee machine as specified, for example, in Figure 7.6. We see that the test case starts with the stimulus *button* in state t_0. In state t_1 we choose to observe a response. The specification prescribes that there should be no output. So if we observe coffee, or tea we add a **fail** label, like in t_2 and t_4. If we observe quiescence (with θ) we continue testing. Again we choose stimulus *button* and arrive in state t_5. Now the specification prescribes that we should observe coffee or tea as response. so, if we observe quiescence we add the **fail** verdict to state t_7. If we observe coffee or tea we stop testing and add **pass** as a verdict to states t_6 and t_8.

Test execution A test run of a test case on an implementation is modeled by synchronous parallel composition (denoted by ∥) of the test case with the implementation under test. This means that inputs of the test case synchronize on outputs of the implementation and vice versa. In case of quiescence, the test case synchronizes on δ with its special θ action. The execution continues until the test case reaches one of its terminal nodes. Because of the special structure of a test case we are sure that the test case will always reach one of its terminal states. An implementation passes the test run if the test case ends in a pass state, if it is not we say that the implementation fails the test case. This means that we have found a possible error. Because an implementation can have non-deterministic behavior, different runs with the same test case can lead to different terminal states (and possibly different verdicts). Therefore, an implementation passes a test case if *all* possible test runs lead to the verdict pass.

Definition 7.32. Let $t \in \mathcal{TEST}(U, I)$ and $i \in \mathcal{IOTS}(I, U)$.

(1) A *test run* of a test case t with an implementation i is a trace of the synchronous parallel composition $t \| i$ leading to a terminal state of t:

σ is a test run of t and i iff $\exists i' : t \| i \overset{\sigma}{\Longrightarrow} \mathbf{pass} \| i'$ or $t \| i \overset{\sigma}{\Longrightarrow} \mathbf{fail} \| i'$.

(2) Implementation i **passes** test case t if all their test runs lead to the pass-state of t:

i **passes** $t =_{\mathrm{def}} \forall \sigma \in L_\theta^*, \forall i' : t \| i \overset{\sigma}{\nRightarrow} \mathbf{fail} \| i'$.

(3) An implementation i passes a test suite T if it passes all test cases in T:

i **passes** $T =_{\mathrm{def}} \forall t \in T : i$ **passes** t.

If i does not pass the test suite, it fails: i **fails** $T =_{\mathrm{def}} \exists t \in T : i$ **passes** t.

Test derivation All the parts of the conformance testing framework are now in place: a conformance relation between implementations and specifications and the execution of a test case on an implementation. We will finish the picture with test derivation (also called test generation). It is especially important that a test case is sound, i.e., if an implementation fails a test case it should be the case that there is really an error according to the specification. If possible we also want to generate a test suite that is exhaustive, i.e., if an implementation has an error then the test suite will detect it. In practice the latter is often impossible because of the (practically) infinite size of the test suite. Below we give the formal definitions of *completeness, soundness and exhaustiveness*. In this definition, we use **ioco** as the implementation relation. **ioco** can be replaced by any of the implementation relations of the previous section.

Definition 7.33. Let s be a specification and T a test suite then:
T is complete $=_{\mathrm{def}} \forall i : i$ **ioco** $s \Leftrightarrow i$ **passes** T
T is sound $=_{\mathrm{def}} \forall i : i$ **ioco** $s \Rightarrow i$ **passes** T
T is exhaustive $=_{\mathrm{def}} \forall i : i$ **ioco** $s \Leftarrow i$ **passes** T

It turns out that a relative simple algorithm can produce a complete test suite for **ioco**. Test generation algorithms for the other implementation relations can be made in a similar way. For the completeness proof we refer to Tretmans [Tre96b]. Note that completeness often means an (practically) infinite test suite (one loop makes a complete test suite infinite). In the definition of the test derivation algorithm we have chosen to use a behavioral definition to make it easier to read (behavioral expression can be transformed to an LTS in a straightforward manner). This means that we do not explicitly create an LTS. To make it easier to understand the relation between the behavior and the LTS we added pictures to represent the way a test case is build up (so the pictures are test cases). Furthermore we give an example of a test case derivation after the definition. Note that we use the notation $\bar{\sigma}$ for a trace in which all δ actions have replaced by θ actions and all input actions have been changed to output actions (only the direction).

Definition 7.34. Let $s \in \mathcal{LTS}(I, U)$ be a specification with initial state q_0. Let S be a non-empty set of states, with initially $S = \{q_0\}$. A test case $t \in \mathcal{TEST}(U \cup \{\theta\}, I)$ is obtained from S by a finite number of recursive applications of one of the following three non-deterministic choices:

(1) ⟶○ pass

$t := \mathbf{pass}$

The test case with only the state **pass** is always a sound test case. This rule stops the recursion in the algorithm.

(2)

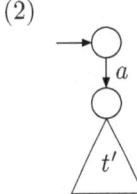

$t := \overline{a}; \ t'$ where $a \in I, S \ \mathbf{after} \ a \neq \emptyset$ and t' is obtained by recursively applying the algorithm for $S' = S \ \mathbf{after} \ a$.

This step in the algorithm adds an input action a to the test case. After applying the input a, the test case behaves as t' which is obtained by applying the test derivation algorithm recursively to S'. t' is depicted as an abstract subtree (triangle) in the figure above.

(3)

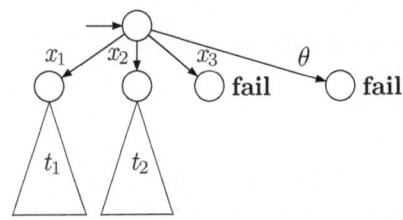

$$
\begin{aligned}
t := \quad & \Sigma \{\overline{x}; \ \mathbf{fail} \mid x \in U, x \notin out(S)\} \\
+ \ & \Sigma \{\theta; \ \mathbf{fail} \mid \delta \notin out(S)\} \\
+ \ & \Sigma \{\overline{x}; \ t_x \mid x \in U, x \in out(S)\} \\
+ \ & \Sigma \{\theta; \ t_\theta \mid \delta \in out(S)\}
\end{aligned}
$$

where t_x and t_θ are obtained by recursively applying the test derivation algorithm for $S' = S \ \mathbf{after} \ x$, $S \ \mathbf{after} \ \delta$, respectively. In this definition $+$ and Σ have the standard process algebraic meaning. $+$ stands for choice and Σ stands for the sum of all expressions in a set.

In this step we add expected outputs to the test case. If the output is incorrect according to the specification we add a transition with the output to a fail state, thus ending that part of the test case. The same holds for

the observation of quiescence where it is not allowed according to the specification. For outputs that are allowed, we continue the test derivation with
t_x, t_θ respectively.

Example. We illustrate the test derivation algorithm with our coffee machine
specification like the one shown on the left hand side in figure 7.6. We will show
how to derive an LTS with the algorithm. We use the same test case as used
to explain the test case definition, see Figure 7.10. When we start, the set S
consists of only the start state q_1 of our specification. We choose one of the three
rules of the test derivation algorithm. Randomly, we start with applying rule 2 of
the test derivation algorithm and apply the input *button*. This is possible, since
q_1 **after** $button = \{q_2\}$ ($\neq \emptyset$). The result is the transition $(t_0, !button, t_1)$ in our
test case. The set S is updated to $S = \{q_2\}$. So we now have a test case with the
stimulus *button*. Now we choose to observe responses from the implementation
under test; we apply rule three. There are three possible responses: *tea*, *coffee*
and quiescence. We compute $out(q_1) = \{\delta\}$ of the specification. So, the only
allowed output is quiescence. Therefore we add a transition with *tea* to a fail-
state $(t_1, ?tea, t_2)$ and a transition with *coffee* to a fail state $(t_1, ?coffee, t_4)$.
For the allowed response δ we add the transition (t_1, θ, t_3). We update S with
S **after** $\delta = \{q_2\}$. We again apply the stimulus *button* which results in the
transition $(t_3, button, t_5)$ and $S = \{q_3\}$. For rule 3 there are now two options,
either the response coffee or tea, since $out(q_2) = \{coffee, tea\}$. We can add the
transitions $(t_5, ?tea, t_6)$, $(t_5, ?coffee, t_8)$ and (t_5, θ, t_7) where t_7 is a fail-state.
Because of non-determinism in the specification we have two possible paths to
continue with. For the "tea" path we update S with $\{q_5\}$ and for the "coffee"
path we update S with $\{q_4\}$. We can in principle continue forever with choosing
between step 2 and three of the test derivation algorithm until we reach a final
state in the specification or until we want to stop. In our case the specification
has reached a final state and we can apply rule 1 to stop the recursion. This
transforms states t_6 and t_8 into pass-states.

7.5.1   Conformance Testing Based on Input/Output State Machine

In practice, system testing is performed with test suites. Each test case of a test
suite is defined to verify that a specific property of the specifications is correctly
implemented, or to detect a precise fault in the implementation. A test case
can be seen as a finite sequence of interactions between a tester and the tested
implementation. This process ends by the assignment of a verdict (usually pass,
fail or inconclusive).

The method of conformance testing introduced by M. Phalippou on IOSM is
different [Pha93]. Indeed, his idea consists in considering in a global way the set
of all interactions and sequences of interactions between the tester and the tested
implementation. According to this principle, a unique object, called canonical
tester, is defined to represent in the one hand all the executions performed by a
given test suite, and in the other hand all its execution.

To implement this approach, it is necessary to define concretely what is a canonical tester, as well as the way of assigning a test verdict with the couple (tester, implementation).

To ensure homogeneity with the specifications and the implementations, the canonical testers are modelled with IOSM. The canonical tester depends directly in the one hand on the implementation relation to be tested, and in the other hand on the trace machine of the specification. The trace machine of a specification S is a deterministic IOSM not comprising any internal action τ and having the same set of traces as the initial IOSM of S.

Definition 7.35 (Trace Machine).
The trace machine of an IOSM $S = \langle S_s, L_s, T_s, s_{0s} \rangle$, noted $TM(S)$, is an IOSM $TM(S) = CC(\langle S_t, L_t, T_t, s_{0t} \rangle)$ defined by:

(1) S_t is the set of subsets of S_s: a state s_t of the trace machine is thus a set of states of the specification $s_t = \{s_{is}\}_{1 \leq i \leq n}$
(2) $L_t = L_s$
(3) $s_{0t} = \{s \mid (s_{0s}, \varepsilon, s)\}$
(4) the transitions of the trace machine are exactly those obtained in the following way: for all $s \in S_t$ and $\mu \in \{!, ?\} \times L_s$, given $s' = \{s_j \mid (\exists\, s_{is} \in S_s)(s_{is}, \overset{\rightarrow}{\mu}, s_j)\}$, if $s' = \emptyset$ then $(s, \mu, s') \in T_t$.

The trace machine generation is similar to the determination of an not-deterministic automaton as introduced by J. Hopcroft and J. Ullman in [HU79]. Thus, from any IOSM, it is possible to calculate a trace machine, which exactly represents the traces of the initial IOSM.

Property 7.36. $Tr(S) = Tr(TM(S))$

The mechanism of verdict assignment is based on an parallel execution of the canonical tester with the implementation to be tested. The verdict is then pronounced according to the properties of the IOSM which represents this parallel composition. Indeed, the canonical tester has one particular state, called *fail*, which indicates that an error has been detected.

Definition 7.37 (Verdict of a canonical tester).
The failure of a tester T applied to an implementation I is defined by: $Fail(T, I)$ iff $(\exists \sigma \in Tr(T))(\overset{\rightarrow}{\sigma} \in Tr(I) \land (T, \sigma, fail))$.
   The verdict is $Succ(T, I)$ iff $\neg(Fail(T, I))$ holds.
   The verdict assigned by the canonical tester is also defined as a global (or total) verdict.

We now present the test theory proposed by M. Phalippou using a concrete example. This example is based on the specification of the coffee machine example. The specification S introduced in figure 7.8 and implementations I_1, I_2, I_3 and I_4 introduced in figure 7.9 are used to illustrate the various steps to apply this testing theory.

First of all, we need to define the canonical tester making it possible to distinguish the IOSM which are implementations in conformity with the initial specification within the meaning of a specific implementation relation. The next definition describes how generate such a tester from the specification S of the coffee machine example and the implementation relation R_1 introduced by the definition 7.26.

Definition 7.38 (Canonical tester for R_1).
Given a specification S and its trace machine $TM(S) = \langle S_s, L_s, T_s, s_{0s} \rangle$, we call canonical tester of S the IOSM noted $T = TCA(S) = \langle S_t, L_t, T_t, s_{0t} \rangle$ such as:

(1) $S_t = S_s \cup \{fail\}$
(2) $L_t = L_s$
(3) $s_{0t} = s_{0s}$
(4) the tester transitions are exactly those obtained by the following rules:

    (a) $(\forall \mu \in \{!, ?\} \times L_s)(\forall s, s' \in S_s)((s, \mu, s') \in T_s \Leftrightarrow (s, \overrightarrow{\mu}, s') \in T_t)$
    (b) $(\forall s \in S_s)(\forall a \in L_s)(\neg(\exists s')((s, !a, s') \in T_s) \Rightarrow (s, ?a, fail) \in T_t)$

This canonical tester of S is thus charged to check that nothing of opposite with what is envisaged can appear. For that, it provides an mirroring image of the traces of the specification. A mechanism to detect the errors is added: if the tester receives one interaction which should not happen in a given state, it reaches the state called *fail*. We can find this detection method in many approaches concerning testing from systems communicating by inputs and outputs, namely an inversion of the inputs and outputs to obtain tests from the specification [RP92]. The structure obtained by inversion of the trace machine determines the tester. This one is then supplemented by adding transitions used to detect errors.

The figure 7.11 introduces the canonical tester on the coffee machine example using the implementation relation R_1. For this example, the set L of all the events which can be received is $L = \{ soup, tea, coffee \}$.

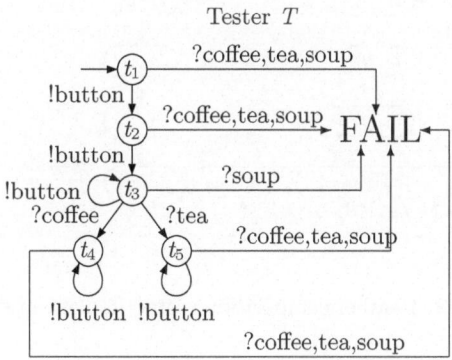

Fig. 7.11. Canonical tester using R_1

In order to assign a verdict, we now introduce the definition of the parallel composition of two IOSM. In fact, this composition makes it possible to model several communication interfaces between various IOSM or several points of interactions.

Definition 7.39 (Parallel composition of two IOSM).
The parallel composition of two IOSM $I_1 = \langle S_1, L_1, T_1, s_{01} \rangle$ and $I_2 = \langle S_2, L_2, T_2, s_{02} \rangle$ is an IOSM $I = I_1 \parallel I_2 = \langle S, L, T, s_0 \rangle$ which is defined by:

(1) $S = S_1 \times S_2$
(2) $L = L_1 \cup L_2$
(3) $s_0 = (s_{01}, s_{02})$
(4) the transitions of the IOSM $I_1 \parallel I_2$ are exactly obtained by means of the following rules:
    (a) $(s_1, \tau, s_1') \in T_1 \Rightarrow \forall s_2 \in S_2 \cdot ((s_1, s_2), \tau, (s_1', s_2)) \in T$
    (b) $(s_2, \tau, s_2') \in T_2 \Rightarrow \forall s_1 \in S_1 \cdot ((s_1, s_2), \tau, (s_1, s_2')) \in T$
    (c) if $a \in L_1 \cap L_2$ then
        $(s_1, ?a, s_1') \in T_1 \wedge (s_2, !a, s_2') \in T_2 \Rightarrow ((s_1, s_2), \tau, (s_1', s_2')) \in T$ and
        $(s_1, !a, s_1') \in T_1 \wedge (s_2, ?a, s_2') \in T_2 \Rightarrow ((s_1, s_2), \tau, (s_1', s_2')) \in T$
    (d) if $a \in L_1 - L_2$ then
        $(s_1, ?a, s_1') \in T_1 \Rightarrow \forall s_2 \in S_2 \cdot ((s_1, s_2), ?a, (s_1', s_2)) \in T$ and
        $(s_1, !a, s_1') \in T_1 \Rightarrow \forall s_2 \in S_2 \cdot ((s_1, s_2), !a, (s_1', s_2)) \in T$
    (e) if $a \in L_2 - L_1$ then
        $(s_2, ?a, s_2') \in T_2 \Rightarrow \forall s_1 \in S_1 \cdot ((s_1, s_2), ?a, (s_1, s_2')) \in T$ and
        $(s_2, !a, s_2') \in T_2 \Rightarrow \forall s_1 \in S_1 \cdot ((s_1, s_2), !a, (s_1, s_2')) \in T$

The IOSM calculated by parallel composition of the R_1 canonical tester and the possible implementations (figure 7.12) show well that the assignment of the verdict consists in checking if a state of the form $(fail, s_i)$ is in the IOSM $T \parallel I_i$. So, the four generated IOSM confirm that, using the implementation relation R_1, only the implementation I_3 does not conform to the specification S.

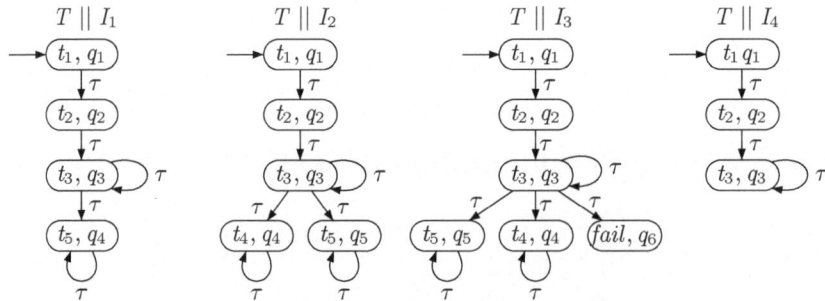

Fig. 7.12. Parallel composition tester/implementation

This global testing approach, already used by E. Brinksma in [Bri89] and introduced by M. Phalippou on IOSM, has the advantage of representing in a

homogeneous way the testing activity without having to pass by the stages of
test suite generation and test case execution as shown in [Pha94a, Pha95].

However, it should be recognized that this approach presents disadvantages
which are the counterpart of the advantages given above. It is for example difficult, without efficient test hypotheses, to study the concepts which are not
defined in the specification, in particular how to connect the test cases to a test
goal, how to add tests to increase the functional coverage of a test suite, or how
to associate the test verdict with a specific diagnosis.

Finally, this method is used in the tool called TVEDA [Ris93, BPR93,
CGPT96]. This tool is developed and used by the telecommunication industry (France Telecom) to automate the design of the test cases for protocol systems [Pha91]. In this area, the complexity of the systems, together with the high
level of fiability which is expected from their global interworking, indeed justify
to bring a great care to the test generation. In this way, TVEDA makes it possible to select a reasonable number of test cases by making some test hypotheses.
Thus, the approach adopted in TVEDA slightly differs from the theory presented
in this section: indeed, it consists, for a given implementation relation, to calculate an approximation of the tester since a rigorous definition is very often too
complex to calculate (see Section 14.2.7 for more details).

7.6   Conclusion

In this chapter we filled in several pieces of the conformance testing framework
for LTS-based testing with inputs and outputs. We started with the introduction
of three models that capture the notion of inputs and outputs: the Input-Output
Automaton, the Input-Output State Machine and the Input Output Transition
System. An interesting characteristic of these models is that they are *input-
enabled*. Next, we have shown several implementation relations over these models. The most important ones are: the fair testing preorder, the may and must
preorder, the **ioco** implementation relation and the R_5 implementation relation.
For the **ioco** theory and the theory of Phalippou we have shown how to derive
test cases and how to execute them against an implementation. For the **ioco**
theory there is a completeness proof for the test generation algorithm.

Finally, it should be stressed that these works are not simply regarded as significant theoretical results, but their practical applications directly contributed
to the development of tools. Thus, an algorithm rising from the **ioco** theory is
implemented in the tool TorX [dVT98], while the R_5 implementation relation is
the base of the tool TVEDA [CGPT96].

8 Test Derivation from Timed Automata

Laura Brandán Briones[1] and Mathias Röhl[2]

[1] University of Twente
brandanl@cs.utwente.nl
[2] University of Rostock
mroehl@informatik.uni-rostock.de

8.1 Introduction

A real-time system is a discrete system whose state changes occur in real-numbered time [AH97]. For testing real-time systems, specification languages must be extended with constructs for expressing real-time constraints, the implementation relation must be generalized to consider the temporal dimension, and the data structures and algorithms used to generate tests must be revised to operate on a potentially infinite set of states.

There are various formalisms that use fictitious clocks for expressing timing constraints. These simplify reasoning about time by recording the timing of events with finite precision only and thereby approximate precise timing of activities. The set of nonnegative integers could be used as a time domain, with the restriction that the sequence of integer times must be non-decreasing. Behavior on a discrete time scale could be modeled with ordinary finite automata by adding a distinguished *tick* event to the set of its actions.

In dense time domains, which could be sub-domains of $\mathbb{Q}^{\geq 0}$ or $\mathbb{R}^{\geq 0}$, events may occur at different time points that lay arbitrarily close together. Detecting arbitrarily small variations would require infinite test cases. However, if two events may occur on different times but for an observer their ordering makes no difference for testing purposes these events may be considered to take place at the same point in time. Henzinger et al. showed that the digitization of clocks allows to distinguish all systems which are distinguishable in the dense time domain if the system can be modeled as a timed transition system [HMP92].

We start with a general introduction to timed automata and associated concepts. The main part presents three different techniques for the generation of real-time black-box conformance tests from timed automata with a dense time domain. The first approach allows for testing (a subclass of) nondeterministic timed automata, the second one concentrates on the exhaustive testing of deterministic timed automata, while the last approach facilitates the testing of deterministic timed automata with silent transitions. An automatic light switch is used as a running example for specifications and test suite derivation.

8.2 Timed Automata

Timed automata extend finite state automata with a finite set of clocks over a dense time domain [AD94]. All clocks increase monotonically at a uniform rate,

M. Broy et al. (Eds.): Model-Based Testing of Reactive Systems, LNCS 3472, pp. 201-231, 2005.
© Springer-Verlag Berlin Heidelberg 2005

and measure the amount of time that has elapsed since they were started or reset. The choice of the next state of a timed automaton depends, in addition to the kind of an input symbol, on the occurrence time of the input symbol relative to the occurrence of previously read symbols. Each transition of the system may reset some of the clocks, and has an associated enabling condition which is a constraint on the values of the clocks. A transition can be taken only if the current clock values satisfy its enabling condition. Timing constraints on clocks may be expressed by the following syntax.

Definition 8.1. For a set C of clock variables, the set $\Phi(C)$ of **clock constraints** φ, where $c \in C$ and $k \in \mathbb{Q}^{\geq 0}$, is defined inductively by

$$\varphi \stackrel{def}{=} c < k \mid c > k \mid c \leq k \mid c \geq k \mid \varphi_1 \wedge \varphi_2$$

Often, $c = k \stackrel{def}{=} c \leq k \wedge c \geq k$ and true $\stackrel{def}{=} 0 \leq c$ are used as abbreviations.

Definition 8.2. A **timed automaton** $\mathscr{A}$ is a tuple $\langle S, S_0, \Sigma, C, Inv, E \rangle$, where

- S is a finite set of locations
- $S_0 \subseteq S$ is a set of initial locations
- Σ is a finite alphabet that denotes the set of actions
- C is a finite set of clocks
- $Inv : S \to \Phi(C)$ associates a clock invariant to each location
- $E \subseteq S \times \Sigma \times \Phi(C) \times 2^C \times S$ gives the set of transitions [Alu99].

A transition $(s, a, \varphi, \lambda, s') \in E$ represents a change of location from $s \in S$ to $s' \in S$ on symbol $a \in \Sigma$. The clock constraint (guard) $\varphi \in \Phi$ specifies when the transition is enabled, and the set $\lambda \subseteq C$ gives the set of clocks to be reset when this transition is taken. Clock invariants constrain how long the automaton is allowed to stay in a certain location.

Example. We adopt the automatic Light Switch from Springintveld et al. as an example [SVD01]. The Light Switch can be specified by a timed automaton $\mathscr{A}$, with

- $S = \{s_0, s_1\}$
- $S_0 = \{s_0\}$
- $\Sigma = \{on, off\}$
- $C = \{c\}$
- $Inv(s_0) = $ true, $Inv(s_1) = c \leq 5$
- $E = \{(s_0, on, \text{true}, \{c\}, s_1), (s_1, on, c < 5, \{c\}, s_1), (s_1, off, c = 5, \emptyset, s_0)\}$

Its behavior can be explained as follows. The state of the system in which the light is off is represented by s_0, and the state s_1 represents the situation where the light is on. The light can be turned on by pushing the *on* button. After five time units the switch turns itself *off*. Before that happens, the *on* button may be pushed again, which will leave the light on (cf. Figure 8.2).

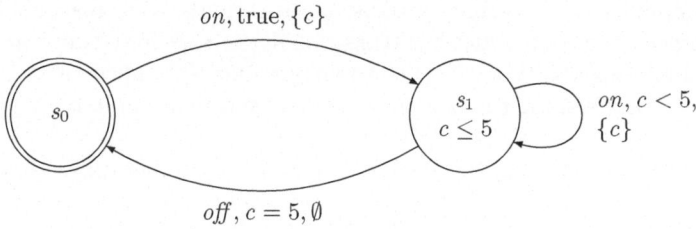

Fig. 8.1. A timed automata specification of an automatic Light Switch

Remark 8.3. Timed automata were introduced by Alur and Dill [AD94] as a generalization of finite-state machines over infinite words [Tho90]. We only consider timed automata without acceptance conditions which are usually referred to as **timed safety automata** [HNSY92]. An introduction to acceptance is given in Section 19.2, whereas a discussion of acceptance conditions in the context of timed automata can be found elsewhere [HKWT95].

The behavior of a timed automaton $\mathscr{A}$ depends on both its current location and the actual values of all its clocks.

Definition 8.4. A **clock valuation** over a set of clocks C is a map ν that assigns to each clock $c \in C$ a value in $\mathbb{R}^{\geq 0}$. With $V(C)$ we denote the set of clock valuations over C. For $d \in \mathbb{R}^{\geq 0}$, $\nu + d$ denotes the clock interpretation which maps every clock c to the value $\nu(c) + d$. For $\lambda \subseteq C$, $\nu[\lambda := 0]$ denotes the clock interpretation for C which assigns 0 to each $c \in \lambda$, and agrees with ν over the rest of the clocks.

A labeled transition system $\mathscr{M}$ with uncountably many states can be used to define the possible behavior of a timed automata $\mathscr{A}$. A state of $\mathscr{M}$ has to be a pair $\langle s, \nu \rangle$ such that s is a location of $\mathscr{A}$ and ν is a clock valuation for C satisfying invariant $Inv_{\mathscr{A}}(s)$. Transitions of $\mathscr{M}$ represent either an elapse of time or a transition of $\mathscr{A}$.

Definition 8.5. The **semantics** of a timed automaton $\mathscr{A}$ is given by the LTS $\mathscr{M} = \langle Q, Q_0, L, \rightarrow \rangle$, where

- $Q = \{\langle s, \nu \rangle \in S_{\mathscr{A}} \times V(C_{\mathscr{A}}) \mid \nu \models Inv_{\mathscr{A}}(s)\}$
- $Q_0 \subseteq Q$ with $\langle s, \nu \rangle \in Q_0$ iff $s \in S_{0_{\mathscr{A}}}$ and $\nu(c) = 0$ for all clocks $c \in C_{\mathscr{A}}$
- $L = \Sigma_{\mathscr{A}} \cup \mathbb{R}^{\geq 0}$
- $\rightarrow \subseteq Q \times L \times Q$, which could be either
  - $(\langle s, \nu \rangle, d, \langle s, \nu + d \rangle)$ iff $d \in \mathbb{R}^{\geq 0}$ and for all $0 \leq d' \leq d$, $\nu + d' \models Inv_{\mathscr{A}}(s)$
  - $(\langle s, \nu \rangle, a, \langle s', \nu[\lambda := 0] \rangle)$ iff $(s, a, \varphi, \lambda, s') \in E_{\mathscr{A}}$ and $\nu \models \varphi$

Due to dense-time clocks, the transition system $\mathscr{M}$ for a timed automaton $\mathscr{A}$ has infinitely many states and operates on infinitely many symbols. Analysis of safety requirements of real-time systems can be formulated as reachability problems for timed automata. Since the transition system $\mathcal{M}$ for a timed automaton $\mathcal{A}$ is infinite, reachability analysis constructs a quotient called the **region automaton** by partitioning the uncountable state space into finitely many regions [Alu99].

A timed automaton can be seen as accepting (or generating) timed words and thereby defining a timed language. Two timed automata are said to be equivalent if they accept the same timed language.

Definition 8.6. A **timed word** over an alphabet Σ is a finite sequence (a_1, t_1) $\ldots (a_n, t_n)$ of symbols $a_i \in \Sigma$ paired with nonnegative real numbers $t_i \in \mathbb{R}^{\geq 0}$ that are nondecreasing $(\forall\, i < n.t_i < t_{i+1})$. A **timed language** over Σ is a set of timed words over Σ.

Remark 8.7. Alur and Dill showed that a Büchi automaton (called region automaton) can be constructed that accepts exactly the set of untimed words that are consistent with the timed words accepted by a timed automaton [AD94]. The construction of the region automaton is PSPACE-complete.

Remark 8.8. Alur and Dill showed the language inclusion problem to be undecidable for nondeterministic timed automata but solvable in PSPACE for deterministic timed automata. The problem of deciding the emptiness of the language of a given timed automaton is PSPACE-complete for deterministic timed automata [AD94].

Deterministic timed automata form an important subclass of timed automata that are strictly less expressive than nondeterministic timed automata [AD94]. For timed automata to be deterministic multiple transitions starting at the same location with the same label are only allowed if their clock constraints are mutually exclusive. Thus, at most one of the transitions with the same action is enabled at a given time.

Definition 8.9. A timed automaton $\langle S, S_0, \Sigma, C, Inv, E \rangle$ is called **deterministic** iff

- $|S_0| = 1$, and
- for all $s \in S$, for all $a \in \Sigma$, for every pair of transitions of the form $\langle s, a, \varphi_1, \lambda_1, s_1 \rangle \in E$ and $\langle s, a, \varphi_2, \lambda_2, s_2 \rangle \in E$, $\varphi_1 \wedge \varphi_2$ is unsatisfiable.

Definition 8.10. Timed automata with **silent transitions** are gained by extending Definition 8.2 such that for a transition $(s, a, \varphi, \lambda, s') \in E$ an action a can be in $\Sigma \cup \tau$, where $\Sigma \cap \tau = \emptyset$. A transition $(s, a, \varphi, \lambda, s')$ is called a silent transition (often called ϵ-transition) when $a = \tau$. If, in addition $\lambda = \emptyset$ then we speak of a silent transition without reset.

Remark 8.11. Whereas silent transition do not increase the expressiveness of untimed automata they strictly increase the power of timed automata. Bérard et al. showed silent transitions with clock resets that lie on a directed cycle to be responsible for this increase in expressiveness [BPDG98].

8.3   Testing Event Recording Automata

Nielsen and Skou present a technique for the automatic generation of *real-time* black-box conformance tests for *non-deterministic* systems [NS03]. They start from a determinizable class of timed automata specifications called ERA, with a dense time interpretation. The tests are generated using a coarse grained equivalence class partition of the specification.

8.3.1   Model

Event Recording Automata (ERA) were proposed by Alur, Fix and Henzinger [AFH94] as a determinizable subclass of timed automata and have language inclusion as a decidable property (like all deterministic timed automata).

Like a timed automaton [AD94], an ERA has a set of clocks which can be used in guards (clock constrains) and be reset when an action is taken. In ERA, however, each action a is uniquely associated with a clock c_a, called the event clock of a. Whenever an action a is executed the event clock c_a is automatically reset. No further clock assignments are permitted. The event clock c_a thus *records* the amount of time passed since the last occurrence of a. No silent τ-actions or location invariants are permitted. These restrictions ensure determinizability [AFH94].

Definition 8.12. An **Event Recording Automaton** (ERA) $\mathscr{A}$ is a tuple $\langle S, s_0, \Sigma, E \rangle$, where

- S is a non-empty (finite) set of locations
- $s_0 \in S$ is the initial location
- Σ is a finite set of actions
- $E \subseteq S \times \Sigma \times \Phi(C) \times S$ is the set of transitions
  where
  - $C = \{c_a \mid a \in \Sigma\}$ is the set of real-valued clocks
  - $\Phi(C)$ is the set of clock constraints (or guards), these guards are generated by the syntax $\varphi ::= \gamma \mid \varphi \wedge \varphi$, where γ is a constraint of the form $c_1 \sim k$ or $c_1 - c_2 \sim k$ with: $\sim \in \{\leq, <, =, >, \geq\}$, k a non-negative integer constant, and $c_1, c_2 \in C$.

All actions are *urgent*, meaning that synchronization between two automata takes place immediately when the parties have enabled a pair of complementary actions. The complementary actions are actions by which the automata synchronize, in our cases input and output actions, denoted as _?, _! respectively. The requirement of *urgent* actions is needed because with non-urgent observable actions the synchronization delay could be unbounded.

Example. Figure 8.2 shows an ERA which describe the behavior of the automatic Light Switch. The initial location is indicated by double circle. Formally, the ERA is given by $\langle S, s_0, \Sigma, E \rangle$, where

- $S = \{s_0, s_1\}$
- s_0 is the initial state

- $\Sigma = \{on?, off!\}$
- $E = \{(s_0, on?, \text{true}, s_1), (s_1, on?, c_{on} < 5, s_1), (s_1, off!, c_{on} = 5, s_0)\}$

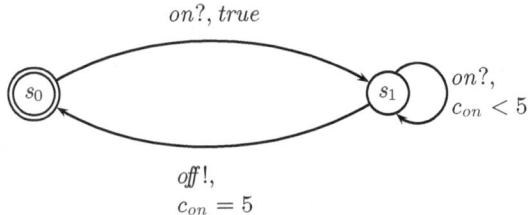

$on?, true$

s_0 s_1 $on?,$ $c_{on} < 5$

$off!,$ $c_{on} = 5$

Fig. 8.2. ERA specification for an automatic Light Switch [SVD01]

The determinization procedure for ERAs is given by Alur, Fix and Henzinger [AFH94], and is conceptually a simple extension of the method used for the untimed case, only now the guards must be taken into account.

8.3.2   Symbolic Representation

Timed automata (a network of ERAs) with a dense time interpretation cannot be analyzed by finite state techniques, since the timed transition system associated with it has infinitely many states. Therefore, it must be analyzed symbolically [NS03]. Similar to the region automaton [Alu99] which partitions the state space into finitely many regions, here *zone* is used instead, in the following way.

The state of a network of timed automata is represented by a pair $\langle \bar{s}, \bar{\nu} \rangle$, where $\bar{s}$ is the vector of the automata's current location, and $\bar{\nu}$ is the vector of their current clock values. A *zone* z is a conjunction of clock constraints of the form $c_1 \sim k$ or $c_1 - c_2 \sim k$ with $\sim \in \{\leq, <, =, >, \geq\}$ or equivalently, the solution set to these constraints. A symbolic state $[\bar{s}, z]$ represents the (infinite) set of states $\{\langle \bar{s}, \bar{\nu} \rangle \mid \bar{\nu} \in z\}$.

Example. The graphical view of the symbolic state $[s_1, z]$ for the ERA of example 8.3.1, with $z = c_{on} < 5$ is shown in Figure 8.3.

Zones can be represented and manipulated efficiently by the *difference bound matrix* (DBM) data structure [Bel57]. The use of zones allows us to compute:

- The symbolic state that results after take a transition from a given source symbolic state
- The reachable state space. Forward reachability analysis starts in the initial state $(\bar{s}_0, \bar{0})$ and computes the symbolic states that can be reached by execute an action from an exists one, or by let time pass. When a new symbolic state is included in one previously visited, no further exploration of the new state needs to take place. Forward the reachability analysis terminates when no new state can be reached

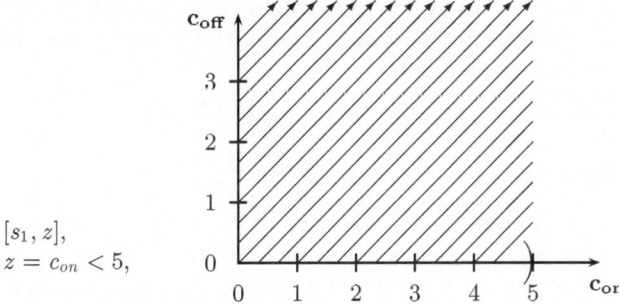

$[s_1, z],$
$z = c_{on} < 5,$

Fig. 8.3. A symbolic state and the solution set corresponding to the zone z

- Given a symbolic path to a symbolic state, a concrete timed *trace* leading to it (or a subset thereof) can be computed by propagating its constraints back along the symbolic path used to reach it, and by choosing specific time points along this *trace*

Remark 8.13. To ensure soundness of the produced tests, symbolic reachability analysis is needed to select only states for testing that are reachable, and to compute only timed *traces* that are actually part of the specification.

8.3.3   Testing

As opposed to exhaustive testing, a test *selection criterion* is used in this case (or *coverage criterion*), i.e. a rule that describe which behavior or which requirements should be tested. *Coverage* is a metric of completeness with respect to a test selection criterion.

For real-time systems it is proposed to partition the clock valuations into domains and ensure that each such domain is tested systematically.

Example. In our example of the automatic Light Switch, a partition domain for c_{on} could be as shown in Figure 8.4.

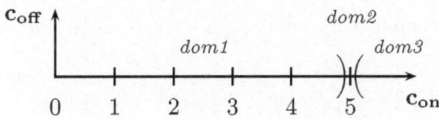

Fig. 8.4. ERA Domains Graph

The selection criterion used here is based on partition the state space of the specification into coarse equivalence classes, and require that the test suite for each class yields a set of required observations of the implementation when it is expected to be a state in that class. Like in the Hennessy's works [HN83], the following abstract syntax is used:

(1) **after** σ **must** A,
(2) **can** σ,
(3) **after** σ **must** $\emptyset$

where $\sigma \in Act^*$ and $A \subset Act$. Informally, (1) is successful if at least one of the observations in A (called a *must* set) can be observed whenever the *trace* σ is served, (2) is successful if σ is a prefix of the observed system, and (3) is successful if this not case (i.e. σ is not a prefix). Using this notation, each class is decorated with the *simple deadlock* observations of the forms **after** ε **must** A (a *must* property), **after** a **must** $\emptyset$ (a *refusal* property), and **can** a (a *may* property) that should be satisfied in that class (this idea was taken from the testing preorder).

A test case consists of a timed *trace* which lead to a desired state in a coarse equivalence class followed by one of the *simple deadlock* observations.

Now, we present the state partitioning definition, which is used to construct the equivalence class graph. This graph is a transformation of the initial automata, which preserve all the information from it. And moreover, the equivalence class graph is what is effectively used in the test derivation process.

The State Partitioning works as follows. Let S' be a vector location in the determinized automaton, note that S' can be a set of locations of the original automaton. Therefore, this control location S' will have the clock valuations partitioned such that two clock valuations belong to the same equivalence class if and only if they enable precisely the same outgoing transitions from S', i.e. the locations are equivalent with respect to the enabled transitions.

An equivalence class is represented by a pair $[S', p]$, where S' is a set of location vectors, and p is the inequation which describe the clock constraints that must hold for that class, i.e. $[S', p]$ is the set of states $\{\langle S', \bar{\nu} \rangle \mid \bar{\nu} \in p\}$. Further, to obtain equivalence classes that are continuous convex polyhedra, and to enable the reuse of existing efficient symbolic techniques (as used in model checking), this constraint is rewritten in disjunctive normal form. Each disjunct form is treated as an equivalence class.

Definition 8.14. State Partitioning $\Psi(S')$
Let S' be a set of location vectors, $E(S')$ the set of transitions from a location in S'. If E is a set of transitions with $\Gamma(E)$ we denote the set of guards of the set E.

$$\Gamma(E) = \{\varphi \in \Phi(C) \mid \bar{s} \xrightarrow{\varphi, a} \bar{s'} \in E\}$$

Let P be a constraint over clock inequations γ composed using the logical connectives ($\wedge, \vee$, or $\neg$). DNF(P) denotes a function that rewrites constraint P to its equivalent disjunctive normal form, i.e. such that $\bigvee_i \bigwedge_j \gamma_{ij} = P$. Each conjunct in disjunctive form can be written as a guard $\varphi \in \Phi(C)$. The disjunctive normal form can be interpreted as a disjunction of guards such that $\bigvee_i \varphi_i = \bigvee_i \bigwedge_j \gamma_{ij}$. Let

$$\Psi(S') = \{P_{E'} \mid E' \in 2^{E(S')} \wedge P_{E'} = \bigwedge_{\varphi \in \Gamma(E')} \varphi \wedge \bigwedge_{\varphi \in \Gamma(E(S')-E')} \neg\varphi\}$$

Then, the set of guards φ_i whose disjunction equals the disjunctive normal form is denoted as GDNF, i.e,

$$\text{GDNF}(P_{E'}) = \{\varphi_i \in \Phi(C) \mid \bigvee_i \varphi_i = DNF(P_{E'})\}$$

and finally $\Psi_{dnf}(S')$ is:

$$\Psi_{dnf}(S') = \bigcup_{P_{E'} \in \Psi(S')} \text{GDNF}(P_{E'}).$$

To make this definition more understandable we show the next example. Using our example of the automatic Light Switch, we present the procedure for find the equivalences classes for $S' = \{s_1\}$.

Example. Let $S' = \{s_1\}$, then the transitions from S' are:

$$E(S') = \{(s_1, on?, c_{on} < 5, s_1), (s_1, off!, c_{on} = 5, s_0)\}$$

the guards of $E(S')$ are:

$$\Gamma(E(S')) = \{c_{on} < 5, c_{on} = 5\}$$

only for simplicity we will present $2^{\Gamma(E(S'))}$ instead of $2^{E(S')}$:

$$2^{\Gamma(E(S'))} = \{\emptyset, \{c_{on} < 5, c_{on} = 5\}, \{c_{on} < 5\}, \{c_{on} = 5\}\}$$

and:

$$\Psi(S') = \{(c_{on} \geq 5) \wedge (c_{on} \neq 5), (c_{on} < 5) \wedge (c_{on} \neq 5), \\ (c_{on} \geq 5) \wedge (c_{on} = 5), (c_{on} < 5) \wedge (c_{on} = 5)\}$$

the disjunctive normal form of $\Psi(S')$ is :

$$\Psi_{dnf}(S') = \{c_{on} > 5, c_{on} < 5, c_{on} = 5, \emptyset\}$$

Then we have: $[s_1, c_{on} > 5], [s_1, c_{on} < 5]$ and $[s_1, c_{on} = 5]$ as states for our equivalence class graph.

The state space of the ERA specification is a graph of equivalence classes. A node in this graph corresponds to an equivalence class. A transition between two nodes is labeled with an action, and represents the possibility of execute an action in a state in the source node, wait some amount of time, and thereby enter in a state in the target node. The graph is constructed by start from an existing node $[S', p]$ (initially the equivalence class of the initial location), and then for each enabled action a, compute the set of locations S'' that can be entered by execute the a action from the current equivalence class. Then the partitions p' of location S'' can be computed according to Definition 8.14. Every $[S'', p']$ is then an a successor of $[S', p]$. Only equivalence classes whose constraints have solutions need to be represented. The equivalence class graph is defined inductively in the Algorithm 11.

Each equivalence class $[S', p]$ is decorated with the action sets M, C, R from the testing preorder, as it is shows in definition 8.15.

Algorithm 11 Equivalence Class Graph

---

input: ERA determinized specification *Spec*
output: A equivalence Class Graph

1   $S'_0 = \{\overline{s_0}\}$
2   $E = \emptyset$ *// E the set of transition*
3   $N = \{[S'_0, p] \mid p \in \Psi_{dnf}(S'_0) \wedge p \neq \emptyset\}$ *// N is the set of nodes*
4   $N' = N$ *// N' is the set of new nodes*
5   **while** $N' \neq \emptyset$ **then**
6       $N''' = \emptyset$
7   **foreach** $[S', p] \in N'$
8   **foreach** $a \in \Sigma$:
9                 $S'' = \{\overline{s'} \mid \exists\ \overline{s} \in S' : \overline{s} \xrightarrow{\varphi, a} \overline{s'}\}$
10   **if** $S'' \neq \emptyset$ **then**
11                    $N'' = \{[S'', p'] \mid p' \in \Psi_{dnf}(S'') \wedge p' \neq \emptyset\}$
12                       $E = E \bigcup \{([S', p], a, [S'', p']) \mid [S'', p'] \in N'' \wedge (p \wedge \varphi) \neq \emptyset\}$
13            $N''' = N''' \bigcup N''$
14       $N' = N''' - (N''' \bigcap N)$
15       $N = N \bigcup N'$

Definition 8.15. Decorated Equivalence Classes
Define $\mathrm{Must}([S', p]) = \{A \mid \exists\ \langle S', \overline{\nu} \rangle : \langle S', \overline{\nu} \rangle \in [S', p] : \langle S', \overline{\nu} \rangle \models$ **after** ϵ **must** $A\}$
$\mathrm{Sort}([S', p]) = \{a \mid \exists\ \langle S', \overline{\nu} \rangle : \langle S', \overline{\nu} \rangle \in [S', p] : \langle S', \overline{\nu} \rangle \xrightarrow{a} \}$

- $M([S', p]) = \mathrm{Must}([S', p])$
- $C([S', p]) = \mathrm{Sort}([S', p])$
- $R([S', p]) = \Sigma - \mathrm{Sort}([S', p])$

where ϵ denote the empty sequence.

If σ is a timed *trace* that lead to $[S', p]$ and $A \in M([S', p])$ then: **after** σ **must** A, is a test to be passed for that class. Similarly: **after** $\sigma \cdot a$ **must** $\emptyset$, is a test to be passed if $a \in R([S', p])$, and **can** $\sigma \cdot a$ if $a \in C([S', p])$. The number of generated tests can be reduced by remove tests that are logically passed by another test, i.e. the **must** sets can be reduced to $M([S', p]) = min_{\subseteq}\mathrm{Must}([S', p])$ (where $min_{\subseteq}(M)$ gives the set of minimal elements of M under subset inclusion), and the actions observed during the execution of a **must** test can be removed from the **may** tests, i.e. $C([S', p]) = \mathrm{Sort}([S', p]) - \bigcup_{A \in M([S', p])} A$.

Example. The equivalence classes graph for the automatic Light Switch are shown in Figure 8.5.

The equivalence class graph preserves all timed traces of the specification, and the required deadlock information for the Hennessy test [HN83] of the specification by the M, C and R action sets is stored in each node. The non-determinism found in the original specification is therefore maintained, but is represented differently, in a way that is more convenient for test generation: a test is composed

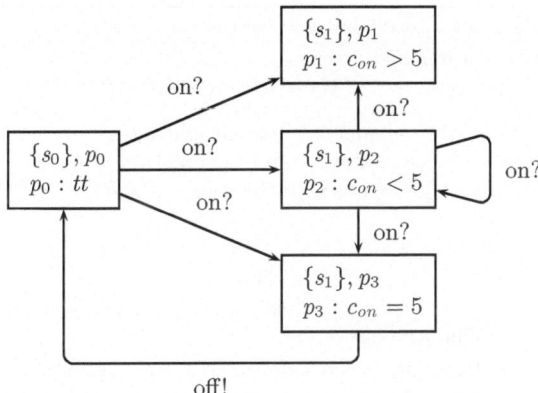

Fig. 8.5. ERA Equivalence Class Graph for the Light Switch

of a *trace* (a deadlock observation possible in the specification thereafter) and its associated verdict. This information can be simply found by following a path in the equivalence class graph.

Even the equivalence class graph have the necessary information for generate timed Hennessy tests, it also contains behavior and states not found in the specification, and use such behavior will result in irrelevant and unsound tests (in the same way as in model checking after use zones it is necessary to make a reachability analysis). To ensure soundness, only *traces* and deadlock properties actually contained in the specification should be used in a generated test. Therefore, the specification is interpreted symbolically, and the tests is generated from a representation of only the reachable states and behavior.

Algorithm 12 represents the test generation procedure. Step 1 constructs the equivalence class graph. The result of step 2 is the *symbolic reachability graph*. Nodes in this graph consist of symbolic states $[S', z/p]$ where S' is a set of location vectors, and z is a constraint characterizing a set of reachable clock valuations also in p, i.e. $z \subseteq p$. A transition represents that the target state is reachable by execute an action from the source state and then wait for some amount of time. The nodes in the reachability graph are decorated with the set M, C and R. Step 4 initializes an empty set *Tested* that contains the symbolic states from which test have to be generated so far. Steps 5 and further contain the test generation process.

This algorithm only generates tests for the *first* symbolic state that reaches a given partition, and uses the set *Tested* to ignore subsequent passes over the same partition. This ensures that all the *may*, *must*, and *refusal* properties are only generated once per partition, thus reduce the number of produced test cases.

This theory and algorithm have been implemented in a prototype tool called RTCAT. RTCAT inputs an ERA specification in AUTOGRAPH format, see [BRRdS96]. A specification may consist of several ERA operating in parallel and communicating via shared clocks and integer variables, but no silent actions (τ)

Algorithm 12 Overall Test Case Generation

---

input: ERA specification *Spec*
output: A complete cover set of timed Hennessy properties

  1   Compute $Spec_p$ = Equivalence Class Graph($Spec$)
  2   Compute $Spec_r$ = Reachability Graph($Spec_p$)
  3   Label every $[S', z/p] \in Spec_r$ with the sets M, C, R
  4   *Tested* := ∅
  5   **foreach** $[S', z/p] \in Spec_r$ // *traverse $Spec_r$*
  6   **if** $\not\exists\ z' : [S', z'/p] \in$ *Tested* **then**
  7   *Tested* := *Tested* $\cup \{[S', z/p]\}$ // *enumerate tests*
  8   Choose $\langle \bar{s}, \overline{\nu} \rangle \in [S', z/p]$
  9   Compute a concrete timed *trace* σ from $\langle \overline{s_0}, \overline{0} \rangle$ to $\langle \bar{s}, \overline{\nu} \rangle$
10   Make Test Cases:
11   **if** $A \in M([S', p])$ **then** *after σ must A,* is a relevant test
12   **if** $a \in C([S', p])$ **then** *can $\sigma \cdot a$,* is a relevant test
13   **if** $a \in R([S', p])$ **then** *after $\sigma \cdot a$ must ∅,* is a relevant test

---

are allowed. The application of this technique to a realistic specification shows "promising results: the test suite is quite small, is constructed quickly, and with a reasonable memory usage" [NS03].

8.4 Testing Deterministic Timed Automaton

Springintveld, Vaandrager and D'Argenio [SVD01] showed that *exhaustive* testing of *trace equivalence* for *deterministic* timed automaton with *dense time* interpretation is theoretically possible, but quite infeasible in practice. A grid algorithm for bounded time-domain automaton is presented, which capture of the real-time behaviors using finitely many points.

8.4.1 Model

The timed I/O automaton model is used here, which is a finite (untimed) automaton together with a timing annotation. This model is equivalent to the original timed automaton [AD94] with some restrictions in order to makes exhaustive test derivation feasible. A timed I/O automaton makes exhaustive test derivation feasible if it does not have silent τ-transitions, is deterministic, is input enabled and has isolated output as we will show later.

A *finite automaton* $\mathscr{A}'$[1] is a rooted labeled transition system with Q (the set of states) and E (the transition relation $\rightarrow$) finite. We will fix some useful notations and definitions. An *execution fragment* of the LTS $\mathscr{A}'$ is a finite or infinite alternating sequence $q_0 a_1 q_1 a_2 q_2 \ldots$ of states and actions of $\mathscr{A}'$ ($a_i \in L_{\mathscr{A}'}$ and $q_i \in L_{\mathscr{A}'}$), beginning with a state, and if it is finite also ending with a state,

---

[1] the reason why we use $\mathscr{A}'$ instead of $\mathscr{A}$ here, is only notational. Then $\mathscr{A}'$ denote a automaton and $\mathscr{A}$ will denote a timed automaton

such that for all $i > 0$, $q_{i-1} \xrightarrow{a_i} q_i$. An *execution* of $\mathscr{A}'$ is an execution fragment that begins with the initial state q_0 of $\mathscr{A}'$. A state q of $\mathscr{A}'$ is *reachable* if it is the last state of some finite execution of $\mathscr{A}'$. σ is a **distinguishing trace** of q and q' if it is either a *trace* of q but not of q', or the other way around (for the definition of *traces* see Appendix: Label Transition Systems). If $\delta \in E$ and $\delta = (q, a, q')$ we denote $\mathbf{src}(\delta) = q$, $\mathbf{act}(\delta) = a$ and $\mathbf{trg}(\delta) = q'$.

Definition 8.16. Let $\mathscr{B}$ be an LTS. A relation $R \subseteq Q_{\mathscr{B}} \times Q_{\mathscr{B}}$ is a *bisimulation* on $\mathscr{B}$ iff whenever $R(q_1, q_2)$, then

- $q_1 \xrightarrow{a} q_1'$ implies that there is a $q_2' \in Q_{\mathscr{B}}$ such that $q_2 \xrightarrow{a} q_2'$ and $R(q_1', q_2')$
- $q_2 \xrightarrow{a} q_2'$ implies that there is a $q_1' \in Q_{\mathscr{B}}$ such that $q_1 \xrightarrow{a} q_1'$ and $R(q_1', q_2')$

States q, q' of LTSs $\mathscr{B}$ and $\mathscr{B}'$, respectively, are *bisimilar* if there exists a bisimulation R on the disjoint union of $\mathscr{B}$ and $\mathscr{B}'$ (with arbitrary initial state) that relates q to q'. In such a case, we write : $q \simeq q'$. LTSs $\mathscr{B}$ and $\mathscr{B}'$ are *bisimilar*, notation $\mathscr{B} \simeq \mathscr{B}'$, if $q_0 \simeq q_0'$ for q_0 the initial state of $\mathscr{B}$ and q_0' the initial states of $\mathscr{B}'$.

It is well known that if $\mathscr{B}$ is deterministic, for all states q, q' of $\mathscr{B}$, $\mathscr{B} : q \simeq q'$ if and only if *traces* $(q) = traces(q')$. As a consequence, two deterministic LTSs $\mathscr{B}$ and $\mathscr{B}'$ are bisimilar iff they have the same sets of traces.

Let C be a set of clocks with $c \in C$, then define $\mathbf{dom}(c) \overset{def}{=} J \cup \{\infty\}$, were J is a bounded interval over $\mathbb{R}$ with infimum and supremum in $\mathbb{Z}$ and $\mathbf{intv}(c) \overset{def}{=} dom(c) - \{\infty\}$. The **terms** over C (denoted as $T(C)$) are expressions generated by the grammar $e := c \mid k \mid e+k$, with $c \in C$ and $k \in \mathbb{Z}^{\infty}$, i.e. $\mathbb{Z} \cup \{\infty\}$. Let $F(C)$ be the boolean combinations of inequalities of the form $e \leq e'$ or $e < e'$ with $e, e' \in T(C)$. A *(simultaneous)* **assignment** over C is a function μ from C to $T(C)$, the set of all these functions is denoted as $M(C)$. If φ is a constraint over C and μ an assignment, then $\varphi[\mu]$ denotes the constraint obtained from φ by replacing each variable $c \in C$ by $\mu(c)$. Finally a **clock valuation** over C is a map ν that assigns to each clock $c \in C$ a value in its domain (this set of valuations is denoted as $V(C)$). We say that ν *satisfies* φ, notation $\nu \vDash \varphi$, if φ evaluates to true under valuation ν.

In the next definition is presented the timing annotation for a finite automaton, which is a set of clocks, a set of invariants for each state, a set of guards, which allowed the transition to be made of not, Ass the assignments for each transition, and ν_0 the initial clock valuation.

Definition 8.17. A **timing annotation** for a given finite automaton $\mathscr{A}' = \langle Q, q_0, E \rangle$ is a tuple $\mathscr{T} = \langle C, Inv, \Phi, Ass, \nu_0 \rangle$, where

- C is a finite set of clocks
- $Inv : Q \to F(C)$ associates an invariant to each state
- $\Phi : E \to F(C)$ associates a guard to each transition

- *Ass* : $E \to M(C)$ associates an assignment to each transition s.t. for each $\delta \in E$:

$$Inv(\mathbf{src}(\delta)) \wedge \Phi(\delta) \Rightarrow \bigwedge_{c \in C} (Ass(\delta)(c) \in dom(c)) \wedge Inv(\mathbf{trg}(\delta))[Ass(\delta)]$$

- $\nu_0 \in V(C)$ is the initial *clock valuation*. It should hold that $\nu_0 \vDash Inv(q_0)$ and, for all $c, \nu_0(c) \in \mathbb{Z}^\infty$.

Above all, we present the timed I/O automata, which, as we already say, is a finite automaton together with a timed annotation and some restrictions. These restrictions are fundamentals to prove future theorems for the discretization of the state space.

Definition 8.18. A timed I/O automaton (TIOA) is a triple $\mathscr{A} = \langle \mathscr{A}', \mathscr{T}, \mathscr{P} \rangle$, where $\mathscr{A}'$ is a finite automaton with $L_{\mathscr{A}'} \cap \mathbb{R}^{>0} = \emptyset$ (to do not confuse labels of actions with labels of time), $\mathscr{T}$ is a timing annotation for $\mathscr{A}'$ and $\mathscr{P} = (\mathcal{I}, \mathcal{O})$ is a partitioning of $L_{\mathscr{A}'}$ in input actions and output actions. The following properties must hold, for all $\delta, \delta' \in E_{\mathscr{A}'}$ and $q \in Q_{\mathscr{A}'}$:

- (Determinism) if $\mathbf{src}(\delta) = \mathbf{src}(\delta')$, $\mathbf{act}(\delta) = \mathbf{act}(\delta')$ and $\Phi(\delta) \wedge \Phi(\delta')$ is satisfiable then $\delta = \delta'$
- (Isolated outputs) if $\mathbf{src}(\delta) = \mathbf{src}(\delta')$, $\mathbf{act}(\delta) \in \mathcal{O}$ and $\Phi(\delta) \wedge \Phi(\delta')$ is satisfiable then $\delta = \delta'$
- (Input enabling) every input is always enabled within the interior of the invariant of each location and only within it
- (Progressiveness) for every state of its operational semantics ($\mathcal{OS}(\mathscr{A})$, defined as follows) there exists an infinite execution fragment that starts in this state, contains no input actions, and in which the sum of the delays diverges.

In order to not confuse, and following the previous implicit convention, in a TIOA $\mathscr{A}$ we will use S as the set of locations and Σ as the set of actions. In contrast to the associated operational semantics $\mathcal{OS}(\mathscr{A})$, where Q is the set of states and L is the set of actions.

Example. Figure 8.6 depicts the timed I/O automaton which represent the Light Switch.

The operational semantics of $\mathscr{A}$ (denoted as $\mathcal{OS}(\mathscr{A})$) is defined as the LTS $\langle Q, L, q_0, \rightarrowtail \rangle$, with Q, L and q_0 similarly as in previous Definition 8.5, and $\rightarrowtail$ being the smallest relation that satisfies the following two rules, for all $(s, \nu), (s', \nu') \in Q$, $a \in \Sigma$, $\delta \in E$ and $d \in \mathbb{R}^{>0}$:

- $$\frac{\delta : s \xrightarrow{a} s', \ \nu \vDash \Phi(\delta), \ \nu' = \nu \circ Ass(\delta)}{(s, \nu) \xrightarrow{a} (s', \nu')}$$

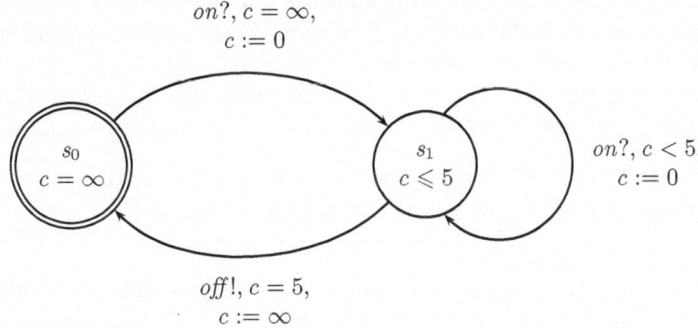

Fig. 8.6. TIOA specification for a Light Switch [SVD01]

- $$\frac{\forall\, 0 \leq d' \leq d \; : \; \nu \oplus d' \models Inv(s)}{(s,\nu) \overset{d}{\rightarrowtail} (s,\nu \oplus d)}$$

where the actions in $\mathbb{R}^{>0}$ are referred to as *time delays* and

$$(\nu \oplus d)(c) \overset{def}{=} \begin{cases} \nu(c) + d & \text{if } (\nu(c)+d) \in intv(c) \\ \infty & \text{otherwise} \end{cases}$$

The following lemma, which is a direct corollary of the definitions, gives four basic properties of the operational semantics of a timed I/O automaton.

Lemma 8.19. *Let $\mathscr{A}$ be a TIOA, then*

- $\mathcal{OS}(\mathscr{A})$ *is deterministic*
- $\mathcal{OS}(\mathscr{A})$ *possesses Wang's time additivity property:*

$$q \overset{d+d'}{\rightarrowtail} q' \text{ iff } \exists\, q'' : q \overset{d}{\rightarrowtail} q'' \wedge q'' \overset{d'}{\rightarrowtail} q'$$

- *Each state of $\mathcal{OS}(\mathscr{A})$ has either*
  - *a single outgoing transition labeled with an output action, or*
  - *both outgoing delay transitions and outgoing input transitions (one for each input action),*

  but no outgoing output transitions
  States of the second type are called **stable**

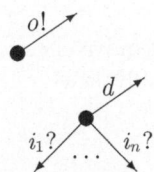

- *For each state $q \in Q_{\mathcal{OS}(\mathscr{A})}$, there exists a unique finite sequence of output actions σ and a unique stable state q' such that $q \overset{\sigma}{\rightarrowtail} q'$.*

8.4.2   Discretization

The construction of a finite subautomaton used, for the discretization of the state space, is based on the fundamental concept of a *region* due to Alur and

Dill [AD94]. The key idea behind the definition of a region is that, even though the number of states of the LTS $\mathscr{OI}(\mathscr{A})$ is infinite, not all of these states are distinguishable via constraints. If two states corresponding to the same location agree on the internal parts of all the clock values, and also in the order of the fractional parts of all the clocks, then these two states cannot be distinguished.

Definition 8.20. The equivalence relation $\cong$ over the set $V(C)$ of clocks valuations is given by: $\nu \cong \nu'$ if and only if $\forall\ c, c' \in C$:

- $\nu(c) = \infty$ iff $\nu'(c) = \infty$
- if $\nu(c) \neq \infty$ then $\lfloor \nu(c) \rfloor = \lfloor \nu'(c) \rfloor$ and $(fract(\nu(c)) = 0$ iff $fract(\nu'(c)) = 0)$
- if $\nu(c) \neq \infty \neq \nu(c')$ then $fract(\nu(c)) \leq fract(\nu(c'))$ iff $fract(\nu'(c)) \leq fract(\nu'(c'))$

where $\forall\,k \in \mathbb{R}$ (in this case a valuation of a clock), $\lfloor k \rfloor$ denotes the largest number in $\mathbb{Z}$ that is not greater than k, and $\lceil k \rceil$ denotes the smallest number in $\mathbb{Z}$ that is not smaller than k and $fract(k)$ is the fractional part of k (so $fract(k) = k - \lfloor k \rfloor$).

A *region* is an equivalence class of valuations induced by $\cong$.

Example. Figure 8.7 shows the 11 regions of the c_{on} clock from the Light Switch.

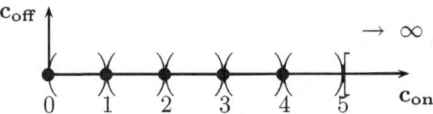

Fig. 8.7. Regions of the c_{on} clock from the Light Switch example

Lemma 8.21. *For all clock constraints φ:*

$$if\ \ \nu \cong \nu'\ \ then\ \ \nu \vDash \varphi\ iff\ \nu' \vDash \varphi$$

The equivalence relation $\cong$ on the clock valuations of a TIOA can be extended to an equivalence relation on states, by defining

$$(s, \nu) \cong (s', \nu') \overset{def}{=} (s = s' \wedge \nu \cong \nu')$$

A *region* of a TIOA is an equivalence class of states induced by $\cong$.

Because testing is based on distinguishing sequences (cf. Chapter 4), it is necessary to have an automaton that can distinguish each sequences that is used. Correspondingly, the Grid Automaton will be presented after present all its necessary ingredients.

Let $\mathbb{G}^n$ be the set of integer multiples of 2^{-n}, for some sufficiently large natural number n. If t is a real number, we use the notation[2] $\lfloor t \rfloor_n$ for the largest

---

[2] do not confuse with the notation $\lfloor\ \rfloor$ without subindice

number in $\mathbb{G}^n$ that is not greater than t, and $\lceil t \rceil_n$ for the smallest number in $\mathbb{G}^n$ that is not smaller than t. We write $[t]_n$ for the fraction $(\lfloor t \rfloor_n + \lceil t \rceil_n)/2$, note that $[t]_n \in \mathbb{G}^{n+1}$. For a TIOA $\mathscr{A}$ and its $\mathscr{OS}(\mathscr{A})$ associated, write Q^n for the set of states $(s, \nu) \in Q$ such that, for each clock $c, \nu(c) \in \mathbb{G}^n \cup \{\infty\}$.

The following lemma shown that given any state (q) in $\mathbb{G}^n$ for all $a \in \Sigma$ and $d \in \mathbb{G}^n$, labels of a transition in the semantic $(\rightarrowtail)$, the target state (q') of that transition is also in $\mathbb{G}^n$.

Lemma 8.22. *Let $q \in Q^n$, then*

- *If $q \xrightarrow{a} q'$ with $a \in \Sigma$ then $q' \in Q^n$*
- *If $q \xrightarrow{d} q'$ with $d \in \mathbb{G}^n$ then $q' \in Q^n$.*

Moreover, for a *distinguishing trace* of length m for two states in Q^n, a *trace* can be derived in which all delay actions are in the grid set $\mathbb{G}^{n+m}$.

Theorem 8.23. *Let $\mathscr{A}, \mathscr{B}$ be TIOAs and theirs associated semantics $\mathscr{OS}(\mathscr{A})$, $\mathscr{OS}(\mathscr{B})$, let $(r, r') \cong (s, s')$ for states $r \in Q_{\mathscr{A}}, r' \in Q_{\mathscr{B}}, s \in Q_{\mathscr{A}}^n$ and $s' \in Q_{\mathscr{B}}^n$, and let $\sigma = a_1 a_2 \ldots a_m$ be a distinguishing trace for r and r'. Then there exists a distinguishing trace $\tau = b_1 b_2 \ldots b_m$ for s and s' such that, for all $j \in [1, \ldots, m]$, if a_j is an input or output action then $b_j = a_j$, and if a_j is a delay action then $b_j \in \mathbb{G}^{n+j}$ with $\lfloor a_j \rfloor \leq b_j \leq \lceil a_j \rceil$.*

This theorem allows to *transform* each *distinguishing trace* into one in which all delay actions are in a grid set, and shown that there is a dependency between the length of the *trace* and the granularity of the grid: the longer the *trace* the finer the grid. This is due to the fact that the distinguish power of a *distinguishing trace* for two states r and r' entirely depends on the regions traversed when applying σ to r and r', respectively. Moreover, we can conclude that the grid size depends on the number of states, not just on the number of clocks.

In order to obtain a grid size that is fine enough to distinguish all pairs of different states, the following theorem establishes an upper bound on the length of minimal *distinguishing traces*.

Theorem 8.24. *Suppose $\mathscr{A}$ and $\mathscr{B}$ are TIOAs with the same input actions, and r and s are states of $\mathscr{OS}(\mathscr{A})$ and $\mathscr{OS}(\mathscr{B})$, respectively : $r \not\simeq s$ (with $\simeq$ denoting bisimilarity 8.16). Then, there exists a distinguishing trace for r and s of length at most the number of regions of $Q_{\mathscr{A}} \times Q_{\mathscr{B}}$.*

Finally, we are in position of define the Grid Automaton. For each TIOA $\mathscr{A}$ and natural number n, the grid automaton $\mathscr{G}(\mathscr{A}, n)$ is defined as the subautomaton of $\mathscr{OS}(\mathscr{A})$ in which each clock value is in the set $\mathbb{G}^n \cup \{\infty\}$, and the only delay action is 2^{-n}. Note that since in the initial state of $\mathscr{OS}(\mathscr{A})$ all clocks take values in $\mathbb{Z}^\infty$, it is always included as a state of $\mathscr{G}(\mathscr{A}, n)$. Moreover, since $\mathscr{G}(\mathscr{A}, n)$ has a finite number of states and actions, $\mathscr{G}(\mathscr{A}, n)$ is a finite automaton.

Definition 8.25. Let $\mathscr{A} = \langle S, \Sigma, s_0, E \rangle$ be a TIOA, its $\mathscr{OS}(\mathscr{A}) = \langle Q, L, q_0, \rightarrowtail \rangle$ and $n \in N$. The grid automaton $\mathscr{G}(\mathscr{A}, n)$ is the LTS $\mathscr{A}'' = \langle Q', L', q_0', \rightarrowtail' \rangle$ given by

- $Q' = Q^n$
- $L' = \Sigma \cup \{2^{-n}\}$
- $q_0' = q_0$
- for all $q, q' \in Q'$ and $a \in L', q \xrightarrow{a}' q'$ iff $q \xrightarrow{a} q'$.

The grid automaton is the restriction of $\mathcal{OS}(\mathscr{A})$ to the time steps in 2^{-n}, therefore $\mathscr{G}(\mathscr{A}, n)$ is finite.

Example. In Figure 8.8 the grid automaton of our example of the Light Switch for $n = 2$ is presented. Here we denote the initial state as $<<\ >>$, for distinguish it from the double circle denoting the initial state in a TIOA.

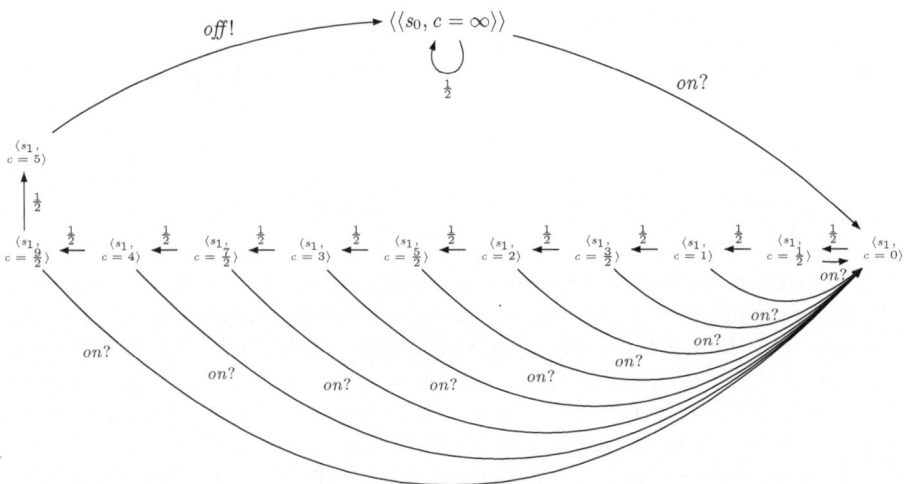

Fig. 8.8. The grid automaton $\mathscr{G}(\mathscr{A}, n)$ with $\mathscr{A}$ as the Light Switch automaton and $n = 2$

Corollary 8.26. *Let $\mathscr{A}$ and $\mathscr{B}$ be TIOA with the same input actions, and let n be at least the number of regions of $S_{\mathscr{A}} \times S_{\mathscr{B}}$, then*

$$\mathscr{A} \simeq \mathscr{B} \quad \text{iff} \quad \mathscr{G}(\mathscr{A}, n) \simeq \mathscr{G}(\mathscr{B}, n).$$

Using the grid automaton with the appropriate degree of granularity the problem of decide bisimulation equivalence of TIOA is reduced to the problem of decide bisimulation equivalence of their finite subautomata.

8.4.3   Testing

A **test sequence** for a TIOA $\mathscr{A}$ is a finite sequence of delays and input actions of $\mathscr{A}$ (we denoted the set of this sequences as Exp). A test sequence σ can be applied to $\mathscr{A}$ starting from any state s of its $\mathcal{OS}(\mathscr{A})$. The application of σ to $\mathscr{A}$ in s uniquely determines a finite, maximal execution fragment in $\mathcal{OS}(\mathscr{A})$.

How to perform a test sequence is shown in the following definition. The outcome of performing a test sequence on $\mathscr{A}$ is described in terms of an auxiliary labeled transition system T.

Definition 8.27. The test sequence is the LTS $T = \langle (Exp \times Q), \Sigma, (\epsilon, s_0), \twoheadrightarrow \rangle$ with $(Exp \times Q)$ as its set of states, where Exp is the test sequence to be executed, Σ is a set of actions, (ϵ, s_0) is (arbitrarily chosen) initial state, and a transition relation $\twoheadrightarrow$ that is inductively defined as the least relation satisfying the following four rules, for all $q, q' \in Q, \sigma \in Exp, i \in \mathcal{I}, o \in \mathcal{O}$ and $d, d' \in \mathbb{R}^{>0}$:

- $$\frac{q \xrightarrow{o!} q'}{(\sigma, q) \xrightarrow{o!} (\sigma, q')}$$

- $$\frac{q \xrightarrow{i?} q'}{(i?\sigma, q) \xrightarrow{i?} (\sigma, q')}$$

- $$\frac{q \xrightarrow{d} q'}{(d\sigma, q) \xrightarrow{d} (\sigma, q')}$$

- $$\frac{q \xrightarrow{d'} q', \sup\{t \in \mathbb{R}^{>0} | q \xrightarrow{t}\} = d' < d}{(d\sigma, q) \xrightarrow{d'} ((d-d')\sigma, q')}$$

The first rule says that output actions are always performed autonomously, i.e. independently of the input of the intended test sequence. Instead, input actions are only performed if they are explicitly specified in the test sequence. This is stated by the second rule. Similarly, the third rule says that a delay can occur only when it is both specified by the test sequence and allowed by $\mathscr{A}$. In some cases, a delay specified in the test sequence cannot occur since it is interrupted by an autonomous output action of $\mathscr{A}$. In such a case, the part of the delay up to the output action is executed, while the rest is postponed until $\mathscr{A}$ stops doing output actions autonomously. This last case is expressed by the fourth rule.

Theorem 8.28. *Let $\mathscr{A}$ a TIOA and T its test sequence, then*

- *each state of T has at most one outgoing transition, and*
- *T does not have an infinite execution fragment.*

Theorem 8.28 allows us to define $exec(\sigma, q)$ as the execution fragment of $\mathcal{OS}(\mathscr{A})$ obtained by projecting the states in the unique maximal execution fragment of T that starts in (σ, q) on their second component. We define $outcome(\sigma, q)$, the *outcome of the sequence σ in state q*, as the *trace* of the execution fragment that is induced by performing the test sequence:

$$outcome(\sigma, q) \overset{def}{=} trace(exec(\sigma, q))$$

Deriving and Applying a Test Suite It is assumed that the behavior of the IUT (Implementation Under Test) is accurately modeled by a TIOA *Impl*. Then the IUT conforms to the specification *Spec* if *Impl* is bisimilar to *Spec*.

The method of building test suites is similar to Chow's classical algorithm for Mealy machines [Cho78] (cf. Chapter 4). A test suite consists of a finite set of test sequences which should be applied to the implementation. Each sequence consists of the concatenation of two sequences. The initial part of a test sequence is taken from a *transition cover* P for a grid subautomaton of *Spec*, i.e. a set of test sequences that together exercise every transition of the subautomaton.

Definition 8.29. Let $\mathscr{A}$ be a TIOA, $n \in \mathbb{N}$, $\mathscr{A}'' = \mathscr{G}(\mathscr{A}, n)$. A *transition cover* for $\mathscr{A}''$ is a finite collection $P \subseteq Exp_n$ of test sequences, such that $\epsilon \in P$ and, for all transitions $q \xrightarrow{a}' q'$ of $\mathscr{A}''$ with q reachable (within $\mathscr{A}''$) and stable (Definition 8.19), P contains test sequences σ and $\sigma \cdot a$ such that $q_0 \xrightarrow{\sigma}' q$.

The trailing part of a test sequence is taken from a set Z, which is a *characterization set* for a grid subautomaton of *Impl*, meaning that for every pair of non-bisimilar grid states, Z contains a sequence that distinguishes between them.

Definition 8.30. Let p a state of $\mathscr{A}$, q a state of $\mathscr{B}$, and let σ be a test sequence for $\mathscr{A}$ and $\mathscr{B}$. σ distinguishes p from q if $\text{outcome}_{\mathscr{A}}(\sigma, p) \neq \text{outcome}_{\mathscr{B}}(\sigma, q)$. If Z is a set of test sequences for $\mathscr{A}$ and $\mathscr{B}$, written $p \approx_Z q$ means that no test sequence in Z distinguishes p from q.

The ability of always being able to bring the machine back to its initial state is used. In the timed case, it is not reasonable to consider the reset as an instantaneous operation: typically, some time will elapse between the moment when it is requested the machine to go to its initial state, and the moment at which the reset operation has been completed. But, it is not difficult to prove that the maximal time that can elapse between the occurrence of a reset action and the time at which the initial state is reached is always less than the number of regions of $\mathscr{A}$.

Then, the test suite is defined for a given TIOA as follows.

Definition 8.31. Let $\mathscr{A}$ be a TIOA and $n \in \mathbb{N}$. Let P be a transition cover for $\mathscr{G}(\mathscr{A}, n)$ and Z a characterization set for the TIOA model of the IUT. The test suite for $\mathscr{A}$ generated from P and Z with grid size n is defined by

$$\text{test-suite}(\mathscr{A}, n, P, Z) \overset{def}{=} P \cdot Z \cdot \{\text{reset max}\}$$

i.e. the concatenation of the transition cover, the characterization set and the reset time.

Definition 8.32. A state of a TIOA is *quiescent* if each execution fragment starting in that state that contains an output action also contains an input action.

Algorithm 13 is the testing algorithm that applies each test case from the test suite to an implementation (the prove of correctness is showed in [SVD01]). This algorithm is restricted to TIOAs with a *quiescent* initial state, where the machine waits for stimulus from its environment before producing any output.

Algorithm 13 Test Generation

---

input: A TIOA *Spec*, the specification automaton, with reset action *reset*,
reset time max, and a *quiescent* initial state.
An Implementation Under Test (IUT), a device that accepts inputs from I_{Spec} and produces outputs in $\mathcal{O}_{\text{Spec}}$.
A natural number n.
A natural number m.
output: A verdict PASS or FAIL

1   Let $X = I_{\text{Spec}} \cup \{2^{-n}\}$
2   Determine a (minimal) finite transition cover P for $\mathcal{G}(Spec, n)$
3   **For all** test sequences $\sigma \in$ test-suite($Spec, n, P, X^{m-1}$) **do**
4   Apply test sequence σ to the IUT
5   Return FAIL and halt if outcome of the IUT differs from
                outcome$_{Spec}(\sigma, s^0_{Spec})$
6   Return PASS and halt

This algorithm results in a huge number of sequences. Therefore, it cannot be claimed to be itself of practical value. Rather, the major contribution here is the TIOA model and the demonstration that an algorithm to derive a (complete) test suite does exist. Moreover, there are ways to reduce the number of tests, and make the time delays within the tests manageable [SVD01].

8.5   Testing Networks of UPPAAL Timed Automata

Cardell-Oliver [CO00] presents a test generation method for networks of *deterministic timed automata* on a *dense time* base. Timed automata are extended with persistent data variables and are allowed to have silent transitions. Test generation is based on test views that partition events into visible (relevant) and hidden events according to a certain test purpose. By only testing for visible events the size of the resulting test suite can be reduced. The work presented is a generalization of previous work by Cardell-Oliver and Glover [COG98] that was applicable only for specifications with a discrete clock model.

8.5.1   Model

For model specification, UPPAAL timed automata [LPY97] are adopted. UPPAAL timed automata (UTA) extend Alur and Dill's model of timed automata with (integer) data variables. With UTA, networks of deterministic timed automata can be specified. This allows for closed world specifications of systems, i.e.

the behavior of an system's environment can be specified explicitly. Synchronization between components takes place by complementary actions of automata, i.e. by simultaneous occurrence of an output event $a!$ and an input event $a?$, with $a \in \Sigma$, respectively. Each automaton $\mathscr{A}_i$ can use a set of integer variables Var_i that is a subset of a set of global integer variables Var. Guards on transitions are extended to apply for both clocks and data variables.

Definition 8.33. An **UPPAAL timed automata** $\mathscr{A}$ is a tuple $\langle S, s_0, \Sigma, C, Inv, E \rangle$, where

- S is a finite set of locations
- s_0 is the initial location
- $\Sigma = \mathcal{I} \cup \mathcal{O} \cup \{\tau\}$ is a finite set of actions, partitioned into input actions, output actions, and the silent action
- C is a finite set of (real-valued) clocks
- $Inv : S \rightarrow \Phi(C)$ assigns clock invariants to locations
- $E \subseteq S \times \Sigma \times \Phi(C, Var_{\mathscr{A}_i}) \times 2^R \times S$ is the set of transitions.

Transitions $(s, a, \varphi, r, s') \in E$ are denoted by $s \xrightarrow{a, \varphi, r} s'$, where a is the action to be performed, φ the guard of the transition, and r a set of assignments for clocks and data variables. Clock variables can be reset to an integer constant $l \in \mathbb{Z} \cup \{-1\}$. A reset to -1 denotes a turn-off of the according clock variable. Data variables can be reset to integer expressions of the form $v := k * v + k'$, where $v \in Var_{\mathscr{A}_i}$ and $k, k' \in \mathbb{Z}$. R is used to denote the set of all possible reset operations.

Remark 8.34. The definition of UTA mainly follows the one presented by Bengtsson et al. [BLL$^+$95]. The definition given here omits urgent synchronization but includes silent transitions as well as location invariants.

For testing purposes, clock constraints in guards and invariants are required to be closed ($<$ and $>$ are not allowed) and domains for clocks and data variables are required to be finite.

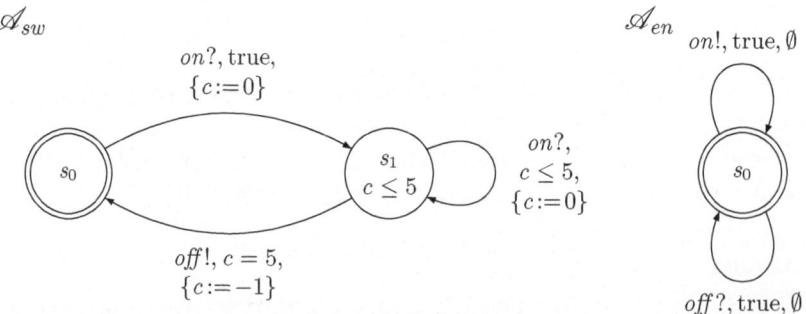

Fig. 8.9. UTA specification of the Light Switch $\mathscr{A}_{sw}$ and its environment $\mathscr{A}_{en}$

Example. The Light Switch can be defined by an UTA
$\mathscr{A}_{sw} = \langle S, s_0, \Sigma, C, Inv, E \rangle$, where

- $S = \{s_0, s_1\}$
- $\Sigma = \{on, off\}$, with $\mathcal{I} = \{on\}$ and $\mathcal{O} = \{off\}$
- $C = \{c\}$
- $Inv(s_0) = $ true, $Inv(s_1) = c \leq 5$
- $E = \{(s_0, on?, $ true$, \{c := 0\}, s_1), (s_1, on?, c \leq 5, \{c := 0\}, s_1),$
$$(s_1, on?, c = 5, \{c := \text{-}1\}, s_0)\}.$$

Specification of the environment can be done analogously (cf. Figure 8.9).

The definition of the semantics of UPPAAL timed automata is based on timed transition systems with an uncountable set of states.

Definition 8.35. A **timed transition system** (**TTS**) over a set of actions Σ and a time domain $\mathbb{R}^{\geq 0}$ is a tuple $\mathscr{M} = \langle Q, L, \longrightarrow, q_0 \rangle$ of a set of states Q, an initial state $q_0 \in Q$, and a set of labels $L \subseteq \Sigma \cup \mathbb{R}^{\geq 0}$, a transition relation $\longrightarrow \subseteq Q \times L \times Q$ that has to satisfy the following properties ($\forall q, q', q'' \in Q \wedge \forall d, d_1, d_2 \in \mathbb{R}^{\geq 0}$):

- *time determinism:* if $q \xrightarrow{d} q' \wedge q \xrightarrow{d} q''$ then $q' = q''$
- *time additivity:* $q \xrightarrow{d_1 + d_2} q''$ iff $q \xrightarrow{d_1} q' \xrightarrow{d_2} q''$
- *0-delay:* $q \xrightarrow{0} q'$ iff $q = q'$.

Since specifications of real-time systems in UPPAAL are generally networks of automata, a LTS $\mathscr{M}$ has to be constructed for parallel compositions of UTA. The set $P = \{p_1, \ldots, p_n\}$ is used to contain the names of all components that are part of the specification, with p_i being the name of the component specified by the automaton $\mathscr{A}_i$. The set of channels usable for synchronization is given by $Ch = (\bigcup_i \mathcal{I}_{\mathscr{A}_i}) \cap (\bigcup_i \mathcal{O}_{\mathscr{A}_i})$.

States of $\mathscr{M}$ are pairs $(\bar{s}, \nu)$, where $\bar{s}$ is a vector holding the current control locations for each component (automaton) and ν maps each clock to a value in the time domain as well as each data variable to an integer value.

Transition labels of $\mathscr{M}$ are either delays $d \in \mathbb{R}^{\geq 0}$ or event triples (p_i, a, r) with p_i being the name of the automaton executing an action a, that could either be a silent action or an output action (which implies the occurrence of an complementary input actions of another automaton). An action a leads to the execution of a set of resets r that contains resets for clocks, variables, and locations. Location resets explicitly denote a change of location of a component which results in an update of the according element in $\bar{s}$. The set of all possible reset statements is given by $\mathcal{R} \subseteq 2^{\bigcup_i R_{\mathscr{A}_i} \cup R_i^s}$, with $R_{\mathscr{A}_i}$ being the usual resets of $\mathscr{A}_i$ and R_i^s being the set of resets for locations of $\mathscr{A}_i$.

Definition 8.36. The semantics of a network of UTA $\mathscr{A}_1, \ldots, \mathscr{A}_n$ is given by the TTS $\mathscr{M} = \langle Q, L, \rightarrow, q_0 \rangle$, where

- $Q = \{\langle \bar{s}, \nu \rangle \mid \bar{s}[i] \in S_{\mathscr{A}_i}, \nu \models Inv_{\mathscr{A}_i}(C_{\mathscr{A}_i})\}, \forall 1 \leq i \leq n$
- $q_0 = \langle \bar{s}_0, \nu_0 \rangle$ with $\bar{s}_0[i] = s_{0\mathscr{A}_i}$ and $\nu_0[i] = 0, \forall 1 \leq i \leq n$

- $L = \mathbb{R}^{\geq 0} \cup (P, Ch \cup \{\tau\}, \mathcal{R})$
- $\rightarrow \subseteq Q \times L \times Q$, that could be either
  - $\langle \bar{s}, \nu \rangle \xrightarrow{d} \langle \bar{s}, \nu \oplus d \rangle$ iff $\forall i : \nu \oplus d \models Inv_{\mathscr{A}_i}(\bar{s}[i])$
  - $\langle \bar{s}, \nu \rangle \xrightarrow{p_i, \tau, r} \langle \bar{s}[s'_{\mathscr{A}_i} / s_{\mathscr{A}_i}], r_i(\nu) \rangle$ iff $(s_i, \varphi, \tau, r_i, s'_i) \in E_{\mathscr{A}_i}$ and $\nu \models \varphi$, with $r = r_i \cup \{s_{\mathscr{A}_i} := s'_{\mathscr{A}_i}\}$
  - $\langle \bar{s}, \nu \rangle \xrightarrow{p_i, a, r} \langle \bar{s}[s'_{\mathscr{A}_i} / s_{\mathscr{A}_i}, s'_{\mathscr{A}_j} / s_{\mathscr{A}_j}], (r_i \cup r_j)(\nu) \rangle$ iff $(s_i, \varphi_i, a!, r_i, s'_i) \in E_{\mathscr{A}_i}$, $(s_j, \varphi_j, a?, r_j, s'_j) \in E_{\mathscr{A}_j}$, $\nu \models \varphi_i$, and $\nu \models \varphi_j$, with $r = r_i \cup r_j \cup \{s_{\mathscr{A}_i} := s'_{\mathscr{A}_i}, s_{\mathscr{A}_j} := s'_{\mathscr{A}_j}\}$

For a variable assignment ν and a delay d, $\nu \oplus d$ denotes the variable assignment after d. $\oplus$ models time-insensitiveness of all data variables and that all enabled clocks progress at the same rate:

$$\forall v \in Var : (\nu \oplus d)(v) = \nu(v), \text{and}$$
$$\forall c \in \bigcup_i C_{\mathscr{A}_i} : (\nu \oplus d)(c) = \begin{cases} \nu(c) + d & \text{if } \nu(c) \geq 0 \\ \nu(c) & \text{if } \nu(c) = -1 \end{cases}$$

Silent transitions result in the change of location of one component. According transitions in $\mathcal{M}$ express this change by replacing the ith element of the location vector $\bar{s}$ by a new location $s'_{\mathscr{A}_i}$ and applying the resets r to ν. Synchronizations between two components involve two location transitions, one for the sender $\mathscr{A}_i$ and one for the receiver $\mathscr{A}_j$. Consequently the ith and the jth element of $\bar{s}$ have to be replaced with $s'_{\mathscr{A}_i}$ and $s'_{\mathscr{A}_j}$ respectively, and the union of transition resets $r_i \cup r_j$ has to be applied to ν.

Remark 8.37. The definition given here follows Bengtsson et al. [BLL⁺95] in defining states as pairs of a location vector $\bar{s}$ and variable valuations ν.

An alternative to the use of a location vector would be to include for every component p_i a special variable loc_i, which holds the current location of the according process, into the set Var. States could then be defined as $S \subseteq (Var \rightarrow \mathbb{Z}) \cup (C \rightarrow \mathbb{R}^{\geq 0})$ [CO00].

Example. The possible behavior of the Light Switch specified by $\mathscr{A}_{sw}$ in the environment $\mathscr{A}_{en}$ is given by a TTS $\mathcal{M}_s = \langle Q, L, \longrightarrow, q_0 \rangle$, where

- $Q = \left\langle \binom{s_{\mathscr{A}_{sw}}}{s_{\mathscr{A}_{en}}}, c \rightarrow [0, 8] \right\rangle$, with $s_{\mathscr{A}_{sw}} \in S_{\mathscr{A}_{sw}}$ and $s_{\mathscr{A}_{en}} \in S_{\mathscr{A}_{en}}$
- $q_0 = \left\langle \binom{s_0}{s_0}, c = 0.0 \right\rangle$
- $L = [0, 8] \cup (\{sw, en\}, \{on, off\}, \{\{c := 0, s_{\mathscr{A}_{sw}} := s_1\}, \{c := -1, s_{\mathscr{A}_{sw}} := s_0\}\})$
  (Resets for locations of the environment are omitted since $\mathscr{A}_{en}$ has only one location.)

For testing we constrain the time domain to $[0, 8]$. Note that due to the dense time domain, $\mathcal{M}_s$ has infinitely many states and infinitely many transitions (cf. Figure 8.10).

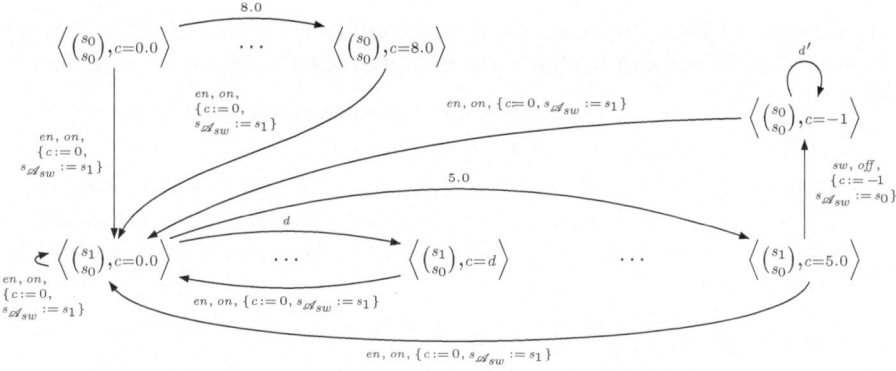

Fig. 8.10. Timed transition system $\mathscr{M}_s$ for $\mathscr{A}_{sw} \| \mathscr{A}_{en}$

8.5.2   Digitization

Timed transition systems are not directly amenable to testing. Besides their infiniteness, TTS *traces* include some *traces* that cannot be observed, e.g. delays that are not followed by visible events. Furthermore, observable TTS *traces* do not contain sufficient information to distinguish between input and output events.

A **testable timed transition systems** is a TTS but also a (deterministic) FSM. A TTTS $Spec = \langle Q, L, \longrightarrow, q_0 \rangle$ uses a subset $Q \subset Q_{\mathscr{M}}$ of states of the original TTS. Labels of the TTTS are timed event 4-tuples (d, io, a, r) with discrete delay $d \in \mathbb{N}$, $io \in \{inp, out\}$, and a and r as in $\mathscr{M}$. It is derived from a TTS $\mathscr{M}$ executing the following steps:

(1) *Digitize clocks*: Each timed *trace* with times in $\mathbb{R}^{\geq 0}$ is mapped onto a set of *traces* with times in $\mathbb{Z}$. For each reachable state q and for each delay $d \in \mathbb{R}^{\geq 0}$ within a lower and upper bound $LB \leq d \leq UB$ after which an event a can occur include for every $i \in \{LB, LB+1, \ldots, UB\}$ a transition from $\langle \overline{s}, \nu \rangle$ to $\langle \overline{s}, \nu \oplus i \rangle$ into the TTTS.

(2) *Distinguish between inputs and outputs of the SUT*: The set of network components can be partitioned into automata specifying the system under test $\mathscr{S}$ and automata describing the environment $\mathscr{E}$ of the SUT, with $\mathscr{S} \cap \mathscr{E} = \emptyset$. Each transition (p_i, a, r) of a TTS becomes in the TTTS $(0, inp, a, r)$ if $\mathscr{A}_i \in \mathscr{E}$, or $(0, out, a, r)$ if $\mathscr{A}_i \in \mathscr{S}$ respectively.

(3) *Distinguish between visible and invisible actions*: Visible events of a TTTS are defined by a test view $\mathcal{V} = (P' \subseteq P, Var' \subseteq Var, C' \subseteq C, Ch' \subseteq Ch)$. In the TTTS all $a \in Ch \backslash Ch'$ are replaced by τ. The reset set is reduced to only contain resets for elements of $\overline{s}$ with $p \in P'$, for variables $v \in Var'$, and for clocks $c \in C'$. All states with equal values for visible variables are considered to belong to the same visible equivalence class ($q =_{\mathcal{V}} q' \overset{def}{=} \forall p_i \in P' \forall v \in (Var' \cup C') : \nu(v) = \nu'(v) \wedge s[i] = s'[i]$, with $q = (\overline{s}, \nu)$ and $q' = (\overline{s}', \nu')$).

(4) *Normalize TTTS:* Not observable events could not be tested. Therefor, silent events are elided and delays of these omitted events are added to their following visible events. Each transition sequence of the form $q_0 \xrightarrow{d_1, inp, \tau, \{\}} q_1 \xrightarrow{d_2, out, a, r} q_2$ is replaced by $q_0 \xrightarrow{d_1 + d_2, out, a, r} q_2$.

Subsequently, the TTTS has to be re-transformed into a deterministic transition system, since omitting events may have introduced non-determinism. Note that, normalization is not allowed to remove cycles of silent actions. At least one of the actions on such a cycle has to be made visible, i.e. the test view $\mathcal{V}$ has to be changed, to get a proper TTTS.

(5) *Minimize TTTS:* remove all states that are redundant, i.e. all but one that are in the same visible equivalence class and have the same set of *traces*. There might be states that are in the same visible equivalence class but do not have the same set of visible *traces*. Such states have to be kept.

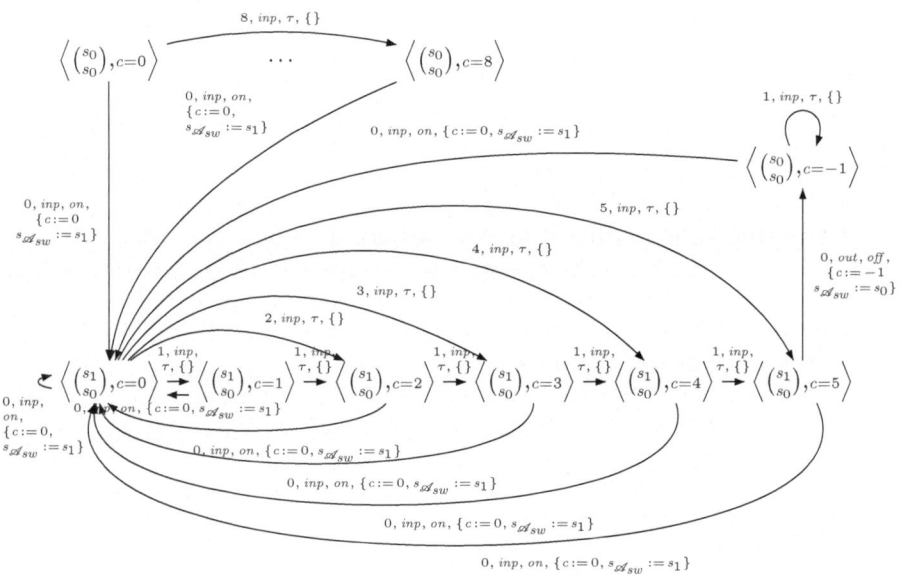

Fig. 8.11. A TTTS gained from TTS $\mathcal{M}_s$ after digitization and label transformation

Example. After digitization the TTS $\mathcal{M}_s$ is reduced to a TTTS with 15 states (cf. Figure 8.11).

Let us now assume a test view $\mathcal{V} = (P', Var', C', Ch')$, where $P' = \{p_{en}\}$, $Var' = Var = \emptyset$, $C' = C = \{c\}$, and $Ch' = Ch = \{on, off\}$. Since $P' \subset P$ does not contain the name of the switch component p_{sw}, valuations and resets of the locations of the Switch become invisible. By using this view, and applying normalization the set of states can be reduced to contain only 3 states. We get the TTTS $Spec = (Q, L, \longrightarrow, q_0)$, where

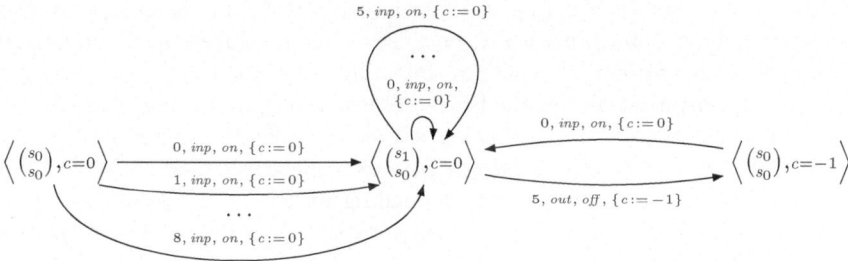

Fig. 8.12. The TTTS *Spec* after the application of a test view, normalization, and minimization

- $Q = \{q_0, q_1, q_2\} = \left\{ \left\langle \binom{s_0}{s_0}, c=0 \right\rangle, \left\langle \binom{s_1}{s_0}, c=0 \right\rangle, \left\langle \binom{s_0}{s_0}, c=-1 \right\rangle \right\}$

- $\longrightarrow = \{t_1, \ldots, t_{16}\} = \Big\{ q_0 \xrightarrow{0, inp, on, \{c:=0\}} q_1, \ldots, q_0 \xrightarrow{8, inp, on, \{c:=0\}} q_1,$

  $q_1 \xrightarrow{0, inp, on, \{c:=0\}} q_1, \ldots, q_1 \xrightarrow{5, inp, on, \{c:=0\}} q_1,$

  $q_1 \xrightarrow{5, out, off, \{c:=-1\}} q_2, \quad q_2 \xrightarrow{0, inp, on, \{c:=0\}} q_1 \Big\}$

(cf. Figure 8.12)

8.5.3 Testing

The conformance relation for testable timed transition systems is trace equivalence. Formally, $\text{Conf}(Spec) \stackrel{def}{=} \{S \mid \text{traces}(Spec) = \text{traces}(S)\}$. A test suite for a TTTS *Spec* consists of one test case for every transition in *Spec*. A test case essentially consists of three parts. The first part reaches the source state of a transition. Secondly, the transition is executed. The third part has to verify that the execution of the transition has resulted in the target state specified by *Spec*, i.e. it is a state verification sequence.

The usage of test views dramatically simplifies the search for these *separating sequences*. With classical FSM testing techniques (without data variables and test views) each state needs to be distinguished form any other in the automaton (cf. Chapter 4). Since the normalization of the TTTS ensures that *Spec* is minimal and does only contain visible events we know exactly in which state we are after the execution of a certain *trace* (except for states that are in the same visible equivalence class). Hence, the third part of a transition test needs only to distinguish the target state of the transition to be tested from other states in their visible equivalence class. There may not exist a unique separating sequence for each such state (cf. Chapter 3), since *traces* of one state may be included in *traces* of other states. To distinguish these states, the *separating sequences* are paired with oracles that states whether the final event of the *trace* shall be observed.

Please note, that even if *Impl* is deterministic, from the tester's perspective it does not behave deterministically, because events produced by the implementation may occur at different points in time. Since the tester has no capability to control when output events of the SUT will eventually occur any possible *trace* has to be considered for both reaching a state and distinguishing a state. One of all possible *reach traces*, or *separating traces* respectively, had to be chosen on the fly during execution of the test, depending on the actual occurrence of an output event. If there is a *trace* that does not depend on the choices of the SUT we only need to consider this one for testing.

The conformance test algorithm (cf. Algorithm 14) takes a TTTS *Spec*, constructed using a View $\mathcal{V}$, as input and produces a finite set of *traces* each accompanied with an oracle (yes/no) for observing its final event.

Algorithm 14 TTTS Conformance Test Algorithm

input: TTTS $Spec = \langle Q, L, \longrightarrow, q_0 \rangle$, Test View $\mathcal{V}$
output: Test($Spec$)

1   $Test(Spec) = \emptyset$
2   **for** every $q \in Q$ **do**
3   // find all acyclic traces, i.e. that visit no state more than once, ending at q
4       $reach(q) = \{\sigma \mid q_0 \xrightarrow{\sigma} q \wedge acyclic(\sigma)\}$
5   **for** every $q \in Q$ that is a transition's destination state **do**
6   **for** each $q' =_\mathcal{V} q$ **do**
7   // distinguish q from all states in the same visible equivalence class
8   **if** $q = q'$ **then** $\sigma = \langle \rangle$
9   **else** // non trivial distinction of states
10   **for** every $\sigma = l_1 \ldots l_n$ with $l_1 \ldots l_{n-1} \in \text{traces}(q) \cap \text{traces}(q')$ **do**
11   **if** $\sigma \notin \text{traces}(q) \cap \text{traces}(q')$ **then** // σ distinguishes between q and q'
12   // pair σ with oracle whether the final event should be observed
13   **if** $\sigma \in \text{traces}(q)$ **then** diff$(q, q')+ = \sigma * $yes
14   **else if** $\sigma \in \text{traces}(q')$ **then** diff$(q, q')+ = \sigma * $no
15 // Compose a test for every transition
16 **for** every $t = (q_1, l, q_2) \in \longrightarrow$ **do**
17   **for** each $q_i =_\mathcal{V} q_2$
18   Testfor(t) $+= \sigma_1 \cdot l \cdot \sigma_i * R_i$, with $\sigma_1 \in reach(q_1)$ and $\sigma_i * R_i \in diff(q_2, q_i)$
19   Test($Spec$) $+=$ Testfor(t)

Previous work did allow implementations to have extra states [COG98]. Now it is claimed that "the assumption of a bounded, small number of extra states is not appropriate for real-time systems" [CO00], because minor changes of a timed automata specification can result in a very large change in the size of its TTTS.

Definition 8.38. Real-Time Faults for TTTS: *Impl* $\in$ NonConf($Spec$) if and only if

- *Impl* has no more states then *Spec* and
- *Impl* has a single transition fault or *Impl* can be transformed to *Spec* by a sequence of single transition faults.

It can be shown that for a TTTS specification *Spec*, the test suite *Test(Spec)* that is generated by the TTTS Test generation Algorithm detects any Impl $\in$ Nonconf(*Spec*) [CO00]. If the implementation satisfies the test hypotheses then all tests for *Spec* will be passed by the implementation if and only if the implementation is trace equivalent to *Spec*.

Example. Spec $= \langle Q_{Spec}, L, \longrightarrow, q_0 \rangle$, $\mathcal{V} = (\{s_{en}\}, \emptyset, \{c\}, \{on, off\})$

(1) *Reach all states*
- reach(q_0) = $\{\langle\rangle\}$
- reach(q_1) = $\{\langle 0, inp, on, \{c:=0\}\rangle, \ldots, \langle 8, inp, on, \{c:=0\}\rangle\}$
- reach(q_2) = $\{\langle 0, inp, on, \{c := 0\} \cdot 5, out, off, \{c := \text{-}1\}\rangle, \ldots, \langle 3, inp, on,$
  $\{c:=0\} \cdot 5, out, off, \{c:=\text{-}1\}\rangle\}$

(2) Distinguish states in the same visible equivalence class: Since q_0 is not a destination state for some transition we do not need to distinguish between q_0 and q_1 although both are in the same visible equivalence class. q_2 has no other state in its visible equivalence class. Therefor, all *distinguishing traces* are trivial, i.e. $\{\langle\rangle\}$

(3) Pair traces with oracles.
- diff(q_1, q_1) = $\{\langle\rangle * yes\}$
- diff(q_2, q_2) = $\{\langle\rangle * yes\}$

(4) Compose tests for every transition.
- testfor(t_1) = $\langle 0, inp, on, \{c:=0\}\rangle * yes$
- . . .
- testfor(t_{10}) = $\langle 0, inp, on, \{c:=0\} \cdot 1, inp, on, \{c:=0\}\rangle * yes$
- . . .
- testfor(t_{15}) = $\langle 0, inp, on, \{c:=0\} \cdot 5, out, off, \{c:=\text{-}1\}\rangle * yes$
- testfor(t_{16}) = $\langle 0, inp, on, \{c := 0\} \cdot 5, out, off, \{c := \text{-}1\} \cdot 0, inp, on, \{c := 0\}\rangle * yes$

Since the tester has control over the event *on* we can choose one trace of all possible *reach*() traces for each state, although the states may be reached by different traces. If *on* were under control of the SUT we had to include all possible *reach*() traces for the according states. Furthermore, if we allowed *off* events to occur between an lower and upper time bound we had to include all possible traces including an *off* event into the according *reach* sets.

Please note, that transitions with yes oracles may be included in longer transitions, e.g. testfor(t_{16}) subsumes testfor(t_1) and testfor(t_{15}).

8.6   Summary

All three approaches use timed automata with a dense time model for testing real-time systems. All need to partition the uncountable state space of the semantics of (networks of) timed automata into a finite number of states considered equivalent.

Nielsen and Skou use coarse-grained domains [NS03]. A fully automatic method for the generation of real-time test sequences from a subclass of timed automata called event-recording automata is proposed. The technique is based on the symbolic analysis of timed automata inspired by the UPPAAL model-checker. Test sequences are selected by covering a coarse equivalence class partitioning of the state space. They argue that the approach provides a heuristic that guarantees that a well-defined set of interesting scenarios in the specification has been automatically, completely, and systematically explored.

Springintveld, Vaandrager and D'Argenio proved that exhaustive testing with respect to bisimulation[3] of deterministic timed automata with a dense time interpretation is theoretically possible [SVD01]. Testing of timed systems is described as a variant of the bounded time-domain automaton (TA). The TA describing the specification is transformed into a region automaton, which in turn is transformed into another finite state automaton, referred to as a Grid Automaton. Test sequences are then generated from the Grid Automaton. The idea behind the construction of the Grid Automaton is to represent each clock region with a finite set of clock valuations, referred to as the representatives of the clock region. However, although being exact, their grid method is impractical because it generates "an astronomically large number of test sequences" [SVD01].

Cardell-Oliver presents a testing method for networks of deterministic timed automata extended with integer data variables [CO00]. Checking of trace equivalence is done only for parts of a system that are visibly observable. In addition to the usual time-discretization test views are used to discriminate between states depending on a test-purpose. Test views partition variables and events into visible and hidden ones. Equivalence on visible clocks and variables induces an equivalence relation on states. States that are evidently different, i.e. that are in different visible equivalence classes, need not be distinguished from each other. This significantly reduces the length of test suites.

	specs	time	det.	τ	network	impl. rel.	based on	exhaustive
[NS03]	ERA	$\mathbb{R}^{>0}$			√	trace inclusion	testing preorder	
[SVD01]	TIOA	$\mathbb{R}^{>0}$	√			bisimulation	W method	√
[CO00]	UTA	$\mathbb{R}^{>0}$	√	√	√	bisimulation	W method	

Table 8.1. Comparison

In practice, time resources used for test case generation and execution should be as small as possible and test coverage as high as possible. This general need on

---

[3] In the case of determinism, bisimulation and trace equivalence coincide [vG01]

effectiveness becomes even more evident in real-time testing. Exhaustive testing becomes infeasible for any system of considerable size. Some approaches for testing real-time systems (cf. Chapter 13) gain practicability by dropping formal rigorousness. However, safety-critical systems require for justified confidence into their behavior. To make timed automata based testing applicable to systems of realistic size, remains to be done.

9 Testing Theory for Probabilistic Systems

Verena Wolf

University of Mannheim
Lehrstuhl für Praktische Informatik II
vwolf@pi2.informatik.uni-mannheim.de

9.1 Introduction

The aim of this chapter is to give a survey of testing relations for probabilistic systems. We summarize the relevant material on probabilistic extensions of the work of De Nicola and Hennessy [dNH84] who defined implementation relations for nondeterministic processes based on a notion of testing (see also Chapter 5). We mainly concentrate on the relative expressive power of the different preorders[1]. All presented relations are primarily of theoretical interest and to the best of our knowledge their usefulness in practical applications has not been shown yet.

Testing can be described as recording the behavior of systems executing in a particularly designed environment. In the classical setting a (testing) environment of a process P is simulated by considering the parallel composition $P \| T$ of P and a test process T (basically another nondeterministic process but equipped with a set of success actions or states). De Nicola and Hennessy define P *may* T if a success state can (*may*) be reached by $P \| T$ and P *must* T if $P \| T$ reaches a success state on *every* run (execution). Two processes P, Q are related if P **may** (**must**, respectively) T implies Q *may* (*must*, respectively) T for all test processes T.

In 1990, Ivan Christoff extended the classical testing theory to fully probabilistic processes that are basically labeled transition systems enriched with probabilistic information [Chr90]. He considered the parallel composition $P \| T$ of a fully probabilistic process P and a nondeterministic process T and analyzed the trace distribution of (the fully probabilistic result) $P \| T$. Two fully probabilistic processes P and Q are related if the trace distributions of $P \| T$ and $Q \| T$ coincide for all possible test processes T. Additionally, Christoff constructed a characterization by extended traces which are a denotational model simplifying the development of algorithms for the computation of the preorder.

Two years later Cleaveland et al. presented a testing approach based on probabilistic test processes [CSZ92]. They argued that the environment of a fully probabilistic process P may also be probabilistic and accordingly, they applied probabilistic test processes T, equipped with success states, and considered the probability of reaching success in $P \| T$. Furthermore, they lifted extended traces

---

[1] We use the term "preorder" as synonym for "testing relation" although it might be the case that the respective relation is not transitive or transitivity has not been shown.

M. Broy et al. (Eds.): Model-Based Testing of Reactive Systems, LNCS 3472, pp. 233-275, 2005.
© Springer-Verlag Berlin Heidelberg 2005

to probabilistic traces and proved that the resulting relation coincides with their testing relation.

The classical theory of testing was also extended to probabilistic processes (also called probabilistic automata [Sto02]) that are, informally stated, a mixture between nondeterministic and fully probabilistic processes. They are more abstract than fully probabilistic processes but enriched with "conditional probabilities".

Five years after the seminal work of De Nicola and Hennessy, Larsen and Skou extended the classical testing theory to probabilistic processes but instead of considering the parallel composition, they defined a set of observations O_T with regard to a nondeterministic test process T and tested a probabilistic process P by recording the probability of an observation $o \in O_T$ occurring in P. Two probabilistic processes P and Q are related if for all test processes T and all observations o the probability of o is equal in P and Q. Their probabilistic extension of ordinary bisimulation coincides with this testing relation.

Jonsson and Yi also constructed testing relations for probabilistic processes [JY95, JY02]. Their testing may-relation boils down to standard simulation for non-probabilistic processes and can be characterized by a notion of probabilistic simulation [JGL91].

Probabilistic processes are also considered by Segala and two preorders (may- and must-testing) are constructed that act as a "natural" extension of the classical may- and must-relations [Seg96]. Segala provides a characterization by the trace and the failure distribution precongruence which is the probabilistic extension of trace inclusion with a congruence property.

Testing relations have also been examined for stochastic process algebras by Bernardo and Cleaveland [BC00]. They are capable of modeling stochastic systems acting in continuous time and their underlying model are action-labeled continuous-time Markov chains that are basically fully probabilistic processes enriched with residence times. Bernardo and Cleaveland extended the testing criteria for fully probabilistic processes by adding a time criterion and obtained a strictly finer testing relation than for fully probabilistic processes.

Further approaches of testing probabilistic systems by Núñez et al., Stoelinga and Vaandrager, Kumar et al., Wu et al. exist [NdFL95, SV03, KCS98, WSS94] but are not treated here. We will describe the most important results of testing probabilistic systems in a unified manner to make a comparison between all the different approaches of probabilistic testing easier and present relationships between the resulting preorders and their characterizations. We do not address computability issues, because most authors use an infinite (or even uncountable) set of tests to define implementation relations[2], but try to find characterizations that are less costly to compute. There are no practical applications mentioned using probabilistic testing relations.

---

[2] In contrast to the some of the previous chapters, we use the term "implementation relation" in a more general way, i.e. it designates all kinds of relations that are constructed to show that one process is more abstract than another where "abstraction" is not defined any further.

Organization of the chapter: This chapter is organized as follows. In Section 9.2 we set up some notations and terminologies. Section 9.3 (9.4 and 9.5, respectively) introduces fully probabilistic processes, probabilistic processes and action-labeled continuous-time Markov chains and in Section 9.6 we discuss different sets of test processes. Section 9.7 (9.8 and 9.9, respectively) presents a compositional way of testing fully probabilistic processes (probabilistic processes and action-labeled continuous-time Markov chains, respectively) and in Section 9.10 we study the relationship between the different testing relations. Section 9.11 describes characterizations for each preorder and in Section 9.12 we treat the testing approach of Larsen and Skou and establish the relation between testing and bisimulation. Section 9.13 concludes the chapter.

9.2   Preliminaries

We start with some definitions used in the following sections.
Processes:

- In the following a *non-probabilistic process* is a rooted LTS[3] $C = (S_C,$ Act, $\rightarrow_C, s_C)$. We fix the set of actions Act for all non-probabilistic processes and briefly write $C = (S_C, \rightarrow_C, s_C)$. Moreover, the subscript of the set of states, the transition relation and the initial state is always equal to the name of the corresponding process. Let us denote by Act_τ the set $\text{Act} \cup \{\tau\}$. In the sequel, we sometimes use the term *nondeterministic process* for a non-probabilistic process. Let *NP* denote the set of all non-probabilistic processes.

- From now on, s, t, u, v, w range over states of a non-probabilistic process and a, b, c, d range over actions. Sometimes primes or indices are added.

- A state s is called *terminal* if it has no outgoing transitions, i.e. $s \not\rightarrow_C$. Otherwise s is called *non-terminal*.

- A non-probabilistic process C is *finitely-branching* if the set of outgoing transitions of all $s \in S_C$ is finite, i.e.

$$\{(s, a, s') \mid s \xrightarrow{a}_C s', a \in \text{Act}_\tau, s' \in S_C\}$$

  is finite for all $s \in S_C$. C is *divergence-free* if there is no infinite sequence $s_0, s_1, \ldots$ with $s_0 = s_C$ and $s_i \xrightarrow{\tau}_C s_{i+1}$ for all $i \in \mathbb{N}$.

- A non-probabilistic process $C = (S_C, \rightarrow_C, s_C)$ is τ-free if $\rightarrow_C \subseteq S_C \times \text{Act} \times S_C$.

- A *finite path* α in C is a sequence

$$\alpha = s_0\ a_0\ s_1\ a_1 \ldots a_{n-1}\ s_n,$$

  where $n \in \mathbb{N}, s_0 = s_C, s_i \xrightarrow{a_i}_C s_{i+1}$ for $0 \leqslant i < n$ and s_n is terminal. Let $lstate(\alpha) = s_n$ denote the last state of a finite path α.

---

[3] Rooted labeled transition systems are defined in the Appendix 22.

- A *finite trace* β is a sequence

$$\beta = a_0 \, a_1 \ldots a_{n-1} \in \mathsf{Act}^*.$$

  Let $trace(\alpha)$ denote the ordered sequence of all external actions occurring in a finite path α. Note that finite paths always end up in a terminal state and start in the initial state whereas traces can be arbitrary sequences of Act^*.

- We use the previous definitions of terminal states, τ-free, finitely-branching and divergence-free non-probabilistic processes also for all the probabilistic extensions that are defined later (the formal definitions are analogous). We will use the term *process* for all kinds of processes considered in the sequel and from now on all processes are divergence-free and finitely-branching.

Weight functions: A *weight function* on a countable set S is a function $\delta : S \to \mathbb{R}_{\geqslant 0}$. Let $Weight(S)$ denote the set of all weight functions on S.

Distributions: $\mu \in Weight(S)$ is a *distribution* on a countable set S if $\sum_{s \in S} \mu(s) = 1$. Let $supp(\mu) = \{s \in S : \mu(s) > 0\}$ and $Distr(S)$ be the set of all distributions on S. If $s \in S$ then χ_s denotes the unique distribution on S with

$$\chi_s(t) = \begin{cases} 1 & \text{if } t = s, \\ 0 & \text{if } t \in S \setminus \{s\}. \end{cases}$$

The product $\mu \times \lambda$ of two distributions μ on a set S and λ on a set T is the distribution on $S \times T$ defined by

$$(\mu \times \lambda)(s, t) = \mu(s) \cdot \lambda(t), \quad s \in S, t \in T.$$

In the following $\lambda, \mu, \pi, \sigma$ will always denote distributions.

Probability spaces: A *probability space* is a tuple $(\Omega, \mathcal{A}, P)$, where

- Ω is a nonempty set of outcomes,
- $\mathcal{A} \subseteq \mathcal{P}(\Omega)$ is a σ-algebra, i.e. $\Omega \in \mathcal{A}$ and $\mathcal{A}$ is closed under countable union and complement,
- $P : \mathcal{A} \to [0,1]$ is a probability measure, i.e. $P(\Omega) = 1$, $P(\emptyset) = 0$ and for countably many pairwise disjoint $A_1, A_2, \ldots \in \mathcal{A}$ we have

$$\textstyle\sum_i P(A_i) = P(\bigcup_i A_i).$$

For $\mathcal{C} \subseteq \mathcal{P}(\Omega)$ let $\sigma(\mathcal{C})$ denote the smallest σ-algebra containing $\mathcal{C}$ defined by

$$\sigma(\mathcal{C}) = \bigcap_{\substack{\mathcal{C} \subset \mathcal{A} \\ \mathcal{A} \text{ is } \sigma\text{-algebra on } \Omega}} \mathcal{A}.$$

A probability measure defined on an appropriate set $\mathcal{C}$ can be extended to a unique probability measure on $\sigma(\mathcal{C})$ (for details we refer to the book of Feller [Fel68]).

Example. Consider $\Omega = [0,1]$ and $\mathcal{C} = \{]a, b] \mid 0 \leqslant a < b \leqslant 1\}$. Then $\sigma(\mathcal{C})$ is the set of all countable unions of closed or open subsets of $[0,1]$ and $P(]a, b]) = b - a$ can be extended to a unique probability measure (the so-called Lebesgue measure) on $\sigma(\mathcal{C})$.

$\square$

9.3   Fully Probabilistic Processes

In this section, we consider *fully probabilistic processes* which are probabilistic extensions of ordinary nondeterministic processes. In a fully probabilistic process the process itself decides which action is performed next with regard to the probabilities associated with the actions (in contrast to non-probabilistic processes where the next action is chosen nondeterministically). So fully probabilistic processes describe aspects of uncertainty or randomness in a system with probability. Fully probabilistic processes can interact by performing actions synchronized with the environment, but in contrast to nonprobabilistic processes no nondeterminism exists to be resolved by an external user. They can also be seen as the action-labeled extension of *discrete-time Markov chains* [KS76].

Definition 9.1. A **fully probabilistic process** is a tuple $P = (S_P, \rightarrow_P, s_P)$ where

- S_P is a countable set of states,
- $\rightarrow_P \subseteq S_P \times \mathsf{Act}_\tau \times [0,1] \times S_P$ is a transition relation such that for all $s \in S_P$

$$\sum_{\substack{a,p,s': \\ (s,a,p,s') \in \rightarrow_P}} p \in \{0,1\},$$

- $s_P \in S_P$ is an initial state.

$\square$

We simply write $s \xrightarrow{(a,p)}_P s'$ if $(s, a, p, s') \in \rightarrow_P$. We call $s \xrightarrow{(a,p)}_P s'$ an *outgoing transition* or an *a-ransition* of the state s. Let *FPP* denote the set of all fully probabilistic processes and let $Pr_P^a(s, s')$ denote the probability of an a-transition from s to s', i.e.

$$Pr_P^a(s, s') = \sum_{s \xrightarrow{(a,p)}_P s'} p.$$

Furthermore, for $A \subseteq \mathsf{Act}_\tau, S \subseteq S_P, s' \in S_P$ let

$$Pr_P^A(s, S) = \sum_{a \in A} \sum_{s' \in S} Pr_P^a(s, s'),$$
$$Pr_P^A(s) \quad = Pr_P^A(s, S_P),$$
$$Pr_P^a(s) \quad = Pr_P^{\{a\}}(s),$$
$$Pr_P^A(s, s') = Pr_P^A(s, \{s'\}).$$

Sometimes we omit the subscript P if P is clear from the context.

Example. Figure 9.1 shows a fully probabilistic process $P = (S_P, \rightarrow_P, s_P)$ with $S_P = \{s_P, u_1, u_2, u_3, u_4, v_1, v_2\}$ and $\rightarrow_P = \{(s_P, a, 0.5, v_1), (s_P, b, 0.5, v_2), (v_1, a, 0.2, u_1), (v_1, a, 0.8, u_2), (v_2, \tau, 0.3, u_3), (v_2, b, 0.7, u_4)\}$. We have $Pr^a(s_P, v_1) = 0.5$ and $Pr^a(v_1) = Pr^{\{a,b\}}(s_P) = 1$, for instance.

$\square$

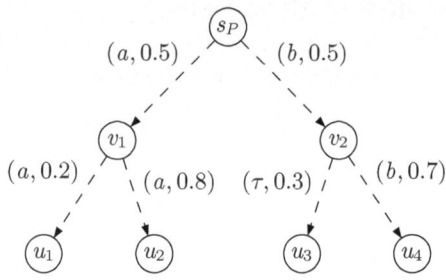

Fig. 9.1. An example of a fully probabilistic process.

9.3.1 Paths and Traces of Fully Probabilistic Processes

Similar as to non-probabilistic processes we define *paths* and *traces* in a fully probabilistic process.

Definition 9.2. Let $P = (S_P, \rightarrow_P, s_P) \in FPP$.

- A **finite path** α of P is a sequence

$$\alpha = s_0 \, a_0 \, s_1 \, a_1 \ldots a_{n-1} \, s_n,$$

  where $s_0 = s_P$, s_n is terminal and $s_i \xrightarrow{(a_i,p)}_P s_{i+1}$, $p > 0$ for $0 \leqslant i < n$. As before, $lstate(\alpha) = s_n$ denotes the last state of a finite path α.

- An **infinite path** α of P is an infinite sequence

$$\alpha = s_0 \, a_0 \, s_1 \, a_1 \ldots,$$

  where $s_0 = s_P$ and for $0 \leqslant i : s_i \xrightarrow{(a_i,p)}_P s_{i+1}$, $p > 0$.

- A **finite trace** β is a sequence

$$\beta = a_0 \, a_1 \ldots a_{n-1} \in \mathsf{Act}^*.$$

- An **infinite trace** β is a sequence

$$\beta = a_0 \, a_1 \ldots \in \mathsf{Act}^\omega.$$

  Let $trace(\alpha) \in \mathsf{Act}^\omega$ be the ordered sequence of all external actions occurring in a finite/infinite path α.

  □

Example. Consider $P \in FPP$ in Example 9.3. We have, for instance, the finite paths $\alpha_1 = s_P \, a \, v_1 \, a \, u_1$ and $\alpha_2 = s_P \, b \, v_2 \, \tau \, u_3$ of P. P has no infinite paths. Furthermore, we have $trace(\alpha_1) = a \, a$ and $trace(\alpha_2) = b$.

  □

We proceed with the construction of a probability space for sets of paths and traces of P. We define the set of outcomes Ω as the set $Path(P)$ containing all finite and infinite paths in P. Furthermore, let $C(\alpha) \subseteq \Omega$ denote the set of all paths starting with the sequence α (also called a *cylinder set*) and let $\mathcal{C}$ be the set of all $C(\alpha)$, where α is an alternating sequence of states and actions. We define a probability measure Pr_P by induction on $\mathcal{C}$ as follows.

$Pr_P(C(s_0)) = 1$ if $s_0 = s_P$ and 0 otherwise,

$Pr_P(C(s_0\ a_0\ s_1\ a_1 \ldots a_{n-1}\ s_n\ a'\ s')) =$

$\quad Pr_P(C(s_0\ a_0\ s_1\ a_1 \ldots a_{n-1}\ s_n)) \cdot Pr_P^{a'}(s_n, s').$

Pr_P can be extended to a unique probability measure Pr_P^{path} on $\sigma(\mathcal{C})$. We briefly write $Pr_P^{path}(\alpha)$ for $Pr_P^{path}(C(\alpha))$.

We have a similar construction for traces of a fully probabilistic process P. The set of outcomes is the set of all traces and the σ-algebra $\sigma(\mathcal{C})$ is built with cylinder sets of traces. We have for the probability of the cylinder set of all traces starting with the sequence $\beta \in \mathsf{Act}^*$:

$$Pr_P'(C(\beta)) = Pr_P^{path}(\{\alpha \in Path(P) \mid \beta \text{ is a prefix of } trace(\alpha)\}).$$

Again it is possible to extend the probability measure Pr_P' to a unique probability measure Pr_P^{trace} on $\sigma(\mathcal{C})$. We briefly write $Pr_P^{trace}(\beta)$ for $Pr_P^{trace}(C(\beta))$. We call Pr_P^{trace} the **trace distribution** of P, although $\sum_{\beta \in \mathsf{Act}^\omega} Pr_P^{trace}(\beta)$ might be greater as one. We have $\sum_{\substack{\beta = trace(\alpha), \\ \alpha \in Path(P)}} Pr_P^{trace}(\beta) = 1$ instead.

Example. For the paths α_1, α_2 in Example 9.3.1 (see also Figure 9.1) we have that

$Pr_P^{path}(s_P\ a\ v_1\ a\ u_1) = 0.5 \cdot 0.2 = 0.1,$

$Pr_P^{path}(s_P\ b\ v_2\ \tau\ u_3) = 0.5 \cdot 0.3 = 0.15,$

$Pr_P^{trace}(a\ a) = 0.5 \cdot 0.2 + 0.5 \cdot 0.8 = 0.5,$

$Pr_P^{trace}(b) = 0.5.$

$\square$

9.4   Probabilistic Processes

Probabilistic processes are another basic model for systems with probabilistic phenomena. Probabilistic processes are the action-labeled extension of *Markov decision processes* [Put94] and are also known (sometimes in a more general form) as *probabilistic automata* [SL94]. Probabilistic processes are more abstract than fully probabilistic processes because they can represent nondeterministic behavior. They combine modeling probabilistic behavior and interaction with

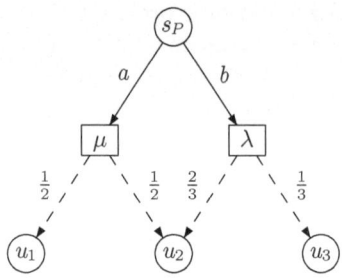

Fig. 9.2. The probabilistic process P.

the environment by resolving nondeterminism. So one probabilistic process P describes a set of fully probabilistic processes (here called *resolutions* of P). We show how to find a way of splitting P into several resolutions, i.e. how to remove nondeterminism and obtain a set of fully probabilistic processes (resolutions) from P. A more detailed comparison between several models for probabilistic systems can be found in the work of Glabbeek, Smolka and Steffen [vGSS95].

Definition 9.3. A **probabilistic process** is a tuple $P = (S_P, \to_P, s_P)$, where

- S_P is a countable set of states,
- $\to_P \subseteq S_P \times \mathsf{Act}_\tau \times Distr(S_P)$ is a transition relation,
- $s_P \in S_P$ is an initial state.

□

We write $s \xrightarrow{a}_P \mu$ for a transition $(s, a, \mu) \in \to_P$ and define PP as the set of all probabilistic processes. A state s can have several nondeterministic alternatives for the next transition. The destination of a transition $s \xrightarrow{a} \mu$ is chosen probabilistically with regard to the distribution μ. For a transition $s \xrightarrow{a} \mu$ the probability $\mu(s')$ for some $s' \in supp(\mu)$ can be seen as the conditional probability of the target state s' given that transition $s \xrightarrow{a} \mu$ is chosen. This is motivated by the idea that the external environment decides which action is performed whereas the probabilistic choice determining the next target state is resolved by the process itself. Of course, the external user cannot choose between two transitions $s \xrightarrow{a}_P \mu$ and $s \xrightarrow{a}_P \mu'$, $\mu \neq \mu'$. We therefore have a kind of "true" nondeterminism in addition. Later on we will remove nondeterminism by adding weights to every transition such that analyzing the process becomes less difficult.

Example. Figure 9.2 shows $P = (S_P, \to_P, s_P) \in PP$ with $S_P = \{s_P, u_1, u_2, u_3\}$, $\to_P = \{(s_P, a, \mu), (s_P, b, \lambda)\}$, $\mu(u_1) = \mu(u_2) = \frac{1}{2}$, $\lambda(u_2) = \frac{2}{3}$ and $\lambda(u_3) = \frac{1}{3}$. States are drawn as circles and distributions as boxes. Transitions $s \xrightarrow{a}_P \mu$ are drawn as solid arrows and probabilistic choices are drawn as dashed arrows.

We can state that the probability of reaching u_1 lies in the interval $[0, \frac{1}{2}]$ because a higher probability than $\frac{1}{2}$ is not possible even if the environment schedules the left transition. Furthermore, this probability can be 0 if the right transition is chosen. In a similar manner we derive that the probability of reaching u_2 lies in the interval $[\frac{1}{2}, \frac{2}{3}]$. In general we can assume that the left transition is taken with probability p_1, the right transition with probability p_2 and that with probability $1 - (p_1 + p_2)$ no transition is chosen (the external user decides to do nothing). Accordingly, in the following section we add weights to every transition.

$\square$

9.4.1   Removing Nondeterminism

The idea of adding weights to nondeterministic alternatives is also known as *randomized policies, schedulers* or *adversaries* [Put94]. Sometimes the possibility of scheduling no transition at all is omitted or all weights take only values in the set $\{0, 1\}$ (also called *deterministic scheduler*).

Adding weights means reducing P to a fully probabilistic resolution of P where the (unique) probability of reaching certain states or performing certain actions can be computed.

Definition 9.4.

- Let $P = (S_P, \to_P, s_p) \in PP$ and $\perp \notin S_P$, $stop \notin \mathsf{Act}_\tau$. We extend Act to the set $\mathsf{Act} \cup \{stop\}$ and P to $Stop(P) = (S_P \cup \{\perp\}, \to, s_P) \in PP$ with

$$\to = \to_P \cup \{(s, stop, \chi_\perp) \mid s \in S_P\}.$$

- Let $Q = (S_Q, \to_Q, s_Q) \in PP$ and let δ be a weight function on $(S_Q \times \mathsf{Act}_\tau \times Distr(S_Q))$ such that for all non-terminal states $s \in S_Q$:

$$\sum\nolimits_{a,\mu:s \xrightarrow{a}_\mu} \delta(s, a, \mu) = 1.$$

In this case δ is called a *weight function for* P and $\delta(Q) = (S_Q, \to, s_Q) \in FPP$ is given by

$$s \xrightarrow{(a,p)} s' \text{ iff } \delta(s, a, \mu) \cdot \sum\nolimits_{\mu:s \xrightarrow{a}_\mu} \mu(s') = p.$$

- Let $fully(P)$ be the set of fully probabilistic processes of $P \in PP$ constructed in the way previously described, i.e.

$$fully(P) = \{\delta(Stop(P)) \mid \delta \text{ is a weight function for } Stop(P)\}.$$

$\square$

The *stop*-action models that no transition of P is chosen. This action always ends in the terminal $\perp$-state and no further executions are possible. Sometimes the $Stop(P)$ extension is called the *halting extension* of P.

Example. Figure 9.3 shows $\delta(Stop(P)) \in fully(P)$ where P is the probabilistic process of Figure 9.2 and $\delta(s_P, a, \mu) = \frac{1}{2}$, $\delta(s_P, b, \lambda) = \frac{1}{3}$, $\delta(s_P, stop, \chi_\perp) = \frac{1}{6}$ and $\delta(u_i, stop, \chi_\perp) = 1$ for $i = 1, 2, 3$.

$\square$

We have already defined paths and traces in fully probabilistic processes. With the help of the previous construction we analyze paths and traces in a probabilistic process P by considering $fully(P)$.

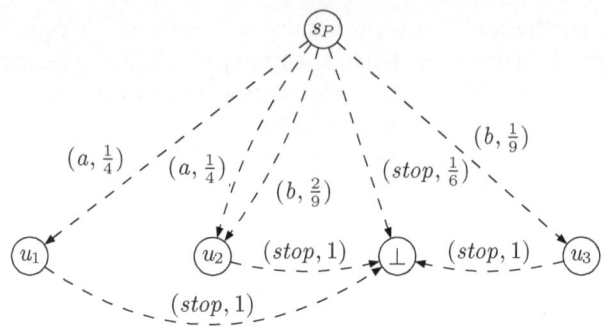

Fig. 9.3. Removing nondeterminism in a probabilistic process.

9.5   Action-Labeled Continuous-Time Markov Chains

Action-labeled continuous-time Markov chains (aCTMCs) are the underlying model of stochastic process algebras like TIPP, EMPA and PEPA [GHR93, BG96, Hil96] and the action-labeled extension of continuous-time Markov chains. The difference between aCTMCs and fully probabilistic processes (as presented in Section 9.3) is that the process acts in continuous time and an exponentially distributed residence time X is associated with each state. Transition probabilities are replaced by rates and the process remains X time units in the corresponding state and chooses a successor state with regard to the probabilities implicitly given by the rates. Thus, aCTMCs model real-world systems with time-dependence and randomness.

Definition 9.5. An **action-labeled continuous-time Markov chain** M is given by a tuple $(S_M, \longrightarrow_M, s_M)$ where

- S_M is a countable set of states,
- $\longrightarrow_M \subseteq S_M \times (\mathsf{Act}_\tau \times \mathbb{R}_{>0}) \times S_M$ is a transition relation and
- $s_M \in S_M$ is an initial state.

Furthermore, for all $s \in S_M$ the exit rate

$$E(s) = \sum_{\substack{s', a, r: \\ (s,a,r,s') \in \to_M}} r$$

is finite.

$\square$

Let $ACTMC$ denote the set of all action-labeled continuous-time Markov chains. We write $s \xrightarrow{(a,r)}_M s'$ for $(s, a, r, s') \in \to_M$. We interpret an aCTMC as follows: Every element $s \xrightarrow{(a,r)}_M s'$ corresponds to an a-transition in the chain from state s to state s'. Every transition has an associated stochastic delay with a duration determined by r. If s has only one successor s', an a-transition to s' can take place after a delay which lasts an exponentially distributed time period. We

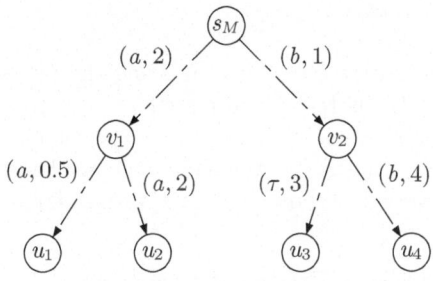

Fig. 9.4. An example of an aCTMC.

use r as parameter of the exponential distribution such that the probability of reaching s' in at most x time units equals $1 - e^{-r \cdot x}$. If s has more than one transition a "race" between all possible outgoing transitions starts after s is entered. For each element $s \xrightarrow{(a,r)} s'$ an exponentially distributed random number with regard to r is generated and the transition with the smallest value wins the race. This means that after the shortest delay which is equal to the smallest value of all generated random numbers, a transition to the corresponding state takes place. Note that the minimum of random variables $X_1, X_2, ...$ governed by an exponential distribution with parameters $r_1, r_2, ...$, respectively, is exponentially distributed with parameter $r_1 + r_2 + ...$ So after entering s the chain remains in s for a time period which is exponentially distributed with parameter $\sum_i r_i$, when $r_1, r_2, ..$ are the rates of all possible outgoing transitions of s.

Example. Figure 9.4 shows an aCTMC $M = (S_M, \to_M, s_M)$ with

$$S_M = \{s_P, u_1, u_2, u_3, u_4, v_1, v_2\} \text{ and } \to_M = \{(s_M, a, 2, v_1), (s_M, b, 1, v_2),$$

$$(v_1, a, 0.5, u_1), (v_1, a, 2, u_2), (v_2, \tau, 3, u_3), (v_2, b, 4, u_4)\}.$$

We have $E(s_M) = 3$ and $E(v_1) = 2.5$, for instance. Note that "Markovian" transitions are drawn with dashed arrows here.

□

Now, we show how to transform an aCTMC to a fully probabilistic process [BHKW03]. After this transformation we are able to use all definitions presented in Section 9.3 for aCTMCs. The transformation is called *embedding* because the continuous-time nature of the aCTMC is embedded into a discrete-time.

Definition 9.6. Let $M = (S_M, \to_M, s_M)$ be an aCTMC. Then the fully probabilistic process $\phi_{em}(M) = (S_M, \to, s_M)$ is given by

$$s \xrightarrow{(a,p)} s' \text{ iff } s \xrightarrow{(a,r)}_M s' \text{ and } p = r/E(s).$$

□

Since embedding does not change the probabilities of paths, only the time information is lost, we define paths and traces in an aCTMC M analogously to paths and traces in $\phi_{em}(M)$. Let $Path(M) = Path(\phi_{em}(M))$ denote the set of all paths in an aCTMC M.

9.6   Test Processes

Testing a process is mostly done by simulating the process environment by another process. The idea is to let the tested process run in parallel with a *test process*. Test processes are special kinds of non-probabilistic, fully probabilistic or probabilistic processes. In the following we consider three different classes of test processes and we will discuss "design criteria" for test processes.

9.6.1   Selection of Test Process Properties

To find a suitable method for simulating the environment of a process by a test process, we have to distinguish between the three probabilistic models we have (fully probabilistic processes, probabilistic processes and aCTMCs). But some decisions are equal for all models:

- A frequently used approach is that *no structural distinction* exists between test processes and tested processes, i.e. the test process and the tested process are both fully probabilistic, probabilistic or aCTMCs, respectively. For fully probabilistic processes some authors applied non-probabilistic test processes [Chr90, LS91], whereas others applied fully probabilistic test processes [CSZ92]. So in the remainder of the chapter we will consider both approaches. For probabilistic processes we will only consider test processes that are probabilistic process [Seg96, JY02]. To the best of our knowledge for aCTMCs only one testing approach has been studied [BC00]. The tested aCTMC is combined with a "passive" aCTMC where the choice between external actions is non-probabilistic and the choice between internal actions is a "race".

- Very often authors restrict to *finite* test processes. It turns out that infinite test processes offer no more distinguishing power than finite test processes (proved for the non-probabilistic and for the probabilistic setting by Segala [Seg96] and by Kumar et al. [KCS98]). This is caused by the fact that every infinite path is considered to be unsuccessful. Thus, we only consider finite test processes here, i.e. a test process is not able to perform an infinite sequence of actions.

- In many approaches test processes are equipped with a set of *success or failure states* reporting whether the test was successful or not. Only Christoff and Larsen et al. analyze the entire observational behavior of the process/test process composition [Chr90, LS91]. For the former approach one can distinguish between success and failure and whether it is reached via an action or a state. A test process can report "success" by containing success actions or success states. It is clear that the difference is of no importance. In our setting we apply test processes equipped with a set of success states. It is also possible to apply a test process with a single success state, though we follow here the more general approach.

- Without loss of generality we can assume that test processes are *acyclic* to ease the computation of success probabilities. Cycles can be removed by copying states, i.e. all states that can be reached by more than one path from the initial state are copied such that the process becomes acyclic. It is easy to verify that this does not change the resulting success or trace probabilities of compositions with processes to be tested. Furthermore, we assume that success states are terminal, i.e. they have no outgoing transitions. The behavior of the process after reaching success is of no interest to us.

- We use test processes that are capable of performing internal actions and test processes that are not. It is easy to see that in the non-probabilistic setting of our chapter τ-actions do not increase the distinguishing power of test processes. However, in the probabilistic setting they do which can be seen by a trivial example (compare Example 9.7.2 on page 251).

Definition 9.7. Let $\mathcal{T}_\tau^{np}$ ($\mathcal{T}_\tau^{pp}$, $\mathcal{T}_\tau^{fp}$, respectively) be the set of all $T \in NP$ (PP, FPP, respectively) that are finite-state and acyclic and have a set of success states in addition. We call $T \in \mathcal{T}_\tau^{np}$ ($\mathcal{T}_\tau^{pp}$, $\mathcal{T}_\tau^{fp}$, respectively) a *non-probabilistic (probabilistic, fully probabilistic) test process*. Let $\mathcal{T}^{np} \subset \mathcal{T}_\tau^{np}$ ($\mathcal{T}^{pp} \subset \mathcal{T}_\tau^{pp}$, $\mathcal{T}^{fp} \subset \mathcal{T}_\tau^{fp}$, respectively) be the set of all non-probabilistic (probabilistic, fully probabilistic) test processes that cannot perform any τ-action.

□

9.6.2   Test Processes for Fully Probabilistic and Probabilistic Processes

Segala, Jonsson and Yi analyze probabilistic processes running in parallel with a probabilistic test process that simulates a "natural" environment for probabilistic processes [Seg96, JY02].
In the parallel composition of a probabilistic process and a probabilistic test process external actions are shared and forced to be performed in parallel and τ-actions are carried out in isolation.

Definition 9.8. The **parallel composition** of $P = (S_P, \to_P, s_P) \in PP$ and $T = (S_T, \to_T, s_T) \in \mathcal{T}_\tau^{pp}$ is the probabilistic process $P \parallel T = (S_P \times S_T, \to, (s_P, s_T))$ with

$$\to \; \subseteq (S_P \times S_T) \times \mathsf{Act}_\tau \times Distr(S_P \times S_T)$$

such that for $a \neq \tau$ the following holds:

$$(s, t) \xrightarrow{a} (\lambda \times \mu) \text{ iff } (s \xrightarrow{a}_P \lambda \wedge t \xrightarrow{a}_T \mu)$$

and

$$(s, t) \xrightarrow{\tau} (\lambda \times \mu) \text{ iff } (s \xrightarrow{\tau}_P \lambda, \mu = \chi_t) \vee (t \xrightarrow{\tau}_T \mu, \lambda = \chi_s).$$

□

Since T has a set of success states, we may have states in $P \parallel T$ where the second component is a success state. We call such states success states as well.

We present two approaches of constructing testing relations for probabilistic processes in Section 9.8.

A fully probabilistic process P is analyzed by running in parallel with a non-probabilistic test process or a fully probabilistic test process. Fully probabilistic test processes have more distinguishing power than non-probabilistic ones as can be seen by Example 6, page 263. We will discuss both approaches here and start with the description of two different classes of non-probabilistic test processes [Chr90].

Definition 9.9. Let $\mathcal{T}^{np,re} \subset \mathcal{T}^{np}$ be the set of all $T = (S_T, \rightarrow_T, s_T) \in \mathcal{T}^{np}$ with

$$(t \xrightarrow{a}_T t' \wedge t \xrightarrow{a}_T t'') \implies t'' = t'.$$

Let $\mathcal{T}^{np,re}_{seq} \subset \mathcal{T}^{np,re}$ be the set of all $T = (S_T, \rightarrow_T, s_T) \in \mathcal{T}^{np,re}$ with

$$(t \xrightarrow{a}_T t' \wedge t \xrightarrow{a'}_T t'') \implies (a = a' \wedge t'' = t').$$

$\square$

$\mathcal{T}^{np,re}$ is the set of "reactive" test processes, reactive in the sense that $T \in \mathcal{T}^{np,re}$ has no internal nondeterminism. $\mathcal{T}^{np,re}_{seq}$ is the set of all sequential test processes because in $T \in \mathcal{T}^{np,re}_{seq}$ there is no choice at all between several transitions.

We apply non-probabilistic test processes here to fully probabilistic processes. The parallel composition is defined as follows.

Definition 9.10. The **parallel composition** of $P = (S_P, \rightarrow_P, s_P) \in FPP$ and $T = (S_T, \rightarrow_T, s_T) \in \mathcal{T}^{np}$ is the fully probabilistic process $P \| T = (S_P \times S_T, \rightarrow, (s_P, s_T))$ with

$$(s, t) \xrightarrow{(a, \frac{p}{v(s,t)})} (s', t') \text{ iff } s \xrightarrow{(a,p)}_P s' \text{ and } t \xrightarrow{a}_T t',$$

$$(s, t) \xrightarrow{(\tau, \frac{p}{v(s,t)})} (s', t') \text{ iff } s \xrightarrow{(\tau,p)}_P s' \text{ and } t = t',$$

where $a \neq \tau$ and $v(s,t) = \sum_{a \in \mathsf{Act}} | \{t \xrightarrow{a}_T t'\} | \cdot Pr_P^a(s) + Pr_P^\tau(s)$.

$\square$

Note that the parallel composition of a fully probabilistic process and a non-probabilistic test process that is able to perform τ-transitions is not sensible here since there is no appropriate probability for an internal move of T in $P \| T$ and we do not want to abstract from the probabilistic information here at all.

Following the approach of Cleaveland et al. the environment of a fully probabilistic process is simulated by a test process which is also a fully probabilistic process [CSZ92]. The parallel composition of $P \in FPP$ and $T \in \mathcal{T}_\tau^{fp}$ is a fully probabilistic process $P \| T$ that executes external actions of P and T synchronously and internal actions in isolation. Here internal actions are treated as "invisible" for the environment and synchronizing over internal actions is not allowed.

Definition 9.11. The **parallel composition** of two fully probabilistic processes $P = (S_P, \rightarrow_P, s_P)$ and $T = (S_T, \rightarrow_T, s_T)$ is $P \| T = (S_P \times S_T, \rightarrow, (s_P, s_T)) \in FPP$ where for $a \neq \tau$

$$(s,t) \xrightarrow{(a,p)} (s',t') \text{ iff } s \xrightarrow{(a,p_1)}_P s' \wedge t \xrightarrow{(a,p_2)}_T t' \wedge p = \frac{p_1 \cdot p_2}{v(s,t)},$$

$$(s,t) \xrightarrow{(\tau,p)} (s',t) \quad \text{iff } s \xrightarrow{(\tau,p')}_P s' \wedge p = \frac{p'}{v(s,t)},$$

$$(s,t) \xrightarrow{(\tau,p)} (s,t') \quad \text{iff } t \xrightarrow{(\tau,p')}_T t' \wedge p = \frac{p'}{v(s,t)},$$

where

$$v(s,t) = \sum_{a \in \mathsf{Act}} Pr_P^a(s) \cdot Pr_T^a(t) + Pr_P^\tau(s) + Pr_T^\tau(t).$$

□

Note that $\frac{1}{v(s,t)}$ acts as normalization factor. The first possibility is that P and T perform action a synchronously and the probability of this common action is the normalized product of each single probability. The other two possibilities are that a τ-action is performed independently. If T contains success states, we may have states in $P \| T$ where the second component is a success state. We call these states in $P \| T$ also success states (as before). All test processes are finite, thus, the parallel composition of a fully probabilistic process and a fully probabilistic test process is finite as well.

9.6.3 Test Processes for ACTMCs

A *Markovian test process* T simulates the environment of an aCTMC M and behaves like a "passive" aCTMC. All rates of external actions in T are zero describing that an enabled transition $s \xrightarrow{(a,0)} s'$ is waiting for synchronization (possibly for an infinite duration) whereas $\tau-$actions must be executed with non-zero rate. Passive rates are replaced by "active" rates, i.e. rates that are greater zero, during synchronization with M. The motivation is that the process to be tested determines the "speed" at which external actions happen whereas the test process imposes no further delays (just observes) except by internal transitions. Of course, a more stochastic environment might be also suitable for an aCTMC but this approach has not been investigated yet.

Definition 9.12. A **Markovian test process** T is a tuple $(S_T, \rightarrow_T, s_T)$ where S_T is a finite set of states, $s_T \in S_T$ an initial state and $\rightarrow_T \subseteq S_T \times \mathsf{Act}_\tau \times \mathbb{R}_{\geqslant 0} \times S_T$ with

$$s \xrightarrow{(a,r)}_T s' \implies \begin{cases} \text{if } a \neq \tau \text{ then } r = 0, \\ \text{if } a = \tau \text{ then } r > 0. \end{cases}$$

Furthermore, T has a set of terminal success states $\mathcal{A} \subseteq S_T$ and is acyclic. Let $\mathcal{T}_\tau^{pa}$ denote the set of all Markovian test processes and $\mathcal{T}^{pa} \subset \mathcal{T}_\tau^{pa}$ the set of all Markovian test processes without the ability to perform an internal action.

□

Note that $\mathcal{T}^{pa}$ is the set of all non-probabilistic test processes (without the ability to perform internal actions), if we ignore the rate component 0 here. The parallel composition of an aCTMC and a Markovian test process is defined as follows.

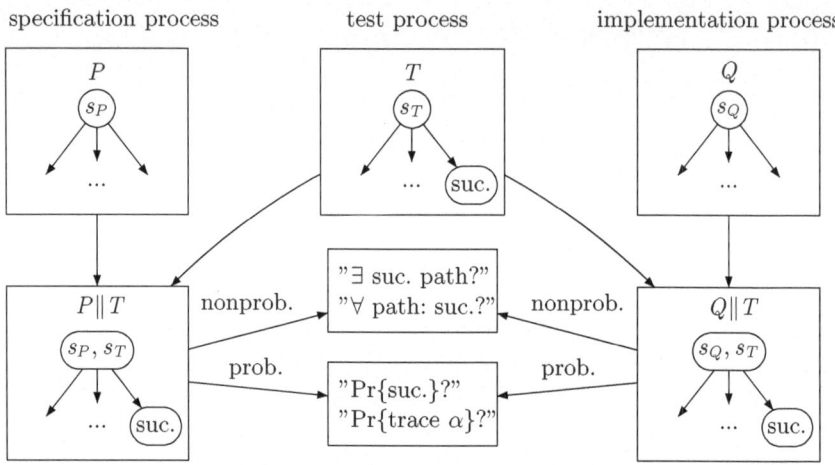

Fig. 9.5. Compositional testing of processes.

Definition 9.13. The **parallel composition** of $M = (S_M, \rightarrow_M, s_M) \in ACTMC$ and $T = (S_T, \rightarrow_T, s_T) \in \mathcal{T}_\tau^{pa}$ is $M \| T = (S_M \times S_T, \rightarrow, (s_M, s_T)) \in ACTMC$ where

$$\rightarrow \subseteq (S_M \times S_T) \times \mathsf{Act}_\tau \times \mathbb{R}_{>0} \times (S_M \times S_T)$$

is a transition relation such that for $r > 0, a \neq \tau$

$$(s, t) \xrightarrow{(a,r)} (s', t') \text{ iff } s \xrightarrow{(a,r)}_M s' \text{ and } t \xrightarrow{(a,0)}_T t',$$

$$(s, t) \xrightarrow{(\tau,r)} (s', t') \text{ iff } (s \xrightarrow{(\tau,r)}_M s', t' = t) \text{ or } (t \xrightarrow{(\tau,r)}_T t', s' = s).$$

□

Note that in $M \| T$ all passive rates of the test process are replaced by active ones and therefore $M \| T \in ACTMC$.

9.7   Compositional Testing of Fully Probabilistic Processes

In the following we introduce the probabilistic extension of classical testing. The idea is that we have an implementation process Q and a specification process P and we want to know if Q implements P. The answer of this question is given by a testing relation which is constructed in the following way (see Figure 9.5): A test process T (with a set of success states) simulates an environment for the two processes by running in parallel with P and Q, respectively. Informally, P and Q are related in the non-probabilistic setting if the following holds (may-testing):

> The existence of a successful path[4] in $P \| T$ implies that a successful path exists in $Q \| T$.

---

[4] Recall that all considered paths here are "maximal", i.e. end up in an terminal state.

or (must-testing):

> If all paths in $P\|T$ are successful then all paths in $Q\|T$ are successful.

For fully probabilistic processes we do not distinguish between may- and must-testing. There are two approaches to relate $P, Q \in FPP$:

> "The probability of all successful paths in $P\|T$ is at most the probability of all successful paths in $Q\|T$."

and

> The probability of any trace α in $P\|T$ is at most the probability of α in $Q\|T$.

Intuitively speaking, an implementation (Q) should be at least as successful as the specification (P).

9.7.1   Testing with Non-probabilistic Test Processes

In this section, we present the approach of Christoff [Chr90]. He presents a testing theory for fully probabilistic processes that is based on reactive, non-probabilistic test processes without internal actions. Two fully probabilistic processes P and Q are related with regard to their trace distributions while running in parallel with a non-probabilistic test process. Note that $\mathcal{T}^{np,re}$ is a proper subset of $\mathcal{T}^{np}$, the set of all non-probabilistic test processes (compare Definition 9.7, page 245).

Definition 9.14. [Chr90] Let $P, Q \in FPP$.

- $P \sqsubseteq_{CH}^{tr} Q$ iff $\forall T \in \mathcal{T}_{seq}^{np,re}$, $\alpha \in \mathsf{Act}^*$:

$$Pr_{P\|T}^{trace}(\alpha) \leqslant Pr_{Q\|T}^{trace}(\alpha).$$

- $P \sqsubseteq_{CH}^{wte} Q$ iff $\forall T \in \mathcal{T}^{np,re}$, $\alpha \in \mathsf{Act}^*$:

$$\sum_{a \in \mathsf{Act}} Pr_{P\|T}^{trace}(\alpha\,a) \leqslant \sum_{a \in \mathsf{Act}} Pr_{Q\|T}^{trace}(\alpha\,a).$$

- $P \sqsubseteq_{CH}^{ste} Q$ iff $\forall T \in \mathcal{T}^{np,re}$, $\alpha \in \mathsf{Act}^*$:

$$Pr_{P\|T}^{trace}(\alpha) \leqslant Pr_{Q\|T}^{trace}(\alpha).$$

□

Recall that $\mathcal{T}_{seq}^{np,re}$ contains only "sequential" test processes, so $\sqsubseteq_{CH}^{tr}$ is coarser than or equal to $\sqsubseteq_{CH}^{wte}$ and $\sqsubseteq_{CH}^{ste}$. It turns out that $\sqsubseteq_{CH}^{tr}$ can be characterized by trace inclusion (hence, the superscript "tr"), i.e.

$$P \sqsubseteq_{CH}^{tr} Q \text{ iff } \{\beta \in \mathsf{Act}^* \mid Pr_P^{trace}(\beta) > 0\} \subseteq \{\beta \in \mathsf{Act}^* \mid Pr_Q^{trace}(\beta) > 0\}.$$

The probabilistic information gets lost due to the restrictions of the test processes. Since $\sqsubseteq_{CH}^{wte}$ compares the sum of the trace probabilities whereas the

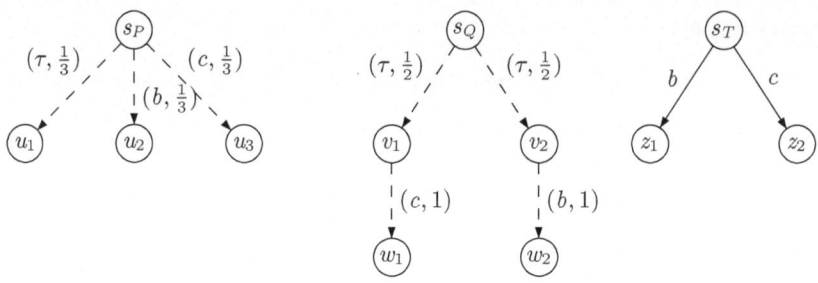

Fig. 9.6. $P \sim_{CH}^{tr} Q$ but $P \not\sim_{CH}^{wte} Q$.

$\sqsubseteq_{CH}^{ste}$ compares each single trace probability, it is clear that $P \sqsubseteq_{CH}^{ste} Q$ implies $P \sqsubseteq_{CH}^{wte} Q$. Hence, for $P, Q \in FPP$ we have

$$P \sqsubseteq_{CH}^{ste} Q \Longrightarrow P \sqsubseteq_{CH}^{wte} Q \Longrightarrow P \sqsubseteq_{CH}^{tr} Q.$$

In the following we will see that these implications can not be reversed. The superscript is chosen due to the fact that $\sqsubseteq_{CH}^{wte}$ is a "weak testing preorder" compared to the finer preorder $\sqsubseteq_{CH}^{ste}$ ("strong testing preorder"). We denote the induced equivalence relations by $\sim_{CH}^{i} = \sqsubseteq_{CH}^{i} \cap (\sqsubseteq_{CH}^{i})^{-1}$ where $i \in \{tr, wte, ste\}$ and sometimes we write $\sqsubseteq_{CH}$ and $\sim_{CH}$ instead of $\sqsubseteq_{CH}^{ste}$ and $\sim_{CH}^{ste}$, respectively.

Example. Figure 9.6 shows two fully probabilistic processes P and Q with $P \sim_{CH}^{tr} Q$ but $P \not\sim_{CH}^{wte} Q$. The latter can be seen by applying the test process T. Then

$$\sum_{a \in \mathsf{Act}} Pr_{P \| T}^{trace}(a) = \tfrac{2}{3} < \sum_{a \in \mathsf{Act}} Pr_{Q \| T}^{trace}(a) = 1.$$

If we apply some $T' \in \mathcal{T}_{seq}^{np,re}$ instead we always have $Pr_{P \| T'}^{trace}(\alpha) = Pr_{Q \| T'}^{trace}(\alpha)$ for all $\alpha \in \mathsf{Act}^*$.

In Figure 9.7 we have $P' \sim_{CH}^{wte} Q'$ but $P' \not\sim_{CH}^{ste} Q'$. The latter can be seen if we apply the test process T in Figure 9.6 to P' and Q'. We have that

$$\tfrac{1}{4} = Pr_{P' \| T}^{trace}(c) < Pr_{Q' \| T}^{trace}(c) = \tfrac{1}{3}.$$

It is easy to see that $P'' \sim_{CH}^{ste} Q''$.

$\square$

Note that we obtain the same relations in Definition 9.14 by replacing the probability distribution $Pr_P^{trace}(\cdot)$ by the conditional probability distribution $Pr_P^{ctrace}(\cdot)$ defined as follows: For $\alpha \in \mathsf{Act}^*$ and $a \in \mathsf{Act}$ let

$$Pr_P^{ctrace}(\alpha\,a) = \begin{cases} Pr_P^{trace}(\alpha\,a)/Pr_P^{trace}(\alpha) & \text{if } Pr_P^{trace}(\alpha) > 0, \\ 0 & \text{otherwise.} \end{cases}$$

This is an important fact, on which the proof of the characterization theorem 9.29 relies.

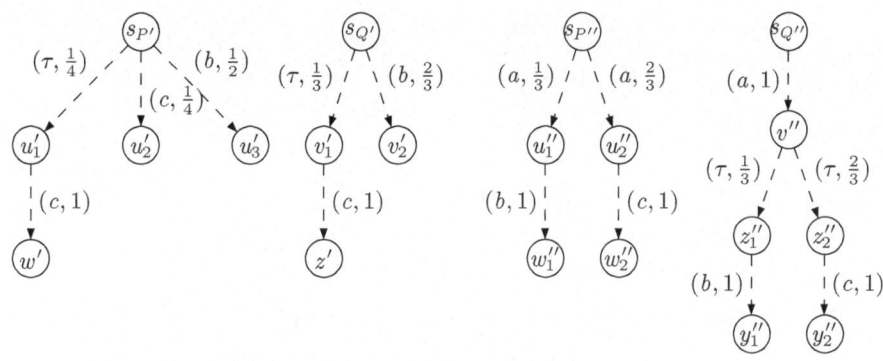

Fig. 9.7. $P' \sim_{CH}^{wte} Q'$ but $P' \not\sim_{CH}^{ste} Q'$ and $P'' \sim_{CH}^{ste} Q''$.

9.7.2   Testing with Fully Probabilistic Test Processes

In this section, we discuss the approach of Cleaveland et al. [CSZ92]. We want to compare two fully probabilistic processes P and Q with regard to their testing behavior in a "probabilistic environment" (simulated by a fully probabilistic test process). The idea is to consider $T \in \mathcal{T}_\tau^{fp}$ running in parallel with P and Q, respectively, and compute the total success probabilities in $P\|T$ and in $Q\|T$. Let $\mathcal{A}$ be the set of success states in $P\|T$. Compute the probability $\mathcal{W}_{P\|T}$ of reaching a success state in $P\|T$, i.e. let

$$\mathcal{W}_{P\|T} = Pr_{P\|T}^{path}(\{\alpha \in Path(P\|T) \mid lstate(\alpha) \in \mathcal{A}\}).$$

Recall that test processes are finite and acyclic here and success states are terminal. Since P is divergence-free and finitely-branching, the previous probabilities are well-defined.

Definition 9.15. [CSZ92] Let $P, Q \in FPP$.

$P \sqsubseteq_{CL} Q$ iff $\forall T \in \mathcal{T}_\tau^{fp} : \mathcal{W}_{P\|T} \leqslant \mathcal{W}_{Q\|T}$.

$\square$

The idea of this relation is that the process P acting in the "environment T" should not have a greater success probability than Q acting in the same environment. Intuitively, we take Q as implementation process and P as specification. So we have $P \sqsubseteq_{CL} Q$ if the implementation is always doing as required or even better than the specification. Let $\sim_{CL} = \sqsubseteq_{CL} \cap (\sqsubseteq_{CL})^{-1}$ denote the induced equivalence relation. Cleaveland et al. showed that $\sqsubseteq_{CL}$ and $\sim_{CL}$ coincide.

Note that a different definition of the parallel composition may result in a different preorder. However, applying test processes T that are capable of performing internal transitions yields (in contrast to the non-probabilistic case) a finer relation than using τ-free test processes which can be seen with the following example.

Example. Consider Figure 9.8 and assume $P, Q, P', Q' \in FPP$, $T \in \mathcal{T}_\tau^{fp}$ (success states are drawn with bold lines here and in later figures). It can be shown

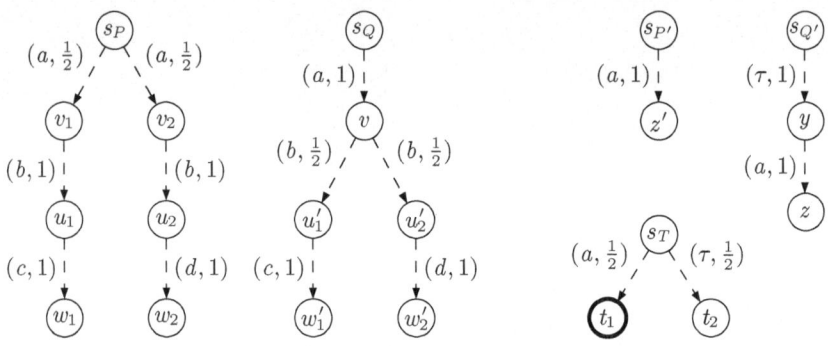

Fig. 9.8. $P \sqsubseteq_{CL} Q$ but $P' \not\sqsubseteq_{CL} Q'$.

that $P \sim_{CL} Q$ but P and Q can be distinguished by the so-called probabilistic bisimulation [LS91], see also Definition 9.32, page 271. Thus, $\sim_{CL}$ is coarser than probabilistic bisimulation. Moreover Figure 9.8 shows that using τ-action in fully probabilistic test processes increases the distinguishing power. P' and Q' can not be distinguished by τ-free test processes but we have $\frac{1}{2} = \mathcal{W}_{P' \| T} > \mathcal{W}_{Q' \| T} = \frac{1}{3}$.

$\square$

9.8   Compositional Testing of Probabilistic Processes

In this section we focus on the approaches of Segala[Seg96] and Jonsson and Yi [JY02, JY95]. We apply a probabilistic test process $T \in \mathcal{T}_\tau^{pp}$ to $P, Q \in PP$. The following steps are necessary to construct a testing relation.

(1) Consider the parallel composition $P \| T \in PP$ and construct the set of fully probabilistic processes $fully(P \| T)$ (as described in Section 9.4.1, page 241).

(2) For every fully probabilistic process $P' \in fully(P \| T)$ construct a probability space for all paths and traces in P' (with probability measures $Pr_{P'}^{path}$ and $Pr_{P'}^{trace}$).

(3) Compute vectors of success probabilities as follows. Let $\mathcal{A} = \{w_1, \dots, w_m\}$ be the set of success states in T. Compute for any $i \in \{1, \dots, m\}$ the probability $\mathcal{W}_{P'}(w_i)$ of reaching a state (s, w_i) in P', i.e. let

$$\mathcal{W}_{P'}(w_i) = Pr_{P'}^{path}(\{\alpha \in Path(P') \mid \exists s \in S_P : lstate(\alpha) = (s, w_i)\}).$$

Note that since T is finite and acyclic and P is divergence-free, no infinite paths in P' exist, so $\mathcal{W}_{P'}(w_i)$ is well-defined.

(4) Compute also the *total success probability* $\mathcal{W}_{P'} = \sum_{i=1}^{m} \mathcal{W}_{P'}(w_i)$.

Definition 9.16. [Seg96] Let $P, Q \in PP$.

- $P \sqsubseteq_{SE}^{may} Q$ iff for all $T \in \mathcal{T}_\tau^{pp}$:

  $$\forall P' \in fully(P\|T) : \exists Q' \in fully(Q\|T) : \mathcal{W}_{P'}(w) \leqslant \mathcal{W}_{Q'}(w)$$

  for all success states w in T.

- $P \sqsubseteq_{SE}^{must} Q$ iff for all $T \in \mathcal{T}_\tau^{pp}$:

  $$\forall Q' \in fully(Q\|T) : \exists P' \in fully(P\|T) : \mathcal{W}_{P'}(w) \leqslant \mathcal{W}_{Q'}(w)$$

  for all success states w in T.

We write $P \sqsubseteq_{SE} Q$ iff $P \sqsubseteq_{SE}^{may} Q$ and $P \sqsubseteq_{SE}^{must} Q$.

$\square$

The motivation of $\sqsubseteq_{SE}^{may}$ is that each resolution of $P\|T$ should have a success probability not greater than at least one resolution of $Q\|T$. This is an implementation relation if we take Q as implementation process and P as specification. It is also possible to interpret success as "error" and motivate it the other way round, i.e. P acts as implementation process and Q as specification.

In the must-preorder the quantifiers over the fully probabilistic processes of $P\|T$ and $Q\|T$ are exchanged (compared with the may-testing relation) and it requires that all elements of $fully(Q\|T)$ have a greater or equal success probability than at least one element of $fully(P\|T)$.

Example. Figure 9.9 shows two probabilistic processes P and Q (similar to Example 9.7.2). Transitions to distributions which assign probability one to a certain state, like (s_Q, a, χ_v), for instance, are omitted in the picture and an arrow is directly drawn from the state s_Q to v instead. It can be seen that $P \not\sqsubseteq_{SE}^{may} Q$ and $P \sqsubseteq_{SE}^{must} Q$ as follows.
If we test P and Q with T, for example, we have to remove two nondeterministic choices in $P\|T$ and one in $Q\|T$ (compare Figure 9.10). Let $x_1, x_2 \in [0,1]$, $x_1 + x_2 \leqslant 1$ and let δ' be a weight function for $Stop(Q\|T)$ with

$$\delta'((v, v''), b, \mu \times \chi_{u_1''}) = x_1,$$

$$\delta'((v, v''), b, \mu \times \chi_{u_2''}) = x_2,$$

$$\delta'((v, v''), stop, \chi_\perp) = 1 - (x_1 + x_2).$$

Then we choose a weight function δ for $Stop(P\|T)$ with

$$\delta((v_1, v''), b, \chi_{(u_1, u_1'')}) = x_1,$$

$$\delta((v_1, v''), b, \chi_{(u_1, u_2'')}) = 1 - x_1,$$

$$\delta((v_2, v''), b, \chi_{(u_2, u_1'')}) = 1 - x_2,$$

$$\delta((v_2, v''), b, \chi_{(u_2, u_2'')}) = x_2.$$

Let $P' = \delta(Stop(P\|T))$ and $Q' = \delta'(Stop(Q\|T))$ be the fully probabilistic result after the *stop*-transformation and applying δ and δ' to $P\|T$ and $Q\|T$, respectively. We have $\mathcal{W}_{P'}(w_1'') = \mathcal{W}_{Q'}(w_1'') = 0.5 \cdot x_1$ and $\mathcal{W}_{P'}(w_2'') = \mathcal{W}_{Q'}(w_2'') =$

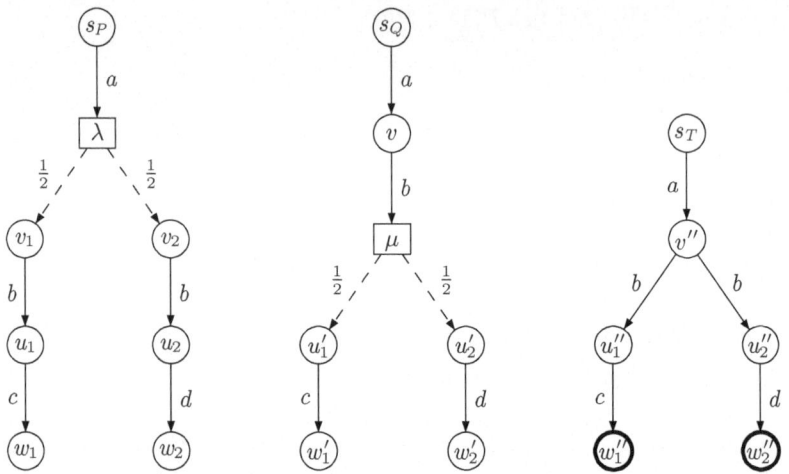

Fig. 9.9. $P \sqsubseteq_{SE}^{must} Q$, but $P \not\sqsubseteq_{SE}^{may} Q$.

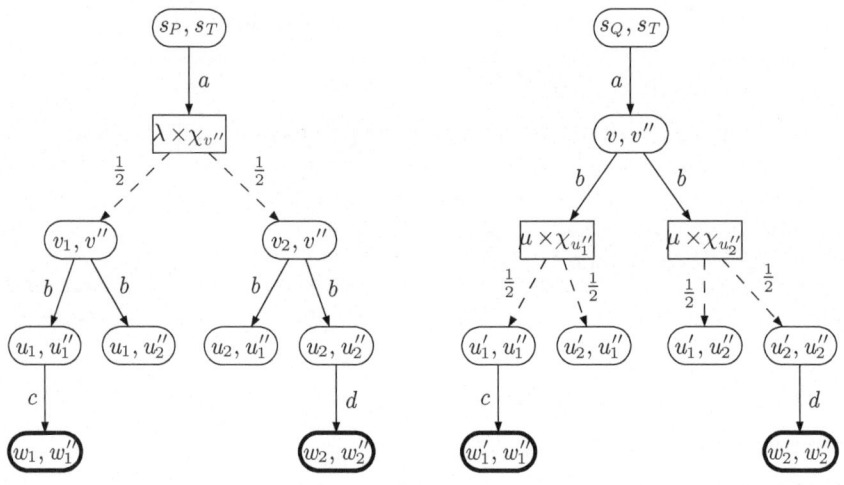

Fig. 9.10. The parallel composition of P, Q with test process T from Figure 9.9.

$0.5 \cdot x_2$. In a similar way we can find for all test processes T' a weight function δ for $Stop(P \| T')$ with regard to all possible weight functions δ' for $Stop(Q \| T')$. Thus we have $P \sqsubseteq_{SE}^{must} Q$.

It is easy to verify that $P \not\sqsubseteq_{SE}^{may} Q$. Let δ be a weight function for $Stop(P \| T)$ with

$$\delta((v_1, v''), b, \chi_{(u_1, u_1'')}) = x_1,$$
$$\delta((v_1, v''), b, \chi_{(u_1, u_2'')}) = 1 - x_1,$$
$$\delta((v_2, v''), b, \chi_{(u_2, u_1'')}) = 1 - x_2,$$
$$\delta((v_2, v''), b, \chi_{(u_2, u_2'')}) = x_2.$$

where $x_1 > 0.5$ and $x_2 \geqslant 0.5$. Then it is not possible to find a weight function for $Stop(Q \| T)$ such that the inequality of Definition 9.16 is fulfilled.

We also have $Q \sqsubseteq_{SE}^{may} P$ and $Q \sqsubseteq_{SE}^{must} P$ which can be seen in a similar way.

□

Segala also provides analogous relations where infinite test processes are applied and showed that the finite and the infinite one, respectively, coincide [Seg96]. Note that $\sqsubseteq_{SE}^{may}$ boils down to the standard may-testing relation of De Nicola and Hennessy and $\sqsubseteq_{SE}^{must}$ boils down to the standard must-testing relation (compare Section 9.10) when omitting probabilities. Furthermore, a characterization for $\sqsubseteq_{SE}^{may}$ is presented in Section 9.11.

The preorders of Jonsson and Yi compare the total success probability of two finite and τ-free probabilistic processes P and Q by applying a probabilistic test process $T \in \mathcal{T}^{pp}$ [JY02]. Their construction of a fully probabilistic process from $P \| T$ and $Q \| T$ is more restrictive than the one presented in Section 9.4.1. The weight function δ takes only values in the set $\{0, 1\}$ and there is no possibility of scheduling no transition at all, i.e. they do not add *stop*-transitions to a ⊥-state. That is, a unique transition is chosen from each state. So if we consider the discussion of Example 9.4, page 240 we are now analyzing the limits of the intervals which are specified by nondeterministic alternatives. In this case there are only two possible weight functions in Example 9.4:

$$\delta_1(s_0, a, \mu) = 1, \ \delta_1(s_0, b, \lambda) = 0 \ \text{ or } \ \delta_2(s_0, a, \mu) = 0, \ \delta_2(s_0, b, \lambda) = 1.$$

Let

$$fully^{\{0,1\}}(P) = \{\delta(P) \mid \delta \text{ is a weight function for } P \text{ with}$$
$$\delta : (S_P \times \mathsf{Act} \times Distr(S_P)) \to \{0, 1\}\}$$

be the set of all fully probabilistic process obtained from P (similar to Definition 9.4 but without the additional ⊥-state and *stop*-transitions). Note that every element of $fully^{\{0,1\}}(P)$ is also an element of $fully(P)$, if we add the ⊥-state and the *stop*-transitions weighted with zero.

It is an interesting open question whether Segala's treatment of nondeterministic choices is more expressive regarding testing relations, because Jonsson and Yi work only with "limits" of intervals of probabilities whereas Segala analyzes all possible probabilities that are provided by the process.

Definition 9.17. [JY95, JY02] Let $P, Q \in PP$ be τ-free.

- $P \sqsubseteq_{JY}^{may} Q$ iff for all $T \in \mathcal{T}^{pp}$:

$$\max_{P' \in fully^{\{0,1\}}(P \| T)} \mathcal{W}_{P'} \geqslant \max_{Q' \in fully^{\{0,1\}}(Q \| T)} \mathcal{W}_{Q'}.$$

- $P \sqsubseteq_{JY}^{must} Q$ iff for all $T \in \mathcal{T}^{pp}$:

$$\min_{P' \in fully\{0,1\}(P\|T)} \mathcal{W}_{P'} \leqslant \min_{Q' \in fully\{0,1\}(Q\|T)} \mathcal{W}_{Q'}.$$

We write $P \sqsubseteq_{JY} Q$ iff $P \sqsubseteq_{JY}^{may} Q$ and $P \sqsubseteq_{JY}^{must} Q$.

$\square$

Two processes P and Q are related in $\sqsubseteq_{JY}^{may}$ if the "best" fully probabilistic resolution of $P\|T$ has a total success probability that is at least the total success probability of the best fully probabilistic resolution of $Q\|T$. Note that $\sqsubseteq_{JY}^{may}$ boils down to ordinary simulation [Jon91] (when probabilities are omitted) which is another implementation relation for non-probabilistic processes [Jon91].

A non-probabilistic process Q simulates a non-probabilistic process P if Q can "simulate" every step of P. The converse must not necessarily hold.

Jonsson and Yi also showed that $\sqsubseteq_{JY}^{may}$ coincides with their probabilistic simulation [JY02].

Note that if $P \sqsubseteq_{JY} Q$ the process Q is bounded in some sense by P (so again we assume that Q has the role of the implementation and P the role of the specification). The total success probabilities of Q have to lie in the interval

$$[\min_{P' \in fully\{0,1\}(P\|T)} \mathcal{W}_{P'}, \max_{P' \in fully\{0,1\}(P\|T)} \mathcal{W}_{P'}].$$

Thus P is a more abstract resolution of Q and the requirements in P are fulfilled in this case because the "worst" resolution of $Q\|T$ is at least as good as the worst resolution of $P\|T$.

Example. Consider P and Q in Figure 9.9, page 254. It can be shown that $Q \sqsubseteq_{JY} P$. The composition with T, for example, yields

$$\{0.5\} = \{\mathcal{W}_{Q'} \mid Q' \in fully\{0,1\}(Q\|T)\}$$
$$\subset \{\mathcal{W}_{P'} \mid P' \in fully\{0,1\}(P\|T)\} = \{0, 0.5, 1\}.$$

$\square$

9.9 Compositional Testing of Markovian Processes

In this section, we briefly sketch a testing theory for action-labeled Markov chains as proposed by Bernardo and Cleaveland [BC00]. The idea of defining a notion of testing for aCTMCs is very similar to the approaches for fully probabilistic processes in Section 9.7 but here two quantities are taken into account when testing $M_1, M_2 \in ACTMC$ with a Markovian test process $T \in \mathcal{T}_\tau^{pa}$:

(1) For $i \in \{1, 2\}$ consider all paths α in the fully probabilistic embeddings $M_i' = \phi_{em}(M_i\|T) \in FPP$ with success state $lstate(\alpha)$ and calculate their probabilities where $Pr_{M_i\|T}^{path} := Pr_{M_i'}^{path}$[5].

---

[5] Here the path distribution of an aCTMC M is equal to the path distribution of the embedded fully probabilistic process $\phi_{em}(M)$

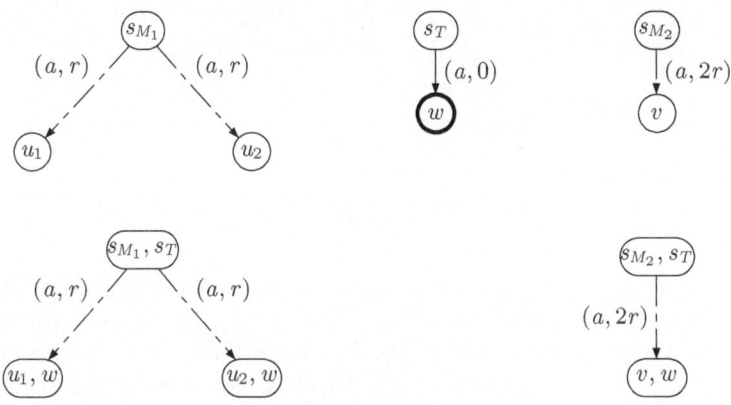

Fig. 9.11. $M_1 \sim_{BC} M_2$.

(2) The *expected duration* $t(\alpha)$ of a path α in $M_i \| T$ is given by:

$$
t(\alpha) = \begin{cases} 0 & \text{if } \alpha = s, \\ \frac{1}{E(s_n)} + t(s_0\, a_0\, s_1\, a_1 \dots a_{n-1}\, s_n) & \text{if } \alpha = s_0\, a_0\, s_1\, a_1 \dots a_{n-1}\, s_n\, a'\, s'. \end{cases}
$$

Recall that $E(s)$ is the sum of all outgoing rates of s. The expected residence time in s is given by $\frac{1}{E(s)}$. Thus, $t(\alpha)$ adds up all expected residence times of states visited by α. Let $\mathcal{W}_{M_i\|T}^{\leq x}$ denote the probability of all paths with expected duration $x \in \mathbb{R}_{\geq 0}$ that end up in a successful state, i.e.

$$
\mathcal{W}_{M_i\|T}^{\leq x} = Pr_{M_i\|T}^{path}(\{\alpha \in Path(M_i\|T) \mid t(\alpha) \leq x \wedge lstate(\alpha) \text{ is a success state}\}).
$$

Definition 9.18. [BC00] Let $M_1, M_2 \in ACTMC$.

$$
M_1 \sqsubseteq_{BC} M_2 \text{ iff } \forall\, T \in T_r^{pa} : \forall x \geq 0 : \mathcal{W}_{M_1\|T}^{\leq x} \leq \mathcal{W}_{M_2\|T}^{\leq x}.
$$

We write $M_1 \sim_{BC} M_2$ iff $M_1 \sqsubseteq_{BC} M_2$ and $M_2 \sqsubseteq_{BC} M_1$.

□

A more natural approach would conceivably be considering the probability of reaching a success state within x time units (instead of using the *expected* duration). This approach has also been considered by Bernardo and Cleaveland and it turns out that the two resulting preorders coincide [BC00].

Example. Consider the two aCTMCs M_1 and M_2 and the Markovian test process T in Figure 9.11. It is obvious that $M_1 \sim_{BC} M_2$ since T is the only "sensible" test for these two chains and the probability of reaching the success state w is 1 for both processes. The expected time of the three possible success paths (two in $M_1\|T$ and one in $M_2\|T$) is $\frac{1}{2r}$. Note that in this example the probability of reaching a success state within x time units equals $1 - e^{-x \cdot 2r}$ for both $M_1\|T$ and $M_2\|T$.

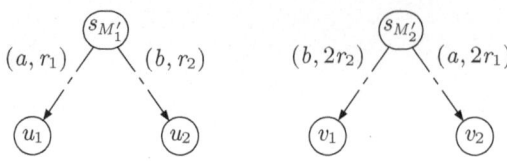

Fig. 9.12. $M_1 \not\sqsubseteq_{BC} M_2$.

The example in Figure 9.12 shows that even processes that differ only by expected duration can be different under $\sqsubseteq_{BC}$. The probability of an a-transition equals $\frac{r_1}{r_1+r_2} = \frac{2r_1}{2(r_1+r_2)}$ in M_1' and in M_2'. The probability of a b-transition is also equal for both. Thus, a preorder solely based on these transition probabilities can never distinguish M_1' and M_2' whereas $\sim_{BC}$ can because the expected residence time is $\frac{1}{r_1+r_2}$ for $s_{M_1'}$ but $\frac{1}{2(r_1+r_2)}$ for $s_{M_2'}$. Hence $M_1' \not\sqsubseteq_{BC} M_2'$.

□

9.10   Relationships Between Different Testing Relations

In this section we look more closely at the relationship between the preorders previously presented and also the relationship between the classical (non-probabilistic) testing relations of De Nicola and Hennessy [dNH84] and the probabilistic extensions in this chapter. Figure 9.14 on page 265 gives an overview of the relationships and is discussed at the end of this section.

We start with the introduction of the classical testing relations where non-probabilistic test processes are applied to non-probabilistic processes (see also Chapter 5).

Definition 9.19. The **parallel composition** of $C = (S_C, \to_C, s_C) \in NP$ and $T \in \mathcal{T}_\tau^{np}$ is a non-probabilistic process $C \| T = ((S_C \times S_T), \to, (s_C, s_T))$ with

$$(s,t) \xrightarrow{a} (s',t') \text{ iff } (s \xrightarrow{a}_C s' \wedge t \xrightarrow{a}_T t' \text{ for } a \neq \tau),$$

$$(s,t) \xrightarrow{\tau} (s',t) \text{ iff } s \xrightarrow{\tau}_C s',$$

$$(s,t) \xrightarrow{\tau} (s,t') \text{ iff } t \xrightarrow{\tau}_T t'.$$

□

Definition 9.20. [dNH84] Let $C_1, C_2 \in NP$ and $T \in \mathcal{T}_\tau^{np}$ with set $\mathcal{A}$ of success states.

- C_1 **may** T iff $\exists \alpha \in Path(C_1 \| T) : lstate(\alpha) = (s,t)$ with $t \in \mathcal{A}$, $s \in S_{C_1}$.
- C_1 **must** T iff $\forall \alpha \in Path(C_1 \| T) : lstate(\alpha) = (s,t)$ with $t \in \mathcal{A}$, $s \in S_{C_1}$.
- $C_1 \sqsubseteq_{DH}^{may} C_2$ iff $\forall T \in \mathcal{T}_\tau^{np} : C_1$ **may** $T \implies C_2$ **may** T.
- $C_1 \sqsubseteq_{DH}^{must} C_2$ iff $\forall T \in \mathcal{T}_\tau^{np} : C_1$ **must** $T \implies C_2$ $must T$.
- $C_1 \sqsubseteq_{DH} C_2$ iff $C_1 \sqsubseteq_{DH}^{may} C_2$ and $C_1 \sqsubseteq_{DH}^{must} C_2$.
- $C_1 \sim_{DH} C_2$ iff $C_1 \sqsubseteq_{DH} C_2$ and $C_2 \sqsubseteq_{DH} C_1$.

□

We call a path successful if its last state is a success state. We are applying elements of $\mathcal{T}_\tau^{np}$ here but it is easy to see that the set of test processes can be reduced to τ-free test processes without loss of expressiveness. The following steps show how to delete τ-transitions in test processes.

- Fix $T = (S_T, \to_T, s_T) \in \mathcal{T}_\tau^{np}$ with a set $\mathcal{A}$ of success states and assume without loss of generality that T has a tree-like structure, i.e. every state $t \neq s_T$ has exactly one predecessor.

- We define $prec : S_T \to S_T$ inductively by

$$prec(s) = \begin{cases} s_T & \text{if } s = s_T, \\ s & \text{if } \exists s' : s' \xrightarrow{a}_T s, a \neq \tau, \\ prec(s') & \text{if } s' \xrightarrow{a}_T s \text{ implies } a = \tau. \end{cases}$$

Note that $prec(s)$ is constructed such that s can be reached from $prec(s)$ with a sequence of internal moves.

- Let $RM_\tau(T) = (\{s \in S_T \mid \exists s' : s = prec(s')\}, \to, s_T) \in \mathcal{T}^{np}$ be a non-probabilistic test process where $\to$ is such that

$$prec(s) \xrightarrow{a} s' \text{ iff } a \neq \tau \text{ and } s \xrightarrow{a}_T s'.$$

Let $\mathcal{A}' = \{prec(s) \mid s \in \mathcal{A}\}$ be the set of success states of $RM_\tau(T)$.

Intuitively speaking, $RM_\tau(T)$ is the τ-free copy of T.

Proposition 9.21. Let $C \in NP$ and $T \in \mathcal{T}_\tau^{np}$.

C **may** T iff C **may** $RM_\tau(T)$,

C **must** T iff C **must** $RM_\tau(T)$.

Informally speaking, for each path α in $C \| T$ there is a corresponding path α' in the process $C \| RM_\tau(T)$ such that the $RM_\tau(T)$-part of α' is the τ-free copy of the T-part of α. In our setting, removing τ-transitions in non-probabilistic test processes does not change the relation $\sqsubseteq_{DH}$. So we apply the set $\mathcal{T}^{np}$ instead of $\mathcal{T}_\tau^{np}$ for $\sqsubseteq_{DH}$ and the resulting relations coincide.

$\mathcal{T}^{np}$ can be decreased to $\mathcal{T}^{np,re}$ by "splitting" a test process in several "reactive" ones:

For $T = (S_T, \to_T, s_T) \in \mathcal{T}^{np}$ with set of success states $\mathcal{A}$ let $RM_{nd}(T) \subseteq \mathcal{T}^{np,re}$ be the set of all test processes $T' = (S, \to, s_T)$ where

- $\to$ is a largest subset of $\to_T$ with

$$s \xrightarrow{a} s', s \xrightarrow{a} s'' \Rightarrow s' = s'',$$

- S is the set of all states in the process $(S_T, \to, s_T)$ reachable from s_T and

- $\mathcal{A}' = \mathcal{A} \cap S$ is the set of success states of T'.

Proposition 9.22. *Let C be a non-probabilistic process and $T \in \mathcal{T}^{np}$.*

C **may** T *iff* $\exists\, T' \in RM_{nd}(T) : C$ **may** T',

C **must** T *iff* $\forall\, T' \in RM_{nd}(T) : C$ **must** T'.

For the "if" part we split each test process $T \in \mathcal{T}^{np}$ in the set $RM_{nd}(T)$ and for the "only if" part we construct T by merging all $T' \in RM_{nd}(T)$.

Theorem 9.23. *Let C_1, C_2 be non-probabilistic processes.*

$C_1 \sqsubseteq_{DH}^{may} C_2$ *iff* $\forall\, T \in \mathcal{T}^{np,re} : C_1$ **may** $T \Longrightarrow C_2$ **may** T,

$C_1 \sqsubseteq_{DH}^{must} C_2$ *iff* $\forall\, T \in \mathcal{T}^{np,re} : C_1$ **must** $T \Longrightarrow C_2$ **must** T.

Proof: The "only if" part follows easily from Proposition 9.21 and 9.22 and the "if" part follows immediate. □

We have an alternative definition for $\sqsubseteq_{DH}$ now and reduced the set of applied test processes. To relate $\sqsubseteq_{DH}$, $\sqsubseteq_{SE}$, $\sqsubseteq_{JY}$, $\sqsubseteq_{CL}$, $\sqsubseteq_{CH}$ and $\sqsubseteq_{BC}$ or just the may and must parts (if existing), respectively, we define functions ϕ_{np} and ϕ_{pp} which map a (fully) probabilistic process P on a non-probabilistic process $\phi_{np}(P)$ and a fully probabilistic process Q on a probabilistic process $\phi_{pp}(Q)$, respectively (compare Figure 9.14), page 265.

Definition 9.24. Let $P = (S_P, \to_P, s_P) \in PP$ and $Q = (S_Q, \to_Q, s_Q) \in FPP$.

- $\phi_{np}(P) = (S_P, \to, s_P) \in NP$ is such that

$$s \xrightarrow{a} s' \text{ iff } \exists\, \mu : s \xrightarrow{a}_P \mu \text{ and } \mu(s') > 0.$$

- $\phi_{np}(Q) = (S_Q, \to', s_Q) \in NP$ is such that

$$s \xrightarrow{a}{}' s' \text{ iff } s \xrightarrow{(a,p)}_Q s' \text{ and } p > 0.$$

- $\phi_{pp}(Q) = (S_Q, \to'', s_Q) \in PP$ is such that

$$s \xrightarrow{a}{}'' \mu \text{ iff } Pr_Q^a(s) > 0 \text{ and } \mu(s') = \begin{cases} p/Pr_Q^a(s) & \text{if } s \xrightarrow{(a,p)}_Q s', \\ 0 & \text{otherwise.} \end{cases}$$

□

The function ϕ_{np} reduces a process P (Q, respectively) to its branching structure and "deletes" the probabilistic information and ϕ_{pp} maps a fully probabilistic process to a probabilistic process and discards the information of the probability of a certain action. The conditional probabilities for the target states of one action are preserved but the probabilities between the different actions are deleted. Note that only a subclass of probabilistic processes is captured by ϕ_{pp} since there is always only one transition for each action in the resulting probabilistic processes. Thus, the result of $\phi_{np}(\phi_{pp}(Q))$ is different from $\phi_{np}(Q)$ because in $\phi_{np}(\phi_{pp}(Q))$ some information about the branching structure may be lost.

Now we will consider the relationships between the preorders depicted in Figure 9.14. The numbers of the arrows connecting the preorders are equal to the numbers in the following enumeration. We have only picked out the most interesting pairs of testing relations here and not all possible combinations. To the best of our knowledge the relationship between pairs (2),(4),(6) and (8) have not been examined before.

Let $M_1, M_2 \in ACTMC$, $P, Q \in FPP$ and $\hat{P}, \hat{Q} \in PP$ and recall that ϕ_{em} maps an aCTMC to a fully probabilistic process.

(1) $(\sqsubseteq_{SE}, \sqsubseteq_{DH})$: Segala states that $\sqsubseteq_{SE}^{may}$ is a "natural" extension of $\sqsubseteq_{DH}^{may}$ [Seg96], i.e.

$$\hat{P} \sqsubseteq_{SE} \hat{Q} \implies \phi_{np}(\hat{P}) \sqsubseteq_{DH} \phi_{np}(\hat{Q}).$$

This can be seen as follows: First observe that

$$\mathcal{T}_{\tau}^{np} = \{T' \in \mathcal{T}_{\tau}^{np} \mid \exists\, T \in \mathcal{T}_{\tau}^{pp} : \phi_{np}(T) = T'\}$$

and $\phi_{np}(\hat{P}) \| T'$ is isomorphic to $\phi_{np}(\hat{P} \| T)$ for all $T \in \mathcal{T}_{\tau}^{pp}$ with $\phi_{np}(T) = T'$. Assume $\hat{P} \sqsubseteq_{SE}^{may} \hat{Q}$ and $\phi_{np}(\hat{P})$ **may** T', i.e. there exists a successful path in $\phi_{np}(\hat{P}) \| T'$. Therefore, there exists a $P' \in fully(\hat{P} \| T)$ and a success state w in T with $\mathcal{W}_{P'}(w) > 0$. But for every $P' \in fully(\hat{P} \| T)$ there exists a $Q' \in fully(\hat{Q} \| T)$ with $\mathcal{W}_{P'}(w) \leqslant \mathcal{W}_{Q'}(w)$ (compare Definition 9.16, page 253). Hence, $\mathcal{W}_{Q'}(w) > 0$ and there exists a successful path in $\phi_{np}(\hat{Q} \| T)$.

Now assume $\hat{P} \sqsubseteq_{SE}^{must} \hat{Q}$ and $\phi_{np}(\hat{P})$ *must* T', i.e. all paths in $\phi_{np}(\hat{P}) \| T'$ are successful. Hence, for all $P' \in fully(\hat{P} \| T)$ all paths in $\phi_{np}(P')$ are successful and $\sum_{w \in \mathcal{A}} \mathcal{W}_{P'}(w) = 1$ where $\mathcal{A}$ is the set of success actions in T. Since it holds for all $Q' \in fully(\hat{Q} \| T)$ that $\mathcal{W}_{P'}(w) \leqslant \mathcal{W}_{Q'}(w)$ for some P', we have $1 = \sum_{w \in \mathcal{A}} \mathcal{W}_{P'}(w) \leqslant \sum_{w \in \mathcal{A}} \mathcal{W}_{Q'}(w) = 1$. Thus all paths in Q' must be successful.

We can conclude that Segala's relations are a natural extension to the probabilistic setting. That the converse of the statement does not hold can be easily seen with Example 9.8. In Figure 9.9, page 254 we have $\phi_{np}(P) \sqsubseteq_{DH} \phi_{np}(Q)$ but $P \not\sqsubseteq_{SE}^{may} Q$.

(2) $(\sqsubseteq_{JY}, \sqsubseteq_{SE})$: We have to consider $\sqsubseteq_{SE}$ in a more restrictive way. Only τ-free probabilistic processes are now of interest and instead of $fully(\cdot)$ we take $fully^{\{0,1\}}(\cdot)$ in Definition 9.16. Furthermore, we do not compare the success probabilities of each single success state rather than the total success probability. Let the resulting relations be denoted by $\preceq_{SE}^{may}$ and $\preceq_{SE}^{must}$. It is easy to see that $\preceq_{SE}^{may}$ is *not* equivalent to $\sqsubseteq_{JY}$ or $\sqsubseteq_{JY}^{may}$. But we have that $\preceq_{SE}^{must}$ is equivalent to $\sqsubseteq_{JY}^{must}$. To see this, consider two τ-free probabilistic processes $\hat{P}$ and $\hat{Q}$ and $T \in \mathcal{T}^{pp}$ with $\hat{P} \preceq_{SE}^{must} \hat{Q}$. Then we have

$$\forall\, Q' \in fully^{\{0,1\}}(\hat{Q} \| T) : \exists\, P' \in fully^{\{0,1\}}(\hat{P} \| T) : \mathcal{W}_{P'} \leqslant \mathcal{W}_{Q'}.$$

Now let Q^{min} be the fully probabilistic process with the smallest success probability, i.e. $W_{Q^{min}} = \min_{Q'}\{W_{Q'} \mid Q' \in fully^{\{0,1\}}(\hat{Q}\|T)\}$. Let P'' be the process such that the equation above holds with $Q' = Q^{min}$. Then we have

$$\min_{P'} W_{P'} \leqslant W_{P''} \leqslant W_{Q^{min}}.$$

So $\hat{P} \sqsubseteq_{JY}^{must} \hat{Q}$. The proof for deriving $\hat{P} \sqsubseteq_{JY}^{must} \hat{Q}$ from $\hat{P} \preceq_{SE}^{must} \hat{Q}$ is similar and omitted here.

(3) $(\sqsubseteq_{JY}, \sqsubseteq_{DH})$: Jonsson and Yi defined a testing relation which boils down to ordinary simulation but not to the ordinary testing relation, i.e.

$$\hat{P} \sqsubseteq_{JY} \hat{Q} \not\Longrightarrow \phi_{np}(\hat{P}) \sqsubseteq_{DH} \phi_{np}(\hat{Q}).$$

It is easy to construct a counterexample where $\hat{P} \sqsubseteq_{JY} \hat{Q}$ and $\phi_{np}(\hat{P}) \not\sqsubseteq_{DH}^{may} \phi_{np}(\hat{Q})$. But $\sqsubseteq_{JY}^{must}$ boils down to $\sqsubseteq_{DH}^{must}$ which is not surprising since we have relationship (1) and (2).

(4) $(\sqsubseteq_{CH}, \sqsubseteq_{DH})$: We show that

$$P \sqsubseteq_{CH} Q \Longrightarrow \phi_{np}(P) \sqsubseteq_{DH} \phi_{np}(Q).$$

Recall that for $\sqsubseteq_{CH}$ test processes $T \in \mathcal{T}^{np,re}$ are applied (compare Definition 9.14) and with Theorem 9.23 also for $\sqsubseteq_{DH}$. Assume $P \sqsubseteq_{CH} Q$ and $\phi_{np}(P)$ **may** T, i.e. there exists a path α in $\phi_{np}(P)\|T$ ending up in a success state w. Since $T \in \mathcal{T}^{np,re}$, we have that $trace(\alpha) = \beta$ corresponds to a single path in T, i.e. there is only a single path α_T in T with $trace(\alpha_T) = \beta$. Furthermore, all paths α' in $Q\|T$ with $trace(\alpha') = \beta$ lead to w. Together with $P \sqsubseteq_{CH} Q$ we derive $0 < Pr_{P\|T}^{trace}(\beta) \leqslant Pr_{Q\|T}^{trace}(\beta)$. So there is at least one successful path in $Q\|T$ with a nonzero probability and $\phi_{np}(P) \sqsubseteq_{DH}^{may} \phi_{np}(Q)$ follows. With a similar argument we can derive that $\phi_{np}(P) \sqsubseteq_{DH}^{must} \phi_{np}(Q)$.

(5) $(\sqsubseteq_{CL}, \sqsubseteq_{DH})$: It holds [CSZ92]

$$P \sqsubseteq_{CL} Q \Longrightarrow \phi_{np}(P) \sqsubseteq_{DH} \phi_{np}(Q).$$

First recall that $\phi_{np}(P)$ is not equal to $\phi_{np}(\phi_{pp}(P))$ in general. So we cannot derive this statement from (1) and (6). We show that this statement is true as follows. First observe that $P \sqsubseteq_{CL} Q$ iff

$$\mathcal{W}_{P\|T} \geqslant p \Longrightarrow \mathcal{W}_{Q\|T} \geqslant p, \,\forall\, T \in \mathcal{T}_\tau^{fp}, \forall\, p \in [0,1].$$

Furthermore, we have that $\phi_{np}(P\|T)$ is isomorphic to $\phi_{np}(P) \| \phi_{np}(T)$ and

$$\mathcal{T}^{np,re} \subset \{T' \in \mathcal{T}_\tau^{np} \mid \exists\, T \in \mathcal{T}_\tau^{fp} : \phi_{np}(T) = T'\}.$$

Moreover, we have that for each $T' \in \mathcal{T}_\tau^{np}$ there exists at least one test process $T \in \mathcal{T}_\tau^{fp}$ with $\phi_{np}(T) = T'$. Hence, if $P \sqsubseteq_{CL} Q$ and $\phi_{np}(P)$ **may** T then there exists a successful path in $\phi_{np}(P\|T)$ and $\mathcal{W}_{P\|T}(x) = p$ with $p \in$

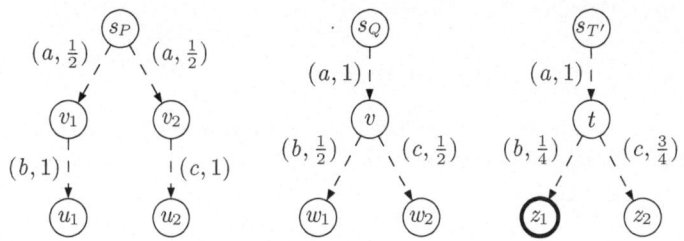

Fig. 9.13. $P \sqsubseteq_{CH} Q$ but $P \not\sqsubseteq_{CL} Q$.

$(0, 1]$ and so $\mathcal{W}_{Q\|T}(x) \geqslant p$ which means that we have also a successful path in $\phi_{np}(Q\|T)$ and $\phi_{np}(Q)$ **may** T. If all paths in $\phi_{np}(P\|T)$ are successful then $\mathcal{W}_{P\|T}(x) = 1 = \mathcal{W}_{Q\|T}(x)$ and we can conclude that all paths are successful in $\phi_{np}(Q\|T)$, so $\phi_{np}(P) \sqsubseteq_{DH}^{must} \phi_{np}(Q)$.

Note that, of course, the opposite of this statement does not hold.

(6) $(\sqsubseteq_{CL}, \sqsubseteq_{CH})$: We show that

$$P \sqsubseteq_{CL} Q \Longrightarrow P \sqsubseteq_{CH} Q$$

holds. First, recall that $\sqsubseteq_{CH}$ compares for each $T \in \mathcal{T}^{np,re}$ the trace distribution of $P\|T$ and $Q\|T$ whereas for $\sqsubseteq_{CL}$ the success probabilities in $P\|T$ and $Q\|T$ are compared for each $T \in \mathcal{T}_{\mathcal{T}}^{fp}$. Now assume $P \sqsubseteq_{CL} Q$ and $T \in \mathcal{T}^{np,re}$. We have to show that for all $\alpha \in \mathsf{Act}^*$

$$Pr_{P\|T}^{trace}(\alpha) \leqslant Pr_{Q\|T}^{trace}(\alpha).$$

For a given trace α in T there is only one single prefix β_1 of a path $\beta = \beta_1\beta_2 \in Path(T)$ with $trace(\beta_1) = \alpha$. Then there exists $T' \in \mathcal{T}^{fp}$ such that $\phi_{np}(T') = T$ and $Pr^a(t) = 1/|\{b \in \mathsf{Act} \mid Pr^b(t) > 0\}|$ for all $t \in S_T = S_{T'}$. Let t' with $\beta_1 = s_0\, a_1 \ldots a_n\, t'$ be the only success state of T'. Then

$$Pr_{P\|T}^{trace}(\alpha) = Pr_{P\|T'}^{trace}(\alpha) = \mathcal{W}_{P\|T'} \leqslant \mathcal{W}_{Q\|T'} = Pr_{Q\|T'}^{trace}(\alpha) = Pr_{Q\|T}^{trace}(\alpha).$$

Hence $P \sqsubseteq_{CH} Q$. Example 6 shows two fully probabilistic processes which are distinguished by $\sqsubseteq_{CL}$ but not by $\sqsubseteq_{CH}$.

Example. Consider Figure 9.13. We have $P \sim_{CH} Q$ but P and Q can be distinguished by $\sqsubseteq_{CL}$ by applying the test process T' because if z_1 is the only success state then $\frac{1}{2} = \mathcal{W}_{P\|T'} > \mathcal{W}_{Q\|T'} = \frac{1}{4}$.

$\square$

(7) $(\sqsubseteq_{BC}, \sqsubseteq_{DH})$: Bernardo and Cleaveland showed that

$$M_1 \sqsubseteq_{BC} M_2 \Longrightarrow \phi_{np}(\phi_{em}(M_1)) \sqsubseteq_{DH} \phi_{np}(\phi_{em}(M_2)) \text{ [BC00]}.$$

Here, this follows also directly from (5) and (8). The strictness follows from either the strictness of (5) or the strictness of (8). For a counter example see also [BC00].

(8) $(\sqsubseteq_{BC}, \sqsubseteq_{CH})$: We show here that

$$M_1 \sqsubseteq_{BC} M_2 \Longrightarrow \phi_{em}(M_1) \sqsubseteq_{CH} \phi_{em}(M_2)$$

holds which has not been considered by Bernardo and Cleaveland [BC00] or Christoff [Chr90]. Assume $M_1 \sqsubseteq_{BC} M_2$. We have to show that for each $T \in \mathcal{T}^{np,re}$, $\alpha \in \mathsf{Act}^*$

$$Pr^{trace}_{\phi_{em}(M_1)\|T}(\alpha) \leqslant Pr^{trace}_{\phi_{em}(M_2)\|T}(\alpha).$$

For a given T we set $T' = (S_T, \to, s_T) \in \mathcal{T}^{pa}_\tau$ where $\to$ is such that

$$t \xrightarrow{a}_T t' \text{ iff } t \xrightarrow{(a,0)} t' \text{ for } a \in \mathsf{Act}.$$

For a given trace α in T there is only one single prefix β_1 of a path $\beta = \beta_1\beta_2 \in Path(T)$ with $trace(\beta_1) = \alpha$. It is easy to verify that

$$Pr^{trace}_{M_1\|T'}(\alpha) = Pr^{trace}_{\phi_{em}(M_1)\|T}(\alpha).$$

So if the last state of the sequence β_1 is the only success state in T', we can derive

$$Pr^{trace}_{M_1\|T'}(\alpha) = \mathcal{W}^{\leqslant x}_{M_1\|T'} \leqslant \mathcal{W}^{\leqslant x}_{M_2\|T'} = Pr^{trace}_{M_2\|T'}(\alpha).$$

Hence we have $\phi_{em}(M_1) \sqsubseteq_{CH} \phi_{em}(M_2)$.

$\sqsubseteq_{BC}$ is strictly finer than $\sqsubseteq_{CH}$ which can be seen by a simple counterexample similar to example 9.7.2 because we can apply test processes with τ-transitions.

(9) $(\sqsubseteq_{BC}, \sqsubseteq_{CL})$: To relate the Markovian testing relation $\sqsubseteq_{BC}$ and the fully probabilistic testing relation $\sqsubseteq_{CL}$, we have to consider the sets of applied test processes. For $\sqsubseteq_{BC}$ some kind of "passive" test processes are used because external actions must have rate zero. Only τ-transitions have nonzero rates. For $\sqsubseteq_{CL}$ all transitions in test processes are equipped with probabilities. Since probabilistic test processes have more distinguishing power than non-probabilistic test processes (see relationship (6)), we have

$$M_1 \sqsubseteq_{BC} M_2 \not\Longrightarrow \phi_{em}(M_1) \sqsubseteq_{CL} \phi_{em}(M_2)$$

in general. It is easy to construct a counterexample (similar to Example 6). Of course, the converse of the statement is also wrong, because of the additional requirement on the expected duration of a successful path for $\sqsubseteq_{BC}$. So $\sqsubseteq_{BC}$ and $\sqsubseteq_{CL}$ are incomparable. Bernardo and Cleaveland defined $\sqsubseteq_{CL}$ in a restrictive way such that the statement holds [BC00].

Figure 9.14 shows a diagram of the relationships discussed above.

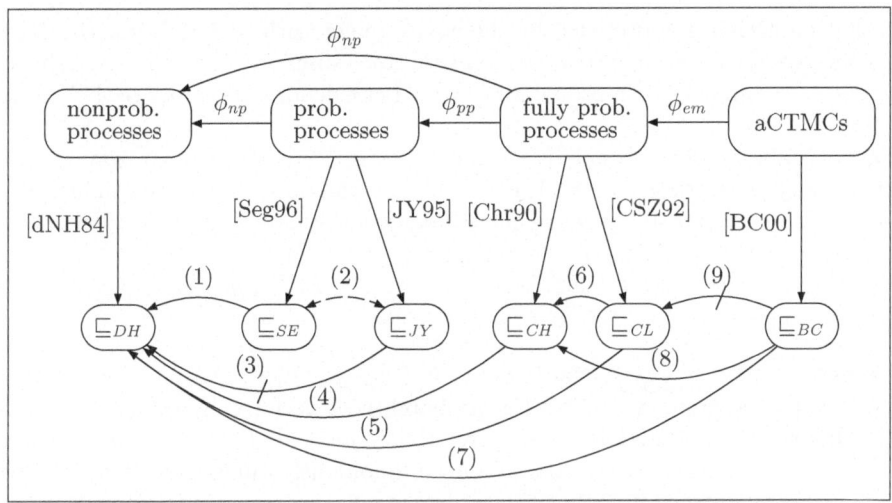

Fig. 9.14. Relationships between the different preorders: The upper horizontal arrows show the mappings between the different classes of processes. The vertical arrows symbolize the different approaches in defining testing relations for each class. A horizontal arrow is drawn from relation A to relation B if A implies B at the corresponding "probabilistic information level". Crossed arrows symbolize that A does *not* imply B and arrows are dotted if the implication is true with further restrictions.

9.11 Characterizations of Probabilistic Testing Relations

In this section, we briefly sketch characterizations for the preorders $\sqsubseteq_{CL}$, $\sqsubseteq_{CH}$ (Section 9.7), $\sqsubseteq_{SE}$, $\sqsubseteq_{JY}$ (Section 9.8) and $\sqsubseteq_{BC}$ (Section 9.9). Cleaveland et al. found a characterization for $\sqsubseteq_{CL}$ by *probabilistic traces* [CSZ92] and a very similar concept is used for $\sqsubseteq_{CH}$ and $\sqsubseteq_{BC}$ which are characterized by *extended traces* [Chr90, BC00]. $\sqsubseteq_{SE}^{may}$ can be characterized by the *trace distribution precongruence* [Seg96] and $\sqsubseteq_{JY}^{may}$ coincides with *probabilistic simulation* [JY02]. Figure 9.15, page 270 gives an overview of the different characterizations and is discussed at the end of this section.

9.11.1 Probabilistic and Extended Traces

Let μ_0 be the weight function on Act_τ with $\mu_0(a) = 0$ for all $a \in \mathsf{Act}_\tau$ and let $\mathcal{D} = Distr^*(\mathsf{Act}_\tau) \cup \{\mu_0\}$, where $Distr^*(\mathsf{Act}_\tau)$ is the set of all distributions μ over Act_τ with a finite support $supp(\mu) = \{s \in S : \mu(s) > 0\}$.

Definition 9.25. A **probabilistic trace** is a sequence

$$\alpha = (a_1, \mu_1)\,(a_2, \mu_2)\,\ldots(a_n, \mu_n),\, a_i \in \mathsf{Act}_\tau, \mu_i \in \mathcal{D} \text{ for } 1 \leqslant i \leqslant n.$$

$\square$

A probabilistic trace represents a trace $a_1\, a_2\,\ldots a_n$ with the restriction that the set of possible actions at step i is $supp(\mu_i)$ instead of Act_τ. The intuitive idea is that an action a is provided by the environment with probability $\mu_i(a)$. The occurrence of the action τ in a probabilistic trace simulates that τ is "performed by the environment" with probability $\mu_i(\tau)$. Let ϵ denote the empty probabilistic trace.

The probability of a probabilistic trace is computed in a similar way as the probability of a trace (see Section 9.3.1) but with a different "normalization factor" in each step because we must take into account the probability of an action in each step. So we have some kind of conditional probability.

We present some helpful definitions now. Let $P \in FPP$, $\mu \in \mathcal{D}$, $s, s' \in S_P$ and $i \in \mathbb{N}$.

- Let $v(s, \mu) = \sum_{a \in \mathsf{Act}} Pr_P^a(s) \cdot \mu(a) + Pr_P^\tau(s) + \mu(\tau)$ be a normalization factor. The first summand denotes the probability of performing an observational action a that is provided with probability $\mu(a)$. $Pr_P^\tau(s)$ is the probability that P performs an internal action autonomously (independent of μ) and $\mu(\tau)$ is the probability that the environment performs τ independently.

- Let $Pr_P^{silent}(s, i, s', \mu)$ denote the probability of reaching s' via i τ-transitions from P "under the condition μ" when starting in s:

$$Pr_P^{silent}(s, 0, s', \mu) = \begin{cases} 1 & \text{if } s = s', \\ 0 & \text{otherwise.} \end{cases}$$

$$Pr_P^{silent}(s, i+1, s', \mu) = \begin{cases} \frac{1}{v(s,\mu)} \cdot \sum_{\hat{s} \in S_P} Pr_P^\tau(s, \hat{s}) \cdot Pr_P^{silent}(\hat{s}, i, s', \mu) \\ \qquad\qquad\qquad\qquad\qquad\qquad \text{if } v(s, \mu) > 0, \\ 0 \qquad\qquad\qquad\qquad\qquad\quad \text{otherwise.} \end{cases}$$

Let

$$Pr_P^{silent}(s, s', \mu) = \sum_{i=0}^{\infty} Pr_P^{silent}(s, i, s', \mu)$$

denote the probability of reaching s' via a sequence of τ-transitions when starting in s "under the condition μ". Note that $Pr_P^{silent}(s, s', \mu)$ is well-defined because P is divergence-free.

- For $a \neq \tau$ let

$$Pr_P^a(s, s', \mu) = \sum_{\hat{s}: v(\hat{s}, \mu) > 0} Pr_P^{silent}(s, \hat{s}, \mu) \cdot Pr_P^a(\hat{s}, s') \cdot \frac{\mu(a)}{v(\hat{s}, \mu)}.$$

be the probability of a "weak" a-transition, i.e. s' is reached via a (possibly empty) sequence of τ-transitions followed by one a-transition when starting in s.

For a "weak" τ-transition performed "by the environment" (simulated by μ) we have

$$Pr_P^\tau(s, s', \mu) = Pr^{silent}(s, s', \mu) \cdot \frac{\mu(\tau)}{v(s', \mu)}.$$

- Let α be a probabilistic trace in P. The probability of α starting in the state s is inductively defined by

$$Pr_P^{ptrace}(s, \alpha) = \begin{cases} 1 & \text{if } \alpha = \epsilon, \\ \displaystyle\sum_{s' \in S_P} Pr_P^a(s, s', \mu) \cdot Pr_P^{ptrace}(s', \alpha') & \text{if } \alpha = (a, \mu) \, \alpha'. \end{cases}$$

- Let $Pr_P^{ptrace}(\alpha) = Pr_P^{ptrace}(s_P, \alpha)$ (where s_P is the initial state of P) denote the probability of a probabilistic trace α in P.

Definition 9.26. [CSZ92] Let $P, Q \in FPP$.

$P \preceq^{ptrace} Q$ iff for all probabilistic traces $\alpha : Pr_P^{ptrace}(\alpha) \leqslant Pr_Q^{ptrace}(\alpha)$.

$\square$

Note that opposed to Cleaveland et al. we do not allow synchronization over τ-actions, so $\preceq^{ptrace}$ is slightly different from the corresponding relation in [CSZ92].

Theorem 9.27. *[CSZ92] For all fully probabilistic processes P, Q:*

$P \preceq^{ptrace} Q$ *iff* $P \sqsubseteq_{CL} Q$.

Proof sketch: The idea for proving $\sqsubseteq_{CL} \subseteq \preceq^{ptrace}$ is to construct $T(\alpha) \in \mathcal{T}_\tau^{fp}$ from a given probabilistic trace α such that the success probability in $P \| T(\alpha)$ (and $Q \| T(\alpha)$, respectively) is equal to the probability of α in P (and Q, respectively).
The proof of $\preceq^{ptrace} \subseteq \sqsubseteq_{CL}$ relies heavily on the fact that only a subset of all possible fully probabilistic test processes is necessary to decide whether $P \sqsubseteq_{CL} Q$ or not. These test processes are called *essential* and an essential test process T contains only paths that are successful in $P \| T$ (and $Q \| T$, respectively) or "stop" after one step when reaching success is impossible. For details we refer to the work of Cleaveland et al. [CSZ92]. Note that the set of essential test processes of P is still infinite. Thus deciding $P \sqsubseteq_{CL} Q$ is not practical. $\square$
Christoff gives a characterization by *extended traces* for his testing relations [Chr90]. Bernardo and Cleaveland show that $\sqsubseteq_{BC}$ can also be characterized by such traces [BC00]. This is not surprising since non-probabilistic test processes (used by Christoff) and Markovian test processes used in [BC00] are very similar and an extended trace "simulates" in fact a non-probabilistic test process. Let $\mathcal{D}'$ be the set of all weight functions σ over Act_τ with $\sigma(a) \in \{0, 1\}$ for $a \neq \tau$ and $\sigma(\tau) = 0$.

Definition 9.28. An **extended trace** is a sequence

$$\alpha = (a_1, \sigma_1)(a_2, \sigma_2) \ldots (a_n, \sigma_n), a_i \in \mathsf{Act}, \sigma_i \in \mathcal{D}' \text{ for } 1 \leqslant i \leqslant n.$$

$\square$

Note that we restrict to τ-free extended traces here because for $\sqsubseteq_{CH}$ we apply τ-free test processes and a characterization of $\sqsubseteq_{BC}$ including test processes that can perform τ-transitions has not been presented by Bernardo and Cleaveland. It is clear that a characterization for $\sqsubseteq_{BC}$ covering $\mathcal{T}_{\tau}^{pa}$ instead of $\mathcal{T}^{pa}$ can be constructed in a similar way as for $\sqsubseteq_{CH}$ by taking weight functions σ_i with $\sigma_i(\tau) \in [0,1]$ and $\sigma_i(a) \in \{0,1\}$ for $a \neq \tau$.

The definition of the probability $Pr_P^{etrace}(\alpha)$ for an extended trace α in P is equal to the definition of $Pr_P^{ptrace}(\alpha)$ as defined just before if the second component σ of each step in α is in $\mathcal{D}'$ instead of $\mathcal{D}$, i.e. by replacing the probabilistic trace α by an extended trace in all the previous definitions we obtain $Pr_P^{etrace}(\alpha)$.

Theorem 9.29. *[Chr90] Let $P, Q \in FPP$.*

- $P \sqsubseteq_{CH}^{tr} Q$ *iff for all finite traces β:*

$$Pr_P^{trace}(\beta) > 0 \text{ implies } Pr_Q^{trace}(\beta) > 0.$$

- $P \sqsubseteq_{CH}^{wte} Q$ *iff for all extended traces α and all $\sigma \in \mathcal{D}'$:*

$$\sum_{a \in \mathsf{Act}} Pr_P^{etrace}(\alpha\,(a,\sigma)) \leqslant \sum_{a \in \mathsf{Act}} Pr_Q^{etrace}(\alpha\,(a,\sigma)).$$

- $P \sqsubseteq_{CH}^{ste} Q$ *iff for all extended traces α:*

$$Pr_P^{etrace}(\alpha) \leqslant Pr_Q^{etrace}(\alpha).$$

$\square$

Note that $\sqsubseteq_{CH}^{tr}$ was defined applying non-probabilistic test processes that are sequential. This kind of test processes distinguish processes with regard to the traces they can perform. The probabilistic information is not taken into account. $\sqsubseteq_{CH}^{wte}$ and $\sqsubseteq_{CH}^{ste}$ are characterized by extended traces since every test process $T \in \mathcal{T}^{np,re}$ can be simulated by an extended trace.

To formulate a characterization for $\sqsubseteq_{BC}$, we have to define an additional function that tells us the expected duration of an extended trace in an aCTMC. The details are omitted here because it is very similar in spirit to calculating the probability of an extended trace. Two aCTMCs M_1 and M_2 are related iff for all extended traces α and all $t \in \mathbb{R}_{\geqslant 0}$ the probability of α in M_1 with a duration $\leqslant t$ is at least the probability of α in M_2 with a duration $\leqslant t$. It turns out that the resulting relation coincides with $\sqsubseteq_{BC}$ [BC00].

9.11.2 Trace Distributions

Let $P \in PP$ and $Pr_{P'}^{trace}$ the probability measure for traces in $P' \in fully(P)$ as defined in Section 9.3. We define the set of all

- trace distributions of P by $tdistr(P) = \{Pr_{P'}^{trace} \mid P' \in fully(P)\}$.
- finite trace distributions of P by

$$ftdistr(P) = \{Pr_{P'}^{trace} \mid P' \in fully(P) \wedge \exists k \in \mathbb{N} : Pr_{P'}^{trace}(C_k) = 1\},$$

where C_k denotes the set of all traces in P' of length at most k. So all the probability is concentrated on finite traces.

Definition 9.30. Let $P, Q \in PP$.

- The **trace distribution preorder** $\preceq^{td}$ is given by

  $$P \preceq^{td} Q \text{ iff } tdistr(P) \subseteq tdistr(Q).$$

- The **finite trace distribution preorder** $\preceq^{ftd}$ is given by

  $$P \preceq^{ftd} Q \text{ iff } ftdistr(P) \subseteq ftdistr(Q).$$

- The **trace distribution precongruence** $\preceq^{tp}$ (**finite trace distribution precongruence** $\preceq^{ftp}$, respectively) is the coarsest precongruence with respect to $\|$[6] that is contained in $\preceq^{td}$ ($\preceq^{ftd}$, respectively).

$\square$

Segala shows that $\preceq^{td}$ and $\preceq^{ftd}$ coincide [Seg96]. This is also stated by Stoelinga and Vaandrager as "Approximation Induction Principle" [SV03]. Furthermore we have that $\preceq^{ftd}$ and $\preceq^{td}$ characterize $\sqsubseteq_{SE}^{may}$.

Theorem 9.31. *[Seg96] Let P, Q be probabilistic processes.*

$$P \sqsubseteq_{SE}^{may} Q \text{ iff } P \preceq^{tp} Q \text{ iff } P \preceq^{ftp} Q.$$

$\square$

Segala also provides a characterization by *failure distributions* for $\sqsubseteq_{SE}^{must}$ [Seg96]. Failures are similar to traces but end in a set of actions that cannot be performed by the last state. The details of this characterization are omitted here because it is similar to the case of trace distributions.

Stoelinga and Vaandrager present an intuitive "testing scenario" (also known as button pushing experiment) and proved that the resulting relation is equivalent to the trace distribution preorder [SV03]. Note that in a sense this also motivates Segala's may-preorder due to theorem 9.31.

We have also a characterization of $\sqsubseteq_{JY}$ by structures called "chains of a process" that are similar to traces [JY02]. A very interesting result is the characterization of $\sqsubseteq_{JY}^{may}$ by probabilistic simulation as briefly presented in the following section.

9.11.3   Probabilistic Simulation

The idea of ordinary simulation is to prove that an implementation Q refines an abstract specification P in such a way that required properties are fulfilled [Jon91]. So Q is simulated by P if "every step in Q can be simulated by a step in P" but not necessarily vice versa. In the probabilistic setting, simulation relations have been defined amongst others by Jonsson [JGL91] and Segala [SL94]. In 2002, Jonsson and Yi proposed an alternative definition of probabilistic simulation which coincides with their probabilistic may-testing preorder [JY02].

---

[6] A relation $\mathcal{R}$ is a *precongruence* with respect to $\|$ if $P \mathcal{R} Q$ implies $(P \| \hat{P}) \mathcal{R} (Q \| \hat{P})$ for an arbitrary probabilistic process $\hat{P}$. Note that $\|$ denotes the parallel composition operator from Definition 9.8 here.

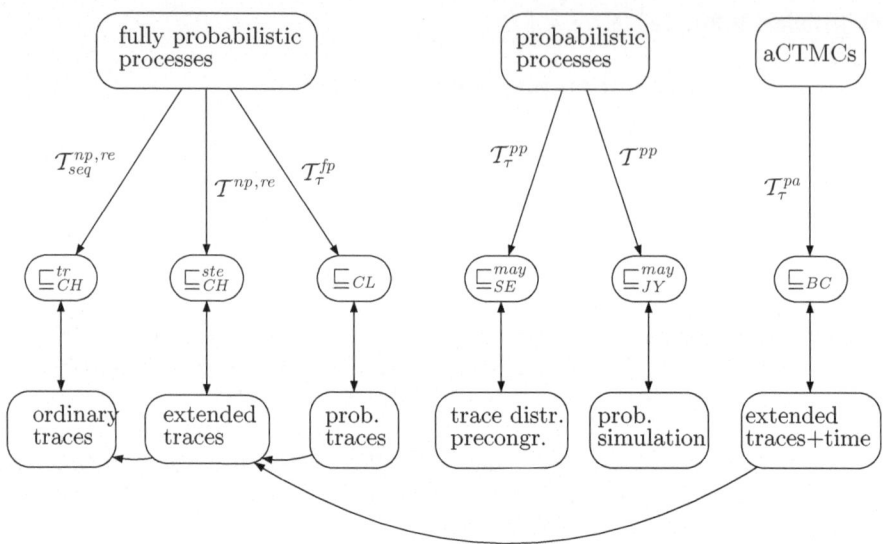

Fig. 9.15. Characterizations for probabilistic testing relations: The upper vertical arrows connect the respective class of processes with the matching testing relation and the label corresponds to the applied set of test processes. The lower vertical arrows connect each testing relation with the respective characterization and the lower horizontal arrows show that extended traces are a special case of probabilistic traces and a special case of extended traces with an additional time requirement. Moreover, ordinary traces are a special case of extended traces.

Figure 9.15 shows the characterizations presented in this section and the applied sets of test processes, respectively. Moreover, the underlying models are depicted. Of course, extended traces, enriched with a time function, boil down to ordinary extended traces and probabilistic traces are the probabilistic extension of extended traces. It is clear that extended traces are an extension of ordinary traces.

9.12   Connecting Testing and Probabilistic Bisimulation

In the following, we discuss the work of Larsen and Skou that connects an intuitive testing approach for a subclass of probabilistic processes with *probabilistic bisimulation* [LS91]. Larsen and Skou apply non-probabilistic test processes to τ-free reactive probabilistic processes . A probabilistic process $P = (S_P, \rightarrow_P, s_P)$ is *reactive* if $s \xrightarrow{a}_P \mu$ and $s \xrightarrow{a}_P \lambda$ implies $\mu = \lambda$ for all $s \in S_P$. The intuitive idea is that in each step the external environment chooses an action and there is no "internal" nondeterminism between two transitions with equal actions. For $s \xrightarrow{a} \mu$ we put $\mu_{s,a} = \mu$. We write $s \xrightarrow{a}\!\!\!\!/ \ _P$ if there exists no $\mu_{s,a}$.

Larsen and Skou defined the probabilistic bisimulation equivalence such that for two bisimulation equivalent states the probability to move with an a-transition to an equivalence class E is equal for all $a \in Act_\tau$.

Definition 9.32. [LS91] Let P be a reactive probabilistic process. An equivalence relation $\mathcal{R} \subseteq S_P \times S_P$ is a **probabilistic bisimulation** iff for all $(s, s') \in \mathcal{R}$ we have that

$$\sum_{v \in E} \mu_{s,a}(v) = \sum_{v \in E} \mu_{s',a}(v) \text{ for all } E \in S_P/\mathcal{R}, a \in \mathsf{Act}_\tau,$$

where $S_P/\mathcal{R}$ denotes the quotient space of $\mathcal{R}$.

Two reactive probabilistic processes P, Q are **probabilistically bisimilar** if there exists a probabilistic bisimulation $\mathcal{R}$ on $(S_P \cup S_Q)$ such that (s_P, s_Q) are in a probabilistic bisimulation in the probabilistic process $(S_P \cup S_Q, \rightarrow_P \cup \rightarrow_Q, s_P)$[7]. We write $P \sim^{bs} Q$ in this case.

□

The probabilistic bisimulation extends the standard bisimulation [HM85] for non-probabilistic processes. It was motivated by a probabilistic modal logic *PML* [LS91] that is a probabilistic extension of the Hennessy-Milner logic *HML*, also introduced by Hennessy and Milner [HM85]. Two non-probabilistic processes (probabilistic processes) are bisimilar (probabilistic bisimilar, respectively) if and only if they satisfy exactly the same *HML* (*PML*, respectively) formulas.

For a more detailed discussion about probabilistic bisimulation see the work of Baier et al. [BHKW03] where also a weak[8] notion of $\sim^{bs}$ is defined and where the relationship between probabilistic (bi-)simulation and probabilistic logics is examined in the discrete-time and also in the continuous-time case.

In the following, we present a testing approach that is, opposed to the previous sections, not based on the parallel composition of a test process and a tested process and it turns out that this approach yields a relation equivalent to probabilistic bisimulation. Without loss of generality we can assume that $T = (S_T, \rightarrow_T, s_T) \in \mathcal{T}^{np}$ has a tree-like structure, i.e. each $t \in S_T, t \neq s_T$ has exactly one predecessor. We define a set of *observations* O_T that are produced if T is applied:

Definition 9.33. Let $O_T(s)$ denote the set of *observations* obtained from the state $t \in S_T$ inductively given by $O_T(t) = \{1_\omega\}$ if t is terminal and

$$O_T(t) = (\{0_{a_1}\} \cup \{1_{a_1} : o \mid o \in O_T(t_1)\}) \times \ldots \times (\{0_{a_n}\} \cup \{1_{a_n} : o \mid o \in O_T(t_n)\})$$

if $t \xrightarrow{a_i}_T t_i, 1 \leqslant i \leqslant n$. Let $O_T = O_T(s_T)$.

□

Note that O_T is well-defined since test processes are finite-state, finitely branching and acyclic. Intuitively, 1_a denotes that action a is observed and 0_a that a is *not* observed. The observed actions are concatenated with ":". The observation $1_a : o$, for instance, means that a is observed and followed by the observation o. If the test process branches, the observation is a tuple. For example, $1_a : (0_a, 1_b)$ means that first action a is observed and then for the a-branch (in T) no a-action is performed (0_a) and for the b-branch a b-action is executed (1_b). Of course, $a = b$ is possible.

---

[7] Without loss of generality we can assume that $S_P \cap S_Q = \emptyset$.

[8] "Weak" in the sense that τ-actions are treated in a special way.

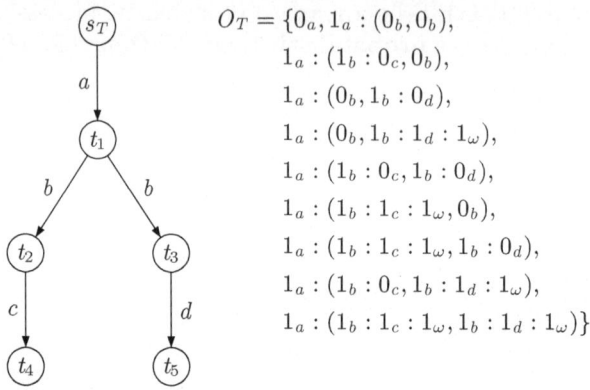

$$O_T = \{0_a, 1_a : (0_b, 0_b),$$
$$1_a : (1_b : 0_c, 0_b),$$
$$1_a : (0_b, 1_b : 0_d),$$
$$1_a : (0_b, 1_b : 1_d : 1_\omega),$$
$$1_a : (1_b : 0_c, 1_b : 0_d),$$
$$1_a : (1_b : 1_c : 1_\omega, 0_b),$$
$$1_a : (1_b : 1_c : 1_\omega, 1_b : 0_d),$$
$$1_a : (1_b : 0_c, 1_b : 1_d : 1_\omega),$$
$$1_a : (1_b : 1_c : 1_\omega, 1_b : 1_d : 1_\omega)\}$$

Fig. 9.16. The set of observations O_T for a test process T.

Example. Figure 9.16 shows $T \in \mathcal{T}^{np}$ and the observations O_T.

□

The probability of an observation can be computed using the following definition.

Definition 9.34. The probability distribution $Pr_{P,T}^{Obs} : (O_T, S_P) \to [0, 1]$ assigns a probability to every observation $o \in O_T$ of a test process $T \in \mathcal{T}^{np}$ applied to a state in a τ-free reactive probabilistic process P. It is defined inductively on the length of o.

$$Pr_{P,T}^{Obs}(1_\omega, s) = 1, \forall s \in S_P.$$

$$Pr_{P,T}^{Obs}(0_a, s) = \begin{cases} 1 & \text{if } s \xrightarrow{a}\!\!\!\!/\;\; P, \\ 0 & \text{otherwise.} \end{cases}$$

$$Pr_{P,T}^{Obs}(1_a : o, s) = \begin{cases} 0 & \text{if } s \xrightarrow{a}\!\!\!\!/\;\; P, \\ \sum_{s' \in S_P} \mu_{s,a}(s') \cdot Pr_{P,T}^{Obs}(o, s') & \text{otherwise.} \end{cases}$$

$$Pr_{P,T}^{Obs}((o_1, \ldots, o_n), s) = \prod_{i=1}^n Pr_{P,T}^{Obs}(o_i, s).$$

Let $Pr_{P,T}^{Obs}(o) = Pr_{P,T}^{Obs}(o, s_P)$ for all $o \in O_T$ and for $O' \subseteq O_T$

$$Pr_{P,T}^{Obs}(O') = \sum_{o \in O'} Pr_{P,T}^{Obs}(o).$$

□

It is easy to see that $Pr_{P,T}^{Obs}$ is indeed a probability distribution, i.e. $Pr_{P,T}^{Obs}(O_T) = 1$.

Definition 9.35. [LS91] Let P, Q be τ-free reactive probabilistic processes.

$$P \sqsubseteq_{LS} Q \text{ iff } \forall T \in \mathcal{T}^{np}, \forall o \in O_T : Pr_{P,T}^{Obs}(o) \leqslant Pr_{Q,T}^{Obs}(o).$$

We write $P \sim_{LS} Q$ iff $P \sqsubseteq_{LS} Q$ and $Q \sqsubseteq_{LS} P$.

□

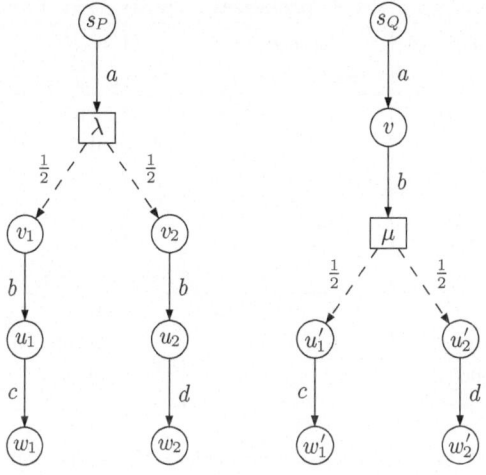

Fig. 9.17. $Q \sqsubseteq_{LS} P$ and $P \not\sqsubseteq_{LS} Q$.

Example. Consider $P, Q \in PP$ shown in Figure 9.17 (see also Example 9.8, page 253). We have $Q \sqsubseteq_{LS} P$ and $P \not\sqsubseteq_{LS} Q$. If we apply the test process T of Figure 9.16, we can derive for $o = 1_a : (1_b : 1_c : 1_\omega, 1_b : 0_d)$

$$Pr_{P,T}^{Obs}(o) = \tfrac{1}{2} \cdot [(1 \cdot 1) \cdot (1 \cdot 1)] + \tfrac{1}{2} \cdot [(1 \cdot 0) \cdot (1 \cdot 0)] = \tfrac{1}{2},$$
$$Pr_{Q,T}^{Obs}(o) = [\tfrac{1}{2} \cdot 1 + \tfrac{1}{2} \cdot 0] \cdot [\tfrac{1}{2} \cdot 1 + \tfrac{1}{2} \cdot 0] = \tfrac{1}{4}.$$

So we obtain $P \not\sqsubseteq_{LS} Q$, but recall we have $P \sim_{JY} Q$, $Q \sqsubseteq_{SE} P$ and $P \not\sqsubseteq_{SE} Q$ (see Example 9.7.2).

□

Larsen and Skou proved that the following relationship between their notion of testing and the probabilistic bisimulation holds:

Theorem 9.36. *[LS91] Let $P, Q \in PP$ be τ-free and reactive. Then*

$$P \sim^{bs} Q \text{ iff } P \sim_{LS} Q.$$

□

Note that the previous theorem also holds for probabilistic processes that are not finitely branching but fulfill the *minimal probability assumption*, i.e. there exists $\epsilon > 0$ such that whenever $s \xrightarrow{a} \mu$ either $\mu(s') = 0$ or $\mu(s') > \epsilon$ for all s'. The difference between $\sim_{LS}$ and the testing preorders defined in the previous sections is that $\sim_{LS}$ considers success or failure "after each step" whereas testing relations for probabilistic processes like $\sqsubseteq_{SE}$ or $\sqsubseteq_{JY}$ take only the success probability after a (maximal) trace into account. So it is clear that $\sim_{LS}$ distinguishes processes that can not be distinguished by $\sqsubseteq_{SE}$ or $\sqsubseteq_{JY}$. To the best of our knowledge this relationship has not been further considered yet.

	model	test processes	boils down to	characterization
$\sqsubseteq_{CH}$	fully probabilistic processes	τ-free, nonprob., reactive $(\mathcal{T}^{np,re})$	classical testing $(\sqsubseteq_{DH})$	extended trace distribution
$\sim_{LS}$	τ-free reactive prob. processes	τ-free, nonprob. $(\mathcal{T}^{np})$	ordinary bisimulation	probabilistic bisimulation $(\sim_{bs})$
$\sqsubseteq_{CL}$	fully probabilistic processes	fully probabilistic $(\mathcal{T}_\tau^{fp})$	classical testing $(\sqsubseteq_{DH})$	probabilistic trace distribution
$\sqsubseteq_{SE}^{may}$	probabilistic processes	probabilistic $(\mathcal{T}_\tau^{pp})$	classical testing $(\sqsubseteq_{DH})$	trace distr. pre-congruence $(\preceq^{ftp})$
$\sqsubseteq_{JY}^{may}$	τ-free prob. processes	τ-free, probabilistic $(\mathcal{T}^{pp})$	ordinary simulation	probabilistic simulation
$\sqsubseteq_{BC}$	action-labeled CTMCs	"passive" $(\mathcal{T}_\tau^{pa})$	classical testing $(\sqsubseteq_{DH})$	extended trace distribution

Table 9.1. Summary table: The first column lists the most important probabilistic testing relations we have discussed in this chapter. In the second column the corresponding class of processes is depict and the third column shows the set of applied test processes. In the fourth column, the resulting relations are listed when the probabilistic information is disregarded. The last columns lists the corresponding characterizations.

9.13   Summary

We have given an extensive survey of the testing theory for probabilistic systems and presented the definitions of different preorders in a uniform style to ease the task of establishing relationships between them. Moreover we saw that in most cases the relations are closely connected with the classical testing relation of De Nicola and Hennessy (see Figure 9.14, page 265) and we discussed characterizations to better reflect the nature of the relations (see Figure 9.15, page 270). Table 9.1 summarizes the main contents of this chapter.

Computational issues: Most authors do not not address computational issues, but from the summary table we can see that some of the relations are decidable. First, consider the characterization by extended traces. If the process is finite, we can determine the (finite) set of extended traces with a non-zero probability and compute the probability of each extended trace with the inductive definitions of section 9.11.1. Christoff presents algorithms for verification of his testing relations in [CC91]. Furthermore, we have a characterization by probabilistic bisimulation that can be computed in polynomial time and space by a partitioning technique [HT92]. To the best of our knowledge, for all other relations no algorithms computing them exist.

Open problems:

- We have only pointed out the most obvious connections between the different preorders presented here. Clarifying which relations are incomparable and which are finer/coarser than others would be helpful to obtain a more complete picture on probabilistic testing relations. For example, the relationship between the following pairs of relations has not been considered yet: $(\sqsubseteq_{CL}, \sqsubseteq_{SE}), (\sqsubseteq_{CL}, \sqsubseteq_{JY}), (\sqsubseteq_{CH}^{wte}, \sqsubseteq_{BC})$ and the $\sqsubseteq_{LS}$ with any of the "compositional testing relations".

- Many relations are not computable because infinite sets of test processes have to be applied, so an interesting problem would be finding the set of "essential" test processes that decide whether two processes are related or not. A good starting point would be defining the "informativeness" of a test process with regard to the tested process. Of course, test processes should be as compact as possible avoiding unnecessary computations.

Part III

Model-Based Test Case Generation

The previous parts of this book have, in general, been concerned with checking models against models. A theoretical underpinning with, among other things, respect to completeness of these approaches has been given.

If correctness of a model w.r.t. another model is to be proved, then the size of their state spaces becomes a crucial problem. It may turn out that with today's technology, mathematical verification is not possible for arbitrary systems. In addition to complexity issues, checking models against models—or properties—is crucially dependent on the assumptions that have been encoded into the models. Mathematically established correctness only holds under the condition that these assumptions do indeed hold.

As a consequence, there is a growing agreement that verification technology such as model checking or deductive theorem proving must hence be complemented with activities that relate the real world to the models. This is particularly true for embedded devices where complex systems interact with an equally complex environment.

The idea of model-based testing is then to have a model of the system, or specification, and use this model to generate sequences of input and expected output. Roughly speaking, the input is applied to the system under test, and the system's output is compared to the model's output, as given by the generated trace. This implies that the model must be valid, i.e., that it faithfully represents the requirements. The apparatus of the previous parts can be seen as a means to increase confidence that a model does indeed conform to the requirements.

Basically, this is achieved by redundancy: two models (state machines, temporal formulae, etc.) are built, and detection of a discrepancy among them points at potential difficulties.

If an artifact that is to be checked is of a purely mathematical nature, then infinite input domains, or infinite runs, can technologically be coped with by means of finite representations. It is hence possible to argue about infinite behaviors. If, on the other hand, this artifact is part of the real world, and includes sensors, actuators, operating systems, and legacy systems, then these arguments cannot be applied. The reason is that in general, reasoning about systems involves reasoning about states, and when hardware is involved, there is no definite knowledge about these states. The consequence is that the comparison between an actual system and a model is incomplete, both for complexity and principal reasons.

Overview This motivates the structure of four chapters in this third part of the book.

Chapter 10 provides a brief overview of methodological issues in model-based testing. Pretschner and Philipps discuss both the need for abstraction in practical applications of model-based testing and different scenarios of model-based testing.

The selection of a few traces of the model can be done w.r.t. functional, structural, and stochastic criteria. The first category seems to be amenable to methodology rather than to technology. In Chapter 11, Gaston and Seifert have a thorough look at the two other criteria, structural and stochastic criteria. While structural criteria have been used for finite state machines (transition coverage, for instance) in previous chapters of the book, they look at coverage criteria at the level of programming languages. This does not contradict the title of this part: models may well be specified by means of programming languages, and code is often used to specify guards and assignments in respective modeling languages. The authors then have a look at stochastic criteria and review the discussion on comparing their fault detecting power with testing that is based on partition the input domain.

In the third Chapter 12 of this part, Lúcio and Samer go one step further. They assume a selection criterion, be it functional, structural, or stochastic, to be given. The selection criterion and the model are then used to generate test cases. The generation process is the subject of their article. Consequently, they investigate the use of model checking, symbolic execution, theorem proving, and logic programming. Tools that rely on these and other mechanisms—on-the-fly testing, in particular—are discussed later in this book, in Chapter 14.

Finally, the fourth Chapter 13 is concerned with a particularly complex class of systems, namely real-time and mixed discrete-continuous, or hybrid, systems. Berkenkötter and Kirner first define the two classes of systems. After showing how real-time systems can be modeled with different formalisms, they show how test cases can be generated for them. As far as hybrid systems are concerned, hybrid statecharts and hybrid variants of process algebras are introduced. Because of the very large state spaces of these classes of systems, they discuss ways to cope with this complexity, namely decomposition approaches and the use of discrete, very abstract models that are connected to more concrete models and that are used for directing the search for test cases.

10   Methodological Issues in Model-Based Testing

Alexander Pretschner[1] and Jan Philipps[2]

[1] Information Security
Department of Computer Science
ETH Zürich
Haldeneggsteig 4, 8092 Zürich, Switzerland
Alexander.Pretschner@inf.ethz.ch

[2] Validas AG
gate
Lichtenbergstr. 8., 85748 Garching, Germany
philipps@validas.de

10.1   Introduction

Testing denotes a set of activities that aim at showing that actual and intended behaviors of a system differ, or at increasing confidence that they do not differ. Often enough, the intended behavior is defined by means of rather informal and incomplete requirement specifications. Test engineers use these specification documents to gain an approximate understanding of the intended behavior. That is to say, they build a mental model of the system. This mental model is then used to derive test cases for the implementation, or system under test (SUT): input and expected output. Obviously, this approach is implicit, unstructured, not motivated in its details and not reproducible.

While some argue that because of these implicit mental models all testing is necessarily model-based [Bin99], the idea of model-based testing is to use *explicit behavior models* to encode the intended behavior. Traces of these models are interpreted as test cases for the implementation: input and expected output. The input part is fed into an implementation (the system under test, or SUT), and the implementation's output is compared to that of the model, as reflected in the output part of the test case.

Fig. 10.1 sketches the general approach to model-based testing. Model-based testing uses abstract *models* to generate traces—test cases for an implementation—according to a *test case specification*. This test case specification is a selection criterion on the set of the traces of the model—in the case of reactive systems, a finite set of finite traces has to be selected from a usually infinite set of infinite traces. Because deriving, running, and evaluating tests are costly activities, one would like this set to be as small as possible.

The generated traces can also be manually checked in order to ascertain that the model represents the system requirements: similar to simulation, this is an activity of *validation*, concerned with checking whether or not an artifact—the model in this case—conforms to the actual user requirements. Finally, the model's traces—i.e., the test cases—are used to increase confidence that the

M. Broy et al. (Eds.): Model-Based Testing of Reactive Systems, LNCS 3472, pp. 281–291, 2005.
© Springer-Verlag Berlin Heidelberg 2005

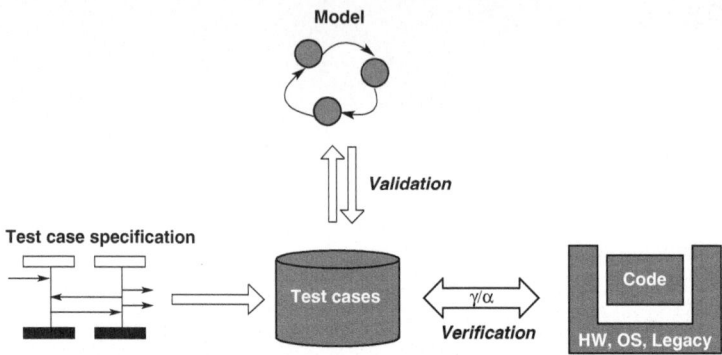

Fig. 10.1. Model-Based Testing

implementation corresponds to the model, or to prove that it does not. Testing is hence an activity of *verification*: the implementation is checked for correctness w.r.t. the model which can arguably be interpreted as a behavior specification, and which represents the formalized user requirements.

This approach immediately raises an array of difficult questions. The issues of test case specifications and generation technology are treated in Chapters 11 and 12 of this book, and are consequently not the subject of this chapter. Instead, we focus on the following two key questions.

(1) Obviously, in the above approach, the model has to faithfully represent the user requirements, i.e., the intended behavior: it has to be valid. Why would one choose to build a costly model, validate it, derive tests and run them on a SUT rather than directly validate the SUT?
(2) Because system and software construction occur—as any engineering activity—under high time and cost constraints, can we build a single model to generate both test cases and production code?

The first question is answered by requiring models to be more abstract, or "simpler", than the SUT. Because they are more abstract, they are easier to understand, validate, maintain, and more likely to be amenable to test case generation. The above approach to model-based testing is then modified as follows. The input part of a model's trace—the test case—is concretized (γ in the figure) before it is fed into the implementation. Conversely, the output of the SUT is abstracted (α in the figure) before it is compared to the output of the model. Note that this approach incurs a cost: aspects of the SUT that were abstracted away can obviously not directly be tested on the grounds of the abstract model.

The second question will be answered by discussing different scenarios of model-based testing that regard different interleavings and flavors of building models and code. Roughly, it will turn out that some sort of redundancy is indispensable: choosing to derive both test cases and implementations from one single model requires one to precisely know what this means in terms of quality assurance: in this way, code generators and assumptions on the environment can be tested.

One might argue that if the model has to be valid anyway, then we could generate code from it without any need for further testing. Unfortunately, this is no viable option in general. Since the SUT consists not only of a piece of code that is to be verified but also of an environment consisting of hardware, operating system, and legacy software components, it will always be necessary to dynamically execute the SUT. This is because the model contains assumptions on the environment, and these may or may not be justified.

Overview

The remainder of this chapter is organized as follows. Sec. 10.2 elaborates on the different levels of abstraction of models and implementations. In Sec. 10.3, we discuss several scenarios of model-based testing and shed light on how to interleave the development of models and of code. Sec. 10.4 concludes.

10.2   Abstraction

Stachowiak identifies the following three fundamental characteristics of models [Sta73].

- Models are *mappings* from a concrete (the "original") into a more abstract (the "model") world;
- Models serve a specific *purpose*;
- Models are *simplifications*, in that they do not reflect all attributes of the the concrete world.

In this section, we take a look at the third point. There are two basic approaches to simplification: omission and encapsulation of details.

10.2.1   Omission of Details

When details are actually discarded, in the sense that no macro expansion mechanism can insert the missing information, then the resulting model is likely to be easier to understand. This is the basic idea behind development methodologies like stepwise refinement, where the level of abstraction is steadily decreased. [1] Specifications at higher levels of abstraction convey the fundamental ideas. As we have alluded to above, they cannot directly be used for testing, simply because they contain too little information. This is why we need driver components that, where necessary, insert missing information into the test cases.

The problem then obviously is which information to discard. That is true for all modeling tasks and, until building software becomes a true engineering discipline, remains a black art which is why we do not discuss it further here.

---

[1] A similar scheme is also found in incremental approaches like Cleanroom [PTLP99] where the difference between two increments consists of one further component that is 100% finished.

In the literature, there are many examples of abstractions—and the necessary insertion of information by means of driver components—for model-based testing [PP04]. These are also discussed in Chap. 15.

This variant of simplification reflects one perspective on model-based development activities. Models are seen as a means to actually get rid of details deemed irrelevant. As mentioned above, no macro expansion mechanism can automatically insert them, simply because the information is given nowhere. Missing information can, in the context of stepwise refinement, for instance, be inserted by a human when this is considered necessary.

10.2.2   Encapsulation of Details

Details of a system (or of parts a system) can be also be referenced. Complexity is reduced by regarding the references, and not the content they stand for. This second kind of abstraction lets modeling languages appear as the natural extension of programming languages (note that we are talking about behavior models only). The underlying idea is to find ways to *encapsulate* details by means of libraries or language constructs.

Encapsulating the assembly of stack frames into function calls is an example, encapsulating a certain kind of error handling into exceptions is another. The Swing library provides abstractions for GUI constructs, and successes of CORBA and the J2EE architectures are, among many other things, due to the underlying encapsulation of access to communication infrastructures. The MDA takes these ideas even further. Leaving the domain of programming languages, this phenomenon can also be seen in the ISO/OSI communication stack where one layer relies on the services of a lower layer. The different layers of operating systems are a further prominent example.

What is common about these approaches is that basically, macro expansion is carried out at compile or run time. In the respective contexts, the involved information loss is considered to be irrelevant. These macros are not only useful, but they also restrict programmers' possibilities: stack frame assembly, for instance, can in general not be altered. Similarly, some modeling languages disallow arbitrary communications between components (via variables) when explicit connectors are specified. The good news is that while expressiveness—in a given domain—is restricted, the languages become, at least in theory, amenable to automatic analysis simply because of this restriction.

Of course, the two points of view on model-based development activities are not orthogonal. There is no problem with using a *modeling language* in order to very abstractly specify arbitrary systems. In the context of testing, the decision of which point of view to adopt is of utter importance. When models of the pure latter kind are taken into consideration, then they are likely to be specified at the same level of abstraction as the system that is to be tested. We then run into the above mentioned problem of having to validate a model that is as complex as the system under test.

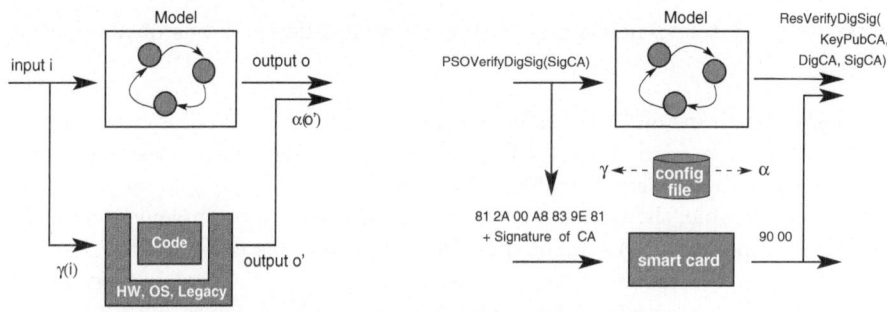

Fig. 10.2. Abstractions and concretizations. The general setting is depicted at the left; an example where α and γ are defined via a configuration file is given at the right.

10.2.3 Concretization and Abstraction

As argued above, with the possible exception of stress testing, it is methodologically indispensable that in terms of model-based testing, models are simplifications of the system under test. Consequently, test cases derived from the model can in general not be directly fed into the system. To adapt the test cases to the system, it is necessary to re-insert the information by means of *driver components*:[2] the input part i of a trace of the model—a test case—is concretized to the level of the implementation, $\gamma(i)$. In general, there will be many choices to select $\gamma(i)$, simply because the model is an abstraction. This choice is left to the test engineer, or a driver component that he or she has to write.

$\gamma(i)$ is then fed into the implementation which reacts by outputting some o'. By construction, o' is not at the same level of abstraction as the output of the model, o. Unfortunately, we cannot in general use γ to compare $\gamma(o)$ to o'. The reason is that as in the case of concretizing input, there are many candidates for $\gamma(o)$, and for comparing the system to the model, a random choice is not an option here.

The classical solution to this problem is to use an abstraction function, α, instead. Since α is an abstraction function, it itself involves a loss of information. Provided we have chosen γ and α adequately, we can now apply α to the system's output and compare the resulting value $\alpha(o')$ to the model's output. If $\alpha(o')$ equals o, then the test case passes, otherwise it fails. In the driver component, this is usually implemented as follows: it is checked whether or not the implementation's output is a member of the set of possible implementation outputs that correspond to the model's output (of course, in non-deterministic settings it might possible to assign a verdict only after applying an entire sequence of stimuli to the SUT).

The idea is depicted in Fig. 10.2, left. Note that the general idea with pairs of abstraction/concretization mappings is crucial to many formally founded ap-

---

[2] Of course, this concretization may also be performed in a component different from the driver.

proaches to systems engineering that work with different levels of abstraction [BS01b].

Example. As an example, consider Fig. 10.2, right. It is part of a case study in the field of smart card testing [PPS+03]. The example shows a case where the verification of digital signatures should be checked. In order to keep the size of the model manageable, the respective crypto algorithms are not implemented in the model—testing the crypto algorithms in themselves was considered a different task. Instead, the model outputs an abstract value with a set of parameters when it is asked to verify a signature. By means of a configuration file—which is part of the driver component—, the (abstract) command and its parameters are concretized and applied to the actual smart card. It responds 90 00 which basically indicates that everything is alright. This value is then augmented with additional information from the configuration file, e.g., certificates and keys, and abstracted. Finally, it is compared to the output of the model.

Further examples for different abstractions are given in Chap. 15.

10.3   Scenarios of Model-Based Testing

Model-based testing is not the only use of models in software engineering. More common is the constructive use of behavior models for code generation. In this section we discuss four scenarios that concern the interplay of models used for test case generation and code generation. The first scenario concerns the process of having one model for both code and test case generation. The second and third scenarios concern the process of building a model after the system it is supposed to represent; here we distinguish between manual and automatic modeling. The last scenario discusses the situation where two distinct models are built.

10.3.1   Common Model

In this scenario, a common model is used for both code generation and test case generation (Fig. 10.3).

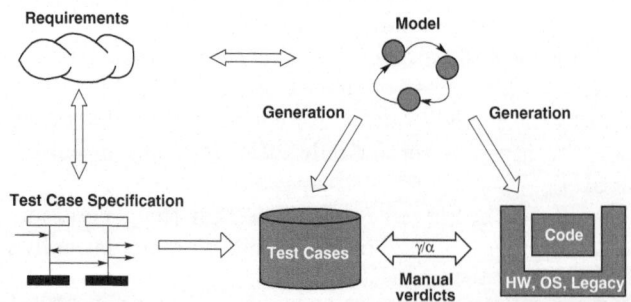

Fig. 10.3. One model is used for both code and test case generation

Testing always involves some kind of redundancy: the intended and the actual behaviors. When a single model for both code generation and test case generation chosen, this redundancy is lacking. In a sense, the code (or model) would be tested against itself. This is why no automatic verdicts are possible.

On the other hand, what can be automatically tested are the code generator and environment assumptions that are explicitly given, or implicitly encoded in the model. This can be regarded as problematic or not. In case the code generator works correctly and the model is valid, which is what we have presupposed, tests of the adequacy of environment assumptions are the only task necessary to ensure a proper functioning of the actual (sub-)system. This is where formal verification technology and testing seem to smoothly blend: formal verification of the model is done to make sure the model does what it is supposed to. Possibly inadequate environment assumptions can be identified when (selected) traces of the model are compared to traces of the system. Note that this adds a slightly different flavor to our current understanding of model-based testing. Rather than testing a system, we are now checking the adequacy of environment assumptions. This is likely to be influential w.r.t. the choice of test cases.

Depending on which parts of a model are used for which purpose, this scenario usually restricts the possible abstractions to those that involve a loss of information that can be coped with by means of macro expansion (Sec. 10.2).

10.3.2   Automatic Model Extraction

Our second scenario is concerned with extracting models from an existing system (Fig. 10.4). The process of building the system is conventional: somehow, a specification is built, and then the system is hand coded. Once the system is built, one creates a model manually or automatically, and this model is then used for test case generation.

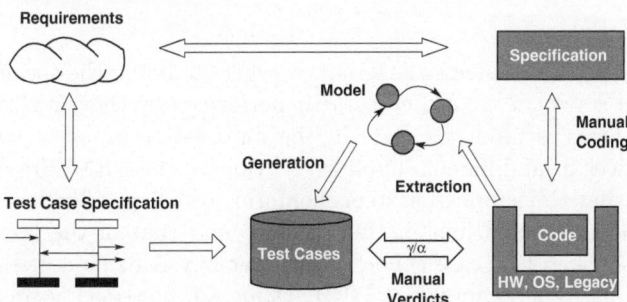

Fig. 10.4. A model is automatically extracted from code

Automatically extracting abstractions from code or more concrete models is a rather active branch of computer science [Hol01, GS97, SA99] which we will not discuss here. The abstractions should be created in a way such that at least some—and identifiable—statements about them should carry over to the more concrete artifact. In the context of testing, it is important to notice that we run into the same problem of not having any redundancy as above. The consequence is that automatic verdicts make statements only about assumptions in the automatic process of abstraction.

Abstractions are bound to a given purpose [Sta73]. Automatic abstraction must hence be performed with a given goal in mind. It is likely that for test case generation, fully automatic abstraction is not possible but that test engineers must provide the abstraction mechanism with domain and application specific knowledge.

10.3.3   Manual Modeling

A further possibility consists of manually building the model for test case generation, while the system is again built on top of a different specification (Fig. 10.5). Depending on how close the interaction between the responsibles for specification and model is, there will in general be the redundancy that is required for automatically assigning verdicts.

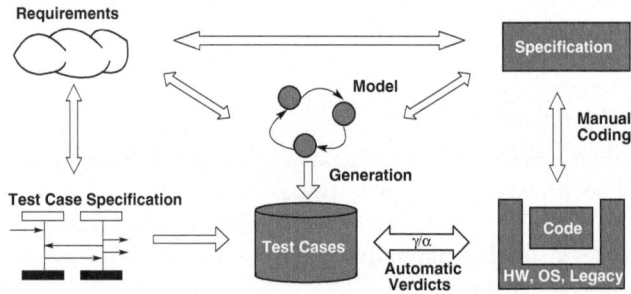

Fig. 10.5. A model is built only for testing purposes

This approach also reflects the situation where building the specification and implementing a system are not necessarily performed by the same organization. For instance, this is often the case in the automotive industry where OEMs assemble devices from different suppliers. Obviously, the OEMs are interested in making sure that the supplied systems conform to the specification.

As an aside, combinations of this scenario and that of the last subsection typically arise when test case generation technology is to be assessed (a recent survey contains some examples [PP04]). Doing so, however, is problematic in that testing is only performed when the system has, in large parts, already been built.

10.3.4   Separate Models

Finally, a last scenario is noteworthy that involves having two redundant and distinct models, one for test case generation, and one for code generation (Fig. 10.6).

This approach allows one to have automatic verdicts. The model for development may be as abstract as desired when the requirement for automatic code generation is dropped.

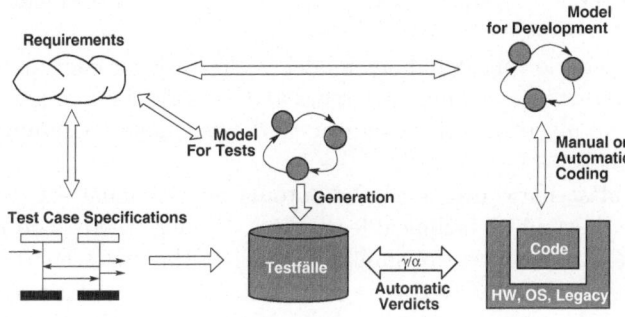

Fig. 10.6. Two models

10.3.5   Interleaving

Except for the last scenario, the above scenarios share the commonality that there is no real interaction between the development processes of the models and that of the code. In iterative development processes with ever changing requirements, this seems unrealistic. With suitable definitions of what an increment is, it is of course possible to interleave the development of two models, or to interleave the development of a model and some code. Of course, this is likely to involve some overhead. We will not discuss this issue any further here since that has been done elsewhere [PLP03] with considerations of the role of regression testing and of compositional testing [Pre03].

10.3.6   Summary

Automatic code generation from models boils down to perceiving models as possibly executable artifacts written in a very high-level programming language. This goes well beyond the use of models for analytical purposes only where, again, it is widely accepted that while it might be too expensive, modeling in itself usually reveals many errors. Currently, the embedded systems industry expresses a high degree of interest in these concepts.

We have shown that one must be careful in ensuring redundancy when models are used for testing and code generation. Models for the further can involve both flavors of simplification that we identified in Sec. 10.2, namely the one where information is encapsulated, and the one where information is deliberately dropped. Models for the latter can obviously only involve encapsulation of details.[3] We consider a thorough discussion of when the use of models for code generation is likely to pay off utterly important but beyond the scope of this paper. Briefly, we see a separation of concerns, multiple views, and restriction as key success factors of modeling languages [SPHP02]. The following captures the essence of the four scenarios and provides a prudent assessment.

- Our first scenario considered one model as the basis for code and tests. This is problematic w.r.t. redundancy issues and a restriction to abstractions that boil down to macros. Code generators and environment assumptions can be checked.
- The second scenario discussed the automatic or manual extraction of abstractions (beyond its technical feasibility). Because there is no redundancy either, the consequences are similar to those of the first scenario.
- The third scenario discussed the use of dedicated models for test case generation only. Because there is redundancy w.r.t. a manually implemented systems and because of the possibility of applying simplifications in the sense of actually losing information, this scenario appears promising. This is without any considerations of whether or not it is economic to use such models. We will come back to this question in the conclusion in Sec. 10.4.
- Finally, the fourth scenario considered the use of two independent models, one for test case generation, and one for development. The latter model may or may not be used for the automatic generation of code. This scenario seems to be optimal in that it combines the—not yet empirically verified— advantages of model-based testing and model-based development. Clearly, this approach is the most expensive one.

10.4   Conclusion

In this brief overview chapter, we have discussed the role of models in the context of testing. Some emphasis was put on a discussion on the methodological need for different abstraction levels of models and implementations. The basic argument is that the effort to manually validate an SUT—checking whether or not it corresponds to the usually informal requirements—must find itself below the effort necessary to build the model, validate the model, and derive test cases from it. Abstract models are easier to understand than very concrete artifacts. On the other hand, abstraction incurs a cost: aspects that were abstracted can usually not be tested. We discussed the role of driver components that, to a certain extent, can re-introduce the missing information.

A further focus of this article is on different scenarios of model-based testing. We have discussed the role of redundancy and the problematics of generating both tests and production code from one single model.

---

[3] When they focus on certain parts of a system only, then this clearly is a loss of information. However, code can obviously only be generated for those parts that have been modeled.

The fundamental concern of model-based testing seems to be whether or not it is more cost-effective than other approaches—traditional testing, reviews, inspections, and also constructive approaches to quality assurance. While first evaluations of model-based testing are available [PPW+05], there clearly is a need for studies that examine the economics of model-based testing.

11   Evaluating Coverage Based Testing

Christophe Gaston[1] and Dirk Seifert[2]

[1] Commissariat a l'energie atomique
     Logiciels pour la Sûreté des Procédés
     christophe.gaston@cea.fr
[2] Technische Universität Berlin
     Software Engineering Research Group
     seifert@cs.tu-berlin.de

Abstract. In the previous chapters, various formal testing theories have been discussed. The correctness of an implementation with respect to a model is denoted by a so-called conformance relation. Conformance relations are relations between mathematical abstractions of implementations and models. Based on these conformance relations, different testing strategies have been defined. In this chapter, we concentrate on formal objects used to select test suites. These formal objects are so-called coverage criteria. A coverage criterion is a property that a selected test suite has to satisfy. We explore to which purposes these coverage criteria can be used for. Then we concentrate on the fault detection ability of a test suite satisfying a given coverage criterion.

11.1   Introduction

All testing methodologies introduced in this book follow the same generic test process. Test cases are generated according to a given model of the implementation. The model results from a requirements analysis and has to be (if testing is done automatically) a formal description of the requirements. Test cases are sequences of input/output pairs and a finite set of test cases is called test suite. For each test case of a test suite, the input specified in the first pair of the sequence is refined with concrete data called test data. Test data are submitted to the implementation through its environment. The implementation generates a result which is captured through its environment. The result is compared (with respect to a conformance relation) to the output specified in the pair. If the conformance relation is not contradicted, the process goes on with the following pair. If generated outputs all correspond to the intended outputs, the test case is executed successfully. If all the test cases of the test suite are executed successfully, a success verdict is assigned to the test process, since no test case of the test suite allows to show that the implementation does not conform to the specification. Figure 11.1 shows this testing framework.

The number of test cases required to obtain confidence in the system under test is usually infinitely large for real life applications. Consequently, a so called *domain expert* is involved in the test process, as he is able to extract interesting test suites due to his knowledge. For automated test case generation, the problem remains unsolved. So, for current testing practices, one of the open questions is: Which test suite should be extracted from a possibly infinite set of test cases?

M. Broy et al. (Eds.): Model-Based Testing of Reactive Systems, LNCS 3472, pp. 293-322, 2005.
© Springer-Verlag Berlin Heidelberg 2005

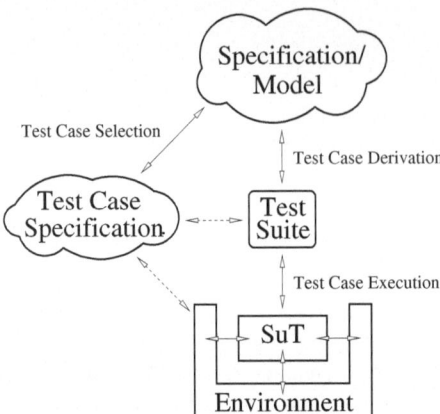

Fig. 11.1. A Usual Test Framework

Information provided by the model to extract test cases can have two different natures. On the one hand, functional aspects can be used. These aspects of the model describe the intended functionality of the implementation. The goal of test purpose based techniques is to generate test suites to validate such kind of properties [FJJV96, BGM91]. On the other hand, structural aspects of the model can be used. These structural aspects can be the *state space* description or the *dynamics* description of the implementation. For example, in *Z*, *VDM*, or *B* specifications, the state space is given by a set of typed variables and predicates describing the invariant. The dynamics description is constituted of operations which map input data and the state before applying the operation to the output data and the state after applying the operation. In Extended Finite State Machines, the state space is expressed by variables and by guards over these variables, while the dynamics description is given by assignments on variables, transition functions, and functions which define the output generated depending on an input received and the current state. In coverage based testing techniques, test suites are selected to cover some structural aspects of the model with respect to given coverage criteria. Coverage criteria can be seen as predicates defined on triples (P, M, T), where P is a program whose associated model is M, and T is a test suite. The meaning of such a criterion can be understood in two ways:

- As an *adequacy criterion*, which is a set of rules used to determine whether or not testing is complete for a given program, specification and criterion.
- As a *selection criterion*, which is a set of rules used to select test cases for a given program and specification.

A selection criterion helps to select a test suite in order to fulfill a goal, whereas an adequacy criterion helps to check that a previously selected test suite satisfies a goal. The notion of coverage criteria has been originally defined for white-box testing techniques. In these techniques, structural aspects to cover are related to programs: for example, a coverage criterion may be to cover all statement sequences in a program. In this book, we focus on coverage criteria related to models: for example, a coverage criterion may be to cover all the states of a model.

This chapter provides an overview of different research activities dealing with the coverage based testing techniques and their evaluation. In Section 11.2, we discuss how coverage criteria can help to select meaningful test suites. In Section 11.3, we present common coverage criteria. In Section 11.4 we concentrate on providing quantitative elements to evaluate the ability to detect faults of coverage based testing techniques. Finally, in Section 11.5, we summarize the main results and present open problems.

11.2   Coverage Criteria

To address the question *Which test cases should be extracted from a possibly infinite set of test cases ?* it is possible to use advanced specifications describing which test cases to choose. Such specifications are usually called test case specifications (cf. Figure 11.1), and are, strictly speaking, selection criteria.

The main reasons for an infinitely large test suite are that a specification can represent an infinite number of traces (e.g., caused by variables ranging over infinite domains) and that a specification can contain infinite traces (e.g., caused by loops). For the first reason the problem is to select traces for the second reason the problem is to chop traces. Basically, the specification (ideally) describes all possible test cases while the test case specification describes which of these test cases are likely to find errors and, consequently, increase the confidence in the correctness of the implementation. Most of the criteria used for selecting test cases can be coarsely classified according to the following three aspects:

(1) The test case specification is a description of a structural criterion which should be covered.
(2) The test case specification is a description of functional aspects, also called scenarios, which should be covered.
(3) The test case specification contains stochastic information about different aspects of the implementation which is be used to concentrate on particular details.

The third variant is also used to restrict a test case specification if this represents an infinite model (for example, if path coverage is required which is usually infeasible to achieve as explained in the following section).

11.2.1   Structural Criteria

Basically, coverage criteria are used to measure the *quality* or, more precisely, the *adequacy* of test suites: A test suite is adequate according to a criterion if a designated percentage of this coverage criterion is reached. Depending on this, testing is continued or stopped. A structural criterion is an assertion about the structure of the specification. For example, in model based specifications states or transitions can be used. In class diagrams, for example, it could be required to use at least one instance of each class in the diagram.

For test case generation this means that test cases are generated according to a structural criterion, and that a test case is selected if this test case increases the coverage of this criterion. In the case of several test cases one can choose the test case with the major contribution.

For example, **transition coverage** requires choosing test cases in such a way that all transitions of the specification are covered. The **boundary interior** test requires that every loop is repeated zero, one and at most k times. The strongest coverage criterion is the **path coverage** criterion. This criterion is satisfied by a test suite if and only if for any possible path in the model, the test suite contains at least one test case which enforces an execution of this path in the implementation. Path coverage is in general impossible to achieve and impractical for real life testing. Reasons for that are loops in the model or infinite data spaces.

11.2.2   Functional Criteria

Another method to select test cases is using a model of the environment. Usually, such a model is called *scenario model*, *use case* or *user profile* and allows to describe scenarios which involve user enabled functionalities. The idea is that the test case specification is used to determine the inputs used to test the implementation and the model is used to estimate the expected outputs of the implementation.

For example, if the system under test is a banking application, usual functionality is the deposit of money into an account, the withdrawal of money from an account, or checking the balance. All these functionalities can be described as scenarios. Another example are the so called attack traces in security engineering. Here, possible ways to attack the system under test by an *unfriendly* user are modeled in scenarios and used to control the test selection process. So, functional criteria restrict the test case generation to particular scenarios and thus restrict the number of test cases.

As mentioned before, further reduction is required in case that the test case specification represents a possibly infinite set of scenarios (for example, if the test case specification is modeled as a state machine containing loops).

11.2.3   Stochastic Criteria

Usually, stochastic criteria[1] result from analysis of the expected user behavior or system usage, respectively. The simplest case is that all parts of the implementation, or all its functionalities have equal probability of execution. In this case, test case selection is done randomly. In contrast, if some functions are frequently used or represent important functionalities, test cases connected to these functionalities are preferred.

---

[1] Note that stochastic criteria can also be referred to as *statistical criteria*.

In the following section we review some usual coverage criteria that are used to select test cases. The aim of the section is to give the reader an intuition of usual criteria. A more exhaustive presentation of coverage criteria can be found elsewhere [FW88, RW85, ZHM97].

11.3   Coverage Based Testing

The problem of tractable coverage criteria that are easier to satisfy than the path coverage criterion, has been studied for a long time in the context of white-box testing. A lot of criteria have been defined [Mey79]. In the following, we present different coverage criteria used in the context of model based testing approaches which are adapted from white-box testing. Most of these coverage criteria can be classified into two main classes: *control flow oriented* coverage criteria and *data flow oriented* coverage criteria.

Control flow oriented coverage criteria are based on logical expressions introduced in the specification which determine the branch and loop structure of the implementation. Data flow oriented coverage criteria focus on the data flow part of the implementation. More precisely, they focus on the way values are associated to their variables and how these assignments affect the execution of the implementation [VB01].

In the following coverage criteria are introduced and explained, keeping in mind the analogy between models and abstract programs. Our discussions fits also for coverage criteria associated to programs with respect to white-box testing (i.e., coverage of code). In this context coverage criteria are usually described as flow graphs. However, we do not need this notion to present control flow criteria. Thus, a flow graph definition is only introduced in Section 11.3.2.

11.3.1   Control Flow Oriented Coverage Criteria

Basically, control flow oriented coverage criteria rely on the notions of *decision* and *condition* [VB01]. A condition is an *elementary* boolean expression which cannot be divided into further boolean expressions. A decision can be seen as a control point in the specification at which the control flow can follow various paths. In programming languages, this is a boolean expression consisting of several conditions combined by logical connectives. An instantiation of the common IF-THEN-ELSE construct in programming languages is an example for a decision. The most basic control flow criterion is the decision coverage criterion.

The **decision coverage** criterion [Mey79], also known as **branch coverage**, requires that each possible outcome (i.e., *true* or *false*) of every decision in the specification is produced at least once. For example, the specification contains a decision D: IF (A∧B) THEN S, where A and B are conditions. It is required that at least one test case makes (A∧B) evaluate to *true* and one makes (A∧B) evaluate to *false*. A test suite which contains two test cases, one such that A is *true* and B is *true* and the other one such that A is *false* and B is *true*, is sufficient to test decision D. The example clearly demonstrates that decision coverage does not ensure test suites which cover all different outcomes of a condition involved in a given decision. For example, the fact that B is failure causing could remain undetected with this criterion. To overcome this weakness, three refined criteria have been introduced.

The **condition coverage** criterion requires that each possible outcome of every condition in each decision is produced at least once. To give an example, we consider again decision D. The condition coverage criterion requires that A and B have taken all possible outcomes. Thus, a test suite which contains two test cases, one such that A is *true* and B is *false* and the other one such that A is *false* and B is *true* is sufficient to test decision D.

Even though the condition coverage criterion captures all conditions, it is not powerful enough to capture coverage of decisions. The test suite described above for condition D illustrates this fact: It consists of two test cases which both make (A∧B) evaluate to false. To overcome this weakness one must combine condition coverage and decision coverage. This is done in decision condition coverage.

The **decision condition coverage** criterion requires that each possible outcome of every condition in each decision is produced at least once and that each possible outcome of every decision in the specification is produced at least once. For decision D, a test suite which only contains two test cases, one such that A is *true* and B is *true* and the other one such that A is *false* and B is *false*, is sufficient to test decision D with regard to decision condition coverage. Decision condition coverage is strictly stronger than both decision coverage and condition coverage in the sense that each test suite which satisfies decision condition coverage satisfies both decision coverage and condition coverage.

The **multiple condition coverage** criterion requires that each possible combination of conditions outcomes in each decision is produced at least once. Again, we consider decision D, a test suite containing four test cases (A is *true* and B is *true*, A is *true* and B is *false*, A is *false* and B is *true* and A is *false* and B is *false*) is necessary to test D with regard to multiple condition coverage.

Note that multiple condition coverage requires full search of various combinations of condition values [VB01]. If the number of conditions in a decision is equal to n, the number of test cases to satisfy multiple condition coverage grows up to 2^n. This becomes unmanageable even for relatively moderate values of n. Decision coverage, condition coverage and decision condition coverage criteria require less test cases. For example, condition coverage requires two test cases per condition. If a decision contains n conditions, the criterion requires at maximum $2n$ test cases. However, a test suite which satisfies one of these three weaker criteria will not cover all combinations of conditions outcomes. The modified condition decision coverage criterion provides an intermediate position.

The **modified condition decision coverage** criterion requires that each possible outcome of every condition in a decision is produced at least once, each possible outcome of every decision is produced at least once and that each condition in a decision has been shown to affect the decision's outcome independently. A condition is shown to affect a decision's outcome independently by varying that condition while all other possible conditions are fixed.

Modified condition decision coverage includes in its definition both decision coverage and condition coverage. Furthermore, decision coverage can be deduced from condition coverage in combination with the independently affect property. Again, we consider decision D. A test suite with three test cases such that A is *true* and B is *true*, A is *true* and B is *false*, and A is *false* and B is *true* satisfies the modified condition decision coverage. Obviously, such a test suite satisfies the condition decision coverage and also the independently affect property. From these two facts, it is easy to see that decision coverage is satisfied. The number of required test cases ranges between $n + 1$ and $2n$ which is manageable even for large values of n. However, there are situations in which it is impossible to vary one condition value while keeping the others unchanged. This is the case if A is *true* implies that B is *true*. To overcome this problem, Vilkomir et. al. provide an improved formal definition of the modified condition decision coverage criterion [VB02]. There it is sufficient to choose any combination that varies both condition and decision even-though other conditions may also vary.

At last, the **full predicate coverage** criterion requires that each possible outcome of every condition in a decision is produced at least once, where the value of a decision is directly correlated with the value of a condition. Intuitively, multiple condition decision coverage is relaxed in the sense that it is not required that conditions in a decision independently affect the decision.

11.3.2   Data Flow Oriented Coverage Criteria

Data flow oriented criteria are based on data flow analysis with respect to compiler optimization activities. They require test cases that follow instruction sequences from points where values are assigned to variables to points where those variables are used. To introduce different criteria, we define *flow graphs* associated to a model. Strictly speaking, we discuss code coverage as used in white-box testing approaches. The relationship between models and code is that *behavioral* models can be compiled into code and that described coverage criteria can be applied to this code. However, there are many possibilities for this relationship; the way criteria are applied depends on the concrete approach. For example, using modified condition decision coverage at level of assembly code does not make sense.

A **flow graph** associated to a model is a directed graph that consists of a set of nodes and a set of edges connecting these nodes. Nodes contain linear sequences of computations (i.e., access to external values, variable assignments, data changes, etc). Edges represent transfer of control between nodes specified in the specification. Additionally, each edge is associated with a boolean expression that is the condition of the corresponding control transfer. A flow graph contains an initial node, which denotes the beginning of an abstract[2] computation, and a set of terminal nodes which denote exit points. Depending on the type of model, initial and terminal nodes have to be chosen or added (for example, extended finite state machine formalisms do not use notions of *beginning* and *ending* of

---

[2] Abstract in the sense that models are abstractions of programs.

computations). In some cases, a data flow graph can be seen as an annotated control flow graph.

In the following, a flow graph is a representation of all statement sequences of the model, and a test case is a possible (instantiated) instance of a path in the flow graph (i.e., inputs which execute the instruction sequence denoted by the path) [ZHM97]. Moreover each occurrence of a variable in a node is classified either as definition occurrence or as use occurrence. The latter can be further divided into computational use or, if it is used within a predicate, into predicate use. In the following necessary definitions are given:

- A *definition clear path* with respect to a variable x in a flow graph is a path where for all nodes in the path there is no definition occurrence of x.
- A definition occurrence of variable x within a node u *reaches a computational use occurrence* of x within a node v, if and only if there is a path $p = (u, w_1, \ldots, w_n, v)$, such that $(w_1, \ldots, w_n)$ is definition clear with respect to x.
- A definition occurrence of variable x in u *reaches a predicate use occurrence* of x on the edge (w_n, v), if and only if there is a path $p = (u, w_1, \ldots, w_n, v)$, such that $(w_1, \ldots, w_n)$ is definition clear with respect to x and there exist a predicate occurrence of x associated to the edge from w_n to v.
- For both predicate and computational use occurrence, a definition occurrence of x in u *feasibly reaches* the use occurrence of x, if and only if there is a path p, such that there exists inputs which enforce the execution of p.

The simplest data flow criteria rely on paths that start with the definition of a variable and end with the use of the same variable. The following criteria are adapted from the work of Frankl and Weyuker [FW88].

A test suite T satisfies the **all definitions coverage** criterion, if and only if for all definition occurrences of a variable x, such that there is a use occurrence of x which is feasibly reachable from the definition, there is at least one element in T which is a numerical instance of a path p, that contains a sub path through which the definition of x reaches some use occurrence of x. Thus, the all definitions coverage criterion ensures that all defined variables will be tested at least once by one of their uses in the model. However, this is insufficient as tester require to test all uses of all variable definitions. It is ensured by the all uses criterion.

A test suite T satisfies the **all uses coverage** criterion, if and only if for all definition occurrences of a variable x and for all use occurrences of x which are feasibly reachable from the definition, there is at least one element in T which is a numerical instance of a path p that contains a sub path through which the definition of x reaches the use occurrence.

The previously described criteria have been specialized to take into account that a use occurrence can be a computational use or a predicate use [RW85]. However, the all uses coverage criterion does not ensure that all possible ways to reach a use occurrence have been tested. As there may be several sub paths which allow a definition occurrence of a variable to reach a use occurrence of this variable. Note that some of these paths may be infinite due to cycles and cannot be covered. A possible solution is to restrain to cycle free sub paths. The only cycles allowed are those that begin and end at the same node. The all definitions uses paths criterion requires each of such cycle free sub paths to be covered by at least one test case.

A test suite T satisfies the **all definitions uses paths coverage** criterion, if and only if for all definition occurrences of a variable x and for all paths q through which a use occurrence of x is reached, there is at least one element in T which is a numerical instance of a path p that contains q as a sub-path. Moreover, q is required either to be cycle free or to be such that the first node is also the last node. This criterion may never be satisfied since such cycle free paths are infeasible to generate. But, more complex criteria (involving several definition and use occurrences) are definable.

Ntafos introduces a family of coverage criteria (required k-tuples) and their definition relies on the notion of k-dr interactions [Nta88]. For $k > 1$ a **k-dr interaction** is a sequence $K = [d_1(x_1), u_1(x_1), d_2(x_2), u_2(x_2), \ldots, d_k(x_k), u_k(x_k)]$ and for all $i < k$:

- A definition occurrence of x_i is $d_i(x_i)$.
- A definition use of x_i id $u_i(x_i)$.
- The use occurrence $u_i(x_i)$ and the definition occurrence $d_{i+1}(x_{i+1})$ are associated with the same node n_{i+1} in a path $p = (n_1) \cdot p_1 \cdot (n_2) \cdot \ldots \cdot (n_{k-1}) \cdot p_{k-1} \cdot (n_k)$ such that the definition occurrence $d_1(x_1)$ is associated to n_1.
- The ith definition occurrence $d_i(x_i)$ reaches the ith use occurrence $u_i(x_i)$ through p_i.

Where p is an interaction path for the k-dr interaction K. The aim of the required k-tuples criteria is to achieve test suites which allow to test j-dr interactions for $j \le k$.

A test suite T satisfies the **required k-tuples** criterion, if and only if for all j-dr interactions L with $1 < j \le k$, there is at least one test case in T which is a numerical instance of a path p such that p includes a sub path that is an interaction path for L.

The presented criteria are basic coverage criteria. Numerous criteria have been defined elsewhere (for example, criteria that take the number of loogs into account). For further study, the paper of Zhu et. al. provides a presentation of a large number of coverage criteria [ZHM97].

11.4   Coverage Based Testing and Fault Detection Ability

In the following, we concentrate on systems which are non-reactive: that is, they can be seen as functions (taking an input as argument and yielding a result). For these systems, test cases are pairs of inputs and intended outputs. We present contributions which aim at providing quantitative elements to evaluate the ability to detect faults of structural coverage based testing techniques.

We assume that structural coverage based testing techniques can be seen as partition based testing techniques. Partition based testing consists in splitting the whole input domain of the implementation into several subdomains. For example, domain $D = \{0, 1, 2\}$ is separated into two subdomains $D_1 = \{0, 1\}$ and $D_2 = \{2\}$. D_1 and D_2 define together a *partition* (in the mathematical sense) of D. Usually, the terminology of partition based testing is associated to any technique involving a division of the input domain into several subdomains even if these subdomains overlap. For example, if the domain $D = \{0, 1, 2\}$ is divided into the following two subdomains: $D_1' = \{0, 1\}$ and $D_2' = \{1, 2\}$.

Let us consider any structural selection criterion applied on a given model and program. Selecting a test suite implies dividing the whole input domain of the implementation. For example, a model described in a formalism containing the "if-then-else" statement with x ranging over D: *if* $(x \leq 1)$ *then inst$_1$ else inst$_2$*. By using decision coverage, the selected test suite contains at least two test cases: one for which the selected test data is such that $x \leq 1$ and one for which the test data is such that $x > 1$. This example clearly demonstrates that testing techniques in which test case selection processes are based on structural criteria are in fact partition based testing techniques.

The first part of the following section is to compare abilities to detect faults of structural coverage based testing techniques and of random based testing. Random based testing consists in selecting a certain number of test data randomly out of the input domain and evaluating outputs caused by test data with regard to intended results expressed in the model. Following the discussion above, we discuss contributions which compare random based testing and partition based testing techniques. Section 11.4.1 provides a structured presentation of several significant contributions to this aspect.

The second part of the following section is to compare techniques based on different structural criteria on the basis of abilities to detect faults. One of the most well known ways to compare criteria is by the subsume relation. It is a way to compare the severity of testing methods (in terms of adequacy of test suites). In Section 11.4.2 we present several relations derived from the subsume relation. Then, it is studied whether or not these relations impact the fault detection ability. That is, the following question is addressed: If two criteria are involved in one of these relations, what can we say about their respective abilities to detect faults?

11.4.1   Partition Testing Versus Random Testing

Here we focus on contributions which address the problem of comparing respective abilities to detect faults of random based and partition based testing [DN84, HT90, Nta98, Gut99]. All these contributions are based on a common mathematical framework. This framework is called the failure rate model and is now described.

We suppose that an implementation is used for a long period of time with various samples of randomly selected test data. Furthermore we suppose that we are able to observe the number of detected faults at any time. The number of faults will converge towards a constant. We denote θ the ratio between this constant and the total number of possible inputs. The ratio θ is called the failure rate associated to the domain D of the implementation. The probability to randomly select one test data which does not reveal a fault is $1 - \theta$ and the probability to randomly select n test data, none of which reveals a fault, is $(1 - \theta)^n$. The probability to reveal at least one fault for n randomly selected test data can be expressed as follows: $P_r = 1 - (1 - \theta)^n$.

Now let us consider that a partition based testing technique partitions the domain D into k subdomains $D_1 \ldots D_k$. For each D_i, $i \in \{1, \ldots, k\}$, θ_i denotes the failure rate associated to D_i. Now suppose that the testing technique states that n_i test data must be selected in D_i. A total of n test data is selected, therefore $n = \sum_{i=1}^{k} n_i$. The probability to select n_i test data in D_i, none of which reveals a fault, is $(1 - \theta_i)^{n_i}$ and the probability to detect at least one fault when selecting n_i test data in each D_i is $P_p = 1 - \prod_{i=1}^{k} (1 - \theta_i)^{n_i}$.

For each D_i, $i \in \{1, \ldots, k\}$, p_i is the probability that a randomly chosen test data is in D_i, so that $\theta = \sum_{i=1}^{k} p_i \theta_i$. Thus, P_r and P_p can be expressed as follows:

$$P_p = 1 - \prod_{i=1}^{k} (1 - \theta_i)^{n_i} \qquad \text{(for partition based testing), and}$$

$$P_r = 1 - (1 - \sum_{i=1}^{k} p_i \theta_i)^n \qquad \text{(for random based testing).}$$

In the following, contributions introduced can be classified into two different types. In the first type of contributions the results are based on simulation experiments. The idea is to perform comparisons between P_r and P_p with different valuations of their variable parts. In the second type of contributions (the fundamental approaches) the results are based on mathematical proofs. Under particular assumptions, fundamental results are proved.

Simulation Experiments

Duran and Ntafos [DN84] follow the framework described above to address the problem whether or not one of the two testing methods is more efficient at detecting faults than the other. That is, they compare P_r and P_p through various simulation experiments. Moreover the authors compare the two testing methods through another criterion: the expected number of errors that a set of test data will discover. Using an ideal partition scheme in which each subdomain contains at most one fault, the expected number of errors discovered with partition based testing is given by the formula $E_p(k) = \sum_{i=1}^{k} \theta_i$. Here, one test data is randomly chosen out of each subdomain D_i. The expected number of errors found by n random test data $E_r(k, n)$ is given by the formula $E_r(k, n) = k - \sum_{i=1}^{k} (1 - p_i \theta_i)^n$.

The simulation experiments consist of different variations: the number k of subdomains, the number n_i of test data in each subdomain (and thus the overall number n of test data), the failure rate θ_i in each subdomain and the probability p_i that a randomly chosen test data is in the subdomain D_i (and thus the overall failure rate θ). For each variation Duran and Ntafos study the ratio $\frac{P_r}{P_p}$ and $\frac{E_r}{E_p}$. The experiments reported are based on two different assumptions on failure rates. On the one hand, a usual belief about partition based testing is that it allows to obtain homogeneous subdomains. That is, if an input of a subdomain is failure causing, then all inputs of the subdomain have a high probability to be failure causing and conversely. Under this assumption, failure rates should be either close to 0 or close to 1. On the other hand, there are examples of program paths that compute correct values for some, but not all, of their input data. Under this assumption, the failure rate distribution should be more uniform than suggested above.

- In the first experiment, the authors suppose that the partition based testing technique divides the domain into 25 subdomains. It is supposed that the partition based technique requires the selection of one test data per sub-domain. To provide a fair comparison the random based testing method requires to select 25 test data randomly. Several values for θ_i are selected. The θ_i's are chosen from a distribution such that 2 percent of the time $\theta_i \geq 0.98$ and 98 percent of the time $\theta_i \leq 0.049$. These assignments reflect a situation in which subdomains are homogeneous. The p_i are chosen from a uniform distribution. It appears that on a total of 50 trials 14 trials are such that $P_r \geq P_p$. However the mean value of $\frac{P_r}{P_p}$ is 0.932. Under the same hypothesis on failure rates, the experiment is repeated for $k = n = 50$ and the results are even more surprising. Indeed, one could think that increasing the number of subdomains should favor partition based testing. However this experiment does not corroborate this intuition: the mean value of $\frac{P_r}{P_p}$ was 0.949. The mean value of the ratio $\frac{E_r}{E_p}$ is for 25 subdomains and 50 trials it is equal to 0.89, and for 50 subdomains and 50 trials it is equal to 0.836.
- In the second experiment, the assumption on the θ_i distribution is that θ_i's are allowed to vary uniformly from 0 to a given value $\theta_{max} \leq 1$. Several possible values are assigned to θ_{max}. Experiments are performed for $k = n = 25$ and $k = n = 50$. As θ_{max} increases P_r and P_p tend to 1. Random based testing performs better for the lower failure rates and also when the size of the partition is 25 instead of 50. Similar studies are carried out for E_r and E_p. In these studies, the number of randomly selected test data is allowed to be greater than the number of test data selected for partition based testing (100 for random based testing versus 50 for partition based testing): this is consistent with the fact that carrying out some partition based testing scheme is much more expensive than performing an equivalent number of random test data. Under these assumptions, random based testing performed better than partition based testing most of the time ($E_r > E_p$).

All these experiments deeply question the value of partition based testing with regard to random based testing. However, these are simulation results. Therefore, the authors concentrate on actual evaluations of random based testing. Duran and Ntafos propose to evaluate random based testing on three programs containing known bugs. The first program contains three errors. The first error is detected 11 out of 50 times, the second error 24 times and the third error 45 out of 50 times. The simple error in the second program is detected by 21 out of 24 times. For the third program 50 test cases were generated. The simple error was detected 18 of 50 times. More programs were tested with similar results.

One of the features of coverage criteria is that they can be used to measure coverage of test suites generated by other methods. The authors evaluate some test suites generated by random based testing, with program based coverage criteria. Test suites are generated for the programs previously used to evaluate random based testing. The idea is to simply generate a test suite and then to use a given criterion to see if the test suite satisfies the requirements stated by the criterion. Several criteria are then considered to measure random based testing adequacy. The number of test data generated ranges between 20 and 120 and five programs from the previous experiments were used. The over-all result is, that for a moderate number of random test data random based testing allows to cover these criteria for coverage percentages ranging from 57 percent up to 94 percent depending on the criterion.

The experiments presented in the paper indicates that it is reasonable to assume that random based testing can find more errors per unit cost than partition based testing, since carrying out some partition based testing scheme is much more expensive than performing an equivalent number of random test data. This holds for homogeneous subdomains and for values of θ_i uniformly distributed. Assumptions on failure rates may be unrealistic but actual evaluations show that random based testing seems to discover some relatively subtle errors without great efforts. Moreover, random based testing seems to ensure a high level of coverage for some usual coverage criteria.

Hamlet and Taylor [HT90] explore the results of Duran and Ntafos more deeply. They perform experiments based on statistical assumptions very similar to those made by Duran and Ntafos.

They compare partition based testing and random based testing with respect to the conventional failure rate model used by Duran and Ntafos. They are compared by different numerical valuations of their respective probabilities to detect faults for the same number of selected test data ($\sum_{i=1}^{k} n_i = n$). Different relationships between θ and θ_i are proposed:

- The first relationship is based on the assumption that if a test data is randomly selected, the probability that this test data is an element of any subdomain is $1/k$. Thus θ is the average of the sum of all θ_i: $\theta = \frac{1}{k}\sum_{i=1}^{k} \theta_i$. The difference between random based and partition based testing in terms of the probability of finding at least one failure will be maximal when the variance of the θ_i has a maximum. If only one test data per subdomain is selected, this occurs if only one subdomain, the jth one, is failure causing ($\theta_j = k\theta$ and $\theta_i = 0$ for $i \neq j$). This situation is studied for different failure rates and different sizes of partitions. To give a significant advantage to partition based testing, the number k of subdomains has to be of the same order of magnitude as the inverse of θ: in the frame of this investigation, the most favorable case is that random based testing is about 0.63 as effective as partition based testing. This result is clearly better than the results obtained by Duran and Ntafos [DN84]. But Hamlet and Taylor also observe that the assumption $p_i = 1/k$ is not realistic.

- The second relationship is introduced by Duran and Ntafos [DN84]. This relationship is based on the assumption that when a test data is randomly selected the probability that this test data is an element of subdomain D_i is an arbitrary number p_i. The influence of the number of subdomains, the distribution of θ_i and of lower and upper bounds for θ_i is investigated by different experiments. This deeper investigation does not contradict previous results given by Duran and Ntafos [DN84] which indicate that there are little differences between partition based and random based testing with regard to their probabilities of revealing failures. Even-though partition based testing is sometimes better, slight advantage for partition based testing can be reduced by using a higher number of random test data.

- The third relationship explores modifications of the relationship described above. The aim is to gain information on the importance of the way the subdomains are chosen and, the impact of homogeneity on the effectiveness of partition based testing. To obtain information on the importance of subdomain selection, one needs a correlation between the probability of a random test data in a given subdomain (p_i) and its failure rate (θ_i). The correlation is denoted by a weight associated to each θ_i. This weight is used to calculate p_i. The higher the weight is, the more subdomains with high failure rates have a low probability that a random test data would fall into them. The model intuitively favors partition based testing if the weight associated to a failure causing subdomain is high. Experiments are consistent with this intuition but the effectiveness of random based testing is not dramatically affected: in the worst case, random based testing is 0.77 as effective as partition based testing. Some other experiments in which failure rates are controlled were conducted. Some subdomains (hidden subdomains) have small probability of being used by random test data while other subdomains (exposed subdomains) have a high probability of being used. Failure rates of subdomains are then varied. When failure rates of hidden subdomains are higher than the overall failure rate, partition based testing is favored. When failure rates of hidden subdomains are lower than the overall failure rate, random based testing is favored. The only result is that the advantage of partition based testing arises from increased sampling in regions where failures occur. Other experiments are performed to obtain information on the importance of the impact of homogeneity on the effectiveness of partition based testing. In these experiments failure rates of hidden subdomains are permitted to vary uniformly from 1 to 0.2 (low homogeneity) and results are compared to the case where they varied from 1 to 0.9 (high homogeneity). The largest impact of low homogeneity is found to be only a 22 percent decrease in the effectiveness of partition based testing. Most of the time experiments do not show that homogeneity is an important factor which impact partition based testing effectiveness.

Besides conventional failure rate model used by Duran and Ntafos [DN84], Hamlet and Taylor also investigate a comparison between partition based and random based testing by the so-called *Valiant's Model* [Val84]. The motivation of this study is that faults are uniformly distributed over the state space of the program code, not over its input space. Valid partitions are therefore those that result from reflecting uniform coverage of program states into the input domain where testing is done. Valiant's Model does not allow to calculate such partition but it allows to relate the number of test data to the probability of missing a failure. Thus, for a given probability of missing a failure, it is possible to compare the number of test test data for both random based and partition based testing. Experimental results indicate that random based testing outperforms partition based testing many times.

Experiments performed in the contribution of Hamlet and Taylor confirm conclusion of Duran and Ntafos: partition based and random based testing are of almost equal value with respect to their ability to detect faults. Hamlet and Taylor explore the impact of homogeneity of subdomains on the ability to detect faults of partition based testing. They are not able to show that homogeneity is an important factor.

Ntafos [Nta98] presents further comparisons between random based and partition based testing. Additionally, the expected cost of failures is taken into account as a way to evaluate the effectiveness of testing strategies. A comparison is made between random based testing and proportional partition based testing. The latter is a partition based testing method where the number of allocated test data for each subdomain depends on the probability that a chosen test data falls into this subdomain. Shortly, the ratio between the number of selected test data for two arbitrary subdomains is equal to the ratio between probabilities that a test data falls into these subdomains.

First of all the power of proportional partition based testing is investigated. A problem here is that occurrences of rare special conditions (subdomains with low probability that randomly chosen test data fall into them) require a large number of test data. Suppose that an input domain is divided into two subdomains and one of them corresponds to a rare special condition which occurs once in a million runs. Then proportional partition based testing would require a total of $1,000,001$ test data to test a program that consist of a single *IF* statement. It is also argued that if the number of required test data grows, proportional partition based testing allocates test data which are the same as randomly selected test data. Thus, even though some experiments show that proportional partition based testing performs at least as well as random based testing, the difference between the respective performances tends to zero while the number of test data grows. Simulation experiments in which P_r and P_p are compared are presented. The allocation of test data in each subdomain is parameterized by the probability that a randomly chosen test data fall into this subdomain. Different failure rates, number of subdomains and test data are used. None of the experiments allows to conclude that one method is better than the other.

Comparisons between proportional partition based, partition based, and random based approaches with regard to the cost of missing a failure are also provided. The measure used is given by the expression $\Sigma c_i(1-\theta_i)^{n_i}$, where for each subdomain D_i c_i is the cost of a failure for test data in D_i, θ_i is the failure rate for D_i, and n_i is the number of test data out of D_i. For various values of k and n, sample simulation results are given that compare proportional partition based, partition based, and random based testing. Random probabilities are assigned to each subdomain. The only interesting result is that uniform partition based testing performs better than the other two strategies.

Fundamental Approaches

Gutjahr [Gut99] proposes a probabilistic approach: in contrast to the previously introduced papers, the contribution is based on mathematical proofs. The mathematical framework is obtained by slightly modifying the one used by Duran and Ntafos [DN84]. These modifications are motivated as follows: from a pragmatic point of view, neither the domain of failure nor the failure rate are known. Therefore the deterministic variables θ and θ_i are considered to be random variables associated to the probability distributions. These probability distributions are supposed to be deduced from knowledge of experts of the domain of interest. This knowledge includes the type of program, its size, the programming language used, etc. Thus θ_i and θ are replaced by $\overline{\theta}_i = E(\theta_i)$ and $\overline{\Theta} = E(\theta)$, where E is the mathematical expectation for the distribution. In this context, the probability of selecting at least one test data which reveals a fault is expressed as follows:

$$\overline{P}_p = E(1 - \prod_{i=1}^{k} (1 - \theta_i)) \qquad \text{(for partition based testing), and}$$
$$\overline{P}_r = E(1 - (1 - \theta)^k) \qquad \text{(for random based testing).}$$

The probabilities depend on a class of programs and models of a given domain and no longer on the program itself. Different results led the authors to draw the following conclusions:

- If no particularly error prone subdomain is identified before testing and if finding out the failure rate of one subdomain does not change estimations of failure rates in other subdomains, then partition based testing techniques for such a partition have a higher probability to detect errors than random based testing techniques. If the failure rate in each subdomain is close to the overall failure rate, fault detection probabilities for both testing techniques are nearly equivalent.
- Under the same assumptions than described above, if the input domain is partitioned in k subdomains and the same number of test data is selected out of each domain, then the fault detection probability of partition based

testing can be up to k times higher than that of random based testing. This is the case whenever:
(a) There are many small subdomains and only one (or a few) large subdomain(s).
(b) Homogeneous subdomains contain either mostly inputs that are correctly processed or essentially inputs that are failure causing.

All results presented in this paper are based on strong assumptions on failure rates and distribution of probabilities: One can not deduce a fundamental superiority of partition based testing over random based testing. However, the author claims that there are arguments for the conjecture that, in some practical applications, both conditions (a) and (b) are at least approximately satisfied. The first argument is that most of structural partition based testing techniques define partitions on the basis of predicates used in the program. These introduce extremely unbalanced subdomain sizes. As a result, condition (a) is lucky enough to be almost true. Concerning condition (b), it is argued that reasonable subdivision techniques bundle up inputs to subdomains that are processed by the program in a similar way. In such context, if one input of a subdomain is recognized as failure causing, this increases the probability that the other inputs are also failure causing. Conversely, this probability is decreased if an input is recognized as correctly processed.

Notes All contributions show that we know very little about the comparison between random based and partition based testing with regard to their respective ability to detect faults. Independently from the technical background (simulation, theoretical approaches), the presented results and conclusion are based on strong assumptions on failure rates. It is difficult to judge the relevance of these assumptions with regard to real failure rates. Random based testing seems to be the most valuable technique to test reliability of software. This is due to the fact that random selection of test data makes no assumption on the inputs. In contrast, partition based selection constrains relations between inputs. Thus, selected test suites have great chances to be non-representatives for usual uses of the software. If one wants to constrain test suites while addressing reliability, the constraints should be based on operational profiles rather than on structure of the model. This increases chances to run test data which are representatives of real use cases. Nevertheless, partition based testing techniques have great value. In particular, it is known that in practice they are the only ones that tackle efficiently the problem of specific fault detection. For example logical faults or boundary faults can be efficiently analyzed by these kinds of approaches. Unfortunately, the failure rate model does not allow to capture the notion of specific fault (common mistakes made by programmers). Thus, this model can not be used to ground theoretically this fact. Contributions allowing to define models that could take into account this notion of specific faults would be of great value. This would allow to compare partition based testing and random based testing with regard to their abilities to detect these specific faults. Concerning the nature of systems under test, all contributions presented here deal with non-reactive systems. Contributions allowing to relate partition based testing and random based testing for reactive systems would be an interesting prospect. However the failure rate model should be adapted to take into account infinite runs.

11.4.2   Structural Criteria and Ability to Detect Faults

In this section, we compare the ability to detect faults for different testing methods involving structural coverage criteria to select test suites. We present a contribution by Frankl and Weyuker [FW93]. They propose to define relations between criteria and to study, for each of these relations, what knowing that a criterion C_1 is in relation with a criterion C_2 tells us about their respective ability to detect faults. One of the most well known way to compare two coverage criteria is the **subsume relation**. A criterion C_1 subsumes a criterion C_2 if and only if for any program and associated model, C_1 is satisfied by a test suite T implies C_2 is satisfied by T. The subsume relation compares constraints imposed by criteria to select test suites. In contrast, relations proposed by Frankl and Weyuker only compares partition induced by criteria. This allows to compare fault detection abilities of criteria by different assumptions on the test data selection process. These assumptions are made explicit in the way fault detection ability is measured. Frankl and Weyuker propose three different measures. We note $\mathcal{SD}_C(P, M) = \{D_1, D_2, \ldots, D_k\}$ the partition induced by a given criterion C for a given program P and associated model M. For $i \in \{1, \ldots, k\}$, we denote $d_i = \mid D_i \mid$ and m_i the number of failure causing inputs in D_i. The measures proposed by Frankl and Weyuker are:

- $M_1(C, P, M) = \max_{1 \leq i \leq k} \left(\frac{m_i}{d_i} \right)$ measures to what extent failure causing inputs are concentrated at subdomains. The only assumption made on the test data selection process is that at least one test data is selected in each subdomain. With this assumption, $M1(C, P, M)$ is a lower bound of the probability that a test suite will expose at least one fault.

- $M_2(C, P, M) = 1 - \prod_{i=1}^{k} \left(1 - \frac{m_i}{d_i} \right)$ measures the exact probability that an adequate test suite exposes at least one fault, assuming that the test data selection process requires exactly one selection per subdomain.

- $M_3(C, P, M, n) = 1 - \prod_{i=1}^{k} \left(1 - \frac{m_i}{d_i} \right)^n$ measures the exact probability that an adequate test suite exposes at least one fault, provided that the test data selection process requires n selections per subdomain.

For each relation R defined between criteria, for every program P and every model M, the authors investigate the following questions:

(A) Does $R(C_1, C_2)$ imply $M_1(C_1, P, M) \geq M_1(C_2, P, M)$?
(B) Does $R(C_1, C_2)$ imply $M_2(C_1, P, M) \geq M_2(C_2, P, M)$?
(C) Does $R(C_1, C_2)$ imply $M_3(C_1, P, M, 1) \geq M_3(C_2, P, M, n)$ where $n = \frac{|\mathcal{SD}_{C_1}(P,M)|}{|\mathcal{SD}_{C_2}(P,M)|}$?

Let us comment the last question. One problem with using M_2 as a measure is that one criterion C_1 may divide the domain into k_1 subdomains while another criterion C_2 divides the domain into k_2 subdomains where $k_1 > k_2$. Then, M_2 gives C_1 an unfair advantage since C_1 will require k_1 test data while C_2 will only require k_2 test data. M_3 allows to overcome this problem by comparing $M_3(C_1, P, M, 1)$ and $M_3(C_2, P, M, \frac{k_1}{k_2})$.

We now introduce five relations defined by Frankl and Weyuker.

The Narrows Relation (1)

> C_1 **narrows** C_2 **for** (P, M) if for every subdomain $D \in \mathcal{SD}_{C_2}(P, M)$ there is a subdomain $D' \in \mathcal{SD}_{C_1}(P, S)$ such that $D' \subseteq D$. If for every (P, S) C_1 narrows C_2, one says that C_1 **universally narrows** C_2.

Example: We consider a program P whose input domain is the set of integers between $-N$ and $+N$, with $N > 1$. C_1 is a criterion that requires the selection of at least one test data that is 0 and at least one test data that is different of 0. C_2 is a criterion that requires the selection of at least one test data that is greater than or equal to 0 and at least one test data that is less or equal to 0. Therefore C_1 uses two subdomains: $D_1 = \{0\}$ and $D_2 = \{x \mid -N \leq x \leq N \wedge x \neq 0\}$. C_2 uses two subdomains: $D_3 = \{x \mid 0 \leq x \leq N\}$ and $D_4 = \{x \mid -N \leq x \leq 0\}$. Since D_3 and D_4 both contain D_1, C_1 narrows C_2.

Relation to the subsume relation: Consider that for any (P, M), C_1 and C_2 give rise to the same set of subdomains, but C_2 requires selection of two test data out of each subdomain whereas C_1 only requires selection of one test data out of each subdomain. Trivially, C_1 universally narrows C_2. However, C_1 does not subsume C_2, since a test suite consisting of one element out of each subdomain is C_1-adequate but not C_2-adequate. However, we have the following theorem:

Theorem 11.1. *Let C_1 and C_2 be two criteria which explicitly require the selection of at least one test data out of each subdomain, then C_1 subsumes C_2 if and only if C_1 universally narrows C_2.*

Proof. Assume C_1 universally narrows C_2. Let T be a test suite that is C_1-adequate for some program P and model M. T requires the selection of at least one test data out of each subdomain of $\mathcal{SD}_{C_1}(P, M)$. Thus, since each subdomain in $\mathcal{SD}_{C_2}(P, M)$ is a superset of some subdomains belonging to $\mathcal{SD}_{C_1}(P, M)$, T is a test suite which requires the selection of at least one test data out of each subdomain of $\mathcal{SD}_{C_2}(P, M)$. We conclude that C_1 subsumes C_2.

Conversely, assume C_1 does not universally narrow C_2. There exists a program P and a model M such that some subdomain $D \in \mathcal{SD}_{C_2}(P, M)$ is not a superset of any subdomain of $\mathcal{SD}_{C_1}(P, M)$. Thus for each $D' \in \mathcal{SD}_{C_1}(P, M)$, $D' - D \neq \emptyset$. Let T be a test suite which requires the selection of exactly one test data out of $D' - D$ for each $D' \in \mathcal{SD}_{C_1}(P, M)$. T is C_1-adequate but not C_2-adequate. So C_1 does not subsume C_2.

Relation to the three measures: We consider questions (A), (B) and (C) introduced in the introduction of this section. In order to answer these questions we consider the following example. Domain D of a program P is $\{0, 1, 2\}$. M is the model associated to P. We suppose that $\mathcal{SD}_{C_1}(P, M) = \{\{0, 1\}, \{0, 2\}\}$ and $\mathcal{SD}_{C_2}(P, M) = \{\{0, 1\}, \{0, 1, 2\}\}$. Since $\{0, 1\} \subseteq \{0, 1\}$ and $\{0, 2\} \subseteq \{0, 1, 2\}$, C_1 narrows C_2.

(A) Does C_1 narrow C_2 imply $M_1(C_1, P, M) \geq M_1(C_2, P, M)$?

We answer in the negative. Suppose that only 1 and 2 are failure causing: $M_1(C_1, P, M) = \frac{1}{2}$ while $M_1(C_2, P, M) = \frac{2}{3}$ and thus $M_1(C_1, P, M) < M_1(C_2, P, M)$.

(B) Does C_1 narrow C_2 imply $M_2(C_1, P, M) \geq M_2(C_2, P, M)$?

We answer in the negative. Suppose that only 1 and 2 are failure causing: $M_2(C_1, P, M) = 1 - (1 - \frac{1}{2})(1 - \frac{1}{2}) = \frac{3}{4}$, $M_2(C_2, P, M) = 1 - (1 - \frac{1}{2})(1 - \frac{2}{3}) = \frac{5}{6}$ and thus $M_2(C_1, P, M) < M_2(C_2, P, M)$.

(C) Does C_1 narrow C_2 imply $M_3(C_1, P, M, 1) \geq M_3(C_2, P, M, n)$ where

$$n = \frac{|\mathcal{SD}_{C_1}(P, M)|}{|\mathcal{SD}_{C_2}(P, M)|}?$$

We answer in the negative. Since in our example $n = 1$, question (C) is equivalent to Question (B).

As stated above, the narrows relation does not necessarily induce a better fault detection ability for each of the three measures considered. Thus from Theorem 11.1, it is naturally deduced that the subsume relation does not necessarily induce a better fault detection ability for each of the three measures considered.

The Covers Relation (2) The narrows relation can be strengthened to impose that each subdomain of the partition induced by C_2 can be expressed as a union of some subdomains of the partition induced by C_1. This gives rises to the following definition:

C_1 **covers** C_2 **for** (P, M) if for every subdomain $D \in \mathcal{SD}_{C_2}(P, M)$ if there is a non-empty collection of subdomains $\{D_1, \ldots, D_n\}$ belonging to $\mathcal{SD}_{C_1}(P, M)$ such that $D_1 \cup \cdots \cup D_n = D$. If for every (P, M) C_1 covers C_2, one says that C_1 **universally covers** C_2.

Example: We consider criteria C_1 and C_2 and Program P used to illustrate the narrow relation. Since D_3 and D_4 both contain D_1, C_1 narrows C_2. However, since $D_3 \neq D_1$, $D_3 \neq D_2$ and $D_3 \neq D_1 \cup D_2$, C_1 does not cover C_2.

In contrast, we consider a program P' whose input domain are the integers between $-N$ and N ($N > 0$). Suppose that criterion C_1' induces a partition into two subdomains: $D_1' = \{x \mid -N + 1 \leq x \leq N\}$ and $D_2' = \{x \mid -N \leq x \leq N - 1\}$ and that criterion C_2' induces a partition into one subdomain: $D_3' = \{x \mid -N \leq x \leq N\}$. Since $D_3' = D_1' \cup D_2'$, C_1' covers C_2'.

Relation to the subsume relation: The following theorem is obvious:

Theorem 11.2. *Let C_1 and C_2 be two criteria. C_1 universally covers C_2 implies C_1 universally narrows C_2.*

From Theorem 11.1, we immediately have the following theorem:

Theorem 11.3. *Let C_1 and C_2 be two criteria which explicitly require the selection of at least one test data out of each subdomain, then C_1 universally covers C_2 implies C_1 subsumes C_2.*

Relation to the three measures: In order to answer questions (A), (B) and (C), we consider the following example. Domain D of a program P is $\{0, 1, 2, 3\}$. M is the model associated to P. We suppose that $\mathcal{SD}_{C_1}(P, M) = \{\{0, 1\}, \{1, 2\}, \{3\}\}$ and $\mathcal{SD}_{C_2}(P, M) = \{\{0, 1, 2\}, \{1, 2, 3\}\}$. Since $\{0, 1, 2\} = \{0, 1\} \cup \{1, 2\}$ and $\{1, 2, 3\} = \{1, 2\} \cup \{3\}$, C_1 covers C_2.

(A) Does C_1 cover C_2 imply $M_1(C_1, P, M) \geq M_1(C_2, P, M)$?

We answer in the negative. Suppose that only 0 and 2 are failure causing: $M_1(C_1, P, M) = \frac{1}{2}$ while $M_1(C_2, P, M) = \frac{2}{3}$ and thus $M_1(C_1, P, M) < M_1(C_2, P, M)$.

(B) Does C_1 cover C_2 imply $M_2(C_1, P, M) \geq M_2(C_2, P, M)$?

We answer in the negative. Suppose that only 2 is failure causing. $M_2(C_1, P, M) = 1 - (1 - \frac{1}{2}) = \frac{1}{2}$ while $M_2(C_2, P, M) = 1 - (1 - \frac{1}{3})(1 - \frac{1}{3}) = \frac{5}{9}$ and thus $M_2(C_1, P, M) < M_2(C_2, P, M)$.

(C) Does C_1 cover C_2 imply $M_3(C_1, P, M, 1) \geq M_3(C_2, P, M, n)$ where $n = \frac{|\mathcal{SD}_{C_1}(P, M)|}{|\mathcal{SD}_{C_2}(P, M)|}$?

We answer in the negative. It is obvious that for $n \geq 1$, $M_3(C_2, P, M, n) \geq M_2(C_2, P, M)$. Now $M_3(C_1, P, M, 1) = M_2(C_1, P, M)$. Since we have proven that there exists P and M such that $M_2(C_1, P, M) < M_2(C_2, P, M)$, we deduce that there exists P and M such that $M_3(C_1, P, M, 1) < M_3(C_2, P, M, n)$.

As for the narrows relation, the covers relation does not necessarily induce a better fault detection ability for each of the three measures considered. Thus, ensuring that each subdomain of the partition induced by C_2 can be expressed as a union of some subdomains of the partition induced by C_1 is not sufficient to gain a superiority of C_1 over C_2 (at least with respect to the three measures considered).

The Partitions Relation (3) The cover relation is then strengthened to ensure that for each subdomain of the partition induced by C_2, a partition consisting of pairwise disjoint subdomains induced by C_1 may be defined.

C_1 **partitions** C_2 for (P, M) if for every subdomain $D \in \mathcal{SD}_{C_2}(P, M)$ there is a non-empty collection of pairwise disjoint subdomains $\{D_1, \ldots, D_n\}$ belonging to $\mathcal{SD}_{C_1}(P, M)$ such that $D_1 \cup \cdots \cup D_n = D$. If for every (P, M) C_1 partitions C_2, one says that C_1 **universally partitions** C_2.

Example: Let us consider criteria C_1' and C_2' and the program P' used to illustrate the covers relation. Since $D_3' = D_1' \cup D_2'$ C_1' covers C_2' and, since $D_1' \cap D_2' \neq \emptyset$, C_1' does not partition C_2'.

In contrast we consider a program P'' whose input domain are the integers between $-N$ and N ($N > 0$). Suppose that a criterion C_1'' induces a partition into two subdomains: $D_1'' = \{x \mid 0 \leq x \leq N\}$ and $D_2'' = \{x \mid -N \leq x < 0\}$ and that criterion C_2'' induces a partition into one subdomain: $D_3'' = \{x \mid -N \leq x \leq N\}$. Since $D_3'' = D_1'' \cup D_2''$ and $D_1'' \cap D_2'' = \emptyset$, C_1'' partitions C_2''.

Relation to the subsume relation: The following theorem is obvious:

Theorem 11.4. *Let C_1 and C_2 be two criteria. C_1 universally partitions C_2 implies C_1 universally covers C_2.*

From Theorem 11.2, we have the following theorem:

Theorem 11.5. *Let C_1 and C_2 be two criteria. C_1 universally partitions C_2 implies C_1 universally narrows C_2.*

From Theorem 11.1 we have the following theorem:

Theorem 11.6. *Let C_1 and C_2 be two criteria which explicitly require the selection of at least one test data out of each subdomain, then C_1 universally partitions C_2 implies C_1 subsumes C_2.*

Relation to the three measures:

(A) Does C_1 partition C_2 imply $M_1(C_1, P, M) \geq M_1(C_2, P, M)$?

The answer is positive, as stated in the following theorem:

Theorem 11.7. *If C_1 partitions C_2 for a program P and a model M then $M_1(C_1, P, M) \geq M_1(C_2, P, M)$.*

Proof. Let $D_0 \in \mathcal{SD}_{C_2}(P, M)$. Let $D_1, \ldots, D_n$ be disjoint subdomains belonging to $\mathcal{SD}_{C_1}(P, M)$ such that $D_0 = D_1 \cup \cdots \cup D_n$. Then $m_0 = m_1 + \cdots + m_n$ and $d_0 = d_1 + \cdots + d_n$. Thus $max_{i=1}^{n}(\frac{m_i}{d_i})$ is minimized when each $\frac{m_i}{d_i} = \frac{m_0}{d_0}$. So $max_{i=1}^{n}(\frac{m_i}{d_i}) \geq \frac{m_0}{d_0}$ and therefore $M_1(C_1, P, M) \geq M_1(C_2, P, M)$.

(B) Does C_1 partitions C_2 imply $M_2(C_1, P, M) \geq M_2(C_2, P, M)$?

We answer in the negative. Domain D of a program P is $\{0, 1, 2, 3\}$. M is the model associated to P. We suppose that $\mathcal{SD}_{C_1}(P, M) = \{\{0\}, \{1, 2\}, \{3\}\}$

and $\mathcal{SD}_{C_2}(P, M) = \{\{0, 1, 2\}, \{1, 2, 3\}\}$. Since $\{0, 1, 2\} = \{0\} \cup \{1, 2\}$, $\{0\} \cap \{1, 2\} = \emptyset$, $\{1, 2, 3\} = \{1, 2\} \cup \{3\}$, and $\{1, 2\} \cap \{3\} = \emptyset$, C_1 partitions C_2. Suppose that only 2 is failure causing. $M_2(C_1, P, M) = 1 - (1 - \frac{1}{2}) = \frac{1}{2}$ while $M_2(C_2, P, M) = 1 - (1 - \frac{1}{3})(1 - \frac{1}{3}) = \frac{5}{9}$ and thus $M_2(C_1, P, M) < M_2(C_2, P, M)$.

(C) Does C_1 partitions C_2 imply $M_3(C_1, P, M, 1) \geq M_3(C_2, P, M, n)$ where $n = \frac{|\mathcal{SD}_{C_1}(P,M)|}{|\mathcal{SD}_{C_2}(P,M)|}$?

We answer in the negative. For $n \geq 1$, $M_3(C_2, P, M, n) \geq M_2(C_2, P, M)$. Now $M_3(C_1, P, M, 1) = M_2(C_1, P, M)$. Since we have proven that there exists P and M such that $M_2(C_1, P, M) < M_2(C_2, P, M)$, we deduce that there exists P and M such that $M_3(C_1, P, M, 1) < M_3(C_2, P, M, n)$.

The partitions relation ensures a better fault detection ability for measure M_1 (if C_1 partitions C_2 then C_1 is better at detecting faults than C_2 with regard to M_1) but not necessarily for the two others. Recall that measure M_1 is a lower bound of the probability that a test suite will expose at least one fault. Thus Theorem 11.7 only ensures that if C_1 partitions C_2, this lower bound of the probability that a test suite will expose at least one fault is greater for C_1 than for C_2. Another intuitive way to understand this result is that a partition induced by C_1 concentrates more failure causing inputs in one specific subdomain than a partition induced by C_2 does.

The Properly Covers Relation (4) In order to obtain a better fault detection ability regarding measure M_2, the cover relation is specialized so that each subdomain D of the partition $\mathcal{SD}_{C_1}(P, S)$ is used only once to define a partition of a subdomain of $\mathcal{SD}_{C_2}(P, S)$.

Let us note $\mathcal{SD}_{C_1}(P, S) = \{D_1^1, \ldots, D_m^1\}$ and $\mathcal{SD}_{C_2}(P, S) = \{D_1^2, \ldots, D_n^2\}$.

C_1 **properly covers** C_2 for (P, M) if there is a multi-set

$$\mathcal{M} = \{D_{1,1}^1, \ldots D_{1,k_1}^1, \ldots, D_{n,1}^1, \ldots D_{n,k_n}^1\}$$

such that $\mathcal{M} \subseteq \mathcal{SD}_{C_1}(P, M)$ and $D_i^2 = D_{i,1}^1 \cup \cdots \cup D_{i,k_i}^1$ for $i \in \{1, \ldots, n\}$. If for every (P, M) C_1 properly covers C_2, one says that C_1 **universally properly covers** C_2.

Example: Consider a program P with integer input domain $\{x \mid 0 \leq x \leq 3\}$, and criteria C_1 and C_2 such that $\mathcal{SD}_{C_1} = \{D_a, D_b, D_c\}$ and $\mathcal{SD}_{C_2} = \{D_d, D_e\}$, where $D_a = \{0\}$, $D_b = \{1, 2\}$, $D_c = \{3\}$, $D_d = \{0, 1, 2\}$, and $D_e = \{1, 2, 3\}$. Then $D_d = D_a \cup D_b$ and $D_e = D_c \cup D_b$, so C_1 covers (and also partitions) C_2. However, C_1 does not properly cover C_2 because subdomain D_b is needed in to cover both D_d and D_e, but only occurs once in the multi-set $\mathcal{SD}_{C_1}$.

On the other hand consider criterion C_3 where $\mathcal{SD}_{C_3} = \{D_a, D_b, D_b, D_c\}$. C_3 does properly cover C_2. It is legitimate to use D_b twice to cover both D_d and D_e, since it occurs twice in $\mathcal{SD}_{C_3}$.

Relation to the subsume relation: The following theorem is obvious:

Theorem 11.8. *Let C_1 and C_2 be two criteria. C_1 universally properly covers C_2 implies C_1 universally covers C_2.*

From Theorem 11.2 we have the following theorem:

Theorem 11.9. *Let C_1 and C_2 be two criteria. C_1 universally properly covers C_2 implies C_1 universally narrows C_2.*

From Theorem 11.1 we have the following theorem:

Theorem 11.10. *Let C_1 and C_2 be two criteria which explicitly require the selection of at least one test data out of each subdomain, then C_1 universally properly covers C_2 implies C_1 subsumes C_2.*

Relation to the three measures:

(A) Does C_1 properly cover C_2 imply $M_1(C_1, P, M) \geq M_1(C_2, P, M)$?

We answer in the negative. Domain D of a program P is $\{0, 1, 2, 3\}$. M is the model associated to P. We suppose that $\mathcal{SD}_{C_1}(P, M) = \{\{0, 1\}, \{1, 2\}, \{3\}\}$ and $\mathcal{SD}_{C_2}(P, M) = \{\{0, 1, 2\}, \{3\}\}$. Since $\{0, 1, 2\} = \{0, 1\} \cup \{1, 2\}$ and $\{3\}$ is an element of $\mathcal{SD}_{C_1}(P, M)$, C_1 properly covers C_2. We suppose that only 0 and 2 are failure causing. Therefore, $M_1(C_1, P, M) = \frac{1}{2}$ and $M_1(C_2, P, M) = \frac{2}{3}$. We conclude $M_1(C_1, P, M) < M_1(C_2, P, M)$.

(B) Does C_1 properly cover C_2 imply $M_2(C_1, P, M) \geq M_2(C_2, P, M)$?

The answer is positive as stated in the following theorem:

Theorem 11.11. *If C_1 properly covers C_2 for program P and model M, then $M_2(C_1, P, M) \geq M_2(C_2, P, M)$.*

Proof. The proof requires some intermediate lemma.

Lemma 11.12. *Assume $d_1, d_2 > 0$, $0 \leq x \leq d_1$, $0 \leq x \leq d_2$, $0 \leq m_1 \leq d_1 - x$ and $0 \leq m_2 \leq d_2 - x$. Then we have:*

$$\frac{m_1 + m_2}{d_1 + d_2 - x} \leq (1 - (1 - \frac{m_1}{d_1})(1 - \frac{m_2}{d_2})).$$

Proof. Since

$$(1 - (1 - \frac{m_1}{d_1})(1 - \frac{m_2}{d_2})) = \frac{m_1 d_2 + m_2 d_1 - m_1 m_2}{d_1 d_2}$$

it suffices to show that

$$0 \leq (m_1 d_2 + m_2 d_1 - m_1 m_2)(d_1 + d_2 - x) - (m_1 + m_2)(d_1 d_2)$$
$$= m_2 d_1 (d_1 - m_1 - x) + m_1 d_2 (d_2 - m_2 - x) + m_1 m_2 x$$

This follows immediately from the assumption that $(d_1 - m_1 - x)$, $(d_2 - m_2 - x)$, d_i, m_i, and x are all non negative.

Lemma 11.13. *Let $D_3 = D_1 \cup D_2$. Then $\frac{m_3}{d_3} < (1 - (1 - \frac{m_1}{d_1})(1 - \frac{m_2}{d_2}))$.*

Proof. For any set $\{D_1, \ldots, D_n\}$ of subdomains, let us note $f(D_1, \ldots, D_n) = \prod_{i=1}^{k} (1 - \frac{m_i}{d_i})$.

We want to show that: $1 - f(D_3) < 1 - f(D_1, D_2)$ or that $f(D_3) > f(D_1, D_2)$.

We start by showing that for given values d_3 and m_3, the value of $f(D_1, D_2)$ is maximized when $D_1 \cap D_2$ contains as few failure causing inputs as possible. This is clear intuitively, since points in the intersection are more likely to be selected. Thus when as many of them as possible are not failure causing, the probability to select an input which does not cause a fault is maximal (that is if $f(D_1, D_2)$ is maximal).

Formally, let $D_a = D_3 - D_2$, $D_b = D_3 - D_1$ and $D_c = D_1 \cap D_2$. Let d_a, d_b, d_c and x_a, x_b, x_c be the size and the number of inputs which does not cause a fault of D_a, D_b and D_c respectively. The following equation holds:

$$f(D_1, D_2) = (\tfrac{x_a + x_c}{d_a + d_c})(\tfrac{x_b + x_c}{d_b + d_c})$$

Suppose it is possible to swap one non failure causing input out of D_a with one failure causing input of D_c. Let us call D_1' and D_2' the subdomains obtained from D_1 and D_2 by applying this operation. Doing so leaves the values d_a, d_b, d_c, and x_b unchanged but decrements x_a and increments x_c, yielding

$$f(D_1', D_2') = (\tfrac{x_a - 1 + x_c + 1}{d_a + d_c})(\tfrac{x_b + x_c + 1}{d_b + d_c}) > f(D_1, D_2).$$

Similarly, swapping a non failure causing input of D_b with a failure causing input of D_c leads to two subdomains D_1'' and D_2'' such that $f(D_1'', D_2'') > f(D_1, D_2)$.

Thus, to prove the lemma, it suffices to consider the following two cases.

Case 1: D_c consists entirely of non failure causing inputs. In this case, letting $x = d_c = |\, D_1 \cap D_2 \,|$, the hypotheses of Lemma 11.12 are satisfied, so:

$$\tfrac{m_1 + m_2}{d_1 + d_2 - d_c} \le (1 - (1 - \tfrac{m_1}{d_1})(1 - \tfrac{m_2}{d_2})) \text{ holds.}$$

Since $m_3 = m_1 + m_2$ and $d_3 = d_1 + d_2 - d_c$, it gives the desired result.

Case 2: D_a and D_b consist entirely of failure causing inputs. We want to show that $f(D_3) - f(D_1, D_2) \ge 0$, where

$$f(D_3) = \tfrac{x_c}{d_a + d_b + d_c} \text{ and } f(D_1, D_2) = (\tfrac{x_c}{d_a + d_c})(\tfrac{x_c}{d_b + d_c}).$$

It suffices to show

$$0 \le x_c((d_a + d_c)(d_b + d_c) - x_c(d_a + d_b + d_c))$$

318   Christophe Gaston and Dirk Seifert

that is

$$0 \le x_c(d_a(d_b + d_c - x_c) + d_b(d_c - x_c) + d_c(d_c - x_c))$$

But this follows immediately from the fact that $0 \le x_c \le d_c$.

Lemma 11.14. *Let* $D = D_1 \cup \cdots \cup D_n$. *Then* $f(D) \ge f(D_1, \ldots, D_n)$.

Proof. Proof by induction on n. The base case, $n = 1$ is trivial. Now assuming that

$$D = D_1 \cup \cdots \cup D_k \Rightarrow f(D) \ge f(D_1, \ldots, D_k),$$

we want to show that

$$D' = D_1 \cup \cdots \cup D_{k+1} \Rightarrow f(D) \ge f(D_1, \ldots, D_{k+1}).$$

Since $D' = D \cup D_{k+1}$, from Lemma 11.13 we deduce $f(D') \ge f(D, D_{k+1})$. Now from the definition of f, $f(D, D_{k+1}) = f(D)f(D_{k+1})$. We deduce $f(D') \ge f(D)f(D_{k+1})$. From the inductive hypothesis, we can write $f(D) \ge f(D_1, \ldots, D_k)$.

Thus we deduce $f(D') \ge f(D_1, \ldots, D_k)f(D_{k+1})$. From the definition of f we conclude $f(D') \ge f(D_1, \ldots, D_{k+1})$.

We now prove Theorem 11.11. Assume C_1 properly covers C_2 for a program P and model M. Let us denote $\mathcal{SD}_{C_1}(P, M) = \{D_1^1, \ldots, D_m^1\}$ and $\mathcal{SD}_{C_2}(P, M) = \{D_1^2, \ldots, D_n^2\}$. Let $\mathcal{M} = \{D_{1,1}^1, \ldots D_{1,k_1}^1, \ldots, D_{n,1}^1, \ldots D_{n,k_n}^1\}$ be a set such that such that $\mathcal{M} \subseteq \mathcal{SD}_{C_1}(P, M)$ and $D_i^2 = D_{i,1}^1 \cup \cdots \cup D_{i,k_i}^1$ for $i \in \{1, \ldots, n\}$.

From the definition of f we can write

$$f(D_1^2, \ldots, D_n^2) = \prod_{i \le n} f(D_i^2).$$

From Lemma 11.14, we have

$$\prod_{i \le n} f(D_i^2) \ge \prod_{i \le n,} \prod_{j \le k_i,} f(D_{i,j}^1).$$

Since for all $i \le m$ we have $f(D_i^1) \le 1$, we deduce:

$$\prod_{j \le k_i,} f(D_{i,j}^1) \ge f(D_1^1, \ldots, D_m^1).$$

Thus we deduce:

$$f(D_1^2, \ldots, D_n^2) \ge f(D_1^1, \ldots, D_m^1).$$

We conclude the proof:

$$M_2(C_1, P, M) \ge M_2(C_2, P, M).$$

(C) Does C_1 properly cover C_2 imply $M_3(C_1, P, M, 1) \ge M_3(C_2, P, M, n)$ where $n = \frac{|\mathcal{SD}_{C_1}(P,M)|}{|\mathcal{SD}_{C_2}(P,M)|}$?

We answer in the negative. Assume that the domain of a program P is $\{0, 1, 2\}$. Let us note M the model associated to P. We suppose that $\mathcal{SD}_{C_1}(P, M) = \{\{0, 1\}, \{0, 2\}\}$ and $\mathcal{SD}_{C_2}(P, M) = \{0, 1, 2\}$. Since $\{0, 1, 2\} = \{0, 1\} \cup \{0, 2\}$, C_1 properly covers C_2. Suppose that only 1 is failure causing then $M_3(C_1, P, M, 1) = 1 - (1 - \frac{1}{2}) = \frac{1}{2}$. Now, $M_3(C_2, P, M, 2) = 1 - (1 - \frac{1}{3})^2 = 1 - (\frac{2}{3})^2 = \frac{5}{9} > M_3(C_1, P, M, 1)$.

The properly covers relation ensures a better fault detection ability for measure M_2 (if C_1 properly covers C_2 then C_1 is better at detecting faults than C_2 with regard to M_2) but not necessarily for the two others. Recall that measure M_2 measures the exact probability that an adequate test suite exposes at least one fault, assuming that the test data selection process requires exactly one selection per subdomain. However we answered to question (C) in the negative. This means that if the same number of test data is used for C_1 and for C_2, then nothing ensures that C_1 will be better at detecting faults than C_2 (for measure M_3). Note also that if C_1 properly covers C_2, then nothing ensures that a partition induced by C_1 concentrates more failure causing inputs in one specific subdomain than a partition induced by C_2 does. This is due to the fact that we answered in the negative to question (A).

The Properly Partitions Relation (5) The properly partitions relation constrains the partitions relation exactly as the properly covers relation constrains the covers relation. Let us note $\mathcal{SD}_{C_1}(P, S) = \{D_1^1, \ldots, D_m^1\}$ and $\mathcal{SD}_{C_2}(P, S) = \{D_1^2, \ldots, D_n^2\}$.

C_1 **properly partitions** C_2 **for** (P, S) if there is a multi-set

$$\mathcal{M} = \{D_{1,1}^1, \ldots D_{1,k_1}^1, \ldots, D_{n,1}^1, \ldots D_{n,k_n}^1\}$$

such that $\mathcal{M} \subseteq \mathcal{SD}_{C_1}(P, S)$ and $D_i^2 = D_{i,1}^1 \cup \cdots \cup D_{i,k_i}^1$ for $i \in \{1, \ldots, n\}$. Moreover, it is required that for each i, collection $\{D_{i,1}^1, \ldots, D_{i,k_i}^1\}$ is pairwise disjoint. If for every (P, S) C_1 properly covers C_2 for (P, S), one says that C_1 **universally properly partitions** C_2.

Example: Again, consider criteria C_2 and C_3 used to illustrate the properly cover relation. C_3 also properly partitions C_2 since $D_d = D_a \cup D_b$, $D_e = D_c \cup D_b$, $D_a \cap D_b = \emptyset$, $D_c \cup D_b = \emptyset$

Relation to the subsume relation: The two following theorems are obvious:

Theorem 11.15. *Let C_1 and C_2 be two criteria. C_1 universally properly partitions C_2 implies C_1 universally properly covers C_2.*

Theorem 11.16. *Let C_1 and C_2 be two criteria. C_1 universally properly partitions C_2 implies C_1 universally partitions C_2.*

Either from Theorem 11.8 or from Theorem 11.4, we have the following Theorem:

Theorem 11.17. *Let C_1 and C_2 be two criteria. C_1 universally properly partitions C_2 implies C_1 universally covers C_2.*

From Theorem 11.2 we have the following theorem:

Theorem 11.18. *Let C_1 and C_2 be two criteria. C_1 universally properly partitions C_2 implies C_1 universally narrows C_2.*

From Theorem 11.1 we have the following theorem:

Theorem 11.19. *Let C_1 and C_2 be two criteria which explicitly require the selection of at least one test data out of each subdomain, then C_1 universally properly partitions C_2 implies C_1 subsumes C_2.*

Relation to the three measures:

(A) Does C_1 properly partition C_2 imply $M_1(C_1, P, M) \geq M_1(C_2, P, M)$?

The answer is positive, as stated in the following theorem:

Theorem 11.20. *If C_1 properly partitions C_2 for a program P and a model M then $M_1(C_1, P, M) \geq M_1(C_2, P, M)$.*

Proof. From Theorem 11.16 C_1 partitions C_2. Theorem 11.7 allows us to conclude that $M_1(C_1, P, M) \geq M_1(C_2, P, M)$.

(B) Does C_1 properly partitions C_2 imply $M_2(C_1, P, M) \geq M_2(C_2, P, M)$?

The answer is positive, as stated in the following theorem:

Theorem 11.21. *If C_1 properly partitions C_2 for a program P and a model M then $M_2(C_1, P, M) \geq M_2(C_2, P, M)$.*

Proof. From Theorem 11.15 C_1 properly covers C_2. Theorem 11.11 allows us to conclude that $M_2(C_1, P, M) \geq M_2(C_2, P, M)$.

(C) Does C_1 properly partition C_2 imply $M_3(C_1, P, M, 1) \geq M_3(C_2, P, M, n)$ where $n = \frac{|SD_{C_1}(P,M)|}{|SD_{C_2}(P,M)|}$?

We answer in the negative. Domain D of a program P is $\{0, 1, 2, 3\}$. M is the model associated to P. We suppose that $SD_{C_1}(P, M) = \{\{0\}, \{1\}, \{2, 3\}\}$ and $SD_{C_2}(P, M) = \{0, 1, 2, 3\}$. Since $\{0, 1, 2, 3\} = \{0\} \cup \{1\} \cup \{2, 3\}$ and $\{0\} \cap \{1\} = \{0\} \cap \{2, 3\} = \{1\} \cap \{2, 3\} = \emptyset$, C_1 properly partition C_2. Suppose that only 2 is failure causing. $M_3(C_1, P, M, 1) = 1 - (1 - \frac{1}{2}) = \frac{1}{2}$ while $M_3(C_2, P, M, n) = 1 - (1 - \frac{1}{4})^3 = 1 - (\frac{3}{4})^3 = 1 - \frac{27}{64} = \frac{37}{64}$. Thus $M_3(C_2, P, M, 3) > M_3(C_1, P, M, 1)$

The properly partitions relation ensures a better fault detection ability for measure M_1 and M_2 (if C_1 properly partitions C_2 then C_1 is better at detecting faults than C_2 with regard to M_1 and M_2) but not necessarily for M_3.

Notes Since for most criteria of interest, the universally narrows relation is equivalent to the subsumes relation, one can interpret the presented results by concluding that the subsume relation is a poor basis for comparing criteria. However, it is important to note that the results here are worst case results in the sense that it is only considered whether or not the fact that one criterion subsumes another guarantees improved fault-detecting ability. The question of what C_1 subsuming, or narrowing, or covering, or partitioning C_2 tells us about their relative ability to detect faults in "typical" programs remains open. Moreover, note that the most convincing measure studied is measure M_3, since this measure takes into account the number of test data used. Thus it is possible to compare two criteria for the same number of test data. However none of the relations presented here induces a better fault detection ability for measure M_3.

11.4.3   Remarks

Questions addressed in Section 11.4.1 and Section 11.4.2 can be compared. The way random based testing is modeled in the contributions presented in Section 11.4.1 results in a "partition oriented" view of random based testing. Indeed random based testing can be seen as a partition based technique which partitions the input domain in a single subdomain (the input domain itself). Even-more, random based testing can be seen as a coverage criterion which divides the input domain of a program in one subdomain: the input domain itself. Let us call random criterion this criterion. Consider now any structural criterion. It is easy to see that such a criterion either properly partitions or properly covers the random criterion (depending on the fact that the criterion of interest induces overlapping or non overlapping subdomains). Contributions presented in Section 11.4.1 essentially make the assumption that the same number of test data is used both for random based an partition based testing. Thus comparing random based testing and partition based testing with regard to their ability to detect faults (as expressed in Section presented in Section 11.4.1) is equivalent to associate a criterion C to the partition based testing technique considered, and to compare C with the random criterion with regard to Measure M_3 (as defined in Section 11.4.2). Results introduced in Section 11.4.1 indicates that partition based testing is not better at detecting faults than random based testing. This result is thus totally consistent with the fact that both properly covers and properly partitions relations do not induce a better fault detection ability, with regard to measure M_3.

11.5   Summary

The application of coverage techniques at the model level seems a promising approach. These techniques allow rather easy test selection from executable models, while ensuring (at a certain degree) the coverage of targeted behaviors of the model (e.g. a set of test cases for which all variable definitions of the model are stimulated). Of course, criteria have to be adapted to specification formalisms: for example it makes no sense to talk about data flow criteria for models described in a specification formalism which does not handle variables. However most of the usual criteria can be easily adapted to models, since models' executable aspect makes them "look like programs". Moreover, approaches based on model coverage may be adapted to perform functional testing. This can be done through property coverage by model checking approaches or user profile usages for example. The main point is that this kind of functional testing is still based on coverage considerations, which is very valuable since generated test suites are supposed to cover in a measurable manner behaviors of the model which reflect an abstract scenario (or property).

All these properties make model-coverage-based-testing methods good candidates to detect specific faults at the earliest design level. The strength of coverage approaches relies mainly on their ability to explore in a systematic manner "missing logic" faults: bad treatment of bounds for example. These approaches are the only one to tackle the problem of detecting catastrophic failure causing inputs. However, one must keep in mind that these properties are not sufficient to ensure reliability. In particular, there is no scientific evidence that coverage based testing is better than random testing to reach this purpose. To gain more insight, a further analysis of what is a "typical program under test" is needed, since the usual failure rate model seems unsuitable to provide such evidence. The same problem occurs when one tries to classify criteria with respect to their respective ability to detect faults.

Common belief however seems to be that random testing should systematically complement coverage based approaches. Coverage based approaches should be used to detect specific faults while random approaches aim at providing confidence about programs reliability.

12 Technology of Test-Case Generation

Levi Lúcio[1] and Marko Samer[2*]

[1] Software Modelling and Verification Group
University of Geneva
levi.lucio@cui.unige.ch

[2] Institute of Information Systems
Vienna University of Technology
samer@dbai.tuwien.ac.at

12.1 Introduction

Model based test case generation deals with the generation of test cases based on test case specifications and a model of the system under test (SUT). Since the number of possible test cases is in general too large to be practically useful, test case specifications are used to select *interesting* test cases. Therefore, test case generation can be seen as the search problem of finding appropriate test cases. In the previous chapter, several kinds of test case specifications, in particular coverage criteria, have been presented. In the current chapter, we will show how techniques from various fields in computer science such as program analysis and formal methods can be applied to generate test cases that satisfy such specifications. The input part of each test case can then be fed into the SUT whose output is compared with the output part of the test case in order to detect errors. In particular, we will cover test case generation by *theorem proving*, *symbolic execution*, and *model checking*. Although these techniques are often used in combination, we will describe them separately in order to show their applicability and specific features from different points of view.

Theorem proving can be used to support the generation of test cases from a model that is given as formal specification. The basic assumption behind this approach is that the model can be partitioned into equivalence classes which represent the same behavior with respect to the test; in particular, test data in the same equivalence class are assumed to cause the same error (or no error in the case of success). Each such equivalence class represents one test case. It is therefore sufficient to extract a small amount of test data from each test case. We will present several approaches from the literature of how to find such an appropriate partitioning of a given specification into equivalence classes. In particular, we will show how general purpose theorem provers can be used to transform Z specifications into test cases by syntactic transformations as well as by taking semantic aspects into account. Moreover, we will show how Prolog can

---

* This author was supported by the European Community Research Training Network "Games and Automata for Synthesis and Validation" (GAMES) and by the Austrian Science Fund Project Z29-N04.

M. Broy et al. (Eds.): Model-Based Testing of Reactive Systems, LNCS 3472, pp. 323-354, 2005.
© Springer-Verlag Berlin Heidelberg 2005

324 Levi Lúcio and Marko Samer

be used to extract test cases from specifications given as logic programs, and why correctness proofs can be useful in test case generation.

Symbolic execution is a program verification technique from the 1970s. Differently from the other verification techniques discussed in this chapter, symbolic execution was initially applied to real code rather than to abstract models. Several software verification frameworks using symbolic execution were built in the 1970s. However, their success was limited since the required mathematical machinery was not sufficiently developed. Recently, the principles of symbolic execution have been reused to cope with the problems of state space explosion while searching for execution traces in a software application's abstract model. By replacing actual system inputs with symbols, i.e., variables and sets of constraints over them, symbolic execution allows coping with the problem of unbounded entries – thus reducing state space explosion. There is however a price to pay since traces found in this way are symbolic and need to be instantiated. After introducing the basic concepts of symbolic execution as it was invented in the 1970s for code verification, we will discuss several modern frameworks for test case generation that make use of symbolic execution. The examples are chosen to demonstrate that symbolic execution can be used both with abstract models and concrete code.

Model checking is a method for verifying finite-state systems. Given a system model and a specification written in a temporal logic, the model checker automatically determines whether the model satisfies the specification. In addition to being fully automatic, an important feature of model checking is that in principle a witness resp. counterexample can be supplied when the model succeeds resp. fails to satisfy the specification. There exist several approaches that establish connections between model checking and model-based testing. The main idea of these approaches is that test case specifications can be written in temporal logics such that the problem of test case generation is reduced to the problem of finding a set of witnesses resp. counterexamples to the specification. Since model checking in the context of test case generation is also covered by other chapters in this book, we will give only a short summary and refer to other chapters.

This chapter is organized as follows: In Sec. 12.2, we present test case generation by theorem proving. The use of symbolic execution is then described in Sec. 12.3. Afterwards, in Sec. 12.4, we cover test case generation by model checking. Finally, we summarize in Sec. 12.5. The responsibilities for the two main parts of this chapter, namely *theorem proving* and *symbolic execution*, were splitted in the following way: Marko Samer was responsible for Sec. 12.2 and Levi Lúcio was responsible for Sec. 12.3.

12.2 Theorem Proving

An automated **theorem prover** attempts to construct a proof for a given input conjecture. However, since for complex problems it is rarely possible to construct a proof fully automatically, in most cases – especially in industrial applications – the user has to guide the proof search procedure. Such user controlled theorem provers are called *semi-automated* or *interactive*. In this context, automated **theorem proving** is the process of constructing a proof by an automated or semi-automated theorem prover.

The importance of automated theorem proving arises not only from its mathematical and philosophical relevance, but also from the fact that many problems in artificial intelligence and formal verification can be reduced to theorem proving. In industrial environments, however, theorem proving is rarely used because it is very time consuming and requires expert knowledge. Nevertheless, in some areas of high-quality productions [Sch00, Sch01], there is no adequate alternative to formally prove properties of the system under consideration. Moreover, there exist several attempts to combine theorem proving with model checking in order to compensate the shortcomings of each other [ORR+96, CCG+03]. This can be seen as further evidence for the importance of automated theorem proving.

In this section, we survey how automated theorem proving technology can be used in test case generation. Although theorem proving is often used in combination with other techniques, we focus on approaches where theorem proving is the dominating technique. The typical method in this context is based on formal specifications which model the SUT. Such a model resp. specification is then partitioned into equivalence classes which are assumed to satisfy a **uniformity hypothesis**, i.e., they are assumed to represent the same behavior concerning the test; in particular, test data in the same equivalence class are assumed to cause the same error (or no error in the case of success). Each such equivalence class is then interpreted as one test case. Hence, because of the uniformity hypothesis, it suffices to extract a small amount of test data from each test case. Note that the test cases generated by the approaches presented in this section are single instances and not sequences of test cases as would be necessary for testing reactive systems. Extensions for generating test case sequences are described in the referred literature or are topic of future research.

Our aim in the following is to show how theorem provers can be applied to construct such test cases from a given specification. There exist three major approaches in the literature to address this issue:

- Use theorem provers to generate test cases from Z specifications
- Translate algebraic specifications into logic programs and use Prolog's theorem proving mechanisms to generate test cases
- Construct formal proofs from which test cases can be extracted

Since our focus will be on the first item, which is mainly based on the specification language Z, we start with a short introduction of some basic concepts of this language.

12.2.1   The Z Specification Language

Z is a commonly used formal specification language based on set theory and first-order predicate logic [Spi92, PST96, ISO02]. As every formal specification language, Z uses mathematical notation to describe the properties a system must satisfy. One of the main concepts of Z is the possibility to decompose specifications into small parts called **schemas**. This allows the user to describe a system by its subsystems, i.e., to present it piece by piece. Schemas in Z are used to specify static as well as dynamic aspects. In general, a schema has the following form:

```
┌─ Name ──────────────────────────────────────────
│  Declaration; ...; Declaration
├──────────────────────────────────────────────────
│  Predicate; ...; Predicate
└──────────────────────────────────────────────────
```

Every schema consists of a schema name, a declaration part (or signature), and a predicate part. The schema name is used to refer to the schema within other schemas, the declaration part consists of the declarations of the free variables occurring in the predicate part, and the predicate part describes the properties the system must satisfy, i.e., the relationship between the variables. Note that the declarations and predicates are usually written among each other within the declaration and predicate part respectively. Moreover, note that there is an implicit conjunction between the predicates in the predicate part.

A system specification in Z usually consists of a specification of the states and a specification of the possible operations, i.e., the state transitions. We will now illustrate these concepts by a simple example of an up-counter modulo four (ring counter).

```
┌─ Counter ───────────────────────────────────────
│  $ctr : \mathbb{N}$
├──────────────────────────────────────────────────
│  $0 \leq ctr < 4$
└──────────────────────────────────────────────────
```

In this schema, the state variable ctr is declared to be a natural number. The predicate part determines the values ctr can take, which can be seen as an invariant the system must satisfy. According to this schema, our system consists of four states, namely the four possible values of ctr. We will now specify the operation to increment the counter:

```
┌─ Increment ─────────────────────────────────────
│  $\Delta Counter$
├──────────────────────────────────────────────────
│  $((ctr < 3) \wedge (ctr' = ctr + 1)) \vee ((ctr = 3) \wedge (ctr' = 0))$
└──────────────────────────────────────────────────
```

In this schema, the declaration part refers to schema *Counter*. The preceding symbol Δ indicates an implicit declaration of the variables of *Counter* before and after the operation *Increment*[1] has been applied. In particular, $\Delta Counter$ declares the variables ctr and ctr', where ctr represents the value before and ctr'

---

[1] Note that for simplicity we identify the operation with its corresponding schema.

represents the value after the application of *Increment*.[2] This allows us to define the effect of the operation *Increment* on *Counter* in the predicate part. In particular, if the value of *ctr* is less than three, then its value after the application of *Increment* must be *ctr* + 1, and if *ctr* is equal to three, then its value after application of *Increment* must be zero.

Finally, let us specify another example: the modulo operation of natural numbers which, given the base and the modulus, returns the common residue.

$$
\begin{array}{l}
\underline{\quad Modulo\ } \\
\quad b?, m?, r! : \mathbb{N} \\
\hline
\quad b? \geq m? \\
\quad (r! < m?) \vee (m? = 0) \\
\quad \exists\, k : \mathbb{N} \bullet b? = m? * k + r!
\end{array}
$$

This schema declares the three variables $b?$, $m?$, and $r!$ to be natural numbers. The suffixes '?' and '!' indicate input and output parameters respectively.

The predicate part consists of three predicates. The first ensures that the base must be greater or equal to the modulus. The second ensures that the specified residue is the common residue, i.e., less than the modulus, or that the modulus is equal to zero. In the latter case, the residue should be equal to the base which is greater or equal to the modulus according to the first predicate. The final predicate specifies the relationship between base, modulus, and residue.

As already mentioned, the above constructs represent only a small fraction of the whole Z specification language. The reader is referred to [Spi92, PST96, ISO02] for a more exhaustive introduction to Z. We will use Z specifications as the basis of test case generation in the following section.

12.2.2   Test Case Generation from Z Specifications

Given a model of the SUT as Z specification, general purpose theorem provers can be used to support the partitioning of the specification into equivalence classes. We will now present some approaches of how to construct test cases from Z specifications in such a way. We start with the *disjunctive normal form approach*, a method that allows us to syntactically transform Z specifications into equivalence classes. Afterwards, we present the *classification-tree method* which enables us to integrate semantic aspects into the partitioning process. Finally, we discuss *partitioning heuristics* which can be seen as a general theoretical framework of syntactic and semantic partitioning methods.

The Disjunctive Normal Form Approach. In the approach of Helke et al. [HNS97], Z specifications are translated into the input language of Isabelle

---

[2] Similarly, a preceding symbol Ξ indicates an implicit declaration of the variables of *Counter* which, in contrast to Δ, remain unchanged, that is $ctr' = ctr$.

[Pau94, NPW02], a generic theorem prover which supports proof tactics[3]. Set operations, predicate logic, and Cartesian products in Z can be directly translated into Isabelle. The representation of schemas in Isabelle can be done in several ways; Helke et al. [HNS97] chose a predicate representation (cf. Kolyang et al. [KSW96]). For instance, the schema *Counter* resp. *Increment* in Sec. 12.2.1 is translated into the predicate *Counter* resp. *Increment* as shown below, where λ identifies the free variables:

$$Counter \equiv \lambda\, ctr.\, [\, ctr : \mathbb{N} \mid 0 \le ctr < 4\,]$$
$$Increment \equiv \lambda(ctr, ctr').\, [\, Counter(ctr) \wedge Counter(ctr') \mid$$
$$((ctr < 3) \wedge (ctr' = ctr + 1)) \vee ((ctr = 3) \wedge (ctr' = 0))\,]$$

With this encoding of Z specifications, Isabelle can be applied to construct test cases in such a way as described in the following. The approach of Helke et al. [HNS97] is based on *disjunctive normal form partitioning* [DF93]. That is, the predicate part of a schema is transformed into disjunctive normal form, where the disjuncts are pairwise disjoint (i.e., the disjunction is equivalent to the exclusive or of its disjuncts). Each of the resulting disjuncts is assumed to define a equivalence class concerning the test behavior, and can therefore be interpreted as a test case. The pairwise disjointness allows us to treat each test case entirely independently. To obtain disjunctive normal form, the usual logical transformation rules can be applied. To obtain pairwise disjointness, however, disjunction, implication, and bi-implication have to be transformed according to:

$$A \vee B \equiv (A \wedge \neg B) \vee (\neg A \wedge B) \vee (A \wedge B) \tag{12.1}$$
$$A \Rightarrow B \equiv \neg A \vee (A \wedge B) \tag{12.2}$$
$$A \Leftrightarrow B \equiv (A \wedge B) \vee (\neg A \wedge \neg B) \tag{12.3}$$

The schemas of our example above are already in such a normal form (cf. Sec. 12.2.1). The schema *Counter* consists of only one disjunct in the predicate part and is therefore trivially in disjunctive normal form. Furthermore, the schema *Increment* is also in disjunctive normal form. In this simple example, it is easy to see that the disjuncts are pairwise disjoint because $ctr < 3$ and $ctr = 3$ are mutually exclusive. Nevertheless, for demonstration purposes, we ignore our knowledge of the disjointness of the disjuncts and apply transformation rule (12.1) to the schema *Increment*. Thus, we obtain the equivalent schema:

---

[3] Proof tactics are "subroutines" written in a metalanguage for the purpose of supporting the proof search procedure. For instance, they can be used to transform proofs or to justify proof steps by autonomously performing detailed proof steps.

Increment
_____

Δ*Counter*
_____

$((ctr < 3) \wedge (ctr' = ctr + 1) \wedge \neg(ctr = 3)) \vee$
$((ctr < 3) \wedge (ctr' = ctr + 1) \wedge \neg(ctr' = 0)) \vee$
$(\neg(ctr < 3) \wedge (ctr = 3) \wedge (ctr' = 0)) \vee$
$(\neg(ctr' = ctr + 1) \wedge (ctr = 3) \wedge (ctr' = 0)) \vee$
$((ctr < 3) \wedge (ctr' = ctr + 1) \wedge (ctr = 3) \wedge (ctr' = 0))$

The predicate part in this schema can be simplified by removing unsatisfiable disjuncts and unnecessary literals. For instance, the final disjunct is unsatisfiable because $ctr < 3$ and $ctr = 3$ are contradictory. The remaining four disjuncts can be simplified by removing redundant literals. For instance, the literal $\neg(ctr = 3)$ in the first disjunct can be removed because it is already implied by $ctr < 3$. When continuing these simplifications, we finally obtain the original definition of the schema *Increment* in Sec. 12.2.1. This is not surprising because, as mentioned above, the original definition was already in the desired normal form. In general, however, this need not to be the case. The generation of test cases in this approach consists of two steps:

(1) Compute disjunctive normal form with mutually exclusive disjuncts
(2) Remove unsatisfiable disjuncts and simplify the remaining test cases

For the computation of the disjunctive normal form, an optimization to avoid redundancy was used by Helke et al. [HNS97]. In particular, the predicate part P of each schema is initially transformed into a conjunction of the form $P = R \wedge Q$, where R is a meta-variable consisting of those schema predicates that do not contain disjunctions (implicitly or explicitly), and Q is a meta-variable consisting of the remaining predicates that contain at least one disjunction. For instance, $P = a \wedge (c \vee (d \wedge e)) \wedge b$ can be transformed such that $R = a \wedge b$ and $Q = (c \vee (d \wedge e))$, where a, b, c, d, and e denote atoms. The disjunctive normal form is then computed for Q while R is ignored. Hence, the resulting representation of the predicate part P consists of a purely conjunctive part R and an expression Q in disjunctive normal form. This avoids that purely conjunctive predicates appear in each disjunct of the disjunctive normal form which would lead to much redundancy.

The preparing partitioning of the predicate part and the computation of the disjunctive normal form can be implemented by Isabelle's proof tactics. To detect unsatisfiable disjuncts, Isabelle's conditional rewrite mechanisms are used, i.e., a special parameterized tactic called *simplifier*. It allows to define rewrite rules which are able to find contradicting disjuncts and makes it possible to rewrite them to *false*. For instance, the final disjunct in the above schema *Increment* contains $ctr < 3$ as well as $ctr = 3$. An application of rewriting yields $3 < 3$ which is obviously false. Hence, the disjunct is unsatisfiable and can be removed. A side effect of such rewritings to find contradicting disjuncts is that redundancy is reduced, i.e., the test cases are simplified. On the other hand, how-

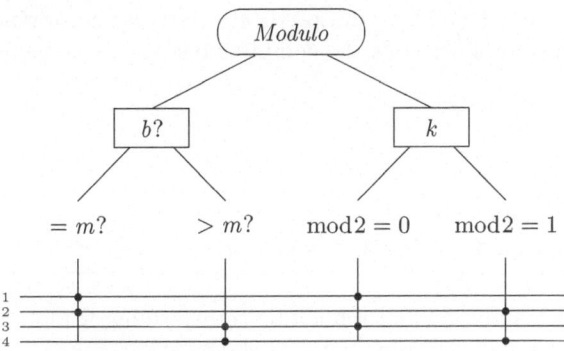

Fig. 12.1. Classification-tree of *Modulo*

ever, new disjuncts maybe introduced. This can be corrected by post-processing the disjuncts after the elimination step.

As already mentioned, each of the disjuncts obtained by this procedure represents a test case. Thus, the disjuncts can be separated into schemas for each test case with the same declaration part as the original schema and one of the disjuncts as predicate part respectively. Case studies by Helke et al. [HNS97] have shown that most of the generated test cases after the first step are not satisfiable. Therefore, the second step, i.e., the simplification by removing unsatisfiable disjuncts and reducing redundancy, is the most expensive part in this approach.

The Classification-Tree Method. The drawback of such purely syntax-oriented approaches as proposed by Helke et al. [HNS97] is that the user has only little influence on the generation of *relevant* test cases. Therefore, a combination with the semantic-oriented approach of classification-trees [GG93] was investigated by Singh et al. and Sadeghipour [SCS97, Sad98]. In the *classification-tree method*, the test object is analyzed with respect to properties which are considered to be relevant for the test. For each such property, a disjoint partitioning is performed. The partitions can then be further classified until a sufficiently refined partitioning is reached. It is easy to see that this refinement process can be graphically represented as a tree, the **classification-tree**.

For instance, the classification-tree of the schema *Modulo* in Sec. 12.2.1 concerning the variables $b?$ and k is shown in Fig. 12.1. In this tree, $b?$ is partitioned depending on being equal to or greater than $m?$, and k is partitioned depending on being even or odd. Each combination of the leaves of different classifications in such a tree represents a *high-level* test case. In our example, each row in the combination table below the classification-tree represents such a high-level test case (according to the marked points in the table).

Since these test cases contain only variables occurring in the classification-tree, we have to add them as additional predicate to the original schema in order to obtain complete test cases. For instance, if we add the fourth test case

$(b? > m?) \wedge (k \bmod 2 = 1)$ to the predicate part of the original schema, we obtain after some simplifications the complete test case schema:

$\textit{Modulo\_(Partition4)}$ _____
$b?, m?, r! : \mathbb{N}$

$b? > m?$
$(r! < m?) \vee (m? = 0)$
$\exists\, k : \mathbb{N} \bullet (k \bmod 2 = 1) \wedge (b? = m? * k + r!)$

This test case can be further refined by transforming it into disjunctive normal form as in the previous approach, which yields two refined test cases:

$$(b? > m?) \wedge (r! < m?) \wedge \exists\, k : \mathbb{N} \bullet ((k \bmod 2 = 1) \wedge (b? = m? * k + r!))$$
$$(b? > m?) \wedge (m? = 0) \wedge \exists\, k : \mathbb{N} \bullet ((k \bmod 2 = 1) \wedge (b? = m? * k + r!))$$

Note that in addition to the semantic aspects, the classification-tree method provides a hierarchical structuring of the test cases, while test cases in the pure disjunctive normal form approach are completely unstructured. An application of theorem proving to support this approach was presented by Sadeghipour [Sad98]. In particular, the theorem prover Isabelle [Pau94, NPW02] is used as integral part of a tool environment for test case generation based on the classification-tree method. The theorem prover is applied, e.g., for simplification tasks, for checking test data consistency, and for test evaluation.

Partitioning Heuristics. An approach with the objective of building a uniform theoretical foundation and generalizing the above methods was presented by Burton et al. [BCM00, Bur00, Bur02]. This approach is based on CADiZ [TM95, Toy96, Toy98], a Z type checker and theorem prover. Since the input language of CADiZ is Z itself, there is no necessity for translating Z specifications. The main difference to the approaches of Helke et al. [HNS97], Singh et al., and Sadeghipour [SCS97, Sad98] is that various partitioning heuristics are supported in the work of Burton et al. [BCM00, Bur00, Bur02]. In particular, the test case generation of Helke et al. [HNS97] is based on disjunctive normal form partitioning as shown above. This partitioning, however, can be generalized by other partitioning heuristics such as heuristics based on boundary value analysis or type analysis. For instance, the predicate $m \geq 0$ can be partitioned by boundary value analysis into $(m = 0) \vee (m = 1) \vee (m > 1)$, and the domain of the variable $n \in \mathbb{Z}$ can be partitioned by type analysis into $(n < 0) \vee (n = 0) \vee (n > 0)$.

In addition, the partitioning can also be based on fault-based heuristics which take the experience of faults detected in previous builds into account. For instance, if the specified operation n^2 is assumed to be incorrectly implemented as $2 * n$, where $n \in \mathbb{N}$, then the partitioning would be $(n = 1) \vee (n > 2)$ because n^2 and $2 * n$ cannot be distinguished by $n = 0$ and $n = 2$.

Of course, these partitionings can also be performed by the classification-tree method of Singh et al. and Sadeghipour [SCS97, Sad98]. However, as we will see in the following, partitioning and fault-based heuristics can be seen as a uniform theoretical framework.

Partitioning heuristics can in Z be formulated as theorems which describe the equivalence between the original predicate and the partitions. In particular, there are two components of this equivalence: **completeness**, which ensures that the union resp. disjunction of the partitions covers the original predicate, and **disjointness**, which ensures that the partitions are pairwise disjoint. The corresponding generic partitioning heuristics are

$$\forall \, \mathrm{Vars}(P) \, \bullet \, P \, \Leftrightarrow \, P_1 \vee P_2 \vee \ldots \vee P_n$$
$$\forall \, \mathrm{Vars}(P) \, \bullet \, \forall \, i, j : 1..n \, \bullet \, i \neq j \, \Rightarrow \, \neg(P_i \wedge P_j)$$

where P denotes the original predicate, P_i with $1 \leq i \leq n$ denotes a partition, and *Vars* denotes a function that returns the declarations of all variables occurring in its argument. To obtain partitioning heuristics, the above templates have to be instantiated. Examples of such instantiations concerning disjunctive normal form have already been shown above (see transformation rules (12.1), (12.2), and (12.3)). An instantiation of a boundary value analysis heuristic is given by:

$$\forall \, A, B : \mathbb{Z} \, \bullet \, A \geq B \, \Leftrightarrow \, (A = B) \vee (A = B + 1) \vee (A > B + 1)$$

To obtain concrete test cases, such a heuristic has to be applied to a selected predicate in a specification, i.e., it has to be instantiated with the parameters of the predicate. For instance, let us apply the above boundary value heuristic to the first predicate of the schema *Modulo* in Sec. 12.2.1. To this aim, we first have to prove within CADiZ that the heuristic is a tautology. If this is the case, the heuristic's instantiation with respect to the predicate (A and B are instantiated by $b?$ and $m?$ respectively) is computed by CADiZ's pattern matching mechanisms within a tactic. The resulting equivalence is:

$$b? \geq m? \, \Leftrightarrow \, (b? = m?) \vee (b? = m? + 1) \vee (b? > m? + 1)$$

Now, the predicate $b? \geq m?$ in the schema can be replaced by the right hand side of this equivalence, which yields:

Modulo _____

$b?, m?, r! : \mathbb{N}$

_____

$(b? = m?) \vee (b? = m? + 1) \vee (b? > m? + 1)$
$(r! < m?) \vee (m? = 0)$
$\exists \, k : \mathbb{N} \, \bullet \, b? = m? * k + r!$

Finally, the predicate part of this schema can be transformed into disjunctive normal form. Each of the resulting six disjuncts represents one test case. Thus, the disjuncts can be separated into schemas for each test case.

Fault-based heuristics can be divided into *necessary conditions* and *sufficient conditions*. **Necessary conditions** are able to distinguish between different (mutated) subexpressions. This, however, is not always sufficient to detect faults because, for example, two mutated subexpressions may cancel each other out such that the fault does not propagate to the output. The generic fault-based heuristic for the necessary condition is

$$\exists \, \mathit{Vars}(E_i) \; \bullet \; \exists \, \mathit{Vars}(E_j) \; \bullet \; \neg(E_i = E_j)$$

where E_i and E_j denote two subexpressions and *Vars* is as above. For instance, to distinguish between multiplication and addition of natural numbers, the following instantiation can be used as heuristic:

$$\exists \, A, B : \mathbb{N} \; \bullet \; \neg(A * B = A + B)$$

For example, if we assume that the multiplication in the schema *Modulo* in Sec. 12.2.1 is incorrectly implemented as addition, we choose the following instantiation of the necessary condition for detecting this fault:

$$\exists \, m?, k : \mathbb{N} \; \bullet \; \neg(m? * k = m? + k)$$

Sufficient conditions, on the other hand, restrict the range of the values the variables can take such that the fault is observable at the output. The generic fault-based heuristic for the sufficient condition is given by

$$\exists \, \mathit{Vars}(P) \; \bullet \; \exists \, \mathit{Vars}(P') \; \bullet \; \neg(P \Leftrightarrow P')$$

where P and P' denote two predicate parts and *Vars* is as above. The same fault assumption in schema *Modulo* as above would lead to the following instantiation:

$$
\begin{aligned}
\exists \, & b?, m?, r!, k : \mathbb{N} \; \bullet \\
& \neg(((b? \geq m?) \wedge ((r! < m?) \vee (m? = 0)) \wedge (b? = m? * k + r!)) \\
& \Leftrightarrow ((b? \geq m?) \wedge ((r! < m?) \vee (m? = 0)) \wedge (b? = m? + k + r!)))
\end{aligned}
$$

The sufficient condition is obviously much harder than the necessary condition because the whole predicate part has to be considered. On the other hand, it contains more information about the testing domain and has therefore stronger failure detection capabilities. However, the construction of satisfiable sufficient conditions is not always possible. The relation between necessary and sufficient fault detection conditions is analogous to weak and strong mutation testing [Bur00].

It is easy to see that each test case generated by the above techniques can be seen as a set of constraints on the variables. Thus, CADiZ's built-in constraint solver can be used to randomly select test data satisfying these constraints. A case study of this approach can be found in [BCGM00], and a combination with graphical notations such as Statecharts from which abstract finite state machines (AFS machines) can be extracted in order to generate test sequences by finding counterexamples during model checking the AFS machines is presented in [BCM01, Bur02].

12.2.3   Logic Programming

One of the most important representatives of declarative programming languages is *Prolog*. Due to its high abstraction level, Prolog seems also adequate as specification language. In particular, many formal specification notations have straightforward translations to logic programs, nondeterminism appears naturally in logic programming, and specifications in Prolog are executable [Den91]. Prolog can be seen as a general framework that uses the underlying theorem proving techniques, extended by some control mechanisms, to construct test cases from specifications given as logic program.

Bernot et al. [BGM91] presented a general theoretical framework and implementation issues of how to use Prolog for test case generation. Essentially, their implementation, given an algebraic specification and some auxiliary parameters, returns uniformity sub-domains and test data. The approach is based on a translation of algebraic specifications into Horn clause logic, Prolog's resolution principle, and some specific control mechanisms to ensure, for instance, termination and finite domains.

The theoretical framework is based on **testing context refinements**[4], i.e., refinements of a triple containing a set of hypotheses, a set of test data, and an "oracle". The hypotheses describe the assumptions on the testing environment such that the success of the test data ensures the correctness of the SUT with respect to the specification, and the oracle is a decision procedure for the success of the test data when submitted to the SUT. The starting point of the refinement process is an initial testing context which is guaranteed to be *valid* and *unbiased*, where *valid* means that incorrect programs are rejected, and *unbiased* means that correct programs are accepted. This initial testing context is then successively refined by operations that preserve validity and unbias. Note that, although we finally want ground formulas, formulas in the test data set of the initial and intermediate testing contexts can contain variables.

The basic assumption on the underlying algebraic specification[5] is that every formula is a positive conditional equation of the form

$$(v_1 = w_1 \wedge \ldots \wedge v_k = w_k) \Rightarrow v = w,$$

where v_i, w_i, v, and w for all $1 \leq i \leq k$ are terms with variables. We will show how a set of such formulas can be used to generate test cases with Prolog. The first step is to transform every equation in both preconditions and conclusions into an equation of the form $f(t_1, \ldots, t_n) = t$, where f is a defined operator and t, t_1, ..., t_n contain only basic operators, called *generators*, but no defined operators. This transformation is achieved by four syntactic transformation rules [BGM91]. The resulting formulas are of the form

$$(f_1(t_{1,1}, \ldots, t_{1,n_1}) = r_1 \wedge \ldots \wedge f_m(t_{m,1}, \ldots, t_{m,n_m}) = r_m) \Rightarrow f(t_1, \ldots, t_n) = r.$$

---

[4] Note that a *testing context* is not the same as a *test context* as defined in the glossary.
[5] In this approach, a specification is defined as a set of formulas.

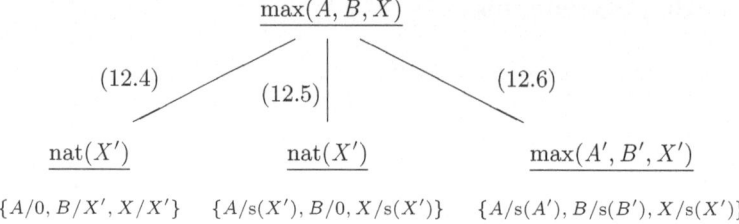

Fig. 12.2. Resolution tree of $\max(A, B, X)$

It is easy to see that every equation of the form $f(t_1, \ldots, t_n) = t$ can be replaced by a literal $\tilde{f}(t_1, \ldots, t_n, t)$ with arity $n + 1$. Hence, we obtain a Horn clause resp. Prolog rule of the form

$$\tilde{f}(t_1, \ldots, t_n, r) \leftarrow \tilde{f}_1(t_{1,1}, \ldots, t_{1,n_1}, r_1), \ldots, \tilde{f}_m(t_{m,1}, \ldots, t_{m,n_m}, r_m).$$

Therefore, we have transformed the initial specification into a Prolog program. It remains to show how test cases can be generated with this program. Two important properties in this context are *completeness* and *termination*. To ensure a complete proof search strategy, iterative deepening can be used instead of Prolog's standard depth-first search. This, however, does not guarantee termination because some unsatisfiable goals cannot be detected. To solve this problem, rewriting is used by Bernot et al. [BGM91] to simplify goals before each resolution step in order to alleviate the detection of unsatisfiable goals.

The refinement resp. unfolding process to obtain a suitable decomposition of the specification into sub-domains is implemented by recursively replacing each defined operator by the cases corresponding to its definition. This is already provided by Prolog's resolution principle. For instance, consider the predicate max/3 defined by the following three clauses, where s denotes the successor function:

$$\max(0, X, X) \leftarrow \text{nat}(X). \tag{12.4}$$
$$\max(s(X), 0, s(X)) \leftarrow \text{nat}(X). \tag{12.5}$$
$$\max(s(A), s(B), s(X)) \leftarrow \max(A, B, X). \tag{12.6}$$

For example, $\max(s(0), s(s(s(0))), s(s(s(0))))$ is true since the maximum of $s(0) \doteq 1$ and $s(s(s(0))) \doteq 3$ is $s(s(s(0))) \doteq 3$. The resolution tree shown in Fig. 12.2 is obtained when applying one resolution step to the goal $\max(A, B, X)$. The leaves of this tree obviously represent a decomposition of max/3 according to its definition. For the first two clauses we obtain the resolvent $\text{nat}(X')$, and for the third clause we obtain the resolvent $\max(A', B', X')$ together with the corresponding unifiers. These resolvents can now be further decomposed. The crucial point is to decide when the refinement process has to be stopped, i.e., to control the degree of decomposition. To this aim, meta-clauses are used by Bernot et al. [BGM91]. The literals are chosen for resolution according to a selection

heuristic in order to stop resolution when a sub-domain is reached which seems
to satisfy a uniformity hypothesis. Each branch of the resulting resolution tree
represents one test case. Starting from the instantiations of the predicates at the
leaves, test data of the original predicate can be computed using the unifiers on
the corresponding branch.

To obtain ground formulas which represent the executable test data, two
kinds of instantiation hypotheses have to be implemented. The first is called
regularity hypothesis and means that it is sufficient to consider test cases
below some maximal complexity. For instance, it may be sufficient to instantiate
list variables with lists up to a maximal length. This can be realized in Prolog
by a predicate implementing an appropriate complexity measure which ensures
that variables are instantiated only below a fixed complexity. For the remaining
variables, the **uniformity hypothesis** can be applied, i.e., an instantiation
within the domain is randomly chosen. This can be implemented in Prolog by
using a random choice strategy for the clauses during resolution and selecting
the first solution found in this way.

A more implementation oriented approach to test case generation with Prolog was presented by Denney [Den91]. He has shown how the technical problems
occurring in the context of test case generation with Prolog can be solved by
a meta-interpreter. The main idea is to dynamically construct a specification
automaton by Prolog's goal-reduction procedure during the specification execution. Uniform sub-domains of the specification input and output domains are
obtained by special sets of arcs of the specification automaton called *routes*, i.e.,
all paths over a route are considered to be equivalent. In particular, a **route**
is a "set of arcs over which there is at least one path through the automaton
corresponding to a path through the specification that uses all and only those
arcs in that route". The meta-interpreter tries then to generate one test case
for each route by using some heuristics (e.g., to control recursion/termination).
Since term ordering may affect the test case generation process and the user
should not need to take care of term ordering when writing specifications, the
meta-interpreter uses a constraint list which contains insufficient instantiated
goals until they can be evaluated.

12.2.4   Extracting Test Cases from Proofs

In principle, the intention of formal proofs is to ensure the correctness of an
abstract model of a system. Therefore, at first sight, one might probably say that
testing of a system is unnecessary if such correctness proofs exist. However, what
guarantees that the abstract model is a correct representation of the concrete
system, i.e., what guarantees that there have been no mistakes in the model
building process? On the other hand, if we assume that testing of the concrete
system is unavoidable, why should we construct correctness proofs? An approach
of answering these questions was presented by Maharaj [Mah99, Mah00].

The main idea in this approach is that theorem proving procedures often
perform a detailed analysis of the input domain of the given model. This anal-

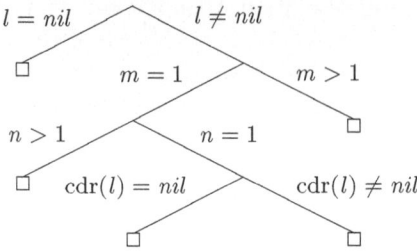

Fig. 12.3. Proof structure of *select*

ysis is then reflected in the structure of the resulting formal proof. Thus, the partitioning of the input domain in order to obtain sub-domains which satisfy a uniformity hypothesis is done as by-product of the proof process, i.e., the domain analysis is implicitly available in the proof structure and need not to be done by special test case generation procedures as usual. Test cases extracted from correctness proofs can then be used for verifying the SUT.

A small case study to justify this approach was also presented by Maharaj [Mah99]. It discusses a small program implementing the function *select* which, given a list and two integers m and n, returns the sublist from the m-th element to the n-th element. The specification of this function is given by two properties. We consider the first of them which specifies the length of the returned sublist:

$$\forall l : \text{List} \bullet \forall m, n : \mathbb{N} \bullet (0 < m \le n) \wedge (n \le \text{length}(l)) \qquad (12.7)$$
$$\Rightarrow \text{length}(\text{select}(l, m, n)) = n - m + 1$$

The function has to be implemented in a high-level programming or specification language about which it is easy to reason. In the case study, the functional programming language Miranda was used. The resulting program can be seen as an executable specification of a low-level language implementation that has to be tested. The theorem prover PVS [ORS92] was used to prove the correctness of the Miranda implementation regarding both specified properties.

Property (12.7) was proved by induction on the length of the list. The corresponding proof structure is shown in Fig. 12.3, where cdr : List $\rightarrow$ List is a function that maps a list to its tail. This structure arises from the case distinctions during the proof process. Since the proof is done by induction on the list length, the first branching distinguishes between the induction start ($l = nil$) and the induction step ($l \ne nil$). The other branchings result from the proof of the induction step.

The test cases can be extracted from this tree by combining the conditions on the variables that occur on the branches from the root to the leaves. Since each branch represents a test case, we obtain five test cases. For instance, the test case corresponding to the right most branch is given by:

$$\{0 < m \le n, n \le \text{length}(l), l \ne nil, m > 1\}$$

These test cases can then be simplified, and well known unfolding techniques can be applied. Maharaj [Mah99] also has shown that, in this simple example, test cases generated by conventional test case generation methods from specifications are subsumed by the test cases extracted from the proof.

12.3   Symbolic Execution

Symbolic execution is a program verification technique born in the 1970s. One of the first papers in the area by King [Kin76] describes the technique as being somewhere between the informal and the formal approaches. The informal approach may be described as follows: the developer creates test cases which are sets of input values to be provided to the application; these test cases are ran against the application which will output the results; the test results are tested for correctness against the expected results. In what concerns the formal approach, it means describing the application by means of a **specification language** and then using a **proof procedure** to prove that the program will execute as expected. While the informal approach involves actual execution of the application, the formal one can be applied even before a prototype for the system exists.

Symbolic execution was invented to fill the gap between the two above mentioned techniques. While the informal approach completely disregards input values that are not taken into consideration in the test cases, the formal one requires an exhaustive mathematical description of the application which is not easy to produce.

The first goal of symbolic execution is to explore the possible execution paths of an application. The difference between symbolic execution and informal testing with sample input values is that the inputs in symbolic execution are symbols representing classes of values. For example, if a numeric value is expected by the application, a generic x representing the whole set of numerical values is passed. Obviously, the output of the execution will be produced as a function of the introduced input symbols.

Given that symbolic execution is done over non-defined values, the **control paths** that are covered have to be defined either by heuristics or by humans at run-time. In particular, the symbolic execution of conditional structures is of great interest: when a symbolic condition is evaluated, the result may be true, false or not decidable. In case of true or false, it is clear which control path should be followed. If the symbolic execution environment is not able to decide unambiguously which branch of the condition should be taken, then both control paths can be followed and the symbolic execution of the program splits. From the above, one can imagine that to each possible program control path corresponds a conjunction of conditions accumulated by the decisions taken during the execution. The set of conditions that defines a control path is called its **path condition**.

It is now possible to talk about test case generation. As for the other two techniques mentioned in this section (*model checking* and *theorem proving*), test cases can be generated as by-products of symbolic execution. The main goal of symbolic execution is to analyze the control structure of a program and possibly discover errors in it. However, by finding a solutions to the equations that describe control paths it is possible to extract values that can be used as test cases. These values will clearly force the application to follow the control path that defines that path condition.

From the above it can be understood that symbolic execution was invented mainly for **white-box testing**. Despite, nothing prevents from applying the same techniques starting from an abstract specification such as a state machine. Symbolically searching a state space helps coping with state space explosion since it reduces the number of possible paths by associating classes of inputs. Several authors [PPS+03, LP01, LPU02] provide interesting examples of the usage of symbolic execution for generating test cases from an abstract model. From here on in this text we will use the term **model** to mean both program and abstract specification.

In this section we will provide an account of the above described topics. In particular in Sec. 12.3.1 we will go through the technique of symbolic execution, showing both how it works and what problems it raises. In Sec. 12.3.2 the topic of test case generation from symbolic execution is discussed. Since in our days test case generation is mainly done using a conjunction of techniques, we will discuss several test case generation methods where symbolic execution plays a significant role.

12.3.1   The Technique

As already discussed in the introduction, **symbolic execution** started to be as a technique to help debugging programs by instantiating input variables with symbols. Each symbol represents the whole range of values a given input variable may assume. As an illustration, consider the code in Fig. 12.4 which is a C translation of an example that can be found in [Cla76]:

```
    int foo(int a,int b) {
1       a++;
2       if (a > b)
3           a = a - b;
4       else
5           a = b - a;
6       if (a <= -1)
7           a = -a;
8       return a
    }
```

Fig. 12.4. *foo* C code

In order to execute this piece of code symbolically, we start by assuming the instantiation of the input variables a and b of the *foo* routine by the symbols $\alpha 1$ and $\alpha 2$.

The instruction labelled *1* is an **assignment** which increments the value of $\alpha 1$. In this case it is simple to see that after this statement is executed we have $\alpha 1 = \alpha 1 + 1$.

The symbolic execution of a **conditional** statement is however more complicated. If we take the statement labelled *2* from the *foo* routine, there are two cases to consider:

- $\alpha 1 > \alpha 2$: the next instruction is the one labelled *3*;
- $\alpha 1 \leq \alpha 2$: the next instruction is the one labelled *5*.

Since both $\alpha 1$ and $\alpha 2$ are symbolic and represent the whole range of numeric values the input variables to the program may assume, it is impossible to decide whether the program should follow label *3* or label *5*. It is thus necessary to follow both of them and to split the execution in two separate control paths. Each of these control paths will however have a condition attached to it: the control path associated to the fact that $a > b$ is *true* has the $a > b$ condition attached to it; the control path associated with the fact that $a \leq b$ is *true* has the $a \leq b$ condition attached to it. These conditions are called **path conditions**. If we generalize, a path condition can be seen as a set of arbitrary constraints on input variables.

In Fig. 12.5 it is possible to observe the partial symbolic execution of *foo* by means of a directed graph. The nodes of the graph correspond to the state of the input variables and of the path condition while the edges correspond to the next statement in line for execution.

From *foo's* symbolic execution much information can be retrieved:

- At each state of the symbolic execution three data are known: the input variable's symbolic value, the path condition's symbolic value and the next statement to be executed;
- Each leaf in the symbolic execution tree corresponds to the end of a control path. The path condition on each leaf is the conjunction of all the assumption made about the input values as the program executes. At the tree's leaves, the path condition fully documents the followed control path;
- This method enables the detection of control paths that are never executed in a model. For example, in *foo* the control path *(1-3,6-8)* is associated with the path condition $(\alpha 1 - \alpha 2 > -1) \wedge (\alpha 1 - \alpha 2 \leq -2)$. There is no solution for these equations so no input values will ever make the program follow this control path.

The example from Fig. 12.5 only deals with **assignments** and **conditional** statements, no **loop** statements are included. We will not go into the details of how to symbolically execute a loop statement since the algorithm can be extrapolated from the one for symbolically executing a conditional statement:

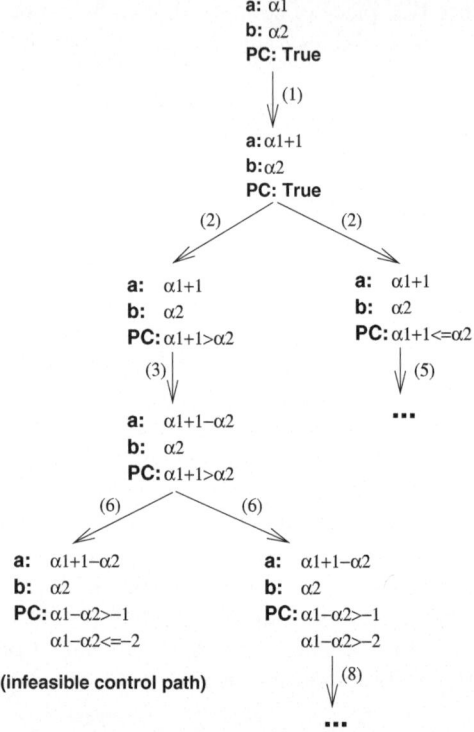

Fig. 12.5. Symbolic execution tree of *foo*

- if from the path condition it can be deduced that the loop condition is
    - *true* then the control path is directed to the beginning of the loop statements;
    - *false* then the control path is directed to the first statement after the loop.
    - both *true* and *false*, then the control path is split in two as described in the first two bullets.

An interesting case is when the condition expression of a conditional statement involves a subroutine or method call. As an example, imagine instruction *2* of the *foo* routine has the following condition: $f(a) > b$, where f is a function or a method defined elsewhere in the application. In that case two different strategies may be used: consider the return value of the function call as one or multiple symbolic expressions (resulting from the symbolic execution of the f subroutine); consider the $f(a)$ expression as another symbolic variable over the possible return values of f.

Proving Program Correctness It is possible to extract relevant information only from symbolically executing an application model. For example, infeasible control paths may be identified or errors in the code can be detected by looking at the path conditions for each control path. However, using symbolic execution it is possible to go further than that into the domain of proving **program correctness**.

King [Kin76] discusses the similarities between proving program correctness and symbolic execution. In order to prove that a program is correct it is necessary to state a **precondition** that constraints input variables and a **postcondition** that will be required to be true after program execution. It is possible to perform these proofs with symbolic execution since:

- the precondition can simply be conjunct with the path condition at the beginning of the execution;
- the postcondition can again be conjunct with the path condition at the end of the execution of each control path. If there is no solution for the equations posed by the conjunction of a control path's path condition and the postcondition, then that path should not exist.

The proof can also be done in a compositional fashion by making pre and postconditions cover relevant segments of the program. Proving the program is correct corresponds in this case to proving all the specified segments. This technique is used in [Kin76] to show that EFFIGY (one of the first symbolic executors) could be used to prove program correctness.

The authors of [KPV03] use a similar technique for verifying object oriented concurrent programs with complex data structures. Their approach consists of annotating source code with method pre and postconditions and performing symbolic execution using a model checker. Each time the model checker fails to verify one of the preconditions the search backtracks (the path is infeasible) and an alternative execution path is tried out.

Issues Related to the Approach Several difficulties arise when trying to execute a model symbolically. As with other verification techniques, the main problem is linked to the fact that the state space for control path verification is usually infinite, as well as the range of values of each input. Despite the advantage offered by symbolic execution of abstracting sets of input values into symbols, solving the *path condition* equations is still necessary in order find which input values yield a given control path. The following bullets discuss these problems and how some authors approached them.

- *Dealing with infinite control paths* If we consider models which comprise loops - which means all the programming languages and virtually all state spaces generated by abstract specifications - there is an infinite number of control paths with infinite states. When a loop depends on symbolic input values it is a difficult problem to automatically understand when the loop execution should stop. Several solutions may be envisaged:

- simply prompt the user at each iteration of the loop for directions;
- establish an upper limit on the amount of iterations to be performed on each loop (automatically or by human intervention). This limit is an heuristic and will have an impact on the quality of the generated control paths;
- Try to automatically find a fixed point to the loop. This is however not trivial and may require human assistance.

The usual approach implemented in symbolic executors is to provide an upper limit on the number of symbolic executions to be performed (e.g. CASEGEN [RHC76], DISSECT [How77]). In DISSECT another approach to controlling control path length is to provide an upper limit for the total control path length, as well as for the total amount of generated paths.

- *Solving path condition equations* This is crucial both for the symbolic execution itself and for test case generation. During symbolic execution it will be necessary to constantly evaluate the path condition equations of in order to decide whether the control path being explored is feasible or not. If there is no solution to the equations at some moment, the path is infeasible.

  In what concerns test case generation, for each feasible control path the *path condition* provides the relation between input variables that will direct execution through that particular path. If it is possible to generate values that satisfy that relation, then it is possible to extract a test case.

- The *path condition* holds a general system of equalities and/or inequalities, for which any algorithm will not be complete. Clark [Cla76] presents a linear programming algorithm that can be applied in the case where the equations are linear constraints. Ramamoorthy et al. [RHC76] deal with non-linear equations using a systematic trial and error procedure. This procedure assigns random values to input variables until a solution is found (which is not always possible). Much more recently in [PPS+03], random trial and error is also used, in conjunction with limit analysis.

In this subsection we have discussed the fundamentals of symbolic execution. This knowledge provides the basis for understanding the next section - an overview on test case generation using symbolic execution.

12.3.2   Test Case Generation Using Symbolic Execution

While going through the available literature on test case generation using symbolic execution we found that the models used to specify the application vary wildly. We have thus opted by describing in this section three examples that have their starting point in three different abstract models: B [Abr96], AUTO-FOCUS [FHS96] and CO-OPN [OBG01].

More than that, we also found that some interesting techniques that make use of symbolic execution for test case generation don't use abstract models but rather start directly from code. We explore in this section also one of these techniques coming from white-box testing. We find that the example described enriches this survey since it can also eventually be used in test case generation from abstract models.

Another axis where we based this survey on are the synergies between symbolic execution and other program verification techniques in the context of test cases generation. As we have shown in Sec. 12.3.1, symbolic execution started out as a pure white-box testing technique during the 1970s. Later, it has been recycled to help reducing state-space explosion problems associated with formal verification techniques such as *model checking* (Sec. 12.4) or *theorem proving* (Sec. 12.2).

The examples that follow encompass the application of several techniques for program verification, including obviously symbolic execution. For each of the examples the several techniques employed for test case generation are identified, so that the synergies between them are exposed.

We start with three frameworks for model based test case generation where symbolic execution is heavily used. We then pass onto one example of code based test case generation which we find particularly interesting since it uses model checking to perform symbolic execution.

Abstract Model-Based Test Case Generation The three following examples are relatively similar in the way they approach the problem of test case generation. They all start from an abstract specification and perform searches through the execution state space of the specified application by using a **constraint logic programming** language or simply **Prolog**. This search is done in a symbolic fashion in the sense that each state of the model corresponds not to a single concrete state but rather to a set of constrained model input variables. The constraints for the model input variables at a given state are calculated by symbolically executing the path until that state - the same way we have shown in Sec. 12.3.1.

At this point it seems important to also define what a constraint logic programming (CLP) language is. CLP languages are declarative logic languages, such as Prolog, but particularly enabled to deal with arbitrary constraints. Examples of constraints could be for example $X > 0$ or $Y + Z < 15$. Intuitively, while Prolog's inference engine only understands syntactic unification, a CLP engine includes semantic knowledge about constraints while performing unification. This makes CLPs more efficient than Prolog for performing searches through variable constrained state spaces such as the ones we are considering in this text.

We will start by an example that builds test cases starting from a **B** specification. This approach called BZ-TT (BZ-Testing-Tools) is described by Legeard and Peureaux in [LP01, LPU02, LPU04] and consists essentially of three steps:

- *translating a B specification into their custom **CLPS-B** constraint logic programming language*: B is a specification language related to **Z** that supports the development of C code from specifications. In B a software application can be seen as a state machine in which each state is defined by a number of state variables and transitions are defined by the operations the state machine accepts for each state.

  The translation step generates CLPS-B prototypes of the operations described in B to allow the animation of the specification. With CLPS-B it is then possible to generate the execution state space for the specified application and to search it for traces that are interesting to be tested. The translation from B into CLPS-B can be seen as a first (abstract) prototyping of the system under test;

- *calculate the **boundary states** for each state variable in the specification*: Boundary states consist of states of the specification execution which are considered to be particular hence should be tested. In order to find these states the test case generation framework relies on symbolic execution. In what follows, please keep in mind that this approach is limited to finite enumerated domains.

  Boundary states are calculated in the following fashion: each state variable's[6] value domain is partitioned by symbolic execution of the B specification (by means of the CLPS-B translation). In fact, in a B specification properties of state variables are defined both in the preconditions and the body of operations by structures such as "SELECT...THEN", "IF...THEN...ELSE" or "ANY...WHERE". For each possible execution (each possible trace) of the specification there is a *path condition* associated. The difference with normal symbolic execution is that this time the interest is not on all the conditions posed on all the state variables, but rather on the conditions posed on one single state variable. For example, if we consider that a given execution trace implies the following conditions over state variable x with domain 1,2,...,9,10:

$$x \in \{1, 2, 3, 4, 5\} \wedge x \neq 3$$

then x's value domain would be partitioned in the following way:

$$x \in \{1, 2, 3\} \cup \{3\} \cup \{3, 4, 5\} \cup \{5, ..., 10\}$$

From this union of sets called *P-Domain* it is possible to calculate an intermediate product called *boundary values*. These are the values belonging to the extremes of each of the subsets in the *P-Domain* set. If we take the example above, the *boundary values* for $x \in \{1, 2, 3\} \cup 3 \cup \{3, 4, 5\} \cup \{5, ..., 10\}$ would be $\{1, 3, 5, 10\}$. It should be said that we have not taken into consideration state variables over non-numeric sets, although the computation of boundary values for these sort of variables is relatively similar to the previous description.

---

[6] State variables are related to what we described in Sec. 12.3.1 as *input variables*

It is now possible to calculate the *boundary states*. These correspond to states in the execution space of the specification where at least one of the state variables assumes a *boundary value*. Symbolic execution is again necessary at this stage given that in order to know the ranges of all the other state variables that define a *boundary state* it is necessary to know the *path condition* for that state.

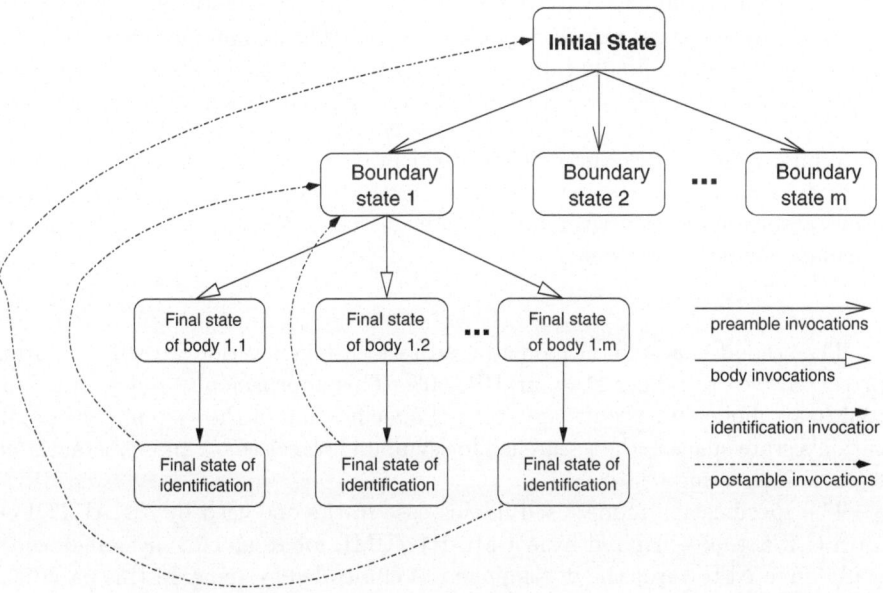

Fig. 12.6. Trace construction for boundary testing

- *generate the test cases (traces through the state space)*: this activity may be resumed to the following:

  - *Calculate the preamble trace to the boundary state*: this consists of calculating the sequence of operations that leads the system to a *boundary state*. Given that the *path condition* for the boundary state is already known, this can be considered trivial;
  - *Calculate the "critical invocation" step*: the authors of the approach define *critical invocation* as the execution of the operations which are possible from the *boundary state*. The execution of these operations in is clearly sensitive since is implies the manipulation of a boundary value. For that reason the input parameters for the operations under analysis are decomposed into subdomains as was done in order to find the *boundary values*. We can say that the operations accessible from the *boundary state* are then symbolically executed over their entry parameters, yielding a subdivision of the *preamble trace* (see Fig. 12.6);

– *Calculate the identification traces and the postamble after the "critical invocation"*: The identification trace consists of one or more operations to be executed in order to observe the behavior of the system after the critical step. The postamble trace is a sequence of operations that resets the state machine to the initial state from where new test cases can be again searched for.

It is then possible to concatenate the *preamble trace* with the *critical invocation* traces with the *identification traces*. The remaining symbolic parts of the traces are finally fully instantiated in order to generate real test case scripts that can be applied to a concrete implementation of the application.

While trying to discriminate the verification techniques used in this framework we can identify clearly the usage of *symbolic execution*, but also of *theorem proving* since a logic programming language (i.e. a *theorem prover*) is used to calculate the *boundary states*.

The second example on model-based test case generation we will discuss is presented by Pretschner *et al.* in [PPS$^+$03]. This approach also relies on a CLP tool to symbolically execute the abstract specification of the system. The application's state space is then searched for symbolic traces that can be instantiated to form interesting test cases.

The specification model used in this case in the one used by the AUTOFO-CUS CASE tool - inspired from UML-RT (UML for Real-Time systems), especially directed towards the development of embedded systems. In this paradigm the system's structure is defined as a network of components. Each of the bottom level component's behavior is described by a state machine. Composition of the bottom level state machines generates higher level state machines and so on until the full system's state machine is reached. As in the previous example, states are defined by state variables and the transitions are possible via commands (or operations) that are issued to the system.

Before describing how the test cases are generated, it is useful to mention that the authors of the approach consider different kinds of coverage of the execution state space. In [PPS$^+$03] they describe three different coverage classes:

- *Functional coverage*: this sort of coverage implies generating test cases that exercise precise execution scenarios given in the specification. Both positive as well as negative test cases are interesting to validate the system;
- *Structural coverage*: structural criteria implies for example issuing sequences of commands that selectively test critical components of the system. Another example is the coverage of states that may be considered dangerous or unsafe;
- *Stochastic coverage*: using this approach random traces are generated through the execution state space of the application. Despite the search not being directed, this sort of coverage may still produce relevant test cases.

The generation of test cases is done by translating the AUTOFOCUS model into a CLP language so that it can be symbolically executed by a constraint logic engine. The idea is that a bottom level transition of a component K is modelled into a formula of the following type:

$$step^K(\overrightarrow{\sigma}_{src}, \overrightarrow{\iota}, \overrightarrow{o}, \overrightarrow{\sigma}_{dst}) \Leftarrow guard(\overrightarrow{\iota}, \overrightarrow{\sigma}_{src}) \wedge assgmt(\overrightarrow{o}, \overrightarrow{\sigma}_{dst})$$

This means that upon reception of input $\overrightarrow{\iota}$, component K can evolve from control and data state $\overrightarrow{\sigma}_{src}$ to $\overrightarrow{\sigma}_{dst}$ while outputting $\overrightarrow{o}$. In order for this to happen however the transition's guard has to hold. Also, the data state of the component after transition is determined by the assignment function $assgmt$. If we consider a component K that is not a bottom level one, then a transition of component K shall be composed of a set of lower-level transitions of K's subcomponents.

The CLP program representing the application's specification is then executed to calculate interesting traces through the execution's state space. We can say symbolic execution is used here since the traces are built not with actual input values for each transition - rather with constraints over variables representing input values. One of the interesting feature of this particular framework is the possibility of annotating the abstract AUTOFOCUS specification with coverage criteria. These annotations are also translated into the CLP model of the application in order to allow heuristics for trace construction.

Clearly, at the end of the search the symbolic traces need to be instantiated in order to build real test cases that can be used to verify a concrete implementation of the system. This instantiation is done either at random or by limit analysis.

As in the previous example, we can clearly identify in this approach the presence of the *symbolic execution* and the *theorem proving* verification techniques.

The final example on test case generation from an abstract model we describe in this text is presented by Peraire, Barbey and Buchs in [CPB98]. The starting point for the framework is a formal specification language called CO-OPN (Concurrent Object Oriented Petri Nets), also developed by the same group. CO-OPN uses algebraic structures to define data types and the Petri Net formalism to handle concurrency. From a specification in this language an axiomatization in Prolog is produced automatically. The role of this axiomatization is dual:

- it allows the generation of test cases by composition of operations of the SUT's interface. Since there is an infinite random amount of these compositions, the test engineer can apply hypotheses on the behavior of the system in order to reduce the initial number of tests. This is done using a special purpose language;
- on the other hand the axiomatization of the specification in Prolog also makes it executable (at a level which is necessarily more abstract than the SUT). This high level prototype makes it possible to validate the generated

tests, i.e. checking whether the transitions between the operations in the test sequence are possible. If they are not, then that sequence of operations should not be applicable to the implementation - this type of tests are negative but also relevant to verify the correctness of the SUT.

The next step in the approach is to define a set of hypotheses that will direct the symbolic execution of the axiomatized prototype. Unlike other frameworks described in this section, this one relies on human intuition during test case selection. Despite the fact that some of the possible automation during this step is lost, the high-level language used to describe hypotheses about interesting test cases provides a basis to generate tests which are semantically meaningful.

The test engineer can express two types of hypotheses concerning the tests that will be generated:

- *Regularity hypotheses*: this type of hypotheses stipulates that if a test containing a variable v if valid for a subset of v satisfying an arbitrary complexity criteria, then it is valid for all of v's domain of greater complexity. The notion of variable in a test is very generic, including not only input variables but also constraints on the shape of the sequence of operations that form the test. This is however a complex topic and the reader is referred to [Per98] for details;
- *Uniformity hypotheses*: the uniformity hypotheses state that if a test containing a variable v is valid for one value of v, then it is valid for all of v's domain.

After introduction in the system of hypotheses by the test engineer, the prolog adapted engine (the resolution is not pure SLD[7]) symbolically executes the uninstantiated tests against the axiomatic definition of the application. The idea behind the approach is to extract from path condition of a given test the constraints on the variables corresponding to the input values of the operations present in that test. Given this knowledge it becomes possible to calculate the subdomains of the uninstantiated input variables and apply uniformity hypotheses in a way that the operation behaviors described in the specification are taken into consideration. This activity is somehow equivalent to what is performed by Legeard and Peureaux in [LP01] while calculating the *P-Domains*.

Again, as with the previously described approaches, both theorem proving and symbolic execution techniques are used in this test case generation framework.

Code-Based Test Case Generation In the last example of this section we will be describing a framework by Khurshid *et al.* [KPV03] that generates test

---

[7] SLD is the standard mechanism used in logic programming languages in order to compute goal solutions

cases not from an abstract model as the ones described in 12.3.2, but from Java code directly. We chose to take this detour from the main topic of this section in order to discuss a technique that:

- generates test cases from "real code" in a modern programming language;
- takes advantage of a model checker (Java PathFinder) to overcome some of the difficulties of symbolic execution;
- takes advantage of symbolic execution to overcome some of the difficulties of model checking.

Java PathFinder is a model checker (see Sec. 12.4) built specifically for Java. As all model checkers, it allows verifying that a model of an application (or, in this case the application itself) satisfies a set of logic formulas specifying given properties of the application. An interesting property to be verified with Java PathFinder is for example that no exception is left unhandled in a given method. As a result of the model checking we can obtain either execution trace witnesses of the validity of the formulas or execution trace counter-examples if the formulas do not hold. Clearly, witnesses are positive test cases and counter examples are negative ones.

There is a fundamental difference between this approach and the ones described before. In fact, all the previous frameworks were based on the fact that a model of the application, assumed correct, existed. The implementation could then be verified against that model. In the present case, the model does not exist explicitly: it is provided implicitly with the temporal logic formulas. The expected correct and incorrect behaviors of the implementation are described by the test engineer using temporal logic. The simple fact that the witnesses or counterexamples to these formulas exist already provides information about the correctness of the implementation.

One of the main issues around model checking software applications is the state space explosion problem. In order to be model checked efficiently, an application needs to be bounded on its input variables. Symbolic execution may help in this point, by replacing explicitly valued states by symbolic states representing large domains.

On the other hand, model checking provides a number of built-in facilities that allows exploring a state space efficiently. In particular, goodies like the handling of loops, recursion or method invocation can be hidden from the symbolic execution part. The handling of infinite execution trees is handled by the model checker by exploring the state space using either iterative deepening depth first or breadth first techniques. Heuristic based search is also supported.

In what concerns the technique itself, it requires that the Java code passes through a first instrumentation phase. Since Java PathFinder takes in pure Java code, the model checking is done over all possible values of input variables of the system. In order for the model checker to be able to manipulate symbols rather than real values the code needs to be instrumented. This is done at three levels:

- Basic typed variables (e.g. integers) are replaced by objects of an *Expression* type that will be able to keep track of symbolic values. Objects that are static or dynamic can be seen as compositions of the basic types and can thus be represented symbolically by replacing the basic typed fields with *Expression* objects;
- Code instrumentation is also necessary in order to build the *path condition* for each of the traces the model checker explores. To do this a *PathCondition* class is provided that allows modifying the conditional statements of the code so that the path condition may be built as the application is executed;
- Finally, code instrumentation is used to add method pre and postconditions. Method preconditions are used to constrain the method's input values. This is relevant in order to constrain the search space and avoid execution traces that will never exist.

For each of the types of instrumentation described above, the framework provides the necessary Java libraries.

The most interesting aspect of this approach is the symbolic execution algorithm that allows dealing with methods that take as inputs complex unbounded data structures. This algorithm uses what the authors of [KPV03] call *lazy initialization* since it initializes data structures as the they are accessed. In Fig. 12.7 the algorithm for lazy initialization is described.

```
if (f is uninitialized) {
    if (f is a reference field of type T) {
        nondeterministically initialize f to
            1. null
            2. a new object of class T (with uninitialized field values)
            3. an object created during a prior initialization of a field of type T
        if (method precondition is violated)
            backtrack();
    }
}
```

Fig. 12.7. Lazy initialization algorithm

The algorithm allows the construction of path conditions that take into consideration not only conditions over basic types, but also over complex data structures involving a dynamic number of objects. Fig. 12.7 only shows how the algorithm deals with initializing references to objects, being that primitives types are given symbolic values. The *backtrack()* instruction in the algorithm points out the fact that since the initialization of a reference is non-deterministic, the algorithm backtracks when the selected initialization is not allowed by the precondition of the method. It can then continue searching for other solutions at the last decision point.

Finally, the test cases are obtained by running the Java PathFinder model checker over the instrumented code. For each of the criteria specified in logic formulas, witnesses or counter-examples traces are generated. As in the previous approaches, the path conditions for these traces may then be used the build the actual input values to test the concrete system.

12.4   Model Checking

In the next few paragraphs we will describe the application of model checking for test case generation. Given that the topic is explored in depth in Chap. 19 of the present volume, we limit ourselves to giving a short overview of the subject.

Several approaches exist that establish connections between model checking and model-based testing (see [CSE96, EFM97, GH99, GRR03, HLSU02, HCL$^+$03, RH01a, RH01b]). In all these approaches the problem of test case generation is reduced to finding witnesses or counterexamples to a set of temporal logic formulas. These temporal logic formulas express control flow oriented test coverage criteria (see [GH99, GRR03, RH01a, RH01b]) or data flow oriented test coverage criteria (see [HLSU02, HCL$^+$03]). The capability of model checkers to find witnesses and counterexamples to the logic formulas allows then test case generation to be fully automatic. The obtained execution traces are obtained from a simplified model of the application and can be used to test a real implementation either for correct traces or for error situations.

In [CSE96, EFM97], the authors propose similar approaches that use test purposes instead of test coverage criteria. Differently from test coverage criteria which capture structural entities of a model, test purposes express behavioral properties of a model. Examples are properties of certain states or a sequence of states to be traversed.

The authors of [ABM98, AB99] apply model checking to test case generation for mutation analysis-based test coverage criteria. By applying mutation operators to either a system model or a property, mutants are produced. A test suite is then generated to cover the inconsistent behaviors exhibited by the mutants. The capability of model checkers to construct counterexamples is used to find such inconsistent behaviors.

Model checking-based test case generation provides several relevant features in comparison to other test case generation techniques. First, all details on test case generation are hidden inside the model checkers. This allows the test engineer to focus on only high-level specifications of test purposes or coverage criteria written in temporal logic. On the other hand, test case generation is language independent in the sense that the temporal logic formulas can be applied to various specification and programming languages without having to build a dedicated tool for each language. Finally, test case generation can be performed on large and complex models since model checking is a relatively mature technology.

12.5   Summary

In this chapter we have shown how the search problem of finding test cases that satisfy given test case specifications can be solved by applying well known techniques from computer science. After introducing the basic terminology and the used formalisms in each section, we have shown how techniques and tools from *theorem proving, symbolic execution*, and *model checking* can be applied to perform, improve, or support test case generation based on a model of the SUT.

At first, we have presented some approaches from the literature of how test case generation can be done by *theorem proving*. A formal specification of the SUT is transformed into equivalence classes, which are assumed to represent the same behavior with respect to the test. Therefore, each equivalence class can be interpreted as one test case. We have shown how such transformations into equivalence classes resp. partitions can be performed using theorem proving technology. In particular, we described how general purpose theorem provers can be applied to generate test cases from Z specifications. Starting at the purely syntactic disjunctive normal form approach, we have shown how to integrate semantic aspects by means of the classification-tree method, and how partitioning resp. fault-based heuristics can be used. Afterwards, we have covered test case generation by logic programming, i.e., we have shown how algebraic specifications can be translated into Horn clauses from which test cases can be extracted by Prolog's resolution principle. Finally, we have shortly described test case extraction from correctness proofs. Topics for future research in this area are extensions regarding test case sequencing and concurrency, broader constraint solving abilities, and applications to a wider range of graphical notations.

We have also shown that *symbolic execution* is a relevant technique to help coping with state space explosion while generating test cases. Symbolic execution is generic enough to be applied to abstract models as well as to concrete code. In particular, we have described three test case generation frameworks. The first two start by performing a translation of their respective abstract models (in the B and AUTOFOCUS modelling language) into a constraint logic programming language. The resulting CLP model is then symbolically executed in order to search for traces that represent interesting test cases. In both examples a synergy between symbolic execution and theorem proving is established, given that logic programming is used to perform state space exploration. The third example framework demonstrates generating test cases starting from Java code. A very interesting feature of this approach is that it uses model checking to symbolically search the state space. In a way, this example comes to reinforce the notion that symbolic execution is not used on its own to generate test cases – rather it is merged with other techniques in order to overcome their shortfalls, as well the ones in symbolic execution itself.

Finally, we have shortly described the application of *model checking* in model-based test case generation. Specifically, we have covered the relation between control flow resp. data flow oriented coverage criteria and the capability of model checkers to construct witnesses and counterexamples. There still remain a number of open questions in this context. Most research efforts in model checking focus on efficient model checking algorithms for a single temporal logic formula. In model checking based test case generation, however, we are given a set of temporal logic formulas from dozens to hundreds and are interested in both determining the satisfiability of the formulas and generation of witnesses and counterexamples.

13   Real-Time and Hybrid Systems Testing

Kirsten Berkenkötter[1] and Raimund Kirner[2]

[1] Department of Computer Science
   University of Bremen
   kirsten@informatik.uni-bremen.de
[2] Real-Time Systems Group
   Vienna University of Technology
   raimund@vmars.tuwien.ac.at

13.1   Introduction

Real-Time and Hybrid Systems A system whose functionality is not only dependent on the logical results of computation but also on the time in which this computation takes place is called **real-time system**. We speak of **hard real-time** if timing constraints always have to be met exactly. In contrast, **soft real-time** allows lateness under specified conditions.

Similarly, **hybrid systems** also consider time to determine if computation works correctly. They are called hybrid as both time-discrete and time-continuous observables exist as well as time-discrete and time-continuous behavior. Variables may have dense values that change with respect to time while events occur discretely. Assignments to variables are also made at discrete points in time. Therefore the behavior of a hybrid system consists of time-continuous parts where variable evaluations change with respect to time and of time-discrete parts where events occur and assignments to variables are performed.

Both kinds of systems are used, e.g. in avionics, in automotive control, and in chemical processes control systems. They are often embedded systems with a probably safety-critical background. This leads to high demands on both modeling and testing for providing high quality.

Testing As stated above, both real-time and hybrid systems are potentially hazardous systems. Obviously, temporal correctness is an important issue of real-time systems. As a result, testing real-time systems is more complex than testing untimed systems as time becomes an additional dimension of the input data space. In case of hybrid systems, complexity increases again as the value domain is continuous instead of discrete.

For model-based testing, the main goal is handling this complexity. On the one hand, this means building models that allow to abstract from details to reduce complexity in a way that test cases can be generated. On the other hand, test cases must be selected in a meaningful way to achieve a manageable number out of them.

Outline In Section 13.2, we will discuss test automation in general and with respect to the special needs of real-time and hybrid systems. We then focus on

M. Broy et al. (Eds.): Model-Based Testing of Reactive Systems, LNCS 3472, pp. 355-387, 2005.
© Springer-Verlag Berlin Heidelberg 2005

model-based test case generation in Section 13.3. Different modeling techniques like timed process algebras and timed automata are discussed for real-time and hybrid systems as well as their application in test case generation. After that, evolutionary testing is introduced as a method for improving generated test suites with respect to testing timing constraints in Section 13.4. We conclude with a discussion of the presented techniques in Section 13.5.

13.2   Test Automation

Testing is one of the most time consuming parts of the software development process. Hence, a high degree of **automation** is needed. The general structure for a test automation system is the same for untimed, timed, and hybrid systems. In contrast, the internals of the different parts of a test automation system differ, as the specific characteristics of timed and hybrid systems must be considered.

13.2.1   Overview

First, we have to introduce some testing terminology. **Testing** itself means the execution of the system to be tested which we call **system under test (SUT)**. The SUT is fed input data while the output data is monitored for checking its correctness.

A **test case** is a set of test inputs, execution conditions, and expected results. This does not mean that the test case necessarily gives explicit input data, it may also specify rules for generating test data. The set of test cases for a SUT is called **test suite**. The **test procedure** gives detailed information about the set-up and execution of test cases and the evaluation of the test results. If only the interfaces of the SUT are accessible, a test is called **black-box test**. In contrast, if also internal states can be observed and influenced, a test is called **white-box test**.

As stated in Peleska et al. [PAD+98], a test automation system consists of several logical building blocks as depicted in Figure 13.1:

- MODEL The **test model** represents the required functionality of the SUT. More precisely, it abstracts the functionality to a sensible size to allow the generation of a test suite with manageable size. Different representations can be chosen, e.g. automata or process algebra.
- TEST GENERATION The **test generator** uses the model for deriving test cases. In addition, more specific **test case specifications** that describe a test case or a set of test cases can be used for this purpose. The test generator is responsible for achieving a manageable number of test cases out of the infinitely many possible ones. Therefore it plays an important role in the test automation system.
- TEST MONITORING The execution of test cases must be monitored to keep track of inputs and outputs. This is done by the **test monitor**. On the one hand, this is needed for documentation purposes. On the other hand, results

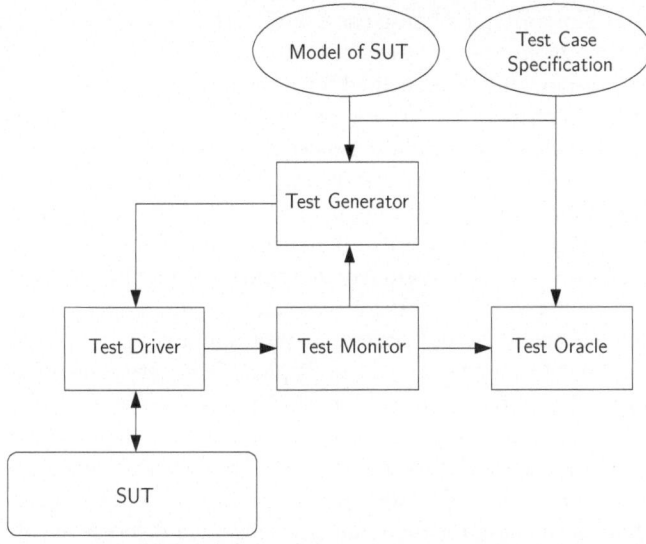

Fig. 13.1. Test automation system

may be needed during execution. To give an example, nondeterminism can occur. Then the output of the SUT is needed to decide which input can be sent next. It is also desirable to know if a test case fails during execution as the test can be aborted then. This holds especially for long time tests.

- TEST EVALUATION Either after or during test execution, the test result has to be assessed. This is the task of the **test oracle**. According to the monitored test data, SUT model, and test specifications, it calculates the **test verdict**. **Passed**, **failed**, and **inconclusive** are frequently used as verdicts.
- TEST DRIVER The parts of the test automation system converge in the **test driver**. It executes the generated test cases, i.e. it posts input to the SUT and receives corresponding outputs. This includes providing interfaces from and to the SUT. Therefore, the test driver works hand in hand with the test monitor.

13.2.2   From Untimed to Timed to Hybrid Models

Due to the time-dependent behavior of a real-time system, new problems arise when testing it as time is a relevant factor. For hybrid systems, also dense-valued variables must be considered. These problems must be analyzed to find suitable abstractions for the SUT model as done in Peleska et al. [PAD+98].

With respect to testing, the sequential components of an untimed system are obviously best understood. Correct behavior is surveyed by looking at the initial and final states of such a component. Concurrent components are more difficult to test as not only the data processed must be correct but also the order in which it is processed. Furthermore, the interactions between the processes lead to many internal states. The amount of test cases and test data to be evaluated can be reduced by describing not only the system under test but also the environment. In this way, input and output are specified for a certain environment, so the number of possible values is reduced to a more manageable size. Also redundancy checks are performed that delete redundant test sequences.

Adding time to the requirements of a system means adding complexity to testing. In addition to the correct sequencing of inputs and outputs, the time at that they occur is crucial. If only **discrete time** is considered, time can be abstracted as a counter that is regularly incremented. The fuzziness of measuring time must be considered in the test automation system. This is the case for real-time systems with both discrete time and data domain.

If it becomes hard to define time as multiples of discrete time intervals, **dense time** has to be taken into account. This is closer to reality as time is naturally dense. Timing constraints are then given with respect to the real numbers. Data is still considered **discrete**. Nevertheless, a model that uses dense time increases complexity even more, so this must be taken into account, e.g. for test case generation. This is the case for real-time systems with discrete data domain and dense time domain.

The last step to be taken is regarding also **dense-valued**, i. e. analog data as done for hybrid systems. This is an abstraction for both analog sensors and actuators and also sensors and actuators that are discrete but have very high sampling rates. In the model,the evaluation of dense-valued variables is specified by piecewise continuous functions over time that may be differential. Therefore the time domain and and the value domain of hybrid systems are both dense.

13.2.3   Real-Time and Hybrid Systems

The different components of the test automation system that has been described in Section 13.2.1 have to be modified as the time and value domain of real-time and hybrid systems must be considered. As described in Section 13.2.2, there are real-time systems with discrete time domain, real-time systems with dense time domain, and hybrid systems with both dense value and dense time domain. These different abstractions of the SUT have to be mirrored in the corresponding test automation system.

- MODEL Obviously, adequate modeling techniques have to be chosen for testing real-time and hybrid systems. For real-time systems, there are several types of timed automata and timed process algebras that consider either discrete time or dense time in modeling. In case of hybrid systems, dense values for variables must also be taken into account. Here, hybrid automata and hybrid process algebra can be used for describing the SUT. It is important to notice that appropriate abstractions from the SUT must be found to obtain a manageable model.
- TEST GENERATION In comparison with untimed systems, test generation is much more difficult for timed and hybrid systems as the search space of the model increases with discrete time, dense time, and (in case of hybrid

systems) dense values. Therefore the algorithms needed for generating test cases have to be chosen carefully to gain a meaningful and manageable test suite.

- TEST MONITORING Again, the important factor is time. For monitoring the execution of test cases, not only inputs and outputs to and from the SUT are relevant, also the time at that these inputs and outputs occur must be logged adequately.

- TEST EVALUATION Test evaluation also depends on time. Not only the correct order of inputs and outputs is needed for deciding if a test has failed or passed, the correct timing is also a crucial factor. An unavoidable fuzziness for measuring time must be considered. The same holds for measuring dense-valued data with respect to hybrid systems.

- TEST DRIVER For real-time systems, the test driver must be capable of giving inputs at the correct time, i.e. it must be fast enough for the SUT. For hybrid systems, the same holds for dense data values, e.g. differential equations have to be processed fast enough to model the valuation of data values over time. If analog, i.e. dense-valued, data is expected as input from the SUT, this must be generated. The most important function of the test driver for real-time and hybrid systems is therefore bridging the gap between the abstract model and the corresponding implementation, i.e. the SUT. On the one hand, it has to concretize the input from the model to the SUT. On the other hand, it has to abstract the output from the SUT for the test monitor and test oracle.

All in all, we can identify two main issues for testing real-time and hybrid systems:

- Building manageable and meaningful models from the SUT.
- Finding manageable and meaningful test suites.

Test oracle, test monitor, and test driver are more a challenge in implementation. They have in common that they depend on the model and the test case generation to work efficiently. Therefore, the focus in the following chapters is on modeling and test case generation.

13.3   Model-Based Test Case Generation

The aim of model-based testing is to derive test cases from an application model that is an abstraction of the real behavior of the SUT. As described in Section 13.2.2, time can be abstracted either as discrete or dense time for real-time systems. Values are considered discrete. For hybrid systems, the time domain is dense just as the value domain. There are approaches for modeling each of these systems as well as test case generation algorithms based on these models. These are described in the following.

13.3.1   Real-Time Systems – Discrete Time and Discrete Values

First, we focus on real-time systems that consider both time and value domain as discrete. Different modeling techniques can be used here, e. g. process algebras as the **Algebra of Communicating Shared Resources (ACSR)** [LBGG94, Che02] or **Timed Communicating Sequential Processes (TCSP)** [DS95, Hoa85] or different variants of **Timed Automata** [AD94].

In this section, we will discuss ACSR as a process algebra and **Timed Transition Systems (TTS)** as an example for automata as test case generation algorithms for these exist. Timed CSP has also been used for testing purposes, but here research has been done with regard to test execution and test evaluation and not test case generation [PAD+98, Pel02, Mey01]. Test case specifications are written in Timed CSP and then executed instead of deriving a test suite from a Timed CSP model of the SUT.

Describing Real-Time Constraints Before describing the formalisms used in testing frameworks to model real-time applications, we introduce a more intuitive graphical language to describe real-time constraints called **constraint graph** language. We use it to present a simple example of a real-time application that is used throughout this chapter.

A constraint graph (CG) is a directed graph $G(V, E)$ with a distinguished starting node $\varepsilon \in V$. The nodes of a CG represent I/O events where input events are given by there name while output events are marked with a horizontal line above their name, e.g. $\overline{event}$. The edges E of CG are illustrated as $f \xrightarrow[F]{T} g$, where f denotes the source I/O event and g denotes the target I/O event. T is the time constraint that guards the edge. It can be an interval $[t_1, t_2)$ or a fixed delay t. F denotes the possibly empty set of forbidden I/O events that may not occur before receiving the target event g to allow the edge to be taken. Multiple edges starting from a single node have the semantics of alternative executions, except multiple edges that are marked with a common diamond at their origin. These represent concurrent execution. The constraints of concurrent edges must be valid simultaneously.

Edges with a given timing constraint where the target event is an input event are called **behavioral constraints**. These limit the rate at which inputs are applied to a system. In contrast, edges with a given timing constraint where the target event is an output event are called **performance constraints** that dictate the rate at which outputs are produced by a system.

Real-Time Monitor Example For a better understanding of the described modeling techniques, we will use in this section a simple real-time monitor example called *RTMonitor*. The task of *RTMonitor* is to observe whether events occur within a certain time interval after triggering the monitor application. Such a tool could be, for example, used to monitor whether a robot arm moves correctly by sampling its temporal position at two control points. The initial state of *RTMonitor* is denoted as ε while the start of *RTMonitor* is triggered by event *Start*. The incidents of two control points are reported by signals *Pos1* respectively *Pos2*.

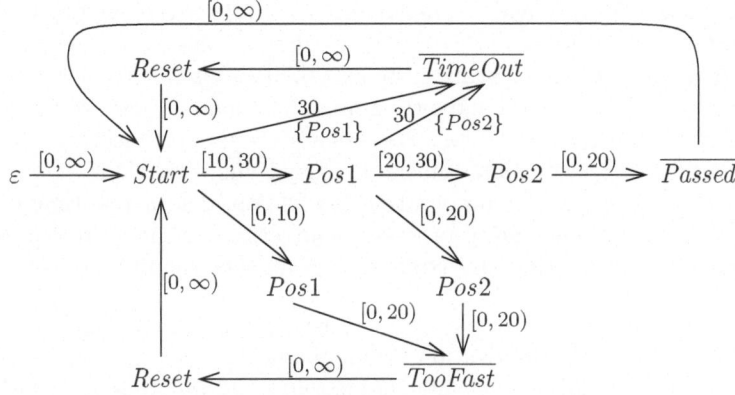

Fig. 13.2. Constraint graph of the real-time monitor example

The constraint graph of *RTMonitor* that shows the relative timing constraints is given in Figure 13.2. The start of monitoring can be triggered at an arbitrary time instant. Once it is triggered:

- The first event *Pos1* has to be reported within time interval $[10, 30)$.
- The second event *Pos2* has to be reported within time interval $[20, 30)$ after the first event.
- If one of these two events occurs too early, event $\overline{TooFast}$ has to be triggered.
- In case that one of these two events has not been observed after passing the time interval, event $\overline{TimeOut}$ has to be stimulated.
- After output event $\overline{TooFast}$, respectively $\overline{TimeOut}$, has been used to indicate an incorrect timing, the input event *Reset* can be used to restart the monitoring.
- If both events have occurred with a correct timing, event $\overline{Passed}$ will be triggered within time interval $[0, 20)$ after event *Pos2*.
- The monitoring application is restarted by waiting again for trigger event *Start*.

There is no timeout mechanism for the time constraint $[0, 20)$ of the event $\overline{Passed}$. $\overline{Passed}$ is an output event and therefore its time constraint $[0, 20)$ is the allowed delay introduced between processing the previous event and generating the output event $\overline{Passed}$. However, for testing the real-time behavior of the SUT, the validity of such a performance constraint also has to be tested on the SUT.

To exemplify the semantics of a constraint graph's edge with forbidden I/O events we describe the meaning of the edge "$Start \xrightarrow[\{Pos1\}]{30} \overline{TimeOut}$". It implies that the last received input event was *Start*. Then, this edge is taken if for the time interval of $[0, 30)$ the application receives no input event Pos_1. In this case, the output event $\overline{TimeOut}$ will be emitted.

ACSR-based Test Case Generation ACSR is based on the Calculus of Communicating Systems (CCS) [Mil89], a process algebra to specify untimed, concurrent, and communicating systems. ACSR adds several operators to describe timed behavior and handle the communication and resource consumption of concurrent real-time processes. These operators support mechanisms for modeling bounded execution time, timeouts, delays, and exceptions.

Modeling: The ACSR computation model considers a real-time system as a collection of communicating processes competing for shared resources. Every computation step is either an **event** or a resource consuming **action**:

- EVENT (e_i, p_i): An event e_i having a priority level p_i is denoted as (e_i, p_i). It serves as a synchronization or communication mechanism between processes. The execution of events does not consume any time in contrast to the execution of actions. The example event (e_i, p_i) describes an input event in contrast to an output event that is drawn with a top bar above its name: $(\bar{e}_i, p_i)$.
- ACTION $\{(r_i, p_i)\}^t$: An action is a set of consumptions of resources r_i at corresponding priority level p_i $(1 \leq i \leq n)$ that needs t time units to execute. A resource consumption is denoted by a pair $(r_i, p_i)^t$.

A process P can be one of the following expressions:

NIL	– process that executes no action (deadlock).
$A^t : P_1$	– executes action A for t time units and proceeds with process P_1. The action $\emptyset^t$ represents idling for t time units.
$e.P_1$	– executes event e and proceeds with process P_1.
$P_1 + P_2$	– nondeterministic selection among the processes P_1 and P_2.
$P_1 \parallel P_2$	– concurrent execution of processes P_1 and P_2.
$P_1 \triangle_t^a (P_2, P_3, P_4)$	– temporal scope construct that binds the execution of event a by process P_1 with a time bound t. If P_1 terminates successfully within time t by executing the event a, the "success-handler" P_2 is executed. If P_1 fails to terminate within t, process P_3 is executed as a "timeout exception handler". Lastly, the execution of P_1 may be interrupted by the execution of a timed action or an instantaneous event of process P_4.
$[P_1]_I$	– process P_1 that only uses resources in set I.
$P_1 \backslash F$	– process P_1 where externally observable events with labels in F are disallowed while P_1 is executing.
$P_1[R_e, R_a]$	– relabels the externally observable events of P_1 according to the relabeling function R_e and the resources of P_1 according to the relabeling function R_a.

$recX.P_1$ – process P_1 that is recursive, i.e. it may have an infinite execution. Every free occurrence of X within P_1 represents a recursive call of the expression $recX.P_1$.

X – recursive call of the surrounding recursive process $recX.P_1$.

RTMonitor Example: We will now model the RTMonitor example according to the constraint graph given in Figure 13.2. An ACSR model of $RTMonitor$ is shown in Figure 13.3. It does not use any actions as resources are not considered in this example. The model excessively uses the concept of temporal scopes to model the allowed time intervals.

$$
\begin{aligned}
RTMonitor &= recX.((Start,1).P_{MA_1}) \\
P_{MA_1} &= \emptyset^\infty \triangle_{10}^{(Pos_1,1)} (P_{early}, P_{MA_2}, NIL) \\
P_{MA_2} &= \emptyset^\infty \triangle_{20}^{(Pos_1,1)} (P_{MB_1}, P_{miss}, NIL) \\
P_{MB_1} &= \emptyset^\infty \triangle_{20}^{(Pos_2,1)} (P_{early}, P_{MB_2}, NIL) \\
P_{MB_2} &= \emptyset^\infty \triangle_{10}^{(Pos_2,1)} (P_{ok}, P_{miss}, NIL) \\
P_{ok} &= (\overline{Passed},1).X \\
P_{miss} &= (\overline{TimeOut},1).(Reset,1).X \\
P_{early} &= (\overline{TooFast},1).(Reset,1).X
\end{aligned}
$$

Fig. 13.3. ACSR model of the real-time monitor example

First, process $RTMonitor$ is defined as a recursive process where the recursion is performed in subprocess P_{ok}. $RTMonitor$ is waiting an unlimited time period for the occurrence of event $(Start,1)$ and continues then with process P_{MA_1}. Process P_{MA_1} together with process P_{MA_2} checks whether event $(Pos_1,1)$ occurs within time interval $[10,30)$ and continues then with process P_{MB_1}. If the event comes too early respectively too late, the corresponding output events $(\overline{TooFast},1)$ or $(\overline{TimeOut},1)$ are generated by process P_{early} respectively P_{miss}. After receiving an input event $(Reset,1)$ process $RTMonitor$ is recursively called. Analogous to P_{MA_1} and P_{MA_2}, processes P_{MB_1} and P_{MB_2} check whether event $(Pos_2,1)$ occurs within time interval $[20,30)$. After that, control is taken over by process P_{ok} that emits the output event $(\overline{Passed},1)$ and then recursively calls $RTMonitor$.

The use of a process algebra like ACSR allows to abstract from the real application behavior by modeling only the dynamic aspects of interaction. In case of ACSR these aspects of interaction include events as well as resource consuming actions. Mechanisms like temporal scope and time consuming actions can express the temporal behavior of the application. ACSR does not support the modeling of numerical calculations or direct communication of parameters. Therefore, the use of ACSR is adequate in cases where the behavior of event communication and resource consuming actions of concurrent processes are the only interesting aspects.

<u>Test Case Generation:</u>   As stated above, ACSR describes the interaction of concurrent processes. Testing such a system of concurrent processes is done by expressing a test as a separate process that we call T. The application of a test T to a process P is denoted as $T \triangleright P$ as done by Clarke and Lee [CL95, CL97a, CL97b]. The test operator $\triangleright$ is introduced for testing purposes and is not part of the ACSR specification itself. It implies an auxiliary sink process that absorbs unsynchronized output events between the tester process and the process under test. For testing the ACSR model of the SUT a test T written in ACSR can be directly applied to the model. But for model-based testing the test T has to be translated into another language so that it can be applied to the SUT, i.e. it must be executable.

A test T indicates by signaling whether a test was a success or failure. The notion of success or failure of a test is modeled by the special event labels $\overline{success}$ and $\overline{failure}$. Since the generality of ACSR's syntax obscures some common testing operations, the following notational conventions have been introduced by Clarke and Lee [CL97a]:

$\top$ – process that signals successful termination of a test: $\top \equiv (\overline{success}, 1).recX.(\emptyset : X)$.

$\bot$ – process that signals the failing of a test: $\bot \equiv (\overline{failure}, 1).recX.(\emptyset : X)$.

$\delta.T$ – *unbounded wait* for the occurrence of an action or event of test process T: $\delta.T \equiv (recX.(\emptyset : X)) \triangle_\infty (NIL, NIL, T)$.

$T_1 \triangle_t T_2$ – simplified *timeout notation*: $T_1 \triangle_t T_2 \equiv T_1 \triangle_t (NIL, T_2, NIL)$.

$T_1 ; T_2$ – sequential composition of tests $T1$ and T_2: $T_1 ; T_2 \equiv (T_1[\{e_{sccs}/success\}, \emptyset] \parallel \delta.(e_{sccs}, 1).T_2) \backslash \{e_{sccs}\}$ where event e_{sccs} is not used in T_1 or T_2.

$(e, p)!T$ – applies event (e, p) as input to the SUT and proceeds with T: $(e, p)!T \equiv (\overline{e}, p).T$.

$(e, p)?T$ – the specific output event (e, p) from the SUT must be received; if it is not received, the *required response* is a failed test: $(e, p)?T \equiv (e, p).T + (\tau, 1).\bot$ where $p > 1$.

The constraint graph given in Figure 13.2 can now be used to derive a test suite to verify whether the temporal behavior of the application conforms to the ACSR model given in Figure 13.3. The test suite is then transformed by a trivial rewriting step into a test language suitable for testing the SUT. We have to notice that this test case generation method does not deal with infinite application behavior.

Two kinds of constraints in the SUT are tested by this approach: **behavioral constraints** and **performance constraints**:

- PERFORMANCE CONSTRAINT This kind of constraint describes a delay interval that ends when a required output is produced.
- BEHAVIORAL CONSTRAINT This kind of constraint describes a delay interval that ends when a required input is applied.

A *performance constraint* is tested by a simple test that verifies that the correct response is received during the required interval. Figure 13.4 shows the three situations of an erroneous implementation of a sample constraint S. Implementation I_1 shows the case that the required output $\overline{E_1}$ is not produced within the interval $[t_1, t_2)$. In contrast, output $\overline{E_1}$ occurs to early in implementation I_2. I_3 demonstrates the situation in which an output is produced within the required interval $[t_1, t_2)$ but the event associated with the output is incorrect. Since the quantity being tested is the delay introduced by the SUT, there are no input parameters for the tester to vary. Therefore, it also does not make a difference whether the time domain boundaries are open or closed ones.

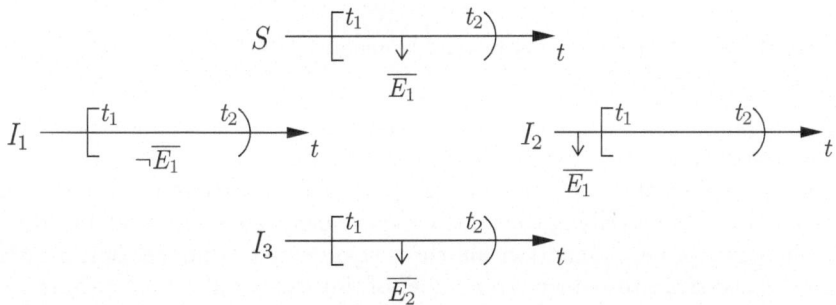

Fig. 13.4. Erroneous implementations of performance constraints

For *behavioral constraints* each of the two time domain boundaries is verified by up to two test points. As shown in Figure 13.5, the number and position of the test points for each domain boundary depends on its type and value. In contrast to the performance constraints, for behavioral constraints it makes a difference whether the time domain boundaries are open or closed ones, because test points have to be used close to these boundaries. One test point is always placed directly on the domain boundary. For closed domain boundaries the second test point is placed at a distance of ϵ outside the boundary. For open domain boundaries the second test point is placed at a distance ϵ inside the boundary. For the special case where the upper boundary is ∞, it is not possible to place a test point at the domain boundary. It is approximated by placing a test point at time T_{max} after the start of the interval, where T_{max} is the longest constraint interval in the system specification. For both open and closed interval boundaries, the up to two tests per boundary are sufficient to verify that the required change in system behavior has occurred within ϵ time units with respect to the required point in time.

A test suite can be derived by generating test cases so that both coverage criteria are fulfilled. The following three steps are used for test case generation:

(1) Deriving test process templates from the constraint graph. These templates will supply inputs at some time within the required interval, observe the outputs of the SUT to verify that they are generated within the correct time interval, and terminate with $\top$ if the test is successful or $\bot$ if the test fails.

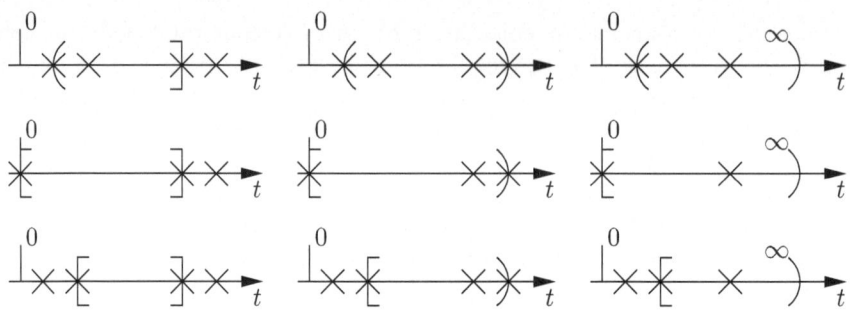

Fig. 13.5. Test points to test interval boundaries of behavioral constraints

(2) Derive input delay values that must be covered by the test in order to satisfy the intended coverage requirements.
(3) The output of the two previous steps is used to determine all test case candidates. As describing each delay requirement separately would lead to a high degree of redundancy within the test processes, a further optimization pass is necessary to reduce the number of test cases. Since this optimization problem is NP-hard, the usage of heuristics is necessary.

Since a process may also contain recursive elements (i.e. loops in the constraint graph), a full depth-first traversal of the constraint graph in step 1) and step 2) is not feasible. Therefore, the traversal must be bounded to a maximum depth.

Summary: The test framework described by Clarke and Lee has already been applied to real applications such as a relatively simple communication protocol [CL97b]. However, there is still room for further research in improving this method. A useful extension would be the development of coverage criteria that address interactions between different timing constraints (such as race conditions). Furthermore, coverage metrics that exploit the ACSR's focus on resource requirements and priorities in interactions would improve the generality of the test case generation framework.

An extension of the framework of Clarke and Lee to handle also infinite executions of processes is necessary for testing typical reactive systems that are nonterminating. The critical aspect of this extension is the design of the required test coverage criteria. For applications that can be expressed by a finite constraint graph without loops, it is sufficient to use coverage criteria that guarantee local coverage across the constraint graph. In case of infinite executions, it is required to define the coverage criteria such that the overall amount of test cases that are required for testing is limited. One possible method is giving a fixed upper bound for the length of test sequences. This strategy can be directly combined with the coverage criteria described by Clarke and Lee.

TTS-based Test Case Generation Test case generation with discrete time and value domain has also been done based on timed automata. Originally, timed automata work with a dense time domain [AD94]. In contrast, we present here results from Cardell-Oliver that use discrete time [CO00]. In this approach, it is argued that events cannot be observed at arbitrarily close times even if this can be specified in the dense time domain. Therefore digital clocks that model discrete time are used.

In the original algorithm, the basic assumption is that the implementation does not possess more states than its model. In this case, it can be proven that the generated test suite detects non-conformance between model and SUT and is furthermore complete. We do not believe that this is always guaranteed as the model is generally derived from the requirements of the SUT and not from the SUT itself. We refer to Chapter 8 for theoretical background. However, we believe that the presented ideas for generating a manageable test suite are useful as their focus is decreasing the amount of test cases.

Modeling: The basis for this approach are **Timed Transition Systems** (**TTS**) that mainly consist of three components:

- STATES Each TTS owns a finite set of states.
- INITIAL STATE One of these states is the initial state, where execution starts.
- LABELED TRANSITION RELATIONS Source and a target states are connected by labeled transition relations. The label is discussed with respect to the used timed automata definition.

The timed transition system itself is described by a network of communicating timed automata as used in the tool UPPAAL [LPY97]. These automata further consist of:

- VARIABLES Each automaton owns a finite set of data and clock variables. All variables are bounded. Clocks have to be reset if the specified bound is reached.
- GUARDS Guards are predicates that are conjunctions of constraints on clock and data variables. They are used for labeling transitions. If the guard evaluates to true, the transition is enabled and can be taken.
- EVENTS Each automaton owns a finite set of events. Different automata communicate via these events over synchronization channels. For this purpose, each event is classified either as input or as output. If a is the name of a synchronization channel, $a!$ is the corresponding output event and $a?$ the corresponding input event. Like guards, events are used to label transitions. Two transitions are involved and must therefore be enabled: one that emits event $a!$ and one that receives event $a?$.
- ASSIGNMENTS With assignments both data and clock variables can be reset. They are also used to label transitions.
- CLOCK INVARIANTS Each state of the automaton can own an invariant that specifies when the state has to be left due to a given timing constraint.

With respect to transitions, labels are composed of guards, events, and assignments in this order. The initial state is marked with an inner circle in the state symbol as shown in Figure 13.6. The network of communicating automata

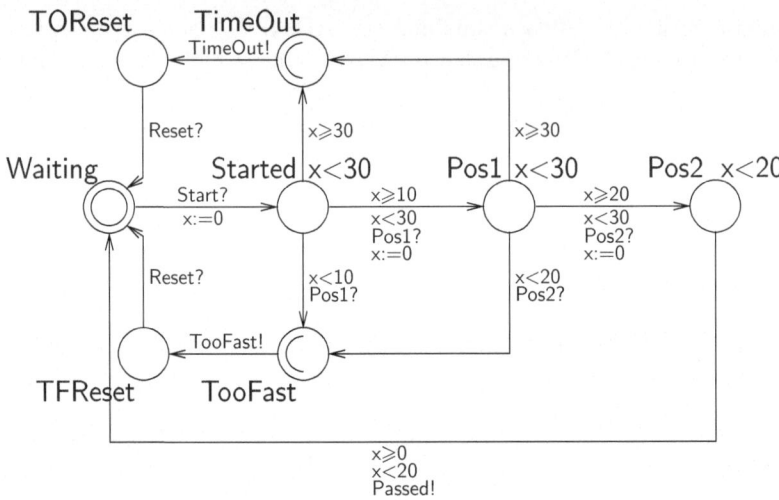

Fig. 13.6. UPPAAL timed automaton model of the real-time monitor example

is merged to a product automaton that is given as a TTS enriched with the clock invariants that are not included in the general TTS notation.

RTMonitor Example: Again, we will look on the RTMonitor example. It is realized by an UPPAAL timed automaton in Figure 13.6. In the initial state, we wait until event *Start* is received. After that, event *Pos*1 should occur in time interval $[10, 30)$. If this has been received correctly, we wait again if event *Pos*2 occurs in time interval $[20, 30)$. In this case, event *Passed* is generated in time interval $[0, 20)$.

If events *Pos*1 or *Pos*2 occur too early, event *TooFast* is generated and control is switched to state *TFReset*. Vice versa, event *TimeOut* is generated and control is switched to state *TOReset*, if these events do not occur in their specified time intervals. After *TooFast*, respectively *TimeOut*, has been generated, we wait for event *Reset* to restart the RTMonitor.

The states *Started* and *Pos*1 own both an invariant $x < 30$, so after 30 time units these states must be left. The same holds for state *Pos*2 where the invariant is $x < 20$. States *TooFast* and *TimeOut* are marked committed which is shown with the symbol C inside the state. A committed state must be left immediately after entering it, i.e. events *TimeOut* and *TooFast* are sent immediately.

In this example, we have seen that real-time systems can be modeled adequately with timed automata. By using states and transitions, the control flow of the modeled application can be easily captured. The timed automata variant of UPPAAL also allows modeling inputs and outputs explicitly. This further simplifies understanding of the automaton. However, large systems become intractable by using this modeling technique. Hierarchical structuring of models can help here.

Test Case Generation: The central idea of the approach of Cardell-Oliver is using **test views** for transforming a given TTS to a **Testable TTS (TTTS)**. As described above, the model used for test case generation is given by a TTS that is derived from a network of UPPAAL automata. In combination with this model, different **test views** can be used that each describe a specific test purpose. The TTS is transformed to a smaller TTS by a view. This is the TTTS that is used for test case generation.

Each test view is designed to fulfill a given test purpose. This is described by different parameters:

- INTERFACE With respect to the TTS, we have to identify events that are produced from the test driver and are therefore input events for the SUT and events that are produced by the SUT for the test driver and are therefore output events. That is, we identify the interface between the test driver and the SUT.
- DISCRETE CLOCK The digital clock used in the test automation system must be specified. The clock grain must be chosen according to the needed precision to distinguish between observed and stimulated events and the possibilities of the used hardware.
- HIDING The set of events can be divided into observable and hidden events. Therefore, only the events of interest with respect to the test purpose are observable in the TTTS. This can reduce the search space of the system as also less states are visible if traces to and from them are not observable any more.

With the help of the test view, the test designer can control the size of the test suite. The TTTS can be detailed if important test cases are generated and less detailed if the test purpose is not crucial. The size of the search space is determined by the discrete clock as its granularity influences the search space and by the hidden and observable events that lead to less observable transitions. In general, the search space is decreased as states cannot be distinguished anymore after eliding invisible transitions. Only under specific circumstances it is increased.

This happens if a state has n incoming transitions that are all hidden and m outcoming transitions that are all visible. Before hiding, the number of visible edges in the TTS is $n + m$, after hiding, the number of visible edges in the transformed TTTS is $n * m$. The test designer can react to this by using a different test view where these events are not hidden. A similar problem is a cycle of transitions where all events are hidden. This is not allowed for creating a test view as the SUT may cycle forever in this loop without a possibility of observation when test cases are executed, i.e. unbounded nondeterminism occurs. Here, at least one event must be made visible in the test view.

Another problem in this context is that the resulting TTTS may have redundant states. These could be distinguished in the TTS before the transformation by different distinguishing traces of inputs, outputs, and delays. After the transformation, these distinguishing traces can be equivalent due to hidden events. In this case the TTTS can be minimized before test case generation. This is not necessary but helpful as test case generation can be performed more efficiently if the size of the TTTS is further reduced.

The test case generation algorithm itself is based on the W method [Cho78] discussed in detail in Chapter 4. It works in the following way:

(1) For each state all acyclic traces that lead to that state are generated. It is possible that one or more of these traces are tester controlled, i.e. the inputs of the test driver to the SUT produce deterministic outputs of the SUT. If such a trace exists, this can be used as a test case in the following. If nondeterminism is possible, the correct test case is selected out of all generated ones during testing with respect to the output of the SUT.

(2) After that, we have to check that the reached state is really the state we expected. As the underlying TTS has persistent variables, it may be possible to identify states based on variable values. If this is not possible, distinguishing sequences as introduced by Chow [Cho78] can be used. Again, tester controlled test cases are preferred as this reduces the test suite. Else all possible test cases must be present to be chosen during test execution.

(3) Furthermore, not just every state but also every transition should be visited. Therefore one test case for every transition is generated.

(4) At least, the test suite is created based on the test cases produced in step 1 to 3. We check for redundant test cases as a short test trace may be included in a longer one. In this case, the short traces can be elided from the test suite. It is expected that the nondeterministic test cases are all executed at least once if testing the implementation is performed long enough. In practice, this may not happen but cannot be prevented. The test suite can be further reduced if it is possible to limit the possible set of input values to the SUT by making assumptions about the possible ones. Often, a system is expected to run in a specific environment so some input values can never occur.

Summary: The main idea of this test case generation algorithm is obviously the usage of test views. These specify the interface between the SUT and the test driver, the clock granularity, and the amount of observable events based on the test purpose. By using UPPAAL automata that differentiate between sending and receiving events, interfaces can be easily specified. The clock grain can be chosen with respect to the used timing constraints in the model and the used hardware. The art of creating test views is the subdivision of the event set into hidden and observable events. The amount of test cases generated by the algorithm depends mainly on these. Therefore the test designer has to consider carefully which events should be observed in a test view and which not.

As we cannot guarantee that the set of states is equivalent in the implementation and the model, the completeness results for the generated test suite is not relevant. However, test views are a means to reduce the set of test cases and are therefore useful. Moreover, the usage of persistent variables helps reducing the amount of test cases as states can be often distinguished based on variable values. If we do not consider time in test views, these can also be used to reduce test suites of untimed systems.

The obvious drawback is that test views must be chosen carefully. The created test suites for each view may overlap and hence increase the overall testing time unnecessarily. Worse, parts of the system may never be tested as no test view covers them. Therefore, the generated test suites must be compared before using them for testing.

13.3.2   Real-Time Systems – Dense Time and Discrete Values

For modeling real-time systems, also dense time can be used as this is the natural way time is passing. This approach is used in the original **Timed Automata** approach by Alur and Dill [AD94] and also in the more restricted **Event Recording Automata** (**ERA**) [AFH94]. As the different timed automata variants do not differ significantly we reuse the RTMonitor example from Section 13.3.1 and focus on test case generation with respect to the differences in using discrete and dense time.

ERA-based Test Case Generation   In Section 13.3.1 we already presented one technique for generating test cases based on timed automata models. However, this approach is working with a discrete time domain. It is also possible to use a dense time domain for test case generation. This approach is driven by the natural flow of time that is not discrete but dense [Nie00]. Furthermore, processor clocks are discrete but their granularity is so fine that it can be regarded as dense.

The test case generation algorithm is based on Hennessy's testing theory for untimed systems, i.e. it is based on preorder relations. This is described in more detail in Chapter 5, Chapter 6, and Chapter 8. We are interested here in the ways the test cases in a test suite are chosen out of the possible ones.

Modeling: The timed automaton model ERA [AFH94] chosen by Nielsen is very similar to the one presented in Section 13.3.1 but more restricted [Nie00]. Due to these restrictions, ERA can be determinized. Briefly, there are states and transitions labeled with guards, actions, and assignments to clock variables. Actions are partitioned into hidden and observable ones that are either input or output actions used for synchronization while transitions are either urgent or non-urgent.

The characteristic feature of ERA is that clocks and actions are coupled as each action has an associated clock. This clock is reset every time the action is performed, other resets are not allowed. Therefore, a clock measures the time between two occurrences of its associated event. Similar to UPPAAL automata, input and output actions are always synchronized. The environment has control over clock resets as it performs the complementary actions to the ones of the model of the SUT, so clock valuations are determined. The environment is the test driver as it stimulates and records inputs and outputs to and from the SUT.

For test case generation, ERA are further restricted by permitting only observable and urgent actions and forbidding clock invariants in states. Urgent and non-urgent actions were not distinguished by Alur et. al. for ERA but are introduced by Nielsen for testing purposes. With only urgent actions, transitions must be taken immediately if they are enabled and their action synchronization can be performed. Therefore, it is determined when a transition must be taken. ERA are enhanced by allowing integer variables that can be shared between automata in a network just as clock variables.

RTMonitor Example: On the first sight, the RTMonitor model created with ERA shown in Figure 13.7 does not differ very much from the one created with UPPAAL automata in Section 13.3.1. We have to keep in mind that all clocks are associated to an event and are automatically reset. Therefore, there are no clock assignments shown. Clock names are given with respect to their associated action. To give an example, for event *Start* the corresponding clock is named *StartC*. The initial state has a further inner circle.

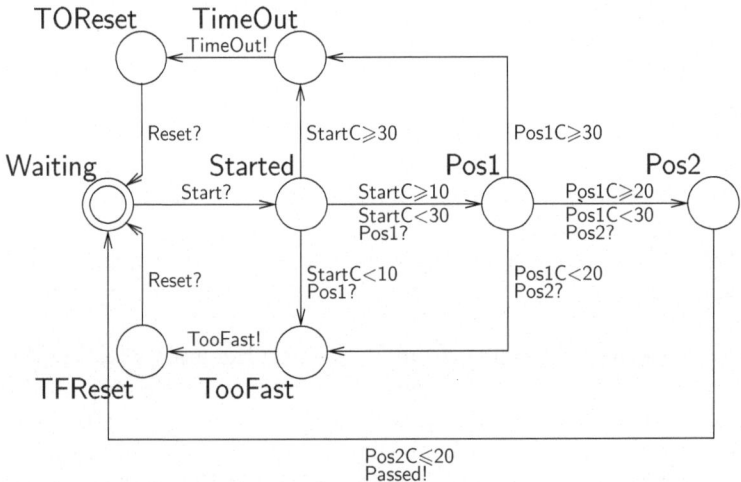

Fig. 13.7. ERA model of the real-time monitor example

The time intervals in which signals *Pos*1 and *Pos*2 should occur, respectively in which signals *TooFast*, *TimeOut*, and *Passed* must be sent, are obviously the same as in the example using discrete time in Section 13.3.1. Nevertheless, they are expressed differently as all clocks are related to events. The most important difference between the two examples using discrete respectively dense time is that in ERA events can be sent and received at any time and not only at fixed time points. To give an example, event *Start* can be received at time unit 1, 2, 3, ... in an UPPAAL automaton using discrete time. In contrast, *Start* can be received at time point 1.5, 1.578, or 2.3 in an ERA with dense time domain. Therefore this model is closer to reality.

Test Case Generation: In the test case generation algorithm presented by Nielsen [Nie00], two main principles are used: partitioning of the state space for decreasing it and using coverage criteria for selecting test cases out of the possible many ones. Determinized ERA automata serve as a basis.

The first step to be taken is partitioning the overall state space by grouping states into sets of equivalent states. These serve as a basis for testing. The motivation for this is that it is more interesting to test inequivalent states then testing equivalent states multiple times. It is also necessary as the underlying TTS of the ERA has infinitely many states due to the dense time domain.

The partitioning is done with respect to the **stable transition criterion**. Nielsen calls it stable edge criterion, but for homogeneity throughout this chapter we prefer the term transition instead of edge. Two sets of states are considered equivalent if they consist of the same states and enable the same set of transitions. A transition is enabled if its guard evaluates to true. A change in the enabled set of transitions may also induce a change in the enabled actions for synchronization. Therefore, different deadlock situations can be detected with respect to the different enabled transitions. Furthermore, guards may be dependent on clock valuations, so the set of enabled transitions changes with respect to time. This behavior requires corresponding test cases. Hence, using the set of enabled transitions is more convenient for testing than just considering transitions.

After partitioning the original ERA, respectively its underlying TTS, into sets of equivalent states, we can visualize the result as a **partition graph**. The equivalent sets of states are called **symbolic states**. Each partition should be tested by at least one test case in a test suite. Before generating it, the reachable parts of each partition are computed. A **symbolic reachability graph** for the partition graph is the result. This is created by starting at the initial state of the partition graph and traverse the graph with respect to symbolic states. Each trace is followed as long as new symbolic states are found.

Test cases are generated from the symbolic reachability graph in the following way:

(1) For each symbolic state, create a concrete trace leading to it with the initial state as a starting point. To do this, a **strengthened symbolic state** is created that consists of all states that will lead to the target state. This is necessary as not all states inside a partition will lead to the target partition. We do this by starting at the target transition and follow the trace back to the initial state so that all constraints in the transitions of the trace will evaluate to true. This proceeding is called **back propagation**.

(2) The strengthened traces created in step 1 are transformed to specific traces with concrete values for delays.

Delays can be chosen according to different strategies:

- PROMPTNESS The smallest possible delay is chosen. This is useful to stress the SUT with the shortest possible interval between inputs and outputs.
- PERSISTENCE A delay somewhere in the middle of the possible values is chosen. This is useful to check the persistence of the SUT.
- PATIENCE The largest possible delay is chosen. Here, the patience of the SUT is tested.

Nielsen claims that many bugs are found near extreme values of inputs and therefore choosing delays with respect to promptness and patience is preferable.

In principle, the test case generation algorithm depends on the reachability graph as the traces represented by this are concretized during test case generation. If the reachability graph or even the partition graph is too large further strategies have to be applied based on pragmatic reasons. These can be:

- TRACE LENGTH LIMITATION One possibility is limiting the trace length of a test case to a certain length. After that, processing of reachable states is aborted.
- RANDOMIZED STATE SPACE EXPLORATION Another way of limiting the size of the partition or reachability graph is choosing the successor states of one state randomly out of all possible ones. This is done until a fixed number of states is reached or a specific time limit exceeds.
- BIT-STATE HASHING It is also possible to use a hash table with fixed length. Each state is stored there with respect to a key value that must be computed based on a given algorithm. Therefore, different states may be related to the same key. As only one bit is used for hashing, there can exist exactly one entry for each key value. If a state with an already used key is reached, it overwrites the hash entry. Exploration from the former state is stopped then.

A generated test suite can be reduced further be eliminating redundant test cases as one test case can be included in another, longer one. To perform this reduction, the test suite is transformed to a tree structure called **test tree**. This is also helpful for nondeterministic tests where new inputs must be chosen with respect to the nondeterministic output of the SUT. Obviously, this technique is also applicable to testing untimed systems.

Summary: The presented test case generation algorithm for models based on a dense time domain relies mainly on the partitioning of state sets into equivalent sets called partitions. Partitions are chosen with respect to state sets that enable the same transitions and consist of the same states. Therefore, the infinitely many states in the TTS underlying an ERA are grouped so that a symbolical finite partition graph is the result. This can be used for test case generation.

The generated test suite can still be very large as it depends on the size of the partition graph. If this is very large, heuristics must be used. Three possibilities are suggested, namely trace length limitation, randomized state space exploration, and bit-state hashing.

The delays used in timed traces also depend on heuristics. Stressing the SUT with the shortest possible delay values as well as testing its patience by choosing the largest delays are claimed to be most important for testing as extreme values are considered best for finding errors.

The chosen modeling language ERA restricts the original timed automata by using only event clocks and urgent transitions. However, this seems not to be a drawback as the resulting model is still expressive. The main problem with this approach is that the partition graph may be still too large to generate a test suite with practicable size without using further heuristics.

13.3.3   Hybrid Systems – Dense Time and Dense Values

The last step is taking also dense values into account as done in **hybrid** systems. These have been studied in many ways during the last ten years. There are different attempts for modeling them and applying concepts known from the formal methods community to them, like model checking or theorem proving, e.g. by Henzinger [Hen96], Alur et al. [ACH$^+$95], Zhou et al. [CJR96], Kapur et al. [KHMP94], Ábrahám-Mumm et al. [ÁMHS01], Lynch et al. [LSV01], or Larsen et al. [LSW97]. Hence, models of hybrid systems are well understood today. In contrast, there are only few attempts for using hybrid models in model-based testing.

We focus on Hybrid Automata [Hen96] and their extension to CHARON [ADE$^+$01, AGLS01, ADE$^+$03] and HybridUML [BBHP03] here. There exists also approaches for hybrid process algebras, e.g. Hybrid CSP as a further extension of Timed CSP [CJR96, Amt00]. Here, research with respect to testing deals with test case specifications and their execution as e.g. in Peleska et al. [PAD$^+$98]. Test case generation based on a model of the SUT is not covered in detail.

Thermostat Example To give an idea of hybrid systems, we will use the thermostat example taken from Alur et al. [ACH$^+$95] throughout this section. The thermostat continuously measures the room temperature x. It turns a heater on and off due to the current temperature. The initial temperature is named θ, K and h are constants describing the power of the heater and the room. The following requirements hold for the SUT and must be considered in the SUT model:

- If the heater is off, x is decreasing according to $x(t) = \theta * e^{-Kt}$.
- If the heater is on, x is increasing in the following way:
  $x(t) = \theta * e^{-Kt} + h(1 - e^{-Kt})$.
- The heater is turned *on* if the temperature falls below m.
- The heater is turned *off* if the temperature rises above M.

Hybrid Automata-Based Test Case Generation With considering dense values in addition to dense time, the state space further explodes. Nevertheless, also hybrid automata can be used for test case generation if appropriate abstractions are found. We can build up on the techniques for discrete- and dense-timed automata presented in Section 13.3.1 and Section 13.3.2.

Modeling: For modeling hybrid systems, **Hybrid Automata** as developed by Henzinger [Hen96] can be used. In general, the time-discrete part of the system is described by transitions while the time-continuous part is modeled inside states. Automata are enriched with flow conditions for describing the evolution of dense-valued variables over time. Clocks are modeled in the same way with a constant rate of change of *1*.

In general, a hybrid automaton H consists of five components:

- VARIABLES A finite set of real-valued variables.
- CONTROL GRAPH The system is described by a finite directed graph with vertices called control nodes and edges called control switches. As long as control resides inside one node, time is passing and the values of the dense variables evolve according to time. This is a continuous change called **flow**. When an edge is taken, control switches to another mode, i.e. a discrete change is performed called **jump condition**. Discrete changes do not consume time.
- INITIAL, INVARIANT, AND FLOW CONDITIONS Three different predicates can be attached to control nodes. First, the **initial condition** specifies the initial values of variables inside a node. Second, an **invariant** can be assigned that describes under which conditions the node has control. If the invariant is violated, control must be switched to another node. At last, a node may have a **flow condition** that describes the evaluation of analog variables over time.
- JUMP CONDITIONS A control switch can be labeled by a predicate called **jump condition**. The edge is enabled if the condition evaluates to true. Only then, the control switch can be taken.
- EVENTS Furthermore, an edge can also have an assigned **event**. If the jump condition of an edge holds and the associated event occurs, the edge is taken and control is switched to the target node. Different hybrid automata $H1$ and $H2$ can interact via events, i.e. they synchronize over event a if a is both an event of $H1$ and of $H2$.

CHARON is a further development of hybrid automata as described by Alur et al. in [ADE$^+$01], [AGLS01], and [ADE$^+$03] with two main improvements. First, not only behavior but also structure of a system can be modeled. This is done in an agent whose behavior is described in a mode. Second, both structure and behavior may be built hierarchically. This allows better structuring of models as large systems become unmanageable with flat structures. A further enhancement is **HybridUML**, a profile of the **Unified Modeling Language** 2.0 (**UML**) with formal semantics [BBHP03]. In addition to the possibilities of CHARON, HybridUML gives better support for datatypes and allows communication not only via shared variables but also via signals. The specification of datatypes, structure, and behavior is handled in different UML diagrams, so no confusion between the different aspects of modeling occurs.

Thermostat Example: We assume that the thermostat consists of a controller and a heater. In Figure 13.8 we can see a hybrid automaton describing the behavior of the controller. This is switching the heater on and off via events named *on* and *off*. The evaluation of the temperature is described by flow conditions. If the temperature falls below m or rises above M, jump conditions will trigger the switch from state *On* to state *Off*. θ is set to 20 here, while $K = 0.1$, $h = 5$, $m = 20$ and $M = 22$. The heater can be modeled as a separate hybrid automaton which has two states *On* and *Off* that have control if the heater is on, respectively off. The switch from one state to another one is triggered by events *on* and *off* that are sent by the controller's hybrid automaton, i.e. the two automata synchronize over these events.

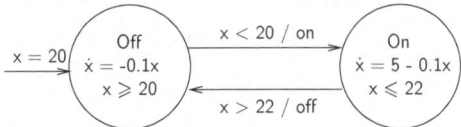

Fig. 13.8. Hybrid automaton for the thermostat controller

For comparison, we look at the same controller as a HybridUML model. The structure of the thermostat is modeled as an agent in Figure 13.9. The thermostat consists of a heater and a controller that communicate via signals *on* and *off*. Temperature x is measured by the controller and is also visible in the thermostat itself, e.g. to monitor the temperature from the environment. Therefore x is a shared variable. Sending of a signal, respectively write access to a shared variable, is shown as a black-filled box, while receiving a signal, respectively read access to a shared variable, is shown as a white-filled box. These boxes are connected to visualize communication structures.

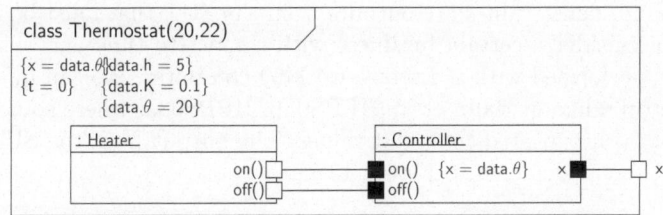

Fig. 13.9. Composite structure diagram for the thermostat agent

In the upper left corner, parameters m and M are set to 20, respectively 22. Both values are given as parameters for better reusability of the thermostat model. Furthermore, variables and constants of the thermostat must be initialized. Constants K, h, and θ are all included in structure *data* and are set to 5, 0.1, and 20. Shared variable x that measures the temperature is set to the initial value θ in both the thermostat and the controller. At last, t is a global clock that must be set to 0 in the beginning.

The behavior of the controller is visualized in Figure 13.10, similar to the hybrid automaton modeled above, i.e. states and transitions coincide in both variants of the thermostat example. Here, flows and invariants are marked explicitly with keywords *flow*, respectively *inv*. Jump conditions of transitions are given in brackets while events are given after a slash.

As we have seen, hybrid automata offer the possibility to model time-discrete and time-continuous behavior. As they are based on well-known automata, they

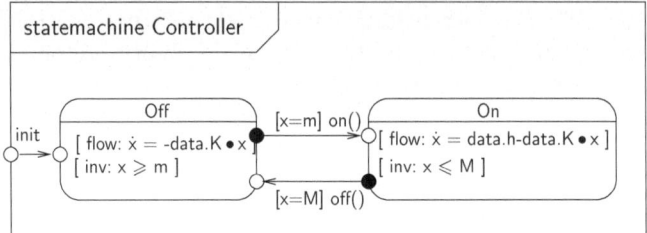

Fig. 13.10. Statechart diagram for the thermostat controller mode

are easy to understand. Hybrid Automata themselves have been introduced for theoretical purposes. In contrast, CHARON and HybridUML have been designed for practical purposes and are able to model both structure and behavior of a system.

Test Case Generation: New problems appear for test case generation based on hybrid systems. In addition to the problems that arise when dense time is considered as described in Section 13.3.2, new problems occur due to the dense value domain. On the one hand, the SUT expects dense values in form of curves as input, e.g. the velocity of a car. The SUT must receive these during test execution from the test driver. Such curves must be selected from the infinitely many possible ones. This is a problem that has not been tackled until now. On the other hand, dense values are outputs from the SUT that must be evaluated. We have to consider a certain fuzziness with respect to time and values as the test itself is performed with a discrete-working computer. We can image this as a tolerance tube like in Hahn et al.[HPPS03b, HPPS03a] where some tolerance is added for both expected time and values. The output from the SUT must lie inside this tube as depicted in Figure 13.11.

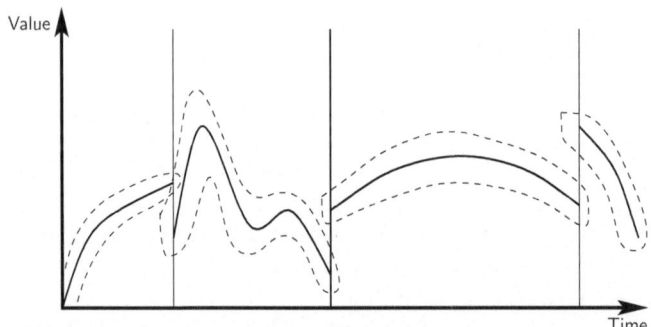

Fig. 13.11. Tolerance tubes for time and values [HPPS03a]

Until now, there is one attempt for test case generation based on hybrid systems. In this approach, two models instead of one are used as done by Hahn et al. [HPPS03b, HPPS03a]. The first model describes the hybrid system, i.e.

the discrete and the continuous part of the SUT. The second model is a purely discrete model that describes abstract control flow in the SUT. This reduces the problem of test case generation for hybrid systems to the one for real-time systems with dense time. This is possible as the hybrid part of the model is always hidden inside states while the discrete part is modeled by transitions. These transitions, respectively their triggers, are needed for generating test cases.

At this point, we have to ask ourselves, why we have not built a discrete model beforehand if this is used for the generation process. We must reconsider that the hybrid model is the most exact model for mirroring the required behavior of the SUT. The pure discrete model is too imprecise for testing the hybrid system. We therefore use the test suite created by the discrete model and feed both the SUT and the hybrid model the generated inputs.

We first consider an **open loop** system, i.e. we do not model the environment of the SUT and feedback from the environment to the SUT as in the closed loop system described in the next paragraph. Here, we have to compare the calculated output given by the hybrid model with the output from the SUT. The hybrid model is used to evaluate if a test has passed or failed as shown in Figure 13.12.

The situation is slightly different for **closed loop** systems. Here, the environment of the SUT is explicitly modeled due to the fact that most systems are required to work correctly in one specific environment and not in all possible ones. Therefore, values of inputs to the SUT can be restricted to possible inputs in the specified environment. As inputs often depend on the output of the SUT, a feedback construction is needed, so outputs of the SUT can be considered to calculate the next input, again with respect to the environment. The advantage of this approach is that complexity is reduced as the possible search space is restricted.

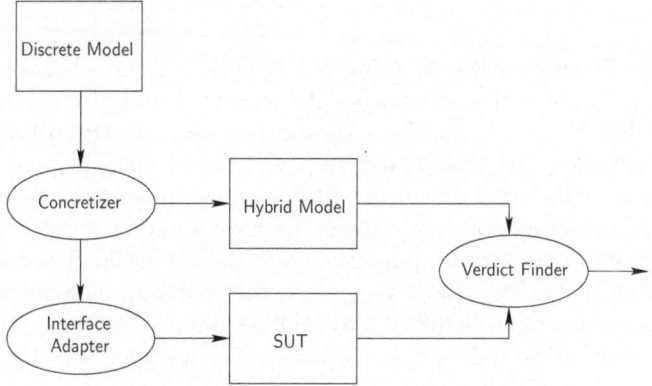

Fig. 13.12. Open loop test [HPPS03a]

Problems occur here with respect to the required feedback construction to the discrete model. The outputs we expect during testing are calculated in the hybrid model. Hence, this is used to give feedback to the discrete model as shown in Figure 13.13. New inputs to the SUT must be given with respect to this feedback, the modeled environment, and the modeled control flow of the SUT. We associate control flow with the hybrid model that defines it according to states and transitions in this model. If the hybrid model has reached a new state, i.e. control has switched from one state to another one, the discrete model must also perform a control switch to a new state, so inputs to the SUT are calculated with respect to the correct state of the system and the corresponding behavior of the environment that may be different in different states. Therefore, the discrete model, the hybrid model, and the environment model have to be synchronized to guarantee correctly generated test cases. This is done by using the output of the hybrid model to differentiate between its states. The output value space is split up into partitions that are related to states.

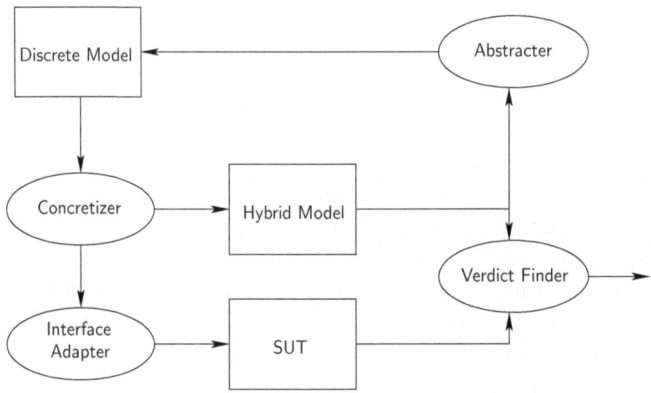

Fig. 13.13. Closed loop test [HPPS03a]

Summary: To summarize, by using one hybrid and one abstracted discrete model we can combine the advantages of the hybrid and discrete approaches. On the one hand, we can calculate results precisely, on the other hand, we are able to generate test traces efficiently. In case of open loop test systems, we just compare the results from the SUT and the hybrid model by the test oracle. In case of closed loop test systems, we have a feedback construction that requires more effort from test automation and test execution. The advantage of this proceeding is that the search space is further reduced. The problem is that the feedback construction is difficult to built as discrete model, hybrid model, and environment model must be synchronized. Partitioning the output space of the hybrid model to fulfill this task may be infeasible or not possible without ambiguities.

Obviously, the multiple model approach increases the modeling effort as we have to built two models instead of one. The key to the usability of this approach is designing a good discrete model. For one, it must mirror the hybrid model to guarantee working test traces, but in the same time, it has to be very abstract to take advantage of the discrete nature, i.e. generating a manageable set of test traces. If the discrete model is too detailed we would again get too much test cases. Another problem not tackled here is generating time-continuous input data as we have infinitely many possibilities for this.

13.4   Optimizing Test Suites by Evolutionary Testing

As we have seen in Section 13.3, there exist different techniques for model-based test case generation for real-time and hybrid systems. They have in common that they adapt algorithms known from testing theory to achieve a manageable test suite that consists of a finite set of test cases. Nevertheless, the number of test cases can still be very large. In that case, further reduction is required. Moreover, we do not know if the test cases derived are "good" test cases, i.e. they are able to find errors in the SUT or increase our confidence in the correct behavior of the SUT. We will present a possible way for improving this situation.

With respect to real-time systems, time is an important factor to guarantee correct behavior. Hence, we are also interested in the best-case execution times and especially in the worst-case execution times to see if deadlines are met. To test the timing constraints imposed by the SUT, the algorithms presented in Section 13.3 do not help since the values for delays generated by them are chosen according to a certain test strategy, e.g. promptness. They do not depend on the real behavior of the SUT.

Evolutionary algorithms can be adapted to optimize the size of the test suite or to test timing constraints imposed by the SUT.

13.4.1   Iterative Refinement Using Evolutionary Testing

Evolutionary testing is a testing technique where test data can be generated automatically by using search techniques. It is called **iterative refinement** because the test data to be optimized is iteratively refined due to a specified quality criterion.

Evolutionary testing has not been explicitly developed as a model-based method for test case generation, but it can be used in combination with this. As shown in Figure 13.14, the test model used in evolutionary testing is quite simple. It basically consists of a start state l_0 and an end state l_1 where the state l_0 can have an initial property p_0 assigned to it. Beside the initial property p_0, the only application specific part of the model is the property p_1 of the end state l_1. p_1 encodes certain aspects of the application that one is interested to be verified by testing. These aspects are typically maximum allowed boundaries such that the system is considered correct as long as it stays within these boundaries.

Reactive systems potentially run endlessly and therefore it is not possible to designate an end state of the system. To apply evolutionary testing, one idea is to identify an interesting intermediate state of the overall system model and use it as end state for the testing model. This allows testing the value of property p_1 when reaching state l_1.

$\langle l_0, p_0 \rangle$ $\langle l_1, p_1 \rangle$

Fig. 13.14. Formal model for evolutionary testing of real-time systems

Though the application model used by evolutionary testing is quite simple, the challenge is to define an effective process of iterative test case generation together with a useful encoding of relevant system aspects by property p_1.

Evolutionary testing as described above assumes a model with a given boundary for the property of the end state p_1. The test goal is to increase the confidence whether this property is an invariant of the system respectively to show by counter-example whether it is invalid. If one is not interested to test a specific boundary of the property p_1, it is also possible to use evolutionary testing to get an idea of the feasible boundary of p_1.

Test Case Generation: As described above, the generation of test cases by evolutionary testing is a process that performs an iterative improvement of the test data. To achieve this, the test results of the previous test run are abstracted by using a fitness calculation. The calculated fitness values are used on the one side to decide whether the iterative test case generation can be stopped and on the other side to guide the calculation of new test data for the next test round. This is a typical optimization problem that can be solved, for example, by **evolutionary algorithms**. A characteristic of evolutionary algorithms is that there exists a whole population of solutions instead of only one current solution.

The choice of a certain search technique is often a question of the compromise between efficiency and robustness to generic problems. The difficulties of searching test data with maximum fitness are demonstrated in Figure 13.15. Figure 13.15(a) shows a relatively simple fitness distribution where even local search methods like *hill climbing* will find the solution easily. A more complex example is given in Figure 13.15(b) where the fitness distribution has more than one local maximum. Evolutionary algorithms have mechanisms to avoid getting stuck on a local maximum.

In the following, evolutionary algorithms are described as a technique for the iterative test case generation.

The iterative process of test-data generation based on evolutionary algorithms is shown in Figure 13.16. The algorithm starts with an initial set of test cases which is called **population**. Each member of the population is called **individual**. Each individual must be a valid parameter of the SUT. During **fitness evaluation** each individual is weighted according to a specified optimization criterion. The test can be stopped if the **exit test** has determined that the best fitness value has been reached or that the number of iterations has exceeded a certain value. In case of termination, the individual with the best fitness value is reported as final result. Otherwise, individuals from the current population are selected to create new individuals out of them. The new individuals will be

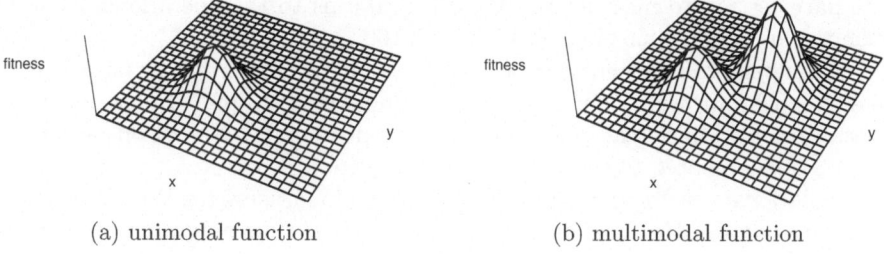

(a) unimodal function   (b) multimodal function

Fig. 13.15. Examples of fitness functions with different difficulty

the population for a new cycle of the evolutionary algorithm. This proceeding is explained in more detail by Goldberg [Gol89].

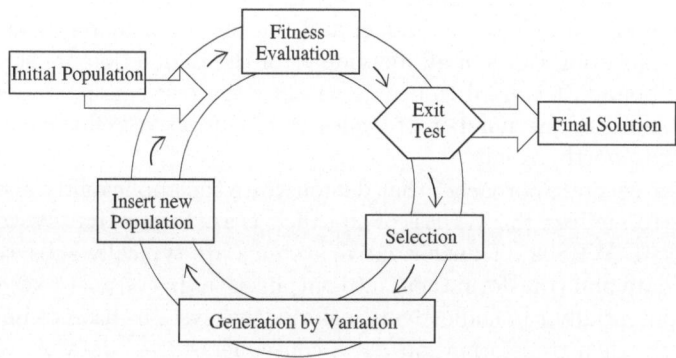

Fig. 13.16. Operational cycle of evolutionary algorithms

With respect to testing, the test case generator must be able to derive test cases. Furthermore, it has to be able to evaluate the fitness of each individual and to perform exit tests. This may require to collect and merge values of several observations into one fitness value.

Testing the Worst-Case Execution Time: To demonstrate the application of evolutionary testing, we describe its application to measurement-based timing analysis of real-time systems. Testing real-time systems means ensuring the correctness in the value and time domain. In contrast to other methods that test both properties in combination, the aim of the test method described in this section [PN98, Weg01, AHP99, GW98] is testing only the time domain. The value domain can be tested separately by other test methods. The property p_1 of the end state of a real-time system we are interested in is the tuple $\langle \text{BCET}, \text{WCET} \rangle$ where the **BCET** means the **best-case execution time** and **WCET** the **worst-case execution time**. In the following we will just describe test case generation for WCET as BCET can be handled similar. The application of evolutionary testing to measure the WCET conforms to the operational cycle of evolutionary algorithms given in Figure 13.16.

Testing the timing behavior of tasks individually requires that each task is free of synchronization points, i.e. it is a simple task [Kop97]. In the following we call the SUT just real-time program without making assumptions about its granularity compared to the whole real-time system.

Evolutionary testing for generating test cases to measure the WCET depends on **fitness evaluation** and the encoding of the real-time program's input variables. The fitness evaluation is realized as a black-box test that measures the execution time for concrete input test data. The execution time measurement is performed for each generated test case while the fitness value is calculated by comparing the relative execution time of each test result. The technical realization of the execution time measurement can be arbitrary.

As evolutionary testing is an iterative process, we also need a **stoppage criterion**. The simple case is that the fitness evaluation provides an execution time that is higher than the specified WCET bound. In this case the test has found a counter-example to the model and the test immediately stops. But as long as the execution times of all individuals of the population are smaller than the WCET bound, it is hard to decide whether the test can be stopped. Using an upper bound of the number of cycles in the iterative refinement does not provide a trustworthy result.

There are several approaches that demonstrate the applicability of evolutionary testing to analyze the WCET of so-called **transformative systems**, e.g., [PN98, Weg01, WBS02]. Transformative systems are typically subsystems that take input data and transform them into output data. In contrast to *reactive systems* that potentially run endlessly, transformative systems have to be triggered separately for each transformation. As a consequence, test data of transformative systems consist of a single test vector while test data of reactive systems consist of a sequence of test vectors.

The application of evolutionary testing based on evolutionary algorithms to reactive systems is not obvious as concrete techniques like *genetic algorithms* operate with individuals having a fixed length. A possible approach would be to test only test sequences of a fixed length, a method that is also used to limit the search space of test cases. However, in case of testing *performance constraints* (described in Section 13.3.1), the presented technique of WCET testing can be applied. This allows to reason at least whether a reactive system can perform its transitions within a certain time period. The verification of *behavioral constraints* (Section 13.3.1) of reactive systems would need another testing technique.

Summary: Evolutionary testing allows the iterative refinement of input data for testing. There exist several works on how to apply evolutionary testing for so-called *transformative systems*. The application of evolutionary testing to reactive systems has not been done and is not obvious. However, we have sketched in this section how evolutionary testing can be applied to test performance constraints of reactive systems. This can be done by applying the methods of WCET testing.

13.5   Summary

In this chapter, we have discussed test case generation for real-time and hybrid systems. As we have seen in the beginning, test automation for real-time and hybrid systems differs from that for untimed systems. The time domain has to be taken into account as well as the dense value domain for hybrid systems, e.g. for test evaluation. The model of the SUT must abstract from the real behavior of the SUT to allow sensible test case generation. In contrast, the test driver concretizes the generated inputs to feed the SUT. Vice versa, the concrete outputs of the SUT are abstracted again so that test evaluation can be done with respect to the abstract model.

Process Algebra vs. Automata Different modeling techniques can be used for this purpose. We have discussed ACSR as a process algebra and different variants of automata that already have been used for test case generation. A process algebra is capable of modeling a system consisting of processes that communicate with each other via events. Concurrency can be modeled explicitly as there are operators for interleaving and parallel execution with synchronization. Time is considered discrete. One problem of process algebras is that this modeling technique has no support in industry where graphical modeling is preferred. Nevertheless, testing based on process algebra has been proven useful and practicable.

In contrast, automata based modeling has more support as this is very popular, e.g. with respect to UML where state machines are used as automata variants. Timed automata introduce either discrete or dense time to be capable of modeling timing constraints. Graphical models are in principle easy to understand as control flow can be captured at one sight. However, large models become intractable in graphical representation. Hierarchy or different abstraction levels must be used to better this situation.

Discrete vs. Dense Time With respect to time, this is either modeled discrete or dense. In the first case, a timer is a counter that is incremented continuously. As the computer itself is working discrete, this seems appropriate. In contrast, time is naturally dense so modeling based on dense time is closer to reality, e.g. when analog sensors and actuators are used. For real-time systems, it must be chosen if the model represents natural time or computer time beforehand. For hybrid systems, time must be modeled dense as the continuous parts of the system rely on this.

Discrete vs. Dense Values Another aspect is the value domain that has to be tested. This is considered discrete for real-time systems. We have seen that test case generation builds up on methods for untimed systems and enhances the generated test cases with timing information. Discrete values for inputs and outputs to respectively from the SUT can be easily generated and evaluated. Time points and intervals for generating inputs and outputs are chosen with respect to the selected test case generation method. For hybrid systems, this situation differs as we have dense-valued variables. Until now, nobody has tackled the problem of generating curves as input data if time-continuous input is needed. With respect to output data, fuzziness is considered for test evaluation.

Test Case Generation Algorithms We presented two different test case generation algorithms for real-time systems that are based on discrete time and one algorithm that is based on dense time. Also one algorithm for creating test suites for hybrid systems was discussed. The most important function of these algorithms is the way in which the size of the test suite is reduced to a manageable size, i.e the way in which test cases are selected.

The first test case generation algorithm discussed is based on the process algebra ACSR where test cases are derived from the constraint graph of the ACSR model. Test data is selected to cover two type of timing constraints, namely performance constraints and behavioral constraints. To handle also applications with recursive elements, upper bounds on the length of tested execution scenarios have to be introduced.

Furthermore, test case generation for systems with discrete time can be done with timed automata models. Here, the central idea is using test views that restrict the model of the SUT to a specified test purpose. Test views are composed by parameters like clock granularity and the division of actions into observable and hidden actions. Therefore the task of the test engineer is creating test views that lead to manageable test suites. This must be done carefully as parts of the system may never be tested while other test views overlap. One important advantage of this approach is that the size of test suites is scalable.

With respect to dense time, the main idea is finding equivalent parts in the model called partitions. Due to the dense time domain, the model has infinitely many states with respect to the infinitely many possible time values. Partitions group these values so that a finite graph is the result that can be used for test case generation. As this may be too large for full exploration, heuristics must be used to limit the size of the state space.

For hybrid systems, the presented algorithm is based on the results of test case generation for real-time systems. In addition to the hybrid model, a second, discrete, model is created that abstracts from the hybrid system. This can be used in combination with the test case generation algorithms for real-time systems presented. The original hybrid model is needed to derive correct evaluations for variables as the discrete model being only an abstraction is not capable of doing this. The selection of dense input curves is not tackled.

Optimization of Test Suites Testing timing constraints is still a difficult topic as delays for stimulating the SUT must be chosen and the correctness of outputs of the SUT must be accessed. First attempts with using evolutionary theory based test case generation methods have shown that these can improve the test suite with respect to determining best- and worst-case-execution times. This can be helpful to prove if a SUT meets its timing requirements.

All other algorithms presented built up on results of testing untimed systems. In contrast, evolutionary testing has a different background and therefore provides a new point of view for future work in the field of real-time and hybrid systems testing.

Future Work Model-based test case generation for real-time and hybrid systems has been successfully applied in relatively small examples. More effort has to be put into this to prove the practicability of test case generation algorithms. There is also only few tool support for test case generation and execution for real-time systems and no tool support for hybrid systems. New techniques like evolutionary testing to test timing constraints must be further surveyed. Also cross-fertilization between the different approaches seems useful to improve the presented algorithms as each has its advantages and disadvantages.

Part IV

Tools and Case Studies

The previous parts of this book have shown how to relate models to models, and how to relate models to actual systems running in their actual environments. This included the theoretical background as well as pragmatic and technological considerations when it came to reducing the number of test cases to a "sufficient" number.

The two articles of this part are concerned with tools and case studies that are, in a way or another, based on the observations of the previous papers. It is concerned with both technology, as reflected in tools, and with methodology, as reflected in a survey of a few selected real world case studies.

Overview Belinfante, Frantzen, and Schallhart provide an overview of tools for test case generation in Chapter 14. They are structured w.r.t. the modeling formalism. The authors take into account tools for test case generation with time-synchronous languages, with extended finite state machines, and with labeled transition systems. Their paper shows that there is an increasing body of tools for automated model-based testing. While this appears very promising, of course, existing tools are limited by the complexity of the systems for which test cases are to be generated. The authors provide arguments for their assessment that test case generation technology has matured to a point at which it is capable of coping with systems that are not toy examples any more.

This claim is even strengthened by El-Ramly, Horstmann, and Prenninger in Chapter 15. They review case studies that actually relied on abstract models that have been successfully used for test case generation. Application domains include processor architectures, protocols, operating systems, and smart cards. In particular, they are interested in the underlying abstraction mechanisms— a result of the observation that the endeavor of checking a system against a model at the same level of abstraction is a dubious endeavor, because the model has to be validated. Roughly, the bottom line of this article is that model-based testing is particularly successful in domains where predefined levels of abstraction (VHDL, RTL) exist.

14　Tools for Test Case Generation

Axel Belinfante[1], Lars Frantzen[2]*, and Christian Schallhart[3]

[1]　Department of Computer Science
University of Twente
Axel.Belinfante@cs.utwente.nl
[2]　Nijmegen Institute for Computing and Information Sciences (NIII)
Radboud University Nijmegen
lf@cs.kun.nl
[3]　Institut für Informatik
Technische Universität München
schallha@cs.tum.edu

14.1　Introduction

The preceding parts of this book have mainly dealt with test theory, aimed at improving the practical techniques which are applied by testers to enhance the quality of soft- and hardware systems. Only if these academic results can be efficiently and successfully transferred back to practice, they were worth the effort.

In this chapter we will present a selection of model-based test tools which are (partly) based on the theory discussed so far. After a general introduction of every single tool we will hint at some papers which try to find a fair comparison of some of them.

Any selection of tools must be incomplete and might be biased by the background of the authors. We tried to select tools which represent a broad spectrum of different approaches. Also, to provide some insight into recent developments, new tools such as AsmL and AGEDIS have been added. Therefore, the tools differ a lot with respect to theoretical foundation, age, and availability. Due to commercial restrictions, only limited information was available on the theoretical basis of some of the tools. For the same reason, it was not always possible to obtain hands-on experience.

Relation to Theory

The preceding chapters of this book discuss theory for model-based testing. One could raise the question: what does all this *theory* bring us, when we want to make (or use) model-based testing *tools*? A possible answer could be that theory allows us to put different tools into perspective and to reason about them.

The formal framework described elsewhere in this book in the introduction to Part II (page 113) allows to reason about, and classify, all model-based testing

---

*　Lars Frantzen is supported by the Netherlands Organisation for Scientific Research (NWO) under project: STRESS – Systematic Testing of Realtime Embedded Software Systems.

M. Broy et al. (Eds.): Model-Based Testing of Reactive Systems, LNCS 3472, pp. 391-438, 2005.
© Springer-Verlag Berlin Heidelberg 2005

approaches, even those that are not aware of it. An example is given in Section 14.3.1, where the error-detecting power of a number of model-based testing tools is compared by looking at the theory on which the tools are based.

The formal framework also allows to reason about correctness, not only of the implementation that is to be tested, but also of the testing tool itself, as we will see below.

The key concept of the formal framework is the *implementation relation* (or *conformance relation*). It is the most abstract concept of the framework, since it has no "physical" counterpart in model-based testing, unlike concepts like *specifications, test suites* or *verdicts*. The implementation relation relates the result of test execution (so, whether execution of tests generated from the model failed or passed) to conformance (or non-conformance) between the model and the SUT. The idea is the following. Suppose a user has a model, and also an idea of which (kind of) implementations the user will accept as valid implementations of the model – an implementation that according to the user is a valid one is said to *conform to* the model. The user will then derive (generate) tests on the basis of (from) the model. The idea is that if the SUT *conforms to* the model, then the execution of all tests that are generated on the basis of the model must be successful. Here *conforms to* is formalized by the implementation relation. Therefore, any tool defines an implementation relation, explicitly or implicitly. If the implementation relation is defined implicitly, it may still be possible to make it explicit by analyzing the test derivation algorithm implemented in the tool, or maybe even by experimenting.

The implementation relation is embodied in the test derivation algorithm. This is reflected in the theoretical framework by the concept of *soundness*, which says that the generated test cases should never cause a fail verdict when executed with respect to a correct (conforming) implementation. A related concept is *completeness* (or *exhaustiveness*) which says that for each possible SUT that does not conform to the model, it is possible to generate a test case that causes a fail verdict when executed with respect to that SUT.

If one knows that a tool implements a test derivation algorithm that is *sound*, analyzing unexpected test execution results may be easier, because one knows that the tool will never generate test cases that cause a fail verdict that was not deserved. The unexpected result may be caused by an error in the SUT (this is what one hopes for), but it may also be caused by an error in the model, or by an error in the glue code connecting the test tool to the SUT. However, (as long as the test derivation algorithm was implemented correctly) it *can not* be caused by the test derivation tool. Without this knowledge, the error can be anywhere.

Also *completeness* of the test derivation algorithm has important practical implications. In practice one is only able to execute a limited number of tests, so one may be unlucky and no distinguishing test case is generated. However, if one does know that the test derivation algorithm is complete, one at least knows that it does not have any "blind spots" that *a priori* make it impossible for it to find particular errors. So, if one has a SUT that is known to be incorrect (non-conforming), and one tries hard and long enough, one should eventually generate a test case that causes a fail verdict for the SUT. In contrast, if one applies a test derivation algorithm for which one knows that it is not complete, one also knows that there are erroneous implementations that one can never distinguish from correct ones, and it makes no difference whether or not one tries long or hard, because the inherent blind spots in the test derivation algorithm simply make it impossible to generate a test case that causes a fail verdict.

14.2   Tool Overview

Tool	Section	Page	Languages	CAR	Method
Lutess	14.2.1	394	Lustre	A	
Lurette	14.2.2	399	Lustre	A	
GATeL	14.2.3	402	Lustre	A	CLP
AutoFocus	14.2.4	406	AutoFocus	A	CLP
Conformance Kit	14.2.5	408	EFSM	R	FSM
Phact	14.2.6	409	EFSM	R	FSM
TVEDA	14.2.7	410	SDL, Estelle	R	FSM
AsmL	14.2.8	412	AsmL	R	FSM?
Cooper	14.2.9	414	LTS (Basic LOTOS)	A	LTS
TGV	14.2.10	417	LTS-API (LOTOS, SDL, UML)	A	LTS
TorX	14.2.11	420	LTS (LOTOS, Promela, FSP)	A	LTS
STG	14.2.12	424	NTIF	A	LTS
AGEDIS	14.2.13	427	UML/AML	CAR	LTS
TestComposer	14.2.14	429	SDL	C	LTS/EFSM?
AutoLink	14.2.15	431	SDL	C	

Table 14.1. Test Tools

Table 14.1 lists the tools that will be presented in more detail below. From left to right, the columns contain the name of a tool, the section in which it is discussed, its starting page number, the input languages or APIs, its origin or availability (whether it was developed by an **A**cademic institute, by a non-university **R**esearch institute, or whether it is **C**ommercially available), and the test derivation method used in the tool (*CLP* stands for testing based on *Constrained Logic Programming*, *FSM* stands for testing of *Finite State Machines* and *LTS* stands for testing of *Labeled Transition Systems*). For some tools we left the *Method* entry open because the method implemented in the tool differed too much from those discussed in the theoretical chapters.

From top to bottom the table shows the tools in the order in which we will present them. Unfortunately, there is no simple single criterion to order them. Therefore, we ordered them by input language and test derivation method. We start with tools for models based on time-synchronous languages. Next, we discuss tools for (extended) finite state machine models. Finally, we discuss tools based on labeled transition system models. For each of those categories, we try to follow the flow of development, so we go from the earlier tools, based on more simple theory, to the later ones, based on more advanced theory. With *AutoFocus* we refer to the testing facilities (for which we do not know a separate name) of the modeling tool *AutoFocus*. The tool *AGEDIS* was developed in a European project. It is commercially available, and freely for academic purposes.

For most of these tools, the theory on which they are based has already been discussed in the previous chapters, and we will just refer to it. For the other tools, we will try to give a brief overview of the relevant theory when we discuss the tool.

Each of the following tool presentations contains an introduction (which also tells where the tool originated, if known), followed by discussions of its test generation process and its interfaces (which also lists its input and output languages), and concluded by a summary and, for the interested reader, a categorized list of literature references.

14.2.1   Lutess

Introduction

Lutess [dBORZ99] is a testing environment for synchronous reactive systems which is based on the synchronous dataflow language Lustre [HCRP91].

It builds its test harness automatically from three elements, a test sequence generator, the SUT, and an oracle. Lutess does not link these elements into a single executable but is only connecting them and coordinating their execution. The test sequence generator is derived from an environment description and test specification. The environment description is given in terms of a synchronous observer, i.e., as synchronous program which observes the input/output stream of the SUT. The environment description determines whether a test sequence is realistic wrt. the environment, and the oracle determines whether the sequence is correct or not.

The SUT and the oracle might be given as synchronous programs, Lutess is able to handle them completely as black-boxes. Optionally, they can be supplied as Lustre programs, which are automatically compiled to be integrated into the test harness.

The test sequence generator is derived by Lutess from the environment description written in Lustre and from a set of constraints which describe the set of interesting test sequences. Lustre has been slightly expanded such that these constraints can be expressed in Lustre, too. Lutess allows one to state operational profiles [Mus93], properties to be tested, and behavioral patterns.

All three components of a test harness must not have any numerical inputs or outputs – this might be the most serious restriction of Lutess: It is only working with Boolean variables.

The test sequences are generated on the fly while the SUT is executed. First the test sequence generator provides an initial input vector for the SUT. Then the SUT and test sequence generator compute in an alternating manner output vectors and input vectors respectively. The oracle is fed with both, the input and the output stream, and computes the verdict. If the SUT is deterministic, i.e., a sequence of input vectors is determining the corresponding sequence of output vectors, then the complete test sequence can be reproduced based on the initial random seed given to the test sequence generator.

Lutess is aimed at two goals – first it supports a monoformalistic approach, i.e., the software specification, the test specification and the program itself can be stated in the same programming language. Second, the same technology should support verification and testing techniques [dBORZ99].

Lustre

Lustre is a high-level programming language for reactive systems [HCRP91, CPHP87] which combines two main concepts, namely it is a dataflow oriented as well as a time-synchronous language.

Lustre is based on the synchrony hypothesis, i. e., a Lustre program is written with the assumption that every reaction of the program to an external event is executed instantaneously. In other words, it is assumed that the environment does not change its state during the computation of a reaction. This allows the use of an idealized notion of time where each internal event of a program takes place at a known point in time with respect to the history of external events.

To make this concept usable in practice, Lustre is designed such that each Lustre program can be compiled into a finite IO-automaton where each state transition is compiled into a piece code without branches. A transition of this automaton corresponds to an elementary reaction of the program. Thus, it is possible to give an accurate upper bound on the maximum reaction time of the program for a given machine. This structuring of compiled synchronous programs was introduced in the context of the Esterel language [BC85]. Taken together, this approach allows to *check* the synchrony hypothesis.

Many reactive systems are easily and naturally modeled in terms of dataflows. Each dataflow is a mapping of discrete time to values, i.e., a dataflow X represents a sequence of values $x_1, x_2, \ldots$. In Lustre, reactive systems are composed of flows of data which are recombined and transformed by a set of operators. In fact each variable in Lustre represents a dataflow. So for example, in Lustre the statement $X = Y + Z$ means that each element of the flow X equals the sum of the corresponding elements of the flows Y and Z, i.e., if $Y = y_1, y_2, \ldots$ and $Z = z_1, z_2, \ldots$ then $X = x_1, x_2, \ldots$ with $x_i = y_i + z_i$.

Advantages of the dataflow approach are that it is functional and parallel. Functional programs are open to automated analysis and transformation because of the lack of side-effects. Parallel components are naturally expressed in Lustre by independent dataflows. Synchronization is implicitly described by data dependencies between the different dataflows.

The following piece of code implements a counter as a so called node.[1] A node recombines a set of dataflows into a new one. In this case val_init is used as initialization of the new flow which is then incremented by val_incr in each cycle.

---

[1] This example has been taken from [HCRP91].

```
node COUNTER(val_init, val_incr : int; reset : bool)
returns (n : int);
let
   n = val_init -> if reset then val_init else pre(n)+val_incr;
tel;
```

This example shows the two more fundamental time operators of Lustre[2]. The first operator `->` is the followed-by operator. If A and B have the respective sequence of values $a_0, a_1, \ldots$ and $b_0, b_1, \ldots$ then A `->` B declares the sequence $a_0, b_1, b_2, \ldots$. Therefore, in the example, the flow of n starts with the first value of val_init.

The second time operator in the example is pre. Given a flow A with the values $a_0, a_1, \ldots$, pre(A) is the flow with the values $nil, a_0, a_1, \ldots$. So in the code above, we find that if reset is true, then n is set to the current value of val_init. Otherwise n is set to the previous value of n plus the increment val_incr. Two simple applications of this node are the following two sequences.

```
even=COUNTER(0,2,false);
mod5=COUNTER(0,1,pre(mod5)=4);
```

The first sequence generates the even numbers, and the second cycles through the numbers between 0 and 4. Note that the reset input is indeed fed with another flow.

To approximate the position of an accelerating vehicle, we can use the following two flows

```
speed=COUNTER(0,acceleration,false);
position=COUNTER(0,speed,false);
```

Note that speed used as input in the second statement is a flow which is changing over time. E.g. if acceleration is the constant flow with value 4, then speed would be the sequence 0,4,8,12,16,..., and position would start with 0,4,12,24,40,...

Testing Method

The construction of the test sequence generation is formally described in the paper [dBORZ99]. Basically, a test sequence generator built by Lutess is based on an environment description given in Lustre and a set of further (probabilistic)

---

[2] Lustre also offers two other operators, namely when and current. These operators allow the manipulation of the clock of a dataflow. Each dataflow in Lustre has an associated clock which determines when a new value is added to the corresponding flow. For example, a flow with the clock true, false, true, ... would be expanded by a new value every second cycle. The when operator allows to declare a sequence which runs with a slower clock, while the current operator allows to interpolate a flow with a slow clock such that it becomes accessible for recombination with faster flows.

constraints to guide the test sequence generation. The environment description computes a predicate which indicates whether the test sequence is relevant or not. The test sequence generator inverts this predicate, i.e., it computes the set of inputs for the SUT which satisfy the environment description. In every step, the oracle is provided with the last input/output pair of the SUT to compute a pass or fail verdict for the sequence tested so far.

Random Testing The behavior of the environment is restricted by a set of constraints which must be satisfied unconditionally by the whole test sequence. For example, an environment description for a telephone-system will allow a test sequence such as $on_i, dial_i, off_i, on_i, dial_i, off_i \ldots$, where on_i is the event of picking up the phone i, $dial_i$ is the event of dialing a number, and off_i is the event of hanging up. A sequence starting with $on_i, on_i, \ldots$ would not be allowed by the environment description, since it is physically impossible to pick up the same phone twice.

Random testing is the most basic mode of operation, where Lutess generates test sequences which respect the environment constraints based on a uniform distribution.

Operational Profile-Based Testing Although random test sequences are possible interactions between the SUT and the environment, the arising test sequences lack realism, i.e., most sequences which occur in the target environment are not generated since they unlikely happen at random. To obtain more realistic test sequences, Lutess allows to add operational profiles to the environment description. An operational profile $CP(e) = \langle (p_1, c_1), \ldots, (p_n, c_n) \rangle$ associates conditional probabilities (p_i, c_i) with an input e. If the condition c_i evaluates to true, then the input e of the SUT will be set to true with probability p_i in the next step. Therefore, operational profiles do not rule out unexpected cases, but they are emphasizing more common sequences of events.

Property-Guided Testing Next, Lutess provides property guided testing. In this case, Lutess will try to generate test sequences which test safety properties. For example, if a property of the form $a \Rightarrow b$ should be an invariance, then Lutess will set a to true if such a setting is consistent with the basic environment constraints. However, Lutess is only able to provide this feature for expressions that do not involve references into the past. For example $pre(a) \Rightarrow b$ cannot be used for property guided testing, since $pre(a)$ is refers to the value of the expression a in the last step.

Pattern-Based Testing Finally, Lutess provides pattern-based testing. A pattern $BP = [true] cond_0 [inter_1] cond_1 \ldots [inter_n] cond_n$ is a sequence of conditions $cond_0, \ldots,$
$cond_n$ with associated interval conditions $inter_1, \ldots, inter_n$. Lutess probabilistically generates test sequences which match the pattern, i.e., if the environment

allows to generate an input such that $cond_0$ becomes true, such a choice is taken with higher probability. Then, Lutess will take choices which are biased to either maintain the first interval condition $inter_1$ or to match the next condition $cond_1$. The concrete probabilities are given as part of the specification. This process is continued until the test sequence has passed the pattern entirely or until the test sequence becomes inconsistent with the pattern.

Test Sequence Generation

Given the internal state of the environment description and the last output of the SUT, the test sequence generator must produce an input vector for the SUT, such that the environment constraints will be satisfied. For random testing, the generator has to determine the set of input vectors which are relevant wrt. the environment description. Then it has to choose one such vector randomly in an efficient way according to the current testing method (random, operational profile-based, property-guided, or pattern-based).

To determine the set of relevant input vectors efficiently, Lutess constructs a Binary Decision Diagram (BDD) [Bry85] to represent all state transitions which are valid within the environment. This BDD contains all valid transitions in all possible states of the environment. To allow efficient sampling on the set of possible input vectors for the current state of the environment description, all variables which determine the next input vector for the SUT are placed in the lower half of the BDD, while all other variables (describing the state and last output of the SUT) are placed in the upper part of the BDD. Given the current state and the last output vector, the generator can quickly determine the sub-BDD which describes all possible input vectors to be sent to the SUT in the next step.

Then this sub-BDD is sampled to determine the next input for the SUT. The sampling procedure is supported by further annotations. Depending on the employed testing methods, the sampling is implemented in different ways, see [dBORZ99] for details on the sampling procedure.

Summary

Lutess allows to build the test harness for fully automated test sequence generation and execution in the context of synchronous reactive systems. The harness is constructed from a SUT, a test specification, and an oracle. The SUT and the oracle can be given as arbitrary synchronous reactive programs. The test sequence generated is based on an environment description given in Lustre. Optionally, the test sequence generation can be controlled by operational profiles, safety properties to be tested, and behavioral patterns to be executed. Lutess has been applied to several industrial applications [PO96, OP95].

However, Lutess is not able to deal with SUTs which have numerical inputs or outputs. Also, it is not possible to express liveness properties in Lutess. Furthermore Lutess does not provide any means to generate test suites based on coverage criteria.

14.2.2   Lurette

Introduction

The approach of **Lurette**[3] is generally comparable to Lutess which has been presented above [RNHW98]. Lurette is also based on the synchronous dataflow language Lustre. Both tools build their test harness from three elements, namely the SUT, a test sequence generator, and an oracle. Moreover, both tools derive the test sequence generator from an environment description written in Lustre while the SUT is tested as a black box. Finally, both tools utilize environment descriptions and oracles given as synchronous observers. Synchronous observers are programs which implement acceptors for sequences. A synchronous observer used as environment description will output true as long as the sequence presented to the observer represents a valid sequence of events in the environment.

However, in contrast to Lutess, Lurette allows to validate systems which have numerical inputs and outputs. On the other hand, Lurette is only offering a single mode for test sequence generation. The randomly generated sequences are based on a uniform distribution. Also, Lurette requires that the SUT is given as a C-file which implements a predefined set of procedures.

The test sequence is generated on the fly during the execution of the SUT. An initial input is provided by the test sequence generator and fed into SUT. From then on, the SUT and the test sequence generator compute outputs and inputs in an alternating fashion.

Testing Method

The testing method of Lurette is relatively simple. The environment description is used to express both relevant and interesting test sequences. In [RNHW98], the term relevance refers to those properties which constrain the environment itself and the term interest refers to the test purpose. The constraints which represent the relevance and the interest are expressed within the same synchronous observer, i.e., there is no distinction between the environment description and the test purpose. This observer is fed with the inputs and outputs of the SUT and evaluates to true, if the sequence so far is relevant and interesting.

A test sequence generated by Lurette is constructed uniformly and randomly such that the observer evaluates to true in every single step of the sequence. In other words, Lurette has to invert the environment description to compute a new input vector for the SUT based on the current state of the environment and the last output of the SUT. The oracle is also fed with the inputs and outputs of the SUT to evaluate the correctness of the sequence. The result of the oracle is either a fail or pass verdict.

Test Sequence Generation

In each step of the test sequence generation, Lurette has to compute an input vector for the SUT based on the internal state of the environment description

---

[3] See also http://www-verimag.imag.fr/SYNCHRONE/lurette/lurette.html.

and the last output of the SUT, such that the environment constraints will be satisfied. The approach is completely analogous to the test sequence generation of Lutess, however, Lurette has to deal with linear constraints over integers and reals.

Abstracting the Observer To solve this problem with numerical constraints, Lurette computes an abstract version of the original observer. In this abstract observer, all numerical constraints have been replaced by new Boolean Variables. These new variables are treated as further inputs of the observer. Consider the following observer with a number of numerical constraints:

```
node RELEVANT(X,Y,Z : int; A,B : bool)
return (relevant : bool)
let
   relevant = (X=0) -> if A then (B or (X>Y))
                       else (X+Y<=Z) and (Z* pre(Y)<12);
tel
```

Note that $pre(Y)$ can be treated as constant, since its value has been determined in the last step. Assuming that we are not in the initial state, Lurette would replace this observer by a new abstract observer with three additional Boolean variables C_1, C_2, C_3 to represent the numerical constraints.

```
node ABSTRACT_RELEVANT(A,B,C1,C2,C3 : bool)
return (relevant : bool)
let
   relevant = (A and (B or C1) or
              ((not A) and C2 and C3);
tel
```

where C_1, C_2, C_3 represent the conditions $X > Y$, $X + Y \leqslant Z$, and $Z * pre(Y) < 12$ respectively.

This abstracted observer is then represented as BDD. The BDD can be inverted effectively, i.e., it is easy to expand a partial truth assignment to a complete satisfying truth assignment. Assigning the last output of the SUT, we have a partial assignment which must be completed such that ABSTRACT_RELEVANT evaluates to true, i.e., the associated BDD evaluates to true.

Choosing the Next Input Lurette chooses one of the Boolean assignments which satisfy the BDD randomly according to a uniform distribution. This assignment determines the set of numerical constraints to be satisfied. This set of linear constraints on integers and reals establishes a convex polyhedron which is explicitly constructed. If the polyhedron is empty, then the Boolean assignment lead to numerical infeasibility – another Boolean assignment must be chosen to repeat the process. If the polyhedron is non-empty, a point is selected within the polyhedron according to a specified strategy, [RNHW98] mentions limited vertices and random selection within the polyhedron. The assignments to the Boolean and numerical variables obtained by this procedure are used as input vector to the SUT.

An Optimization Lurette does not only test linear test sequences. In each step of a test sequence generation and execution, Lurette tests several inputs with the SUT. More precisely, it computes the output of the SUT for a whole set of input vectors and checks whether each of the correspondingly continued test sequences would be correct. This is possible, since the SUT is required to provide one method to produce the next output of the SUT without changing its state, and a separate method to advance the state of the SUT. If an error is found, the test sequence which provoked the error is returned along with a fail verdict and Lurette terminates. If no error is detected, then the test sequence is continued with one of the tested inputs. This is possible, since Lurette is requiring the SUT to be given in a way that allows to compute the output of the SUT on a given input vector without advancing its internal state.

SUT Program Format

To test a program with Lurette, this program must be given as a C-file which implements a synchronous reactive program. In particular, the C-file must implement a specific interface to be integrated into the test harness. This interface must allow to access the following elements:

- The names and types of the inputs and outputs of the SUT, such that the test harness can connect to the SUT with the test case generator.
- The initialization procedure $init_P$ must bring the SUT P into its initial state.
- The output procedure $o = out_P(i)$ has to compute the output of P based on the current internal state of P and the input i. Note that a call to out_P is not allowed to change the state of P.
- Finally, the procedure $next_P(i)$ has to bring P into the next state, again on the basis of the current internal state and the input i.

The Lustre compiler which is provided for free by Verimag produces C-files which are suitable for Lurette. Alternatively, the code generator of the SCADE environment[4] can be used to obtain appropriate input files for Lurette. Other synchronous languages are probably adaptable to Lurette by wrapping the generated code into the above described procedures.

To integrate an oracle into a test harness, it must be provided in the same form as the SUT P.

---

[4] SCADE is a suite for developing dependable software, including tools to facilitate specification, code generation, and code validation. It is based on a graphical implementation of the Lustre language. See http://www.esterel-technologies.com.

Summary

Lurette is targeted at the fully automated testing of synchronous reactive systems. It builds a test harness from an environment description, a SUT, and an oracle. The SUT and the oracle must be given in terms of a C-file which implement a specific set of procedures. The environment description must be given in Lustre. It describes the environment and the test purpose simultaneously. The generated test sequence is chosen randomly such that relevance and interest constraints are satisfied.

Lurette allows to test SUTs which have numerical inputs and outputs. However, Lurette is only able to deal with linear constraints between these numerical parameters. Each step in the test sequence generation is subdivided into two phases, first an abstracted environment description is used to obtain a set of linear constraints to be satisfied. Then the obtained constraint set is solved.

On the other hand, Lurette is *not* able to deal with liveness properties and it only allows to specify test purposes in terms of safety properties.

14.2.3   GATeL

Introduction

The third Lustre-based tool which is described here is **GATeL**[5] [MA00]. Its approach is quite different from the two other Lustre related tools (Lutess and Lurette) presented in this chapter. Lutess and Lurette start the test sequence generation from the initial state. Then the sequence is generated on the fly, i.e., in each step the outputs of the SUT are used to compute a new input for the SUT based on the environment description and the test purpose. This process is iterated either until a negative test verdict is produced, or until the maximum test sequence length is reached. In contrast, GATeL starts with a set of constraints on the last state of the test sequence to be generated. This set of constraints can contain invariant properties as well as any other constraint on the past which can be expressed in Lustre. The latter amounts to a test purpose since it allows to state a predicate on all sequences which are of interest. During the test sequence generation, GATeL tries to find a sequence which satisfies both, the invariant and the test purpose. To find such a sequence, GATeL employs constraint logic programming (CLP) in a search process which extends the sequence backwards, i.e., from the last state to the first one.

Testing Method

GATeL requires the SUT or a complete specification of the SUT, an environment description, and a test objective. All three elements must be supplied as Lustre source code. All three components of the test harness are not allowed to use real variables or tuples.

---

[5] See also http://www-drt.cea.fr/Pages/List/lse/LSL/Gatel/index.html.

The test objective allows to state properties and path predicates. Safety properties are expressed with the `assert` keyword of Lustre. An asserted property must hold in each step of the generated test sequence. To state a path predicate, GATeL employs a slightly expanded Lustre syntax. GATeL allows to express path predicates with the additional keyword `reach`. The statement `reach Exp` means that `Exp` must be reached once within the test sequence. More precisely, GATeL will try to find a test sequence which ends in a state where *all* expressions to be reached evaluate to true.

The SUT and the environment are only allowed to contain assertions. An assertion in the SUT is used by Lustre compilers to optimize the generated code. Assertions within the environment description are used to constrain the possible behavior of the environment – as usual.

As an example, consider the following program and test objective. The node COUNT_
SIGNAL is counting the number of cycles when `signal` is true. Let us further assume that `signal` is part of the input.

```
node COUNT_SIGNAL(signal : bool)
returns (n : int);
let
    base = 0 -> pre(n);
    n = if signal then base + 1 else base;
tel;

assert true -> not ( signal and pre(signal) )
reach COUNT_SIGNAL(signal)>1;
```

The assertion requires `signal` to be true in two consecutive steps. The subsequent `reach` statement requires GATeL to generate a test sequence such that COUNT_SIGNAL(signal) becomes greater than 2.

Based on the SUT (or its specification) and the environment description, GATeL will try to find a test sequence which satisfies the path predicate expressed in the `reach` statement and which satisfies the asserted invariance expressions in every cycle. If such a test sequence can be found, it will be executed with the SUT. The output values computed by the SUT are compared with the corresponding values of the precomputed test sequence. If the two sequences match, the test case passed, otherwise it failed.

Test Sequence Generation

Consider again the node COUNT_SIGNAL with the test objective

```
assert true -> not ( signal and pre(signal) );
reach COUNT_SIGNAL(signal)>1;
```

To find a sequence which satisfies the test objective, GATeL starts with the final cycle of the test sequence to be generated. Using the notation signal[N] to denote the Nth value of the flow `signal`, the constraints on this final cycle N are the following:

- `true -> not ( signal[N] and signal[N-1] ) = true`
- `COUNT_SIGNAL(signal[N]) > 1`

Then GATeL tries to simplify this constraint set as far as possible without instantiating further variables. In this example, GATeL would derive the three constraints shown next, where `maxInt` is a user tunable parameter.

- `true -> not ( signal[N] and signal[N-1] ) = true`
- `COUNT_SIGNAL[N] in [2,maxInt]`
- `COUNT_SIGNAL[N] = if signal[N] then base[N] + 1 else base[N]`

This set cannot be simplified further without instantiating a variable. GATeL has to choose one variable to instantiate – it tries to find a variable with a maximum number of waiting constraints and a minimal domain size. In the example above the first and second constraints are waiting for `signal[N]`, i.e., these constraints can be simplified further once `signal[N]` has been instantiated. The domain of `signal[N]` contains only two values since `signal[N]` is Boolean. Therefore, GATeL would choose to instantiate this variable. The value to be assigned to `signal[N]` is chosen *randomly* wrt. the uniform distribution. This process leads to the following set of constraints (assuming that GATeL chooses to assign true).

- `signal[N] = true`
- `true -> not ( signal[N-1] ) = true`
- `base[N] in [1,maxInt]`
- `base[N] = 0 -> COUNT_SIGNAL[N-1]`

In this situation, GATeL has to decide whether the Nth cycle is the initial one or not. Internally, GATeL uses an implicit Boolean variable to represent this decision. Again, the assigned value is chosen randomly. Assuming that GATeL would choose that the Nth cycle is non-initial, we would find the constraint set shown next.

- `signal[N] = true`
- `signal[N-1] = false`
- `true -> not ( signal[N-2] ) = true`
- `COUNT_SIGNAL[N-1] in [1,maxInt]`
- `COUNT_SIGNAL[N-1] = if signal[N-1] then base[N-1] + 1`
  `                              else base[N-1]`

Note that the third constraint listed above is instantiated from the invariance property which has been expressed as an assertion.

This process of backward constraint propagation is continued until either a test sequence has been found which satisfies all initial constraints or until a contradiction arises. In the latter case, GATeL starts to backtrack. If a test sequence is generated successfully, some variables might be still unassigned. The corresponding values are chosen randomly again to obtain a complete test sequence.

The test sequence generation is implemented in Prolog and based on the ECLiPSe package [ECLb].

Domain Splitting

The basic testing method described above allows to generate a single test sequence. GATeL offers the possibility of "domain splitting", i.e., to replace the domain (described by the current constraint set) with two ore more sub-domains (again described by constraint sets) which are special cases of the original domain (see Section 12.2 on page 324).

For example if the constraint set contains the condition A = B <= C, then GATeL offers two possibilities to split the domain. The first possibility is to split the domain into B <= C and B > C. The second possibility is to split the domain into B < C , B = C, and B > C. Domain splitting can be applied recursively to obtain a tree of sub-domains of the original domain.

Once the user decides to stop the domain splitting, GATeL will produce a test sequence for each sub-domain (if possible).

Summary

GATeL does not only allow to state invariance properties but allows to state path predicates to express the test purpose. To support path predicates, GATeL has to construct its test sequences backwards, i.e., it has to start with the final state to be reached by the test sequence. Thus the test sequence is not generated during the execution of the SUT, but before the SUT is executed.

This backward search is implemented in terms of a backtracking algorithm. The backtracking algorithm has to guess appropriate assignments when the current constraint set does not enforce a particular assignment or does not allows further simplification.

Moreover, GATeL requires the SUT to be given as Lustre source code, representing either the actual implementation or its complete specification. Again, this is necessary, since GATeL has to construct its test sequences backwards.

The feature of domain splitting allows to further subdivide the domain of interesting test sequences interactively. Moreover, it requires human intervention, which does not allow to generate a large number of sub-domains automatically. Finally, the domain splitting applies to the initial constraint set, which primarily constrains the very last cycles of the test sequence. Consequently, the domain splitting as implemented by GATeL only allows to split the domain wrt. the end of the test sequence.

14.2.4   AutoFocus

Introduction

Autofocus[6] is a graphical tool that is targeted at the modeling and development of distributed systems [HSE97]. Within AutoFocus, distributed systems are described as collections of components which are communicating over typed channels. The components can be decomposed into networks of communicating subcomponents. More specifically, a model in AutoFocus is a hierarchically organized set of time-synchronous communicating EFSMs which use functional programs for its guards and assignments. A model in AutoFocus can be used for code generation and as basis for verification and testing.

The testing facilities [PPS+03] of AutoFocus require a model of the SUT, a test case specification, and the SUT itself. The test case specification might be functional, structural, or stochastic. Functional specifications are used to test given properties of the SUT, structural specifications are based on some coverage criterion, and stochastic specifications are used to generate sequences randomly wrt. some given input data distributions. Based on the model and the test case specification, a set of test cases is generated automatically with the help of a constraint logic programming (CLP) environment.

To execute a suite of test sequences, the SUT needs to be adapted to the abstraction level of the model which underlies the test sequences. The adaption has to translate the IO between the conceptual level of the model and the concrete implementation level of the SUT.

The testing environment for smart cards used in [PPS+03] is automatically executing the complete test suite and reports deviations between the expected and actual IO-traces of the SUT.

Test Method

Functional Specifications Functional test purposes are used for testing of a particular feature, i.e., test sequences have to be generated which trigger the execution of a certain functionality. AutoFocus employs a nondeterministic state machine to represent the set of sequences which are of interest, i.e., trigger the functionality in question. In many cases, there is more than one way to exercise a specific feature. In such situations, nondeterministic state machine allow to represent the set of possible test sequences in a natural way. Also, it is possible to add transitions that will cause a failure in the protocol represented by the state machine.

The composition of the model and the functional test specification yields a generator which enumerates test sequences for a given length exhaustively or stochastically.

---

[6] See also http://autofocus.informatik.tu-muenchen.de.

Structural Specifications Structural specification can exploit the hierarchical modeling within AutoFocus, i.e., it is possible to generate suites independently for different components and to use these unit tests to generate integration tests [Pre03]. Also, it is possible to require the generated test sequences not to contain given combinations of commands or states.

In addition, AutoFocus allows to incorporate coverage criteria into the test specification. More precisely, coverage criteria can be applied to the model of the SUT or on the state machine which is used as functional test specification.

Statistical Specifications In the case of statistical testing, test sequences up to a given length are generated randomly. Because of the huge number of test sequences that would be almost identical, the generated sequences can be required to differ to certain degree.

Test Generation

Like GATeL, the test generation of AutoFocus is based on constraint logic programming (CLP). The AutoFocus model is translated into a CLP language and is executed symbolically (see Section 12.3 on page 338 for further details).

Each component K of the model is translated into a corresponding set of CLP predicates $next_K(S_K, i, o, D_K)$. $next_K$ is the next state relation, i.e., $next_K(S_K, i, o, D_K)$ holds if the component K has a transition from state S_K to state D_K with input i and output o. The next-state predicates are composed of the predicates of the subcomponents mirroring directly the decomposition of the model at hand. Executing the generated logic program yields the set of all possible execution traces of the model. The formulation as constraint logic program allows to reduce the size of this set because of the compact symbolic representation of the traces. E.g., if the concrete command i sent to a model is unimportant as long as it is not the *Reset* command, only two traces will be generated, one where the command i is fixed to *Reset*, and another one where the command is left uninstantiated with the constraint $i \neq Reset$. To further reduce the number of generated test sequences, the testing environment allows to prohibit test sequences which contain the same state more than once. In such an approach, the detailed prohibition mechanism must be chosen carefully. Moreover the technique which is used to store and access the set of visited states is crucial to the overall performance. See [Pre01] for details.

To generate the test sequences according to a given test specification, the specification is also translated into or given directly in CLP and added to the CLP representation of the corresponding model. The specification guides the test sequence generation, determines its termination, and it restricts the search space.

The result of this process is a set of symbolic test sequences, i.e., test sequences which contain uninstantiated variables. For example, a symbolic test sequence might contain a command $AskRandom(n)$. The concrete value of n might be free but bound to the interval $[0, 255]$. However, each of these variables might be subject to some of the constraints which are collected during the symbolic execution.

These variables can be instantiated randomly or based on a limit analysis. After instantiation, the test sequences can be used for actual testing.

Summary

AutoFocus allows to model a system as a collection of communicating components which can be decomposed hierarchically into further subnetworks of synchronously communicating components. The testing environment of Auto-Focus provides the possibility to translate its models into a CLP language and to symbolically execute these transformed models. The model can be associated with functional, structural, and stochastic test specifications to generate test sequences based on the symbolic execution within the CLP environment. In addition AutoFocus is able to generate test cases that conform to a given coverage criteria to the model itself, or on a functional test specification. The generated test sequences can be employed to drive a SUT which implements or refines the model which underlies the generated test sequences.

14.2.5   Conformance Kit

Introduction

At KPN Research [KPN] the **Conformance Kit** was developed in the early nineties to support automatic testing of protocol implementations. It is not publicly available. (E)FSMs serve as specifications. Beside the typical EFSM concepts like variables and conditions (predicates) on transitions, some additional notions like gates are introduced to facilitate the mapping to the SUT. The gate concept allows to split a specification into several EFSMs which communicate through such gates.

The first fundamental tool of the Kit is a converter which transforms an EFSM into an equivalent FSM (i.e. same input/output behavior) via enumeration of the (necessarily finite domain) variables. In a next step the resulting FSM is minimized. A basic syntax check is embedded into these steps which is capable of detecting nondeterministic transitions and input-incomplete specifications. Furthermore, EFSMs can be simulated and a composer allows to assemble communicating EFSMs into a single one with equal behavior.

Test Generation Process

The test suite generation tool offers several FSM techniques to derive test cases. A **transition tour** is possible if the FSM is strongly connected. The disadvantage of this method is that only the input/output behavior is tested, the correctness of the end-states of the transitions is not checked. To overcome this disadvantage a tour including unique input/output (UIO) sequences is offered which does check the end-states. It is called **partition tour** because it does not yield one finite test sequence covering all transitions but a set of single sequences for each transition. Each such sequence consists of three parts:

(1) A **synchronizing sequence** to transfer the FSM to its initial state.
(2) A **transferring sequence** to move to the source state of the transition to be tested.
(3) A **UIO sequence** which verifies the correct destination state of the transition.

Note that a partition tour is only possible if the utilized sequences exist, which is not always the case. See Part II of this book for a more detailed description of the FSM-based algorithms. Also a **random sequence** can be computed in which a random generator is used to produce stimuli. Statistics ensures that the whole specification is covered given that a real random generator is used and that the produced sequence is of infinite length. This is of course not practicable but at least these sequences can always be constructed and additional control mechanisms, which allow an explicit exclusion of transitions, may give quite usable results.

Tool Interfaces

A textual representation of the specification (E)FSM is needed. All the necessary information including special features like guards are described here. After a test suite is generated it is expressed in TTCN-MP, the syntactical notation of TTCN-2. A graphical representation in the common TTCN table form (TTCN-GR) is possible via a transformation from TTCN-MP to LATEX.

The Kit has been integrated into several tools and approaches. Below we will introduce two major ones.

14.2.6   PHACT

Philips [Phi] developed in 1995 a set of tools called **PHACT** (PHilips Automated Conformance Tester) which extends the Conformance Kit with the ability to execute the computed TTCN test cases against a given SUT. To link the abstract events of the specification to the corresponding SUT actions, a so called **PIXIT** (Protocol Implementation eXtra Information for Testing, this is ISO9646 terminology) has to be written. The executing part of PHACT consists basically of three components, the *supervisor*, the *stimulator* and the *observer*. The latter two give stimuli to the SUT respectively observe its outputs, hence they must be customized for each system. The supervisor utilizes these two components to execute the TTCN test suite and to give a pass/fail verdict based on the observed behavior. A test log is generated which can be processed by the commercial tool SDT from Telelogic, which in turn can present the log as a Message Sequence Chart.

To execute tests against an SUT, several modules are compiled and linked with the observer and simulator. This results in an executable tester which can be separate from the SUT or linked with it. To compile a tester, modules in C, VHDL (Very High Speed Integrated Circuit Hardware Description Language) and Java are supported. Also the TTCN test suite is translated into one of these languages. This makes it possible to download a whole test application on a ROM-emulator and carry out the test in batch mode.

Other extensions comprise additional test strategies extending the ones offered by the Conformance Kit (partition and transition tour). To do so a test template language is defined. Such templates correspond basically to regular expressions over sequences of input actions that are allowed by the FSM when starting from the initial state. PHACT is not publicly available but several research groups had access to it and used it to conduct case studies, see e.g. [HFT00].

Testing VHDL Designs

In [MRS+97] the authors report about a generic approach to use PHACT for hardware testing. More precisely not real hardware is tested here, but its VHDL model. VHDL can be simulated and is therefore suited for serving as the SUT. After a test suite is generated by the Conformance Kit, a generic software layer is used to interface with the VHDL design. The main problem here is to map the abstract ingredients of the test cases to the model which consists of complex signal patterns, ports, etc. The aim of the approach is to automate this mapping as much as possible. Small protocol examples were used as case studies.

Summary

The Conformance Kit and the tools built upon it such as PHACT made it possible to do several interesting industrial case studies. Furthermore the PHACT implementation was used for a comparative case study involving other tools like TGV and TorX. We return to that in section 14.3.

Related Papers

- Case Studies: [MRS+97, HFT00]

14.2.7   TVEDA

Introduction

The R&D center of France Telecom [Fra], formerly called CNet, developed the TVEDA [CGPT96] tool from 1989 to 1995. The final version TVEDA V3 was released 1995. The main goal was to support automatic conformance testing of protocols. Not a formal test theory but empirical experience of test design methodology formed the base of the TVEDA algorithms. Care has also been taken to let the tool generate well readable and structured TTCN-2 output. The approaches of TVEDA and TGV (see 14.2.10) have been partially incorporated into the tool TestComposer (see 14.2.14) which is part of the commercial tool ObjectGeode from Telelogic [Tel].

Test Generation Process

The notion of test purpose in TVEDA basically corresponds to testing an EFSM-transition. Achieving a complete coverage here is its test approach. This strategy originates from (human) test strategies for lower layer protocol testing. TVEDA basically offers two test selection strategies: single tests for each transition or a transition tour.

To test transitions the tool has to find paths to and from their start-, respectively end-states. One main problem of state-based testing is state explosion when building the complete state graph of the specification (e.g. when transforming a EFSM into a FSM, or a LOTOS specification into its LTS-semantics). In particular the problem consists of finding a path from one EFSM-state to another while satisfying given conditions on the variables. Instead of doing a (prevalently infeasible) raw analysis, TVEDA implements two main approaches to compute feasible paths: symbolic execution and reachability analysis using additional techniques. Only the latter method has been applied effectually and hence found its way into TestComposer. One hindrance of the symbolic attempt is that path computations are time-exponential w.r.t. the length of the path to be computed.

The reachability technique is based on an (external) simulator/verifier. In a first step the EFSM is reduced. Here all the parts which do not concern reaching the demanded target transitions are excluded, i.e. specification elements which do not influence firing-conditions of transitions. After that the simulator is exerted using three heuristics:

(1) A limited exhaustive simulation. A typical limit is 30000 explored states. A major part of the paths is found here. Because of a breadth-first search the discovered paths are also the shortest ones.
(2) Transitions not reached during the first step are tried to be caught during a second exhaustive simulation using a concept of a state-distance. When the distance increases during the exploration, the current path is given up and the next branch is taken. This may yield some new paths which have not been found in step 1.
(3) Finally TVEDA tries to reuse an already computed path which brings the specification to a state which is close to the start state of a missing transition. Another exhaustive search is initiated until the transition is is reached.

This heuristic reachability analysis is used by the offered test selection strategies to produce the resulting test suites. See [CGPT96]for a detailed description of the algorithms.

Tool Interfaces

Estelle[7] or SDL[8] serve as specification languages. A (sequential) SDL specification can be represented as an EFSM. In that case an EFSM-transition corre-

---

[7] ISO9074
[8] ITU Recommendation Z.100

sponds to a path from one SDL-state to the following next state. The resulting test suite is expressed in TTCN.

Summary

TVEDA was successfully applied to several protocol implementations, mostly specified in SDL. Meanwhile it has partly found it's way into TestComposer, which is addressed in section 14.2.14. Most of its underlying empirical principles were later justified theoretically in terms of well elaborated I/O theories, see [Pha94b].

Related Papers

- Underlying Theory: [CGPT96, Pha94b]

14.2.8   AsmL Test Tool

Introduction

At the beginning of the nineties the concept of **Evolving Algebra** came up due to the work of **Yuri Gurevich** [Gur94]. He was driven by the ambition to develop a computation model which is capable of describing any algorithm at its appropriate abstraction level. Based on simple notions from universal algebra an algorithm is modeled as an evolution of algebras. The underlying set corresponds to the machines memory and the algebra transformation is controlled by a small selection of instructions. Later on Evolving Algebra was renamed to **Abstract State Machine**, short **ASM**. ASMs have been used for defining the semantics of programming languages and extended in several directions like dealing with parallelism. See the ASM Homepage [ASMa] for detailed information.

At Microsoft Research a group called *Foundations of Software Engineering* [MSF] is developing the **Abstract State Machine Language**, short **AsmL**, which is a .NET language and therefore embedded into Microsoft's .NET framework and development environment. Based on ASMs it is aimed at specifying systems in an object-oriented manner. AsmL and the .NET framework can be freely downloaded at [ASMb].

Test Generation Process

AsmL has a conformance test facility included which is based on two steps. Firstly the specification ASM is transformed into an FSM before subsequently well known FSM-based algorithms (rural Chinese postman tour, see Part II of this book) are applied to generate a test suite. The whole testing process is bounded by the .NET framework, hence the SUT must be written in a .NET language. The ASM specification is aimed at describing the behavior of the SUT, abstracting away from implementation details.

Generating FSMs out of ASMs

In the following we will try to sketch the extraction process which generates an FSM out of a given ASM specification. This is the crucial step because it highly depends on user-defined and domain-specific conditions to guide the extraction. The quality of these conditions determines whether the resulting FSM is an appropriate abstraction of the ASM and if the extraction algorithm terminates at all.

If one is not familiar with ASMs just think of it as a simple programming language with variables, functions/methods, some control structure like an `if-then-else`, loops, etc. Now every action of the SUT is specified as follows:

> if g_1 then R_1
> ...
> if g_k then R_k

where the g_i are boolean guards and the R_i are further instructions which are not allowed to make use of the `if-then-else` construct anymore (this is a kind of normal form, one can be less strict when specifying). As expected the initial values of the variables determine the initial state of a program run. When an action a is executed the program moves to a next state, which can be seen as a transition with label a between two program states.

The main problem is that such an ASM has usually an infinite number of reachable states (unless all possible runs terminate). Hence it is necessary to reduce the number of states by grouping them according to a suitable equivalence relation. To get a satisfying result this relation must guarantee that firstly the number of resulting equivalence classes (also called *hyperstates*) is finite, otherwise the algorithm does not terminate. Secondly the number should not be too small, i.e. the result does not reflect a meaningful test purpose anymore. In fact you can consider the definition of the equivalence relation as a kind of very general test purpose definition, respectively test selection. The resulting hyperstates basically become the states of the generated FSM.

The equivalence relation is based on a set of boolean conditions $\{b_1, \ldots, b_n\}$. Two states of the ASM lay in the same class iff none of the b_i distinguishes them. Therefore at most 2^n hyperstates are possibly reachable. For example take the g_i of the action specifications as mentioned above as a base for the condition-set. Using them one can define that states differ (represent different hyperstates) iff their sets of executable actions differ. Other obvious selections are conceivable. Beside the potentially exponential number of resulting hyperstates the problem of computing the so called *true-FSM*, which covers all reachable hyperstates, is undecidable (and in a bounded version still NP-hard).

The extracting algorithm which computes the FSM does a kind of graph reachability analysis. A pragmatic solution to the stated problems is to additionally define a so called *relevance condition* which tells the extraction algorithm if the actually encountered ASM-state is worth being taken into account for further traversing, even if it does not represent a new hyperstate. Such a relevance condition usually demands a certain domain specific knowledge to produce a good result, i.e. a FSM which is as much as possible similar to the true-FSM.

The resulting FSM represents the specified behavior of a system based on the offered method calls. Hence the method calls constitute the input actions and their return values correspond to the output actions. For further information see [GGSV02].

Tool Interfaces

The close embedding of AsmL into .NET enables it to interact with the framework and other .NET languages. Guidance by the user is necessary to construct test cases as paraphrased above. This process is supported by a GUI and a parameter generator which generates parameter sets for methods calls. In addition to the mentioned abstractions (hyperstates, relevance condition), filters can be used to exclude states from exploration and a branch coverage criteria can be given to limit the generation process. To carry out the test cases, the SUT must be given as any managed .NET assembly, written in a .NET language. The binding of the specification methods with the implementation methods is supported by a wizard. A test manager is then able to carry out the generated test cases, see [BGN+03].

Summary

The process of generating an FSM out of an ASM is a difficult task which requires a certain expertise from the tester for firstly defining a hopefully suitable equivalence relation and secondly giving a relevance condition which prunes the state space into something similar like the true-FSM. It is also problematic that the resulting FSM may become nondeterministic (even if the specification ASM is not). This makes FSM-based test generation complicated and the AsmL test generator can not handle it. Dealing with nondeterminism seems to be the main focus of current research activities. In [BGN+03] one application of the FSM sequence generator is mentioned but no papers about case studies exist yet. Note that ASM based testing is a quite new topic and ongoing research may produce results which extenuate the actual obstacles.

Related Papers

- Tool Overview: [BGN+03]
- Underlying Theory: [Gur94, GGSV02]

14.2.9   Cooper

Introduction

Cooper [Ald90] is a prototype implementation of the Canonical Testers theory [Bri89]. It was developed in the LotoSphere project [BvdLV95, Lit]. Cooper has never been applied to case studies; its main function is educational, to illustrate the Canonical Tester theory and the Co-Op method [Wez90, Wez95] to derive canonical testers. The underlying theory is discussed in Section 6.4.2 (page 166).

Test Generation Process

(Most of the following is quoted/paraphrased from [Wez95].)

Cooper implements the implementation relation **conf** of [Bri89]. In this notion a process B_1 conforms to B_2 if and only if B_1 contains no unexpected deadlocks with respect to traces of B_2. So, if B_1 performs a trace that can also be done by B_2, and at a certain point B_1 deadlocks, then also B_2 should be able to perform the same trace and deadlock at the same point. This notion of conformance allows B_1 to perform traces that are not in B_2. But when we place B_1 in an environment that expects B_2, it will not deadlock unexpectedly with the environment.

A canonical tester is then a process that can test whether an implementation conforms to a specification with respect to the **conf** relation. To test whether a process P conforms to B we place a canonical tester $T(B)$ in parallel with P. The tester synchronizes with P, as explained below.

In the initial version of the Co-Op method on which Cooper is based, we only have basic actions (events) without values. There is no partitioning in input and output actions, and interaction between tester and implementation is by synchronizing on observable actions. This means that an action can only "happen" if both the tester and the implementation can "do" it. If only one of them (tester and implementation) is willing (or able) to do an action, and the other one can not do the action, then it can not happen. If at a given moment the tester or the implementation has no actions that it can do, or if the intersection of the sets of actions that they can do is empty (which means that there are no actions that they can do together), then they deadlock. There is the notion of an unobservable, internal (τ) action. And, from there, there is the notion of stable and unstable states. Stable states are those from which the implementation will only move after an interaction with its environment. Unstable states are states from which the implementation can move by itself, by performing some internal action.

If the tester tries to test an action x that is performed from an unstable state, it is possible that the implementation has moved to a different state and no longer wants to do x. So, x can be seen as an action that is (for the given state) optional in the implementation (the implementation may want to do it, but it also possible that the implementation no longer can do it because it moved to a different state where the action is not possible). However, in general, after the implementation has moved (by doing an internal action) "through" zero or more unstable states, it will end up in a stable state from which it cannot move by itself (there are no internal actions possible). For such a stable state, the tester must be willing to do at least one of actions that the implementation wants to do from there. Otherwise the tester might deadlock with a correct implementation. The Co-Op method of deriving a canonical tester is based on the above observations.

To slightly formalize the above we can say that the outgoing transitions from a state s can be divided in two sets: $Options(s)$ is the set of actions that s can perform from its unstable states, and $Compulsory(s)$ is a set of of sets of actions, where each of the sets of actions corresponds to a stable state that can be reached from B, and contains exactly the outgoing actions of that stable state.

The initial behavior from the tester is constructed using $Compulsory$ and $Options$. The tester may initially try to test any of the actions in $Options(s)$. The implementation may interact, but this is not guaranteed. Alternatively (or after trying several $Options$), the tester may internally move to a state from which it offers to interact with any of a set of actions: this set is chosen such that it contains exactly one action of each of the elements of $Compulsory(s)$. We assume that eventually the implementation moves to one of its stable states, and from there must be able to perform at least one of the actions offered by the tester. An implementation that does not interact within some limited time is not regarded as conforming. If a process s may, after performing a series of internal actions, enter a deadlocking state from which it cannot perform any actions, $Compulsory(s)$ will contain the empty set. The tester may then try to do any of the observable outgoing transitions of s, but no interaction is guaranteed. The tester may then, after trying zero or more actions, deadlock.

The behavior of the tester after doing an action is computed by first collecting all states subsequent that can be reached by doing that transition, computing the initial behavior for the tester from those states (using $Compulsory$ and $Options$ as above), and combining these initial behaviors.

To paraphrase: this is about who takes the initiative to force a decision in the case of non deterministic choices. If the specification can decide to do something, the tester must be able to follow, but if the specification leaves the choice to its environment, the tester can make (force) the decisions. This means that in the resulting tester, we see internal steps where the tester may make a decision (to select between multiple actions offered from stable states of the implementation), and actions directly offered (without preceding internal step) where the tester must be able to interact directly with actions from unstable states.

User Interaction

Cooper is started with a given specification. It then shows the user this specification, together with the initial canonical tester for it, which is the canonical tester derivation function T applied to the whole expression of the specification.

The user can then zoom in and step by step apply the canonical tester derivation function on expressions and subexpressions, every time replacing a sub expression by its initial tester, which leaves the canonical tester to be applied on the sub expressions that follows the initial actions in initial tester, from which can then in turn the initial tester can be computed, etc.

Cooper allows the user to select a behavior expression, and then computes the corresponding canonical tester by computing the tester for the left-hand side (prefix) of the expression, and combining that with the recursive application to the remaining parts of the expression.

Tool Interfaces

Cooper is part of the toolkit Lite (LOTOS Integrated Tool Environment) [Lit] that was developed in the LotoSphere project for the specification language LO-TOS. All tools in this toolkit work on LOTOS. Cooper only accepts a restricted version of LOTOS, called basic LOTOS, that does only contain actions, without data. [Wez95] extends the theory to full LOTOS, but this has not been implemented.

The canonical tester that Cooper (interactively) generates also has the form of a LOTOS specification. Test execution is not possible, except by taking the LOTOS text from a specification or implementation and the LOTOS text of a tester and manually combining these into a new specification. In this new specification the behaviors of the original specification (or implementation) and the tester are put in parallel composition, synchronizing on all actions (this is actually just a small matter of text editing).

Summary

Even though Cooper is not useful for practical work, it nicely demonstrates the canonical tester theory underlying it, and the way in which the Co-Op method allows compositional derivation of canonical testers.

Related Papers

- Tool Overview: [Ald90]
- Input Language: [ISO88, BB87]
- Underlying Theory: [Bri89, Wez90, Wez95]

14.2.10   TGV

Introduction

TGV [JJ02] has been developed by Vérimag and IRISA Rennes, France. It is a test generator that implements the **ioco** implementation relation[9] [Tre96c] (see Section 7.4, page 178).

TGV is available as part of the Caesar Aldebaran Development Package (CADP) [FGK+96]. It has also been integrated as one of the two test generation engines in the commercial tool TestComposer of ObjectGéode(for SDL), and it is used as test generation engine in AGEDIS, discussed in Section 14.2.13 (page 427).

Different versions of TGV have been used for a number of case studies in various application domains and with different specification languages.

---

[9] We think that TGV has always implemented **ioco**, notwithstanding an earlier publication [FJJV96] that refers to **ioconf** [Tre96a] as the implementation relation.

Test Generation Process

The underlying model of TGV is an Input Output Labeled Transition System (IOLTS). An IOLTS is like an LTS, but with the labels partitioned into three sets: one containing stimuli, another containing observations, and a third containing (invisible) internal actions.

The implementation relation implemented is **ioco**. Hence, the assumption is made that the SUT is input complete, which means that we assume that it will never refuse a stimulus, as long as the stimulus is taken from the set from stimuli.

The input to TGV consists of a specification and a test purpose. Both are IOLTSes. The generated test cases are IOLTSes with three sets of trap states: Pass, Fail and Inconclusive, that characterize the verdicts.

The authors of the papers about TGV define test purposes as follows. Note that this differs from the definition in the glossary. Formally, a test purpose is a deterministic and *complete* IOLTS, equipped with two sets of *trap states* Accept and Refuse, with the same alphabet as the specification. *Complete* means that each state allows all actions (we will see below how this is accomplished), and a *trap* state has loops on all actions. Reaching a state in Accept means that the wanted behavior has been seen; the Refuse set is used to prune behavior in which we are not interested. In a test purpose the special label "*" can be used as a shorthand, to represent the set of all labels for which a state does not have an explicit outgoing transition. In addition, regular expressions can be used to denote sets of labels. For states where the user does not specify outgoing transitions for all labels, TGV completes the test purpose with implicitly added "*" loop transitions. This increases the expressive power of the test purposes, but at the same time may make it (at least for the inexperienced user) more difficult to come up with the "right" test purpose that selects the behavior that the user had in mind (because the implicitly added "*" may make it harder to predict the result). As mentioned in [RdBJ00], in practice, usually some iterations are needed in which one defines or refines a test purpose, generates a test suite, looks at it, and modifies the test purpose, etc.

The test generation process consists of a number of steps; we will briefly describe them below.

From the specification and the test purpose first a synchronous product is computed, in which the states are marked as Accept and Refuse using information from the test purpose. In the next step the visible behavior is extracted, after which quiescent states (states in which no observations from the SUT are expected) are marked. To the quiescent states special δ loop transitions are added. These δ transitions represent an observation of quiescence: the absence of output from the SUT.

The result is determinized by identifying meta-states. Determinization is needed to be able to deal with states that have multiple outgoing transitions with the same label. Then, test cases are extracted by selecting accepted behaviors, i.e. selection of traces leading to Accept states is performed. TGV can generate both a complete test graph, containing all test cases corresponding to the test purpose, and individual test cases. To compute the complete test graph, the traces not leading to an Accept state are truncated if possible, and an Inconclusive verdict is added. Pass verdicts are added to traces that reach Accept. Fail verdicts are implicit for observations not explicitly present in the complete test graph. Finally, from the complete test graph a *controllable* subgraph is extracted. This controllable subgraph no longer has states that offer the choice between stimuli and observations, or that offer the choice between multiple stimuli. In the controllable subgraph each state offers either a single stimulus, or one or more observations. If the result should be a single test case, it can be derived from the complete test graph, by making similar controllability choices.

TGV does most of the steps in an *on the fly* manner, and here on the fly means the following. The steps of the algorithm are executed in a lazy (demand driven) way, where earlier steps are driven by the demand of the later ones, to avoid doing work in earlier steps that will not be used by later ones. So, it is not the case that each step is run to completion, after which the complete result of the step is passed on to the next step. This use of on the fly should not be confused with the use of the words on the fly for the other tools like Lutess, Lurette or TorX: there it refers to continuously alternating between generation of a test step, and execution of the test step (after which the next test step is generated, and executed, and the next, etc.).

Tool Interfaces

To interface with the outside world (both for specification and test purpose, and for generating formalism in which the resulting test suite is presented) TGV uses APIs, which makes it quite flexible.

The specification languages accepted by TGV include LOTOS (via CADP [FGK+96], needs an additional file specifying input/output partitioning), SDL (either using the simulator of the ObjectGéode SDL tool, or using the commercial tool TestComposer [KJG99] that integrates TGV), UML (using UM-LAUT [UMLb, HJGP99] to access the UML model) and IF (using the simulator of the IF compiler [BFG+99]). TGV also accepts specifications in the other formats/languages made accessible by the open/caesar interface [Gar98] (API) of the CADP tool kit. It is also used as test generation engine in AGEDIS (see Section 14.2.13). The resulting test suite can be generated in TTCN or in one of the graph formats (.aut and .bcg) of CADP.

Summary

TGV is a powerful tool for **ioco**-based test generation from various specification languages. New specification languages or test suite output formats can relatively easy be connected thanks to the open APIs TGV uses. The main contribution of TGV lies in the algorithms that it implements, and in its tool architecture.

TGV uses test purposes to steer the test generation process; coming up with the "right" test purposes to generate the tests envisioned may take some iterations.

A limitation lies in the non-symbolic (enumerative) dealing with data. Because all variables in the specification are instantiated for all possible values (or, in the case of infinite data types, for a finite subset), the resulting test cases can be big and therefore relatively difficult to understand (compared to what could be the result if more symbolic approaches would be used).

Related Papers

- Tool Overview: [JJ02]
- Related Tools: [FGK+96, Gar98, UMLb, HJGP99, KJG99, BFG+99]
- Underlying Theory: [Tre96c]
- Case Studies: there is an overview in [JJ02]

14.2.11   TorX

Introduction

In the late nineties the Dutch academic-industrial research project *Côte de Resyste* [TB02] had as its goal to put into practice the (**ioco**) testing theory that had been developed so far. The way to put the theory in practice was by developing a testing tool based on this theory, by applying the tool to case studies to evaluate it, and by forcing it to progress by offering it new challenges. The case studies ranged from toy examples to (not too big) industrial applications [BFdV+99, dBRS+00, dVBF02].

The testing tool result of this project is **TorX**. TorX is both an architecture for a flexible, open, testing tool for test derivation and execution, and an implementation of such a tool. The **ioco** implementation relation that it implements has already been discussed in Chapter 7 (page 173) and will be revisited when we discuss the test generation algorithm of TorX.

TorX can freely be downloaded [Tor], its license file lists the conditions for use.

Test Generation Process

TorX is both a testing tool architecture and an implementation of a testing tool. With "TorX" we refer to the testing tool; unless we explicitly say otherwise. TorX can be used both for test generation and test execution. TorX, the architecture, offers two modes of operation: *batch* and *on the fly* generation and execution. TorX, the testing tool, does not implement all possibilities offered by the TorX architecture.

Batch Mode The batch mode works with two separate phases in which first a test suite is generated, and then executed. The batch generation mode has not been implemented in TorX. The batch execution mode is implemented as on the fly generation and execution (as discussed below) from degenerate models (that only describe a single test case). The batch execution mode has been used to execute test cases generated by TGV [dBRS+00].

On the Fly Mode The on the fly generation and execution mode works in a different way. In this mode generation and execution go hand in hand. Or, phrased differently, during execution the test suite is generated on demand (comparable to lazy evaluation in functional programming languages). As soon as a test step is generated, it is also executed, after which the next test step is generated, and executed, etc. The advantage of this approach is that it is not necessary to expand the complete state space during test generation – in on the fly mode TorX expands only that part of the state space that is needed for a particular test run. How a particular test run is chosen will be discussed below.

Implementation Relation TorX implements the implementation relation **ioco** [Tre96c]. The underlying model is that of Labeled Transition Systems (LTS). The visible labels (L) in the LTS are partitioned into stimuli (I) and observations (U). There are two special labels (actions), τ and δ. τ represents the internal (invisible) action. δ represents *quiescence*, the observation of the absence of output (the observation that there is nothing to observe). How quiescence is actually observed depends on the (interfaces to) the implementation. For message-based interfaces, usually a timer will be set, and when no message is received by the time the timer expires, it is assumed that no message will come at all (until a further stimulus is send), so quiescence has been observed. In other cases there may be other ways to observe quiescence.

The main characteristic of **ioco** is that for any trace of actions allowed by the specification, the output (in $U \cup \delta$) that can be observed from the implementation after doing this trace is allowed in the specification. The assumption is that the implementation is input-enabled, which means that it will be able to consume all stimuli that the tester sends to it. On the other hand, the tester is able to consume all outputs (observations) of the implementation.

TorX Algorithm From the above we can come to an informal description of the algorithm implemented in TorX. We do a walk through the state space of the specification. For now we assume a random walk, so whenever the algorithm has to make a choice, the choice will be made randomly; in the next section we will discuss how the walk (rephrased: how the choices made by the algorithm) can be guided by test purposes (test case specifications). Elsewhere it has been discussed why random walks are effective in protocol validation [Wes89] – similar reasons apply to testing. For a comparison of random walk and other approaches for testing see Section 11.4 (page 301).

If the specification contains nondeterminism, we simply follow multiple paths at the same time.

We start at the initial state of the specification. We choose between stimulating and observing. If we want to observe, we get an observation from the SUT and check if it is allowed by the specification. If we want to stimulate, we derive a stimulus from the specification (if there are multiple possibilities, we choose one) and we send the stimulus to the implementation. We do this until we find an inconsistency (an observation from the implementation was not allowed by the specification), or until we have done a given (pre-decided) number of test steps. In the first case, we give the verdict *fail*, in the second, the verdict *pass*.

If we make the choices randomly, so each test run maps to a random walk in the specification, and we do this often enough, and/or long enough, we should be able to find all errors (provided the random walks are indeed random so we do not consistently ignore certain parts of the specification). The case studies done with TorX, where choices were made randomly, seem to confirm this. Note that for this approach we do not need a test purpose – however, we cannot control the random walk through the specification, other than by deciding on the seed for the random number generator.

Test Purposes To have more control over which part of the specification is walked, the TorX architecture, and the tool, allow the use of a test purpose. In TorX, a test purpose can be anything that represents a set of traces over $L \cup \{\delta\}$. During the random walk, the random decisions to be made (the choice between stimulating and observing, and, when stimulating, the choice of the stimulus from a set of them) are constrained by the traces from the test purpose. If the test purpose traces allow (at a certain point) only stimuli, or only observations, the choice between stimulating and observing is decided by the test purpose. In the same way, the choice of a stimulus is constrained by those that are allowed by the test purpose. If (at a certain point in the random walk) the intersection of the actions allowed by the test purpose and the actions allowed by the specification becomes empty, the test purpose has not been observed (we have *missed* it [VT01]) (there is one exception to this which we will discuss below). This corresponds to the traditional *inconclusive* verdict. On the other hand, if we reach the end of one of the traces of the test purpose, we have successfully observed (*hit* in [VT01]) (one of) the behavior(s) of the test purpose.

The one exception mentioned above is the following. One can think of a test purpose that triggers an error in an erroneous implementation. The last action of such a test purpose can be the erroneous output (observation) triggered by the test purpose. Running such a test purpose with the specification and an erroneous implementation will yield a *fail* verdict, but the last (erroneous) output of the implementation will be the last action in the test purpose, so the test purpose is *hit*, even though the intersection between the (correct) behavior specified in the specification and the incorrect behavior described in the test purpose is empty. The result of the execution will be the tuple $\langle fail, hit \rangle$.

As implicitly suggested above, correctness (pass and fail verdicts) and the success (hit or miss) of observing a desired (or undesired) behavior are treated as two different dimensions, such that when a test purpose is used, the verdict of TorX is a tuple from $\{pass, fail\} \times \{hit, miss\}$, which is slightly more informative than the traditional singleton verdict from $\{pass, fail, inconclusive\}$.

Tool Interfaces

In principle, TorX can be used for any modeling language of which the models can be expressed as an LTS. As much as possible, it tries to connect to existing tools that can generate an LTS for a particular specification language. So far, it has been connected to the Caesar Aldebaran Development Package (CADP, offering .aut, LOTOS) [FGK+96], to Trojka (a program, based on SPIN [Hol91], that derives test primitives from systems described in Promela) [dVT98]. to the LTSA tool (giving access to the language FSP) [MK99], and to the LOTOS [ISO88] simulator Smile [EW92, Eer94].

In this way, TorX can be used with specifications written in the languages LOTOS, Promela [Hol91] and FSP, and in a number of the formats made available via the open-caesar interface of the CADP tool kit [Gar98] (Aldebaran (.aut), binary coded graphs (.bcg)).

For the test purposes TorX uses a special regular expression-like language and tool, called jararaca. The tool jararaca gives access to the LTS (i. e. the traces) described in the test purpose. Also other languages can be used to describe test purposes; initial experiments have been done by describing test purposes in LOTOS and accessing the LTS via the connection to CADP.

The interfaces between the components in TorX are documented, so the user is free to connect his or her own specification language to TorX (as long as it can be mapped onto an LTS).

TorX expects the user to provide the connection to the SUT, in the form of a program (glue code) that implements the TorX Adapter interface. In this interface abstract input and output actions are exchanged. It is the users responsibility to provide in the glue code the encoding and decoding functionality, and the connection to the SUT.

Summary

TorX is a flexible, open tool that is based on the **ioco** implementation relation. It allows (non-deterministic) specifications in multiple languages (in principle any language which can be mapped on an LTS can be connected). It can use but does not need test purposes. It has an open, well defined interface for the connection to the SUT; however, the end user has to provide the glue code to make this connection.

Related Papers

- Tool Overview: [TB02]
- Input Languages: [ISO88, BB87, Hol91, MK99]

- Related Tools: [FGK+96, Gar98, dVT98, MK99, EW92, Eer94]
- Underlying Theory: [Tre96c, VT01]
- Case Studies: [BFdV+99, dBRS+00, dVBF02]

14.2.12 STG

Introduction

STG (Symbolic Test Generator) [CJRZ02] has been developed at IRISA/INRIA Rennes, France. It is a tool that builds on the ideas on which TGV and TorX are based, and adds *symbolic* treatment of variables (data) to these. In TorX and TGV all variables in the specification are instantiated for all possible values[10]. In contrast, variables in STG are treated in a symbolic way, leading to symbolic test suites that still contain free variables, which are then instantiated during test execution. So, STG supports both generation of symbolic test suites, and execution of these.

STG is a relatively new tool. The theory underlying it has been published in 2000 [RdBJ00]; the tool was reported first in 2002 [CJRZ02]. STG has been used to test simple versions of the CEPS (Common Electronic Purse Specification) and of the 3GPP (Third Generation Partnership Program) smart card. The results of the CEPS case study are summarized in [CJRZ01]. STG was used to automatically generate executable test cases, and the test cases were executed on implementations of the systems, including mutants. Various errors in the source code of the mutants were detected.

At the time of writing, STG is not publicly available (this may change in the future).

Test Generation Process

As mentioned in the introduction, STG supports both test generation, and test execution, where the test cases that are generated and executed are symbolic. It implements a symbolic form of **ioconf** [Tre96a] but without quiescence (for an overview of implementation relations see Section 7.4, page 178).

STG takes as input a specification in the form of an (*initialized*, discussed below) Input Output Symbolic Transition System (IOSTS) and a test purpose and produces from these a symbolic test case. Such a symbolic test case is a reactive program that covers all behavior of the specification that is targeted by the test purpose.

For execution, the abstract symbolic test case is translated into a concrete test program that is to be linked with the implementation. The resulting executable program is then run for test execution, which can yield three possible results: Pass, Fail or Inclusive, with their usual meaning.

An IOSTS differs from an LTS in the following way. An IOSTS has specification parameters and variables. Actions are partitioned into input, output and

---

[10] Except when Promela, or LOTOS with Smile, are used in TorX.

internal actions. With each action a signature (a tuple of types) is associated (the types of the messages exchanged in/with the action). An IOSTS does not have states, but (a finite set of) locations. A state is now a tuple consisting of a location and a valuation for the variables and parameters. Transitions now not only associate a source (origin) location with a destination location and an action, but also have a boolean guard, a tuple of messages (the messages sent/received in the action), and a set of assignments. An IOSTS can be *instantiated* by providing values for its parameters. An instantiated IOSTS can be *initialized* by providing an initial condition that assigns a value to each variable. In a *deterministic* IOSTS the next state after execution of an internal action only depends on the source state, and the next state after execution of a valued input or valued output action only depends on the source state and the action. Rephrased, once we know which action is executed, we also know the successor state. So, in an initialized, deterministic IOSTS we resolve the free variables as we execute the actions, i.e. for each transition, the free variables that it introduces are resolved (bound) when the action is executed. Free variables in subsequent behavior only originate from actions that still have to be executed – once these actions are executed as well, also those free variables are bound.

The authors of the STG papers define test purposes as follows (note that this differs from the definition in the glossary, but is relatively close to the test purposes of TGV discussed in Section 14.2.10 on page 417). The test purpose is also an IOSTS. This IOSTS can refer to parameters and variables of the specification to select the interesting part of the specification. A test purpose has two specially named locations: *Accept* and *Reject*. Reaching the Accept location means that the test purpose has been successfully passed. The Reject location is used to discard uninteresting behavior. The user does not have to write a "complete" test purpose, because it is implicitly completed, as follows. For each "missing" outgoing action a self loop is added, and for each outgoing action with guard G, a transition to Reject, with guard $\neg G$, is added. Nevertheless, Rusu et al. mention that according to their experience with the tool TGV, the development of "good" test purposes is an iterative process in which the user writes down a test purpose, examines the result, modifies the test purpose and repeats until a satisfactory result is obtained [RdBJ00].

From a specification and a test purpose a test case is generated by taking the product of the specification and the test purpose. We will skip the details here, and just mention the steps in test case generation. In a first step, the product of specification and test purpose is computed. From this product, the internal actions are removed, which may involve propagating guards of internal actions to the nearest observable actions. In a subsequent step, nondeterminism is eliminated, to avoid that verdicts depend on internal choices of the tester. The last step consists of selecting the part that leads to the Accept locations, and of adding transitions to a new location *fail* for "missing" observation actions. The result should be an initialized, deterministic, observation-complete, sound test case. These properties are proven in the paper.

The test case can still contain parameters and variables, these are filled in during test execution. How the parameters and variables are selected is not discussed in the papers describing STG. Formally, a test case is an initialized, deterministic IOSTS together with three disjoint sets of locations *Pass*, *Inconclusive* and *Fail*.

During test generation and test execution, STG has to do symbolic evaluation of guards, to be able to prune actions that have conflicting guards. If STG would have implemented (a symbolic form of) **ioco**, it would not only have been important for efficiency, to avoid exploring parts of the specification that are "unreachable" anyway, but also for correctness, to be able to mark the right states as quiescent.

The IOSTS model is defined such that it can be easily translated to the input languages of tools like the HyTech model checker [HHWT97] and the PVS theorem prover [ORSvH95]. Rusu et al. demonstrate this by showing how HyTech and PVS can be used to simplify generated tests to prune parts that are unreachable due to guards that contain conflicts [RdBJ00]. STG has been used in conjunction with PVS for combined testing/verification [Rus02].

Tool Interfaces

The tool STG [CJRZ02] can be seen as an instantiation of the approach to symbolic test generation described by Rusu et al. [RdBJ00].

STG accepts specifications and test purposes in the LOTOS-like language NTIF [GL02], a high-level LOTOS-like language developed by the VASY team, INRIA Rhône-Alpes. The specification and the test purpose are automatically translated into IOSTS's, after which the test generation process produces a symbolic test case, which is also an IOSTS. For test execution the symbolic test case is translated into a C++ program which is to be linked with the (interface to the) SUT. The test case C++ program communicates with the (interface to the) SUT via function calls.

For each action of the test case, the (interface to the) SUT should implement a function that has the same signature as the action, such that the messages of the action are passed as parameters to the function.

STG uses OMEGA [KMP+95] for symbolic computations (to compute satisfiability of guards). As a consequence, the data types that are allowed in the specification are limited to (arrays of) integers, and enumerations.

Summary

STG builds on existing theory and tools (algorithms) of mostly TGV, and adds symbolic treatment of data to this, which results in smaller and thus more readable test cases than achieved with the enumerative approaches used so far.

The ability to do symbolic computation (e.g. to detect conflicts in predicates, such that behavior can be pruned) is non-trivial. STG uses the tool OMEGA to do this. The capabilities of OMEGA (what data types does it support) are reflected in the input language for STG.

Related Papers

- Tool Overview: [CJRZ02]
- Input Language: [GL02]
- Related Tools: [KMP+95, ORSvH95, HHWT97]
- Underlying Theory: [RdBJ00]
- Case Studies: [CJRZ01, CJRZ02]

14.2.13   AGEDIS

Introduction

AGEDIS [AGE] (Automated Generation and Execution of test suites for DIstributed component-based Software) was a project running from October 2000 until the end of 2003. The consortium consisted of seven industrial and academic research groups in Europe and the Middle East, headed by the IBM Research Laboratory in Haifa. The goal was the development of a methodology and tools for the automation of software testing in general, with emphasis on distributed component-based software systems. Starting from a specification expressed in a UML-subset, basically the TGV algorithms are used for the test generation. Another tool which partly found its way into AGEDIS is GOTCHA from IBM.

Test Generation Process

An open architecture was a fundamental principle of the AGEDIS design. Therefore interfaces play a vital role. The main interfaces are as follows:

- Behavioral modeling language
- Test generation directives
- Test execution directives
- Model execution interface
- Abstract test suite
- Test suite trace

The first three constitute the main user interface while the last three are more of internal interest. In the following the actual instantiations of the interfaces are shortly introduced.

AML (AGEDIS Modeling Language), which is a UML 1.4 profile, serves as the behavioral modeling language. Class diagrams together with associations describe the structure of the SUT. The behavior of each class is fixed in a corresponding state diagram, where Verimags language IF serves as the action language. Attached stereotypes are used to describe the interfaces between the SUT and its environment. A full description of AML is available at the AGEDIS web page [AGE].

Test purposes are given in the test generation directives which are modeled with system level state diagrams or MSCs. Also simple default strategies are possible. As TestComposer (which also builds on TGV), AGEDIS allows here to use wildcards to specify abstract test purposes which are completed by the tool in every possible way to allow abstraction from event-ordering. AGEDIS offers five predefined strategies to generate test purposes:

- Random test generation
- State coverage – ideally cover all states of the specification
- Transition coverage – ideally cover all transitions of the specification
- Interface coverage – ideally cover all controllable and observable interface elements
- Interface coverage with parameters – like interface coverage with all parameter combinations

The abstract specification parts like classes, objects, methods and data types have to be mapped to the SUT. This, and the test architecture itself, is described in an XML schema which instantiates the test execution directives interface.

The model execution interface encodes all the behavior models of the SUT, i.e. the classes, objects and state machines. Again IF is used to do so. See also here the web site for a detailed description.

Both the abstract test suite and test suite traces are described by the same XML schema. A test suite consists of a set of test cases, zero or more test suite traces and a description of the test creation model. Each test case consists of a set of test steps which in turn may consist of stimuli (method calls), observations, directions for continuation or verdicts. Several stimuli may occur in one test step and they can be executed sequentially or in parallel. The common verdicts pass, fail and inconclusive are possible. Alternative behavior within a test case is used to model nondeterminism. Test cases can also be parameterized to be run with different values and other test cases can be evoked within a test case. AGEDIS is restricted to static systems, i.e. objects can not be created or destructed during test case execution.

The AGEDIS tools are written in Java. Currently, the specification modeling in AML and the creation of test generation directives are only supported using the commercial Objecteering UML Editor together with an AML profile. The designed model can be simulated with an IF-simulator. Test generation based on the model and the test generation directives is done by the TGV algorithms.

AGEDIS also allows an execution of the generated test suite. The execution framework is called Spider. It is able to execute test cases on distributed components written in Java, C or C++. Spider takes care of the distribution of the generated test objects. Furthermore it controls the whole test run, i.e. providing synchronous or asynchronous stimuli, observing the outputs, checking them against the specification and writing the generated traces in the suite as XML files. Two tools are provided for test analysis, a coverage and a defect analyzer. The first one checks for uncovered data value combinations and method calls. It generates new test cases to cover these missed parts and a coverage analysis report. The defect analyzer tries to cluster traces which lead to the same fault and generates one single fault-trace out of them to ease the analysis when many faults are detected.

Tool Interfaces

As outlined above, AGEDIS is based on a specification given in AML. It is able to execute the generated test suite in a distributed environment with components written in Java, C or C++. Widely accepted formats like XML and the open interface structure of AGEDIS offer easy access to extensions and variations of the framework.

Summary

AGEDIS is currently not obtainable for academic use. The list of available publications is also rather small, basically only the motley selection from the AGEDIS website is accessible. Decisions regarding further propagation and succeeding projects will determine the progression of the toolset. The main strength of AGEDIS is its open and user friendly embedding of the theory in a UML-based environment. A related modeling concept is the U2TP (UML Testing Profile) which is about to find its way into UML 2.0 and will therefore gain a great attention by the test-tool vendors. See chapter 17 for more information. Furthermore it is based on UML 2.0 concepts and in that sense better equipped to become the favored test-related modeling language in the UML community. Nonetheless the open concept of AGEDIS may pay off and further development (e.g. regarding dynamic object behavior, converge to U2TP) can make AGEDIS an interesting UML-based testing environment for distributed systems.

14.2.14   TestComposer

Introduction

TVEDA and TGV constitute the basis of TestComposer, which was commercially released in 1999 as a component of **ObjectGeode** by Verilog. In December 1999 Telelogic acquired Verilog. Together with the Tau toolset, in which AutoLink is the test component (also Telelogic), they form the two major SDL toolsets. TVEDA was integrated in the test purpose generation process. Some extensions were applied to facilitate the processing of multi-process specifications (TVEDA was only designed for single-processes). The test case generation was taken over by the TGV algorithms.

Test Generation Process

The whole testing process is based on an SDL specification of a (possibly distributed) system. Any block within the SDL specification can be identified as the SUT. The channels which are connected to the block become PCOs (Points of Control and Observation). In the case of a distributed system TestComposer is restricted to a monolithic tester, i.e. one tester takes care of the whole testing process.

To generate a test suite a set of test purposes is needed, which represent sequences of input and output events exchanged between the SUT and its environment (black box testing). Two modes are offered to generate them. In the interactive mode the user can define test purposes with the help a SDL-simulator. Guiding a stepwise simulation of the system one can construct a sequence of interest.

Based on the SDL specification the tool can automatically complete a set of test purposes based on a state space exploration to achieve a given percentage of system-coverage. As in AutoLink the coverage unit is an observational step, i.e. a sequence of events connecting two states in which the only possible actions are an input stimuli or a timeout of an internal timer (so called stable states). A test purpose corresponds to such an observational step which again corresponds to one or many basic blocks, i.e. blocks of SDL instructions without branching. It is the same approach as the one from AutoLink and hence there is the same problem with nondeterminism, see 14.2.15.

In addition to depth-first and supertrace algorithms TestComposer offers a breadth-first search to traverse the reachability graph. To narrow the search it is possible to exclude parts of the SDL specification (like transitions, processes or whole blocks) from the state exploration. To automatically generate postambles which bring the SUT back to a suitable idle-state, TestComposer allows to manually define boolean expressions that signalizes such idle states and therefore allow a search back to them. Test purposes are automatically partitioned into preamble, test body and postamble. Observer processes can also be used as abstract test purposes. They do not have to be transformed into MSCs like in AutoFocus. Such an observer can be used to prune paths of the state space or generate reports when a given condition holds.

A test purpose does not have to cover a complete sequence of observable events, it can be incomplete (respectively abstract). TestComposer computes the missing events needed to bind the specified ones together. There can be many ways to complete the abstract sequence which allows an abstract test purpose to describe the set of all possible completions. This is especially useful when the order of signals does not matter which is a common situation when different communication channels are involved.

To generate test cases, paths in the SDL specification have to be found which correspond to the test purposes. Here come the TGV algorithms into operation which perform also the postamble computation.

Tool Interfaces

SDL specifications serve as inputs. An API (Application Programming Language) allows the user to construct interfaces with arbitrary test specification languages. A module for TTCN is already included.

Summary

TestComposer is very similar to AutoLink. Some of the comparative results of [SEG00] will be addressed in 14.3.

Related Papers

- Case Studies: [SEG00]

14.2.15   AutoLink

Introduction

autolink [KGHS98, SEG00] is a test generation tool that has been developed at the Institute for Telematics in Lübeck and is based on the former work of the SaMsTaG project [GSDH97]. It has been integrated in (added to) the Tau tool environment of Telelogic in 1997.

AutoLink has been used extensively within the European Telecommunications Standards Institute (ETSI) for the production of the conformance test suite for the ETSI standard of the Intelligent Network Protocol (INAP) Capability Set 2 (CS-2).

Attention has been given to the production of readable output (TTCN) – the resulting test suite is not something that is just to be given to a (TTCN-) compiler to produce an executable test program, it is also to be meant to be amenable to human apprehension.

Test Generation Process

AutoLink uses test purposes to guide the test generation process. It does this by exploring the state space of the specification. These test purposes can be written by hand, obtained by simulation, or generated fully automatically. The automatic generation of test purposes is based on state space exploration, where the decisive criterion is to get a large structural *coverage* of the specification. Each time a part of the specification is entered that has not been covered by a previous test purpose, a new one is generated. The basic unit of coverage is a single symbol of the specification. To avoid generating many identical test cases, larger sequences of coverage units that lead from one stable state to another are examined. A stable state is a state in which the system either waits for a new stimulus from its environment or the expiration of a timer. Such sequences are called observation steps. Each automatically generated test purpose contains at least one observation step. In most cases, an observation step includes a stimulus from the tester and one or more responses from the SUT.

Due to non-determinism, a single observation step can correspond to multiple parts of the specification, i.e. one cannot be sure that an observation step indeed tests the intended part of the specification. Schmitt et al. claim that the computation of Unique Input/Output sequences would solve this problem, but that in practice it is most of the time not necessary to prove that a test includes UIO sequences [SEG00] .

To explore the state space, both depth-first and supertrace algorithms are offered. The user can also provide a path from the initial state to a point from which automatic exploration is done. Also other strategies/heuristics are implemented.

AutoLink also allows test generation using observer processes. The observer process runs in parallel with the specification, and has access to all internal elements of the specification. This seems similar to the power of the test purposes in other test tools discussed here like e.g. STG, TGV, TorX, Lutess. However, the observer process has first to be transformed to a set of message sequence charts, because AutoLink requires (complete) Message Sequence Charts for test purposes.

AutoLink can also generate test cases from only test purposes, so, without specification. Schmitt et al. mention that this can be beneficial, because it is not always possible to simulate a test purpose [SEG00]. One reason for this could be that the specification is incomplete and only partial specifications are available, and thus the behavior one wants to test is not present in the (partial) specification [KGHS98]. We did not study this in detail, but we are worried about the correctness (soundness) of the resulting test cases, because, how can you be sure that the tests that you generate in this way will not reject a correct implementation?

Once the test purposes are available, the test generation from them is divided in three steps. In the first step the data structures for a new test case are initialized, the test purpose is loaded, etc. In the second step the actual state space exploration is performed, and a list of *constraints* is constructed. Constraints are definitions of data values exchanged between the tester and the SUT; one could say that these definitions impose constraints on, for example, values for message parameters, hence the name which originates from TTCN terminology. Basically, for each send and receive event in the test case a constraint with a generic name is created. Usually, these generic names are not very informative. Therefore, a mechanism has been added to AutoLink to allow the user to control the naming and parameterization of these constraints via a configuration file in which rules can defined using a special language. Finally, in the third step the data structure for the resulting test case may be post processed, and identical constraints are merged. Usually, this greatly reduces the number of constraints, and this increases the readability of the generated test suite.

AutoLink supports a generic architecture for distributed testers. The user has to explicitly state synchronization points in the test purpose, after which coordination messages can be generated automatically.

Schmitt et al. state that AutoLink uses on-the-fly generation in the same way as TGV.

Tool Interfaces

AutoLink accepts specifications in SDL. Test purposes should be provided as Message Sequence Charts (MSCs). The resulting test suite is generated in the form of TTCN-2. The constraints (see above) are provided (generated) into separate files, which can be modified by the user before the complete TTCN test suite is generated.

A TTCN compiler can then be used to translate the generated TTCN into an executable test program.

Summary

AutoLink is an (industrial strength) test generator to generate (readable) TTCN test suites from SDL specifications. The test suite generation is guided by test purposes that can be supplied by the user, or also generated fully automatically. Unfortunately, a theoretical underpinning of the algorithms used in AutoLink was not present in the papers we studied. Fortunately, it turned out to be possible to reverse engineer the conformance relation definition for AutoLink [Gog01]. AutoLink has been used in a number of case studies.

Related Papers

- Tool Overview: [KGHS98, SEG00]
- Related Tools: [GSDH97]
- Underlying Theory: [Gog01]

14.3   Comparison

Many aspects can be addressed when comparing tools. Below we name just a few, grouped by separating theoretical aspects from more practical ones.

- Theoretical aspects
  - Are the test generation algorithms based on a sound theory? How do these theories relate to each other?
  - Which error-detecting power can be achieved theoretically?
  - What is the time/space complexity of the underlying algorithms?
  - Is the theory suited for compositional issues? Can models be congruently composed?
  - Is the theory suited for distributed issues? Is it possible to generate several distributed testers or is only a monolithic one possible?
  - How is data handled by the formalisms? Is the theory restricted to simple sets of actions or is there support for complex/symbolic data, e.g. infinite domains? How is this handled?
  - Is there a notion of time? Is it possible to guarantee time constraints during the test execution (which is necessary for real time systems)?
  - Can it deal with nondeterministic SUTs, or only with deterministic ones?
  - Can it deal with non nondeterministic specifications?
- Practical aspects
  - Which error-detecting power can be achieved practically (case studies)?
  - Is it only possible to generate test suites or also to execute them on a real SUT?
  - How user-friendly is the tool? Is there a GUI facilitating the usage? Are graphical models used (e.g. UML)?
  - Which are the supported test case specifications?
  - How difficult is it to create a suitable input (e.g. defining test purposes)? Are many parameters needed and does the tool help in setting them?

- Are the interfaces open or proprietary? Are widely accepted standards used?
- To which operational environment is the tool restricted?
- What practical experience is there (what test cases are performed) with the tool?

We will focus on two comparison approaches that we found in the literature: *theoretical analysis* and *benchmarking*. In a theoretical analysis, one compares the test generation algorithms implemented in the tools, and tries to deduce conclusions from that. In benchmarking, one does a controlled experiment, in which one actually uses the tools to find errors, and tries to deduce conclusions from that.

Below we discuss each of the approaches in more detail. In the discussion we will mainly focus on theoretical and practical error-detecting power. Regarding the other aspects, we have tried to give as much information as possible in the individual tool descriptions, and leave it to the interested reader to follow the references.

14.3.1   Theoretical Analysis

Goga analyzes the theory underlying the tools TorX, TGV, AutoLink and PHACT [Gog01]. For PHACT, the theory underlying the Conformance Kit is analyzed; it implements a UIO test generation algorithm. Goga maps the algorithms used in the tools onto a common theory in order to compare the conformance relations that they use. To be able to do so, he also constructs the conformance relation for AutoLink. Then, by comparing their conformance relations, he can compare their error-detecting power. The rough idea is that, the finer the distinction is that the conformance relation can make, the more subtle the differences are that the tool can see, and thus, the better its error-detection power is. For the details we refer to [Gog01].

The result of this comparison is the following (here we quote/paraphrase [Gog01]). TorX and TGV have the same error-detection power. AutoLink has less detection power because it implements a less subtle relation than the first two (for certain kinds of errors TGV and TorX can detect an erroneous implementation and AutoLink can not).UIO algorithms (PHACT) have in practice less detection power than AutoLink, TGV and TorX. In theory, if the assumptions hold on which UIOv is based, it has the same detection power as the algorithms of the other three tools. These assumptions are:

A) the specification FSM is connected
B) the specification FSM is minimal
C) the number of states of the implementation is less than or equal to the number of states of the specification.

Because in practice assumption C) rarely holds, we conclude that in practice the three other algorithms are in general more powerful than UIOv algorithms.

These theoretical results coincide with the results obtained with the benchmarking experiment discussed below.

Regarding the other theoretical aspects we have tried to give as much information as possible in the tool descriptions. Not all facts (especially complexity issues) are known for every tool and some aspects are still actual research topics. Examples of the latter are compositionality, complex data and real time issues.

14.3.2   Benchmarking

The benchmarking approach takes the view that, as the proof of the pudding is in the eating, the comparison (testing) of the test tool is in seeing how successful they are at finding errors. To make comparison easier, a controlled experiment can be set up. In such an experiment, a specification (formal or informal) is provided, together with a number of implementations. Some of the implementations are correct, others contain errors. Each of the tools is then used to try to identify the erroneous implementations. Ideally, the persons doing the testing do not know which implementations are erroneous, nor do they know details about the errors themselves. Also, the experience that they have with the tools should be comparable (ideally, they should all be expert users, to give each tool the best chance in succeeding).

In the literature we have found a few references to benchmarking or similar experiments.

Other disciplines, for example model checking, have collected over time a common body of cases or examples, out of which most tool authors pick their examples when they publish results of their new or updated tools, such that their results can be compared to those of others.

In (model-based) testing this is much less the case, in our experience. Often papers about model-based testing tools do refer to case studies done with the tools, but usually the case studies are one-time specific ones. Moreover, many of the experiments done for those cases cannot be considered *controlled* in the sense that one knows in advance which SUTs are erroneous. This does make those experiments more realistic – which is no coincidence since often the experiments are done in collaboration with industry – but at the same time it makes it hard to compare the results, at least with respect to error-detecting power of the tools.

Of course, there are exceptions, where controlled model-based testing experiments are conducted and the results are published. In some cases those experiments are linked with a particular application domain. For example, Lutess has participated in a Feature Interaction contest [dBZ99].

Also independent benchmarking experiments have been set up, like the "Conference Protocol Benchmarking Experiment" [BFdV+99, HFT00, dBRS+00] that we will discuss in more detail below. The implementations that are tested in such an experiment are usually much simpler than those that one has to deal with in day-to-day real-life testing – if only to limit the resources (e.g. time) needed to conduct or participate in the experiment. There is not much one can do about that.

Conference Protocol Benchmarking Experiment The Conference Protocol Benchmarking Experiment was set up to compare tools where it counts: in their error-detecting capability. For the experiment a relative simple conference (chat box) protocol was chosen, and a (reference) implementation was made for it (hand written C code). This implementation was tested using "traditional means", after which it was assumed to be correct (we will refer to this one as the correct implementation from now on).

Then, the implementor of the correct version made 27 "mutants" of it by introducing, by hand, small errors, such that each mutant contains a single error that distinguishes it from the correct version. The errors that were introduced fall in three groups.

The errors in the first group are introduced by removing a program statement that writes an output message. The effect of these errors is visible as soon as the (now removed) statement is reached during program execution.

The errors in the second group are introduced by replacing the condition in an internal check in the program by "true". The effect of these errors may not be immediately visible.

The errors in the third group are introduced by removing a statement that updates the internal state of the program. The effect of these errors is not immediately visible, but only when a part of the program is reached where the absence of the preceding internal update makes a difference. So, the error has to be triggered first by reaching the code where the internal update has been removed, and then the error has to be made visible by reaching a part of the program where the erroneous internal state causes different output behavior.

Then, the informal description of the protocol, the source of the implementation and the mutants, and a number of formal specifications were made available via a web page.

Finally, several teams took a model-based testing tool (usually, their own, that they mastered well), reused, or adapted a given specification, or wrote a new one, if necessary, tried to devise test purposes, and tried to detect the incorrect implementations, without knowing which errors had been introduced to make the mutants. To our knowledge, this has been done with the following tools (and specification languages): TorX (LOTOS, Promela); TGV (LOTOS); AutoLink (SDL); Kit/PHACT (FSM). We will briefly mention the results here; for the discussion of the results we refer to the papers in which the results have been published.

TorX and TGV With TorX and TGV all mutants have been detected[11]. With TorX all mutants were found using the random walk testing strategy, so no test purposes were used. With TGV it turned out to be pretty hard to come up (by hand) with the right test purposes to detect all mutants; one mutant

---

[11] That is, all 25 mutants that could be detected with respect to the specification that was used. It turned out that two mutants needed behavior outside the specification to be detected. As a consequence, these mutants are **ioco**-conformant with respect to the specification used.

was detected by a test purpose that was not hand written, but generated by a random walk of a simulator. Elsewhere it has been discussed why random walks are effective in protocol validation [Wes89] – similar reasons apply to testing. For a comparison of random walk and other approaches for testing see Section 11.4 (page 301).

AutoLink With AutoLink not all **ioco**-erroneous mutants were detected: it detected 22 mutants. Here, most likely, the lack of complete success had to do with the test purposes that were hand written[12]. Only after the experiment, the (inexperienced) user of the tool learned of the possibility to let the simulator generate a set of test purposes fully automatically, so unfortunately this feature has not been evaluated.

Kit/PHACT With Kit/PHACT the fewest mutants (21) were detected. Here, no test purposes were needed, but a test suite was automatically generated using the partition tour strategy.

All test cases of the test suite were executed as one large single concatenated test case, without resetting the implementation between individual test cases. This actually helped to detect errors. In some of the test cases an error was triggered in one test case, without being detected there. However, some of the mutants contained an error that made the synchronizing sequence fail to do its job, which thus failed to bring the implementation to its initial state. As a result, it happened that much later, in a different test case, the implementation responded erroneously as a consequence of the error triggered much earlier.

Analysis of the mutants that were not detected showed that in two cases, due to the error, the mutant contained a state not present in the specification. Such non-detected errors are typical for the partition tour method used by PHACT [HFT00]. One other mutant was not detected because the decoding function in the glue code to connect to the SUT was not robust for incorrect input and thus the test execution was aborted by a "core dump". The remaining undetected mutant was not found, because only the explicitly specified transitions were tested. A PHACT test suite that tests all transitions (which is a possibility with PHACT) would probably detect this mutant.

Conclusions with respect to the Benchmarking Approach Performing a controlled benchmarking experiment allows comparison of testing tools where it counts: in their error-detecting capability. However, doing a fair comparison is difficult, because it can be hard to find experimenters that have comparable experience with the tools and specification languages involved. As a consequence, the absolute comparison results should be taken with a grain of salt.

Such benchmarking can also provide information about some of other practical aspects that we listed. For example, the experimenters in the Conference

---

[12] To be more precise, obtained by taking the traces of manual simulation of the specification.

Protocol Benchmarking Experiment also gave estimations of the amount of time invested by humans to develop specifications and test purposes, versus the computer run time needed to generate and execute the tests [BFdV$^+$99, dBRS$^+$00]. Such estimations give some idea of the (relative) ease with which errors can be found with the respective tools.

14.4   Summary

System vendors focus more and more on the quality of a system instead of increasing functionality. Testing is the most viable and widely used technique to improve several quality aspects, accompanying the entire development cycle of a product. Motivated by the success of model-based software development and verification approaches, model-based testing has recently drawn attention of both theory and practice.

System development tools reflect this tendency in many ways, automatic model-based generation of test suites has incipiently found its way into practice. TestComposer and AutoLink are the dominating design tools in the SDL community. The UTP serves the need for test support within UML-based software development, and Microsoft's AsmL is another example for the effort major companies make to benefit from the existing theory.

But whatever theory is chosen as a basis, none of them can belie the dominating problem of system complexity. Even simple behavioral models like FSMs or LTSs can generally not be specified or exploited exhaustively. In that sense testing is always a David vs. Goliath struggle, even when pragmatical approaches were chosen.

Nevertheless it is worth the effort of improving the theory w.r.t. practicability. Furthermore there are system criteria which are not treated satisfactorily yet, like real-time constraints or symbolic data, e.g. infinite data domains.

Although automatic testing is still in the fledgling stages it can already be exerted successfully to improve the quality of real world systems. Further research is needed to improve and ease its application. It is a promising field where formal methods find their way into practice.

15 Case Studies

Wolfgang Prenninger[1], Mohammad El-Ramly[2], and Marc Horstmann[3]

[1] Institut für Informatik
  Technische Universität München
  prenning@in.tum.de
[2] Department of Computer Science
  University of Leicester, UK
  mer14@le.ac.uk
[3] Institut für Verkehrssicherheit und Automatisierungstechnik
  Technische Universität Braunschweig
  m.horstmann@tu-bs.de

15.1 Introduction

In this chapter, we review and analyze some of the significant case studies published on the application of model-based testing. We focus on case studies done in industrial contexts in order to evaluate how model-based testing is applied in practice and how far it is applied. But we also review a few proof of concept and benchmarking case studies. We review case studies on model-based testing of processors [DBG01, SA99, FKL99], smart cards [PPS+03, CJRZ01], protocols [KVZ98, BFdV+99], Java and POSIX [FHP02]. This list is not exhaustive; but it is a good representation of the range of applications, methods and tools used in the available model-based testing case studies. There could be other case studies which we did not detect or have been published recently.

We shall observe that all case studies follow a similar process for model-based testing. Thus, we structure the chapter as follows: Sec. 15.2 gives the big picture and provides a fast overview of the abstract model-based testing process which all case studies have in common. Sec. 15.3 describes the different application domains and their characteristics where model-based testing has been applied. Sec. 15.4 through Sec. 15.8 document in detail which techniques and methodologies are used by the different approaches to instantiate the different phases of the abstract process. Sec. 15.9 summarizes and concludes this chapter.

For technical foundation about test case generation we refer to Chap. 11 and 12. For a thorough overview about test generation tools we refer to Chap. 14.

15.2 The Abstract Process

By studying the reviewed case studies listed in Sec. 15.1 and described in Sec. 15.3 we observe that the underlying process is very similar. All case studies start with an abstract formal test model which is derived either (semi-)automatically out of system development models or manually out of the systems requirements specification. In the later case, manual validation of the test model against system requirements specification should be done first in order to find possible errors

M. Broy et al. (Eds.): Model-Based Testing of Reactive Systems, LNCS 3472, pp. 439–461, 2005.
© Springer-Verlag Berlin Heidelberg 2005

in the test model, otherwise the derived test cases may be significantly flawed. Together with an equally formal test specification, where the selection criteria of how to choose test cases is covered, the automatic generation of test cases can be performed. After that, a concretization of test cases has to be done. This is because the derived test cases are on the same abstraction level as the test model but have to be executed on concrete System Under Test (SUT) level. At last, the test evaluation is done either on SUT level or on abstract test case level.

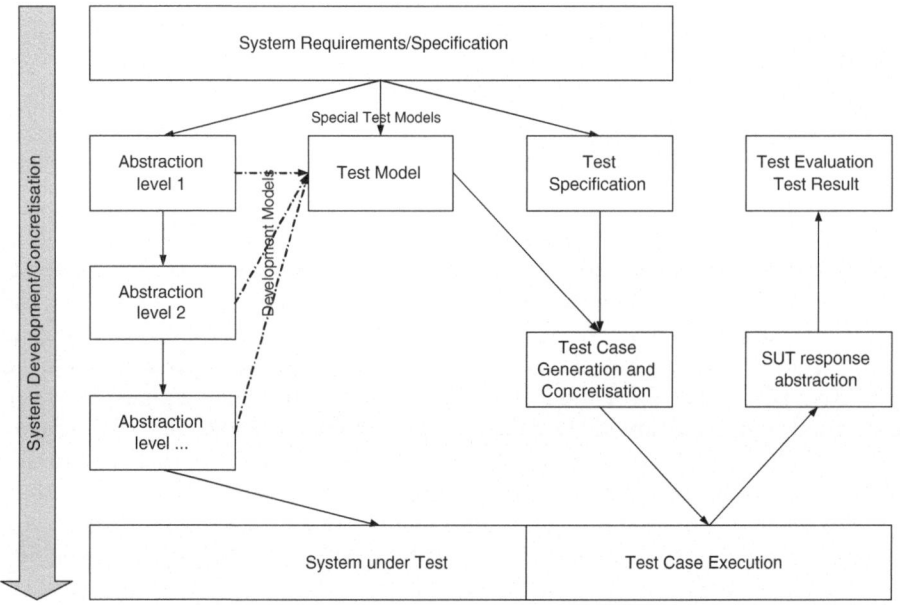

Fig. 15.1. The Abstract Process of Model-based Testing

Fig. 15.1 shows the different activities and results of model based testing in the context of the SUT development process. The arrow at the left side symbolizes the progress in development and concretization of the SUT, where different abstraction layers can exist between the system requirements specification and the SUT. The test model can either be based on the requirement specification by building a special test model or it can be derived out of a certain abstraction level in case that a suitable model exists. A second interface between system development and model based testing is the test purpose that should be defined in the requirement specification and has to be formalized into a test specification. After generation and concretization of test cases the third interface is given by applying the test cases to the SUT and executing them. In the following paragraphs the activities and results of model based testing will be described in an abstract manner before the other sections will explain them in more detail.

Test Model Since the term test model is not part of the glossary it will be introduced here. We call the abstract formal behavior model of the SUT, which is used in conjunction with the test specification to derive test cases, a test model (also abstract test model or sometimes if the context is defined only model). In principle there are two ways for deriving test models. The first is to benefit from an existing model, whether it is a formal specification or a system development model of the SUT. For example, usually in the case studies that involve a hardware SUT, a design model is available that is then abstracted to build a test model. The abstraction becomes necessary due to constraints given by the test case generator and the potential available test model traces, which have to be limited. The second way is to build the test model manually, based on information from the natural language specification of the SUT. For both cases a validation of the test model has to be assured. Sec. 15.4 illustrates both ways in more detail.

Test Specification Besides a test model, a test specification is necessary in order to direct the test case generation. It has two aims, first to define formally what will be tested and second to restrict the amount of resulting test cases. The test specification defines which of the potential available test model traces will form the test suite. Based on a test purpose, which can exist in different degrees of formalization, the test specification has to be in an operational state in order to use it in conjunction with the test model as input for the test case generator. The type of test specification for the considered case studies can be categorized into functional, structural or stochastic specifications (cf. also Chapter 11):

- Functional specifications represent a set of environment behaviors or use cases in order to constrain the behavior of the test model to certain functionalities.
- Structural specifications can be applied to decomposed components, where different coverage criteria starting from simple statement coverage up to path coverage are available.
- Stochastic specifications select test cases by random or by a probability distribution and have been observed to be also useful in some fields, e.g. in partition testing [Nta98].

Test Case Generation Once the test model and test specification are defined, test case generation can be started which results in a test suite. A test case is generated by constructing an execution path of the test model which complies also to the restrictions of the test specification. This process continues until all specified test cases are found.

Test Case Instantiation In order to concentrate on the essential aspects of the SUT to be verified and to handle, in a lot of cases, the state explosion problem of the considered SUTs, the test models have to be on an abstract level. Thus the generated test cases/test suites are also at this abstraction level. Before the execution of these test cases, a concretization of the previously done abstractions has to be performed. Abstraction mechanisms used in the considered case studies are

- Functional Abstraction
- Data Abstraction
- Temporal Abstraction
- Communication Abstraction

which are described in more detail in Sec. 15.7.

Test Execution and Test Evaluation The aim of the test execution and test evaluation is to detect whether a test case passes or not. To determine this, the expected and actual behaviors have to be compared. While the expected behavior is specified in the test model, the actual behavior is determined by the SUT. The problem of test evaluation is that expected and actual results are at different abstraction levels. To overcome this difference, two possibilities exist:

- Evaluation on the level of the SUT makes it necessary to translate the complete test consisting of inputs and outputs to the level of the SUT.
- Evaluation on the level of test model implies to apply again abstraction mechanism and to perform the test evaluation at the abstract level.

15.3 Application Domains

This section provides an overview of some of the domains that have reported success in applying model-based testing. Naturally, applications that involve systems described in formal specifications are better candidates for model-based testing. However, in other cases, model-based testing was applied successfully to systems with natural language specifications. The case studies covered in this chapter include testing processor architectures, protocols, operating systems, part of the Java language specification and smart card applications. In this section, we elaborate on each of these domains.

Processor Architectures Typically, processor architectures are described at a high level of abstraction using a hardware description language, e. g., Verilog HDL or VHDL. Languages like VHDL offer different levels of abstraction for hardware design. The highest is the behavior abstraction level, which is similar to writing a computer program in a high level language. One more concrete level down is the dataflow abstraction. At this level, the design is described in terms of how data move through the system. At the heart of most digital systems today are registers. Dataflow abstraction describes how information is passed between registers in the system. Thus this level is called Register Transfer Level (RTL). The lowest and third level of abstraction, structure abstraction. It is used to describe a system in terms of its components, e.g., gates, flip-flops, etc. Designers simulate and debug the system at the behavior level and then use a top-down approach to refine and debug the system gradually down to the structure level.

Different studies in model-based testing of hardware systems use hardware specifications at different levels of abstraction as the basis for modeling the SUT. In [DBG01] for example, the SUT was the Store Data Unit (SDU) block of ST100, a high performance digital signal processor (DSP). The SDU is a block of the Data Memory Controller that is responsible of storing data to memory. In this study, the design was described at behavior abstraction level in MμALT (Modeling Micro-architecture Language for Traversal), which is a VHDL-based language.

In [SA99], the SUTs were two general-purpose microprocessors. The first is GL85, which is a model of the Intel 8085 processor, designed in VHDL. The second is ARM, which is a downscaled model of the commercial ARM-2 processor. ARM is designed in Verilog. In both cases, the SUT was described at the RTL level.

What is common in these studies is that a full formal description of the SUT is available at one level or another. This opens the door to introduce some automation during model abstraction via a tool that can take the formal description as input and partially infer a state machine from it. This idea was implemented only in [SA99].

In [FKL99], an Architecture Validation Suite (AVS), which is a suite of tests to verify the compliancy of an architecture implementation against the architecture specifications, was built for IBM PowerPC processor architecture. Like the cases above [SA99, DBG01], a formal description of PowerPC architecture was built. But additionally, a behavioral simulator that implements PowerPC architecture was used as a reference model. The simulator is a software that simulates a PowerPC processor. So, given a certain state for the processor and an input, the simulator determines the next state and the output. The basic idea of using the simulator is that a behavioral simulator can be viewed as a formal, correct and complete representation of the architecture. This is because very early in the verification phase, the simulator was used heavily, debugged and tested. Hence, generating an AVS for the SUT can be reduced to generating an AVS for the simulator.

Protocols A protocol is a formal description of the message formats and the rules that two devices or parties must follow to exchange those messages. A number of case studies were done for automatic generation of test suites for protocols. In [KVZ98], the SUT was an implementation of the cache coherency protocol of Bull's CC-NUMA (Cache-Coherent Non Uniform Memory Architecture) multiprocessor architecture. Bull's CC-NUMA consists of a scalable interconnection of modules; the memory is distributed among different modules. Each module contains a set of processors. The key feature of Bull's CC-NUMA architecture is its distributed directory-based cache coherency protocol, which uses a Presence Cache and a Remote Cache in each module.

In [BFdV$^+$99], the SUT was an implementation of the Conference Protocol described in [Pir95]. The conference provides a multicast service, resembling a chat box, to the users participating in a conference. A conference is a group of users that can exchange messages with all conference partners in that conference.

The partners in a conference change dynamically, as users are allowed to join and leave a conference. Multiple conferences can exist at the same time, but a user can participate only in one conference at a time. This experiment [BFdV+99] is one of a few benchmarking experiments done to compare model-based testing tools using the conference protocol [BFdV+99, HFT00, dBRS+00]. A summary of these experiments is introduced in Sec. 14.3.2.

Operating Systems and Language Specifications In these applications [FHP02], model-based testing was applied to automatically generate test cases for parts of the Portable Operating System Interface (POSIX) System API and Java exception handling standards. POSIX defines an operating system interface and environment based on UNIX operating system. This interface supports application portability at the C language source level. The operational behavior of the Java exception handling facility is part of the Java language specification [GJS97]. In both case studies, the available specification of the standard (POSIX System API and Java) was an English language document, with some diagrams and tables. This document specifies the valid stimuli to the software and its excepted responses.

Smart Cards Smart cards are becoming increasingly popular and used in telephones, transportation, banking, and healthcare transactions, and so on. A smart card is basically a one-chip computer with microprocessor, RAM, ROM, EEP-ROM, a serial interface for communication with a terminal, e.g., an ATM or a cellular phone, and possibly a coprocessor for cryptography operations. Smart card applications are command-driven. The card processor reads a command from its input channel, executes it and transmits the response via its output channel.

A number of studies on model-based testing for smart card applications were conducted with documented success. For example, in [CJRZ01], a study on automated test generation for a feature of the CEPS e-purse specifications is reported. CEPS (Common Electronic Purse Specification) is a standard for creating interoperable multi-currency smart card e-purse systems [CEP00]. It was developed by the leading smart card industry players to leverage existing investments by making use of the banks' current payment infrastructure.

In [PPS+03], a case study was performed on the WAP Identity Module (WIM), which is used in the wireless access protocol extension of the GSM standard [CEP95] for cellular phones to provide transport level security, digital signatures and, in general, public key cryptography. The WIM is deployed as a smart card application. Both the CEPS and WIM specifications are written in English language.

15.4   Building an Abstract Model of the System Under Test

This section is an overview of the different methods used for abstracting the SUT into a test model. Obviously, abstraction methods vary depending on whatever system specifications are available. The more formal the system specifications are, the better the chance of automating this step. In the following, we divide the case studies reviewed in this chapter into two categories. The first includes the case studies where the test model was driven from formal specification and/or implementation description of the SUT. The second includes the case studies where the model was driven from natural language specifications of the SUT.

Modeling from Formal Specifications and Implementation Descriptions In the cases where a formal description of the system was available, e.g., the processor architectures tested in [DBG01, SA99], a test model of the SUT could be extracted manually or semi-automatically. In [DBG01], the MμALT design is translated manually to an FSM in GOTCHA Definition Language (GDL) which formed the test model [HN99]. GOTCHA (an acronym for Generation of Test Cases for Hardware Architectures) is a tool for generating an abstract test suite from a test model of the SUT and a set of testing directives, i.e., a test specification. It is part of IBM GOTCHA-Spider (previously known as GOTCHA-TCBeans) [IBM]. The GOTCHA compiler builds a C++ file that contains the embodiment of the FSM.

In [KVZ98], the test model is a formal specification in LOTOS (Language of Temporal Ordering Specifications) of Bull's CC-NUMA cache coherency protocol. The LOTOS specification was manually produced, while the multiprocessor architecture was under design. Then the specification was checked using the CADP (CAESAR/ALDEBARAN Development Package) verification tools, a toolbox with formal verification capabilities. The specification consisted of 2000 LOTOS lines where 1000 lines describe the control part and the other half defines the ADT (Abstract Data Types) part. The specification was debugged and verified with appropriate formal verification techniques and then used as a test model of the SUT. This model is then input to TGV (Test Generation with Verification technology). TGV is a prototype for the generation of conformance test suites for protocols (cf. Sec. 14.2.10). TGV translates the LOTOS test model into an Input Output Labeled transition System (IOLTS).

In [SA99], a test model of the microprocessor was built semi-automatically. A microprocessor RTL model is usually partitioned into datapath and control parts. Abstracting the whole complex processor into a single FSM is infeasible. So, since products of events in control modules are sources of hard-to-discover bugs, the authors focused on modeling control logic. The control part in the initial design is generally implemented using an FSM that encapsulates the description of control behavior. The states of this FSM are naturally selected as candidates of the test model states. The authors developed an algorithm to extract these states automatically from the microprocessor RTL Verilog or VHDL design. The idea is to construct a control flow graph for the Verilog or VHDL description, with multi-way branching statements taken as decision nodes. Then, the algorithm selects variables in the controlling expressions of the decision nodes that are assigned values in all branches as candidate state variables. The candidate variables that change most frequently are selected as control state variables.

The control flow graph is searched for the transition conditions between the different states of each selected variable.

The abstract FSM has the same timing as the original processor. It encapsulates the same control behavior in terms of the movement of instructions through the processor. In complex designs, the control might consist of multiple communicating FSMs. In this case, the FSM that changes most frequently, its states are chosen as the primary control states. For example if the cycle of an FSM needs 5 cycles of another FSM, then the control states of the later are chosen as the primary control states. Other variables or inputs, which affect the control state transition or the datapath operation at different states of the FSM, are selected and added to the FSM manually.

In [FKL99], an Architecture Validation Suite (AVS) was generated for IBM PowerPC architecture using Genesys. Genesys is a directed-random test generator developed by IBM for verification of various processor architectures. Genesys dynamically generates tests using a generation-simulation cycle for each instruction. Genesys needs two models of the SUT. The first is a formal test model of the SUT. This is created manually from PowerPC architecture books. The second is an implementation description in the form of a behavioral simulator for the SUT, which is used to predict the results of instruction execution. Result prediction is done automatically by just running the simulator to execute the desired instruction sequence. However, the simulator itself was built manually.

Modeling from Natural Language Specifications In cases where the SUT was specified in natural language with no formal specifications, hand-built test models needed to be constructed. In [FHP02], this was done for parts of POSIX standard and Java exception handling facility. In both cases, the model was crafted as an FSM in GDL. At this stage, specification defects and inconsistencies were discovered.

In [CJRZ01], the test model was a hand crafted FSM for the part of CEPS that was tested, using IOSTS (Input-Output Symbolic Transition Systems). IOSTS is a modeling language for reactive programs with symbolic processing of variables, parameters and inter-process value passing. IOSTS is rather low level. So, using a higher level language that translates to IOSTS would ease the modeling process.

In [BFdV+99], the SUT is an implementation of the Conference Protocol described in Sec. 15.3. The purpose of this study was to study the feasibility of automatic test derivation and execution from a number of formal specifications and different test execution approaches. Test generation was done with TorX, a generic model-based testing environment. TorX allows plugging in different test generation tools, which accept models of the SUT in different formal languages (cf. Sec. 14.2.11). Since this is a benchmarking experiment, three formal models of the same SUT were built for this study in LOTOS , SDL and PROMELA, each to use with a different test tool. More details of this experiment were introduced in Sec. 14.3.2.

In [PPS+03], the modeling language of AutoFocus was used to build a test model for the WAP Identity Module (WIM). AutoFocus is a tool for developing graphical specifications for embedded systems based on concise description techniques and a simple, formally defined clock-synchronous semantics, which makes it rather well suited for the command/response sequences of smart cards (cf. Sec. 14.2.4). A model in AutoFocus is a hierarchically organized set of time-synchronous communicating EFSMs which use functional programs for its guards and assignments.

Manual development of a test model for a SUT from natural language specifications is labor intensive. This raises the question of cost-effectiveness of applying model based testing in this case. However, if a decision is made to do it, manual modeling comes with an advantage. For the WIM, abstracting the textual requirements and transforming them into a deterministic, complete and executable model exposed some contradictions and ambiguities in the specifications.

To conclude this section, Tab. 15.1 classifies the reviewed case studies according to the type of specification used to build the test model and the abstraction method (manual or semi-automatic) used.

	Modeling from Formal Specifications and Implementation Description	Modeling from Natural Language Specifications
Manual Modeling	[DBG01] SDU of ST100 DSP [KVZ98] Cache Coherency Protocol [BFdV⁺99] Conference Protocol [FKL99] Power PC	[FHP02] POSIX/Java [CJRZ01] Smart Cards: CEPS [PPS⁺03] Smart Cards: WIM
Semi-automatic Modeling	[SA99] Microprocessors	

Table 15.1. The Specifications and Methods Used for Building an Abstract Model of the SUT

15.5   Test Specification

In order to obtain test cases from the test model, a test specification is required. The specification defines what is to be tested. The aim is to find a reasonable number of meaningful test sequences. As listed in Sec. 15.2 and defined in the glossary three main classes of test case specifications can be identified:

- Functional specification
- Structural specification
- Stochastic specification

Tab. 15.2 gives an overview of the used test specification classes in the considered case studies, which will be discussed in details in this section.

Functional Specification The idea of functional specifications is to extract test cases concerning certain functionalities of the SUT to be tested. This is achieved by focusing on a special part or a special view of the system. By doing so, the

	Functional specification	Structural specification	Stochastic specification
[BFdV+99] Conference Protocol			X
[CJRZ01] Smart Cards: CEPS	X	X	
[DBG01] SDU of ST100 DSP		X	
[FHP02] POSIX/Java	X	X	
[FKL99] PowerPC	X	X	
[KVZ98] Cache Coherency Protocol	X	X	
[PPS+03] Smart Cards: WIM	X	X	X
[SA99] Microprocessors		X	

Table 15.2. Test specification classes used in the reviewed case studies

number of possible test traces is reduced by defining additional functional constraints concerning the system itself or its environment. Functional specifications cover I/O relations which refer either to scenarios of specification documents as described in Philipps et al. [PPS+03] or other more special views that result from experience, like fault intensive known sections as described in Fournier et al. [FKL99]. In the majority of cases these requirements describe sequences which can be completed to a state diagram, for example. The state diagram on its own forms only one part of the specification, additional declarations about the traces to be generated are necessary, for instance a restriction of the path length. Otherwise, test cases of infinite size can be found. To overcome this problem, often a functional specification is used in conjunction with structural or stochastic test specifications. Functional specifications are used by three case studies [FHP02, KVZ98, PPS+03].

Structural Specification For the structural specifications, typical code coverage criteria can be used which are lifted to the level of the test model. The spectrum of coverage criteria varies from statement coverage [FKL99], state coverage [DBG01], the MC/DC criterion [PPS+03] up to path coverage [SA99] (for an overview about existing coverage criteria cf. Sec. 11.3). Regardless of how the test model is derived (SUT abstraction, manual modeling), the options of which coverage criteria can be used depend on the complexity of the test model. Those case studies where the resulting test model is already strongly tailored to main test purposes, e.g. by an additional functional test specification or by focusing on a special system part, use path coverage with a given trace length [KVZ98]. Other studies using complex test models have to use more simple criteria like state coverage [DBG01] or the MC/DC criterion [PPS+03]. If structural specification is used in combination with functional specification, then, it is important that the structural criteria are applied to the model of the system and the environment model with the defined constraints.

Stochastic Specification In Philipps et al. [PPS+03] additional stochastic specifications are applied to the result of structural specifications in order to reduce the number of test cases. Belinfante et al. [BFdV+99] use only this type of criterion. Stochastic test specifications can be equally distributed, e.g. every second test case of a randomly generated set will be chosen, or non-equally distributed following a certain distribution function, cf. also Sec. 11.2.

Formalisms used for test specifications In most of the considered case studies, the formalism used for the test specification and the formalism for the test model are identical. Here, we brief the list of formal notations used in the case studies.

- Conference Protocol [BFdV+99]: Since in this case study only stochastic test specifications are used where a random number generator selects the test cases, a special additional formalism is not necessary, but configuration parameters concerning input and output gates or the random number generator have to be defined.
- Smart Cards - CEPS [CJRZ01]: Test model and test specification are expressed in the Input/Output Symbolic Transition System (IOSTS) formalism.
- SDU of ST100 DSP [DBG01]: Here first the MμALT (Modeling micro-Architecture Language for Traversal) language is used. A coverage model is basically determined by adding special attributes to interesting signals or variables. These test constraints restrict the way targeted states are reached. Second, the test generation tool GOTCHA (Generator of Test Cases for Hardware Architecture) is used for generating test cases as execution paths to the state coverage task and continuing to a final state.
- POSIX/Java [FHP02]: GOTCHA and its definition language (GDL) are used to describe a set of coverage criteria and test constraints to form the test specification. As in [DBG01], GOTCHA is also used for test case generation.
- PowerPC [FKL99]: A tool named Comet which is developed at IBM is used. The definition of the coverage model is written in SQL.
- Cache Coherency Protocol [KVZ98]: In this case study different formalisms for test model and test specification are used. LOTOS is used for the test model. Automata in Aldebaran format are used for the test specification. Both are inputs for the test case generator TGV.
- Smart Cards - WIM [PPS+03]: The CASE tool AutoFocus is used where graphical description techniques that are loosely related to the notations of UML-RT form the test model and test specification. For test case generation, the test model and the test specification are automatically translated to CLP (constraint logic programming).
- Microprocessors [SA99]: FSMs where interesting control states and interesting events as state associative control signals are specified, from the test specification. The formalism used therefore is not mentioned.

15.6 Abstract Test Case Generation

This section covers the different methods used for test case generation in the case studies reviewed in this chapter, assuming that a test model of the SUT and a formal description of the test specification are available. Clearly, whenever existing tools are used, there is not much freedom in selecting a test case generation method, as the study is then constrained by the methods supported by the tool. All the methods used employ some search algorithm(s). The output of a test case generation algorithm is a suite of abstract test cases that still need to be instantiated as described in the next section. In the following we elaborate on the different methods used for test case generation in the case studies reviewed. We focus on the methods and tools not covered in Sec. 14.2.

In [SA99], the authors used their own system prototype for test generation. The prototype enumerates all the possible paths on the FSM (i.e. the test model) of the SUT of a given finite length. Despite the small size of the FSMs extracted in this case study, it is infeasible to enumerate all possible state transition paths from the initial state due to the presence of loops. Each generated path is an abstract test case, consisting of a sequence of processor instructions with different events at different stages. In this study, two types of abstract test cases were generated: snapshot and temporal test cases. In a snapshot test case the exact timing of events is considered, while in a temporal test case, only the order of events matters.

Abstract Test Case Generation Using TGV As indicated in [CJRZ01] and [KVZ98], TGV was used for abstract test case generation in these two studies. TGV outputs a test case DAG (Directed Acyclic Graph). The paths of this DAG represent possible system runs of the SUT. Detailed discussion of TGV is in Sec. 14.2.10.

Abstract Test Case Generation Using GOTCHA In [DBG01] and [FHP02], the process of test generation is automated by GOTCHA [HN99], which explores the state space described by the input GDL model. The test engineer has several alternative test generation strategies, including performing breadth-first search and coverage-directed search, from each of the start states. Coverage-directed search involves giving priority to exploring states that lead to new coverage tasks. Coverage is a measure of the completeness of a test suite, i.e., the percentage of a program exercised by the test suite. This will typically involve collecting information about which parts of a program are actually executed when running the test suite in order to identify which branches of the conditional statements have been taken. The most basic level of test coverage is code coverage testing and the most methodical is path coverage testing. A coverage task is a task specified in the test specification that the test suite must satisfy. This is done by including in the test suite a set of test cases that satisfy the task. Coverage-directed search aims to find paths through the FSM model that satisfy each coverage task. To do so, GOTCHA starts by constructing a search tree that explores the entire state space. This is done by traversing all the reachable states of the FSM model. After enumerating the entire reachable state space, a random coverage task is chosen from those that have not yet been covered or proved to be uncoverable. A test case is generated by constructing an execution path to the coverage task (state in this case) then continuing on to a final state. At the point when the recommended test length is exceeded or a final state is reached, the test is output. If the randomly chosen coverage task cannot reach a final state then no test is generated. GOTCHA outputs abstract test cases, each consists of a sequence of states.

Abstract Test Case Generation with Constraint Logic Programming In the case study of model-based test case generation for smart cards described in [PPS+03], Constraint Logic Programming (CLP) was used to compute the set of all possible execution traces of finite length. First, the test model developed in AutoFocus is translated into a CLP program. Second, the test specification is also translated into the CLP language and added to the CLP program of the model. Finally, a logic programming engine solves the program using depth-first search with backtracking and computes the set of all possible execution traces of the model up to a certain length. These traces are the abstract test cases. More details on the use of CLP for test case generation in this case study [PPS+03] were presented in Sec. 12.3.2. More details on AutoFocus are available in Sec. 14.2.4.

Abstract Test Case Generation Using Genesys In [FKL99], Genesys was used to generate an architecture validation suite for PowerPC architecture to be used for testing PowerPC implementations. Genesys is specifically designed for testing processor architectures.

The inputs to Genesys are a test model and a behavioral simulator for the SUT and a test specification. The test specification allows the incorporation of complex heuristic testing knowledge in the form of generation and validation functions coded in C by test engineers. These functions serve many purposes, e.g., they enable adjusting the probability distribution of the targeted test space. As a simple example, the result of zero for an ADD instruction is typically of special importance while its relative probability to occur randomly is practically inexistent. A generation and validation function can be implemented to inform the test generator that the result of zero is important, and should thus be generated with a reasonable probability. More generally, these functions can be used to give adequate weights to corner cases which otherwise would be occurring with negligible probability.

Genesys directly generates executable test cases by combining abstract test generation and concretization. Genesys outputs a test file, which consists of a sequence of instructions starting from a given initial state, and a section of expected results describing the expected values of the various processor resources.

Test case generation is done using depth-first search with backtracking and checking against validation functions. First, the test model has the PowerPC instructions modeled as trees at the semantic level of the processor architecture. An instruction tree includes the instruction's format and a semantic procedure at the root, operands and sub-operands as internal nodes and length, address and data types of each operand as leaves of the intermediate node representing this operand. Second, generation of an instruction instance is done by traversing the instruction tree in a depth-first order. Traversing a node involves invoking all the generation and validation functions associated with it.

Finally, to generate a sequence of instructions, the test generation procedure accepts the required number of instruction instances as input and activates the instruction tree traversal. It also interleaves instruction generation with instruction execution using the behavioral simulator. The intermediate processor state is checked after the new instruction instance has been executed and a decision is taken whether to include the new instance in the test or reject it. If the simulator state after an executed instruction is undesirable, then it is rejected and the state of the simulator is reverted.

15.7   Test Case Instantiation

Let us recall the following part of the model-based process described in Sec. 15.2: A test model together with a test specification is used to generate one or more test cases. Since the test model is an abstraction from the SUT the generated test cases are abstract, too. In order to be able to execute the generated test cases with the SUT they have to be instantiated. With this part of the process in mind we describe the following aspects in this section:

- What is the motivation for the abstract test models and what abstraction techniques are used in the literature?[1]
- What limitations for testing are implied by these abstractions?[1]
- What structures of test cases can be found in the literature?
- What methods are used to translate an abstract test case to a concrete one?

Note that the abstraction of the test model in respect to the SUT arises three times in the model-based testing process: firstly, when building the abstract test model, secondly, when bridging the abstraction gap between abstract test cases and the SUT by instantiating the test cases, and finally, when evaluating the test executions by comparing the abstracted system runs of the SUT with the expected ones of the test model.

15.7.1   Abstractions in the Test Model

The purpose of the test models is: to support the validation process and the verification process of the system under development. On the one hand the model is used to formalize and to validate the system's requirements. On the other hand the model serves as specification and is used to test a system's implementation in order to verify the implementations behavior. Due to these requirements the models abstract as far as possible from implementation details and concentrate on the main aspects of the system. In this section we summarize briefly the motivation for specifying abstract test models and we describe the different abstraction techniques which are used in the reviewed literature.

---

[1] the corresponding paragraph is partly taken from [PP04].

Motivations for the Abstractions The test models of the SUTs described in the literature are all abstractions of the SUTs. Note that the test model must be an abstraction and a simplification of the SUT because if not one could validate directly the SUT without spending extraordinary efforts to build and validate a model. Generally the description techniques for modeling are independent of the implementation languages of the SUTs. The models represent artifacts of the the SUT symbolically in order to be more human readable and comprehensible.

The most important motivation is probably that models are specified to support the validation process. Because the test models concentrate on the parts or certain aspects of the SUT that are to be verified, they are simpler and easier to understand than the whole complexity of the SUT. Hence they can be managed intellectually, validated by reviews and maintained more easily. Even formal methods like model checking or theorem proving are applicable to them sometimes. In other words, we get the confidence more easily that the model meets the requirements of the system and thus the model serves as an abstract reference implementation of the SUT.

Another important motivation is a technical one: generally the test generators suffer from the state explosion problem. In order to support efficient test case generation the models have to be as simple i.e. as abstract as possible.

Yet another aspect is that in some cases the models should be platform independent, i.e. independent from, respectively, the test framework, the simulation environment or the implementation language of SUT. This is achieved by modeling the SUT's artifacts symbolically and by building an adaptor which translates the abstract test cases to concrete ones (cf. Sec. 15.7.3). Hence the models can be used to test several implementations realized on different platforms because the model leaves unchanged and only the adaptor has to be adjusted. Clearly, in this case, platform-specific issues cannot be tested.

Functional Abstraction The purpose of functional (or behavior) abstraction is to concentrate on the "main" functionality of the SUT which has to be verified. This leads to an omission of cumbersome details in the test model that are not in the focus of the verification task.[2] By doing so the model often implements only parts of the complete behavior determined in specification documents, i.e., the model does not completely define the intended behavior of the SUT but models significant aspects only. In addition, functional abstraction supports the model-based testing process: if the SUT's functionality can be divided into independent parts, one can build a separate model for each part in order to verify each functionality separately. An obvious drawback is that only the modeled parts of the specification can be tested and that special care must be taken to detect feature interactions between different functionalities.

Examples for functional abstraction The case study described by Philipps and Pretschner [PPS+03] concentrates on testing the protocols between a smart card

---

[2] This does *not* necessarily mean that special cases are omitted—if these have to be tested, they have to be modeled.

and its environment, a terminal. Therefore the test model abstracts from the complex realization of all cryptographic functions implemented by a smart card. These functions and their responses are represented only symbolically by yielding data of type `encryptedData` when a command `encrypt(data)` is issued. No cryptographic computations are performed in the model. Instead, these computations are performed at the level of the test platform (cf. Sec. 15.8).

The approach described by Farchi, Hartman, and Pinter [FHP02] uses separate models for testing different functionalities of the POSIX standard. The first model was developed for testing the byte range locking interface `fcntl`. This interface provides control over open files in order to deal with processes which are accessing the files. The model restricts the POSIX standard by allowing the extension of a file only once. The paper mentions a second model which was developed for testing the POSIX `fork()` operation.

Other examples for partial modeling i.e. omitting parts of the behavior of the SUT in the test model are that the model does not determine its behavior in certain states for some input values, or the model abstracts completely from exception handling.

Data Abstraction The idea of data abstraction is to map concrete data types to logical or abstract data types in order to achieve a compact representation or a reduction of data complexity at the abstract level. A frequently cited example for data abstraction is to represent binary numbers with integers at the abstract level. However, this example changes only the representation of numbers but does not cause any information loss between the levels of abstraction in the sense that it is trivial to have translations in both directions. A common data abstraction technique with information loss is to represent only equivalence classes of concrete data values in the model. Examples that involve information loss are described below. As mentioned above the key of data abstraction is to construct a mapping between concrete and abstract data types and their elements. Since the abstract data types are used to specify the behavior of the model one test goal is that the operations performed by the SUT on concrete values are correctly implemented with respect to the (abstract) operations on abstract values in the model.

Examples for data abstraction In the case study described by Dushina et al. [DBG01], the SUT is the Store Data Unit (SDU) of a Digital Signal Processor (DSP). The behavior of the DSP depends heavily on the fill level of an SDU's queues. Therefore the status of a queue has been represented in the test model by the abstract data type `empty`, `valid`, `quasifull` or `full`. Then testing discovered a performance bug in the SUT because it turned out that the SDU fills its queues only to quasifull status and does not exploit the full capacity of the queues.

For smart card testing [PPS+03], a radical data abstraction was applied in the test model by abstracting from the file contents of a smart card. The files of the smart card were only represented by symbolic names in the model. This led to a heavy simplification in the model but on the other side it could only test if the fixed file lengths of the smart card conformed to the specifications.

Shen and Abraham [SA99], Philipps and Pretschner [PPS+03] apply another form of data abstraction. They abstract the data types of operands to equivalence classes in the model. For test case instantiation, these symbolic operands are substituted by concrete values which are randomly selected or determined by means of a configuration file.

Communication Abstraction The most prominent application of the communication abstraction principle is the ISO-OSI reference model. Here a complex interaction at a concrete level is abstracted to one operation or message at the more abstract level. At the abstract level, this operation is treated atomically. This is even though in general the corresponding operations at a concrete level can be interleaved with other operations. Using this abstraction principle, one can aggregate handshaking interactions or sequences of causally dependent operations to one operation at an abstract level. For test case instantiation these abstract operations can simply be substituted by the corresponding interaction. For building models, communication abstraction is often combined with functional abstraction.

Examples for communication abstraction In hardware verification [BCG+00] and processor testing [DBG01], a concrete aggregation of pin values, several consecutive signals of different buses, or recurring sequences of processor instructions are abstracted to one symbolic operation in the test model.

In protocol testing [KVZ98], causally dependent operations concerning the same transaction are collapsed into one atomic operation in the test model although the concrete representation can be interrupted by other operations.

Sometimes communication abstraction is combined with data abstraction: Philipps and Pretschner [PPS+03] abstract the concrete byte string commands of a smart card (represented by sequences of hex numbers) to symbolic and human readable messages in the smart card model.

Temporal Abstraction The idea of temporal abstraction is that only the ordering of events is relevant for modeling, i.e., the precise timing of events at the concrete level is deemed irrelevant. We consider abstractions in which the ordering of certain events is irrelevant—as used with partial order reductions—as communication abstractions.

One kind of temporal abstraction is that the test model and the SUT use different granularities of discrete time. Then the granularity of time at the abstract level is coarser than it is at the concrete level. Ideally, a mapping between abstract time steps and the corresponding intervals of lower level time steps is given. This can be a challenging task because in many cases one abstract step does not always correspond to a constant or predictable time interval at the concrete level. This form of temporal abstraction is often used in hardware verification and testing [DBG01, SA99, BCG+00, Mel88] by relating one clock cycle in the model to many clock cycles at the implementation level. Temporal abstraction can be effectively combined with communication or/and functional abstraction.

Another form of temporal abstraction is that the test model abstracts from physical time. For example, the concrete implementation may depend on using a timer of 250 ms duration. This timer is abstracted in the model by introducing two symbolic events—one for starting the timer, and one for indicating expiration of the timer. By doing so, the physical duration of the timer is abstracted away even if the duration of certain timers changes over runtime at the concrete level.

One might well argue that this kind of abstraction is the special case of a more general abstraction, namely abstraction from quality-of-service.

In Tab. 15.3 we summarize the abstraction principles which were used in the documented case studies. The table entry *yes* indicates that the abstraction principle was used in the case study and *no* indicates the opposite. We marked the entry with *?* if we could not find any hint if the abstraction principle was used or not. It turns out considerably that most of the case studies explicitly mentioned that functional abstraction and data abstraction was used.

	functional abstraction	data abstraction	temporal abstraction	communication abstraction
[DBG01] SDU of ST100 DSP	yes	yes	no	yes
[SA99] Microprocessors	yes	yes	yes	yes
[FKL99] PowerPC	yes	?	?	?
[PPS+03] Smart Cards: WIM	yes	yes	yes	yes
[CJRZ01] Smart Cards: CEPS	?	?	?	?
[KVZ98] Cache Coherency Protocol	yes	?	?	yes
[BFdV+99] Conference Protocol	?	yes	?	?
[FHP02] POSIX/Java	yes	yes	?	?

Table 15.3. Used abstraction principles

Limitations of the Abstractions It is crucial that the modeler is aware of the limitations, and therefore decides for the right trade off between abstraction and precision when building appropriate test models for testing the critical aspects of the SUT. There is an inherent complexity in real systems. If some of them are abstracted in the test model in the sense that it cannot be compensated afterwards by the test driver component there is no way to detect faults in the SUT concerning these abstractions. In the following we mention a few limitations and consequences.

Often enough, test models suffer from a more or less distinct and implicit "happy world assumption" which stems from functional abstraction. A typical example is that models assume that parameters of input messages or input operations are within allowed bounds or have the permitted length or arity. With the aid of such models, it is not possible to test the SUT's behavior if it receives messages with illegal parameters. For example, in the smart card domain an operation including its operands is represented by a byte string at the concrete level. In the test model, an operation and its operands are conveniently symbolized by a string (a name). With this kind of model, the behavior of the smart cannot be tested directly if it receives byte string which are for example one byte too short or too long, respectively. It is up to the test engineer to decide whether to cope with such illegal input at the level of the model, or at the level of the driver component.

Intense data abstraction can lead to information loss that cannot be coped with for test case generation. For example the smart card model developed by Philipps and Pretschner [PPS+03] abstracts completely from file contents, and symbolizes files and operations on them without any implementation in the model. Hence the contents of the files and their evolution over runtime could not be tested with this model. Only static properties like file length could be verified.

It is hard to detect feature interaction if functional abstraction is applied to build separate test models for testing distinct functionalities. For instance, Farchi et al. [FHP02] use separate models to test different operations of the POSIX standard. These models help to verify the correct functioning of these operations in a stand-alone manner, but do not help to verify the behavior of the whole SUT where these operations are used in combination. In other words unmeant behavior (bad feature interaction) of the SUT caused by combination of operations which were verified separately cannot detected by this approach.

Finally, problems can arise if temporal abstraction is intensively used in the test model. Obviously, in the domain of distributed real time systems a rigorous use of temporal abstraction can prohibit the detection of faults which stems from the sensitive interleaved timing behavior of the separate components. As a counterexample, Dushina et al. [DBG01] explicitly do not use temporal abstraction in their test model. In order to trace generated test cases and to check the expected performance a clock cycle in the test model corresponds exactly to a clock cycle in the real processor design.

15.7.2   Structure of Test Cases

A test case generated from the abstract test model and a test specification contains inputs for the SUT and expected outputs and observable states from the SUT. In the literature we find the different kinds of structuring a test case as follows:

Test case is a trace In most model-based testing approaches an abstract test case is a trace of the abstract test model. The test generator computes them according to the test specification. In the approach described by Philipps and Pretschner [PPS+03] it is trace of input and output signals, in other approaches [SA99, FKL99, DBG01, FHP02] it is a trace of the model's FSM containing actual states of input, output and internal variables. Overall, the trace describes inputs/stimuli for the SUT and expected outputs or observable states of the SUT for the verdict definition. Roughly, one abstract test case corresponds to one concrete system run of the SUT.

Test case is an automaton In the case studies described by Clarke et al. [CJRZ01] and Kahlouche et al. [KVZ98] an abstract test case is an automaton or a tree-like structure, respectively. Here, the paths in the automaton correspond to system runs of the SUT. Hence one test case describes an set of possible system runs of the SUT. The advantage of this approach is seen being able to encode nondeterminism in the test case, i.e. the SUT is partly allowed to choose the order in which the operations are executed.

Inner structure of test case Some approaches distinguish different parts of a test case. They distinguish between preamble, test body, verdict and postamble (synonyms are prologue, epilogue etc.):

- A *preamble* at the beginning of a test case initializes the SUT, i.e. after the preamble has been executed the SUT has reached the state being the origin for the actual test.
- The *test body* contains operations and stimuli corresponding to the actual test purpose.
- The *verdict* defines a criteria which determines upon outputs or observable states of the SUT if the test passes or fails. The verdict is often a part of the test body.
- The *postamble* at the end of the test case releases the SUT in a defined final state. For example the postamble prepares the SUT for the next test case or resets the SUT. Furthermore it may be used to check the inner state of the SUT by observing certain behaviors.

15.7.3   Translation of Abstract Test Cases to Concrete Test Cases

In Sec. 15.6 we described the generation of test cases. Since the generated test cases are abstract like the test model, i.e. significant information is missing in the generated test cases to be executable with the concrete SUT, the abstract test cases have to be concretized. For example, due to temporal abstraction on the one side an abstract test case contains no timing constrains but on the other side the behavior of the SUT depends on the timing of some events. Hence the precise timing of events has to be introduced in the test case. Due to this fact the model-based testing approaches use a component (we call it tc-translator) which translates the abstract test cases to concrete ones. Then the concrete test cases are applicable to the test platform of the SUT which is, respectively, a simulation environment, a test framework or directly the SUT itself. In other words the tc-translator's task is to bridge the abstraction gap between the test model and the SUT by adding missing information and translating entities of the abstract test case to concrete constructs of the test platform's input language.

For example, if the data type values of an operation's operand are abstracted to equivalence classes in the test model, the tc-translator randomly selects a concrete and type-correct operand for that operation [SA99]. Some model-based testing approaches use a configuration file or table to configure the tc-translator [PPS+03, FHP02, SA99]. This table contains the translation relation between abstract entities (states, operations etc.) of the model and concrete instructions for the SUT's test platform. By doing so, the tc-translator can easily be adjusted for different test platforms. Often one operation in the model is a macro for the tc-translator and is substituted by many instructions at concrete level (communication abstraction). Furthermore the table may specify how to determine the precise timing of operations in a concrete test case if the test model abstracts from timing issues.

Other approaches pre-process the abstract test case before they translate them. For example, Dushina et al. [DBG01] remove all variables of the abstract test sequence not corresponding to inputs of the SUT from the generated test sequence. Furthermore they extend the test sequence with reset instructions before it translated in micro code.

15.8   Test Execution and Test Evaluation

In general, a simulation environment or a test framework (we call it test platform) of the SUT executes and evaluates the concrete test cases. A test case is evaluated to the verdicts *pass* or *fail*. Pass means that SUT conforms with the abstract test model restricted to the behavior specified by the executed test case. Fail means the reverse, i.e., an error was detected during test case execution. Clarke et al. [CJRZ01] introduce in addition to pass and fail a third verdict called *inconclusive*. Inconclusive means that test execution reached a point where no error has occurred but the test purpose cannot be satisfied any more.

Test evaluation is based on a abstraction/concretization relation between the traces of the abstract test model and the concrete system runs of the SUT that has to be determined. None of the reviewed papers defines this relation explicitly. Only Belinfante et al. [BFdV$^+$99] state that it is important to have it but do neither describe it nor declare it. Nevertheless this relation is indicated implicitly in the literature by the description of the applied test evaluation method. We found the following approaches:

- The approach of Farchi et al. [FHP02] translates the complete abstract test case consisting of inputs and expected outputs or observable states of the SUT. The abstract inputs are translated to concrete stimuli of the SUT. The abstract outputs and states are translated to executable verification statements (verdicts) which decide if the output of the SUT conforms with the test model or not. Thus the evaluation of the test is done at the concrete level within the concrete test case.
- The approaches of Philipps et al. [PPS$^+$03] and Dushina et al. [DBG01] translate only the inputs of the abstract test case to concrete level. These concrete stimuli are injected in the SUT by the test platform. The test platform monitors the outputs of the SUT, abstracts them to the abstract level of the test model and compares them with the expected outputs encoded in the abstract test case. Hence the test evaluation in done at the abstract level by comparing the abstracted SUT outputs with the expected output of the test model.

- Kahlouche et al. [KVZ98] describe a special case which does not fit in any of the previous two. Here, the SUT is stimulated with inputs and the observable behavior of the SUT is monitored and saved completely during test execution. Then the monitored trace is translated to the abstract level. Since in this approach the abstract test case has a tree-like structure, the test is evaluated to pass iff the monitored trace is a branch of the test case structure.

As stated above, the abstraction/concretization relation is only indicated in the literature. The main part is hidden in the mechanisms which concretizes the abstract test cases or abstracts the monitored behavior, respectively. There is no information about what advantages each of the approaches has, e.g., concerning scalability or performance.

15.9   Conclusion

In this chapter we reviewed eight case studies from different domains applying model-based testing mostly in an industrial context. In conclusion, we make four important observations.

First, application of model-based testing is motivated by the fact that real world systems (SUTs) are getting more and more complex. Currently, most systems are tested in an unstructured way by manually written test cases. Due to the increasing complexity, it is getting more and more difficult to achieve sufficient test coverage by this approach effectively. Additionally, test suites are growing huge. For example, in [FKL99], the Architecture Validation Suite (AVS) developed for PowerPC architecture consisted of about 87,000 test cases for the 32-bit design and 150,000 test cases for the 64-bit design. More general, it is getting too hard to validate systems against their requirements directly and effectively.

Second, we observed that all case studies follow a common abstract process. The process builds an abstract test model of the system's behavior, which incorporates only the crucial aspects of system in an abstract way. Due to the reduction of complexity in the test model, validating the test model is considerably easier and more effective than directly validating the complex SUT. Then, by means of test case specification, generation, concretization, execution and evaluation, the behavior of the SUT is verified against the abstract test model. This approach leads to a structured test process and enables wide and measurable test coverage. For building abstract test models, we identified four classes of abstraction techniques that were applied in the case studies.

Third, we observed that model-based testing starts to be broadly applied in industry in the domain of processor verification. This stems from the fact that there is a well-understood development process with well-defined abstraction levels (e.g., from VHDL down to RTL) in this domain. Actually, this enables partial automation of the abstract test model building. In the other case studies the test models are built in an ad-hoc manner due to the lack of well-defined abstraction levels in their domains. Nevertheless these case studies are promising proofs of concept.

Finally, we observed that none of the case studies provides results in terms of an rigorous assessment of model-based testing. They do not contain any statements about effectiveness and costs in comparison with traditional testing techniques or other quality assurance techniques like reviews or inspections.

Overall the case studies revealed that a common model-based testing process is settled and the model-based technology for generating test cases is mature enough for industrial application. Yet for a full scale industrial application, domain specific abstraction methods integrated in the development process have to be developed in order to support model-based testing effectively and the assessment of model-based testing has to be investigated.

Acknowledgments: The authors are grateful to Alexander Pretschner for valuable discussions and comments and to the anonymous referees for their insightful remarks and suggestions.

Part V

Standardized Test Notation and Execution Architecture

The previous parts of this volume dealt mainly with test case generation. We have presented methods or finite-state machines and for transition systems and reviewed tools and case studies. In this part, we give two examples for formal test notations. While the two description methods have been designed for specifying test cases manually, it is in general possible to use these notations also for automatically generated test cases, which gives the link to the previous parts.

Chapter 16 gives an introduction to TTCN-3, the Testing and Test Control Notation, which is a standardized language to formulate tests and to control their execution.

In Chapter 17, the standardized UML 2.0 test profile is explained. It provides means to use UML both for system modelling as well as test case specification.

16 TTCN-3

George Din

Fraunhofer Fokus – Institute for Open Communication Systems
din@fokus.fraunhofer.de

16.1 Introduction

This chapter presents **TTCN-3**, the Testing and Test Control Notation, which is the most used technology in the protocol testing field. Many of the previous chapters concern the problem of how to create tests for a system we want to test. In this chapter we consider the problem of test execution. Test execution comprises the following activities: test data is applied to a SUT, the behavior of the SUT is monitored, and expected and actual behaviors are compared in order to yield a verdict.

Before presenting details about test execution with TTCN-3 we consider it is worth presenting shortly the evolution of TTCN-3. The creation of TTCN-3 was an incremental process starting from a version which was adequate only for protocol testing and finishing with a standardized, full-featured language applicable for many testing domains.

16.1.1 Evolution of TTCN-3

The design process of TTCN language is presented by ITU (International Organization for Standardization) in [ITU02]. TTCN was first published in 1992, as an ISO standard. Since then, TTCN language has been intensively used to specify tests for different technologies like Global System for Mobile Communication (GSM), Digital Enhanced Cordless Technologies (DECT), Inteligent Network Application Protocol (INAP), Integrated Services Digital Network (N-ISDN, B-ISDN). This first version of TTCN was not a proper language, but a tabular notation. It was not possible to describe concurrent behaviors within the test system, which was an impediment to apply TTCN to test in parallel the different facets of the system under test. There were missing concepts like packaging, encapsulation and there was also no support for manipulating external data like ASN1[1] (Abstract Syntax Notation One). All these became possible in the **TTCN-2** (Tree and Tabular Combined Notation) version proposed in ISO/IEC (International Organization for Standardization and International Electrotechnical Commission) and in ITU-T (International Telecommunications Union-Telecommunications Standard Sector) in 1998.

Although the language was improved, TTCN-2 was rather associated with conformance testing and was not suitable for various kinds of testing such as

---

[1] ASN.1 is the language used by the Open System Interconnection (OSI) protocols for describing abstract syntax.

M. Broy et al. (Eds.): Model-Based Testing of Reactive Systems, LNCS 3472, pp. 465-496, 2005.
© Springer-Verlag Berlin Heidelberg 2005

inter-operability testing, robustness testing, regression testing, system testing. It was even more difficult to apply it in the areas of mobile protocol testing, service testing or CORBA-based platform testing.

In 1998, as a consequence of a urging need for a proper test language, ETSI (European Telecommunication Standards Institute) proposed a Specialists Task Force to develop a new version of TTCN, namely TTCN-3. The development of TTCN-3 was encouraged by key players of the telecommunication industries and science to define a common test notation for all black-box testing needs. The standardization process, lead by ETSI PTCC (Protocol and Testing Competence Center), finished in 2000. The new language is a text-based language and has the form of a modern programming language, which is obviously easier to learn and to use. TTCN-3 inherits the most important typical programming language artifacts, but additionally it includes important features required for test suite specification. It can be easily used as interchange format between TTCN tools and has a well defined syntax and semantics. TTCN-3 was submitted to ITU-T as Z.140 series and was approved in July 2001[2]. Currently, all ETSI test specifications are written in the TTCN-3 language as Wiles presents in [Wil01].

16.1.2 Practical Importance of TTCN-3

Wiles presents in [Wil01] the testing activities of ETSI which mainly concentrate on testing with TTCN-3. The TTCN-3 language was created due to the imperative necessity to have a universally understandable language syntax to describe test behavior specifications. Its development was imposed by industry and science to obtain a single test notation for all black-box testing needs. In contrast to earlier test technologies, TTCN-3 encourages the use of a common methodology and style which leads to a simpler maintenance of test suites and products. In TTCN-3, the tester specifies the test suites at an abstract level and focuses on the test purpose itself rather then on the test system adaptation and execution. A language which is standard, is an advantage for both test suite providers and users; the test suite providers concentrate on the test specification standardization and accuracy, making them available to everybody in order to certify the quality of products. Moreover, the use of a standard language reduces the costs for education and training, since a great amount of documentation and examples is available. It is obviously preferred to use always the same languages for testing, than learning different technologies for distinct test classes. Constant use and collaboration between TTCN-3 consumers ensures a uniform maintenance and development of the language.

TTCN-3 enables systematic, specification-based testing for various kinds of tests including functional, scalability, load, inter-operability, robustness, regression, system and integration testing. It is a language to define test procedures to be used for black-box testing of distributed systems. It allows an easy and

---

[2] In this chapter we use the terminology defined by ITU for testing. The same terminology was adopted also in the ETSI documents related to TTCN-3. Thus, definitions like "test case", "test system" differ from the glossary of this book

efficient description of complex distributed test behaviors in terms of sequences, alternatives, and loops of stimuli and responses. The test system can use a number of test components to perform test procedures in parallel. TTCN-3 language is characterized by a well-defined syntax and operational semantics, which allow a precise execution algorithm. The task of describing the dynamic and concurrent configuration is easy to perform. The communication between the test system and system under test can be realized either synchronously or asynchronously. To validate the data transmitted between the entities composing the test system, TTCN-3 supports definition of templates which ensure a powerful matching mechanism. To validate the described behaviors, a verdict handling mechanism is provided. The types and values can be either described directly in TTCN-3 or can be imported from other languages (i.e. Abstract Syntax Notation (ASN.1), Extended Markup Language (XML), Interface Definition Language (IDL)). Moreover, in TTCN-3, the parameterization of types and values is allowed. The selection of the test cases to be executed can be either controlled by the user or can be described within the execution control construct.

16.1.3   Related Standards

Figure 1.1 shows an overview of the TTCN-3 language. TTCN-3 is based on a core language which provides interfaces to reference data defined in other description languages. As the figure shows, one can import types and values specified in non-TTCN-3 languages. The front-end can be either the core language itself or one of the presentation formats (tabular format, graphical format etc).

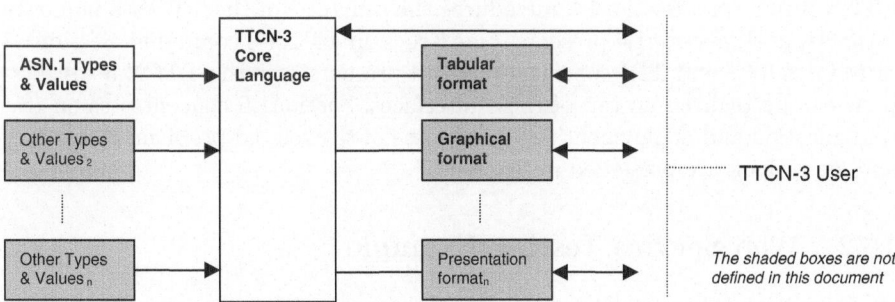

Fig. 16.1. The overall view of the TTCN-3 core language.

The ETSI standard for TTCN-3 comprises six parts which are grouped together in the "Methods for Testing and Specification; The Testing and Test Control Notation version 3" document (all parts are cited in the enumeration below).

- TTCN-3 Core Language. This document specifies the syntax of TTCN-3 language [Ins03].

- Tabular Presentation Format. TTCN-3 offers optional presentation formats. The tabular format is similar in appearance and functionality to earlier versions of TTCN. It was designed for users that prefer the TTCN-2 style of writing test suites. A TTCN-3 module is presented in the tabular format as a collection of tables [Ins03].
- Graphical Presentation Format. It is the second presentation format of TTCN-3 and is based on the MSC format [ITU99] (Message Sequence Charts). The graphical format is used to represent graphically the TTCN-3 behavior definitions as a sequence of diagrams [Ins03].
- Operational semantics. This document describes the meaning of TTCN-3 behavior constructs and provides a state oriented view of the execution of a TTCN-3 module [Ins03].
- The TTCN-3 Runtime Interface (TRI). A complete test system implementation requires also a platform specific adaptation layer. The TRI document contains the specification of a common API interface to adapt TTCN-3 test systems to SUT [Ins03].
- The TTCN-3 Control Interfaces (TCI). This part provides an implementation guide-line for the execution environments of TTCN-3. It specifies the API the TTCN-3 execution environments should implement in order to ensure the communication, management, component handling, external data control and logging [Ins03].

16.1.4   Chapter Overview

The rest of the chapter is structured as it follows: Section1.2 introduces a web-service test example which will be used among all sections to exemplify the TTCN-3 concepts, Section1.3 introduces the semantic of the TTCN-3 language artifacts, next, Section1.4 presents some issues on TTCN-3 compiling. Section1.5 introduces TCI and TRI specifications and presents how the TTCN-3 test systems can be realized on top of these interfaces. Section1.6 concentrates on test configuration and deployment revealing some of the related problems. Summary and an outlook are presented in Section1.7

16.2   Web Service Testing Example

In this section we try to show how easy or how complex it is to use TTCN-3 by using an web service test as example. The main idea is to define a test system for interaction with the system under test (the web service) and validate its basic functionality (i.e. simple queries). TTCN-3 test components are used to emulate system clients. These test components perform the basic functional tests in order to evaluate the reaction of the system to selected service requests or complex service request scenarios. The combination of test components performing different basic functional tests and their parallel execution leads to different test scenarios for the system under test.

In our example we use a dinosaurian database web service (Dino web service) which contains dinosaurian information stored in form of database entries. A dinosaur entry is given as a collection of information about the dinosaur. It is described in terms of the name, time, place, length and location. The web service interface offers different functionalities like search, add, remove, update of dinosaur registrations. The purpose of our TTCN-3 based test system is to validate the correct behavior of these operations. In TTCN-3 we define the test data which the test cases interchange with the SUT, the test configuration by means of test components and ports, and the validated test behavior.

The data format of the entries in the Dino web service is given in form of XML Schema. All entries in the Dino web service must follow this structure.

```
<schema>
    <element name="dinosaur">
        <complexType>
            <sequence>
                <element name="name" type="string"/>
                <element name="length" type="string"/>
                <element name="location" type="string"/>
                <element name="place" type="string"/>
                <element name="time" type="string"/>
            </sequence>
        </complexType>
    </element>
</schema>
```

A web service is a URL-addressable resource returning information in response to client requests. Web services are integrated into other applications or web sites, even though they exist on other servers. So for example, a web site providing quotes for car insurance could make requests behind the scenes to a web service to get the estimated value of a particular car model and to another web service to get the current interest rate.

This example will be used in all following sections in order to exemplify the presented concepts. We will introduce the language by enumerating its main elements and in parallel we will design a complete test system for our web service example. Similarly, we describe the components of the execution environment by showing, on top of this example, how these components are applicable in practice.

16.3   TTCN-3 Based Test Specification

This section is an overview of the TTCN-3 core language and it introduces almost all its key elements. The chapter groups the concepts in four parts: Section 1.3.1 presents the structure of a TTCN-3 test suite, 1.3.2 discuses the test system configuration, 1.3.3 groups together all possibilities to specify test data in TTCN-3, and 1.3.4 describes how the test behavior can be defined in TTCN-3.

16.3.1   Test Building Blocks

The top-level building-block of TTCN-3 is the module. A module contains all other TTCN-3 constructs, but cannot contain sub-modules. It can import completely or partially the definitions of other modules. The modules are defined with the keyword `module`.

In our web service example we define the WebServiceModule. This module imports all definitions from UtilsModule. The module parameter `serviceId` is a parameter which can be configured by the tester at execution and which indicates the service to be tested (`serviceId` takes the default value "0".

```
module WebServiceModule {

  // imports some util functions from another module
  import from UtilsModule all;

  // module parameter -> the id of the tested service
  modulepar { integer serviceId := 0; };

  // other definitions ...
}
```

The modules can be parameterized; parameters are sets of values that are supplied by the test environment at runtime. A parameter can be initialized with a default value which can be changed, later, at execution time.

A module has two parts: the module definition part and the module control part. The definition part contains the data defined by that module (functions, test cases, components, types, templates), which can be used everywhere in the module and can be imported from other modules. The control part is the main program of the module, which describes the execution sequence of test cases or functions. It can access the verdicts delivered by test cases and, according to them, can decide the next steps of execution.

We define, in our example, a control part which tests if a Dino entry exists in the web service database. If the verdict is fail, which means that the entry does not exist, another test case is started. The float values in the `execute` commands represent the maximal time the execution environment must wait until the test cases finish. If the test case does not finish in the indicated period of time, the test case is stopped with the verdict `inconc`.

```
// CONTROL PART
control {
  verdicttype v;
  v := execute(SeparateSearchFunctionalTest(serviceId), 1.0);
  if(v == fail){
      v := execute(SeparateAddFunctionalTest(serviceId), 2.0);
  }
}
```

The control part of a module may call any testcase or function defined in the module to which it belongs. Testcases may call functions or altsteps, but they are not allowed to call other test cases. Similarly, functions are allowed to call other functions or altsteps but no test cases. (function and altstep constructs are defined in Section 1.3.4).

16.3.2 Test System Configuration

TTCN-3 allows the specification of dynamic and concurrent test systems (i.e. the test components can be created dynamically at runtime, the execution of the test behavior can be influenced by the reactions of the SUT). Figure 1.2 shows the conceptual view of a *test system configuration*. A system configuration is the specification of all test components, ports, connections and test system interface involved in the test system. Every test system shall have only one Main Test Component (MTC). The MTC is created automatically by the system at the start of any test case execution. The MTC is the component on which the behavior of test cases is executed. The other test components defined within the test system are called parallel test components (PTC). PTCs can be created dynamically at any time during the execution of a test case. The tested object is called System Under Test (SUT) and the interface to communicate with it is the Abstract Test System Interface.

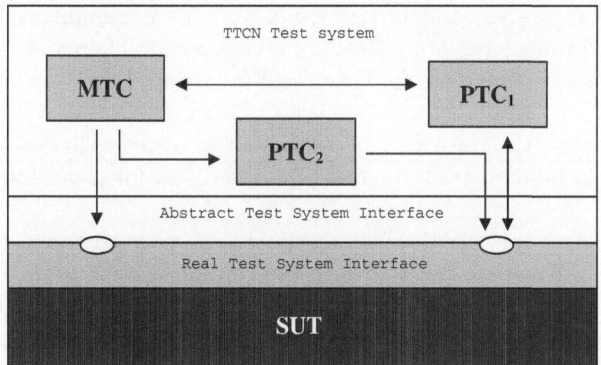

Fig. 16.2. The conceptual view of a test system configuration

The test case execution terminates when the MTC terminates. Before termination of MTC, all other PTCs, which are still running, are stopped by the execution environment. At termination, the MTC collects all PTC verdicts and computes the final verdict.

The test components are defined in the module definition part (which was introduced in 1.3.1). A test component definition may contain a list of ports used for communication, timers, variables and constants. The declarations made for a component are visible to all behaviors which run on that component. The

Abstract Test System Interface can also be defined as a component, since its definition is the same as a component definition: a collection of ports used to connect and communicate with other components.

For Dino web service test we define the MTCType, PTCType and SUTType components. The SUTType component defines a component type which contains an array of ports. This component represents, at an abstract level, the SUT. According to SUTType definition the SUT provides many connection ports which implies that many PTCs can interact with the SUT at the same time.

```
type component MTCType {}

type component PTCType {
    port httpTestPortType httpPort;
    timer localTimer := 3.0;
}

type component SUTType {
    port httpTestPortType httpTestSystemPort[NUMBER_OF_PTCS];
}
```

The communication between test components as well as the one between test components and test system interface are realized over ports. There are two types of communication: message based (the communication is based on asynchronous interchange of messages) and procedure based (the communication is realized in form of synchronous remote procedure invocations). Therefore, TTCN-3 supports two types of ports: message-based and procedure-based ports. Data transmission directions can be defined for each port: in (the received data), out (the sent data), inout (the data can be both sent or received). Ports can also be mixed; they can be used both for message-based and for procedure-based communication.

In our example, we use the httpTestPortType port to connect a test component to the web service (SUT). Since the communication with the SUT is an asynchronous one, we define this port of type message. This port allows to send request messages like *search, update, add* or *remove*. The incoming messages can be of type *dinosaur, updateAck, addAck* or *removeAck*.

```
type port httpTestPortType message {
    out search;
    out update;
    out add;
    out remove;
    in dinosaur;
    in updateAck;
    in addAck;
    in removeAck;
}
```

The system configurations are set by using *configuration operations*. These operations are used in test cases, functions and altsteps, and regard the test components creation and the ports connections. The ports of a component can be connected to other ports by using `connect` or `map` operations. When connecting ports of two PTCs, the operation used is `connect`. When connecting a port of a PTC to a port of SUT, the operation used is `map`. To disconnect ports the opposite operations are used, namely `disconnect` or `unmap`. For our web service test we define the following system configuration:

```
var PTCType PTC := PTCType.create;
map (PTC: httpPort, system: httpTestSystemPort[portNumber]);
PTC.start (SeparateSearchFunctional(system, serviceId));
PTC.done;
unmap(PTC: httpPort, system: httpTestSystemPort[portNumber]);
```

In this example we create the PTC component of type PTCType. The map operation is than used to map the httpPort to one of the system ports httpTest-SystemPort (indexed by portNumber). With `start` operation we run the SeparateSearchFunctional behavior on the PTC component. The `PTC.done` statement determines the execution of the test case to wait until the behavior of the PTC component finishes. `unmap` operation disconnects the ports.

16.3.3 Describe Test Data

Any test system needs to exchange data with the SUT. The communication with the SUT can be either asynchronous, by sending/receiving messages to/from SUT or synchronous, by calling procedures of the SUT. In both cases, the test data must be described within the test system, according to the SUT specification. TTCN-3 offers different constructs to describe the test data: types, templates, variables, procedure signatures etc. They can be used to express any type of protocol message (PDU) or procedure signature. Besides this, TTCN-3 offers also the possibility to import data described in other languages (i.e. ASN.1, IDL, XML).

To describe basic data types, TTCN-3 provides types which are similar to basic types of well-known programming languages (Java, C). Some of them are only testing domain specific, and should be further detailed:

- verdicttype is an enumeration which defines the possible verdicts that can be associated to a test case: `pass, fail, inconc, error, none`.
- anytype is a union of all known TTCN-3 types; the instances of anytype are used as a generic object which is evaluated when the value is known.
- default is used for default handling and represents a reference to a default operation.

TTCN-3 supports ordered structured types such as: record, record of, set, set of, enumerated and union.

A record is a structured type which contains fields. These fields can be of almost all known types: basic types, structured types or user defined types. A field can be marked as `optional`, which indicates that the field can be omitted when setting the record.

In our example we use record to define a dinosaurian type. The dinosaur entry is a record of five charstrings which represents the characteristics of the dinosaur.

```
type record dinosaur {
    charstring name,
    charstring len,
    charstring mass,
    charstring time,
    charstring place
}
```

We use the record type to define also the requests we send to the SUT. An update request shall contain the URL of the service (the web service), the name of the dinosaur and the characteristics we want to change. Please note that len, mass, time and place are optional as it might be possible that we do not want to change all of them (thus we may set the value of the fields we want to change and leave the others optional).

```
type record update {
    url serviceURL,
    charstring name,
    charstring len optional,
    charstring mass optional,
    charstring time optional,
    charstring place optional
}
```

To define a record value, each field of the record must be assigned a value. There are two possibilities to assign values to fields: by using *assignment notation* where each field is assigned a value or by using *value list notation* where the values are enumerated in a list. The fields which were defined optional may not be assigned, they are just marked with the "-" symbol or with the **omit** keyword. The fields of a record are accessed by using the *dot notation*: `RecordValue.ElementId`, where `ElementId` is the name of a field of the record `RecordValue`.

In the web service example we define the variable D of type dinosaur and initialize it by using the *value list notation*. The value of len field is changed again by using the *assignment notation*.

```
var dinosaur D := {"Brachiosaurus", "22 m", "30 tonnes",
                   "Kimmeridgian", "Portugal"};

D.len := "23 m";
```

Templates Templates are data structures used to define message patterns for the data sent or received over ports. They are used either to describe distinct values that are to be transmitted over ports or to evaluate if a received value matches a template specification.

The code below defines the `Brachiosaurus` template used to validate the data received from web service as result of a `search` query. The template says that the Brachiosaurus entry must have the length of 22 m, the values of mass and time must be present and the place can be present or omitted.

```
template dinosaur Brachiosaurus := {
    name := "Brachiosaurus",
    len := "22 m",
    mass := ?,
    time := ?,
    place := *
}
```

Templates can be specified for any type or procedure signature. They can be parameterized, extended or reused in other template definitions. The declaration of a template contains a set of possible values. When comparing a received message with a template, the message data shall match one of the possible values defined by the template.

The templates used in send operations declare a complete set of values which are sent over the test ports; this kind of templates are similar to variables, since the templates are here rather values of the template type. The templates used in receive operations define the data patterns applied to match the incoming data.

The `updateRequest` is a template used to request the web service to update the `Brachiosaurus` entry.

```
template update updateRequest := {
    serviceURL := requestURL,
    name := "Brachiosaurus",
    len := "22 m",
    mass := "30 tonnes",
    time := "Kimmeridgian",
    place := "Portugal, Spain"
}
```

Templates can be used also to express instances of procedure parameters. In this case, the templates reference the associated signature definition. In call or reply operations, the signature templates define complete sets of values which are used for remote procedure invocation. In getcall operations, templates are used to define patterns for the accepted values in the parameter list of a procedure.

For both type and signature templates, TTCN-3 offers several specific constructs which make the template definition very flexible:

- pattern: defines a pattern for a string
- ?: wildcard for any value

- omit: the value is omitted
- *: wildcard for any value or no value at all
- (...): list of valid values
- complement(...): complement of a list of values
- ifpresent: for matching of optional field values
- length: restrictions for string length for string types

16.3.4   Test Behavior

The program elements provided by TTCN-3 are: test case, function and altstep. They are used to structure and express test behaviors, to define default behaviors and to organize items of functionality, which are used in other behaviors.

Test Cases The test cases define the behaviors that are to be validated; they check if the SUT fulfills a requirement or not. Each test case has an associated verdict, which can be set at runtime. A test case runs always on a test component. The test cases can be parameterized and can access the variables, timers or ports of the test component on which they are executed.

We define `SeparateSearchFunctionalTest` test case to test if the dino web service contains entries the user chooses. The test case runs on MTC component and creates a PTC. On PTC we start the SeparateSearchFunctional behavior. In TTCN-3 any function started from a test case is allowed to set the verdict of the test case which started it. Thus the `SeparateSearchFunctional` is allowed to set the verdict of `SeparateSearchFunctionalTest`.

```
testcase SeparateSearchFunctionalTest(in integer serviceId)
runs on MTCType system SUTType {
    var PTCType PTC := PTCType.create;
    integer portNumber := getNextPortNumber();
    map (PTC: httpPort, system: httpTestSystemPort[portNumber]);
    PTC.start (SeparateSearchFunctional(system, serviceId));
    PTC.done;
}
```

Functions Functions are used to express behaviors (like test cases), but also to structure computations in a module. When the functions are used to describe behaviors, similarly to test cases, they must run also on a test component. A function may return a value which is denoted by the `return` keyword. If the function does not access variables, timers or ports that are declared in a component type definition, the `runs on` clause can be omitted. A function can be defined inside the module (its body is defined also in the module) or externally (only the interface is specified in the module). If the function is declared external, then the user should implement the function in the test adapter of that module.

In our example, we define `SeparateUpdateFunctional` functions which runs on a component of PTCType type. It activates the Default() altstep as default behavior (see next Section) and sends an `updateRequest` template to the SUT. The `localTimer` time of the PTC component is started in order to measure the response time. In the alt construct we validate if the SUT responds and if the response matches the `BrachiosaurusAck` template. If the SUT does not answer or the response does not match the `BrachiosaurusAck` template, then the `Default()` altstep is called.

```
function SeparateUpdateFunctional(SUTType sys, integer serviceId)
runs on PTCType

    ... // identify service by serviceId

    activate(Default());

    httpPort.send (updateRequest);

    localTimer.start;
    alt {
        [] httpPort.receive (BrachiosaurusAck) {
            localTimer.stop;
            setverdict (pass);
        }
    }

    deactivate(Default());
}
```

Altsteps Altsteps are used also for describing and structuring component behaviors. An altstep defines an ordered set of alternatives and is called from an alt construct. The body of altsteps is similarly to alt statements; it contains a set of alternative behaviors which are called *top alternatives*. It may also invoke further functions or altsteps; optional statements may also be specified. If the altstep uses ports, timers or variables of a test component or invoke other altsteps or functions with `runs on` clause then it must be defined with the `runs on` clause.

Altsteps can be defined also as default behaviors to handle communication events which may occur, but which are not important for the test. To use an altstep as default behavior `activate` is used. With `deactivate` the default is deactivated. The default behavior is specified at the end of an alt construct and is called if for the current alt statement no alternative is selected.

In our example we use the `Default()` altstep as default behavior. We define in `SeparateUpdateFunctional` an alt statement with one alternative. If that alternative does not match, the Default altstep is also executed. Thus, the runtime checks if the httpPort received other data than `BrachiosaurusAck` or if the timer `localTimer` timed-out.

```
altstep Default() runs on PTCType {
    [] httpPort.receive {
        localTimer.stop;
        setverdict (fail);
    }
    [] localTimer.timeout {
        setverdict (fail);
    }
}
```

Program Statements A program element (test case, function or altstep) may contain different types of statements and operations:

- program statements: expressions, assignments, loop constructs
- behavioral statements: sequential behavior, alternative behavior, interleaving, defaults
- communication operations: send, receive, call, getcall
- timer operations: start, stop, running
- verdict handling: set

Snapshot Semantic One of the most important features of TTCN-3 is the snapshot mechanism which allows the definition of complex interleaved or parallel behaviors. Alternatives are complex behaviors whose sequences of statements are defined as multiple alternatives. To define a branch in an alternative behavior, the alt statement is used.

The execution environment will execute the alternatives by using snapshots. Each branch of an alternative has an associated guard. The guard represents one or more conditions (boolean expressions) that must be fulfilled in order to enter a branch. A snapshot is a state of the test system that includes all information necessary to evaluate the guard of an alt branch. A snapshot is taken when executing an alt statement; that means that all relevant information is collected and used for evaluation of guards. This information contains the states of the components, the timer events and the port enqueued messages. The test system may change its configuration, but the alt statement is evaluated accordingly to the snapshot. The execution environment selects only the branches whose guard conditions are fulfilled. If there is more than one valid guard, then the first one is chosen. If none is valid, then the alt is reevaluated with a new snapshot.

Communication Operations The communication operations are some of the most important operations used to specify test behaviors. TTCN-3 supports message-based and procedure-based communication. The communication operations can be grouped into two parts: stimuli which send information to SUT (send, call, reply raise) and responses used to describe the reaction of the SUT (receive, getreply, trigger, catch).

To apply a sending operation (stimuli) there shall be specified a port used to send the data, the value to be transmitted, and optionally an address to identify a particular connection if the port is connected to many ports. Additionally, at procedure based communication the response and error operation are needed; they are specified by using the getreply and catch operations.

These operations are

- send: send a message to SUT,
- call: to invoke a remote procedure,
- reply: to reply a value when an own procedure is called,
- raise: to report an exception when an own procedure is called an something is wrong in the procedure call.

The message based communication is asynchronous communication. The sending operations are non-blocking; after sending the data, the system does not wait for response. The receive operations block the execution until a matching value is received.

A receiving operation specifies a port at which the operation takes place, defines a matching part for selection of valid receiving values and optionally specifies an address to identify the connection (if the port is connected to many ports).

These operations are

- receive: receive a message from SUT
- getreply: specifies that a method is invoked
- trigger: specifies a message that shall receive in order to go to the next statements
- catch: to collect an exception reported at remote procedure invocation.

Timer Operations The behavior specification may use timers. A timer is used as a type; therefore instances of it can be declared. The operations with timers are start, stop, read (to read the elapsed time), running (to check if the timer is running) and timeout (to check if timeout event occurred). At the declaration of a timer, a value can be assigned; the value is of type float. The start command may be used with parameter (the duration for which the timer will be running) or without parameter (when the default value specified at declaration is used).

In our example, we define a timer on PTCType component and use it in the SeparateSearchFunctional behavior. In general, timers are used to measure the time between sending a stimuli and the SUT's response. If the SUT's answer does not come in a predefined period of time, usually the verdict is set to fail.

Verdict Handling The verdicts can be set and retrieved by using the setverdict and getverdict operations respectively. These operations are allowed in test cases, functions and altsteps. For verdict declaration and instantiation, TTCN-3 provides the verdicttype type. This type is an enumeration of five values: pass, fail, inconc, none and error.

```
alt {
    [] httpPort.receive (BrachiosaurusAck) {
        localTimer.stop;
        setverdict (pass);
    }
}
```

Each test component has an associated verdict; this is called local verdict. The local verdict is handled during execution by using the verdict operations. Additionally, there is a global verdict which is updated when a PTC terminates its execution. The global verdict cannot be accessed with getverdict or setverdict operations. The global verdict is returned always when the test execution of a test case terminates. This verdict can be assigned to a verdict variable in the control part (remember, the testcases can be started only from the control part). If the control part does not collect the verdict, this information is lost.

```
verdicttype v;
v := execute(SeparateSearchFunctionalTest(serviceId), 1.0);
if(v == fail){
    v := execute(SeparateAddFunctionalTest(serviceId), 2.0);
}
```

16.4   TTCN-3 Compiling

TTCN-3 is an abstract notation; the code written in TTCN-3 is usually called **ATS** (Abstract Test Specification). A compiler translates the ATS and produces a program/library called **ETS** (Executable Test Specification). The ETS can be any known language: Java, C, C++, etc. The user is not aware of the translation, as this process is supplied by a TTCN-3 compiler provider. The ETS is deployed into an execution environment whose architecture and design is presented in the next Section.

16.5   TCI and TRI Based Execution Environment

ETSI standardized also the architecture of the execution environment of TTCN-3, besides the core language, semantic and presentation formats. The standard architecture of a test system consists of several entities which communicate mutually through predefined interfaces. The ETSI specification is comprised in two documents: TTCN-3 Runtime Interface (TRI) which is the fifth part of the standard [Ins03] and TTCN-3 Control Interfaces (TCI) which is the sixth part of the standard [Ins03]. The Runtime Interface and Control Interfaces provides an unified model to realize the TTCN-3 based systems [SVG02], [SVG03].

This section explains the implementation of TTCN-3 based test systems. Here are presented the architecture of a Test System, the main system subcomponents which build a test system and the standard APIs defined for the communication between the subcomponents.

16.5.1   Test System Architecture

The general structure of a distributed TTCN-3 Test System is depicted in Figure 1.3. A TTCN-3 Test System is build up of a set of interacting entities which manage the test execution (interpret or execute the TTCN-3 code), realize the communication with the SUT, implement external functions and handle timer operations.

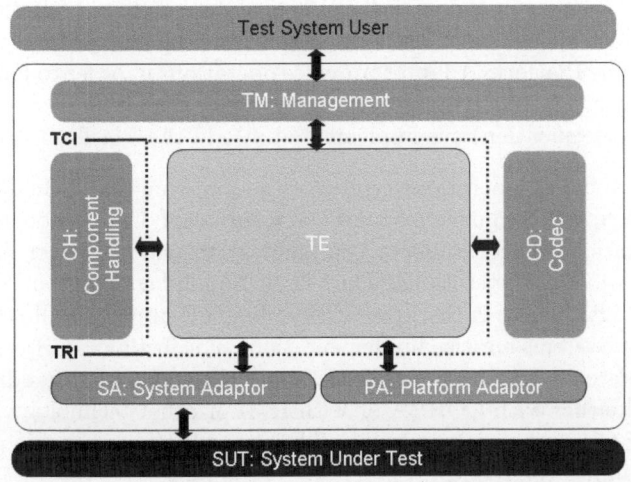

Fig. 16.3. Test System Architecture.

The test system contains the executable code produced during compilation - TTCN-3 Executable (TE), which communicates with the Test Management (TM), the Component Handling (CH) and the Codec (CD) via the TTCN-3 Control Interfaces. The communication with the System Under Tests is realized by using the TTCN-3 Runtime Interfaces (TRI) which define the interfaces between the TE, the System Adapter (SA) and the Platform Adapter (PA).

The main components of the test system are:

- TTCN-3 Executable (TE) interprets or executes the compiled TTCN-3 code. This component manages different entities: control, behavior, component, type, value and queues, entities which are the basic constructors for the executable code.
- Component Handler (CH) handles the communication between components. The CH API contains operations to create, start, stop test components, to establish the connection between test components (map, connect), to handle the communication operations (send, receive, call and reply) and to manage the verdicts. The information about the created components and their physical locations is stored in a repository within the Execution Environment.

- Test Management (TM) manages the test execution. It implements operations to execute tests, to provide and set module parameters and external constants. The test logging is also realized by this component.
- Coding/Decoding (CD) encodes and decodes types and values. The TTCN-3 values are encoded into bitstrings which are sent to the SUT. The received data is decoded back into the TTCN-3 values.
- System Adapter realizes the communication with the SUT. The communication operations *send, receive, call, getcall, reply*, used to interact with the SUT, are defined and implemented by the System Adapter.
- Platform Adapter implements the timers and the external functions. Timers are platform specific elements and have to be implemented outside the test system. The Platform Adapter provides operations in order to handle timers: *create, start, stop.* External functions (whose signature is specified in the TTCN-3 specification) are implemented also in the Platform Adapter.

The TCI and TRI operations represent the mapping to a technology specific interface description language (ex. IDL) of a subset of TTCN-3 operations. The test configuration, intercomponent communication and the timer handling belong to this subset of operations. They shall be implemented outside the Test Executable (TE), which is the generated code. This approach allows the use of different Test Systems entities implementations. For instance, CH (which implements the intercomponent communication and the component handling) can be implemented either with CORBA or with RMI or other technology. The implementation of CH is transparent to TE; TE just calls the operations provided by CH which handles the request.

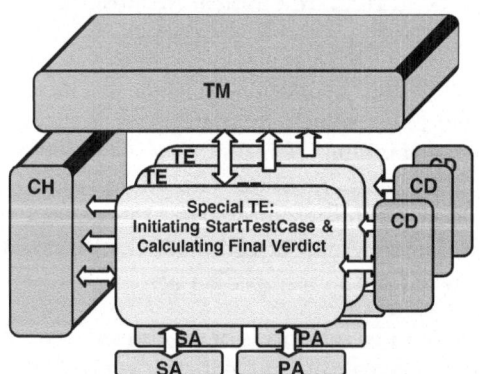

Fig. 16.4. Distributed Test System Architecture.

TTCN-3 tests can be distributed over several test devices. Figure 1.4 shows the distributed perspective of the test system architecture. The TE is instantiated on each test device. The handling of components, which may be created on different nodes, is realized by CH. The TM is responsible for the logging of the distributed tests and for the presentation of the results to the test system user. The CD, SA and PA entities are instantiated on each device because their implementation may differ depending on their underlying heterogeneous devices.

16.5.2 Test Control Interfaces

The TTCN-3 Control Interfaces provide a standardized adaptation for the management and the handling of test components and for the encoding/decoding of a test system to a particular test platform.

The 6th part of the ETSI TTCN-3 standard defines the interaction between three main entities: Test Management (TM), Test Component Handler (CH) and Coder/Decoder (CoDec). The test can be distributed over many test hosts and different test behaviors can be executed simultaneously. As it is conceived within the standard, on each host, an instance of the test system is created. The Test Execution (TE) must be distributed on each host with its own codec (CD), System Adapter (SA) and Platform Adapter (PA). The Component Handling (CH) supplies the communication between the test components created, that run on different hosts. The Test Management coordinates and manages the execution of the test.

The interaction between the main entities is defined as a set of interfaces. The API, conceived within the interfaces, defines operations which the entities either provide or use. For this reason, there are two classes of interfaces: provided and required. Provided interfaces contain operations which are offered by an entity; the required interfaces contain operations that an entity expects from the other entities.

Data Types The TTCN-3 data described in the test module must be transformed into concrete data values which are handled by the entities implementing the test system. TE contains the data values which are generated at compilation. In order to maintain a common data model, the TCI standard defines the *Abstract Data Type Model*, which describes the interfaces that handle the TTCN-3 data from TE. Each abstract data type has associated a set of operations which defines its functionality.

The *Abstract Data Type Model* contains two parts: the data type Type, which represents all TTCN-3 types of a module, and data types that represent TTCN-3 values (instances of TTCN-3 types). All TTCN-3 types provide the same interface. One may obtain for a type the module where it was defined, its name or class and the type of encoding. Any type can be instantiated by using the newInstance method. The different types of values, which can appear in a TE, are presented in Figure 1.5.

All types of values inherit the Value type and provide the core operations: getValueEncoding, getType and notPresent. The Value types represent the mapping of the abstract TTCN-3 values to concrete ones. There are three categories of values: a) basic types (integer, float, boolean etc), b) string based values (hexstring, octetstring, charstring etc) and c) structured types (union, record, verdict). All of them provide additional operations (besides the operations extended from Value) to access their functionality.

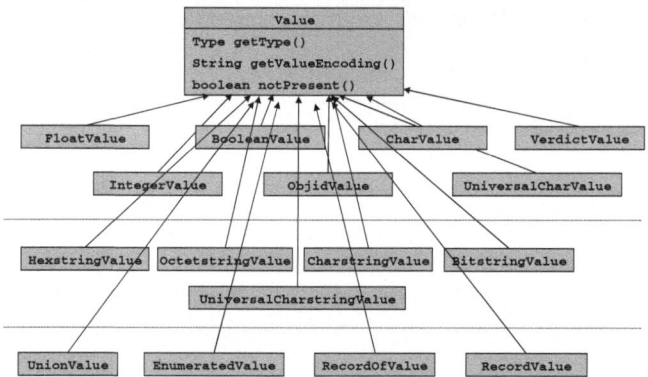

Fig. 16.5. The TTCN-3 Value Types which can appear in a TE.

Management of the Test Execution The overall management of a test system is realized by the Test Management entity (TM). The TM operations can be split into two parts: operations which are used by the user to control the test execution and operations provided to TE in order to notify the user about changes in the execution status.

The user may start or stop the test cases and the control part. This functionality is implemented in TE. In response, the TE may notify the TM when a test case or the control started or terminated. As presented in Section 1.3, the test cases can be parameterized. This is also reflected in the TM - `tciStartTestCase` method which has a `TciParamterListType` as argument. The TE, where the MTC is executed, is called *special* TE and is used to start the test cases or the control part.

The values of the parameters of a module are transferred to TE also via TM interface. TE may ask TM about the value of a parameter by using the `tciGetModuleParameter`.

A user may obtain information about the content of a module. With the `tciGetTestCases` and the `tciGetModuleParameters` methods, the user may acquire the list of test cases and module parameters.

Test Configuration The abstract operations used in the TTCN-3 test specifications in order to define test configurations (create, connect, disconnect, start, stop etc) are mapped to concrete operations in the CH interface. All the configuration operations are reflected by the CH API. The configuration operations are called from behaviors (test cases, functions, control) which are contained by TE. Since the TE does not know where to create or start components, the request is sent to CH. Conceptually, CH has knowledge about every component. The requests from TE are analized on the basis of the CH knowledge; CH decides if the requests are to be handled locally or remotely (a component can be created either locally or remotely). If the request is executed locally, it is sent back to the local TE. If the request is to be executed on a remote node, the CH sends the request to the remote TE. CH keeps track of the modifications in the test system configuration; it stores the references of the components, knows about the running behaviors and manages the component connections. CH can also be asked if a component is running or done. Whenever an error at execution inside of a TE occurs, the `tciReset` operation is called in order to stop all the other components (of all TEs).

Component Communication The communication operations between components are realized also by CH. CH provides to TE a set of operations which are called whenever data is transmitted between components. The CH communication operations represent the mapping of the TTCN-3 communication operations: send, receive, call, getcall etc. When a component sends data to another component, the request is forwarded to CH. CH has the global view over the distributed configuration and knows the host of the receiving component as well. If the host is a remote one, the message is send to the remote TE. TTCN-3 supports two types of communication: asynchronous and procedure based. Consequently, CH supports also the two types of data communication by providing methods like `tciSendConnected`, `tciEnqueueMsgConnected` for asynchronous communication, but also methods like `tciCallConnected`, `tciEnqueueCallConnected` for procedure based communication.

Verdict Handling CH is informed about the termination of the components; for this task, TE calls the `tciTestComponentTerminatedReq` method with the verdict of type `VerdictType` as parameter. CH delivers all the verdicts to the special TE, which computes the global verdict.

Errors, Logging In addition, TM provides methods to log the errors and the log messages reported by TE. These messages are presented to the user by the tciLog and tciError operations.

Data Encoding The TTCN-3 values must be converted to SUT specific data. This task is solved by CD, which provides the `tciEncode` and the `tciDecode` operations. The encoding operation is called by TE before the data is sent to the Test Adaptor. The decoding operation is used by TE when data is received from TestAdapter. To be able to decode, CD requires some information from TE; this information is the *decoding hypothesis*. The behavior running in TE knows the type of data that is to be received, so it asks CD to try to decode the received data according with a certain expected type. If the decoding fails, CD is called again with a new decoding hypothesis.

Test Control Interfaces Implementation In the previous sub-sections we introduced the standard Test Control Interfaces used to execute and control the test execution. These interfaces have to be implemented in the execution environments, thus the user does not have to be aware about their implementation.

This task is rather tool specific and the tool provider must consider them as a general layout for the implementation of the TTCN-3 execution environment.

Consequently we also do not have to do anything with respect to our web-service example. We just take an execution tool (TCI complient) and run the tests specified in TTCN-3. But before running we need to care about the adapter to the SUT which is presented in detail in the next section.

16.5.3   Test Adaptation

The 5th part of the ETSI TTCN-3 standard [Ins03] defines the Test Runtime Interfaces by means of communication of TE with the System Adapter (SA) and with the Platform Adapter (PA). This part describes two tasks; firstly, the way the TE sends data to SUT or manipulates timers, and secondly, the way the SA + PA notify the TE about the received test data and timeouts.

The TTCN-3 specifications use the operation system to access the SUT. The component returned by the system operation is conceptually similar to the other PTCs and is usually called *system* component; it may contain ports, variables, timers etc and can be connected to other components. In contrast to normal components, the ports of the *system* component are connected with the ports of other components by using the map operation. As far as the test execution is concerned, the *system* is handled differently. The configuration operations map, unmap are not sent to CH, but to the Test Adapter. The communication operations of the *system* component are handled in the Test Adapter as well.

Timer Operations The timer handling operations, used in the TTCN-3 specifications, are implemented in PA. The TTCN-3 timer operations are correlated to the PA operations: triStartTimer, triStopTimer, triReadTimer and triTimerRunning.

Communication with SUT SA implements all message and procedure based communication operations. The SA interface defines the mapping of the TTCN-3 communication operations (send, receive, call etc). The data received from SUT has to be transmitted to TE. The enqueue operations are implemented by TE, so the Test Adapter implementation shall be concerned with the task of using the enqueue operations to deliver the received data to TE.

Adapter Example A minimal example of a TestAdapter implementation is shown in the next fragment of code. It is by no means complete, it is rather provided to explain what the user should implement in order to execute the ATS. This piece of code will be called by the execution environment whenever the SUT is addressed. Before the first statement of the MTC will be executed by the TE it will call the triExecuteTestcase() operation within SA, to indicate that the referenced test case will be executed. The map and unmap operations used in the TTCN-3 ATS are reflected in the adapter by the triMap() and triUnmap()

methods. They are called when the runtime environment is executing the `map` and `unmap` operations from ATS. These operations give the possibility to the user to connect the abstract ports to concrete physical ports, in our case SOAP ports (SOAP is the protocol used to connect to the web-service). The `triSend()` is called whenever the TTCN-3 `send` operation is executed in ATS. It takes over the task of sending the data to the SOAP port.

```
public class WebServiceSA implements TriCommunicationSA {
    public TriStatus triExecuteTestcase( TriTestcaseId tcId,
                                         TriPortIdList tsiPorts ) {
        // do nothing
        return new TriStatus(TRI_OK);
    }
    public TriStatus triMap( TriPortId compPortId,
                             TriPortId tsiPortId ) {
        mapTTCNPortToSOAPPort(compPortId, tsiPortId);
        return new TriStatus(TRI_OK);
    }
    public TriStatus triUnmap( TriPortId compPortId,
                               TriPortId tsiPortId ) {
        unmapTTCNPortToSOAPPort(compPortId, tsiPortId);
        return new TriStatus(TRI_OK);
    }
    public TriStatus triSend( TriComponentId componentId,
                              TriPortId tsiPortId,
                              TriAddress address,
                              TriMessage sendMessage ) {
        findSOAPPort(tsiPortId).sendMessageOverSOAP(sendMessage);
        return new TriStatus(TRI_OK);
    }
}
```

16.6   Test Deployment and Configuration

16.6.1   Deployment

Test Deployment is related to the activities of installing, updating, configuring and removing of Test Executables (TE). TE is the part generated by the compiler which must be integrated within the execution environment built up of TM, CH, CD, SA and PA. Any TE comes with a descriptor (usually automatic generated) describing the user options of installation (test adapter configuration, module and test cases configuration and component distribution options).

We assume that the execution environment is distributed, that means that the Test Executable shall be deployed on all hosts of the execution environment. Consequently, the test deployment shall consider the distributed aspects of loading code for execution into hosts, of managing the hardware resources on remote hosts, of preparing and configuring the communication platform (i.e CORBA, sockets etc), of controlling the data transport layer and managing the control data between hosts.

The characteristic operations required for deploying tests are:

(1) Packaging of the test component code and its descriptors into a test suite archive.
(2) Assignment of one or more potential target nodes (component homes) for each test component to install on. Assignment of just the initial main test component (MTC) to a selected target node.
(3) Code upload and installation of the code of each component on the assigned target node(s).
(4) Start of the component's execution environment and instantiation of the main test component as the only initial component. All further component instances are created dynamically by the TTCN-3 mechanisms (TTCN-3 control part).
(5) Connection configuration step where the connections between components are realized.
(6) Dynamic creation and connection of further component instances during the run-time of the test suite by the TTCN-3 control part.

The architecture of a platform designed to handle these aspects is presented in Figure 1.6.

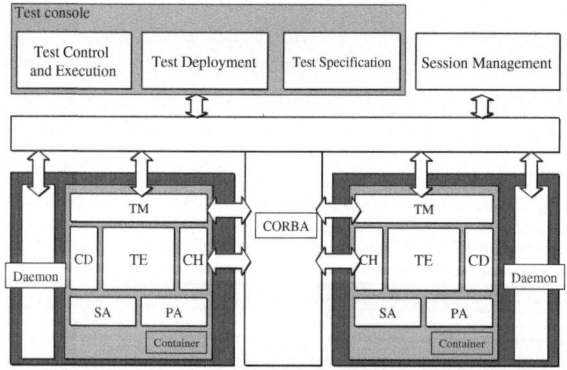

Fig. 16.6. Architecture of a Distributed Test Deployment and Execution Platform

The Test Console is the control point of the platform; it provides support to specify TTCN3 test cases, create test sessions, deploy test suites into containers and control the test execution. The tests are deployed, configured and executed in the context of a test session. The test session has the major role to coordinate the distribution aspects (to compute the hosts of the components according to user preferences, performance requirements, distribution algorithms etc). It collects also the information which must stay persistent after termination of the test execution (when the Test Executable is removed). The persistent information consists usually of the verdict of the test execution, the errors occurred and the logging information.

Daemons are standalone processes installed on any hosts. They manage the containers which belong to test sessions. Containers intercede between Test Console and components, providing services transparently to both of them, including transaction support and resource pooling. The containers are the hosts of Test Executable; they manage installation, configuration and removal of the test components.

As for the tests, containers are the target operational environment and comply with the TCI standard for TTCN3 test execution environment. Within the container, one recognizes the specific test system entities: TM, CH, CD etc. The container subsystems are functionally bound together by the TCI interfaces and communicate with each other via the CORBA platform. The Session-Manager mediation allows many component behaviors to be specified at deployment time, rather than in program code.

16.6.2   Toward Component Distribution

The flexibility of the distribution criteria and mechanisms plays an important role for efficiency, which depends on the mode the components are distributed over the nodes. Test distribution defines which components are to be distributed and where they should be deployed.

To explain better the motivation for test distribution, a simple example is presented. A typical test execution environment consists of heterogeneous resources (computers with different capabilities: memory, CPU, bandwidth etc). The execution environment considered for this example is depicted in Figure 1.7. There are several assumptions for test execution:

- the SUT has different access points. They are accessed via different network cards (of type X and Y)
- the host A has no connection to SUT.
- the host C has 128 MB memory while the hosts B and D have 256 MB
- the host B and C have network cards of type X (so that they can access the access point X of SUT) while host D has network card of type Y so that it may access the SUT at access point Y.

From the example, it is obvious that several distribution combinations are not possible, while other may influence the efficiency of the system. It is not possible to deploy components on host D which need to communicate via access point X. It is also not possible to distribute components on host A which need to communicate to SUT. The two hosts which allow communication with SUT via access points of types X have different memory capacities. If the components are distributed equally (for a huge number of components), then the host C may be overloaded while host B still runs at optimal performance. In this case the distribution should consider the amount of memory consumed by a component

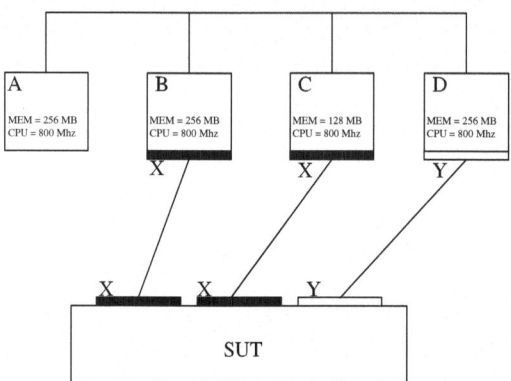

Fig. 16.7. Example of a heterogeneous distributed execution environment

during the execution and distribute them between B and C according to their memory capabilities.

Distribution of components is a mathematical function of different parameters. This function is applied either at deployment time for each component (when its deployment is required) or for all components at once (if known)

In the following function definition, D is the distribution function, p1, p2, ... pn are the parameters which influence the distribution and h1 is the home where the test component should be distributed.

```
h1 = D(p1, p2, ..., pn)
```

Sometimes, it is also possible to compute the homes for all components (h1, h2, ..., hm).

```
{h1, h2, ... hm} = D(p1, p2, ..., pn)
```

There are two types of parameters which are taken into consideration when distributing test components:

- external parameters: bandwidth, CPU, memory
- internal parameters: the number of components, type of components, type of behaviors, connections

The external parameters are application independent parameters whose values depend on the execution environment and are constant for all applications running on that environment. The internal parameters are related to the component based application itself and are different for each application.

The TTCN-3 test components are distributed on different hosts. Unfortunately, in TTCN-3 it is not possible to recognize a component by its id. This problem appears when creating test components without names like in the following example:

```
for (i := 0; i < 100; i := i + 1) {
    var PTCType c := PTCType.create;
    map(c:port1, system:port1);
    c.start(someBehavior1());
}
```

In this example, the component name c is always overwritten, so that the execution environment can not decide which instance is c (the first, the second or the last one). But there are some other characteristics of components in TTCN-3 which can be used at execution to recognize the components. These characteristics are of two categories:

- behavior independent; there are taken into account only parameters which are not defined at the execution of the behavior. They are parameters which can be accessed at the setup phase of the test (component creation, port mapping), before the test behavior is executed.
  - a component has a type which can be retrieved at execution
  - on a component can be started a behavior
  - number of the instance
  - the ports belong to components, so at map operation, one can decide where a component should be deployed.
- behavior dependent; these are characteristics which are considered for distribution, after the behavior is started. This is the case when the home of a component is chosen during the behavior execution; the distribution criteria depends on a particular state of the behavior. Of course, this task is very difficult to realize technically, since the deployment is supposed to be performed after the start of the execution. This implies use of migration mechanism for the components which require other hosts (at execution time). Another approach is based on analyzing the TTCN-3 code before starting the execution and decide where the components should be deployed; but there are situations where this approach cannot be applied, so the only possibility is using of migration mechanisms.

According to the previous assumptions, there are several items which are to be considered for the distribution of TTCN-3 test components:

- component type
- component instance number
- behavior id
- port connections
- content of the behavior
- memory used
- bandwidth used
- CPU

A hardware load monitor is necessary in order to monitor the hardware resource consume. This is a standalone subsystem of the execution environment with the main task to monitor the hardware usage and to be able to report at a certain time the status of resource usage. According to this report, the test component distribution algorithms are able to decide how to deploy the test components.

16.6.3 TTCN-3 Component Distribution Language

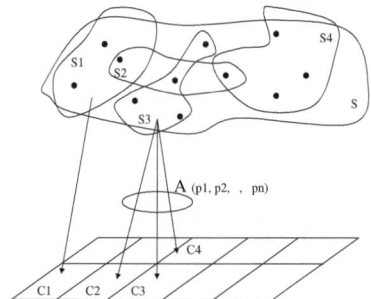

Fig. 16.8. Distribution of test components

The distribution aspects (i.e component and behavior distribution) are not taken into account by TTCN-3 notation. Distribution is considered rather tool specific and should be specified outside the test specification. TTCN-3 describes only test data and test behaviors, it does not specify how the components are distributed on nodes, though distributed setups can be defined in TTCN-3. The advantage of this approach is that the distribution configuration is abstract and it does not depend on a particular test environment. The same test specification (distributed one) can be executed on different hardware environments and diverse distribution setups. For example, a test case which runs a behavior on 10 test components can be distributed on 5 hosts, but it can run on 3 or 2 hosts as well.

As stated before, a component distribution language is required. A minimal language for this purpose was defined by the author of this chapter when implementing a distributed platform for test execution. To better understand the concepts related to test component distribution, some examples written in this language are presented here.

The distribution specification is the process of assembling components to hosts (see Figure 1.8). The assembling process groups all components to be deployed, in a big set. The assembling rules shall define sub-sets of components with a common property (i.e. all components of type *T1*). A (sub-)set defines a *selector* of components and the *homes* where the selected components are placed. The filtering criteria of the *selector* handles component types, component instance numbers, port connections and behavior IDs. The *homes* are the possible locations where the components may be distributed; the homes reflect the user constraints for distribution.

The next piece of XML code is an example of a component assembly file. The *special* tag indicates the host where the MTC component is deployed. The selector defines a filter to select all components of type *ptcType*. The selected components can be deployed either on container1 or on container2. One can define deployment constraints for each container (ex. do not allow deployment of more than 100 components on container2). The user can constrain the memory usage, the CPU load, the number of components etc.

```
<component_assembly>
    <!-- Description of the file -->
    <description>Example to use TCDL language</description>

    <!-- This sets the special container where the mtc will
         be deployed -->
    <special container="container1"/>

    <!-- Example of a set -->
    <set>
        <component_selectors>
            <componenttype>ptcType</componenttype>
        </component_selectors>
        <homes distribution="">
            <container id="container1">
                <max_components>10</max_components>
            </container>
            <container id="container2"/>
                <max_components>100</max_components>
            </container>
        </homes>
    </set>
</component_assembly>
```

Usually, the definition of constraints is a difficult task; for complex setups it may be very difficult to describe an efficient distribution. Therefore, the task of hardware options and constraints should be realized by the execution environment. It should provide services, which implement distribution algorithms that are designed to be efficient for a certain type of problems. The task of the user remains to select the algorithm which solves the problem best. The code below shows a set which deploys the components of types ptcType2, ptcType3 and the instances 1, 2 and 5 of type ptcType4 on the container2 and container3, according with the *mem50* algorithm. The *mem50* is an example of an algorithm which allows to deploy components on a container until the limit of 50 percent of memory is reached.

```
<set>
        <component_selectors>
            <componenttype>ptcType2</componenttype>
            <componenttype>ptcType3</componenttype>
            <instance type="single">
                <componenttype>ptcType4</componenttype>
                <number>1</number>
                <number>2</number>
                <number>5</number>
            </instance>
        </component_selectors>
        <homes distribution="mem50">
            <container id="container2"/>
            <container id="container3"/>
        </homes>
</set>
```

The components which are not accepted by any set selector are deployed in a default home. This home is defined by *collector* tag.

```
<collector>
    <container id="container1"/>
</collector>
```

16.6.4   Stress Test for Dino Web Service

Let suppose we want now to run a stress test for our Dino web-service. In TTCN-3 the test specification is independent on the platform where it will be executed and no distribution option can be configured.

The next TTCN-3 code defines a stress test which creates a big number of PTCs and starts on each one the SeparateSearchFunctional behavior. The PTCs will try to access in parallel the SUT (Dino web-service), thus some stress will be created.

```
testcase SeparateStressTest()
runs on MTCType system SUTType {
    var integer numberOfPTCs := NUMBER_OF_PTCS;
    var integer requestsPerPTC := 1;
    var PTCType PTC[numberOfPTCs];
    var integer i;

    for (i := 0; i < numberOfPTCs; i := i + 1) {
        //create the PTCs
        PTC[i] := PTCType.create;
    }
    for (i := 0; i < numberOfPTCs; i := i + 1) {
        //start the PTC's behavior
```

```
        PTC[i].start (SeparateSearchFunctional(system, i));
    }
    for (i := 0; i < numberOfPTCs; i := i + 1) {
        //wait for the PTCs to terminate
        PTC[i].done;
    }
}
```

The SeparateStressTest can be executed either on one host or on many. In our example we choose a simple distribution scenario which supposes that the PTCs are distributed equally on two test nodes. The below XML code provides the distribution configuration for the chosen scenario. We select the container1 as special container where the MTC component will be installed. The other test components of type ptcType will be installed equally (according to the bestfit algorithm) on the two test nodes.

```
<component_assembly>
    <special container="container1"/>
    <set>
        <component_selectors>
            <componenttype>ptcType</componenttype>
        </component_selectors>
        <homes distribution="bestfit">
            <container id="container1"/>
            <container id="container2"/>
        </homes>
    </set>
</component_assembly>
```

16.7   Summary

In this chapter a detailed introduction into TTCN-3 is provided. It argues why TTCN-3 language was created and presents its practical importance. The chapter sums up in several sections the concepts behind TTCN-3, the TTCN-3 core language, the implementation and execution of TTCN-3 test systems.

A complete example describes the steps the user shall follow in order to run a TTCN-3 test system. First, the user defines the test cases in TTCN-3 language. It uses components, ports and connections in order to define a *test configuration*, defines *data types* (records, sets, basic types etc), defines *test data* (templates) and describe test behaviors (testcases, functions, altsteps). In Section1.3 we concentrated on the most important concepts and constructs used in TTCN-3 abstract test specifications. In parallel, a minimal test suite was developed to the Dino web-service in order to exemplify the practical use of the language. Secondly, an Adapter must be implemented. The adapter implements the TRI (TTCN-3 Runtime Interface). The adapter is SUT specific and shall be implemented for each tested SUT. It contains basically all needed operations to communicate with the SUT (call, send, etc). Third, the user must specify how to distribute the tests if many hosts are used. A particular solution was introduced and discussed (note that the distribution language is only an example not a standard).

Beside the main flow (how to develop test systems with TTCN-3) we discussed several important issues related to implementation of TTCN-3 execution environments based on TCI (TTCN-3 Control Interfaces), deployment and distribution.

Nowadays, TTCN-3 is more and more used, its applicability being extended to many domains. Thanks to its powerful constructs it is perhaps the most suitable technology for testing and makes it easy to apply to any testing needs.

17   UML 2.0 Testing Profile

Zhen Ru Dai

Fraunhofer Fokus - Institute for Open Communication Systems
Kaiserin-Augusta-Allee 31, 10589 Berlin
dai@fokus.fraunhofer.de

17.1   Introduction

The Unified Modeling Language (UML) is a visual language to support the design and development of complex object-oriented systems [RJB99]. While UML models focus primarily on the definition of system structure and behavior, they provide only limited means for describing test objectives and test procedures. In 2001, a consortium was built by the Object Management Group (OMG) in order to develop a UML 2.0 profile for the testing domain [OMG02, UMLa].

A UML profile provides a generic extension mechanism for building UML models in particular domains. The UML 2.0 Testing Profile (U2TP) is such an extension which is developed for the testing domain. It bridges the gap between designers and testers by providing a means to use UML for both system modeling as well as test specification. This allows a reuse of UML design documents for testing and enables test development in an early system development phase [SDGR03, DGNP04].

After two years' work, the U2TP specification [U2T] has finally been adopted by the OMG. Since March 2004, the profile has become an official standard at the OMG [U2T04].

In the U2TP specification, the consortium does not only introduce new concepts which extends the usability of UML regarding test perspectives. Further thoughts have been made on the test execution of the test model. For that, the U2TP specification provides mapping rules of U2TP concepts to two well-known test languages called JUnit and TTCN-3 (Testing and Test Control Notation, version 3) [Ins03]: JUnit is a popular test framework within the eXtreme Programming community for Java unit tests. A JUnit test suite is written in Java. Thus, the executable code can be compiled by Java compilers. In Chapter 16.3, TTCN-3 and its execution environment have already been introduced. By means of a compiler, a TTCN-3 abstract test suite (ATS) is translated into executable test suite (ETS). By means of the standardized TTCN-3 execution environment, the ETS is able to communicate with the system under test.

Besides the test concepts and the mapping rules, the U2TP specification defines two meta-models. One meta-model is based on UML 2.0 [UML03b, UML03a] meta-classes and the second meta-model is a MOF-based (Meta-Object Facility) meta-model. The intention to build the MOF-based meta-model is to have a UML 2.0 independent meta-model. The meta-modelling aspects in the

M. Broy et al. (Eds.): Model-Based Testing of Reactive Systems, LNCS 3472, pp. 497–521, 2005.
© Springer-Verlag Berlin Heidelberg 2005

U2TP document is not introduced in this seminar booklet since it is out of the scope of this seminar[1].

This chapter is structured as follows: in Section 17.2, we will explain the main concepts of the U2TP. The mapping rules from U2TP concepts to JUnit and TTCN-3 concepts are introduced in Section 17.3. In Section 17.4, a case study is depicted, where U2TP concepts are applied to test a Bluetooth device with roaming functionalities. The chapter concludes with a summary.

17.2   The U2TP

The UML 2.0 Testing Profile provides concepts to develop test specifications and test models for black-box testing [Bei95]. The profile introduces four concept groups covering the following aspects: *test architecture, test behavior, test data and time*. Figure 17.1 shows the main concepts of U2TP [U2T04]. Together, these concepts define a modeling language to visualize, specify, analyze, construct and document a test system. In the following, the four concept groups are introduced:

Test Architecture Concepts	Test Behavior Concepts	Test Data Concepts	Time Concepts
SUT	Test objective	Wildcards	Timer
Test context	Test case	Data pool	Time zone
Test component	Defaults	Data partition	
Test configuration	Verdicts	Data selection	
Test control	Validation action	Coding rules	
Arbiter	Test log		
Scheduler			

Fig. 17.1. U2TP Concepts

Architecture Concepts The test architecture group contains the concepts needed to describe elements involved in the test and their relationships.

The system or object to be tested is called the *System Under Test* (SUT). One or more objects within a test specification can be specified as the SUT. As the profile only addresses black-box conformance testing, the SUT provides only a set of operations via publicly available interfaces. No information on the internal structure of the SUT is available for use in the specification of test cases using the U2TP.

Two test elements are defined in U2TP: *test context* and *test component*. A *test context* declares variables, contains a collection of test cases of the same initial test configuration, specifies the test configuration and the test control. *Test components* are the various elements which interact with the SUT to realize the test cases defined in the test context.

---

[1] For more information, please read the U2TP spec.

A *test configuration* as an internal structure of a test context is used to enable the definition of test components realizing a test case, it describes the initial setup of the test components and the connection to the SUT and between each other.

A *test control* is a specification for the invocation of test cases within a test context. It is a technical specification of how the SUT should be tested with the given test context. Often, decisions about further test case executions are made within the test control specification in order to prevent spare time and resource, e.g. if test case #1 fails, the whole test should be stopped, even if there are more test cases specified which also should be performed, but are dependent of the execution result of test case #1.

An *arbiter* is a denoted test component which calculates the final test result derived from temporal test results. This is done according to a particular arbitration strategy, which is provided in the implementation of the arbiter interface. This interface provides two operations for use in verdict setting: *getVerdict* and *setVerdict*. The *setVerdict* operation is used to provide updated information to the arbiter by a test component regarding the current status of the test case in which it is participating. Every validation action invokes the *setVerdict* operation on the arbiter. Every test context should have an implementation of the arbiter interface. If there is no specific arbiter interface implemented, a default arbiter will take into account.

A *scheduler* controls the execution of the different test components. The scheduler will keep information about which test components exist at any point in time, and it will collaborate with the arbiter to inform it when it is time to issue the final verdict. It keeps control over the creation and destruction of test components and it knows which test components take part in each test case.

Behavior Concepts The test behavior group includes concepts to specify test behavior in the context of a test context.

A *test objective* allows the test designer to express the aim of a test. The implementation of a test objective is a *test case* which is an operation within a test context specifying how a set of cooperating components interact with the SUT. The public test case operations of a test context are the test cases. In addition, there may be other private or protected test cases that are used as utilities within the concrete realization of the public test cases. The implementation of test cases is specified by a test behavior. A test case always returns a test verdict.

A UML specification is not necessarily complete, i.e. it does not specify every possible trace of execution. In a testing context, there is a need to have complete definitions such that the number of erroneous test case executions can be kept to a minimum. A *default* specification is a means to make partial behavior definitions of test components complete. Additionally, a test behavior specification typically describes the normative or expected behaviors for the SUT. However, if during test execution an unexpected behavior is observed, a default is applied. The U2TP associates default applications to static behavioral structures. In Interactions, defaults are applied to interaction fragments, in State Machines to state machines, states or regions, and in Activity Diagrams to actions and activities. Since each default in an Interaction applies only to one test component, defaults are attached on interaction fragments to the intersection between the fragment and the test component. In U2TP, defaults behaviors can be specified on different behavior levels, e.g. on a state, interaction, instance etc.. If the innermost default fail to recognize the observed behavior the default of the next level is tried.

Test *verdicts* specify possible test results, e.g. *pass, fail, inconclusive* or *error*. The definition of the verdicts originate from the *OSI Conformance Testing Methodology and Framework* [ISO94]: *Pass* indicates that the SUT behaves correctly for the specific test case. *Fail* describes that the test case has violated. *Inconclusive* is used where the test neither passes nor fails. An *error* verdict indicates exceptions within the test system itself.

A *validation action* can be performed by a test component to denote that the arbiter is informed of a test result which was determined by that test component. The coordination between arbiter and test components is controlled by the scheduler.

Both a test context and a test case may trace their executions. These traces are behaviors in general and are generated during the execution of a test case. They can be recorded as *test logs* and become part of the test specification. A test log has to be attached to a test context or a test case such that it is specified from which test context or test case that test log has been taken.

Data Concepts This concept group contains concepts needed to describe test data. There are means provided to specify test data for the data transmission between the SUT and the test system.

Wildcards which can denote an omitted value, any value or any value or omit (*** or *?*) are needed to specify test data, especially for data reception.

Test cases are often executed repeatedly with different data values to stimulate the SUT in various ways. Also when observing data, abstract equivalence classes are used to define sets of allowed values. Typically, these values are taken from a partition of test data, or lists of explicit values. For this purpose, a *data pool* provides a means for associating data sets with test contexts and test cases. A data pool contains either data partitions which build equivalence classes, or explicit values.

Data partition is used to define an equivalence class for a given type. By denoting the partitioning of data explicitly U2TP provides a more visible differentiation of data.

Data selectors are typically operations that operate over the contained values or value sets. By means of data selectors, test data can be retrieved out of a data pool or a data partition.

Coding rules are shown as strings referencing coding rules defined outside the U2TP such as by ASN.1, CORBA or XML. Coding rules are basically applied to data value specification to denote the concrete encoding and decoding for these values during test execution.

Time Concepts When specifying tests, time concepts are essential to provide complete and precise specifications. U2TP provides two additional time concepts to the existing UML 2.0 simple time concepts: Timer and time zone.

Timers are utilized to manipulate and control test behavior, as well as to ensure the termination of test cases. A timer is owned by an active class. A timer can be started with a certain time value. The predefined time value of a timer has always to be positive. An timer may be stopped as long as it is still active. The expiration time of an active timer can be read and its live status asked for. When a timer expires after its predefined time, a special timeout message is generated automatically. It is sent immediately to the class which owns the timer.

Timezones serve as a grouping mechanisms for test components within a distributed test system. Each test component belongs at most to one timezone. Test components of the same timezone have the same time value and thus are considered to be time-synchronized. The timezone of a test component can be accessed both in the model and at run-time. Comparing time-critical events within the same timezone is allowed.

17.3   Test Execution Via Mappings

The U2TP document defines mapping rules for the test languages JUnit [JUn] and TTCN-3 [Ins03]. The reason for choosing these two languages is quite simple: Firstly, JUnit is a Java based unit test framework which has become very popular in the eXtreme Programming domain because of its simplicity and user-friendliness and TTCN-3 is well-known in the tele-communication test domain. Secondly, when U2TP is developed, the concepts of JUnit and TTCN-3 served as roots for the U2TP. Therefore, the mapping rules are quite straight-forward, though in some cases not complete. Especially the mapping from U2TP to JUnit is not complete. The reason for that is that U2TP is also defined to specify more complex tests, e.g. integration tests or system tests, whereas JUnit is only suitable for unit tests. Also for TTCN-3, not all concepts can be mapped because U2TP provides some more advanced test concepts than TTCN-3.

Nevertheless, the provided mapping rules defined in the U2TP document are not the only way to map between U2TP and JUnit to TTCN-3, respectively. They only serve as references. In the following, we will firstly introduce JUnit and TTCN-3 briefly and then explain their mapping rules to U2TP.

17.3.1   JUnit

In order to test that their code works, people watch the code using calls like System.out.println or debugger. This approach has three problems: scroll blindness, subjectivity and lack of automation [HL02b]. First, it is hard to tell if a complex system is working because so many System.out.println methods are printing so much garbage. Second, it is hard to follow all the printed lines on the console. Third, when the develper makes changes in the code, things can break in an

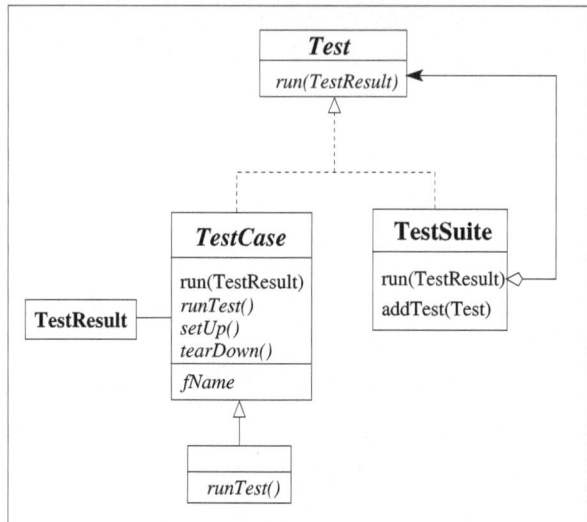

Fig. 17.2. JUnit Classes

unexpected way. If one does not have an automated test, broken subsystems may not be tested. For these reasons, unit-level tests assure that the code a developer has written will be tested automatically, and thus give confidence in the code.

JUnit is a framework for writing unit tests. This section introduces the JUnit framework and provides the mapping from the U2TP concepts to JUnit concepts.

Fundamentals of JUnit JUnit is written by Erich Gamma and Kent Beck. It is an open source framework for automated unit tests. JUnit tests are based on Java. Thus, its execution code is also Java for which there exist various compilers.

By means of the JUnit framework, software developers can derive tests from classes of the JUnit Framework and combine them into a test suite. A unit test checks a single unit of the implementation code, e.g. a method or a class. Unit tests are applied in a test driven design. The tests are developed in parallel to code implementation. In the former, tests are even written before the codes are implemented. The software developer writes the test routines for every piece of code so that the test can be re-run every time the code is changed. For eXtreme Programming [XP], where code integration and code testing are required permanently, unit tests are obligatory. Because of its simplicity, JUnit has become very popular in the XP domain. JUnit is integrated in many toolkits, e.g. Eclipse [ECla] or JBuilder [JBu].

In JUnit, a *test case* is the basic abstraction. A test case can be run in order to check if the test passes. It contains the test methods *setUp()* and *tearDown()*, a *main()* method which runs the test case and an optional *suite()* method which groups test methods in a test suite (Figure 17.2). Usually, every class that is written should have a test case. A JUnit *test suite* is structured in a hierarchical way and is composed of test cases or other test suites. A *test fixture* allows test

U2TP	JUnit
System Under Test (SUT)	not to be identified explicitly.
Test component	Cannot be mapped.
Arbiter	As a property of Test Suite of type TestResult.
Test context	A class inheriting from the TestCase class.
Test control	Overloading the *runTest* operation of the fixture.
Test case	Operation.
Stimulus and observation	Cannot be mapped.
Coordination	Any available synchronization mechanism.
Verdict	Predefined verdicts are pass, fail and error. No inconclusive verdict.
Test configuration	Cannot be mapped.
Wildcards	Cannot be mapped.
Coding rules	Cannot be mapped.
Timezone	Cannot be mapped.
Timer	Cannot be mapped.

Fig. 17.3. U2TP to JUnit Mapping Rules

cases to share common test data and to assure certain pre- and postconditions for every test method. At the end of a test run, JUnit reports a *pass, failure* or *error* as its test result by means of *assertions*. The JUnit framework provides a textual and a graphical test runner.

When putting the concepts into practice, the following steps have to be done[2]:

(1) Derive a subclass from junit.framework.Testcase;
(2) If fixture objects are needed, override the *setUp()* method;
(3) Define a number of tests that return void and whose method name begins with *test;*
(4) *If resources of the fixture need to be released, override the* tearDown() *method;*
(5) *If a related set of test cases need to be grouped, define a test suite.*

Mapping to JUnit JUnit served as one basis for the development of U2TP. Table 17.3 provides the mapping rules from U2TP to JUnit. A lot of the U2TP concepts

---

[2] In Section 17.4.5, an example is shown.

can be mapped to JUnit concepts. But since JUnit is a framework only for unit tests, there are a lot of concepts in U2TP which are not defined in JUnit and also needed for unit tests.

A System Under Test does not need to be identified explicitly in JUnit. Any class in the classpath can be considered as an utility class or a SUT class. An arbiter can be realized as a property of the test suite of a type TestResult. A test context is realized as a class inheriting from the JUnit TestCase class. Test control is defined by overloading the *runTest* operation of he JUnit fixture. A test case is an operation in JUnit. Coordination can be mapped using any available synchronization mechanism available to the test components such as semaphores. In JUnit, predefined verdicts are *pass, fail* and *error*. There is no *inconclusive* verdict. Test components, stimulus, observation, test configuration, timezone are not defined in JUnit since these concepts are only needed for system tests. Also wildcards, coding rules and timers are not concepts of JUnit.

17.3.2   TTCN-3

Fundamentals of TTCN-3 The *Testing and Test Control Notation* - 3rd edition (TTCN-3) is a test specification and implementation language to define test procedures for black-box testing. At time, it is the only accepted standard for test system development in the telecommunication area.

TTCN-3 is a modular language. It comprises concepts suitable for various types of system testings. Additionally to typical programming languages, it also contains features necessary to specify test procedures like test verdicts, matching mechanisms, timer handling, dynamic test configuration specifications, specification of encoding information, synchronous and asynchronous communications.

In a TTCN-3 module, stimuli are sent to the system under test (SUT). Its reactions are observed and compared with the expected behavior defined in the test case. Based on this comparison, the subsequent test behavior is determined and a test verdict is assigned. If the expected and the observed responses differ, a failure test verdict is assigned. A successful test is indicated by a test verdict pass. Since TTCN-3 has been introduced in the last chapter in detail, the reader is requested to read that chapter for a better understanding.

Mapping to TTCN-3 TTCN-3 served as a second basis for the development of the U2TP. Nevertheless, there are concepts which differ from or are added to the Testing Profile. Thus, a mapping from the Testing Profile to TTCN-3 is complete but not the other way around.

Table 17.4 shows an excerpt of the most important mapping rules of the standard. It compares the U2TP concepts with existing TTCN-3 testing concepts. Almost all U2TP concepts have direct correspondence or can be mapped to TTCN-3 testing concepts.

In order to represent the system under test, TTCN-3 provides the indirect definition via ports from the test components to the SUT. Test components are specified by component types. There is a default arbiter built in TTCN-3. If the user wants to specify an explicit arbiter, it must be realized by the main test

U2TP	TTCN-3
System Under Test (SUT)	Indirect definition via ports.
Test component	Component types.
Arbiter	A built-in. User-defined arbiters are realized by the MTC.
Test context	Module definition part.
Test control	Module control part.
Test case	Test case with behavior functions. The MTC creates and starts test components.
Stimulus, observation, coordination	Various TTCN-3 messages.
Verdict	Pre-defined verdicts pass, fail, inconclusive and error. For user-defined verdicts, a special verdict type is needed.
Test configuration	Configuration operations.
Wildcards	Data matching mechanisms.
Coding rules	Encode attributes.
Timer	Timer and timer operations.
Timezone	Cannot be mapped.

Fig. 17.4. U2TP to TTCN-3 Mapping Rules

component (MTC). The test context is mapped to the TTCN-3 module definition part. U2TP test case can be mapped to test cases and functions where the MTC firstly creates test components and start their behavior by functions. Stimuli, observation and coordinations are realized by various kinds of messages. Verdicts are mapped to TTCN-3 verdict types with the predefined verdicts *pass, fail, inconclusive* and *error*. Test configuration are realized by configuration operations. Wildcards can be mapped to wildcards. Coding rules are realized by encoding attributes. Timers and timer operations are present for U2TP as well as for TTCN-3. Timezones are not TTCN-3 concepts. [3]

---

[3] Timezones are introduced in another approach of TTCN-3, called *TimedTTCN* [DGN02]. The change request has already been submitted to ETSI (European Telecommunication Standardization Institution) where TTCN-3 has been developed.

17.4   Test Development with U2TP – A Case Study

In this section, a UML test model [4] is specified based on U2TP. For that, a roaming algorithm for Bluetooth devices [PDGN03] is taken as a case study.

17.4.1   The Application

Bluetooth is an established standard for short-range wireless communication. The Bluetooth specification enables small devices to interact within a short range. The standards related to Bluetooth include both the hardware (radio, baseband and hardware interface) and the basic protocol layers that allow Bluetooth software to run on different Bluetooth enabled devices.

The current Bluetooth standard does not support roaming of Bluetooth devices [Blub]. If a device is losing the link to its master, no provision is made to transfer the connection to another master. Nevertheless, roaming within Bluetooth piconets might be useful when having more than one Bluetooth LAN access point, in order to have a seamless connection when moving. The need for a basic roaming support for Bluetooth devices descends from a project [Blua] situated in the medical domain. Its goal is to replace the traditional cable-based monitoring of patients during surgical treatments with a wireless transmission of the patient's monitoring data using Bluetooth hardware devices.

Roaming for Bluetooth   The an existing roaming approach [PDGN03], it is assumed that all masters (i.e. data receivers) are connected to a fixed network. The mobile devices (i.e. data sending slaves) are usually moving along the masters. If a slave runs the risk of losing connection to its actual master, the connection must be handed over to the next master. The slave prevents the loss by periodically checking the quality of the link to the master by sending a *HCI_Get_Link_Quality* command defined in the Bluetooth standard [Blub]. If the quality drops below a certain threshold value the next master will be chosen. The slave tries to connect directly to the next master, knowing to which master it has to contact to next. Movements of the slave are tracked by a *Location Server*, which updates and provides slave's spacial information in form of a *roaming list* whenever the slave changes its master.

The Activity Diagram in Figure 17.5 shows the activities of a slave necessary for roaming. The slave tries to connect to a master. If the connection is successful, the updated roaming list is transferred to the slave and data can be sent. In parallel, the link quality between slave and master is observed. If the quality gets bad, the slave will look in the roaming list for a new master and try to connect to that master directly. If, for any reason, no connection can be established, a warning message is sent to the user (e.g. by a warning light or a special sound indicating that a problem has occurred). Another warning message is sent to

---

[4] To clarify the terminologies: With *design model*, we mean the system design model in UML. When talking about the *test model*, we mean the UML model enriched with U2TP concepts.

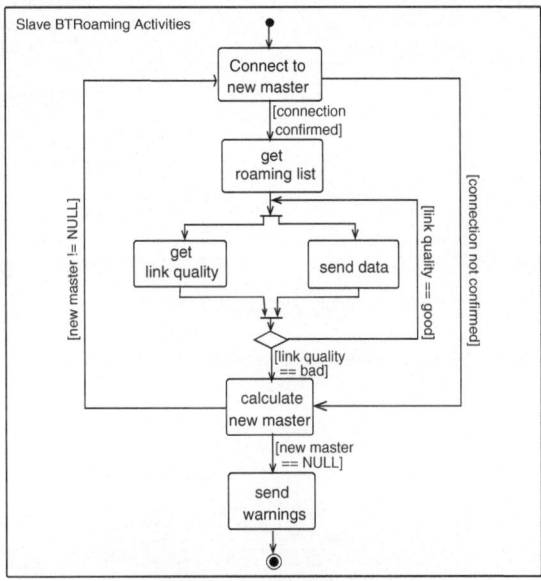

Fig. 17.5. Roaming Algorithm as Activity Diagram

the last master. If the connection to the last master is still alive, the reception of a warning message can be used to initiate appropriate exception handling mechanisms.

Figure 17.6 shows the design of the protocol stack resulting from the proposed roaming approach: Special roaming layers (*Slave Roaming Layer* and *Master Roaming Layer*) are added. They take care of the correct transfer of the connections. Our roaming approach makes no use of the higher protocol stacks of Bluetooth. Therefore, the roaming layers are implemented directly on the hardware interface called *Host Controller Interface* (HCI). The application layers are set upon the roaming layers. The interface from roaming layer to application layer is called *Slave Roaming Interface* (SRI) and *Master Roaming Interface* (MRI), respectively.

Additionally, a master is specified as a fixed network node. Thus, it also embodies the LAN protocol stacks to be able to communicate with the local network. The interface between the *Master Roaming Layer* and the Ethernet is called *Local Network Interface* (LNI).

17.4.2   Test Preparation

Before specifying the test model, the focus of the test must be defined, i.e. which classes should be tested and which interfaces does the tester need in order to get access to these classes.

Figure 17.7 presents a test configuration with one slave and two masters. The focus of the tests is the Slave BTRoaming layer of Figure 17.6. Thus, the Slave

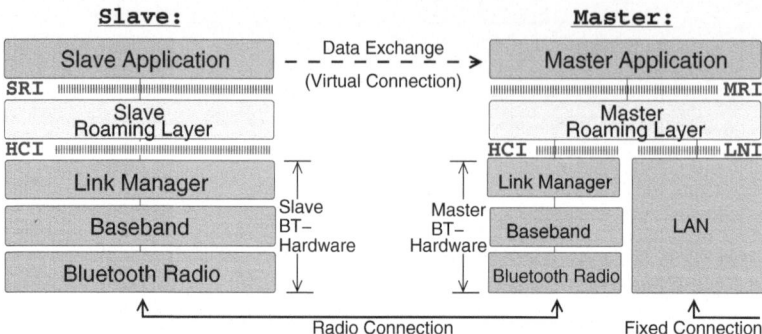

Fig. 17.6. Protocol Stack with Roaming Layer

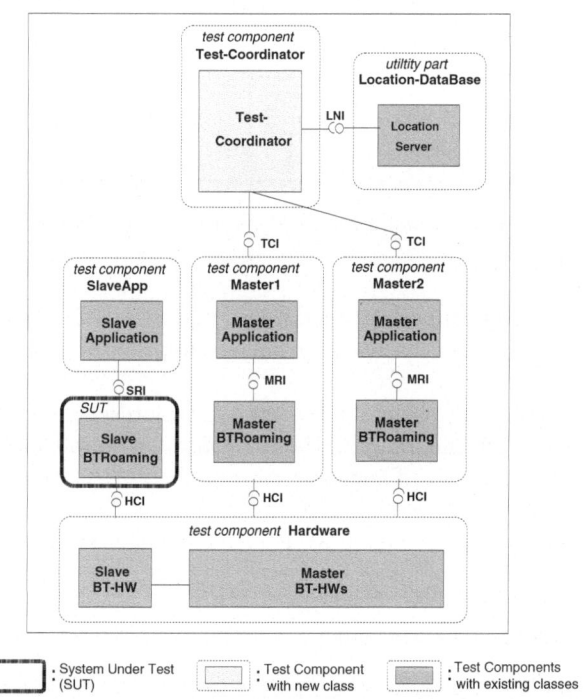

Fig. 17.7. Role Assignment for System Components

Application layer is one test component. Other test components are the underlying Bluetooth Hardware layer and the master components Master1 and Master2.

On the top of the slave and the masters, a new test component of class Test-Coordinator is specified. This test component is the main test component which administrates and instructs the other test components during the test execution. The coordinator is also responsible for the setting of the test verdicts during test case execution. The coordinator has access to the utility part Location-DataBase. This data base embodies the Location Server, which owns the slave roaming lists and the network structure table.

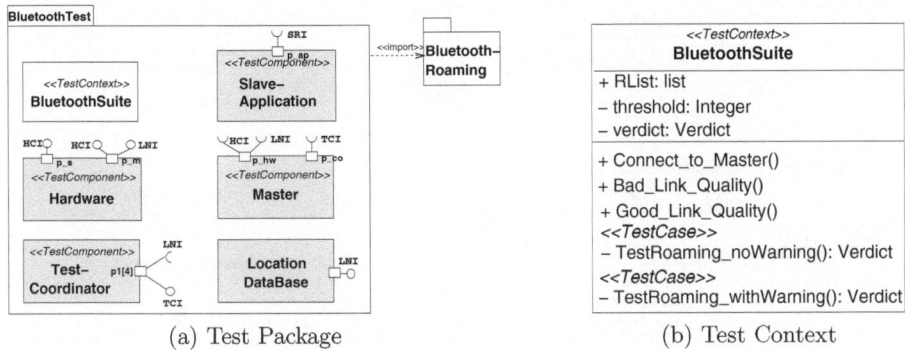

(a) Test Package   (b) Test Context

Fig. 17.8. Test Package & Test Context

In this case study, the following functionalities of the Slave Roaming layer should be tested:

- Is the Slave Roaming layer able to choose a new master by looking up in its roaming list when the connection with its current master gets weak?
- Does the Slave Roaming layer request a connection establishment to the chosen master?
- Does the Slave Roaming layer wait for a connection confirmation of the master when the connection has been established?
- Does the Slave Roaming layer send a warning to the environment, when no master can be found and the roaming list is empty?

These test objectives assume that basic functionalities of the Slave Roaming layer like data forwarding from the application layer to the hardware layer have already been tested in a preceding capability test.

17.4.3   Test Architecture

First of all, a test package for the test model must be defined. The test package is named BluetoothTest (Figure 17.8a). The test package imports the classes and interfaces from a BluetoothRoaming package in order to get access to the classes to be tested.

In Section 17.4.2, the Slave BTRoaming layer is assigned to *SUT* and other system components are assigned to *test components*. The test package consists of five test component classes, one utility part and one test context class. only implicitly specified in the test system. triggered by validation actions in the test cases. The test context class is called BluetoothSuite. It shows various test attributes, some test functions and two test cases (Figure 17.8b).

Test configuration and test control are also specified in the test context class. The *test configuration* (Figure 17.9a) corresponds with the test configuration in Figure 17.7, except that it consists of one slave and four masters m1–m4. Ports with interfaces connect the test components and the SUT to each other.

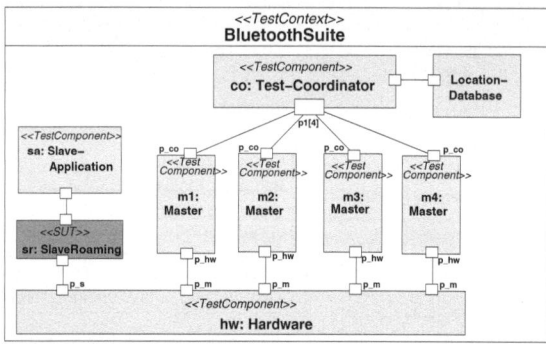 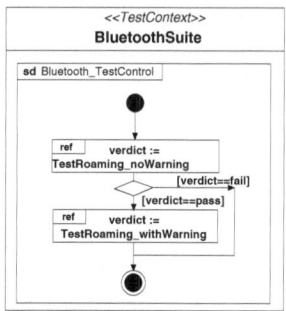

(a) Test Configuration   (b) Test Control

Fig. 17.9. Test Configuration & Test Control

Figure 17.9b illustrates the *test control*, indicating the execution order of the test cases: First, test case TestRoaming_noWarning is executed. If the test result is pass, the second test case TestRoaming_withWarning will also be executed. Otherwise, the test is finished.

17.4.4   Test Behavior

For the specification of test behavior, test objectives for the case study must be defined. As an example, a test case for the following scenario is presented:

> *After the exchange of two data packages, the link quality between Slave and its current master m1 becomes bad. The first alternative master in the roaming list m2 cannot be reached since the link quality is also weak. Thus, after at most two seconds, a further master m3 is chosen from the roaming list and the connection is established successfully.*

Figure 17.10 shows a Sequence Diagram and depicts the test case for the scenario above. Test case TestRoaming_ NoWarning starts with the activation of the timer T1 of six seconds. T1 is a guarding timer which is started at the beginning and stopped at the end of a test case. It assures that the test finishes properly even if, e.g. the SUT crashes and does not respond anymore. In this case, the timeout event is caught by a default behavior.

The function Connect_To_Master, which is referenced at the beginning of the test case establishes a connection between the Slave and Master m1 (see Figure 17.11a): The connection request (con_request) is initiated by the Slave-Application and is forwarded to the master. The master informs the Test-Coordinator about that observation. Then, the master accepts the connection (con_accept), resulting in a confirmation sent from the Bluetooth hardware to both the slave and the master. Thereupon, the master informs the Test-Coordinator about the successful connection, which allows the Test-Coordinator to build a new roaming

list containing the masters (reference makeList) and to transfer it via the master
to the slave using the message roamingList([M2,M3,M4]). The entries of the roaming list indicate that if the connection between slave and its current master gets
weak, master m2 should be tried next. If this connection cannot be established,
master m3 should contacted. As a last alternative, m4 should be chosen. If none
of the alternative masters can be connected to, warnings would be sent out.

When the referenced behavior of Connect_to_Master has finished in Figure
17.10, the slave has successfully connected to master m1 and Slave-Application
starts to send data to the master. Additionally, the link quality is checked periodically. Checking the link quality is specified in the functions Good_Link_Quality
and Bad_Link_Quality in Figure 17.11b. Herein, Slave Roaming triggers the evaluation request and receives the result from the hardware.

In the first evaluation of test case TestRoaming_noWarning (Figure 17.10), the
Hardware has to be tuned to report a good link quality. Thus, further data can
be sent. In the second evaluation, the link quality is determined to be bad.
Therefore, a new master is looked up. According to the roaming list, the new

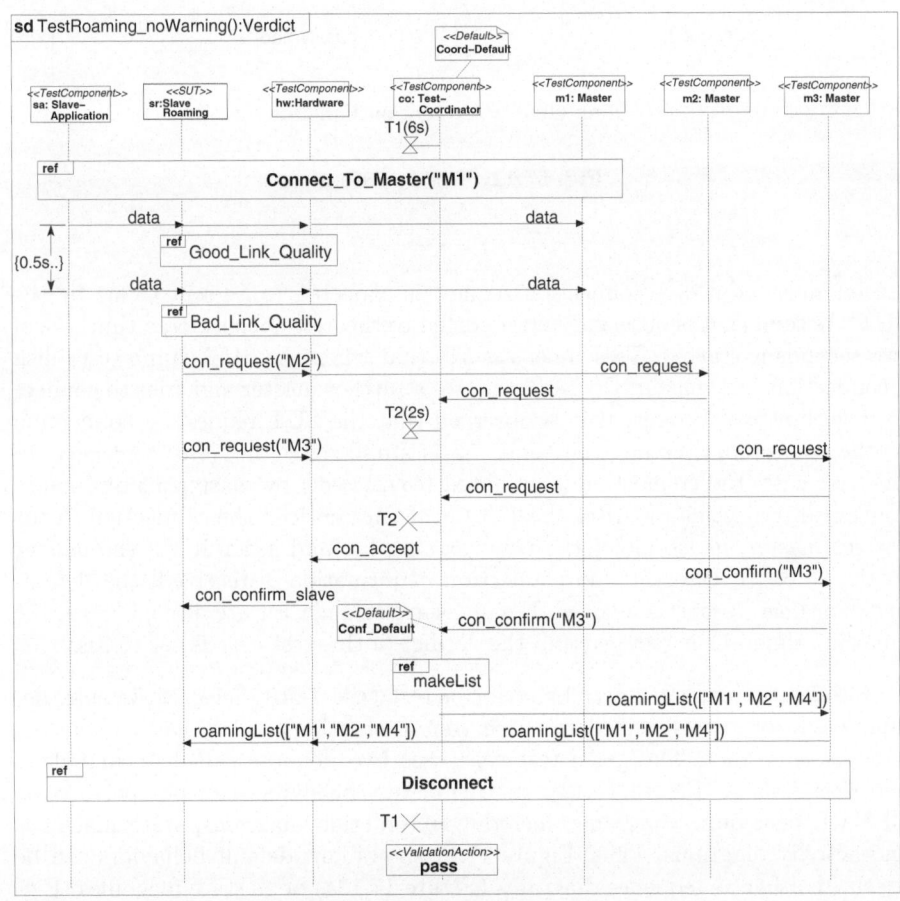

Fig. 17.10. Test Scenario

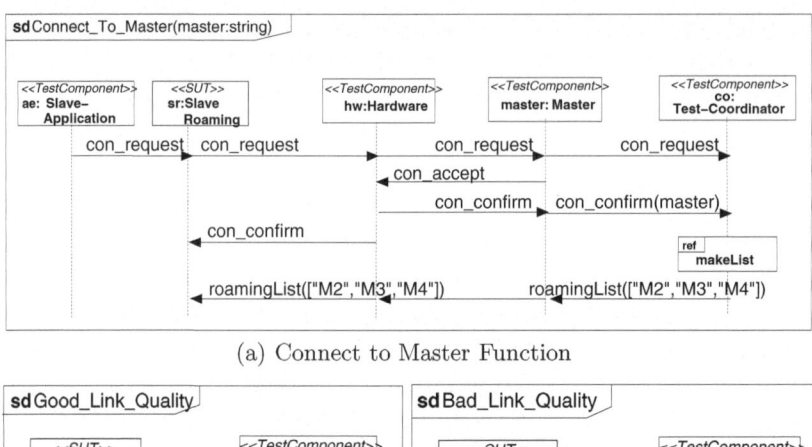

(a) Connect to Master Function

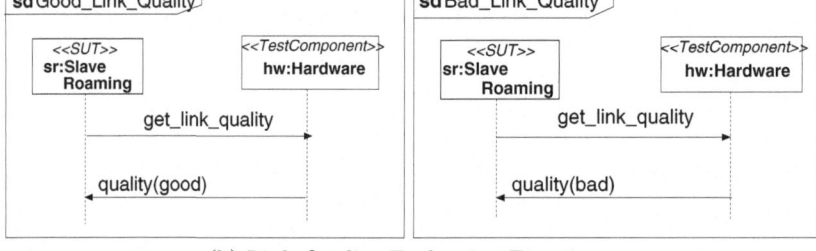

(b) Link Quality Evaluation Functions

Fig. 17.11. Test Functions

master must be m2. A connection request is expected to be sent to m2 by the SUT. As soon as it is observed and reported to the Test-Coordinator, a timer T2 of two seconds is started. This timer assures that when the SUT cannot establish a connection to a master, the SUT chooses a further master and tries to connect to it within two seconds. If it is observed that the SUT requests a connection to the correct master m3, the timer T2 is stopped by the Test-Coordinator. In this test case, the connection is accepted (con_accept) by master m3 and hence confirmed (con_confirm). After the Test-Coordinator noticed the connection to the correct master, it assembles the new roaming list and sends it via the master to the slave. In case that no connection confirmation is received, the default behavior Conf_Default is invoked. Finally, slave and master are disconnected, the guarding timer T1 is stopped and the verdict of this test case is set to pass.

Besides the expected test behavior of test case TestRoaming_NoWarning, default behaviors are specified to catch the observations which lead to a fail or inconclusive verdict. The given test case uses two defaults called Coord_Default and Conf_Default (Figure 17.12). In U2TP, test behaviors can be specified by all UML behavioral diagrams, including interaction diagrams, state machines and activity diagrams. Thus, Figure 17.12 shows how default behaviors can be specified either as sequence diagrams (Figure 17.12a) or as state machines (Figure 17.12b).

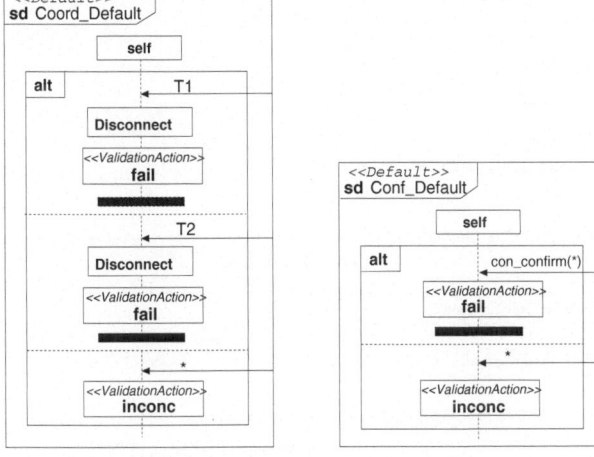

(a) Default as Sequence Diagrams

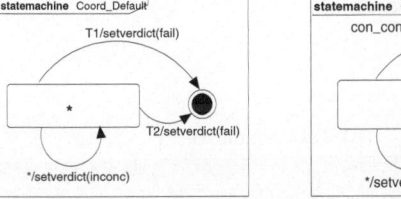

(b) Default as State Machines

Fig. 17.12. Test Defaults

Coord_Default is an instance-specific default applied to the coordinator. It defines three alternatives. The first two alternatives catch the timeout events of the timers T1 and T2. In both cases, slave and master will be disconnected and the verdict is set to fail. After that, the test component terminates itself. The third alternative catches any other unexpected events. In this case, the verdict is set to inconclusive and the test behavior returns back to the test event which triggered the default.

Conf_Default is an event-specific default attached to the connection confirmation event. In the Test-Coordinator, this default is invoked if either the connection confirmation is not sent from the correct master or another message than the connection confirmation is received. In the first case, the verdict is set to fail and the test component finishes itself. In the latter case, the verdict is set to inconclusive and the test returns to main test behavior.

17.4.5   Case Study: Mappings

This section depicts how to map the Bluetooth test model to JUnit and TTCN-3 by applying the introduced mapping rules (Section 17.3).

514   Zhen Ru Dai

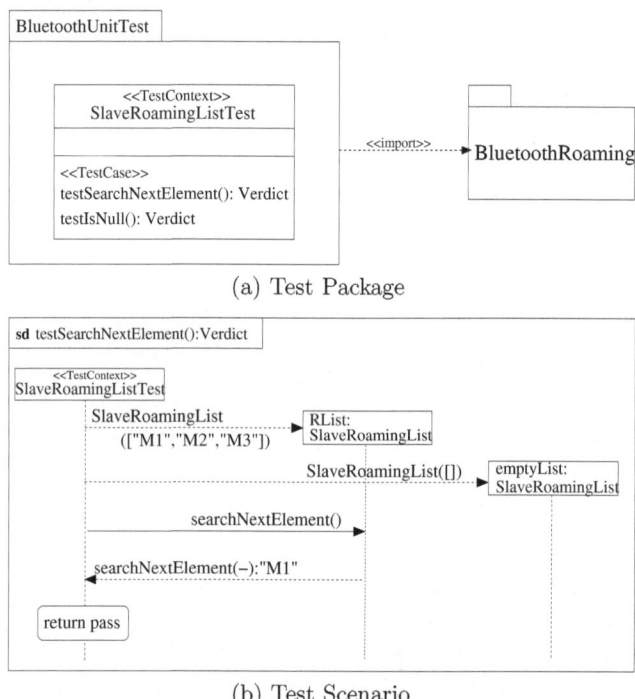

(a) Test Package

(b) Test Scenario

Fig. 17.13. JUnit Test Package and Scenario

Mapping to JUnit In the introduced roaming algorithm, the handling of the
slave roaming list plays an important role in order to guarantee the right choice
of the successory master. Therefore, class SlaveRoamingList will be tested. This
class provides the following methods:

- boolean isNull(): checks if the roaming list is empty. True, if the list is empty,
  otherwise false.
- String searchNextElement(): looks for the next element in the roaming list.

Method isNull() asks whether or not is the roaming list empty, so that no
alternative new master can be found. In case of being empty, warnings will be
sent to the environment. Method searchNextElement() gives out the name of the
new master.

Figure 17.13 shows the unit test specification with U2TP. Figure 17.13a)
depicts a test package called BluetoothUnitTest. The package imports from the
implementation package of the package BluetoothRoaming, in which the methods
isNull() and searchNextElement() are specified. The test context in the test package is called SlaveRoamingListTest, which includes two test cases: testSearchNextEle-
ment() and testIsNull(). The names of the tests are similar to the methods which
should be tested. They just begin with the prefix "test" for a better recognition.

```
/**** BluetoothUnitTest.java ***/

(0) import junit.framework.TestCase;
(1) import BluetoothRoaming;

(2) public class SlaveRoamingListTest extends TestCase {
(3)     private SlaveRoamingList RList;
(4)     private SlaveRoamingList emptyList;

(5)     protected void setUp () {
(6)       RList = new SlaveRoamingList (["M1","M2","M3"]);
(7)       emptyList = new SlaveRoamingList ([ ]);
(8)     }

(9)     public void testIsNull () {
(10)       assertTrue (emptyList.isNull ());
(11)    }

(12)    public void testSearchNextElement () {
(13)      String element = RList.nextElement ();
(14)      assertTrue (element.equals(new String ("M1")));
(15)    }

(16)    public static Test suite () {
(17)      TestSuite suite = new TestSuite ();
(18)      suite.adddTest (new SearchNewMasterTest ("testSearchNextElement"));
(19)      suite.addTest (new SearchNewMasterTest ("testIsNull"));
(20)      return suite;
(21)    }

(22)    public static void main (String args[ ]) {
(23)      junit.textui.TestRunner.run (suite());
(24)    }
(25) }
```

Fig. 17.14. JUnit Code

Figure 17.13b) shows a Sequence Diagram of the test case testSearchNextElement(), which returns a verdict as its result. The test case starts with the test context instance SlaveRoamingListTest and firstly creates two instances RList and emptyList of type SlaveRoamingList. RList has the entries ["M1","M2","M3"] meaning that whenever the link quality between the current master and the slave becomes bad, Master M1 should be the successory master, otherwise Master M2 and M3, respectively. emptyList has no entries. It is created to check whether the method recognizes an empty list and thus send warning messages to the environment.

After the two roaming list instances are created, RList is asked to provide the next element of the roaming list. According to the ordering of the roaming list, the return value is M1. After that, the test is finished and a verdict of value pass is returned to the test context instance. In case the return value is not M1, the verdict will be fail [5].

Figure 17.14 presents the mapped JUnit code of the U2TP diagrams in Figure 17.13. The name of the test file is called *BluetoothTest.java*. In the beginning of the JUnit code, the JUnit framework and the Bluetooth package are imported (lines 0 and 1). An class called SlaveRoamingListTest is built, which corresponds with the U2TP test context instance. Two methods are defined in the JUnit code (lines 9 and 12) which are the test cases in the JUnit test suite. In the test fixture (line 2-4), the objects RList and emptyList are created which is the mapping result of the instance creation in the U2TP instance creations in the beginning of the test case. Figure 17.13b) calls the method testSearchNextElement() (lines 12-15) and asserts a pass verdict, if the test case returns M1 as a result. The lines 16-21 adds the three test cases to the test suite. The last three lines (lines 22-24) calls up the JUnit textual test runner.

Mapping to TTCN-3 After having tested the functionalities of the class Slave-RoamingList, it is time to test the whole *Slave Roaming* layer (Figure 17.6). Therefore, we consider the *Slave Roaming* layer as a black-box, where only actions on the system interfaces can be seen.

The TTCN-3 code in the Figures 17.15, 17.16 and 17.17[6] show the TTCN-3 module in order to test the *Bluetooth Roaming*. The TTCN-3 code derive from the UML diagrams in the Figures 17.8, 17.9, 17.10 and 17.12. They are implemented by means of the mapping rules indicated in Table 17.4. Figure 17.15 embodies the TTCN-3 module called BluetoothTest which imports all types and functions from a BluetoothRoaming module (lines 1-2[7]). After the definition of some external functions and types, various port types are defined. In lines 4-8, a port type called SA2SR_Port_PType is specified with its appropriate message types of data_Type, con_request_Type. Later on, this port type is needed to define the communication port between the *Slave Application* and the *Slave Roaming*[8].

After the port type definitions, test component types with their ports must be specified. Lines 9-15 depicts the test component type SUT_CType, including its port between the *Slave Application* and *Slave Roaming* of type SA2SR_Port_PType and the port between the *Slave Roaming* and the *Hardware* of type SR2HW_Port-_PType .

Two defaults are specified in the test module. Conf_Default is a event-specific default (lines 16-22). Its task is to catch the con_confirm message of any parameter values other than "m3" and set the verdict to fail. Coord_Default (lines 23-34) is a component-specific default which is invoked whenever the *Test Coordinator*

---

[5] This is normally caught be a default behavior, which is defined separately from the actual test case.

[6] The TTCN-3 code in all three tables belong to one TTCN-3 module. They have been separated into three tables for spatial reasons.

[7] Blank lines are not counted.

[8] Various other port types and component types are specified in the TTCN-3 module, which we do not show in the example. The complete TTCN-3 module can be required by the author.

```
                    /*** Bluetooth Roaming Test module ***/

(1) module BluetoothTest {
        import from BluetoothRoaming all;

        /** external functions and type definitions ... **/

        /** Ports **/
    (5)  type port SA2SR_Port_PType mixed {
                            // Port between Slave Application and Slave Roaming
            inout data_Type, con_request_Type }
        /* more port definitions ... */

        /** components **/
(10)    type component SUT_CType {
            // Slave Roaming layer is assigned to SUT
            port SA2SR_Port_PType p_sa;     // port btw. SUT and Slave appl.
            port SR2HW_Port_PType p_sh      // port btw. SUT and hardware
        }
(15)    /* more component definitions ... */

        /** Defaults **/
        altstep Conf_Default () runs on TestCoordinator_CType {
            [] any port.receive (con_confirm_Type:{?}) {
                setverdict (fail) }
(20)        [] any port.receive {
                setverdict (inconc) }
        }

        altstep Coord_Default () runs on TestCoordinator_CType {
            timer T1, T2;
(25)        [] T1.timeout {
                Disconnect_co ();
                setverdict (fail) }
            [] T2.timeout {
                Disconnect_co ();
(30)            setverdict (fail) }
            [] any port.receive {
                Disconnect_co ();
                setverdict (inconclusive) }
        }
```

Fig. 17.15. Bluetooth Test Module: TTCN-3 Types and Defaults

triggers a timeout of the timers T1 and T2 or receives an unexpected message. Both defaults run on the test component type TestCoordinator_CType. Their implementations correspond to the diagrams in Figure 17.12.

Figure 17.16 shows two important functions in the test module. In our test configuration, we determined the *Test Coordinator* to be the main test component (MTC) because the *Test Coordinator* controls the roaming procedure by

```
(1)    /* test configuration function */
       function BluetoothSuite_Configuration
        (inout SUT_CType sut, inout TestCoordinator_CType mtc_comp,
        inout SlaveApplication_CType sa, inout Hardware_CType hw,
(5)     inout Master_CType m1, inout Master_CType m2,
        inout Master_CType m3, inout Master_CType m4)
       runs on TestCoordinator_CType {
                                 // TestCoordinator is assigned to MTC
        sa := SlaveApplication_CType.create;
(10)    map (sut: p_sa, sa: p_sa);
        hw := Hardware_CType.create;
        map (sut: p_sh, hw: p_sh);
        m1 := Master_CType.create;
        connect (hw: p_mh, m1: p_mh);
(15)    connect (m1: p_co, mtc_comp: p_co);
        m2 := Master_CType.create;
        connect (hw: p_mh, m2: p_mh);
        connect (m2: p_co, mtc_comp: p_co);
        m3 := Master_CType.create;
(20)    connect (hw: p_mh, m3: p_mh);
        connect (m3: p_co, mtc_comp: p_co);
        m4 := Master_CType.create;
        connect (hw: p_mh, m4: p_mh);
        connect (m4: p_co, mtc_comp: p_co);
(25)   }

       function NoWarning_master (charstring master) runs on Master_CType {
        var default master_def := activate (Master_Default ());
        if (master == "M1") {
          Connect_to_Master_ma_m1 ();
(30)      while (true) {
            p_hm.receive (data); }
        }
        else if (master == "M2") {
            Connect_to_Master_ma_m1 ();
(35)        p_hm.receive (con_request); // failed request
            p_co.send (con_request);
        }
        else if (master == "M3") {
          Connect_to_Master_ma_m1 ();
(40)      p_hm.receive (con_request); // successful request
          p_co.send (con_request);
          p_hm.send (con_accept);
          p_hm.receive (con_confirm_Type:{"M3"});
          p_co.send (con_confirm_Type:{"M3"});
(45)      p_co.receive (roamingList_Type:{"M1","M2","M4"});
          p_hm.send (roamingList_Type:{"M1","M2","M4"});
        }
        deactivate (master_def);
       }
```

Fig. 17.16. Bluetooth Test Module (ctnd.): TTCN-3 Functions

creating and updating the roaming list of the slave and embodies the whole intelligence of the test system. In TTCN-3, the MTC is responsible for the settlement of the test configuration. Thus, function BluetoothSuite_Configuration (lines 1-25) which is implemented to create test components, including the mapping between the SUT and the test components and connection within the test components, runs on the TestCoordintor_CType.

Function NoWarning_master (lines 26-49) specifies the behavior of the master instances for test case TestRomaing_noWarning (Figure 17.17). Depending on which master (M1, M2 or M3) calls the function, the appropriate behavior is executed. The sequence derive from the message exchanges of the three master instances in the test scenario in Figure 17.10.

In Figure 17.17, test case Test_Roaming_noWarning is specified. This test case runs on the MTC type, which is the TestCoorodinator_CType in the given test configuration. The system under test (SUT) is the *Slave Roaming* layer. After the declaration of some variables and timers, the test configuration is set up by means of the BluetoothSuite_Configuration function. Afterwards, the component-specific default Coord_Default is activated and test component are started with their appropriate functions. A timer T1 is started which assures that the test case terminates properly within a predefined time period of 6 time units. Now the real test behavior can be executed. First of all, *Test Coordinator* connects itself to master M1. The connection of the other test components to master M1 is defined in their individual functions which already started in lines 13-17.

After the connection with M1, two con_request messages are received by the *Test Coordinator*. The first message comes from M2 indicating that master M2 has been asked to connect to the slave. The second connection request comes from M3 to inform that master M2 somehow failed to connect to the slave. Thus master M3 has been asked to. A timer T2 has been started in between to assure that the connection requests are performed periodically, so that the slave will not loose its connection to the current master without having connected to a new master.

Afterwards, the event-specific default Conf_Default is activated. If master M3 accepts the connection request and answers with an connection confirmation (con_confirm) message, the default will be deactivated again. In this case, a new roaming list will be calculated for the slave. The list will be sent to master M3 and the connections will be released. Timer T1 is stopped afterwards and Coord_Default deactivated. Finally, the test verdict is set to pass.

In lines 35-41, the control part is implemented which defines the sequence of test case execution. In this example, the described test case TestRoaming_noWarning will be executed at first. Only if its test verdict is pass, another test case called TestRoaming_withWarning will be executed.

17.5   Summary

In this chapter, the U2TP has been introduced. U2TP is a new UML profile which provides means to specify tests based on UML 2.0. By doing so, a UML

```
(1)    /* test case */
       testcase TestRoaming_noWarning ()
       runs on TestCoordinator_CType system SUT_CType {
                             // TestCoordinator is assigned to MTC
(5)      var SlaveApplication_CType sa;
         var Hardware_CType hw;
         var Master_CType m1, m2, m3, m4;
         var TestCoordinator_CType co;
         timer T1, T2;
(10)     BluetoothSuite_Configuration (system, mtc, sa, hw, m1, m2, m3, m4);
         var default coord_def := activate (Coord_Default ());
                                     // component-specific default
         hw.start (NoWarning_hw);
         sa.start (NoWarning_sa);
(15)     m1.start (NoWarning_master ("M1"));
         m2.start (NoWarning_master ("M2"));
         m3.start (NoWarning_master ("M3"));
         T1.start (6.0);
         Connect_To_Master_co_m1 ();
(20)     p_co.receive (con_request) from m2;        // first request to m2
         T2.start (2.0);
         p_co.receive (con_request) from m3;        // second request to m3
         T2.stop;
         var default conf_def := activate (Conf_Default ());
(25)                             // event-specific default
         p_co.receive (con_confirm_Type: {"M3"}) from m3;
         deactivate (conf_def);
         var roamingList_Type RList := makeList ();
         p_co.send (roamingList_Type: RList) to m3;
(30)     Disconnect_co ();
         T1.stop;
         deactivate (coord_def);
         setverdict (pass);
       }

(35)   /* module control part */
       control {
         if (execute (TestRoaming_noWarning ()) == pass) {
           execute (TestRoaming_withWarning ())
         }
(40)   }
    }
                /* end of Bluetooth Roaming Test module */
```

Fig. 17.17. Bluetooth Test Module (ctnd.): TTCN-3 Test Cases and Control Part

system model may be re-used for testing purposes. This enhances the cooperation between system designers and test designers. Furthermore, existing system models can be provided to the tester for a proper and more detailed test specification. This saves time and reduces cost for test specification.

Besides the test concepts, the U2TP also introduces rules to map U2TP to JUnit and TTCN-3, respectively. By doing so, the test model can be executed based on the mappings and the existing JUnit and TTCN-3 compilers. In the chapter, the usage of the U2TP has been shown by means of a case study. Also, the mappings between the languages are demonstrated on the case study.

Part VI

Beyond Testing

This last part of the book introduces two extensions of the typical testing approach. It describes methods for the continuous testing effort, also at a later run-time of the system. Furthermore, it recalls essentials of model checking, a different powerful technique to get "better" systems, on the one hand to separate model checking and testing, on the other hand, to show possible combinations leading to approaches like *black box checking* or *adaptive model checking*. The latter glue *learning* of automata and model checking to study an underlying system.

18 Run-Time Verification

Séverine Colin[1] and Leonardo Mariani[2]

[1] Laboratoire d'Informatique de l'Université de Franche-Comté (LIFC)
Université de Franche-Comté - CNRS - INRIA
colin@lifc.univ-fcomte.fr
[2] Dipartimento di Informatica, Sistemistica e Comunicazione
Università di Milano Bicocca
mariani@disco.unimib.it

18.1 Introduction

We are going into a ubiquitous computing world, where computation is in every object around us. When that finally happens, when computers finally "disappear into the woodwork" [Dav02], more people will be using computers without realizing they are interacting with computers. This is beginning to happen now. Once people are surrounded by computational artifacts, and when these artifacts are linked together by all forms of networking, both wired and wireless, then the current incipient computer utility will become the predominant aspect.

Implicit in the term utility are such attributes as reliability, flexibility, availability, reserve capacity, and economy. In the long run, the effect of a computer utility system on transforming our basic institutions and social practices may be its most important result. But before that happens, we need to ask the right questions. Are we designing access and data security in our systems? Are reliability and dependability core properties built into these systems?

The question now is how do we build more reliable and dependable computational infrastructures? Dependability has been defined as the property a computer system has so that reliance can justifiably be placed on the service it delivers. The threats to building dependable computing systems include factors such as faults, errors and failures. The means for removing or avoiding such threats include mechanisms that can prevent the faults, remove the errors, and can be used to forecast where the failures are and probably when they occur. Effectiveness of many of these mechanisms can be increased by using data representing the run-time behavior of the target system; in fact these run-time data contain execution samples representing single behaviors of an implemented system. Run-time data is mainly used to check if the system respects requirements, e.g, monitored data can be used to verify temporal constraints. Verification is often performed at run-time, while data is continuously gathered, and therefore called *run-time verification*. In particular, run-time verification can be exploited both during beta testing and during normal use of the software. In the case of beta testing, verification is performed by oracles checking correctness of executions, while during the normal use of software, verification is performed by monitors checking correctness of executions in the deployment environment.

M. Broy et al. (Eds.): Model-Based Testing of Reactive Systems, LNCS 3472, pp. 525-555, 2005.
© Springer-Verlag Berlin Heidelberg 2005

Complete specifications are rarely available, thus it is not realistic to suppose that every behavior can be always classified as positive or negative. However, it is possible to formally specify aspects that are critical for the target application. For instance, temporal constraints can be very important for a car embedded system, but can be of minor importance for a desktop application. On the other hand, in order to ascertain security on desktop applications, unsafe behaviors and unexpected communication events can be more important to detected. Properties that must be checked are often specified by logic formulas, such as in MaC [KKL+01, SSD+03] and PathExplorer [HR01b] that use a three-valued logic and the Linear Temporal Logic (both future and past) respectively [Pnu77]. However, other approaches use mathematical predicates to specify properties, such as in Raz et al.'s anomaly detection technique [RKS02], or implement algorithms addressing specific problems, such as for the Eraser tool that dynamically detects data races [SBN+97].

Recently, run-time verification techniques have been extended with learning mechanisms based on field-data. In particular, data collected in the field is used to infer either an abstract behavior or some properties of the implementation that are then either checked with respect to specification or used during regression testing to match the behavior of new components replacing the observed ones.

In this chapter, first we introduce to the reader the basic concepts of run-time verification (Sections 18.2 and 18.3), and then we present the main verification techniques based on run-time data (Sections 18.4 and 18.5). Furthermore, we present possible extensions of basic run-time verification techniques that can be used when there is no model available (Section 18.6). Finally, we conclude by reporting known case studies (Section 18.7) and by tracing future research directions (Section 18.8).

18.2   The Run-Time Verification Framework

Run-time verification techniques are used to dynamically verify the behavior observed in the target system with respect to given requirements. Requirements are often formally specified and verification is used both to check that the observed behavior matches specified properties and to explicitly recognize undesirable behaviors in the target system.

Since verification is performed while the system is executing, traditional computational intensive verification methods work poorly; therefore, run-time verification techniques are intended as the lightweight counterpart of "off-line" verification techniques.

In particular, a run-time verification technique analyzes the behavior observed in the target system to establish correctness of each single execution by intercepting both important events and observable outputs. Obligations checked at run-time are quite simple in respect to properties that can be verified off-line because the amount of resources that can be employed during system execution is limited and also because conditions checked on single executions, which is the most frequent case, tend to be quite simple.

The point is why check for the fulfillment of obligations at run-time if you can verify the system's formal specification or the system's model? There are several good reasons to use run-time verification:

- if you check the model of your system, you cannot be confident of the implementation since correctness of the model does not imply correctness of the implementation.
- some information is available only at run-time or is convenient to be checked at run-time. For example, it could be not feasible to prove in a reasonable amount of time that your system never reaches a critical status C, even if a formal specification exists, but it could be possible to verify at run-time that your system does not reach status C, at least for observed executions.
- behaviors may depend on the environment where the target system runs; therefore it is not possible to have some necessary information before the system is deployed.
- in the case of systems where security is important or in the case of critical systems, it is useful to verify behaviors that have already been statically proved or tested.

Run-time verification can be compared to testing. In the case of testing, the tester defines a "reasonable" set of test cases that once executed provide a "sufficient level of confidence" on the target system. Test case generation and selection can be performed on different models with different criteria, each one focusing on complementary aspects of the system under test, such as a model of the system's behavior, a specification of a protocol or the software architecture (see Chap. 12 of this book for details on test case generation).

Instead, run-time verification is based on the observation of the dynamic behavior of the target system and on the possibility to establish if the current behavior is correct or not. Run-time verification also provides the possibility to continue to check properties even after the software has been deployed in the final environment, but it requires additional resources in the execution environment and can be intrusive in respect to the target application. On the contrary, testing finishes with the delivery of the application (eventually, in regression testing, it is possible to test a new version of the same application).

Testing and run-time verification are also complementary, in fact one can verify results of the execution of test cases by combining test and run-time verification. Moreover, if one considers that test cases can be generated to stress a property that is verified at run-time, the connection between testing and run-time verification becomes even stronger.

In general, run-time verification is preferred when there are strong requirements on the criticality, dependability and security of the target application, while testing is preferred when it is not possible or convenient to consume resources for creating, and running instrumented applications. Moreover, run-time verification is often used to recognize faulty components and integration errors in hardware systems, such as in the Dynamic Implementation Verification Architecture (DIVA) which exploits run-time verification at intra-processor level [Aus99].

In particular, when the core of a DIVA-based microprocessor completes the execution of an instruction, the operands and the results are sent to the DIVA checker which verifies the correctness of the computation. If errors are detected, the DIVA checker can also fix the errant operation.

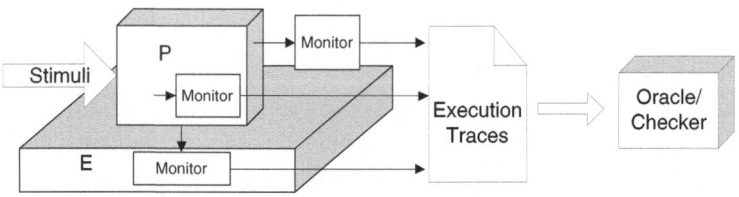

Fig. 18.1. The general scenario in Run-Time Verification

The general scenario that is established when you employ a run-time verification technique of a software system P is shown in Fig. 18.1. The software P runs in the context of an environment E. The environment can be an operating system, such as Windows or Linux, a middleware, such as EJB [MH99] or JXTA [Gon01], or any other framework such as ubiquitous environments or network systems. The software P receives stimuli from either the user of the system or from a test driver and consequently sends events providing information about the behavior of P. Event generation is performed by monitors observing P that are placed inside the environment, inside the target program or outside the target program (see Sec. 18.3 for a detailed explanation of monitors). Events are stored in execution traces that are used as input either for a checker or for an oracle which verifies correctness of the executions. Often, run-time verification techniques do not use execution traces and send events directly to the checker. The term **oracle** is preferred when verification takes place in the testing environment, while checker is more generally used in the other cases.

The environment where verification takes place is an important aspect of a run-time verification technique which is often neglected. It is important to consume a limited amount of resources when you check properties at run-time, since it would be unfeasible to perform complex computations with respect to each single execution and also because the original application will be slowed down too much.

In the case where the verification takes place in the field, hence it is performed at the user site after the system has been deployed, intrusiveness and consumed resources play even a more important role. In fact, it would be annoying for the user to have the system evidently slowing down while verification is taking place. Sometimes, verification of the observed behavior is not just immediate with respect to the execution, but results of the execution are stored in trace files that are then checked. For example, it is possible to build a trace file that is checked when the system is not used, or it is possible to transfer the trace file from a machine to another one before checking takes place, e.g., transferring the file from the client machine to the vendor's site.

To illustrate the runtime verification, a basic example will be used along with the chapter. It is the railroad gate example. It is composed of a *gate* and a *light*. The light can *flash* or be *off*. The gate can be *closed, opened, closing* or *opening*. First the gate is open. Before the door closes, the light flashes to warn the motorists of the imminent closing of the door. The light continues to flash while the door closes until the door is again opened. The program that implements this example is supposed to be instrumented to send information about the state modifications of both the gate and the light. In particular, we suppose that the program can generate the following events at run-time:

- *closing* when the gate begins to close
- *closed* when the gate is closed
- *opening* when the gate begins to open
- *opened* when the gate is open
- *off* when the light is off
- *flashing* when the light begins to flash.

During the execution of the program, a sequence of events is generated. The sequence is an execution trace of the program. For example, three different executions can generate these traces:

(1) *open, off, flashing, closing, closed, opening, open, off.*
(2) *open, off, flashing, closing, closed, off, opening, open.*
(3) *open, off, closing, flashing, closed, opening, open, off.*

A runtime verification technique checks an execution trace against requirements. For example, the requirement that "whenever the gate begins to open, then the gate has been closing in the past, and since then the light has not finished flashing", can be formalized by the past LTL formula [Pnu77]:

$$\uparrow is\_opening \Rightarrow [is\_closing, \downarrow (is\_flashing))$$

Another requirement could be "always in the future whenever the light is off, then the gate will not be closing until the light will be flashing", can be formalized by the future LTL formula:

$$\Box(is\_off \Rightarrow \neg is\_closing \, \mathcal{U} \, is\_flashing)$$

The notations $\uparrow p$ (begin p), $\downarrow p$ (end p), $p \Rightarrow q$ (p implies q), $[p, q)$ (q in the past and not q since p), $\Box p$ (always p), $\neg p$ (not p) and $p \, \mathcal{U} \, q$ (p until a) will be introduced latter in the paper. Propositions *is_opening, is_closing, is_flashing* and *is_off* describe intuitively the state of both the gate and the light, and they correspond to conditions *gate = opening, gate = closing, light = flashing* and *light = off*, respectively.

By matching the formal requirements with the three execution traces, a runtime verification technique can detect a violation of the first requirement in the second trace, since at a given moment the gate is opening, but the light is not flashing; and a violation of the second requirement in the third trace, since at a given moment the light is off, but then, the gate is closing before the light is flashing. These examples will be investigated furthermore in the presentation of the specific techniques.

Before performing verification, it is necessary to obtain traces that must be checked. In the next section we address the problem of generating traces by monitoring executions, while we address verification of formal requirements in Sec. 18.4

18.3   Monitoring Executions

Installation of monitors can be a complex activity since monitors must be less intrusive as possible, but must also generate the necessary events for enabling the verification technique that will be performed. Moreover, monitors must often be installed in many different points of a given system; in fact a specific aspect can be localized in many different parts of the target application. Manual installation of monitors is an error-prone and time consuming activity, hence the installation procedure is often automatic.

Referring to Fig. 18.1, monitors can be installed inside the target program, inside the environment and outside the target program.

In the case of monitors placed inside the target program, the most used approach consists of automatic instrumentation of either the source code or the binary code. In these cases, additional code is placed in strategic points, such as entry points of the procedures or before the execution of specific operations, to generate events [GH03, KKLS01]. There are many programs performing automatic instrumentation of the source code [LLC03], of the binary code [RVL+97] or any intermediate language, e.g., Java bytecode [Fou03, GH03].

Even the oracle can be placed inside the program. This is the case of developers writing assertions in the code while developing the program [BY01]. **Assertions** are boolean expressions that a programmer believes to be true at the time the statement is executed (a false assertion indicates an error). Assertions are checked at run-time and if one assertion is false the event signaling the violation is generated. By using assertions, the software developer places conditions verifying the behavior of the program directly in the program itself, thus facilitating discovering of faulty behaviors. Using assertions instead of *defensive programming* or "`if`" statements gives the possibility to choose between compilation processes that either remove assertions or keep assertions. The program with assertions is generated for testing purposes, while the program without assertions is generated for the deployment in the final environment. There are many languages for assertion specification providing a different expression power. The Java assertion mechanism enables the specification of boolean logic expressions that can be easily checked, while Temporal Rover enables the specification of assertions by using temporal logic [DS03], see Fig. 18.2 for an example. If it is necessary to specify real-time requirements, the Java Run-time Timing Constraint

Monitor [ML97] enables the specification of Real-time Logic [JG90] assertions. Assertion mechanisms have been defined also for other languages such as Eiffel [Mey92] (the language where assertions were originally introduced), C [TJ98] and Ada [SM93].

```
class MyClass {
    static void foo(int x) {
        /*TRBegin
            TRAssert{ Always{x < 0} } =>
            {System.out.println("Violated the assertion x<0 in foo(int x), x=" + x);}
        TREnd*/
        }
}
```

Fig. 18.2. An example of an assertion written by Temporal Rover

In the case where the source code is not available, it is possible to use a modified version of the underlying environment to monitor executions, e.g., a modified JVM [Wol99]. Dynascope is the example of an environment exploiting fine grain monitoring and steering at the cost of expensive executions [Sos92]. These techniques have the advantage that any application running on the target environment is automatically monitored. The drawback is that a modified environment is not always reliable as the original one and monitoring can negatively affect applications that do not need to be monitored. Moreover, the modified environment can be incompatible with the standard environment. Finally, a monitoring environment is not configurable to monitor very specific parts of specific programs, rather it exploits the monitoring capability as a whole. On the contrary, instrumented code and assertions can be enabled or removed in respect to current needs.

Finally, the binding mechanism can be altered to enable monitors to observe communication between components and systems. For example, monitors can observe network communication [DJC94] or inter-component interactions [BS01a]. These approaches have the advantage to be lowly intrusive, but only events and actions implying a communication can be observed. Moreover, installation of these kinds of monitors is often complex [BS01a].

18.4   Concurrency Error Checking

Run-time verification techniques were first used to check classical error patterns, in particular they were used to check concurrent programs. Then, run-time verification techniques were extended to check execution traces against user provided formal requirements written in high-level logics. In this section, we present approaches for checking concurrency errors, while run-time verification of formal requirements will be presented in Sec. 18.5.

Error pattern analysis is conceptually based on analyzing an execution trace by algorithms that are able to detect errors even if those errors do not explicitly occur in the examined execution trace. The goal is to extract as much information as possible from a single execution trace to be able to forecast problems that can occur in executions that have not been explored. In the case of multi-threaded software, debugging is complex since execution of threads is not deterministic and many combinations are possible, thus verification requires specific tools. In this section, we present the application of run-time verification techniques for detecting data races and deadlocks.

18.4.1   Data Races

The Eraser algorithm [SBN+97] is one of the first algorithms that dynamically detects data races in multi-threaded programs. A **date race** occurs when two concurrent threads access a shared variable with at least one write access and threads use no explicit mechanism to prevent accesses from being simultaneous.

The Eraser algorithm takes an unmodified program binary as input and adds instrumentation to produce a new binary that is functionally identical, but includes calls to the Eraser run-time which implements the Lockset algorithm.

The Lockset algorithm enforces the locking discipline requiring that every variable shared between threads is protected by a mutual exclusion lock. As a consequence, the lock must be held by threads accessing the variable. Basically, Eraser instruments standard C, C++ and Unix memory allocation routines and monitors all read and write operations to check whether the program respects or not the locking policy. Eraser does not know which locks are intended to protect which variables, so it must infer the protection relation from the execution history.

In particular, for each shared variable v, Eraser maintains the set $C(v)$ of candidate locks for v. This set contains those locks that have protected v for the computation so far, that is, a lock l is in $C(v)$ if in the current computation every thread that has accessed v was holding l at the moment of the access. When a new variable v is initialized, its candidate set $C(v)$ is considered to hold all possible locks. When the variable is accessed, Eraser updates $C(v)$ with the intersection of $C(v)$ and the set of locks held by the current thread. This process, called lockset refinement, ensures that any lock that consistently protects v is contained in $C(v)$. If $C(v)$ becomes empty, no locks consistently protect v.

A lock is a simple synchronization object used to implement mutual exclusion. Locks can be either *available* or *owned* by a thread. The operations that can be performed on a lock mu are $lock(mu)$ and $unlock(mu)$. Figure 18.3 shows an example taken from the paper presenting the Eraser algorithm [SBN+97] that illustrates how a potential data race is discovered through lockset refinement. The left column contains the program statements that are executed;the column in the middle contains the set of locks held by the considered thread; and the right column contains the set of candidate locks $C(v)$. The example uses two locks mu_1 and mu_2, thus $C(v)$ initially contains both of them. Then, the lock mu_1 is acquired and v is accessed. Thus, $C(v)$ is refined by computing the intersection of $C(v)$ with the set of acquired locks. Later, v is accessed again, when only mu_2 is held. The intersection of the singleton $\{mu_1\}$ with $\{mu_2\}$ is the empty set, therefore no locks protects v. A warning is issued since accesses to variable v are sometimes protected by the lock mu_1 and sometimes by the lock mu_2, thus no locks protects all accesses to v for the whole computation.

	Program	Locks held	$C(v)$
		{}	{mu1,mu2}
	lock(mu1)		
		{mu1}	{mu1,mu2}
	v := v+1		
		{mu1}	{mu1}
Time	unlock(mu1)		
		{}	{mu1}
	lock(mu2)		
		{mu2}	{mu1}
	v := v+1		
		{m2}	{}
	unlock(mu2)		
		{}	{}

Fig. 18.3. Example of the execution progress for the Eraser algorithm in the case of a variable v used by a six statements program.

When a race is reported, Eraser indicates both the file and line number at which the instruction violating the locking discipline is located. The report also includes the thread ID, memory address, type of memory access, and important register values such as the program counter and stack pointer.

The Eraser locking discipline is too strong. There are three very common programming practices that violate the discipline, yet are free from any data races: initialization, read-shared data and read-write locks. These cases have been addressed by Savage et al. who extended the Lockset algorithm to accommodate initialization, read-shared data and read-write locks [SBN+97].

The Eraser algorithm was implemented for Digital Unix and it has been used to detect data races in several programs. In particular, it tackled some large multi-threaded servers written by experienced researchers at Digital Equipment Corporation's System Research Center: the HTTP server and indexing engine from AltaVista, the Vesta cache server, and the Petal distributed disk system. Eraser found undesirable race conditions in three of the four server programs [SBN+97]. A version of the Eraser algorithm which addresses also Java programs has been implemented in PathExplorer [HR01b]. Finally, Compaq provides a run-time debugging and analysis tool for multi-threaded applications called Visual Threads which finds data races by the Eraser algorithm [Har00].

18.4.2   Deadlock Detection

The problem of **deadlock** is common in parallel programs. Deadlock can occur whenever shared resources are required to accomplish a task. For instance, if resource access is not managed correctly, two threads may end up each one holding one resource but waiting for another resource held by the other thread. If neither the first nor the second thread releases the resource until it completes its task, both will wait indefinitely. Both PathExplorer and Visual Threads can detect deadlocks.

The primary unit of data processed by Visual Threads is the event. Events are sent from the application process to Visual Threads and Visual Threads uses these events to model the execution of the application via a state machine. Deadlock is a circularity in the dependency graph of the threads. Deadlock is detected via a simple recursive mark-search algorithm directly applied to the model representation of the program. While detecting deadlocks is useful, observing their occurrence can be quite obvious since a deadlocked application never ends. However, Visual Threads goes beyond this by detecting various conditions that may lead to deadlock. Visual Threads has the capability to detect situations that may not typically have any visible symptom, but that at some point in the future may cause the application to fail. For example, Visual Threads recognizes if locks are acquired in an inconsistent order to forecast the possibility for the application to deadlock.

PathExplorer uses the same idea to detect deadlocks [RH01c]. A *thread map* keeps track of which locks are owned by which thread at any time point. A *lock graph* maintains the information about all locks taken by threads during execution. Nodes of the lock graph represent locks, while edges of the nodes graph represent locking orders; in particular an edge from lock v_1 to lock v_2 is introduced if a thread owning v_1 acquires also v_2. A cycle in the lock graph represents a potential deadlock.

18.5   Checking Temporal Logic Requirements

Instead of verifying a program for checking specific properties, such as deadlocks, it is possible to be more general: verify a program with respect to a formal specification. In this case, user-provided formal requirements are used to unambiguously describe system properties that are intended to be verified. Approaches differ according to both the type of the language and the corresponding verification engine that are used.

18.5.1   PathExplorer and Future LTL

PathExplorer is a run-time verification technique developed by Havelund and Roşu [RH01c]. In PathExplorer, requirements are specified with future Linear Temporal Logic (LTL) formulas and a trace is a finite sequence of events emitted by the observed program. Events indicate when variables are changed. This is slightly different from the traditional view where the trace is a sequence of program states.

Temporal Logic We briefly recall basic notions of **finite trace linear temporal logic** including a recursive definition of the satisfaction relation on a finite trace and a LTL formula.

The satisfaction relation $\models \subseteq$ *Trace* $\times$ *Formula* defines when a trace t satisfies a formula φ, written $t \models \varphi$, and is defined inductively over the structure of the formula as follows: where $p \in$ *Prop* is any atomic proposition, *head* : *Trace* $\rightarrow$ *Trace* and *tail* : *Trace* $\rightarrow$ *Trace* are two functions taking the head and the tail of a trace respectively, *length* is a function returning the length of a finite trace, ϵ denotes a empty trace and φ and ψ are any formulas:

$$
\begin{aligned}
&t \models true && \text{is always true,} \\
&t \models false && \text{is always false,} \\
&t \models p && \text{iff } t \neq \epsilon \text{ and } head(t) \text{ is } p, \\
&t \models \varphi \wedge (\vee, \Rightarrow, \Leftrightarrow)\psi && \text{iff } t \models \varphi \text{ and (or, implied, iff) } t \models \psi, \\
&t \models \circ\varphi && \text{iff } t \neq \epsilon \text{ and } tail(t) \models \varphi, \\
&t \models \Box\varphi && \text{iff } (\forall 1 \leq i \leq length(t))t_i \models \varphi, \\
&t \models \Diamond\varphi && \text{iff } (\exists 1 \leq i \leq length(t)+1)t_i \models \varphi, \\
&t \models \varphi \, \mathcal{U} \, \psi && \text{iff } (\exists 1 \leq i \leq length(t)+1)t_i \models \psi \text{ and} \\
&&& (\forall 1 \leq j < i)t_j \models \varphi.
\end{aligned}
$$

The LTL operators have a slightly different interpretation in the context of finite traces, though similar in spirit to their standard semantics in classical LTL with infinite traces. The formula $\circ\varphi$ (next φ) holds for a finite trace iff the trace is nonempty and φ holds in the suffix trace starting in the next (second) time point. The formula $\Box\varphi$ (always φ) holds if φ holds in all time points, while $\Diamond\varphi$ (eventually φ) holds if φ holds in present or in some future time point. The formula $\varphi \, \mathcal{U} \, \psi$ (φ until ψ) holds if ψ holds in present or in some future time point, and until then φ holds. As an example illustrating the semantics, the formula $\Box(\varphi \Rightarrow \Diamond\psi)$ holds for a finite trace iff for any time point in the trace it holds that if φ is true then eventually ψ is true.

LTL is widely accepted as reasonably good formalism to express requirements of reactive systems. However, there is a tricky aspect of specification-based monitoring which distinguishes it from other formal methods, such as model checking and theorem proving: the end of trace. Sooner or later, the monitored program will be stopped and so does its execution trace. At that moment, the observer needs to make a decision regarding the validity of checked properties. Let us consider the formula $\Box(p \Rightarrow \Diamond q)$. If each p was followed by at least one q during the monitored execution, then, at some extent one could say that the formula was satisfied; but one should be aware that this is not a definitive answer because the formula could have been very well violated in the future if the program had not been stopped. However, there are LTL properties that give the user absolute confidence during the monitoring. For example, a violation of a safety property reflects a clear misbehavior of the monitored program.

In PathExplorer, the fact that the relation $\models$ can be defined recursively in the context of finite traces is crucial to the development of generic dynamic programming algorithms, i.e., algorithms solving optimization problems by caching subproblem solutions rather than recomputing them.

Exercise 18.1 *(Specify requirements with future LTL formula on the railway gate example).*

- Always in the future, when the gate is closing, is closed or is opening, the light flashes
- In the future, the light is off only when the gate is open

Verification in PathExplorer Based on Future LTL The PathExplorer dynamic programming algorithm takes as input a future time LTL formula and generates a special Finite State Machine (FSM), called **binary transition tree finite state machine** (BTT-FSM), which is used as an efficient monitor. We present general concepts of BTT-FSM by using an example; readers interested in details can read the article of Havelund and Roşu [HR04]. A BTT-FSM for the railway gate example formula $\Box(is\_off \Rightarrow \neg is\_closing\, \mathcal{U}\, is\_flashing)$ discussed in Subsec. 18.2 is shown in Figure 18.4.

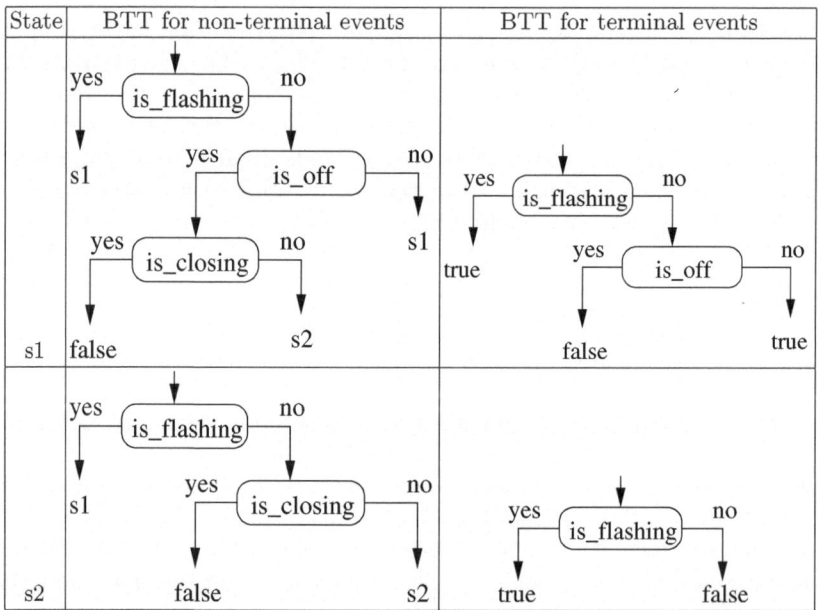

Fig. 18.4. The BTT-FSM for the formula $\Box(is\_off \Rightarrow \neg is\_closing\, \mathcal{U}\, is\_flashing)$

Intuitively, a BTT-FSM is used to derive the next state when an event is recognized; for example, if the BTT-FSM in Figure 18.4 is in state $s1$ and a non-terminal event is received, then it is first evaluate the proposition $is\_flashing$

(propositions are represented by nodes), if the result is true then the BTT-FSM stays in state s_1 else is_off is evaluated; if is_off is false then the BTT-FSM stays in state s_1 else $is\_closing$ is evaluated; if $is\_closing$ is true then the output is "formula violated" else the BTT-FSM moves to state s_2. When a terminal event is received due to termination of monitoring, if the BTT-FSM is in state s_1 then $is\_flashing$ is evaluated; if $is\_flashing$ is true then $true$ is returned, else is_off is evaluated; if is_off is true, $false$ is returned, otherwise is_true is returned. Since only true/false messages are reported on terminal events, the BTT-FSM that is executed when a terminal event is recognized is a Binary Decision Diagram.

gate=open light = off	open	gate=open light = off	off	gate=open light = off	closing	gate=closing light = off
s2		**s2**		**s2**		**false**

Fig. 18.5. Evaluation of the trace *open, off, closing, flashing*

In our example, at the initial state the gate is open and the light is off. Figure 18.5 and 18.6 show the detailed evaluation progress for the traces:

- *open, off, closing, flashing.* (Formula violated)
- *open, off, flashing, closing.* (Formula verified)

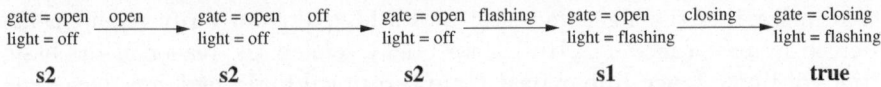

gate = open light = off	open	gate = open light = off	off	gate = open light = off	flashing	gate = open light = flashing	closing	gate = closing light = flashing
s2		**s2**		**s2**		**s1**		**true**

Fig. 18.6. Evaluation of the trace *open, off, flashing, closing*

To simplify evaluation of the propositions in the BTT-FSM's nodes, the value assumed from the abstract state variables at each step is reported in the diagram. The identifier of states traversed during the evaluation process and eventually the verdict are shown below state variables. A transition from a state to the following one is performed by evaluating an event of the execution trace. Events that are successively evaluated are reported as labels of the edges. For example, in the case of the sequence in Figure 18.5, the initial state of the BTT-FSM is obtained by applying the initial state of the system to state s_1. The light is initially off, therefore the value of $is\_flashing$ is false and the value of is_off is true; moreover, the gate is open, thus $is\_closing$ is false, therefore the BTT-FSM evolves to state s_2. Then the event *open* is considered and the BTT-FSM is evaluated again. Now, we are in state s_2 and both $is\_flashing$ and $is\_closing$ are false, hence we remain on state s_2. The evaluation procedure continues in this way until the event *closing* is reached. In this example, the BTT-FSM gets the non-terminal event *closing* while it is in state s_2, with the light set on off and the gate set on closing; *is_flashing* is evaluated to false, *is_off* is evaluated true, *is_closing* is evaluated to true and the final result is false, therefore the formula has been violated.

Exercise 18.2 *(Algorithm Application).* Apply the BTT-FMS of Fig 18.4 on the following traces and determine the resulting truth value:

- *flashing, closing, closed, opening, open, closing, off*
- *flashing, off, closing, closed, opening, flashing, open*

When a new event is received, a BTT-FSM only need to evaluate *at most* all the propositions to compute the next state, so at worst the run-time overhead is linear with respect to the number of distinct variables. The size of the BTT-FSMs can become a problem when storage is a scarce resource, hence particular attention is given to the generation of optimal BTT-FSMs. However, the number of propositions to be evaluated tends to decrease with the number of states, so the overall monitoring overhead is also reduced. This algorithm is recommended in situations where the monitored LTL formulas are relatively small in size.

Future time propositional LTL may not be the most appropriate formalism for logic based monitoring due to the conceptual contradiction between the finite past traces and the logic expressiveness referring to infinite future. Past time LTL can be a more natural logic for run-time monitoring, in fact safety requirements are usually expressed by means of past events.

18.5.2   PathExplorer and Past Time LTL

Before presenting the algorithm used by PathExplorer to verify requirements specified by past time LTL [HR02], we briefly remind the reader of the basic notions of **finite trace linear past time temporal logic**, and introduce some operators used by PathExplorer.

Past Time LTL Syntactically, PathExplorer allows the following formulas, where A is a set of "atomic propositions":

$$F ::= true \mid false \mid A \mid \neg F \mid F \ op \ F \qquad \text{Propositional operators}$$
$$\odot F \mid \diamond F \mid \square F \mid F \ \mathcal{S_S} \ F \mid F \ \mathcal{S_W} \ F \ \text{Standard past time operators}$$
$$\uparrow F \mid \downarrow F \mid [F, F)_\mathcal{S} \mid [F, F)_\mathcal{W} \qquad \text{Monitoring operators}$$

The propositional binary operators *op* are the standard ones, and the other operators should be read :

- $\odot F$ as "previously F",
- $\diamond F$ as "eventually in the past F",
- $\square F$ as "always in the past F",
- $F_1 \ \mathcal{S_S} \ F_2$ as "F_1 strong since F_2",
- $F_1 \ \mathcal{S_W} \ F_2$ as "F_1 weak since F_2",
- $\uparrow F$ as "start F",
- $\downarrow F$ as "end F",
- $[F_1, F_2)$ as "interval F_1, F_2".

A trace is regarded as a finite sequence of abstract states. If s is a state and a is an atomic proposition then $a(s)$ is true if and only if a holds in the state s. If $t = s_1 s_2 \dots s_n$ is a trace then we let t_i denote the trace $s_1 s_2 \dots s_i$ for each $1 \le i \le n$. Then the semantic of these operators is:

$$
\begin{aligned}
&t \models \mathit{true} &&\text{is always true,}\\
&t \models \mathit{false} &&\text{is always false,}\\
&t \models a &&\text{iff } a(s_n) \text{ holds,}\\
&t \models \neg F &&\text{iff it is not the case that } t \models F,\\
&t \models F_1 \mathbin{op} F_2 &&\text{iff } t \models F_1 \text{ or/and/implies/iff } t \models F_2, \text{ when } op \text{ is } \vee/\wedge/\Rightarrow/\Leftrightarrow,\\
&t \models \odot F &&\text{iff } t' \models F, \text{ where } t' = t_{n-1} \text{ if } n > 1 \text{ and } t' = t \text{ if } n = 1,\\
&t \models \Diamond F &&\text{iff } t_i \models F \text{ for some } 1 \le i \le n,\\
&t \models \Box F &&\text{iff } t_i \models F \text{ for all } 1 \le i \le n,\\
&t \models F_1 \, \mathcal{S_S} \, F_2 &&\text{iff } t_j \models F_2 \text{ for some } 1 \le j \le n \text{ and } t_i \models F_1 \text{ for all } j < i \le n,\\
&t \models F_1 \, \mathcal{S_W} \, F_2 &&\text{iff } t \models F_1 \, \mathcal{S_S} \, F_2 \text{ or } t \models \Box F_1,\\
&t \models \uparrow F &&\text{iff } t \models F \text{ and it is not the case that } t \models \odot F,\\
&t \models \downarrow F &&\text{iff } t \models \odot F \text{ and it is not the case that } t \models F,\\
&t \models [F_1, F_2)_{\mathcal{S}} &&\text{iff } t_j \models F_1 \text{ for some } 1 \le j \le n \text{ and } t_i \nvDash F_2 \text{ for all } j \le i \le n,\\
&t \models [F_1, F_2)_{\mathcal{W}} &&\text{iff } t \models [F_1, F_2)_{\mathcal{S}} \text{ or } t \models \neg \Box F,
\end{aligned}
$$

The recursive nature of past time temporal logic is very suitable for dynamic programming; in fact, the satisfaction relation for a formula can be calculated along the execution trace looking only one step backwards:

$$
\begin{aligned}
&t \models \Diamond F &&\text{iff } t \models F \text{ or } (n > 1 \text{ and } t_{n-1} \models \Diamond F),\\
&t \models \Box F &&\text{iff } t \models F \text{ and } (n > 1 \text{ implies } t_{n-1} \models \Box F),\\
&t \models F_1 \, \mathcal{S_S} \, F_2 &&\text{iff } t \models F_2 \text{ or } (n > 1 \text{ and } t \models F_1 \text{ and } t_{n-1} \models F_1 \, \mathcal{S_S} \, F_2),\\
&t \models F_1 \, \mathcal{S_W} \, F_2 &&\text{iff } t \models F_2 \text{ or } (t \models F_1 \text{ and } (n > 1 \text{ implies } t_{n-1} \models F_1 \, \mathcal{S_S} \, F_2)),\\
&t \models [F_1, F_2)_{\mathcal{S}} &&\text{iff } t \nvDash F_2 \text{ and } t \models F_1 \text{ or } (n > 1 \text{ and } t_{n-1} \models [F_1, F_2)_{\mathcal{S}},\\
&t \models [F_1, F_2)_{\mathcal{W}} &&\text{iff } t \nvDash F_2 \text{ and } t \models F_1 \text{ or } (n > 1 \text{ implies } t_{n-1} \models [F_1, F_2)_{\mathcal{W}},
\end{aligned}
$$

Verification in PathExplorer Based on Past Time LTL Safety requirements can be represented as formulas $\Box F$, where F is a past time LTL formula. These properties are very suitable for logic based monitoring because they only refer to the past, and hence their values are always either true or false in any state along the trace, and never *to-be-determined* as in future time LTL.

The dynamic programming algorithm for past LTL formulas takes as input a formula and generates a program that traverses the trace of events while validating the formula. We illustrate the algorithm by using the sample formula $\uparrow \mathit{is\_opening} \Rightarrow [\mathit{is\_closing}, \downarrow \mathit{is\_flashing})_{\mathcal{S}}$ that refers to the railway gate example discussed in Subsec. 18.2.

A formula is first visited top down to assign increasing numbers to subformulas in the order they are visited. Let $\varphi_0, \varphi_1, \dots, \varphi_6$ be the list of all subformulas:

$$
\begin{aligned}
\varphi_0 &= \uparrow \mathit{is\_opening} \Rightarrow [\mathit{is\_closing}, \downarrow \mathit{is\_flashing})_{\mathcal{S}}\\
\varphi_1 &= \uparrow \mathit{is\_opening},
\end{aligned}
$$

$\varphi_2 = is\_opening,$
$\varphi_3 = [is\_closing, \downarrow is\_flashing)_S,$
$\varphi_4 = is\_closing,$
$\varphi_5 = \downarrow is\_flashing,$
$\varphi_6 = is\_flashing.$

The formulas have been enumerated in a post-order fashion, but it is possible to choose a breath-first order, or other enumerations. Because of the recursive nature of past LTL, this enumeration assures that the truth value of $t_i \models \varphi_j$ can be completely determined from the truth value of $t_i \models \varphi_{j'}$ for all $j < j' \leq m$ and the truth values of $t_{i-1} \models \varphi_{j'}$ for all $j \leq j' \leq m$.

The input of the generated program will be a finite trace $t = e_1 e_2 \ldots e_n$ of n events; examples of finite traces for the railway example can be:

- *open, off, flashing, closing, closed, opening, open, off* or
- *open, off, flashing, closing, closed, off, opening, open.*

The generated program evaluates traces by fixing an initial state that is then updated according to events. For the railway gate example, the initial state is defined by the two variables *gate* and *light* that are set to:

$gate = open$
$light = off$

In particular, the generated program will maintain updated the state via the function *update* : **State** $\times$ *Event* $\rightarrow$ **State** that, given both the current state and an event, generates the next state. For example, when the event *flashing* is received, the variable *light* is assigned to *flashing*.

Going into depth of implementation aspects of dynamic programming we can consider how the satisfaction relation is implemented. Generally, a matrix $s[1 \ldots n, 0 \ldots 6]$ of boolean values $\{0, 1\}$, with the meaning that $s[i, j] = 1$ iff $t_i \models \varphi_j$, is defined. However, it is not necessary to store the whole table, which is quite large, because values stored in $s[i, 0 \ldots 6]$ and $s[i-1, 0 \ldots 6]$ are sufficient to evaluate the formula at step i. Therefore, we will refer to $s[i, 0 \ldots 6]$ and $s[i-1, 0 \ldots 6]$ with $now[0 \ldots 6]$ and $pre[0 \ldots 6]$ respectively. At this point is quite simple to understand the algorithm shown in Figure 18.7 which checks the above formula on a finite trace.

As expected, the generated program contains two arrays *pre* and *now*: *pre* contains all subformulas corresponding to the previous state, while *now* contains all subformulas corresponding to the current state. The input is given by the trace of events, which can be read from a file or can be generated on-the-fly without using any storage device. The latter technique is implemented by PathExplorer. In fact the observer and the program interact directly.

The generated program initializes the *state* variable to the value of the first event of the execution trace and then initializes all elements of the *pre* array to the truth value of the corresponding formula. The initial status is supposed to be stationary until monitoring starts, therefore the formulas checking for changes of

```
State state ← {};
bool pre[0 ... 6];
bool now[0 ... 6];
INPUT: trace t = e₁ e₂ ... eₙ;
/* Initialization of state and pre */
state ← update(state, e₁);
pre[6] ← is_flashing(state);
pre[5] ← false
pre[4] ← is_closing(state)
pre[3] ← pre[4] and not pre[5]
pre[2] ← is_opening(state)
pre[1] ← false
pre[0] ← not pre[1] or pre[3];
/* Event interpretation loop */
for i = 2 to n do {
    state ← update(state, eᵢ)
    now[6] ← is_flashing(state);
    now[5] ← not now[6] and pre[6]
    now[4] ← is_closing(state)
    now[3] ← (pre[3] or now[4]) and not now[5]
    now[2] ← is_opening(state)
    now[1] ← now[2] and not pre[2]
    now[0] ← not now[1] or now[3];
    if now[0] = false then output("property violated");
    pre ← now;
};
```

Fig. 18.7. The algorithm generated by PathExplorer for the formula $\uparrow is\_opening \Rightarrow [is\_closing, \downarrow is\_flashing)_S$

the state are false at initialization. In the example, both formulas $\uparrow is\_opening$ and $\downarrow is\_flashing$, that correspond to indexes 5 and 1, are false.

The loop sequentially considers all events, and for each event the current state is first updated, then the *now* array is computed (meaning that the formula is evaluated), and finally the *now* array is copied into the *pre* array (since at next step the current array will be the previous array). If at any step $now[0]$ is false, the formula has been violated. Note that for the way enumeration has been performed $now[0]$ represents the truth value of the whole formula.

Figure 18.8 shows the evaluation progress for the formula $\uparrow is\_opening \Rightarrow [is\_closing, \downarrow is\_flashing)_S$ on the trace *flashing, closing, closed, opening, open, off*. The content of the *pre* array at the end of the loop is reported below each abstract state with the exception of the array of boolean values reported on the first abstract state that denotes the content of *pre* after initialization. We can immediately observe that the trace satisfies the formula $\uparrow is\_opening \Rightarrow [is\_closing, \downarrow is\_flashing)_S$ because $pre[0]$ is true at all steps.

Exercise 18.3 *(Algorithm Application).* Verify that the execution trace *open, off,*

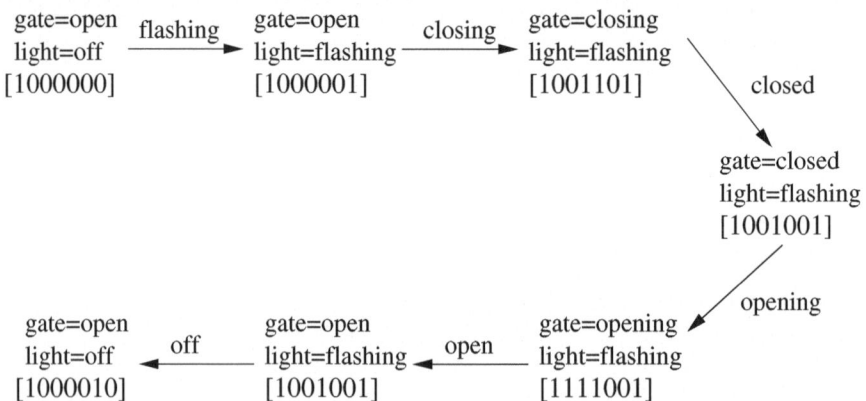

Fig. 18.8. Progress of the algorithm in Figure 18.7 for the trace *flashing, closing, closed, opening, open, off*. The content of the *pre* array is reported below each abstract state. Note that 0 is used for *false* and 1 for *true*.

flashing, closing, closed, off, opening, open violates the formula ↑ *is_opening* ⇒ [*is_closing*,↓ *is_flashing*)$_S$ by simulating the execution of the program shown in Figure 18.7.

Analyzing a fixed past time LTL formula by the PathExplorer dynamically generated algorithm is straightforward, its time complexity is $\Theta(n)$ where n is the length of the input trace, and the required memory is constant since the length of the two arrays is equal to the size of the past time LTL formula. However, if you include the size m of the formula in the analysis, the time complexity is $\Theta(n \cdot m)$, while the required memory is $2 \cdot (m + 1)$ bits. The procedure for enumerating a given formula is linear, thus the algorithm which synthesizes a dynamic programming algorithm from a past LTL formula is linear with the size of the formula.

PathExplorer Architecture PathExplorer can be regarded as consisting of three main modules: an *instrumentation* module, an *observer* module, and an *interaction* module. The instrumentation module performs a script-driven automated instrumentation of the program that must be observed by using the Jtrek Java byte-code engineering tool [Coh]. The instrumented program emits events to the interaction module, which forwards them further to the observation module. If the observer runs on a different computer, events are transmitted over sockets.

18.5.3 Monitoring and Checking (MaC) Method

The Monitoring and Checking (MaC) method [LKK+99, KKL+01] that has been developed at the University of Pennsylvania ensures that a system is behaving correctly with respect to formal requirements. MaC uses two different logics for specifying monitoring scripts and safety requirements. Main phases of the framework are:

(1) system requirements are formalized and a *monitoring script* is written; the monitoring script is used to instrument the code for establishing a mapping from low-level information to high-level events
(2) at run-time, events generated by the instrumented system are checked with respect to requirements

MaC Architecture The run-time monitoring and checking architecture consists of three components: the *filter*, the *event recognizer*, and the *run-time checker*. The filter extracts low-level information from the system, such as both value of program variables and time when those variables change their values, and sends them to the event recognizer. The event recognizer converts received events into both high-level events and conditions that are sent to the run-time checker.

Events delivered to the checker have a timestamp which reflects the actual time of the occurrence of the event. The timestamp enables monitoring of real-time properties of the system. The run-time checker checks correctness of the executions according to the requirement specification, events provided from the event recognizer, and past history. The current prototype of the MaC framework supports instrumentation and monitoring of Java bytecode.

Events and Conditions Monitoring scripts defined by the Primitive Event Definition Language (PEDL) are used to specify both the information that is sent from the filter to the event recognizer, and how this information is transformed into requirement-level events by the event recognizer. In particular, when an "interesting" event occurs in the running system, the filter sends a notification to the event recognizer. Two possible kinds of notification exist: *events* which occur instantaneously during the system execution, and *conditions* which are information holding for a duration of time. Since events are associated with the time of their occurrence and conditions are associated to their duration, it is possible to reason about timing properties of monitored systems.

Sometimes, variables can become undefined because they are out of scope. To support reasoning even on such variables, a three-valued logic is used for PEDL: in addition to true and false, formulas can be evaluated to undefined (the symbol used in such case is $\perp$).

MaC Logic The logic has two sorts: conditions and events. The syntax of conditions (C) and events (E) is as follows, where c is a primitive condition and e is a primitive event:

$$C ::= c \mid \text{defined}(C) \mid [E, E) \mid \neg C \mid C \vee C \mid C \wedge C \mid C \Rightarrow C$$
$$E ::= e \mid \uparrow C \mid \downarrow C \mid E \vee E \mid E \wedge E \mid E \text{ when } C$$

The operators $\neg$, $\vee$, $\wedge$ and $\Rightarrow$ are standard operators (respectively not, or, and, and implies), but they are defined on the domain {true, false, $\bot$}; define(c) allows to know if c is defined, $[c_1, c_2)$ is true if and only if c_2 was never true since the last time c_1 was observed to be true, including the state when c_1 was true; $\uparrow c$ occurs when condition c changes from false to true; $\downarrow c$ occurs when condition c changes from true to false; and "e when c" allows to know if event e occurs when condition c is true.

A model for this logic is a tuple (S, τ, L_C, L_E), where $S = \{s_0, s_1, \ldots\}$ is a set of states, τ is a mapping from S to the time domain (which could be integer, rationale, or real), L_C is a total function from $S \times C$ to {true, false, $\bot$} where C is a countable set of primitive conditions, and L_E is a partial function from $S \times \mathcal{E}$ to $\mathcal{D}_e$ where $\mathcal{E}$ is a countable set of primitive events and $\mathcal{D}_e$ is the domain of the event. Intuitively, L_C assigns to each state the truth value of all the primitive conditions; since conditions are interpreted over a 3-valued logic, the truth value of primitive conditions can be true, false or $\bot$ (undefined). Similarly, in each state s, $L_E(s, e)$ is defined for each event e that occurs at s and gives the value of the primitive event e. The mapping τ defines the time associated to each state, and it satisfies the requirement that $\tau(s_i) < \tau(s_j)$ for all $i < j$, i.e., states are sorted with respect to time.

c_k primitive $\mathcal{D}_M^t(c_k)$	$= L_C(s_i, c_k)$, where $\tau(s_i) \leq t$ and $\forall\, s_j . j > i \Rightarrow \tau(s_j) > t$
defined $\mathcal{D}_M^t(\text{defined}(c))$	$=$ **true** if $\mathcal{D}_M^t(c) \neq \bot$
	false otherwise
pair $\mathcal{D}_M^t([e_1, e_2))$	$=$ **true** if $\exists\, t_0 . t_0 \leq t : M, t_0 \models e_1$ and
	$\forall\, t'. t_0 \leq t' \leq t \Rightarrow M, t' \not\models e_2$
	$=$ **false** otherwise
negation $\mathcal{D}_M^t(\neg c)$	$=$ **true** if $\mathcal{D}_M^t(c) = $ **false**
	$= \bot$ if $\mathcal{D}_M^t(c) = \bot$
	$=$ **false** if $\mathcal{D}_M^t(c) = $ **true**
disjunction $\mathcal{D}_M^t(c_1 \wedge c_2)$	$=$ **true** if $\mathcal{D}_M^t(c_1)$ or $\mathcal{D}_M^t(c_2)$ is **true**
	$=$ **false** if $\mathcal{D}_M^t(c_1) = \mathcal{D}_M^t(c_2) = $ **false**
	$= \bot$ otherwise
conjunction $\mathcal{D}_M^t(c_1 \vee c_2)$	$= \mathcal{D}_M^t(\neg(\neg c_1 \wedge \neg c_2))$
implication $\mathcal{D}_M^t(c_1 \Rightarrow c_2)$	$= \mathcal{D}_M^t(\neg c_1 \wedge c_2)$

Table 18.1. Denotation of conditions

Before defining the semantics of a condition c holding in a given model M at time t, i.e. $M, t \models c$, we define the semantics of the denotation $\mathcal{D}_M^t(c)$ that associates to each condition c its truth value for model M and time t. $\mathcal{D}_M^t(c)$ is defined in a recursive way in the Table 18.1.

The value of $\mathcal{D}_M^t$ for a *primitive condition* c_k is given by the truth value of the condition c_k evaluated on state s_i that is the last discrete state recognized before time t; in the case of *defined*, the result of $\mathcal{D}_M^t$ is *true* if the condition c is defined at state t, otherwise the result is *false*; in the case of *pair*, the value of

$\mathcal{D}_M^t$ is true if event e_1 was true before time t and from that time up to now e_2 has not been ever true; and finally, definitions of *negation, disjunction, conjunction* and *implication* are straightforward; note that $\neg undefined$ is *undefined*.

Table 18.5.3 defines the semantics for conditions and events with respect to model M at time t, the table is self-explanatory.

$M, t \models c$	iff	$\mathcal{D}_M^t(c) = \mathbf{true}$
$M, t \models e_k$ (e_k prim.)	iff	$\exists$ state s_i such that $\tau(s_i) = t$ and $L_E(s_i, e_k)$ is defined
$M, t \models\, \uparrow c$	iff	$\exists s_i.\tau(s_i) = t \wedge M, \tau(s_i) \models c \wedge M, \tau(s_{i-1}) \not\models c$
		i.e, $\uparrow c$ occurs when condition c changes from false to true.
$M, t \models\, \downarrow c$	iff	$\exists s_i.\tau(s_i) = t \wedge M, \tau(s_i) \not\models c \wedge M, \tau(s_{i-1}) \models c$
		i.e, $\downarrow c$ occurs when condition c changes from true to false.
$M, t \models e_1 \vee e_2$	iff	$M, t \models e_1$ or $M, t \models e_2$
$M, t \models e_1 \wedge e_2$	iff	$M, t \models e_1$ and $M, t \models e_2$
$M, t \models e$ when c	iff	$M, t \models e$ and $M, t \models c$
		i.e, event e occurs when condition c is true.

Table 18.2. Semantics of events and conditions

Monitoring Script A PEDL script can monitor any object in the target system, therefore declaration of monitored entities is performed in a language specific manner. In the case of the Railway Gate example, a possible implementation of the system is sketched in Figure 18.9; the PEDL script will monitor the variables *gatePosition* and *lightState* and the methods *open, close, on, off*. For simplicity, we assume that there is only one instance of *GateController* and *LightController* classes.

```
class GateController{                    class LightController{
    public static final int UP = 0;          public static final int OFF = 0;
    public static final int DOWN = 1;        public static final int FLASHING =
    public static final int UPDOWN = 2;  1;
    public static final int DOWNUP = 3;
    int gatePosition;                        int lightState;
    public void open(){...}                  public void on(){...}
    public void close(){...}                 public void off(){...}
    ...                                      ...
};                                       };
```

Fig. 18.9. The implementation of the railway example

Primitive conditions are computed from boolean expressions over monitored variables. An example of primitive condition is:

Cond is_opening = (GateController.gatePosition == GateController.DOWNUP);

PEDL defines also the special primitive condition $InM(f)$ that is true while the method f is executing. Complex conditions are built from primitive conditions using boolean connectives.

Events correspond to updates of monitored variables, calls and returns of monitored methods (several primitive events have been defined in the original paper [LKK$^+$99]). Each event has an associated timestamp and may have a tuple of values containing additional information such as values of the parameters of a call. Events that are defined in the logic are used to construct more complex events from primitive ones.

For the purpose of the railway gate example, we are going to use only the event $StartM(f)$ that is triggered when the flow of control enters method f. The value associated with $StartM$ is a tuple containing the values of all arguments. In particular, we need to monitor closure of the gate (the *closing* event) and conditions corresponding to overture of the gate and flashing of light. Opening of the gate corresponds to condition $gatePosition = DOWNUP$ and flashing of the light corresponds to condition $lightState = FLASHING$. Figure 18.10 shows definition of event *closing* and both conditions *is_opening* and *is_flashing*.

```
export event closing;
export condition is_opening, is_flashing;
Monitored Entities:
    void GateController.close();
    void GateController.gatePosition;
    void LightController.lightState;
EvenDef:
    Event closing = StartM(GateController.close());
CondDef:
    Cond is_opening = (GateController.gatePosition == GateController.DOWNUP);
    Cond is_flashing = (LightController.lightState == LightController.FLASHING);
```

Fig. 18.10. PEDL script for the railway gate example

Safety Requirements The safety requirements (invariants) that need to be monitored are specified by the Meta Event Definition Language (MEDL). MEDL is based on the same logic of PEDL. Primitive events and conditions are imported from PEDL monitoring scripts to MEDL monitoring scripts. For increasing the expressive power of MEDL, the user can define auxiliary variables whose values can be used to define new events and conditions. The MEDL specification is then used by the MEDL compiler to generate the Run-Time checker. The Run-time checker evaluates MEDL expressions on events and conditions received from the event recognizers by using an abstract syntax tree. If a violation is detected, a signal is generated. The Run-time checker evaluates expressions in linear time with respect to the size of the expression.

In the case of the railway gate example, the corresponding MEDL script contains the formula:

$$\uparrow is\_opening \Rightarrow [closing, \downarrow is\_flashing).$$

If we consider the trace $open$, off, $flashing$, $closing$, $closed$, $opening$, $open$, off, the run-time checker will observe the following states:

- s0: $\neg is\_opening$, $\neg is\_flashing$
- s1: $\neg is\_opening$, $is\_flashing$
- s2: $\neg is\_opening$, $is\_flashing$, $closing$
- s3: $is\_opening$, $is\_flashing$
- s4: $\neg is\_opening$, $is\_flashing$
- s5: $\neg is\_opening$, $\neg is\_flashing$

State $s0$ is defined by the pair of events $open$ and off; then s_1 is obtained from s_0 when event $flashing$ takes place. Further states are obtained by considering remaining events. For this trace, the formula $\uparrow is\_opening \Rightarrow [closing, \downarrow is\_flashing)$ is true on all states. The value of this formula is computed for each state using Table 18.1 and 18.5.3:

- s0: true because $\neg is\_opening$
- s1: true because $\neg is\_opening$
- s2: true because $\neg is\_opening$
- s3: true because in s2 the event $closing$ has been triggered and since it, $is\_flashing$ was holding
- s4: true because $\neg is\_opening$
- s5: true because $\neg is\_opening$

Note that it is necessary to store all traces to evaluate MaC formulas.

Exercise 18.4 *(Algorithm Application).* Consider the trace $open$, off, $flashing$, $closing$, $closed$, off, $opening$, $open$, derive information sent to the run-time checker, and evaluate the formula $\uparrow is\_opening \Rightarrow [closing, \downarrow is\_flashing)$ for each state (the formula does not hold in all states) using Table 18.1 and 18.5.3.

Last Work on MaC MaC can detect violation of properties, but cannot provide any feedback to the running system. To overcome this limit, the MaC system has been extended with a feedback capability. The resulting system is called MaCS (Monitoring and Checking with Steering) [KLS⁺02]. The feedback component uses the information collected during monitoring and checking to steer the application back to a safe state after an error occurs.

Computational issues of monitoring by MaC have been investigated by Kim et al [KKL⁺02]. Moreover, Sammapun et al. [SSD⁺03] have defined a formal model of Java MaC safety properties in terms of an operational semantics for Middleweight, which is a considerable subset of the Java language.

18.6   Run-Time Verification of Learned Properties

Often, requirements are not formalized or even are not available, therefore it would be impossible to verify the correctness of observed executions. This scenario would invalidate any run-time verification techniques.

The problem of the lack of formal specifications can be solved by using *program synthesis techniques*. A **program synthesis** technique learns specific aspects[1] of a running system by observing its behavior. In particular, executions are first observed to produce the synthesized properties (learning phase) and then executions are checked with respect to learned properties (verification phase). In some cases, learning continues even during the verification phase.

When a formal specification is not available, program synthesis can automatically produce a specification that can be checked. Program synthesis exploits its potentials when it is used to verify the correctness of an evolving system. In fact, components of a system are often replaced with new components to either extend, modify, remove or correct functionalities of an existing system, but the updated version of the system can contain more faults than the original one, i.e., due to faults contained in the new components (but missing in the existing ones), or due to incompatibilities between new components and the system. The properties inferred from the replaced component can be used at run-time to discover possible faults within the new component. In some cases, new behaviors can be desired, e.g., bug fixes, and thus violations of invariants are ignored.

Furthermore, program synthesis is very effective when applied to a program that is developed with a limited knowledge of the final environment that will host the program itself. In fact, inference can be performed directly in the field so that the learned behavior depends on the context where the system is used. Therefore, the technique automatically takes advantage of information gathered from the field that was not available neither during development nor beta testing. Examples of systems that are developed without "complete" knowledge on the final environment are component-based systems (software components are usually developed in isolation, then are assembled with third-party components, and finally are deployed in unknown environments), mobile systems, agent-based systems, ubiquitous systems, wireless networks and self-adaptable systems. Learned properties can be used also to build test suites [HME03] and to check compliance of the observed behavior with respect to known properties [ECGN01].

A program synthesis technique can be effectively applied at run-time only if it is lightweight, and it is also able to infer meaningful properties that can be further checked. In this chapter, we focus on learning techniques based on *invariant detection*; they consist of techniques that monitor single executions to infer invariants, i.e., properties and relations over measured parameters that hold on all or most of the executions.

---

[1] The learned aspect is dependent on the learning technique that is used, e.g., it could be a behavioral pattern, an interaction protocol, or a relation among stimuli and results.

In the following, we survey over techniques for: detecting pre-conditions, post-conditions and invariants corresponding to specific program points; detecting invariants in component-based systems; and debugging software. The reader interested in learning further techniques can read Chapter 19 which addresses learning state machines.

Invariant Detection over Variables Automatic detection of mathematical properties over monitored variables has been proposed by Ernst et al. [ECGN01] and has been implemented in a tool named Daikon.

The technique requires the instrumentation of the source code of the target program to trace values of interesting variables in specific points, such as the beginning of a procedure, the begin of cycle instructions, and the end of a procedure.

Properties are then inferred by initially assuming that a given set of invariants hold for traced variables. Each execution can respect or violate hypothesized invariants. Violated invariants are deleted, while respected invariants are kept. Once several executions have been monitored, a restricted set of invariants will still exist. These invariants represent the learned properties of the program. Some of these invariants could be casually detected, for example the value of a given variable could be recognized as always positive simply because the user always digits a positive number, but the invariant does not state a property of the program. To reduce number of false invariants, only learned invariants stating relations that have a probability to casually hold below a given threshold are considered.

The initial set of invariants that is supposed to hold for variables in the scope of a point P of the source code is given by applying all relations of the following list for any possible combination of target variables [ECGN01] (x, y and z are used for variables and a,b and c for constant values):

- Invariants over any variable: $x = a$, $x = uninit$, $x \in \{a, b, c\}$
- Invariants over a single numeric variable: $a \leq x \leq b$, $x \neq 0$, $x \equiv a(mod\ b)$, $x \not\equiv a(mod\ b)$
- Invariants over two numeric variables: $y = ax + b$, $x < y$, $x \leq y$, $x > y$, $x \geq y$, $x = y$, $x \neq y$, $x = fn(y)$ or $y = fn(x)$ (where fn is a language specific unary function), any invariant over $x + y$, any invariant over $x - y$
- Invariants over three numeric variables: $z = ax + by + c$, $y = ax + bz + c$, $x = ay + bz + c$, $z = fn(x, y)$ (where fn is a language specific binary function)
- Invariants over a single sequence variable: minimum and maximum sequence value, nondecreasing, nonincreasing or equal, invariant over all elements of the collection
- Invariants over two sequence variables: $y = ax + b$ element wise, $x < y$, $x \leq y$, $x > y$, $x \geq y$, $x = y$, $x \neq y$, x subsequence of y, or vice versa, x is the reverse of y
- Invariants over a sequence and a numeric variable: $i \in s$

The technique provides a small extension for derived variables, thus the set of relations that are checked contain also the following additional list:

- Derived from any sequence: $size(s)$, $s[0]$, $s[1]$, $s[size(s) - 1]$, $s[size(s) - 2]$
- derived from any numeric sequence s: $sum(s)$, $min(s)$, $max(s)$
- derived from any numeric sequence s and any numeric variable i: $s[i]$, $s[i-1]$, $s[0..i]$, $s[0..i - 1]$
- derived from function invocations: number of calls

Since an invariant is checked only if it holds, the cost of computing invariants tends to be proportional to number of invariants effectively discovered [ECGN01].

Despite the wide applicability of the technique, Ernst et al.'s approach has the disadvantage of being applicable only to a restricted set of data types: scalars and collections. Moreover, object-oriented software has been tailored by printing object's attributes into an array [EGKN99], but this approach limits effectiveness of the technique because data can be extracted from objects only if source code is available or object's attributes are declared as public fields.

Invariant Detection in Component-Based Systems In general, invariants are useful to show bugs, e.g., an invariant that should hold is not true, but in the case of component-based systems they can provide further information. For instance, invariants can show limited usage of components, i.e., the invariant describes a particular usage of some features, and can validate program changes, e.g., comparing invariants computed for different versions of the same component.

A technique for checking compatibility of upgrades in component-based systems has been proposed by McCamant and Ernst [ME03]. In this case, invariant detection based on Daikon has been used to discover pre- and post- conditions of services implemented in components. In particular, when a component A used in system S is replaced by a component T, the compatibility of the update is established by (off-line) checking compatibility among pre- and post-conditions. The verified implication is:

$$A_{pre} \Rightarrow T_{pre} \text{ and } (A_{pre} \wedge T_{post}) \Rightarrow A_{post}$$

Pre- and post-conditions of A are computed while the component is used in S, while pre- and post-conditions of T are computed during testing of T.

In several cases, e.g., a weak theorem prover or insufficient testing of T, the technique could classify an update from A to T as unsafe even if it is safe. To detect these cases, whenever there is an unsafe upgrade, the technique checks the possibility to upgrade A with A. We know that this is always a safe upgrade since the behavior is necessarily preserved. If the technique classifies as unsafe the self-upgrade, we know that the response to the upgrade from A to T can be inaccurate.

Raz et al. use invariants to synthesize the behavior of data feed systems [RKS02]. A data feed system provides services based on online data sources; invariants are inferred by observing results gathered from the client-side. In particular, they use techniques from the information extraction field [FK00] to gather data from online services. Then, they compute invariants over multiple numeric fields by Daikon and compute invariants over single numeric fields by statistic estimations [RKS02]. Invariants can be used to monitor the evolution of data feed systems with respect to both updates to implemented functionalities and sensible modifications on data sources. Verification is performed at the client-side and can be used to check multiple data feed systems providing similar services.

The Behavior Capture and Test (BCT) [MP05] technique verifies at run-time learned invariants in the case of component-based and object-oriented software even without requiring source code. BCT uses the Object Flattening technique to automatically extract state data from objects. Object Flattening recognizes non-intrusive methods, named inspectors, of a given object by a heuristic. Selected inspectors are then invoked to get the internal state of the object. In case the internal state is an object, the approach is recursively applied until a given depth or until a primitive data type is obtained. Heuristical selection of inspectors is based on both language introspection, to automatically gather the signature of the methods, and conventions on writing code, to select inspectors by syntactic information. The behavior of the Object Flattening technique is highly configurable and can be adapted to arbitrary enterprise notations. Once state data has been extracted, BCT uses the invariant inference engine implemented in Daikon to derive invariants.

BCT infers also interaction invariants representing the interaction protocol used by components to interact. This protocol is synthesized in a regular expression summarizing all observed behaviors. Letters of the alphabet used to define regular expressions correspond to methods implemented by components of the system, and the language generated by a given regular expression of a component C corresponds to all acceptable behaviors that the component C can perform. In particular, the regular expression is derived by merging the observed interaction patterns and by generating new behaviors as natural generalization of the observed one [MP05].

BCT checks at run-time both interaction and object-oriented invariants by automatically generated monitors which capture both requests and results of performed computations.

Debugging by Invariants The DIDUCE tool [HL02a] instruments the source code to derive invariants that are continuously verified and updated at run-time. The technique seriously takes into consideration the amount of consumed resources, thus lightweight computations of invariants is obtained at the cost of limited expressiveness power of the inferred invariants. In fact, the instrumentation consists of checking equality of object references, static variables, input parameters and return values, with respect to a fixed value. Invariants are relaxed upon violation, in particular a mask defines the bits that must be checked for equality. Each time the equality between the expected value and the observed value is falsified for a bit, the mask is modified and the corresponding bit is not checked anymore. The inference technique consumes little time and memory, but it can specify only invariants stating if a given variable is constant, positive, negative, odd, even or approximatively bounded. This approach has been shown to be particularly effective for debugging [HL02a]; in fact an anomalous behavior often violates several invariants before generating the failure. Thus, the sequence of violated invariants can be used to reach the point storing the fault from the point that has generated the failure.

Other Techniques In the past, other inference techniques have been proposed in the Machine Learning field [RW88], but they are quite complex and rarely can learn programs more complex than a binary function. For instance, Lau et al. [LDW03] proposed a learning technique able to learn program statements from executions, but it learns only procedural programs, requires a heavy instrumentation, and is not suitable to learn programs of non-trivial complexity (the average program length is six statements).

18.7   Case Studies

Theoretical aspects such as language expressiveness, complexity of specifying requirements and intrusiveness of the approach are very important, but the concrete applicability of a run-time verification technique must be demonstrated with industrial case studies.

The Java implementation of PathExplorer, named JPaX, has been essentially developed and used in the NASA Research Center, therefore it has been applied to many programs produced for rovers, spacecrafts and similar devices. In particular, JPaX has been used to verify the planetary rover controller K9's executive subsystem [ADG+03], a space craft fault protection system [ADG+03] and a space craft attitude control system [HR04].

The *K9's executive subsystem* is a multi-threaded system of about 8.000 lines of Java code that executes hierarchical plans. JPaX has been used to discover faults related to concurrency, and produced encouraging results; in fact, the tool discovered all but two concurrency faults, all data races and all deadlocks. The two missed faults are subtle errors involving Java's `wait` and `notify` constructs. More advanced techniques, e.g., model checking, are required to detect such kind of errors.

The *space craft fault protection system* monitors both critical hardware and software components to detect faults and to execute corrective responses. JPaX has been used to check LTL formulas against execution traces and it discovered some bugs and inaccuracies in the documentation. One of the found bugs was even present in the program version that flew on the space craft.

The *attitude control system* is 1850 lines length Java program that was analyzed by the JPaX's concurrency algorithms. Also in this case JPaX found unknown data races and found all artificially generated deadlocks and data races.

Moreover, JPaX has been executed also for verifying several small size programs, such as a discrete-event elevator simulator (about 500 lines of code) and two task-parallel applications (about 250 and 700 lines of code) [AHB03]. JPaX detected some faults, but also false positives[2] demonstrating unsoundness of the technique.

Experimental results show the suitability of the technology for critical applications. The approach is effective in detecting large class of errors, but can produce false warnings [AHB03] and can be ineffective in the case of subtle faults [ADG+03]. Moreover, the computational overhead due to the instrumentation is limited, but applications using large data sets suffer great scalability problems limiting the applicability of JPaX [AHB03]. JPaX is very effective when combined with techniques for the automatic generation of test cases, such as when combined with model-checking, since it is possible to automatically run and verify huge set of test cases.

The MaC approach has been used to implement a fault-tolerant layer for an *inverted pendulum controller* [KLS+02]. The system uses sensors and controllers to monitor the current status of the pendulum and eventually to correct it. The goal is to maintain the pendulum upright. Experimental results demonstrate achievement of the goal, in fact the pendulum is always stabilized after a perturbation is performed. Empirical data show also that the overhead induced in the target system by the instrumentation is very high, however in the case of the pendulum, the instrumented system behaves quickly enough in respect to pendulum cycles.

A simple application of the MaC technique has been used also for monitoring values produced by a program generating *prime numbers* [KKL+02]. The goal of the monitor is to detect prime numbers between 99990 and 100000. This simple program has been essentially used to estimate overhead induced by the MaC technique, results show that MaC slows down the target program from 1.5 to 3.1 times.

More serious experimental work on the MaC technique has been performed for analyzing network protocols [BGK+02] and for monitoring agent formations [GSSL99].

In the first case, MaC has been used together with the NS simulator (a discrete event simulator) for checking properties of a *routing protocol*. Experimental results show the high effectiveness of the approach in detecting faults; on the other hand, experimental results highlight the high overhead induced by runtime verification too. Performance can be sensibly improved by abstracting from some characteristics, for instance by both focusing only on a small set of nodes (population abstraction) and pruning traces including events that do not directly affect the property under verification (packet-type abstraction), it is possible to reduce the computation time from 4 days to 51 seconds.

In the second case, the Mac framework has been used to *monitor the formation of a set of agents* (nanobots, micro-air vehicles, micro-electromechanical systems, ...). Agents are supposed to be monitored from an observer possessing the global knowledge of the formation, e.g., a plane, in contrast with single agents possessing only local knowledge and limited interaction possibility. The formation must keep a fixed geometric shape despite events that can alter the

---

[2] a false positive is an observed inconsistency that does not correspond to a fault

existing structure. The observer recognizes alerts due to wrong positions of some agents and infers the current situation with respect to the number and trend of alerts.

The experimental work focused on the simulation of the effects induced by a blast. Results show that self-repairing mechanisms succeeded in repairing local flaws, but concavities on the overall shape persist. In this case, the observer broadcasts commands for settling up the multi-agent system. Experimental data demonstrate the effectiveness of MaC in checking the current shape of the agent pool.

Experimental results obtained by JPaX and MaC are convincing and benefits are clear, in fact they have been successfully applied for detecting errors, but also for implementing fault tolerant and self-repairing systems.

Time consumed by running the instrumented system instead of the original one is still considerable. Many scenarios justify employment of run-time verification techniques, e.g., critical systems and military systems, but the development of cheaper techniques is still an open issue.

Moreover, techniques based on invariant detection have been employed on systems of different sizes and complexity, e.g., simple routines [ECGN01], data-feed systems [RKS02], commercial systems [MP05] and Perl libraries [ME03]. They are suitable to respond to the lack of formal specifications, but they are expensive to be executed at run-time, especially if it is considered the case where the instrumented application is deployed in the user environment.

Diduce [HL02a] can be considered a nice exception, in fact it both automatically infers invariants and performs checking at cheap cost, but expressiveness of inferred invariants is very limited.

18.8   Summary

For our present computational infrastructures to become computer utility (see [Gru68]), the system elements must be reliable. The move towards open systems, such as ubiquitous computing, peer-to-peer computing, and autonomic computing, means there will be many systems producing interactions that are not predictable at design-time. This trend also means the incipient rise of specialization and standardization of algorithms, of software, and capabilities, and the decline in the historical concentration of general purpose computing. How to build reliability into systems of that kind will involve a lot of intellectual and practical effort. Shipping out systems and waiting for user feedback to correct bugs is simply not plausible any longer.

In *run-time verification*, one expects that, given the specification, and while running an already tested and/or debugged program, a program execution is verified to concur with the specification, and if it does not, the program should automatically be corrected while running. From industrial and exemplar systems, we need to develop theories and use these theories to develop tools that system builders can use to specify, design, build, test, audit, monitor and verify programs.

Although these are very early days, some of the projects already carried out in run-time verification produce tools that, when looked at properly, are simply debuggers with fancy features and/or provide good tracing mechanisms. Examples include, inter alia, Jass [BFMW01], Opium [Duc90], Morphine [DJ01], Coca [Duc99], DynaMICs [GRMD01], Daikon [ECGN01], and ESC/Java [RLNS00]. Some approaches in run-time verification include collecting statistics during run-time to perform some form of debugging later on. However, what is encouraging amongst the majority of these projects and tools is the use of linear time logic (or extensions of it) to describe the monitor that monitors the program behavior [Gei01] or as the basis of a specification language to specify the properties to monitor [DGJV01]. In particular, Hakansson et al. [HJL03] proposed the generation of on-line test oracles with a rich logic which contains past operators, metric time, and can handle data values by means of the quantification construct.

What is needed is a tool (or set of) that software professionals can use to specify requirements, to design the system, to code, to test, to deploy, and to monitor the software while running, something like an integrated development environment (IDE) that combines those attributes. JPAX [HR01a] is going in the right direction. This is an IDE that tries to combine the positive attributes of testing, i.e. in terms of scaling up, and that of formal methods, i.e. by providing temporal formulas for specification. It falls shy to be called a run-time verification tool as it only monitors a program and emits its results, it does not automatically correct the monitored program. MaCS [KLS+02] is going in the right direction towards being called a run-time verification tool. It combines monitoring a program with steering that program if, while running, fails to concur with its specification. There are some obvious problems to tackle in this area, such as how far forward in a running program should a tool look to correct, and the computational complexity that is inherent in tackling such a problem.

19 Model Checking

Therese Berg[1] and Harald Raffelt[2]

[1] Computer Science Department
Uppsala University
thereseb@it.uu.se
[2] Chair of Programming Systems and Compiler Construction
University of Dortmund
harald.raffelt@cs.uni-dortmund.de

19.1 Introduction

When developing hard- or software systems one starts with a collection of requirements. Most requirements arise due to the needs of the customer, others originate from design decisions and further constraints. Of course, the final system should fulfill these requirements. Besides general requirements like scalability and performance, there is often a large number of formal requirements which concern the functionality of the system. Typical requirements of this kind are lifeness requirements (e.g. bad things never happen), fairness requirements (e.g. the system continues doing meaningful things), and in general requirements which prescribe the chronological order of events (e.g. event A may only occur after event B).

A typical approach to meet this goal is to construct a model, to check that the model fulfills the requirements and then to show that the system conforms to the model. For the checking models against formal requirements automatical means have been developed in the past 20 years under the term *model checking*.

Previous chapters have presented various ways of testing. The first and the second part of book introduced some methods for testing finite state machines and labeled transition system. The third part was about model-based test generation. The general assumption of all approaches so far was, that the specification is completely given in form of a model. Then, testing becomes the task of checking whether a system conforms to a given specification or not. But in real life there is unfortunately in most cases no formal model of the system. To make use of, for example, conformance testing presented in Chapter 4 or methods for testing I/O-automata presented in Chapter 7, it is often necessary to build the formal model by hand. This procedure is very error-prone, since in many cases one can only use the informal customer requirement specifications and some expert knowledge of the systems developer to build the model.

One solution to this problem comes from the area of *automata learning*, which provides some methods to generate a formal model out of a black box system. This approach allows at least to compare one version of the system with another one.

However, one can think of a more direct way to the requirements on the final system. After all, the main goal is usually to show that the system fulfills the

M. Broy et al. (Eds.): Model-Based Testing of Reactive Systems, LNCS 3472, pp. 557-603, 2005.
© Springer-Verlag Berlin Heidelberg 2005

requirements and conformance to a hand-made model is just an instrument to achieve.

In this chapter we explain one possible way to check requirements on black boxes. It combines model checking with model learning. It is known under the terms *adaptive model checking* or *black box checking*. The idea is that a (part) of the model of the black box is learned by a machine learning algorithm. This model is then used for model checking the requirements. However, if a counter example is found, it might be because the system does not fulfill the requirement but, it can also be that the model is not adequate. In other words, the bug might be in the model not in the system. Then, the model has to be improved.

To make the chapter self-contained, we recall model checking techniques in the first part of the chapter (Section 19.3) and present learning algorithms in the second part (Section 19.4).

In the last part of the chapter (Section 19.5) the two techniques are combined.

19.2   Preliminaries

Definition 19.1. A **deterministic finite-state automaton (DFA)** is a 5-tuple $\mathcal{M} = (\Sigma, Q, \delta, q_0, F)$, where

- Σ is a finite set of **letters** called **alphabet**
- Q is a non-empty finite set of **states**
- $\delta : Q \times \Sigma \to Q$ is the **transition function**
- $q_0 \in Q$ is the **initial state**
- $F \subseteq Q$ is a set of **accepting states**

The machine starts in the initial state q_0 and reads a **string** or **word** of letters of its alphabet. It uses the transition function δ to determine the next state using the current state and the letter just read. Formally a word w is a sequence of letters $w = a_1 a_2 \ldots a_n \in \Sigma^*$. The **empty word**, which has no letters, is usually denoted by ε. A **prefix** u of a word w is such that $w = uv$, where $w, u, v \in \Sigma^*$. The set of all finite words w with exactly n letters which can be build over an alphabet Σ is defined by $\Sigma^n = \varepsilon$ iff $n = 0$, and $\Sigma^n = \Sigma \cdot \Sigma^{n-1}$. The set of all finite words is denoted by Σ^*, which is defined by $\Sigma^* = \bigcup_{n \in \mathbb{N}} \Sigma^n$.

We denote the number of states Q, the size of the alphabet Σ, and the size of the transition function δ by respectively $|Q|, |\Sigma|$, and $|\delta|$. The latter is defined to be the number of elements of the domain of δ, i.e. $|Q \times \Sigma|$. Furthermore $q_i \xrightarrow{a} q_j$ is a denotation of $\delta(q_i, a) = q_j$.

Definition 19.2. Let $[n] = \{0, \ldots, n\}$. A **finite run** π of a DFA $\mathcal{M}$ on a finite word $w = a_0 a_1 \ldots a_n \in \Sigma^*$ is a sequence of states $\pi = \pi_0 \ldots \pi_{n+1}$, such that

- $\pi_0 = q_0$
- $\forall i \in [n] : \pi_i \xrightarrow{a_i} \pi_{i+1}$

The first state π_0 of the run is the initial state q_0 of $\mathcal{M}$ and each next state π_{i+1} is reached by reading one letter a_i. A run is called **accepting**, if $\pi_{n+1} \in F$. The letters a_i read by a run form a $w = a_1 \dots a_n$. If the run is acceting, then the word read by the run is also said to be accepting. The language a DFA $\mathcal{M}$ recognizes is denoted by $\mathcal{L}(\mathcal{M})$. It is defined as the set of accepting words. We call a language $\mathcal{L}$ **regular** if there is a DFA accepting $\mathcal{L}$.

A different kind of automaton which operates on infinite words was introduced by Büchi [Büc62] for obtaining a decision procedure for the monadic second-order theory of structures with one successor. Later these automata were called Büchi automata. The main idea of Büchi automata is to operate on infinite input words $w = a_0 a_1 \dots \in \Sigma^\omega$, whereas Σ^ω denotes the set of all infinite words over the alphabet Σ.

Definition 19.3. A **Büchi automaton** is a 5-tuple $A = (\Sigma, Q, \delta, q_0, F)$, where

- Σ is a finite set of actions or letters,
- Q is a finite set of **states**,
- $\delta : Q \times \Sigma \rightarrow 2^Q$ is a **transition function**,
- $q_0 \in Q$ is a **initial state** and,
- $F \subseteq Q$ is a set of **accepting states**.

Starting from its initial state the automaton chooses nondeterministically a possible successor state in $\delta(q, a)$ of the current state q.

Definition 19.4. An **infinite run** π of a Büchi automaton A on a word $w = a_0 a_1 \dots \in \Sigma^\omega$ is a sequence $\pi = \pi_0 \pi_1 \dots \in Q^\omega$, such that

- $\pi_0 = q_0$
- $\pi_{i+1} \in \delta(\pi_i, a_i)$.

The first state π_0 of the run is the initial state q_0 of A and each next state π_{i+1} is one of the states reachable by reading one letter a_i. The states that occur infinitely many times in a run are $\inf(\pi) = \{q \mid q \in Q \text{ and } q = \pi_i \text{ for infinitely many } i \geq 0\}$. An infinite run of a Büchi automaton is accepted if it visits accepting states infinitely often. Formally an infinite run $\pi = \pi_0 \pi_1 \pi_2 \dots$ is a accepted iff $\inf(\pi) \cap F \neq \emptyset$. An infinite word $w = a_0 a_1 \dots \in \Sigma^\omega$ is accepted by the automaton, if and only if there is an infinite run of the automaton which accepts the word. The language $\mathcal{L}(A)$ accepted by a Büchi automaton A is the set of all accepted words. The complement of a language $\mathcal{L}(A)$ accepted by a Büchi automaton is the set of all not accepted words, it is defined as $\overline{\mathcal{L}(A)} = \Sigma^\omega \backslash \mathcal{L}(A)$.

The length of a finite run $\pi = \pi_0 \pi_1 \dots \pi_n$ is the number of its elements denoted by $|\pi| = n + 1$. The length of an infinite run is denoted by $|\pi| = \infty$. For $0 \leq i < |\pi|$ the *suffix* of a run $\pi = \pi_0 \pi_1 \dots \pi_n$ starting with element π_i is denoted by $\pi^i = \pi_i \pi_{i+1} \dots$.

19.3   Model Checking

In the last few years model checking has become a powerful and promising approach to automatic verification of systems. In general a model checker is a tool which checks whether a given structure M (called model) satisfies a certain logical constraint ϕ (called property). Typically models are represented by finite automata-like structures and properties are described in temporal logic. In contrast to conventional logics in temporal logics it is possible to describe temporal dependencies like one action must take place before another one. The model checker either confirms that the properties hold or reports that they are not satisfied by the model. Some model checkers can produce a path in the model which does not satisfy the property, a so called counterexample. Counterexamples can be understood as a reason for the unsatisfied property. Besides from providing models and properties no further user interaction is necessary for the entire model checking process. Because of its push-button approach model checking is a powerful verification tool even in large environments like hardware verification.

In Section 19.3.1 we give a brief introduction to models used to describe systems for model checking purposes and in Section 19.3.2 some common formalisms to describe properties of systems are provided. In Section 19.3.3 a common automata-theoretic model-checking algorithm is presented in detail.

19.3.1   Models

Model-checking typically depends on a discrete model of a system which describes the system behavior. Usually these models are graph structures where nodes represent the states of the system and edges represent transitions between the states. For model checking purposes these structures are typically finite, but model checking infinite structures is also possible [BCMS01]. These graphs without any further annotation are not expressive enough to provide an interesting description of the system. Two approaches are in common use: Kripke structures, where the nodes are annotated with so called atomic propositions, and labeled transition systems where the edges are annotated with so called actions. These two descriptions can be combined into so called Kripke transition systems [MOSS99].

In the following we present an introduction into Kripke structures. An introduction into labeled transition systems can be found in Section 22.

Definition 19.5. A **Kripke structure** (**KS**) over a set AP of atomic propositions is a triple (S, R, I), where

- S is a set of states,
- $R \subseteq S \times S$ is a transitions relation and,
- $I : S \to 2^{AP}$ is a labeling function

Each proposition describes a basic local property of the systems states. To each state of the system a set of atomic propositions is assigned by the labeling function $I : S \rightarrow 2^{AP}$, describing which propositions are valid for that state. The labeling function is sometimes called interpretation.

A Kripke structure is called *total* if R is a total relation, otherwise it is called *partial*. A Kripke structure is called *rooted*, if one state $s_0 \in S$ is declared as initial state. For model checking purposes S and AP are usually finite.

Example. In Figure 19.1 a coffee percolator is modeled by a rooted Kripke structure. The set of atomic propositions is defined by $AP = \{coffee, coin\}$.

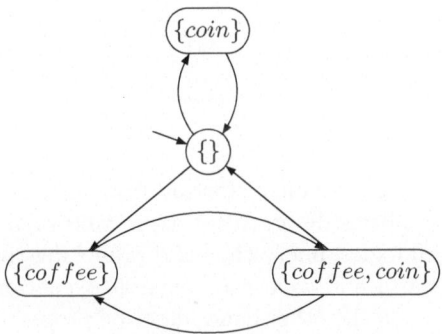

Fig. 19.1. Example Kripke structure

The atomic proposition $coffee$ represents the fact that there is coffee-powder in the machine. In a state which is labeled by the atomic proposition $coffee$, the coffee-percolator is able to brew coffee and to spend it afterwards. The atomic proposition $coin$ represents that there is a coin inside the coin slot and a user has paid for a coffee. Using this extra information one may imagine which actions lead from one state to another. To give a better understanding of the coffee percolator it is also represented as labeled transition system in the next example.

Example. In contrast to Kripke structures were the nodes are labeled with sets of atomic propositions labeled transition systems (compare Section 22) label the transitions with atomic actions. In Figure 19.2 the coffee percolator of the previous example is modeled as labeled transition system. Now one can see that, as long as there is no coffee-powder inserted, every inserted coin will be refused. Once coffee-powder is inserted every insert coin action will be answered by a spend coffee action until the automaton decides internally that one has to insert coffee-powder again.

19.3.2 Temporal Logics

Models describe systems, including their transitional behavior and local properties of the states. In order to model-check these systems, desired global characteristics of the system have to be formalized. For example, one might be interested in reachability properties like: "Is it possible to reach a state where

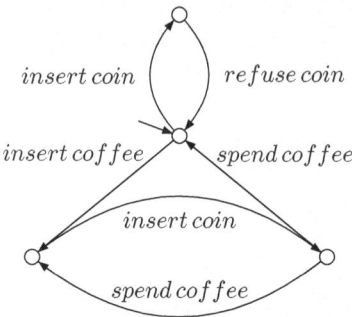

Fig. 19.2. Example Labeled Transition System

a certain atomic proposition holds, starting from the initial state?". Temporal logics are logical formalisms designed for expressing such properties. There are two kinds of temporal logics, linear-time and branching-time. Linear-time logics are concerned with paths and treat each possible execution-path independently, branching-time logics, on the other hand, describe properties that depend on the branching structure of the model. The pros and cons of both logics are compared by Moshe Y. Vardi [Var01]. Both temporal logics have different expressiveness and therefore the kind of properties a model checker can prove depends on the choice of the underlying temporal logic. As an example, consider the two rooted labeled transitions systems in Figure 19.3, showing two different vending machines offering coffee and tea. Both machines serve coffee or tea after a coin has been inserted, but the right machine decides internally whether to serve coffee or tea, in contrast to the left machine which leaves the decision to the customer. Both machines have the same set of computations (maximal paths): $\{(coin,\ coffee),\ (coin,\ tea)\}$. Unfortunately they can not be distinguished in linear-time logics, since in linear-time logics each path is examined separately. Branching-time logic, in contrast, can distinguish these two machines, since it is possible to express properties like "a coffee action is possible after any coin action".

The choice of using linear-time or branching-time logic depends on the properties to be analyzed. Linear-time logics are preferred when only path properties are of interest, as when analyzing data-flow properties, like dead-locks. Branching-time logics are often better for analyzing reactive systems, due to their greater selectivity.

Linear Temporal Logic (LTL)[Pnu77] can be seen as the "standard" linear-time logic. It is often presented in a form to be interpreted over Kripke structures. Its formulas are constructed as follows:

$$\phi ::= \mathsf{true} \mid p \mid \neg\phi \mid \phi \wedge \phi \mid \mathsf{X}(\phi) \mid \phi\mathsf{U}\phi$$

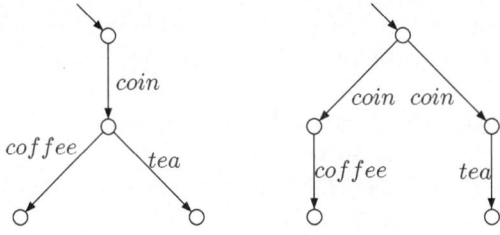

Fig. 19.3. Two vending machines

where p ranges over a set of atomic propositions AP. Note that sometimes true is defined to be a special atomic proposition, which is valid for every state.

The semantics $[\![\phi]\!]$ of a formula ϕ is the set of all runs π for which the property holds: $[\![\phi]\!] = \{\pi \mid \pi \models \phi\}$. The semantics is inductively defined on the structure of the formula.

$$\pi \models \text{true}$$
$$\pi \models p \qquad \Leftrightarrow p \in I(\pi_0)$$
$$\pi \models \neg\phi \quad \Leftrightarrow \pi \not\models \phi$$
$$\pi \models \phi_1 \wedge \phi_2 \Leftrightarrow \pi \models \phi_1 \wedge \pi \models \phi_2$$
$$\pi \models \text{X}(\phi) \quad \Leftrightarrow |\pi| > 1 \wedge \pi^1 \models \phi$$
$$\pi \models \phi_1 \text{U}\phi_2 \Leftrightarrow \exists k \in [|\pi| - 1] : \left(\pi^k \models \phi_2 \wedge \forall i \in [k-1] : \pi^i \models \phi_1\right)$$

Every run π satisfies true and every run π satisfies an atomic proposition, iff the first state π_0 of the run does. The negation and conjunction is interpreted as usual; further Boolean connectives may be introduced as abbreviations. E.g. $\phi_1 \vee \phi_2$, can be introduced as $\neg(\neg\phi_1 \wedge \neg\phi_2)$. The modality $\text{X}(\phi)$ is called "next time ϕ" and requires the property ϕ to hold for the next situation in the run. The modality $\phi_1 \text{U}\phi_2$ is also denoted as $\text{U}(\phi_1, \phi_2)$. It is called "ϕ_1 until ϕ_2" and requires the property ϕ_1 to hold for all situations on the run until finally the property ϕ_2 holds for some situation.

Besides abbreviations of further Boolean connectivities, the following abbreviations are common:

$$\text{F}(\phi) := \text{U}(\text{true}, \phi)$$
$$\text{G}(\phi) := \neg\text{F}(\neg\phi)$$

The modality $\text{F}(\phi)$, called "finally ϕ", requires ϕ to hold for some later situation. The modality $\text{G}(\phi)$, called "globally ϕ", requires ϕ to hold for all situations. The until modality $\phi_1 \text{U}\phi_2$ is sometimes called **strong until** because it requires ϕ_2 to become true finally. In contrast to this modality, there is a different variant, called **weak until**, which holds, even if ϕ_2 never holds while ϕ_1 holds forever. $(\phi_1 \text{WU}\phi_2 := \phi_1 \text{U}\phi_2 \vee \text{G}(\phi_1))$.

Since in system verification one is typically interested whether a specific state satisfies a certain property, there is the following convention: a state $s \in S$ of a transition system satisfies a formula if every run starting at s satisfies it.

Example. To illustrate the meaning of the modalities, here are some examples, that are satisfied by every run of the KS presented in Fig. 19.1:

- $X\,(coffee \vee coin)$ states that in the second step of execution there will be coffee or a coin inside the automaton.
- $G\,(coin \rightarrow X\,(\neg coin))$ states that whenever there is a coin inside the automaton it will be removed in the next step.
- $G\,(coffee \rightarrow (coffee\,\mathsf{WU}\,((coffee \wedge coin) \rightarrow X\neg\,(coffee \vee coin))))$
  states that once there is coffee inside the automaton it will last forever, or it will be removed in a later situation together with a coin in a single step.

Computational Tree Logic Computational Tree Logic (**CTL**) is one of the earliest proposed branching time logics. It can be considered as the branching time counterpart of LTL since it introduces universal and an existential path quantifiers. The syntax of CTL formulas is defined with respect to a KS (S, R, I) over a set AP of atomic propositions.

$$\phi ::= \mathsf{true} \mid p \mid \neg\phi \mid \phi_1 \wedge \phi_2 \mid \mathsf{EX}\,(\phi) \mid \mathsf{E}\phi\mathsf{U}\phi \mid \mathsf{A}\phi\mathsf{U}\phi$$

As mentioned before p is an element of the atomic propositions AP. The semantics of a formula denote the subset of states $s \in S$ for which the formula holds: $[\![\phi]\!]^T = \{s \in S \mid s \models \phi\}$.

Let Π_s^* denotes the set of all runs starting with state s. The semantics of a formula ϕ is inductively defined on the structure of ϕ as follows:

$$
\begin{aligned}
s &\models \mathsf{true} \\
s &\models p && \Leftrightarrow p \in I(s) \\
s &\models \neg\phi && \Leftrightarrow s \not\models \phi \\
s &\models \phi_1 \wedge \phi_2 && \Leftrightarrow s \models \phi_1 \,\wedge\, s \models \phi_2 \\
s &\models \mathsf{EX}\,(\phi) && \Leftrightarrow \exists\, s' \in S : (s, s') \in R \wedge s' \models \phi \\
s &\models \mathsf{E}\phi_1\mathsf{U}\phi_2 && \Leftrightarrow \exists\,\pi \in \Pi_s^* : \exists\, k \in [|\pi|] : \left(\pi^k \models \phi_2 \wedge \forall\, i \in [k-1] : \pi^i \models \phi_1\right) \\
s &\models \mathsf{A}\phi_1\mathsf{U}\phi_2 && \Leftrightarrow \forall\,\pi \in \Pi_s^* : \exists\, k \in [|\pi|] : \left(\pi^k \models \phi_2 \wedge \forall\, i \in [k-1] : \pi^i \models \phi_1\right)
\end{aligned}
$$

Every state s satisfies **true** and every state s satisfies an atomic proposition, iff the proposition is assigned to the state. The negation and conjunction is interpreted as usual, further Boolean connectives may be introduced as abbreviations. The modality EX is called "exists next ϕ". It intuitive means that there is an immediate successor state s' reachable by executing one transition which satisfies ϕ. The modality $\mathsf{E}\phi_1\mathsf{U}\phi_2$, called "exists ϕ_1 until ϕ_2", requires the existence of a run π starting with state s which has a prefix such that ϕ_2 holds for the last state of the prefix and ϕ_1 holds for all other states along the prefix. The modality $\mathsf{A}\phi_1\mathsf{U}\phi_2$ is called "forall ϕ_1 until ϕ_2". It requires that for every computation run π starting with state s, there is a prefix such that ϕ_2 holds for the last state of the prefix and ϕ_1 holds for all other states along the prefix. The following abbreviations are common:

$$\mathsf{AX}\,(\phi) := \neg\mathsf{EX}\,(\neg\phi)$$
$$\mathsf{AF}\,(\phi) := \mathsf{A}\mathsf{true}\mathsf{U}\phi$$
$$\mathsf{EF}\,(\phi) := \mathsf{E}\mathsf{true}\mathsf{U}\phi$$
$$\mathsf{AG}\,(\phi) := \neg\mathsf{EF}\,(\neg\phi)$$
$$\mathsf{EG}\,(\phi) := \neg\mathsf{AF}\,(\neg\phi)$$

The modality $\mathsf{AX}\,(\phi)$, called "forall next ϕ", requires that the property ϕ holds in every reachable successor state of s. The modality $\mathsf{AF}\,(\phi)$, called "forall finally ϕ", requires that the property ϕ holds on every run (starting from the current state s) for some later state. The modality $\mathsf{EF}\,(\phi)$ requires that there is a run starting from state s which satisfies the property ϕ for some later state. It is called "exists finally ϕ". The modality $\mathsf{AG}\,(\phi)$, called "forall globally ϕ", requires that the property ϕ holds on every run for every state. The modality $\mathsf{EG}\,(\phi)$ is called "exists globally ϕ". It requires that there is a run starting from state s which satisfies the property ϕ in every state.

Example. To illustrate the meaning of the modalities, here are some examples, which are satisfied by the KS presented in Figure 19.1:

- $\mathsf{AX}\,(coffee \vee coin)$ states that the automaton can make a step and then there will be coffee or a coin inside the automaton.
- $\mathsf{AG}\,(coin \rightarrow \mathsf{EX}\,(\neg coin))$ states that whenever there is a coin inside the automaton there is a next step which removes the coin.
- $\mathsf{AG}\,(\mathsf{AF}\,(coin))$ states that on every run a coin is infinite often inside the automaton.
- $\mathsf{AG}\,(coffee \rightarrow (\mathsf{E}coffee\mathsf{U}\,((coffee \wedge coin) \rightarrow \mathsf{EX}\neg\,(coffee \vee coin))))$
  states that on every run once there is coffee inside the automaton it will last until it is finally removed in a later situation together with a coin in a single step.
- $\mathsf{EG}\,((coin \rightarrow \mathsf{EX}\,(\neg coin)) \wedge (\neg coin \rightarrow \mathsf{EX}\,(coin)))$ states that there is a run of the coffee percolator where the condition $coin$ and $\neg coin$ is alternating.

Other Temporal Logic Besides LTL and CTL there are a number of other temporal logics. Some of them extend the presented basic version of LTL and CTL to deal with special issues. **Fair computational tree logic** (FCTL) [EL85] for example extends CTL to deal with fairness constraints. Another well known extension to CTL is CTL*, which allows a more general combination of the universal and existential path quantifiers (A, E), and the until and next operator ($\mathsf{X}\,(\phi),\phi\mathsf{U}\phi$). In the following we shortly introduce two other temporal logics which are related to labeled transition systems.

- **Hennessy-Milner Logic (HML)**
  is a simple modal logic introduced by Hennessy and Milner [HM85, Mil89]. In contrast to LTL and CTL it is defined over a set of actions (Act) since it is related to labeled transition systems (see Section 22). HML is build out of the constant **true**, negation, conjunction, and the parameterized existential next operator $\langle a \rangle$ ($a \in Act$). This modality is called "diamond a ϕ" and

holds if there is an a-transitions to a state of the labeled transition system which satisfies ϕ. The important point about HML is that HML-properties can characterize finite automata up to bisimulation.

- **Modal μ-calculus**

  was introduced by Kozen [Koz83] and extends Hennessy-Milner logic by a least fixpoint operator (μ) . In general a fixpoint of a function f is a value x such that $f(x) = x$. Intuitively, the μ-calculus makes it possible to use modalities inside of recursively defined patterns. For example consider the CTL formula $EF(\phi)$. Another way of expressing this is to say that there is a property X such that either ϕ is satisfied in the current state or there is some successor state in which X is true. $X = \phi \vee \Diamond X$. This property can be expressed in μ-calculus as $\mu X.\phi \vee \Diamond X$.

  Due to the extreme power of fixpoint operators the μ-calculus allows to express very complex properties within a sparse formalism. The μ-calculus covers LTL and CTL, and it is even possible to express fairness constraints which is not possible with the basic version of LTL and CTL.

19.3.3   Model Checking Algorithms

Model checking can be realized by several different approaches; prominent examples are the *semantic approach*, the *automata theoretic approach*, and the *tableau approach*.

The idea behind the semantic approach is to inductively compute the semantics of the formula in question to a given finite model, directly. This generates a set of states which satisfy the formula. The semantic approach is typically used for model checking branching time logics. There are efficient algorithms using this approach which operate linear in the size of the model even for the alternation free μ-calculus [CS92].

The automata theoretic approach is used for model checking linear-time logics and branching-time logics as well. This approach reduces the model checking problem to an inclusion problem between automata. An automaton A_ϕ is constructed from the property ϕ which accepts all runs satisfying ϕ. Another automaton A_M is constructed from model M which accepts the executions runs of the model. M satisfies ϕ if the language of the model-automaton A_M is a subset of language accepted by the properties automaton A_ϕ. This problem can be reduced to the problem of deciding non-emptiness of a product automaton which is possible by reachability analysis. As an example, an efficient algorithm for model checking LTL [Var96] is presented later.

The tableau method is used to determine if a certain state s of a given model M satisfies a property ϕ. This approach tries to construct a proof tree that witnesses that a given state satisfies a certain property. If no proof tree can be found, it provides a disproof (counterexample) of the property for the given state. Since the tableau method inspects only a small fraction of the state space [SW91], it combines well with incremental construction of the state space, which is a prominent approach to deal with the state explosion problem.

Another approach of fighting state explosion is to represent the transition relation of the models implicitly with an *ordered binary decision diagram* (OBDD) [BCMD90], since the size of the transition relation is the main limiting factor. By using common model checking algorithms with OBDDs and some refinements, very large examples with up to 10^{120} states have verified [BCL92].

Model Checking LTL To model check Kripke structures with LTL-properties the following approach is proposed. In the first step the model M and the property ϕ are translated into automata models A_M and A_ϕ which represent the structures in a common way. The automaton A_M accepts all computations which are possible in the model and A_ϕ accepts all computations which are allowed with respect to the property. The model checking problem now reduces to the automata theoretic problem of checking that all computations accepted by an automaton A_M are also accepted by the automaton A_ϕ, that is $\mathcal{L}(A_M) \subseteq \mathcal{L}(A_\phi)$. Equivalently, one can check that the language $\mathcal{L}(A_M) \cap \overline{\mathcal{L}(A_\phi)}$ is empty. Instead of building the complement of the language accepted by A_ϕ it is possible to use the language of the complement automaton $\overline{A_\phi}$, which is defined such that it accepts the words of the complement language $\mathcal{L}\left(\overline{A_\phi}\right) = \overline{\mathcal{L}(A_\phi)}$. Complement automata where first studied by Büchi [Büc62], a definition and construction in the context of temporal logics is given by Sistla, Vardi, and Wolper [SVW87].

Since A_ϕ exactly accepts the computations satisfying ϕ the negation $\mathcal{L}(\overline{A_\phi})$ of the automaton can be expressed by negation of the property. $\overline{A_\phi} = A_{\neg\phi}$

There is a number of approaches how to transform an LTL property into an automaton. One basic approach presented in the following model checking algorithm was purposed by Wolper, Vardi and Sistla in 1983 [WVS83], but there are some improved versions. Gastin and Oddoux for example present in "Fast LTL to Büchi Automata Translation" [GO01] a different method which use a variation of Büchi automata (very weak alternating automata) as intermediate step. Etessami and Holzmann suppose a method for "Optimizing Büchi Automata" [EH00] to reduce the size of the automata.

The following basic LTL model checking algorithm presented by Moshe Y. Vardi in 1996 [Var96] is structured in 5 steps:

(1) The Kripke structure M, which represents the model, is translated into a Büchi automaton.
(2) The LTL-property ϕ is translated into an alternating Büchi automaton $\mathcal{A}_{\neg\phi}$ which exactly accepts the computations satisfying $\neg\phi$. (Alternating Büchi automaton are introduced in the later Definition 19.6)
(3) The alternating Büchi automaton $\mathcal{A}_{\neg\phi}$ is translated into a nondeterministic Büchi automation $A_{\neg\phi}$ which exactly accepts the same set of computations.
(4) The language intersection of A_M and $A_{\neg\phi}$ is build, such that $\mathcal{L}(A_M \cap A_{\neg\phi}) = \mathcal{L}(A_M) \cap \mathcal{L}(A_{\neg\phi})$
(5) The language $\mathcal{L}(A_M \cap A_{\neg\phi})$ is checked for emptiness.

If $\mathcal{L}(A_M \cap A_{\neg\phi})$ is empty then $M \models \phi$. On the other hand, if $\mathcal{L}(A_M \cap A_{\neg\phi})$ is not empty there is at least one run of $A_M \cap A_{\neg\phi}$ which is accepted by the model M

but not by the property ϕ. This run can be used as a counterexample, giving a reason why the model does not satisfy the property. In the following we explain each step of the algorithm in detail.

Step 1: The Kripke structure M, which represents the model, is translated into a Büchi automaton.

A rooted Kripke structures $M = (S, s_0, R, I)$ over a set of atomic propositions AP can be viewed as a Büchi automaton $A_M = (\Sigma, Q, \delta, q_0, F)$ where the set of states are equal $Q = S$, the initial states are equal $q_0 = s_0$, every state of the Büchi automation is accepting $F = Q$, each action is a subset of atomic propositions $\Sigma = 2^{AP}$ and the transition function is defined as follows:

$$\delta : (q, a) \in Q \times \Sigma \mapsto \{q' \mid (q, q') \in R \wedge a = I(q)\}$$

Example. In Figure 19.4 the Büchi automaton constructed from the KS in Figure 19.1 is shown.

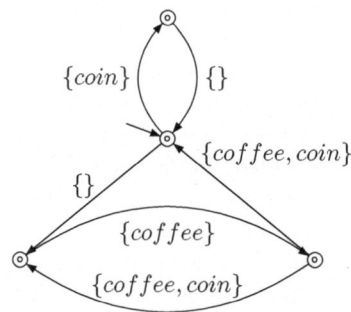

Fig. 19.4. Büchi automaton example

Step 2: The LTL-Property ϕ is translated into an alternating Büchi automaton $\mathcal{A}_{\neg\phi}$ which exactly accepts the computations satisfying $\neg\phi$.

Nondeterminism of (Büchi automata) can be understood as a kind of existential choice; a successor state s' of a state s is one of the states s' in $\delta(s)$. The dual of existential choice is universal choice, and therefore it is natural to consider automata that have the power of existential choice and universal choice. Such automata are called alternating. An alternating Büchi automaton is defined with respect to a set of positive Boolean formulas $\mathcal{B}^+(D)$. Positive Boolean formulas ϕ_B over a set D of variables are constructed as follows where $d \in D$:

$$\phi_B := d \mid \phi_B \dot\vee \phi_B \mid \phi_B \dot\wedge \phi_B \mid \mathsf{true} \mid \mathsf{false}$$

Note that the subscript point of the conjunction $\dot\wedge$ and disjunction $\dot\vee$ of positive Boolean formulas is used to differentiate them from conjunction $\wedge$ and disjunction $\vee$ of LTL formulas. Consider a nondeterministic Büchi automaton which has a transition function including $\delta\left(q_0, a\right) = \{q_1, q_2, q_3\}$. This mapping can be written as $\delta\left(q_0, a\right) = q_1 \vee q_2 \vee q_3$ using positive Boolean formulas. In an alternating Büchi automaton one can have mappings like $\delta\left(q_0, a\right) = (q_1 \wedge q_2) \vee (q_3 \wedge q_4)$, meaning that the automaton starts from its initial state q_0 with an a-transition and can continue in both states q_1, q_2 or in both states q_3, q_4. Note that an alternating Büchi automaton can continue in more than one state at the same time.

Definition 19.6. An **alternating Büchi automaton** $(\Sigma, Q, \delta, q_0, F)$ is a Büchi automaton where the transition function is defined as follows:

$$\delta : Q \times \Sigma \ \rightarrow \ \mathcal{B}^+ (Q)$$

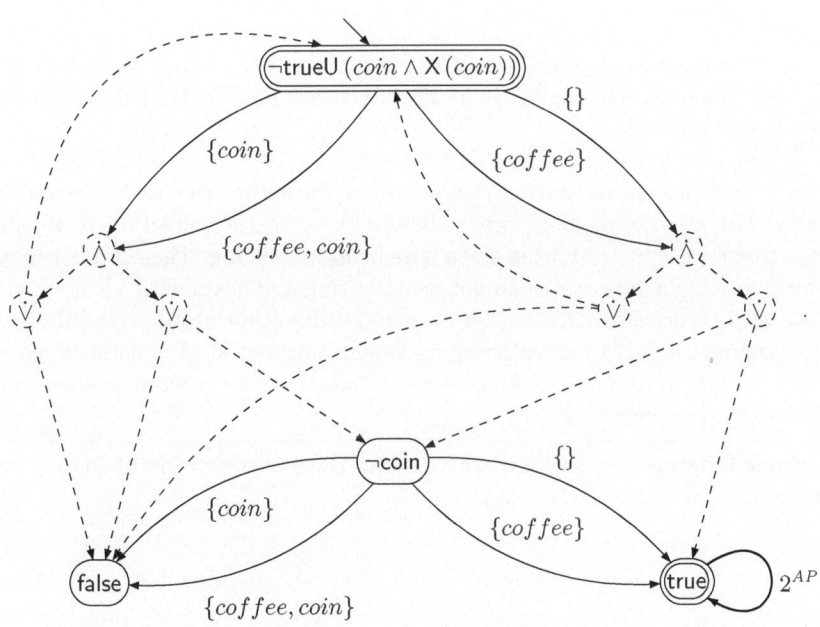

Fig. 19.5. Example Alternating Büchi Automaton

In Figure 19.5 a graphical representation of an alternating Büchi automaton is presented, visualizing the transition function of an automaton in an abstract way. The dotted lines are used to identify edges which belong to positive Boolean combination of states.

Because of the universal choice in alternating transitions, a run of an alternating automaton is a tree rather than a sequence. A *tree* $R = (r, p)$ is an infinite directed acyclic graph where r is a set of nodes and p is a *parent* function. One node designated as the root, denoted by $\varepsilon \in r$. The root ε has no parent and every other node $n \neq \varepsilon$ has a unique parent. The *children* of a node $c(n)$ are the nodes n' which have n as parent. $c(n) := \{n' \mid n = p(n')\}$. The *level* $|n|$ of a node n is the distance from the root ε to the node: the root's level is $|\varepsilon| = 0$ and $|n| = 1 + |p(n)|$. A *branch* $\beta = n_0 n_1 \ldots$ of a tree is a infinite sequence of nodes such that n_0 is the root ε and for all other nodes n_i $(i > 0)$ of the branch the predecessor of a node in the branch is its parent:$n_{i-1} = p(n_i)$.

Definition 19.7. A run of an alternating Büchi automaton on a word $w = a_1 a_2 \ldots \Sigma^\omega$ is a state-labeled tree (R, L), where R is a tree and L is a mapping from the nodes of the tree r to the states, such that $r(\varepsilon) = q_0$ and the following holds:

- Each node n with level $|n| = i |\pi|$ of the tree r has k children $n_1, \ldots, n_k$ such that $\{L(n_1), \ldots, L(n_k)\}$ satisfies¡ $\delta(L(n), a_i)$

Note that the maximal level of a node in R is at most $|\pi|$. Not all branches need to reach such depth, since if $\delta(L(n), a) = \mathsf{true}$, then n does not need to have any children. On the other hand we can not have $\delta(L(n), a) = \mathsf{false}$, since false is not satisfiable.

For an alternating Büchi automaton a run (r, L) is accepting, iff every infinite branch visits accepting states infinitely often. Note that true and false are special states. For any action both states have only a single transition to itself. The state true is accepting and the state false is not accepting. Therefore a run with a branch visiting a false-state can not be accepting and a run with a branch visiting a true-state is accepting if all other branches visit accepting states infinitely often. The language $\mathcal{L}(\mathcal{A})$ of an alternating Büchi automaton $\mathcal{A}$ is determined by all words for which an accepting run exists. Note that for a word w there may be more than one accepting run.

Example. Figure 19.6 outlines a run of the Büchi automation of Figure 19.5 on the infinite word $w = (\{coin\}\{\})^\omega$.

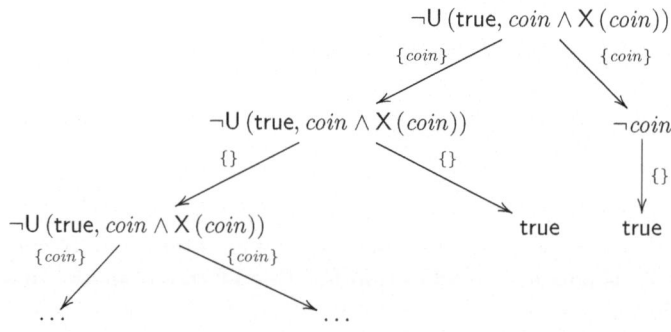

Fig. 19.6. Example run of an alternating Büchi automaton

The alternating Büchi automaton we are going to construct from a property ϕ uses the set of all sub-formulas and their negations as the set of states.

Definition 19.8. The set of sub-formulas $Sub\,(\phi)$ of a property ϕ is inductively defined on the structure of ϕ by:

$$
\begin{aligned}
Sub\,(\text{true}) &= \{\text{true}\} \\
Sub\,(\neg\phi) &= \{\neg\phi\} \cup Sub\,(\phi) \\
Sub\,(\mathsf{X}\,(\phi)) &= \{\mathsf{X}\,(\phi)\} \cup Sub\,(\phi) \\
Sub\,(\phi_1 \vee \phi_2) &= \{\phi_1 \vee \phi_2\} \cup Sub\,(\phi_1) \cup Sub\,(\phi_2) \\
Sub\,(\mathsf{U}\,(\phi_1,\phi_2)) &= \{\mathsf{U}\,(\phi_1,\phi_2)\} \cup Sub\,(\phi_1) \cup Sub\,(\phi_2)
\end{aligned}
$$

The transition function of an alternating Büchi automaton maps states to *positive* Boolean combinations of states. Since properties in LTL may use the negation modality $\neg\phi$ and negation is not allowed in positive Boolean functions, negation of properties is expressed by negation of states. For this reason the negatives of the sub-formulas are included into the set of states of the alternating Büchi automaton. To connect the negation of properties to the negation of positive Boolean combinations of states the following construction is used:

Definition 19.9. The dual $\overline{\phi}$ of a positive Boolean formula is defined inductively on the structure of a formula ϕ as follows:

$$
\begin{aligned}
\overline{\text{true}} &= \text{false} \\
\overline{\text{false}} &= \text{true} \\
\overline{\neg\phi} &= \phi \\
\overline{\phi_1 \vee \phi_2} &= \overline{\phi_1} \dot{\wedge} \overline{\phi_2} \\
\overline{\phi_1 \wedge \phi_2} &= \overline{\phi_1} \dot{\vee} \overline{\phi_2} \\
\overline{\mathsf{X}\,(\phi)} &= \neg\mathsf{X}\,(\phi) \\
\overline{\mathsf{U}\,(\phi_1,\phi_2)} &= \neg\mathsf{U}\,(\phi_1,\phi_2)
\end{aligned}
$$

Given an LTL formula ϕ, one can directly build an alternating Büchi automaton $A_\phi = (\Sigma, Q, \delta, q_0, F)$, such that $\mathcal{L}(A_\phi)$ is exactly the set of computations satisfying the property ϕ. The set of states Q is defined as the set of sub-formulas of ϕ and their negations. The set of actions is defined as $\Sigma = 2^{AP}$. The set of accepting states F consists of all formulas ϕ which have got the form $\neg\mathsf{U}\,(\phi_1,\phi_2)$. The transition function δ is inductively defined on the structure of ϕ as follows:

$$
\begin{aligned}
\delta\,(p, A) &= \begin{cases} \text{true if } p \in A \\ \text{false if } p \notin A \end{cases} \\
\delta\,(\phi_1 \vee \phi_2, A) &= \delta\,(\phi_1, A)\,\dot{\vee}\,\delta\,(\phi_2, A) \\
\delta\,(\phi_1 \wedge \phi_2, A) &= \delta\,(\phi_1, A)\,\dot{\wedge}\,\delta\,(\phi_2, A) \\
\delta\,(\neg\phi, A) &= \overline{\delta\,(\phi, A)} \\
\delta\,(\mathsf{X}\,(\phi), A) &= \phi \\
\delta\,(\mathsf{U}\,(\phi_1,\phi_2), A) &= \delta\,(\phi_2, A)\,\dot{\vee}\,(\delta\,(\phi_1, A)\,\dot{\wedge}\,\mathsf{U}\,(\phi_1,\phi_2), A)
\end{aligned}
$$

The idea behind this recursive definition is: whenever a composed formula is to check it is transformed into a Boolean combination of new formulas. In this way a goal is reduced to several subgoals like in an tableau construction. Since any formula except the one of type $U(\phi_1, \phi_2)$ is turned into smaller sub-formulas, every finite branch of a potential run reaches either **true** or **false**. Every infinite branch has to hit states of the type $U(\phi_1, \phi_2)$ or $\neg U(\phi_1, \phi_2)$ infinitely often. If $U(\phi_1, \phi_2)$ is hit infinitely often it means, that the automaton fails to show that $U(\phi_1, \phi_2)$ holds and ϕ_2 is not satisfied on this branch. Therefore the state $U(\phi_1, \phi_2)$ is not included into the set of accepting states. On the other hand, if $\neg U(\phi_1, \phi_2)$ is hit infinitely often on a branch the automaton is not able to show ϕ_1 or ϕ_2 and $\neg U(\phi_1, \phi_2)$ holds. That is the reason for putting the state of type $\neg U(\phi_1, \phi_2)$ into the set of accepting states.

Example. Consider the property $\phi = G(coin \rightarrow X(\neg coin))$. In the following the construction of the alternating Büchi automaton $\mathcal{A}_\phi$ is presented. The underlying Kripke structure has got $AP = \{coin, coffee\}$ as the set of atomic propositions and therefore the set of actions is:

$$\Sigma = \{\{\}, \{coin\}, \{coffee\}, \{coin, coffee\}\}.$$

Since it is obvious how to get the set of states Q, it remains to calculate the transition function δ. It is easy to see that $\phi = G(coin \rightarrow X(\neg coin))$ is equivalent to $\neg U(\text{true}, coin \vee X(coin))$. Using the definition of the duality and the recursive definition of δ we get:

$$
\begin{aligned}
&\delta\left(\neg U\left(\text{true}, coin \wedge X(coin)\right), \{coin\}\right) \\
=\ &\overline{\delta\left(U\left(\text{true}, coin \wedge X(coin)\right), \{coin\}\right)} \\
=\ &\overline{\delta\left(coin \wedge X(coin), \{coin\}\right) \vee \left(\delta\left(\text{true}, \{coin\}\right) \wedge U\left(\text{true}, coin \wedge X(coin)\right)\right)} \\
=\ &\overline{\delta\left(coin \wedge X(coin), \{coin\}\right)} \dot{\wedge} \overline{\left(\delta\left(\text{true}, \{coin\}\right) \wedge U\left(\text{true}, coin \wedge X(coin)\right)\right)} \\
=\ &\overline{\delta\left(coin, \{coin\}\right) \wedge \delta\left(X(coin), \{coin\}\right)} \dot{\wedge} \left(\overline{\delta\left(\text{true}, \{coin\}\right)} \dot{\vee} \overline{U\left(\text{true}, coin \wedge X(coin)\right)}\right) \\
=\ &\left(\overline{\delta\left(coin, \{coin\}\right)} \dot{\vee} \overline{\delta\left(X(coin), \{coin\}\right)}\right) \dot{\wedge} \left(\overline{\text{true}} \dot{\vee} \neg U\left(\text{true}, coin \wedge X(coin)\right)\right) \\
=\ &\left(\overline{\text{true}} \dot{\vee} \overline{coin}\right) \dot{\wedge} \left(\text{false} \dot{\vee} \neg U\left(\text{true}, coin \wedge X(coin)\right)\right) \\
=\ &\left(\text{false} \dot{\vee} \neg coin\right) \dot{\wedge} \left(\text{false} \dot{\vee} \neg U\left(\text{true}, coin \wedge X(coin)\right)\right)
\end{aligned}
$$

If one calculates the transition function for each (reachable) state and each set of atomic propositions, one gets the alternating Büchi automaton shown in Figure 19.5. Note that some edges have been joined in the graph because of the symmetry of $\{\}$ and $\{coffee\}$ respectively $\{coin\}$ and $\{coin, coffee\}$.

Step 3: The alternating Büchi automaton $\mathcal{A}_{\neg\phi}$ is translated into a nondeterministic Büchi automaton $A_{\neg\phi}$ which exactly accepts the same set of computations.

Two problems arise during the transformation of alternating Büchi automaton $\mathcal{A} = (\Sigma, Q, \delta\ q_0, F)$ into nondeterministic Büchi automaton $A' = (\Sigma, Q', \delta', q'_0, F')$: How to deal with the universal choice and which states should be accepting?

To differentiate states of the alternating Büchi automaton and states of the nondeterministic Büchi automaton we call them alternating states and nondeterministic states.

Obviously the conjunction of states in alternating Büchi automata $\mathcal{A}$ is not directly transferable to nondeterministic Büchi automata A. The solution to this problem is similar to the power-set construction mapping nondeterminism to determinism. If each state of the nondeterministic automaton A consist of a set of states of $\mathcal{A}$ one can translate transitions with conjunction as follows. Consider a transition $\delta\,(q,a) = q_1 \wedge q_2 \vee q_3 \wedge q_4$. Using a power-set construction we can map this transition to a nondeterministic transition $\delta'\,(\{q\}\,,a) = \{\{q_1,q_2\}\,,\{q_3,q_4\}\}$. The idea of this construction is to map the states $\{q\}$ to sets of minimal sets satisfying the transitions positive Boolean condition. If the starting state of a transitions consists of more than one state the transition maps to minimal sets of states which satisfy the conjunction of all transition conditions. Let $U,X \in Q'$ subsets of alternating states. Formally we map $\delta'\,(U,a)$ to a new state X such that $X \models \bigwedge_{q\in U} \delta\,(q,a)$.

This construction is not sufficient to define the accepting states correctly. Surely a set of alternating states has to be accepting if all its states are accepting, but accepting states of alternating Büchi automata do not have to occur in positive Boolean combinations at the same time. A run of an alternating Büchi automaton is accepted if each infinite branch of the run hits accepting states infinitely often, but the accepting states can occur on different levels of each branch of the run. In other words; the (alternating) accepting states of an accepting run can occur one after another on a run of the nondeterministic automaton. The nondeterministic Büchi automaton has to collect the accepting states it has visited. Therefore we define the states for the nondeterministic Büchi automaton as follows: $Q' = 2^Q \times 2^Q$. The first component of this tuple contains non accepting states for which no accepting state was seen recently. The second component is used to collect accepting states and states for which accepting states have been visited. The idea is that successor states of accepting states are shifted from the first component to the second. Thus, the empty set in the first component identifies that for all alternating states of the current (nondeterministic) state accepting states have been visited and therefore we define the set of accepting states as $F' = 2^\emptyset \times 2^Q$.

If the initial state q_0 is not accepting and we have not seen any accepting state initially we define the initial state $q_0' = (q_0,\emptyset)$. If q_0 is an accepting state we define $q_0' = (\emptyset,q_0)$.

For a pair $(U,V) \in Q'$ and an action a let δ' yield the pairs $(U',V') \in Q'$ defined as follows:

- case $U \neq \emptyset$: Let $X,Y \subseteq Q$ be minimal sets satisfying the transitions requested by the states of respectively U and V reading the input symbol then $X \models \bigwedge_{q\in U} \delta\,(q,a)$ and $Y \models \bigwedge_{q\in V} \delta\,(q,a)$. We put non-accepting states in the first component and the accepting states in the second component. Furthermore, we add all members of Y to the second component except the ones which are also in the first component: $U' = Y - F$ and $V' = (X \cap F) \cup (Y - U')$.

- case $U = \emptyset$: Let $Y \subseteq Q$ a minimal set such that $Y \models \bigwedge_{q\in V} \delta\,(q,a)$. Since for all states in U we have seen an accepting state we are going to restart collecting accepting states. Therefore we put all states into U' except the ones which are accepting states. $U' = Y - F$ and $V' = Y \cap F$.

Note that if the minimal set satisfying a transition is empty, the transition is always satisfied and therefore it is identified with the state true.

Step 4: The intersection of A_M and $A_{\neg\phi}$ is build, such that $\mathcal{L}(A_M \cap A_{\neg\phi}) = \mathcal{L}(A_M) \cap \mathcal{L}(A_{\neg\phi})$

Let $A' = (\Sigma, Q', \delta', q'_0, F')$ and $A'' = (\Sigma, Q'', \delta'', q''_0, F'')$ be two nondeterministic Büchi automata. We can build an automaton $A = A' \cap A''$ that accepts $\mathcal{L}(A') \cap \mathcal{L}(A'')$ as: $A = (\Sigma, Q' \times Q'' \times \{0, 1, 2\}, \delta, (q'_0, q''_0, 0), Q' \times Q'' \times \{2\})$. The transition function δ is defined as $\delta((q', q'', x), a) = \{(r', r'', y)\}$ such that both automata read each input symbol simultaneously $\delta'(q', a) = r'$ and $\delta''(q'', a) = r''$ and the third element of the state tuple, counting which automata has visited an accepting state is set as follows:

$$y = \begin{cases} 0 & x = 2 \\ 1 & x = 0 \wedge r' \in F' \\ 2 & x = 1 \wedge r'' \in F'' \\ x & else \end{cases}$$

Since accepting states of both automata may not appear together even if they appear individually infinitely often the setting $F = F' \times F''$ does not work. Therefore the third component is used to ensure that there is an accepting state if and only if both automata have visited an accepting state. The third component is initially 0 meaning that no automaton has visited an accepting state. It changes from 0 to 1 if the first automaton has seen an accepting state and it changes from 1 to 2 if the second automaton has also visited an accepting state. If both states have visited accepting states then there is an accepting state in $A' \cup A''$ and the search for accepting states is restarted with setting the third component back to 0

Step 5: Decide if the intersection of A_M and $A_{\neg\phi}$ is empty.

Since the number of accepting states of a Büchi automaton is finite infinite accepting runs have to visit single accepting states infinitely often. Therefore if an accepting run of a Büchi automaton exists there has to be a cycle in the graph of the automaton which is reachable from the initial state. It is a well known fact that using a depth-first-search algorithm one can search the graph of a Büchi automaton for a reachable cycle in linear time with respect to the number of nodes plus the number of edges. If the states of these cycles intersect with the set of accepting states the language of the automaton is not empty.

19.3.4   Model Checking Tools

In the last few years model checking has become a powerful and promising approach to automatic verification of systems. In order to be suitable for different purposes there are a number of model checking algorithms which work on different types of models and temporal logics. Model checking has become a common technique since in the last two decades a number of model checking tools have been developed.

The first one was *COSPAN* [HK87, HHK96] which has been in use (and continuous development) since 1986. It has been applied to a number of commercial projects, as well as having been licensed to numerous universities for educational use.

Another model checking tool is *Murphi* (Murφ). It focuses on protocol verification and its specification facilities are limited, since it is not possible to define properties of sequential behavior. It is only possible to detect deadlocks, predefined error-states and states that violate a kind of Boolean invariant.

There are two more well-known tools which deal with process specifications written in the verification languages like *Promela* (a Process Meta Language) and *LOTOS*. The model checker *SPIN* [Hol97] is a generic verification system that supported design and verification of asynchronous process systems. It focuses on providing the correctness of process interactions. SPIN accepts models that are described in Promela and properties specified in the syntax of linear time logic. SPIN uses an automata-theoretic approach with on-the-fly construction of the automata. Another model checking tool is *OPEN/CAESAR* [FGM+92]. It was the first model checking tool that supports the standardized process specification language *LOTOS*, but OPEN/CAESAR has a generic API to support other process descriptions as well. OPEN/CAESAR supports the modal μ-calculus and uses an automata theoretic approach with on-the-fly construction as well to fight the state explosion problem.

In contrast to Murφ and SPIN the *Fixpoint-Analysis Machine* [SCK+95] and the *Concurrency Workbench* [CPS93] are designed to support a wide range of applications. The Fixpoint-Analysis Machine can deal with the modal μ-calculus. The tool works not only on labeled transition systems but also on context-free processes (i.e. processes that are given in terms of a context-free grammar). The Concurrency Workbench is designed to incorporate several different verification methods in a modular fashion. As well as the Fixpoint-Analysis Machine it supports the modal μ-calculus.

The model checker *SMV* (Symbolic Model Verifier) was designed to deal with the state explosion problem. It uses an OBDD-based (Ordered Binary Decision Diagram) algorithm and supports properties specified in CTL. It has some extensions to verify fairness constraints. A new variant of *SMV* is the *NuSMV* [CCG+02] project which aims at the development of a state-of-the-art symbolic model checker, designed to be applicable in technology transfer. It is based on SMV and uses essentially the same input language as SMV. The main novelty in this open source project is the integration of model checking techniques based on propositional satisfiability.

19.4   Learning Finite State Machines

Techniques such as model checking and model-based test-generation are a convenient way to automatically improve a system's reliability as a system conforming to its specification. The problem is that in many cases a model of the system does not exist or if it does, it is outdated. If the model is to be constructed by hand this may be time-consuming and it is very much dependent on how familiar the test engineer is with the system under test (SUT). A way to facilitate the test engineer's work and derive a more reliable model, is to automate the generation of a model of the SUT. A proposed procedure to attain this is to apply a technique called *model learning*, sometimes also called model inference.

This section will explain how a so called learning algorithm builds a model of a system under test. The SUT considered is a black box, i.e., we have no information about its internal structure. We do make the assumption that the SUT can be modeled as a deterministic finite state automaton (DFA). We also assume that we know which actions the SUT is able to perform, here called the alphabet Σ. The minimal model of the SUT is the DFA denoted $\mathcal{M}$. The regular language accepted by the finite state automaton is denoted $\mathcal{L}(\mathcal{M})$, also referred to as U.

The basic set-up for all of the variants of the learning algorithm explained in this section is presented in Figure 19.7. The **Learner** represents the algorithm which is trying to estimate U. The Learner estimates U iteratively through gathering enough pieces of information about U until it is able to construct a hypothesis, also called conjecture or approximation of U. The hypothesis is a DFA $\mathcal{A}$ with the language $\mathcal{L}(\mathcal{A})$. If the conjecture is incorrect the learner will continue to collect information until it can construct a "better" conjecture. The Learner iterates in this fashion until the hypothesis is correct.

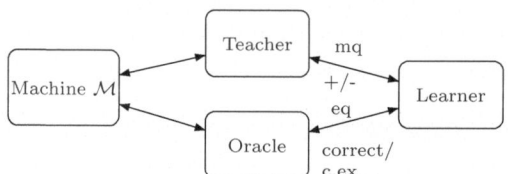

Fig. 19.7. Learning an Automaton.

More specifically, the Learner is able to query the **Teacher** whether a string is accepted by $\mathcal{M}$ or not and the answers will be yes ($+$) or no ($-$), seen in Figure 19.7. A query to the Teacher is called **membership query** (mq). The name refers to the question whether a string is a member of $\mathcal{L}(\mathcal{M})$ or not. Furthermore the Learner can ask an **equivalence query** (eq) to an **Oracle** whether the approximation $\mathcal{A}$ is correct or not. If the Oracle deems that the conjecture is equivalent to $\mathcal{M}$ it confirms the correctness of the hypothesis, otherwise it returns a **counterexample** to $\mathcal{A}$. The counterexample is in the format of a string which is accepted by $\mathcal{M}$ but not by $\mathcal{A}$ or vice versa.

In the following sections we will describe different algorithms for the Learner, all using the setting described above. The first algorithm, *Observation Packs*, abstracts away the data structure in which a Learner stores the gathered information, using sets instead. In the subsequent section, Section 19.4.2, we present Angluin's algorithm, in which the observed information is stored in an *Observation Table*. The *Reduced Observation Table* algorithm, presented in Section 19.4.3, is similar to the Observation Table algorithm except it stores less information. Finally, Section 19.4.4 describes the *Discrimination Tree* algorithm which stores information in a binary tree.

19.4.1   Observation Packs

Balcázar et al. abstract from different data structures and present a unified view on the learning problem studied here, storing information in several, called observation packs sets [BDGW97]. An observation pack can be seen as a way of storing pieces of information the Learner has about an unknown regular set.

One piece of information is a so called *observation*. An **observation** is a pair of the form $(s, +)$ or $(s, -)$ for a word s. The **label** $+/-$ signifies the answer to a membership query on string s. The observations in a set must be consistent, i.e., the same word does not appear with different $+/-$ labels.

The observations are organized in finite sets called **components**, which are not necessarily disjoint. A component is denoted C_k, where $k \in \mathbb{N}$ is the component's index. An **observation pack** $\mathcal{O}$, or pack for short, is a finite sequence of components, $\mathcal{O} = (C_0, \ldots, C_{n-1})$ for some $n \in \mathbb{N}$, for which two conditions must hold:

OP1 Let $s_k \in C_k$ be the shortest word in C_k; then s_k is a prefix of all other words in C_k.

OP2 For each two components C_k and C_l with $l \neq k$, there exists w_{kl} such that both $s_k w_{kl} \in C_k$ and $s_l w_{kl} \in C_l$ but $(C_k, +) \iff (C_l, -)$, i.e., they have different labels.

The string s_k is a word that identifies C_k. The set of suffixes for each s_k is defined as $E_k = \{w \mid s_k w \in C_k\}$. So the word w_{kl} mentioned above is in $E_k \cap E_l$. Furthermore $s_k = s_k \varepsilon$ implies $\varepsilon \in E_k$ by the definition of E_k.

We collect in the set S all the shortest words, s_k, from each component and call them **access strings**. The access strings are then used to index both components and sets of suffixes, so the component C_k is C_s and E_k is E_s where $s = s_k$ for some $s \in S$. An observation pack can be identified with the finite set S of access strings and a mapping from S associating to each s the finite set E_s. The set C_s is the set of words sw, for an access string $s \in S$ and suffix $w \in E_s$.

Definition 19.10. A language U *agrees* with an observation pack $\mathcal{O}$ if all $+$ labels mark words in U, while all $-$ labels mark words not in U.

Assuming that U is a language accepted by a DFA, the suffixes in sets E_s must include evidence (see the second item on the list of conditions on an observation pack) that the access strings belong each to a different equivalence class in the right congruence associated with any regular set U agreeing with the pack. These classes correspond to states of the minimal deterministic finite automaton (DFA) for U: access strings are used to reach the states, hence the name. There can not be any more access strings than states in such an automaton.

Lemma 19.11. *Let $\mathcal{O}$ be a pack, S its set of access strings, U a regular language which agrees with $\mathcal{O}$, and $\mathcal{M}$ the minimal DFA that recognizes U. Then $|S| \leq |\mathcal{M}|$.*

Proof. Let δ^U and q_0^U be the transition function and the initial state of $\mathcal{M}$, respectively. Let the mapping f map S into the states of $\mathcal{M}$ in the natural way: from s to $\delta^U(q_0^U, s)$. We prove that this mapping is injective.

Let s and s' be two access strings in the pack and $s \neq s'$. Assume that they both are mapped by f to the same state via the the transition function δ^U, i.e. f is not injective. So $\delta^U(q_0^U, s) = q_i$ and $\delta^U(q_0^U, s') = q_i$. Let F^U be the set of accepting states for $\mathcal{M}$.

According to the properties of the observation pack, there exists a word $w \in E_s \cap E_{s'}$ such that $sw \in U \iff s'w \notin U$. Either, $\delta^U(q_i, w) \in F^U$ or $\delta^U(q_i, w) \notin F^U$. This means

(1) $\delta^U(q_i, w) \in F^U \implies sw \in U$ and $s'w \in U$, or
(2) $\delta^U(q_i, w) \notin F^U \implies sw \notin U$ and $s'w \notin U$

But this is a contradiction to $sw \in U \iff s'w \notin U$, so f is injective. □

Definition 19.12. Let $\mathcal{O}$ be a pack, with access strings S, and U a set agreeing with $\mathcal{O}$. We say that a word z is *like* $s \in S$ for U if and only if $\forall w \in E_s$ $sw \in U \iff zw \in U$.

To find out whether z is like s we first use the information that sw is labeled $+$ in the pack if $sw \in U$, otherwise $-$. Secondly, for zw we can conduct a membership query and see if $zw \in U$ or not.

Lemma 19.13. *For every word z there is at most one word $s \in S$ such that z is like s for U.*

Proof. Let $s \neq s'$, both in S, and assume z is like s, i.e., $\forall w \in E_s$ $sw \in U \iff zw \in U$. The pack provides a word $w \in E_s \cap E_{s'}$ such that $sw \in U \iff s'w \notin U$. Thus, $zw \in U \iff s'w \notin U$, so that z is not like s' for U. □

Let $\gamma^{\mathcal{O},U} : \Sigma^* \to S$ be the partial function that maps each z to the single access string it is like for U, if there is one; it remains undefined if z is not like any access string for U. From now on, we will use this function in a context in which both $\mathcal{O}$ and U are fixed, so we omit the superscripts and use only γ.

Expanding a Pack Let us now discuss how to extend a pack, evolving to the automaton to learn. We will see the importance of the fact that the function γ can be partial. Let us start by stating that for a given pack we say that a word z is *escaping* when $\gamma(z)$ is undefined.

We can use the knowledge of some escaping string z to adjust the observation pack and get closer to U. In this case we can collect the appropriate observations and expand the pack by adding a new component to it.

The fact that z escapes implies that, for each access string s in the pack, there is a word $sw \in C_s$ providing the suffix w that distinguishes z from s, in the sense that $sw \in U \Longleftrightarrow zw \notin U$. A set formed by all such words zw, additionally including z itself, and each labeled by the corresponding $+/-$ label, forms a component that can be added to the pack preserving two mentioned necessary properties OP1 and OP2. Each expansion by one component brings the pack one state closer to the minimal automaton representing U.

Now we want to have a so called *closed pack*, which means that for an access string s and letter a there is no such word sa that escapes. The transition on a from the state represented by s would be undefined if sa escaped. If we discover an escaping word we expand the pack and when there are no more escaping words of this kind we say that the pack is closed.

Definition 19.14. A pack $\mathcal{O}$ agreeing with U is **closed for** U if:

- $\gamma(\varepsilon)$ is defined;
- $\forall s \in S, \forall a \in \Sigma, \gamma(sa)$ is defined.

Note that the definition depends on U since $\gamma = \gamma^{\mathcal{O},U}$ depends on U. Definition 19.14 actually gives rise to a deterministic finite automaton, whose states are the access strings of the pack, the initial state is $\gamma(\varepsilon)$ and the accepting are states those access strings labeled $+$. We define the transition function to be $\delta(s,a) = \gamma(sa)$ and we extend the transition function δ in a rather common way by, $\delta(s,\varepsilon) = s$, and $\delta(s,wa) = \delta(\delta(s,w),a)$, for $s \in S$, $w \in \Sigma^*$, and $a \in \Sigma$.

Theorem 19.15. *If $\mathcal{O}$ is a pack, U is regular and agrees with $\mathcal{O}$, and $\mathcal{O}$ has as many components as $\mathcal{M}$ (the minimal DFA that recognizes U) has states, then $\mathcal{O}$ is closed for U so that an automaton can be obtained from $\mathcal{O}$ in the manner above, and furthermore this automaton is isomorphic to $\mathcal{M}$.*

Proof. By Lemma 19.11, no pack agreeing with U can have more than $|\mathcal{M}|$ components. Therefore, it is not possible to expand $\mathcal{O}$ preserving the agreement with U, and thus it must be closed. Besides, by the cardinality condition, the function f defined and used in Lemma 19.11 becomes bijective. It is routine to show that this function is an isomorphism, that is: 1) it maps $\gamma(\varepsilon)$ to the initial state of $\mathcal{M}$; 2) it maps exactly those $s \in S$ with $s \in U$ to the final states; and 3) it commutes with $\mathcal{M}$'s transition function.   □

Once we are able to form an automaton from our pack, we can make an equivalence query to the Oracle to find out if it is equivalent to $\mathcal{M}$. If we receive the answer 'yes', we are finished and the automaton is the minimal automaton that exactly accepts U, otherwise we receive a word that behaves different then the constructed automaton but agrees with $\mathcal{M}$; a so called counterexample. Let us study how to process a counterexample.

Counterexample A counterexample is used to correct the hypothesis $\mathcal{A}$ we have about the machine. From the counterexample we will get a word that, when added to the pack, will escape.

Let t be the counterexample of length m, $t = a_0 \ldots a_{m-1}$. For $0 \leq i \leq m$ let u_i be the prefix of length i of t and v_i the corresponding suffix, i.e. $t = u_i v_i$.

Let $s_i = \delta(\gamma(\varepsilon), u_i)$ be the state of the automaton based on the pack that is reached by computing on u_i, the initial state be $s_0 = \gamma(\varepsilon)$ and $s_{i+1} = \delta(s_i, a_i)$. The acceptance of t by this automaton is given by whether the final state s_m is accepting, which corresponds to whether $s_m \in U$.

Since the set of strings that are accepted from a state distinguishes a state from another we look upon suffix v_i as an experiment on corresponding state s_i and through membership queries we find out whether $s_i v_i \in U$. The fact that t is a counterexample means that $t \in U \Longleftrightarrow s_m \notin U$, where $t = s_0 v_0$ and $s_m = s_m v_m$. So consequently there must exist one or more **breakpoint** positions i such that $s_i v_i \in U \Longleftrightarrow s_{i+1} v_{i+1} \notin U$. Since $s_i v_i = s_i a_i v_{i+1}$, the suffix v_{i+1} is an experiment that distinguishes $s_i a_i$ from $s_{i+1} = \delta(s_i, a_i) = \gamma(s_i a_i)$. Now add $s_{i+1} v_{i+1}$ with the appropriate label to the component $C_{s_{i+1}}$. Consequently $\gamma(s_i a_i)$ is not anymore s_{i+1}, hence $s_i a_i$ escapes and we can go on with the pack expansion process.

Example of Observation Pack Let us study the observation pack algorithm applied to the example of the DFA $\mathcal{M}_{ex}$ with the alphabet $\{a, b\}$, shown in Figure 19.8. Initially we conduct an experiment for the empty string. The result of a membership query for ε is $+$ and the first component is initialized with this observation, $C_0 = \{(\varepsilon, +)\}$. The component's corresponding suffix-set is $E_0 = \{\varepsilon\}$. The evolution of $\mathcal{O}$ for this example can be viewed in Table 19.1. The sign $-$ in the table means that the component is unchanged.

In the next step we want to close the pack, therefore we ask membership queries for εa and εb. The results are the observations $(a, +)$ and $(b, +)$, whose strings are like ε, the access string for component C_0. The pack is now closed and we can construct a corresponding automaton $\mathcal{A}^0$, which can be seen in Figure 19.9.

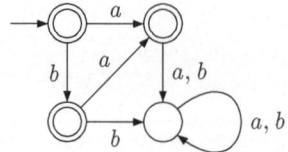

Fig. 19.8. The machine $\mathcal{M}_{ex}$

We conduct an equivalence query for $\mathcal{A}^0$ in order to see if the conjecture is correct. As answer we get a counterexample $t = ab$, we see that $ab \notin \mathcal{L}(\mathcal{M}_{ex})$ but $ab \in \mathcal{L}(\mathcal{A}^0)$. The counterexample can be divided into prefix and suffix, $u_0 = \varepsilon$ and $v_0 = ab$ in order to find the breakpoint where $\mathcal{M}_{ex}$ and $\mathcal{A}^0$ behave differently. A state in a hypothesis is called s_i, for this counterexample $0 \le i \le 2$. We see that a breakpoint can be found for $i = 0$ since $s_0 ab \notin \mathcal{L}(\mathcal{M}_{ex})$ but $s_1 b \in \mathcal{L}(\mathcal{M}_{ex})$ (Recall that $s_1 = \delta(s_0, a)$). Thus b is the experiment that distinguishes $s_0 a = \gamma(\varepsilon)a = a$ from $s_1 = \gamma(\varepsilon a) = \varepsilon$.

	Step 0	Step 1
C_0, E_0 C_1, E_1 C_2, E_2 C_3, E_3	$C_0 = \{(\varepsilon, +)\}$, $E_0 = \{\varepsilon\}$	$C_0 = \{(\varepsilon, +), (b, +)\}$, $E_0 = \{\varepsilon, b\}$ $C_1 = \{(a, +), (ab, -)\}$, $E_1 = \{\varepsilon, b\}$
	Step 2	Step 3
C_0, E_0	–	–
C_1, E_1	–	$C_1 = \{(a, +), (ab, -), (aa, -)\}$, $E_1 = \{\varepsilon, b, a\}$
C_2, E_2	$C_2 = \{(aa, -)\}$, $E_2 = \{\varepsilon\}$	–
C_3, E_3		$C_3 = \{(b, +), (ba, +), (bb, -)\}$, $E_3 = \{\varepsilon, a, b\}$

Table 19.1. The observation pack

It is now enough to add $(b, +)$ to the component C_ε, so $C_0 = \{(\varepsilon, +), (b, +)\}$ and $E_0 = \{\varepsilon, b\}$. Now $\gamma(a)$ is no longer s_0 since a escapes and therefore we expand the pack with a new component C_1, where $C_1 = \{(a, +), (ab, -)\}$ and $E_1 = \{\varepsilon, b\}$, see Step 1. The mapping of b to an access string is now changed to $\gamma(b) = a$.

The next step is to make the pack closed, the missing words are aa and ab. Using membership queries we try to discover an existing access string aa behaves like, but we cannot find one, so it escapes. From the observation $(aa, -)$ we create a new component, $C_2 = \{(aa, -)\}$, whose corresponding suffix set is $E_2 = \{\varepsilon\}$, see Step 2. (The suffix ε differentiates s_2 from all other access strings, so no further suffixes need to be added to C_2.) The next word to map into an access string is ab and we see that $\gamma(ab) = aa$.

Since we now created a new component C_2 we must make sure that the pack is closed, hence we have to check to what access strings the strings aaa and aab are be mapped. Checking these yields $\gamma(aaa) = aa$ and $\gamma(aab) = aa$. The observation pack is now closed and it is possible to form a hypothesis, $\mathcal{A}^1$, about the machine, see Figure 19.9.

Now we conduct an equivalence query for the hypothesis $\mathcal{A}^1$. The Oracle returns a counterexample $t = ba$. Again we perform the search for a breakpoint in t, we initialize the prefix and suffix of t to be $u_0 = \varepsilon$ and $v_0 = ba$, respectively. The breakpoint is found for $i = 0$ where $s_0 ba \in \mathcal{L}(\mathcal{M}_{ex})$ but $s_1 a \notin \mathcal{L}(\mathcal{M}_{ex})$.

In order to adjust $\mathcal{A}^1$, we add $(aa, -)$ to component $(C_{s_1} = C_a =)C_1$, transforming it into $C_1 = \{(a, +), (ab, -), (aa, -)\}$. Now $\gamma(b)$ is not anymore a (it does not behave as a on suffix a) but is instead undefined. This implies that we

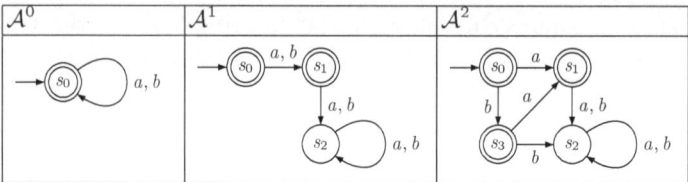

Fig. 19.9. The machine's approximations

have to create a new component, C_3, based on the escaping string b, and add it to $\mathcal{O}$. In order to distinguish the access strings s_0 and s_1, we add to E_3, the suffix a to distinguish b from s_1, and the suffix b to distinguish b from s_0. (The string ε distinguishes b from s_2.) The new component is $C_3 = \{(b, +), (ba, +), (bb, -)\}$ with corresponding suffix set $E_3 = \{\varepsilon, a, b\}$, see Step 3.

We are now able to create our next hypothesis $\mathcal{A}^2$ and conduct an equivalence query for it. The answer to this query is 'yes' and the algorithm terminates and outputs the correct automaton $\mathcal{A}^2$, seen in Figure 19.9.

19.4.2   Angluin's Algorithm

The learning algorithm by Balcázar et al is rather abstract, putting the selected information in sets. In this section we discuss a learning algorithm that still puts information into sets but uses a more concrete data structure: a table. The observation pack algorithm does not tell us how to store exactly all information we query for. In the algorithm we will introduce next, we see how it is possible to store all information in an easy manner. We will now present the *Angluin Algorithm*, which we will also refer to as the *Observation Table Algorithm* [Ang87].

The algorithm, or Learner, makes use of the same environment and plays the same roll as described in Section 19.4. Initially the algorithm has no knowledge of the SUT's regular language, but the information it accumulates about the behavior of the machine, is entered into a so called *observation table*. Due to the table the algorithm has at any point in time information about a finite collection of strings over a known finite alphabet Σ, classifying them as members or non-members of some unknown regular set U.

Angluin's algorithm will make sure that the observation table fulfills some criteria before it constructs a deterministic finite-state machine $\mathcal{A}$ from information in the observation table. This hypothesis of what the language of the SUT is, is the Learner's conjecture which will be sent to the Oracle.

The Observation Table   The information accumulated by the algorithm is a finite collection of observations, which is organized into an observation table. The table is defined as follows:

Definition 19.16. An **Observation Table** over a given alphabet Σ is a tuple $\mathcal{OT} = (S_A, E_A, T_A)^1$, where

---

[1] The index A signifies that the sets belong to Angluin's algorithm.

- $S_A \subseteq \Sigma^*$ is a nonempty finite prefix-closed set,
- $E_A \subseteq \Sigma^*$ is a nonempty finite suffix-closed set, and
- $T_A : ((S_A \cup S_A \cdot \Sigma) \times E_A) \to \{+, -\}$ is a (finite) function

satisfying the property that $se = s'e'$ implies $T_A(s, e) = T_A(s', e')$ for $s, s' \in S_A \cup S_A \cdot \Sigma$ and for all $e, e' \in E_A$.

The words in $S_A \cup S_A \cdot \Sigma$ are called *row labels* and the words in E_A are called *column labels*. The entries consists of signs $(+/-)$ representing whether a word is accepting or not.

The observation table is divided into an upper part and a lower part. The upper part of the observation table is indexed by row labels in S_A. They play a role similar to access strings in the observation pack algorithm, see Section 19.4.1. The lower part's row labels are indexed by all strings of the form sa, $a \in \Sigma$ and $s \in S_A$, unless they already appear in the upper part. Moreover the table is indexed column wise by a suffix-closed set E_A of strings. The suffixes are used in the same fashion as in Section 19.4.1, to distinguish a access string/row from another. The function T_A maps a row label s and a column label e, i.e. $T_A(s, e)$, to the set $\{+/-\}$, it is defined to be $+$ if $se \in U$ and $-$ otherwise. (Note that T_A is total.)

A function $row(s)$ for every $s \in (S_A \cup S_A \cdot \Sigma)$ denotes the finite function $f : E_A \to \{+, -\}$ defined by $f(e) = T_A(s, e)$. In other words, $row(s)$ is the row of entries in the observation table for index s.

It is possible that there exists an entry on a string in several places in the table due to the fact that a string can be divided into different suffixes and prefixes, i.e. row and column labels. Of course, these labels have to agree. This is required by Definition 19.16.

A distinct row in $\mathcal{OT}$ characterizes a state in the automaton which can be constructed from $\mathcal{OT}$. All the row labels to unique rows must be kept in S_A. The rows labeled by elements of $S_A \cdot \Sigma$ are used to create the transition function for the automaton.

To construct a DFA from the observation table it must fulfill two criteria. It has to be *closed* and *consistent*.

Definition 19.17. An observation table $\mathcal{OT}$ is **closed** if for each $s \in S_A \cdot \Sigma$ there exists an $s' \in S_A$ such that $row(s) = row(s')$.

Definition 19.18. An observation table is **consistent** if whenever $row(s) = row(s')$ for $s, s' \in S_A$ then $row(sa) = row(s'a)$ for all $a \in \Sigma$.

When the observation table (S_A, E_A, T_A) is closed and consistent it is possible to construct the corresponding DFA $\mathcal{A} = (\Sigma, Q, \delta, q_0, F)$ as follows:

- $Q = \{row(s) \mid s \in S_A\}$,
- $q_0 = row(\varepsilon)$,
- $F = \{row(s) \mid s \in S_A \text{ and } T_A(s, \varepsilon) = +\}$,
- $\delta(row(s), a) = row(sa)$.

The corresponding DFA constructed in this manner from table (S_A, E_A, T_A) is denoted $\mathcal{A}(S_A, E_A, T_A)$. The first property, closed, holds if a row representing a successor state of some state in Q, the successor state is also in Q. The second property, consistent, ensures that if two rows represent the same state, then they must also have the same successor state on all input symbols.

The Learning Algorithm The learning algorithm, Algorithm 15, maintains the observation table $\mathcal{OT}$. The sets S_A and E_A are both initialized to $\{\varepsilon\}$. Next the the algorithm performs membership queries for ε and for each $a \in \Sigma$, the result is a label for each queried string. The observation table $\mathcal{OT}$ is initialized to (S_A, E_A, T_A).

Algorithm 15 Angluin's Learning Algorithm.

```
 1  Function Angluin()
 2  begin
 3    Initialize  S_A and E_A to {ε}.
 4    Ask membership queries for ε and each a ∈ Σ.
 5    Construct the initial  observation table (S_A, E_A, T_A).
 6
 7    repeat:
 8      while (S_A, E_A, T_A) is not closed or not consistent:
 9        if (S_A, E_A, T_A) is not consistent,
10          then find s and s' in S_A, a ∈ Σ, and e ∈ E_A such that
11          row(s) = row(s') and T_A(sa, e) ≠ T_A(s'a, e),
12          add ae to E_A,
13          and extend T_A to (S_A ∪ S_A · Σ) · E_A using membership queries.
14
15        if (S_A, E_A, T_A) is not closed,
16          then find s ∈ S_A and a ∈ Σ such that
17          row(sa) is different from row(s') for all s' ∈ S_A,
18          add sa to S_A,
19          and extend T_A to (S_A ∪ S_A · Σ) · E_A using membership queries.
20
21      Once (S_A, E_A, T_A) is closed and consistent, let A = A(S_A, E_A, T_A).
22      Make an equivalence query to the Oracle with the hypothesis A.
23        if the Oracle replies  with a counterexample t,
24          then add t and all its prefixes to S_A
25          and extend T_A to (S_A ∪ S_A · Σ) · E_A using membership queries.
26    until the Oracle replies 'yes' to the hypothesis A.
27    return A.
28  end
```

Next the algorithm makes sure that $\mathcal{OT}$ is closed and consistent. If $\mathcal{OT}$ is not consistent, one inconsistency is resolved through finding two strings $s, s' \in S_A$, $a \in \Sigma$ and $e \in E_A$ such that $row(s) = row(s')$ and $T_A(s, ae) \neq T_A(s', ae)$ and adding this new suffix ae to E_A. The observation table is consistent when no more strings as these can be found. The algorithm fills the missing entries in the new column by asking membership queries.

If $\mathcal{OT}$ is not closed the algorithm finds $s \in S_A$ and $a \in \Sigma$ such that $row(sa) \neq row(s')$ for all $s' \in S_A$. The algorithm makes the table closed by adding sa to S_A. When no more such strings can be found the table is closed. The missing entries in $\mathcal{OT}$ are inserted through membership queries.

When $\mathcal{OT}$ is closed and consistent the hypothesis $\mathcal{A} = \mathcal{A}(S_A, E_A, T_A)$ can be formed and its correctness checked through an equivalence query to the Oracle. The Oracle can either reply with a counterexample t, such that $t \in \mathcal{L}(\mathcal{M}) \Longleftrightarrow t \notin \mathcal{L}(\mathcal{A})$, or 'yes'. If the answer is 'yes' the algorithm halts and outputs the correct conjecture $\mathcal{A}$. Otherwise t is a counterexample. In contrast to finding a breakpoint as in the observation pack algorithm, Angluin's approach is to add t and all its prefixes to the table. Then all missing entries are filled. In this way, also the prefix that would be identified by finding the breakpoint is processed.

Example of Observation Table The machine $\mathcal{M}_{ex}$ we want to learn using Algorithm 15, is shown in Figure 19.8. The algorithm initializes $\mathcal{OT}$ (lines 3–5) to A^0 in Table 19.2. Table A^0 is closed and consistent (line 8). Therefore the algorithm can form an automaton based on it (line 21), resulting in $\mathcal{A}^0$, Figure 19.10.

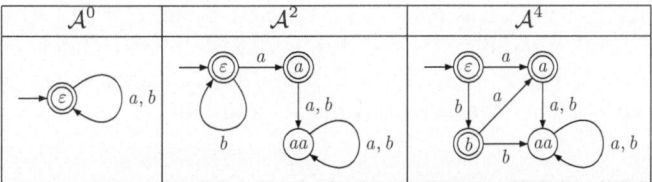

Fig. 19.10. The machine's approximations

The next step is to do an equivalence query for $\mathcal{A}^0$ (line 22). The answer from the Oracle is the counterexample aa since $aa \notin \mathcal{L}(\mathcal{M}_{ex})$ but $aa \in \mathcal{L}(\mathcal{A}^0)$. The counterexample and its prefixes are added to S_A, in the table representation the upper part of the table, and the lower part of the table is extended. The strings in S_A are a and aa and in $S_A \cdot \Sigma$; are b, ab, aaa and aab, see A^1 in Table 19.2. The membership queries for the new entries are made and the answers inserted.

Step 0		Step 1		Step 2			Step 3			Step 4			
A^0	ε	A^1	ε	A^2	ε	a	A^3	ε	a	A^4	ε	a	b
ε	+	ε	+	ε	+	+	ε	+	+	ε	+	+	+
a	+	a	+	a	+	−	a	+	−	a	+	−	−
b	+	aa	−	aa	−	−	b	+	+	b	+	+	−
		b	+	b	+	+	aa	−	−	aa	−	−	−
		ab	−	ab	−	−	bb	−	−	bb	−	−	−
		aaa	−	aaa	−	−	ab	−	−	ab	−	−	−
		aab	−	aab	−	−	ba	+	−	ba	+	−	−
							aaa	−	−	aaa	−	−	−
							aab	−	−	aab	−	−	−
							bba	−	−	bba	−	−	−
							bbb	−	−	bbb	−	−	−

Table 19.2. The observation tables

The algorithm returns (line 8) to check again that the observation table is closed and consistent. This time it will discover an inconsistency in A^1 due to $row(\varepsilon a) \neq row(aa)$, the lefthand side being $+$ and the right hand side being $-$. A new suffix a, which distinguishes the two inconsistent rows a and ε, are added to E_A (line 12). The empty entries in the new columns are filled and the result is A^2 in Table 19.2.

Table A^2 is next checked that it is closed (line 15). Since no row label in the lower part of the table does not already exist in the upper part it is closed. It is now possible to form the automaton $\mathcal{A}^2$, showed in Figure 19.10.

Next the algorithm performs an equivalence query to the Oracle with the hypothesis $\mathcal{A}^2$ (line 22). The response given is again a counterexample, this time $t = bb$, since $bb \notin \mathcal{L}(\mathcal{M}_{ex})$ but $bb \in \mathcal{L}(\mathcal{A}^2)$. The string bb and its prefixes are added to S_A. The lower part of the table is extended by adding the new row labels ba, bba and bbb. The algorithm fills all the empty entries by executing membership queries. This yields table A^3 in Table 19.2.

In the last step the algorithm finds one more inconsistency, due to $row(\varepsilon b) \neq row(bb)$. Solving the inconsistency yields the new column label b, which is added to E_A. The resulting table A^4, see Table 19.2, is closed and consistent and the corresponding hypothesis, $\mathcal{A}^4$ in Figure 19.10, returns a 'yes' in the final equivalence check. The algorithm returns $\mathcal{A}^4$ and halts.

19.4.3   Reduced Observation Tables

We have so far seen two proposals of learning algorithms, the observation pack and the observation table (or Angluin's) algorithms. The next algorithm we will present is a Learner closely related to Angluin's algorithm.

In the setting of the observation table algorithm, see Section 19.4.2, the observation table is likely to contain several rows representing one state. The algorithm presented here is based on the observation table algorithm but contains a smaller version of the table. We will refer to this algorithm by the name *Reduced Observation Table Algorithm*, introduced by Rivest and Schapire [RS93].

Many notions of Angluin's algorithm can directly be transfered to the reduced observation table algorithm. In view of how a table is constructed the sets S_A, E_A, and the table function T_A correspond directly to S_R, E_R, and T_R, respectively. The entries, row labels, column labels and rows are also to be interpreted as in Angluin's algorithm. As in the case of the observation table algorithm, the information the Learner accumulates is a finite collection of observations, which is organized into a *reduced* observation table, denoted $\mathcal{ROT}$. The table is defined as follows:

Definition 19.19. A tuple $\mathcal{ROT} = (S_R, E_R, T_R)$ over a given alphabet Σ is a **Reduced Observation Table**, where

- $S_R, E_R \subseteq \Sigma^*$ are nonempty finite sets,
- $T_R : ((S_R \cup S_R \cdot \Sigma) \times E_R) \to \{+, -\}$ is a (finite) function,

- $se = s'e'$ implies $T_R(s, e) = T_R(s', e')$ for $s, s' \in S_R \cup S_R \cdot \Sigma$ and for all $e, e' \in E_R$, and
- $row(s) = row(s')$ implies $s = s'$ for all $s, s' \in S_R$.

Thus, a reduced observation table differs from an observation table in two ways. First, S_R does not need to be prefix-closed. Second, every row appears only once in the upper part of the table.

Since there cannot be two row labels in S_R that map to the same row, there is no need to check a reduced observation table for consistency. In other words, there cannot be any inconsistency.

The reduced observation table algorithm contains only the access strings, recall Section 19.4.1, which results in a smaller table than Angluin's. This in turn is the cause for using less membership queries. The definition of a **closed** $\mathcal{ROT}$ is as for the observation table. From a closed $\mathcal{ROT}$ we can can construct an automaton in the same manner as in Angluin's algorithm. Besides containing a smaller observation table, a second source of efficiency, compared to Angluin's algorithm, is the faster processing of counterexamples.

Processing a counterexample $t = u_i v_i$ of length m, recall Section 19.4.1, means finding a breakpoint i such that $s_i v_i \in U \iff s_{i+1} v_{i+1} \notin U$, where the $s_i = \delta(row(\varepsilon), u_i)$ are the states visited by t along the automaton and v_i are the corresponding suffixes of t. Some such breakpoint must exist since $s_0 v_0 \in U \iff s_m v_m \notin U$, so that a sequential search will find, say, the first one with m membership queries. Rivest and Schapire show how a binary search finds a breakpoint with $\log m$ queries.

The reduced table is kept small by not adding all prefixes of the counterexample as rows. This means that the new automaton may still classify the previous counterexample incorrectly, so the same counterexample can potentially be used to answer several equivalence queries. Two equal counterexamples can also occur in an algorithm which uses so called discrimination trees, to be discussed in Section 19.4.4.

The Learning Algorithm The reduced observation table algorithm is basically constructed in the same manner as the observation table algorithm. The difference is that since only unique rows are contained in the upper part of the table of the reduced observation table algorithm there is no need to check for consistency. The handling of a counterexample is different to Angluin's algorithm. In this algorithm we search for a breakpoint in the counterexample and add only one row to the upper part of the table, not every prefix of the counterexample as in the case of the other algorithm. The Reduced Observation Table algorithm is given in Algorithm 16.

Example of Reduced Observation Table We will here present an example how the reduced observation table evolves when learning the same example as in Section 19.4.2 shown in Figure 19.8. The table is initialized in the same manner as in Angluin's algorithm so S_R and E_R is set to ε (line 3). For all actions in

---

Algorithm 16 Reduced Observation Table Learning Algorithm.

```
 1  Function Reduced − Observation − Table()
 2  begin
 3   Initialize S_R and E_R to {ε}.
 4   Ask membership queries for ε and each a ∈ Σ.
 5   Construct the initial reduced observation table (S_R, E_R, T_R).
 6
 7  repeat:
 8    while (S_R, E_R, T_R) is not closed:
 9      then find s ∈ S_R and a ∈ Σ such that
10         row(sa) is different from row(s′) for all s′ ∈ S_R,
11         add sa to S_R,
12         and extend T_R to (S_R ∪ S_R · Σ) · E_R using membership queries.
13
14    Once (S_R, E_R, T_R) is closed, let A = A(S_R, E_R, T_R).
15    Make an equivalence query to the Oracle with the hypothesis A.
16    if the Oracle replies with a counterexample t
17      then let the counterexample t be u_i v_i, where u_0 = v_m = ε and v_0 = u_m = t
18      and t = u_i a_i v_{i+1} for i < m, and m is the length of t.
19      Find a breakpoint position i for which s_i a_i v_{i+1} ∈ U ⟺ s_{i+1} v_{i+1} ∉ U holds,
20      where s_i are the states visited by t along A.
21      Add v_{i+1} to E_R
22      and extend T_R to (S_R ∪ S_R · Σ) · E_R using membership queries.
23  until the Oracle replies 'yes' to the hypothesis A.
24  return A.
25  end
```

Σ and ε we perform membership queries and add them to the lower part of the table (lines 4–5), see result in A^0 in Table 19.3. Since the table always is consistent we only have to check that the reduced observation table is closed (line 8). There is no row in the lower part of the table which is not already contained in the upper part, hence the table is closed. It is now possible to form an automaton from the information in the table (line 14), the result is shown in A^0, Figure 19.11.

Step 0		Step 1			Step 2			Step 3			Step 4			
A^0	ε	A^1	ε	b	A^2	ε	b	A^3	ε	b	A^4	ε	b	a
ε	$+$	ε	$+$	$+$	ε	$+$	$+$	ε	$+$	$+$	ε	$+$	$+$	$+$
a	$+$	a	$+$	$-$	a	$+$	$-$	a	$+$	$-$	a	$+$	$-$	$-$
b	$+$	b	$+$	$-$	b	$+$	$-$	aa	$-$	$-$	b	$+$	$-$	$+$
					aa	$-$	$-$	b	$+$	$-$	aa	$-$	$-$	$-$
					ab	$-$	$-$	ab	$-$	$-$	ab	$-$	$-$	$-$
								aaa	$-$	$-$	ba	$+$	$-$	$-$
								aab	$-$	$-$	bb	$-$	$-$	$-$
											aaa	$-$	$-$	$-$
											aab	$-$	$-$	$-$

Table 19.3. The reduced observation tables

The Learner will thereafter make an equivalence query to the Oracle, which returns a counterexample $t = ab$, which we divide into prefix $u_0 = \varepsilon$ and suffix $v_0 = ab$ (lines 17–18). We search for the breakpoint in the counterexample and find it for $i = 0$ since $s_0 ab \notin \mathcal{L}(\mathcal{M}_{ex}) \iff s_1 b \in \mathcal{L}(\mathcal{M}_{ex})$. Now we can add the new column label b (line 21). The result of this operation is shown as A^1 in Table 19.3, now $row(\varepsilon) \neq row(a)$.

Next we check whether table A^1 is closed. The Learner discovers that there is one row in the lower part of the table which is not in the upper part (lines 9–10). In order to rectify this we add the row of a to the upper part and in the lower part we add its successor states, shown in Table 19.3, Table A^2. The extension to the table gives rise to a non-closed table again. So for this reason we move row of aa in the same manner to the upper part, see the result in Table A^3. Now the table is closed and automaton $\mathcal{A}^3$ can be formed, shown in Figure 19.11. The Learner queries the Oracle with this hypothesis, but the Oracle answers with a counterexample.

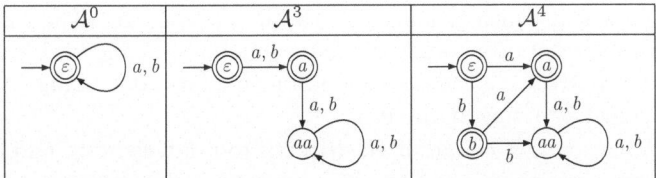

Fig. 19.11. The machine's approximations

The counterexample is $t = ba$, where $ba \in \mathcal{L}(\mathcal{M}_{ex})$ but $ba \notin \mathcal{L}(\mathcal{A}^3)$. Finding the breakpoint is the process of following $\mathcal{A}^3$ along t and discovering where the mistake of not accepting t is made. The breakpoint in this case is found for $i = 0$ since $s_0 ba \in \mathcal{L}(\mathcal{M}_{ex})$ but $s_1 a \notin \mathcal{L}(\mathcal{M}_{ex})$ where the states s_0 and s_1 are represented by ε and a, respectively. We add the new column label a to $\mathcal{ROT}$ and extend the lower part of the table.

In the loop of checking if $\mathcal{ROT}$ is closed, the Learner will discover that the row of b does not exist in the upper part of the table. This row is moved to the upper part of the table and the lower part is extended. The result shown in A^4, Table 19.3. This table is closed and with a final equivalence check with the corresponding automaton $\mathcal{A}_4$ in Figure 19.11 as hypothesis the answer from the Oracle is a 'yes' and the algorithm terminates.

19.4.4   Discrimination Trees

In this section we will discuss a fourth approach to implementing the Learner in the setting described earlier. Instead of using sets for storing the Learner's observations, as in the observation pack algorithm, we will show how it is possible to use a tree.

The Learner's data structure is in this case a binary tree with labeled nodes.

Definition 19.20. Given an alphabet Σ, a **discrimination tree** is tuple $\mathcal{DT} = (S_D, E_D, t)$ where

- $S_D, E_D \subseteq \Sigma^*$ are nonempty finite sets of access strings and suffixes, respectively,
- t is an $S_D \cup E_D$-labeled binary tree where,
  - non-leaf nodes are labeled with suffixes in E_D, and
  - leaves are labeled with access strings in S_D.

The information about whether a string is accepted or not is contained in the structure of a discrimination tree. The computation of the function $\gamma(w)$ for a string w - recall that $\gamma(w)$ maps w to the only access string w is like - becomes simple with the use of discrimination trees; traverse the tree on w in the following manner. Query wv for membership in each node labeled v and enter the right child node on a positive answer and left otherwise. The calculation of $\gamma(w)$ stops in a leaf which is labeled with an access string. The function γ is total since the computation can be done for any input string w. Let $Sift$ be the function that traverses a given discrimination tree for input string w in the just described manner, starting at the root.

A discrimination tree is initialized with the root labeled by ε and two leaves, one labeled by ε and the other one with a string which answers the opposite to ε on a membership query.

The discrimination tree is always closed and consistent, therefore escaping strings can only be obtained through counterexamples. Given a discrimination tree $\mathcal{DT}$, the escaping string is taken via the shortest prefix u_i for which $s_i a_i v_{i+1} \in U \iff s_{i+1} v_{i+1} \notin U$ holds, where $s_i = Sift(u_i, \mathcal{DT})$, see Section 19.4.1 on how to handle counterexamples. The leaf s_{i+1} is replaced by an internal node labeled v_{i+1} which will separate the old leaf representing state s_{i+1} from the new one $s_i a_i$. The algorithm can now start its next iteration with another equivalence query. Altogether, note that equivalence queries are used to modify the tree in order to derive a hypothesis of the automaton to learn, while membership queries are used in the translation from the tree to an automaton and for processing a counterexample.

The Learning Algorithm The discrimination tree algorithm consists of the main function $Discrimination\text{-}Tree$ and auxiliary helper functions; $Sift$, $Hypothesis$, and $Update\text{-}Tree$. The complete algorithm is shown in Algorithm 17, [KV94, BDGW97].

The main function $Discrimination\text{-}Tree$ (line 1) first initializes the discrimination tree. It performs a membership query for ε and if the answer to this query is positive, meaning $\varepsilon \in U$, then the first hypothesis $\mathcal{A}$ has one accepting state, otherwise one non-accepting. This state is the initial state. All the actions from this state will loop back to this state.

The next step for the Learner is to execute an equivalence query with this conjecture. With the information about the counterexample, which the Learner receives, the discrimination tree will be initialized, the root labeled with ε and the leaves labeled with ε and the counterexample, t, from the Oracle.

Henceforth the main function will enter a loop; construct a hypothesis from the discrimination tree and conduct an equivalence query on it. The function processes a counterexample or stops if the Oracle accepts the hypothesis.

The helper function *Sift* (line 31) returns an access string for a given string w by simply sifting down the given tree $\mathcal{DT}$ on w, as described earlier.

The helper function *Hypothesis* (line 44) constructs the hypothesis given a discrimination tree. The hypothesis $\mathcal{A}$ has for each leaf a state, the states are labeled with the access strings, and ε is the initial state. The transitions are constructed in the following manner. For each state s and each $a \in \Sigma$ sift down the discrimination tree on sa, direct the outgoing edge labeled a to the result of the sift action.

The last helper function *Update-Tree* (line 56), updates the discrimination tree given a counterexample t and a discrimination tree $\mathcal{DT}$. The function finds the breakpoint in the counterexample and replaces the erroring leaf by a new node. The replaced leaf becomes one leaf to the new node and the other leaf is a suffix of t.

Example of Discrimination Trees We will here present an example of how the discrimination tree algorithm works. The example machine we will learn is shown in Figure 19.8. The alphabet for the machine is as mentioned earlier $\{a, b\}$.

The first step in the algorithm is to do a membership query for ε to determine whether it is accepting or not, see function *Discrimination-Tree* in Algorithm 17 (line 3). In the succeeding step we construct the automaton $\mathcal{A}^0$, shown in Figure 19.12, with one state where the transitions of a and b loop back to the initial state (line 4). The state is accepting since ε is accepting. Now we can conduct an equivalence query for the first hypothesis $\mathcal{A}^0$.

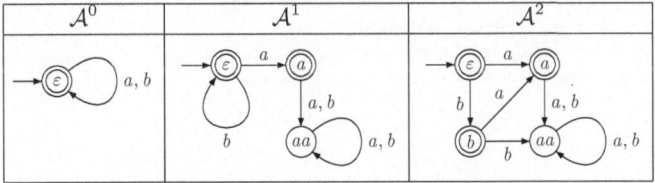

Fig. 19.12. The machine's approximations

An equivalence check for $\mathcal{A}^0$ yields a counterexample $t = aa$. We now have the information we need in order to initialize the discrimination tree (line 8). The root is set to be labeled with the distinguishing string ε and two leaves with ε and the counterexample aa, see tree A^0 in Figure 19.13. After we update the tree with the counterexample we get the discrimination tree A^1 shown in Figure 19.13.

We now construct the automaton corresponding to A^1. It is created by letting every leaf in the tree be a state in the automaton. Given a discrimination tree

---

Algorithm 17 Discrimination Tree Learning Algorithm.

```
 1   Function Discrimination − Tree()
 2   begin
 3   Ask a membership query for ε.
 4   Construct hypothesis A with one state and self−loops for all a ∈ Σ.
 5   If ε is accepted the state  is  accepting, otherwise not.
 6   Make an equivalence query with A; If unsuccessful let the counterexample be t.
 7
 8    Initialize  the tree DT to have the root labeled with ε and the leaves labeled with ε and t.
 9   Update − Tree(t, DT).
10   repeat:
11     Let DT be the current discrimination tree and,
12     let  A = Hypothesis(DT).
13     Make the equivalence query with A.
14     if yes,
15         then halt and output A.
16     else
17           let  t be the counterexample.
18     Update − Tree(t, DT).
19   end
```

```
31   Function Sift(w, DT)
32   begin
33   Set the current node to be the root node of DT.
34   repeat:
35     Let v be the distinguishing string at the current node in the tree.
36     Make a membership query for wv.
37     if wv is accepted,
38         then update current node to be the right child of the current node.
39     else
40         update current node to be the left  child of the current node.
41     if current node is a leaf  node,
42         then return the access string stored at  this  leaf.
43   end
```

```
44   Function Hypothesis(DT)
45   begin
46   for each leaf (access  string) of DT,
47     create a state  in  A that is labeled by that leaf (access  string).
48   Let the  initial  state be ε.
49
50   for each access  string  s of A and each a ∈ Σ,
51   compute the a−transition from state s as follows:
52     Let s′ = Sift(sa, DT) and,
53       let  δ(s, a) = s′.
54   return A.
55   end
```

```
56   Function Update − Tree(t, DT)
57   begin
58   Let the counterexample t be u_i v_i, and t = u_i a_i v_{i+1} for i < m, where m is the length of t.
59   Find the shortest  prefix  u_i for which s_i a_i v_{i+1} ∈ U ⟺ s_{i+1} v_{i+1} ∉ U holds,
60   where s_i = Sift(u_i, DT) and s_{i+1} = Sift(u_{i+1}, DT).
61
62   Replace the leaf  s_{i+1} by an internal node labeled v_{i+1},
63   let one of the leaves be the replaced leaf's label and let the other be s_i a_i.
64   end
```

$\mathcal{DT}$, the transition for an action a in state s is $\delta(s,a) = (\gamma(sa) =)Sift(sa, \mathcal{DT})$. The tree A^0 has the corresponding automaton $\mathcal{A}^1$ in Figure 19.12.

In the next step we make an equivalence query for $\mathcal{A}^1$ to investigate if the hypothesis is correct. We receive a counter example $t = bb$ since $bb \notin \mathcal{L}(\mathcal{M}_{ex})$ but $bb \in \mathcal{L}(\mathcal{A}^1)$. The example is divided into prefix and suffix where $u_0 = \varepsilon$ and $v_0 = bb$. The breakpoint is found for $i = 0$, where $s_0 bb \notin \mathcal{L}(\mathcal{M}_{ex})$ but $s_1 b \in \mathcal{L}(\mathcal{M}_{ex})$. Now we will update the tree in order for it to act correct in relation to the counterexample.

As described in function *Update-Tree* we sift down the tree on b and stop in the leaf ε. We replace this leaf by a node labeled b and let the leaves of b be the replaced leaf ε and b, see resulting tree A^2 in Figure 19.13. The corresponding automaton for the updated tree is $\mathcal{A}^2$ in Figure 19.12.

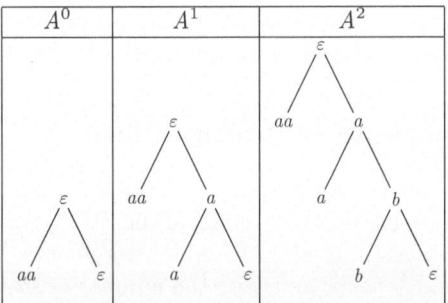

Fig. 19.13. The discrimination trees

Finally, we conduct a equivalence query for hypothesis $\mathcal{A}^2$. We receive the answer 'yes' from the Oracle and the algorithm terminates.

19.4.5   Equivalence Check

The Oracle resolves an equivalence check in the learning setting that we discuss. To learn automata in practice, a realization of such an oracle has to be provided.

The VC-algorithm Vasilevskii and Chow presented independently a method for comparing the language of two automata where one is given as a black-box, provided an upper bound on the number of states is given [Vas73, Cho78].

Of course, two languages L_1 and L_2 are equal, iff they contain the same strings. Comparing an infinite number of strings, however, yields no effective algorithm.

For a regular language, we know that if the length of a string exceeds the number of states of the automaton defining the language, at least one state must be visited twice. In other words, the language of a finite state machine can be described by a finite set of strings together with some "pumping" information.

Using this observation, one can show that it suffices to compare L_1 and L_2 for all strings up to some length linearly bounded by the sizes of the two automata. Vasilevskii and Chow further show that if one automaton is given explicitly, the number of comparisons can be slightly improved.

Details can be found in Chapter 4.7.

A Probabilistic Approach Angluin [Ang87] proposes an equivalence check that yields a correct answer up to some given failure probability.

An Oracle can be realized as a function picking strings randomly and comparing the machine and the hypothesis for those. If a mismatch is found, the corresponding string is a counterexample. If no mismatch is found, the two systems are classified as identical. This conclusion might be wrong with a certain probability. However, if we know the probability distribution of strings being accepted, one can compute the number of comparisons needed to guarantee that this failure probability is below a given limit. See [Ang87] for details.

19.4.6   Query Complexity of the Algorithms

We discuss only the query complexity of the algorithms, i.e., the number of queries needed to construct a correct model of the SUT's regular language. Their time complexity can be estimated with similar arguments.

In this subsection, let n, m, and k be the number of states of $\mathcal{M}$, the length of the longest counterexample returned in a counterexample, and the size of Σ, respectively.

For all algorithms discussed, the number of equivalence queries is at most n: each counterexample processed immediately adds at least one new state to the current hypothesis. Note however, that this number is an upper bound and can be expected to vary in practice for the different algorithms. For example, in the discrimination tree algorithm one needs exactly n equivalence queries, since a new state can only be found with such a query. In Angluin's algorithm, on the other hand, the consistency check that is based on membership queries might give rise to new states as well.

The algorithms differ in the number of membership queries. We first discuss the complexity of the algorithm based on observation packs.

In the observation pack algorithm membership queries are performed for two different purposes: to check for closedness and to process a counterexample.

Consider the first type of membership queries. The observation pack is closed when, for every access string s_i and letter a, $s_i a$ is like some other access string. This is easily determined with membership queries. If the check fails, it provides a witness of non-closedness. If it succeeds, a DFA can be built from the answers of the queries.

Each component contains an access string plus at most $n-1$ strings used to separate it from the other at most $n-1$ components. Therefore, in the worst case, checking for closedness means asking at most n queries for each of (n) strings s_i and (n) queries for each of (kn) strings $s_i a$, giving a total of $O((k+1)n^2)$

queries. At this point we can implement the observation pack algorithm in two different ways:

(1) Check for closedness (and rebuild the automaton) from scratch every time. This means $n(k+1)n^2$ queries.
(2) Use the fact that access strings are never removed from the pack. This means that the set of queries asked in one closedness check is a subset of the queries to be asked in the next one. So, the total number of different queries over all checks is at most $(k+1)n^2$. We can avoid repeating queries by recording all answers to membership queries, at the expense of using more memory.

Now consider the queries used to process the counterexample. If we do not insist on obtaining the shortest distinguishing experiment, we can use Rivest and Shapire's binary search. This means using $O(\log m)$ queries for each counterexample, hence $O(n \log m)$ for the at most n counterexamples.

In total, the algorithm that records all answers uses at most $O(kn^2 + n \log m)$ membership queries.

This is also the cost of the reduced observation table algorithm, if precisely the data structure recording all answers to membership queries is employed.

The discrimination tree algorithm, as described in [KV94], rebuilds the automaton from scratch every time and processes the counterexample sequentially, so it uses $O(kn^3 + nm)$ membership queries. It is not difficult, however, to make it record previous queries and use binary search to process the counterexample. This modified version will have cost of $O(kn^2 + n \log m)$.

In the observation table algorithm, the number of columns in the table is at most n, but the number of rows can be as large as $O(knm)$ because all prefixes of counterexamples are added as rows. Consequently, the number of queries can be up to $O(kn^2m)$.

It can be shown that for any algorithm, making only $O(n)$ equivalence queries, at least $\Omega(kn \log n)$ membership queries have to be made. Further results on lower bounds can be found in [BDGW97].

Note however, that the results are worst-case estimations. One might might in practice trade membership queries for equivalence queries. Experiences with learning algorithms are given in Section 19.4.8.

19.4.7   Domain-Specific Optimizations

The number of queries can be expected to be a limiting factor in practice. Let us study optimizations for learning that are possible when certain further information about the system to learn is provided. The rationale of the presented approach is that in practice, one is often concerned with learning a certain reactive system that can be understood as a special deterministic finite state automaton [HNS03].

The general concept of the optimizations presented here is that instead of the Teacher, an **Assistant** is queried that might either answer a query by consulting the Teacher, or, when possible, deduces the answer to the query using the currently observed information plus the domain specific knowledge about the system to learn.

We present the concept of Assistants using Angluin's algorithm. It might be transferred to the other learning algorithms in a similar manner. However, since not every algorithm stores the result of all membership queries, the effect might be limited.

The Assistants We present different types of assistants, which differ by the provided context information.

Assistant 1. The first property of reactive systems that we consider is prefix-closedness. If the system enters an error state, it will never recover on further input. So if the system enters a non-accepting state, a sink in the corresponding automaton, it will never leave it. Hence, the automaton's language is prefix-closed. In other words, prefixes of accepted strings are also accepted and extensions of rejected strings are rejected.

This is used by the first Assistant which states that if a string is a prefix of a string already in $\mathcal{OT}$ with the entry + then the prefix-string will also be entered as +, without consulting the Teacher. Similarly, a query for a string that is an extension of a string already classified as rejecting is answered negatively without consulting the Teacher.

Assistant 2. Sometimes, one deals with systems that provide a sequence of output symbols to a given sequence of input symbols. These systems may be modeled as deterministic finite state machines (see also Chapter 21 or Part I of this book) where the input alphabet comprises sequences of input symbols and the output alphabet contains sequences of output symbols. These systems can be understood as DFAs over an alphabet comprising actions that are pairs of sequences of input and output symbols. However, such an alphabet is large and the learning algorithm will be expensive. To eliminate the problem we can split an edge labeled by a sequence of input and output symbols into a sequence of edges where each edge is labeled with a single symbol, first the input symbols and then the output symbols. In this way, the number of states increases but the alphabet is kept small.

Often, these systems are deterministic for a given input. The system under test always produces the same output on any given sequence of inputs. So replacing just one output symbol in a string of an input-deterministic language cannot yield another string of this language. An Assistant can use this knowledge to determine that a membership query should be answered with a − for a certain string if in $\mathcal{OT}$ the same string with the modification of one output symbol has the entry +.

Assistant 3. The next Assistant uses the fact that the number of output events in a given situation is determined, and that we wait with feeding new input until the system has produced all its responses. Assume that we have in $\mathcal{OT}$ a string labeled + that ends with an input symbol. Then every string that emerges by changing this input-symbol to any output symbol, will always be rated as −. This can be checked by a further Assistant.

Assistant 4. Often, systems are built-up by independent components, executing actions independently. If a and b are such independent actions, an Assistant can deduce that a query $uabv$ to the Teacher will produce the same result as the query $ubav$.

Assistant 5. Furthermore, the system might be built-up by many identical components. Consider there are two identical components A and B of the system. Component A processes the letters $a_1, a_2, \ldots a_n$ whereas component B processes the letters $b_1, b_2, \ldots b_n$ in a symmetrical way. An Assistant which uses this symmetry information can deduce that a query $a_1 b_1 b_2 a_1$ to the Teacher will produce the same result as the query $b_1 a_1 a_2 b_1$.

The concept of Assistants is also used in extensions of these learning algorithms to timed systems [GJL04].

19.4.8 Practical Experiences

The presented results on the worst-case complexity of the algorithms introduced gives only limited understanding of their practical performance.

In [BJLS03], Angluin's algorithm has been implemented in a straightforward way in order to gain further insights to practical applicability. Furthermore, its performance on randomly generated automata has been analyzed. The experiments focused on the impact of the alphabet size and the number of states on the needed number of membership queries. Additionally, the optimization for prefix-closed systems mentioned in the previous section (Assistant 1) has been implemented and analyzed.

In general, it turned out that learning is a challenging problem. One obstacle is memory consumption. For example, the observation table for a system of 100 states over 25 letters needed about 160 MB of memory. An arbitrary random system of this size took about 40000 membership queries. A prefix-closed system of the same size required even 110000 queries. In general, it turned out that prefix-closed languages are relatively hard to learn compared to arbitrary regular languages. The optimization, however, showed positive results. Figure 19.14 gives an impression of the number of membership queries needed for learning systems of different sizes.

Further experiences are reported in [HNS03] gained in the process of testing a telecommunication system.

Their experiments have been performed on four finite installations, each consisting of the telephone switch connected to a number of telephones. The systems learned varied in the kind of actions the telephones were able to perform, ranging from simple on-hook and off-hook actions of the receiver to actually performing calls. The output events indicate which actions the telephone switch has performed on the particular input. The assistants mentioned in Section 19.4.7 (called *filters* in [HNS03]) have been employed as well.

In this setup, the automatic execution of a single test needs only a few seconds, but in some exceptional cases it took up to 1.5 minutes to execute the test and to collect the output generated by the system. This is due to the large

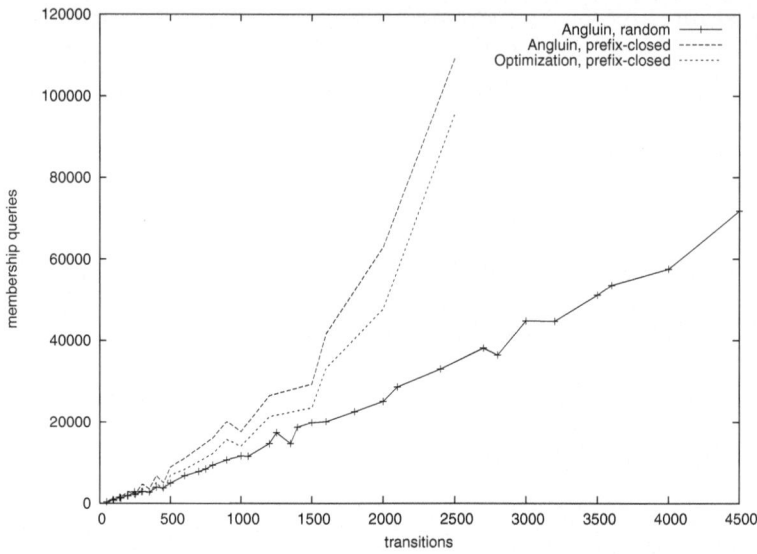

Fig. 19.14. Learning random examples with Angluin's algorithm

timeout values that are specified for telecommunication systems. Thus, reducing the number of membership queries has a huge impact.

For the measurements, the assistants are used in a cumulative way: First Assistant 1 is used, then Assistant 2 and 3 are added. In the last set of measurements, all assistants have been employed.

The result of adding the assistants are measured in terms of a factor of the number of membership queries saved in comparison to learning the example without any assistants. The factor of reduction varies between 8 to 460 in total when all the assistants are added, depending on the example.

Assistant 1 has a similar impact in all considered scenarios, while Assistant 2, 3, and 4 vary much more in their effectiveness, the saving factor increases with the number of states. The number of outputs and the lengths of output sequences between inputs have a particular high impact on the effects of Assistant 2 and 3. More outputs and longer sequences give a better saving factor.

The impact of Assistant 4 and 5, which covers the partial-order and symmetry aspects, increases, as expected, with the number of independent devices. The number of states does not seem to have any noticeable impact on the effectiveness of these assistants.

19.4.9   Further Learning Algorithms

Let us assume that we want to create a model of a system that cannot be reset to a start state. Of course, this setting is not meaningful for systems that contain states from which they can never escape once they are entered, since it would not be able to explore the rest of the automaton. Rivest and Schapire [RS93] have created a learning algorithm for systems without reset that are strongly connected.

Moreover Berman and Roos [BR87] present a learning algorithm for a subclass of context-free languages accepted by counter machines and Freund et al. [FKR+93] give algorithms for learning finite automata on the basis of a single long walk in an average-case setting. Maler and Pnueli [MP95] study the problem of learning sets of infinite strings. In [DH03a, DH03b], learning of regular tree languages is studied. Learning of timed systems is addressed in [GJL04].

Looking at Angluin's algorithm, it becomes obvious that there is a trade-off between membership and equivalence queries. Instead of performing an equivalence query for a closed and consistent table, one could compare the row labels of equal rows on further suffixes by membership queries. This might reveal an inconsistency, yielding a separation of the previously equal rows, and thus more states. For every such case, an equivalence query could be saved. This idea is worked out in [BDGW94] and [BGHM96].

19.5   Adaptive Model Checking

In the first section of this chapter, we have studied automatic means for verifying SUTs based on model checking. However, model checking requires a model. If the system under test is a black box, one can use the learning techniques explained in the previous section to learn a model of the box. Then model checking can be applied.

In [GPY02] a method that integrates learning a model of the black box and verifying it is presented. It is termed **Adaptive Model Checking** (AMC). It is similar to the method previously studied in [PVY99] under the term **black box checking**.

Adaptive model checking is a method that deals with the problem of having an inaccurate model of a SUT. Given a property that the system must satisfy, model checking is performed on a preliminary model and if a counterexample is found it is compared with the system under test. The result of the comparison is either that the SUT does not satisfy the property or an automatic refinement of the model.

First, we present an overview of the algorithm in Figure 19.15. The algorithm used for learning is Angluin's algorithm [Ang87] and the algorithm for performing the equivalence check between the model and the SUT is the Vasilevskii-Chow (VC) algorithm [Vas73, Cho78]. Note that there are two sorts of counterexamples in this setting, videlicet counterexamples produced by the model checker, called mc-counterexamples, and counterexamples produced by the VC algorithm, called vc-counterexamples.

In the black box checking scenario no initial model is assumed to exist and Angluin's algorithm starts from scratch. The AMC algorithm starts with the model learned so far. This model might be inaccurate. The AMC algorithm applies model checking to this model. There are two possible outcomes of this check:

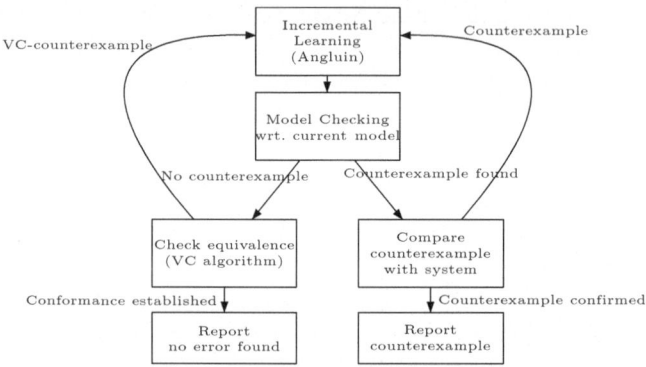

Fig. 19.15. Overview of the Adaptive Model Checking Algorithm.

(1) If the model checker finds a mc-counterexample for the checked property, the SUT runs the counterexample in order to see if it is indeed a sequence of actions that can be performed by the SUT.

- If the SUT accepts the mc-counterexample we have an input sequence that shows that the SUT does not satisfy the property. Then the mc-counterexample is reported and the AMC algorithm terminates.
- In the second scenario where the sequence can not be performed by the SUT, the mc-counterexample will be given to the learning algorithm and the model will be refined.

(2) In the second case, if the model checker does not produce a mc-counterexample, one has to investigate whether the model corresponds to the SUT. Applying the VC algorithm resolves this question. As before, if a vc-counterexample is found, the counterexample is given to Angluin's algorithm and the model is refined. If no vc-counterexample is found the AMC algorithm concludes that the SUT satisfies the property and the AMC algorithm terminates.

We will now present the AMC algorithm in more detail.

Model The model of the SUT is constructed by Angluin's algorithm in the AMC method. The AMC method assumes that the SUT gives information whether an input can be currently executed by the SUT. Therefore the language of the SUT is assumed to be prefix-closed and hence the model as well. The model is a finite automaton and its runs represent only the successful experiments (strings) in the SUT. The learning algorithm used in AMC to learn this model is Angluin's algorithm. We assume that we know an upper bound on the number of states, n, of the SUT.

Property The property is given as an LTL formula, and this can be translated into a Büchi automaton. So the property can be expressed in Linear Temporal

Logic (see Section 19.3.2 on Linear Temporal Logic) and transformed into a finite automaton $A_{\neg \phi}$ on infinite words not accepting the property, usually a Büchi automaton. The algorithm for model checking LTL is presented in detail in Section 19.3.3. LTL is used since it delivers counterexamples in the format of a sequence of actions. Since Computational Tree Logic is not suitable to describe properties of regular languages and counterexamples in CTL are not just words of a language, CTL cannot be used in the AMC algorithm.

Initialization Let $\mathcal{M}$ be the SUT and $\mathcal{A}_{init}$ an initial model of $\mathcal{M}$ in the following section. The AMC algorithm is initialized by providing Angluin's algorithm with the information of the initial model so that fewer calls to the (time expensive) VC algorithm are needed. In [GPY02], three ways to use the initial model are proposed.

(1) A false negative mc-counterexample t found (i.e., a sequence t that was considered to be a counterexample, but has turned out not to be an actual execution of the SUT $\mathcal{M}$). This corresponds to a counterexample in Angluin's algorithm. Following Angluin's algorithm we perform membership queries for all prefixes of t.
(2) The runs T of a spanning tree of the model $\mathcal{A}_{init}$ as the initial set of row labels S_A (access strings). We initialize Angluin's algorithm by adding each $s \in S_A$ to $\mathcal{OT}$ and perform membership queries for the missing entries.
(3) A set of separating sequences $DS(\mathcal{A}_{init})$, see Section 4.4, calculated for the states of $\mathcal{A}_{init}$ as the initial set of column labels E_A. Thus, we initialize Angluin's algorithm by setting $\mathcal{OT}$ to be empty, and $E_A = DS(\mathcal{A}_{init})$.

So this three ways of initializing the sets S_A and E_A account for the attempt to speed up learning, but with the entries in $\mathcal{OT}$ queried for on the SUT at hand now.

Note that when using all three initializations and if $\mathcal{A}_{init}$ models $\mathcal{M}$ accurately with these choices of S_A and E_A then this will allow Angluin's algorithm to learn $\mathcal{A}_{init}$ correctly, without the assistance of the expensive equivalence check (VC algorithm).

Handling Model-Checking Counterexamples The model checker can construct two types of mc-counterexamples to a LTL formula, finite and infinite. In the first case there is no extra work in handling it: The counterexample is given directly to Angluin's algorithm. In the second case we must make the counterexample finite in order for Angluin's algorithm to use it.

An infinite counterexample is an ultimately periodic word of the form $w_1 w_2^\omega$ where $w_1, w_2^\omega \in \Sigma^*$. Assuming that the automaton being checked has n number of states, the counterexample given to Angluin's algorithm is $w_1 w_2^{n+1}$. Running w_1 in $A_{\neg \phi}$ it needs to terminate in an accepting state s. Starting from s the second part w_2 needs to terminate in s as well. For each such pair, we apply the second part n more times. That is, we try to run the string $w_1 w_2^{n+1}$. If we succeed, this means that there is a cycle in $A_{\neg \phi} \cap \mathcal{M}$ through a state with s

as the $A_{\neg\phi}$ component. This is the case since there are at most n ways to pair up s with a state of $\mathcal{M}$. In this case, there is an infinite accepting path in the intersection.

Experiments and Discussion In [GPY02], an experimental implementation of the algorithm is analyzed. Two CCS models [Mil89] are learned and two properties are checked. The two selected properties do not hold, and the correct models are tampered with in order to experiment with finding a (false negative) mc-counterexample. This counterexample is in all experiments, using the AMC method, utilized to initialize the observation table in Angluin's algorithm. This is the initialization mentioned in Section Initialization, case 1. The model checker checks the properties sequentially. The experiments have been performed on SUTs with approximately 500 and 100 states, respectively.

The experiments aim to compare the black box checking method (in which Angluin's observation table is not initialized) and the AMC method. Experiments are performed in the AMC method with different combinations to initialize Angluin's observation table, choices (1) and (2) (then $E_A = \{\varepsilon\}$), (1) and (3) (then $S_A = \{\varepsilon\}$) and (1), (2), and (3) are used.

The results can be summarized as follows. Comparing the different ways of initializing $\mathcal{OT}$ we see that learning from scratch are in these experiments slower then using initialized tables. The results also indicate that AMC method give rise to more states in the model than the black box checking method. Furthermore, the counterexamples are shorter when learning from scratch than those when initialized tables are used, if the number of states of the initialized tables are large.

The adaptive model checking methods is applicable for models that are inaccurate but not completely irrelevant. When comparing an algorithm learning from scratch, and using an initial model to guide the learning of the modified SUT (AMC) the different benefits over each other are unveiled. The learning from scratch method can be useful when there is a short error trace that identifies why the checked property does not hold. In this case, it is possible that the learning from scratch method will discover the error after learning only a small model. The AMC method is useful when the modification of the SUT is simple or when it may have a very limited affect on the correctness of the property checked.

However, it has to be said that adaptive model checking is still a mainly unexplored area that further theory as well as practical insights are needed.

19.6   Summary

In this chapter an introduction to model checking and model learning was given. Furthermore, it was shown how to combine both techniques to an approach in which properties of a SUT are verified directly.

First of all we have presented Kripke transition systems which build a simple basis for temporal logics used in model checking. The essential difference between linear time logics and branching time logics was made plain on the basis of an example. Subsequently we presented *linear time logic* (LTL) and computational tree logic (CTL) which are widely used for model checking purposes. Since the combination of model checking and model learning for testing purposes is only meaningful with linear time logics we presented a basic model checking algorithm for linear time logic.

In the second part of the chapter we first gave an introduction to the general ideas of model learning algorithms. Continuing in the same subject, we presented a number of learning algorithms; the observation pack algorithm, Angluin's algorithm, the reduced observation table algorithm and, the discrimination tree algorithm. Subsequently we discussed the algorithms' query complexity and presented some domain specific optimizations to reduce the number of queries. We rounded the model learning part off with some experimental results.

The final part in this chapter presented the adaptive model checking algorithm, which combines model checking and model learning into one approach. The approach try to make use of information in an existing model of the SUT in order to save effort in the learning procedure. If no model exist or the existing model is irrelevant compared to the current SUT, the approach is still applicable.

Although model checking and model learning are both established research areas, a lot of work remains to be done when considering testing. The combination of model checking and testing techniques should be clarified. Models to be used for testing might ask for different characteristics of the learning procedures than they currently have. For example, the construction of an abstract model of a SUT using learning algorithms might ask for a new approach. Issues in this area need to be examined from a theoretical as well as practical point of view.

Part VII

Appendices

20　Model-Based Testing – A Glossary

Alexander Pretschner and Martin Leucker

Overview The idea of model-based testing is to compare the I/O behavior of a valid behavior model to that of a system one wants to test (the system under test, SUT). In order to do so, a few I/O traces of the model are fixed. Picking "interesting" traces is a demanding task, and it is reflected in test purposes and test case specifications. The input part of a test case is applied to the SUT, and the output of the SUT is compared to the output of the model (this expected output is part of the the test case).

Since models are abstractions, or simplifications, it may be necessary to bridge the different levels of abstraction between the model and the SUT. Before being applied to the SUT, the input part of the test case may have to be concretized to its level of abstraction. Output of the SUT may well have to be abstracted before being compared to the output of the test case (that is, output of the model). Sometimes it is the case that the levels of abstraction are identical.

When considering real-time or continuous systems, then often it is not possible to predict the exact values. Instead, small deviations (so-called jitter) may be acceptable in both the time and the value domains. A test case then represents a whole family of runs of the SUT.

Terminology

- **Test case** A test case is a structure of input and expected output behavior.
  - The structure is a finite sequence in case of (quasi-)deterministic systems. A test case then corresponds to one or many intended runs of the SUT, which is a consequence of acceptable jitter in the time and value domains (this is why we call these systems quasi-deterministic, or deterministic, for short).
  - It is tree-like (of possibly infinite branching but finite length) in case of nondeterministic systems. As in the case of deterministic systems, each path in the tree corresponds to one or many runs of the SUT because of jitter.
- **Test data** Test data is the input part of a test case.
- **Test suite** A test suite is a set of test cases. The notion of a test suite may comprise a set of execution conditions: assumptions on the environment, configuration of the SUT, etc. Test suites may be infinite or even uncountable. However, when tests are actually performed, only a finite amount of input can obviously be applied.
- **Test purpose** A test purpose is a property one wants to test. Examples include "conformance", "statement coverage", "invariant ψ". These properties can be expressed informally or formally. In general, they cannot directly be used for testing a system because

M. Broy et al. (Eds.): Model-Based Testing of Reactive Systems, LNCS 3472, pp. 607-609, 2005.
© Springer-Verlag Berlin Heidelberg 2005

  – they specify possibly infinitely many runs of a system, or
  – it is not clear how to derive a test suite.

• **Test case specification** A test case specification formally represents a test
  suite. The notion of a test case specification is bound to that of a test case
  generator. While it is not necessarily clear how to derive a test suite from a
  test purpose, it must be well-defined how to derive a test suite from a test
  case specification. A test case specification gives an operational flavor to a
  test purpose, and it is a demanding task to find good test case specifications:
  since it describes possibly infinitely many traces of possibly infinite length,
  how should an invariance property be tested? Many test case specifications
  can correspond to the same test purpose. Many test cases can correspond to
  the same test case specification.

  Obviously, a test case specification requires knowledge of the intended behavior (or **specification**, or behavior **model**) of a SUT. If an explicit behavior
  model exists, then the test case specification can be understood as a selection
  criterion on the set of model traces. Since this seminar is on model-based
  testing, we always tacitly assume the existence of such a model, and we
  hence define test case specifications as selection criteria on this model. In
  particular, this is implies that a model of the SUT is not part of the test
  case specification. However, environment models that are tailored to a given
  test purpose may well be included in the test case specification.

  Test case specifications can be **functional** (concerned with a given requirement), **structural** (concerned with the structure of of a model or the SUT's
  code), **stochastic**, or combinations thereof. They can be defined on the
  model of a SUT or on the model of the SUT's environment, or both.

• **Test case generator** A test case generator takes a test case specification
  and a model of the SUT as input and yields a test suite as output.

• **Testing** Testing comprises the activities of defining test purposes and test
  case specifications as well as that of generating test suites and test execution.
  In the context of model-based testing, test cases are generated from a model.

• **Test execution** Test execution comprises the following activities. Test data
  is applied to a SUT, the behavior of the SUT is monitored, and expected
  and actual behaviors are compared in order to yield a verdict. Bridging the
  different levels of abstraction of the model and the SUT can be done before or
  during test execution. "Running a test" and "executing a test" are synonyms
  for test execution.

• **Test system** The real system which includes the test engine, executable
  tests, adaptors, and the test equipment.

• **Verification** Verification is the process of checking up to which point formal
  documents describe the same behavior: "Are we building the system right?"
  With this definition, testing is an activity of verification. There is no general
  agreement on this point.

• **Validation** Validation is the process of checking whether or not a system
  does what it is supposed to do: "Are we building the right system?" Validation connects informal and vague requirements with a system.

- **Conformance** Conformance is a relation between the observable behavior of a SUT and that of its specification, or model. The idea is that model and implementation exhibit the "same" behavior. However, the granularity of this relation may vary.
- **Monitor** A monitor observes those parts of the behavior of a SUT that should be compared to the intended behavior as provided by a test case.
- **Verdict** The verdict is the result of the comparison of intended and actual behaviors of a SUT (parts of the intended behavior are provided as test cases). Generally, verdicts can be either of *pass* (behaviors conform), *fail* (they don't), and *inconclusive* (don't know).
- **Black-Box Testing** Black-Box Testing denotes testing activities that do not take into account knowledge of the inner structure (the code) of the SUT.
- **White-Box Testing** White-Box Testing denotes testing activities that do take into account knowledge of the inner structure (the code) of the SUT.
- **IUT, Implementation under Test** A IUT is the implementation one wants to test. In many cases, it is not possible to access the IUT directly, but only via a *test context*.
- **SUT, System under Test** An SUT is the implementation that one wants to test (IUT) together with those things that one does not want to test, but needs to access the IUT (test context).
- **Model** A model is an abstraction, i. e., a simplification, of a SUT or of its environment, or both. In model-based testing, a model of the SUT is, among other things, used for determining expected output.
- **Test Context** A Test Context consists of things that one does not want to test, but are "in the way" between the tester and the thing that one wants to test. For example, things like communication channels, or parts of the system of which the IUT is a part that cannot easily be removed from the system. A test context may "blurr" the view that one can have of an implementation, and therefore (parts of) the test context may have to be part of the model. Usually, one assumes that the test context is correctly implemented.

Acknowledgment Axel Belinfante provided valuable comments.

21 Finite State Machines

Bengt Jonsson

In this appendix, we review basic definitions and the Mealy machine model. The definitions and most of the notation follow [LY94, LY96].

21.1 Basic Definitions

Definition 21.1. A **Mealy machine** is a quintuple $\mathcal{M} = \langle I, O, S, \delta, \lambda \rangle$ where

- I and O are finite nonempty sets of *input symbols* and *output symbols*, respectively,
- S is a finite nonempty set of *states*,
- $\delta : S \times I \rightarrow S$ is the *state transition function*,
- $\lambda : S \times I \rightarrow O$ is the *output function*.

An intuitive interpretation of a Mealy machine is as follows. At any point in time, the machine is in one state $s \in S$. It is possible to give inputs to the machine, by applying an input symbol a. The machine responds by producing an output symbol $\lambda(s, a)$ and transforming itself to the new state $\delta(s, a)$. We can depict Mealy machines as directed labeled graphs, where S is the set of vertices. For each state $s \in S$ and input symbol $a \in I$, there is an edge from s to $\delta(s, a)$ labeled by "a/b", where b is the output symbol $\lambda(s, a)$. See Figure 21.1 for an example of a Mealy machine (due to Sven Sandberg). Note that the letters a and b are used in two ways. In the text they are metasymbols denoting arbitrary input and output symbols, whereas in examples they denote specific input or output symbols.

Applying an input sequence $x = a_1 a_2 \cdots a_k \in I^*$ starting in a state s_1 takes the machine successively to a sequence of states $s_2, s_3, \ldots, s_{k+1}$, where $s_{i+1} = \delta(s_i, a_i)$ for $i = 1, \cdots, k$, and produces a sequence of output symbols $b_1 b_2 \cdots b_k \in O^*$, where $b_i = \lambda(s_i, a_i)$ for $i = 1, \cdots, k$. We extend the transition and output functions from input symbols to sequences of input symbols, by defining $\delta(s_1, x) = s_{k+1}$ and $\lambda(s_1, x) = b_1 b_2 \cdots b_k$. A more precise recursive definition is as follows:

$$
\begin{aligned}
\delta(s, \varepsilon) &= s \\
\delta(s, xa) &= \delta(\delta(s, x), a) \\
\lambda(s, \varepsilon) &= \varepsilon \\
\lambda(s, xa) &= \lambda(s, x)\lambda(\delta(s, x), a)
\end{aligned}
$$

We further extend the transition and output functions from states to sets of states, by defining $\delta(Q, x) \stackrel{\text{def}}{=} \{\delta(s, x) : s \in Q\}$ and $\lambda(Q, x) \stackrel{\text{def}}{=} \{\lambda(s, x) : s \in Q\}$ where $Q \subseteq S$ is a set of states.

The number $|S|$ of states is usually denoted n.

M. Broy et al. (Eds.): Model-Based Testing of Reactive Systems, LNCS 3472, pp. 611-614, 2005.
© Springer-Verlag Berlin Heidelberg 2005

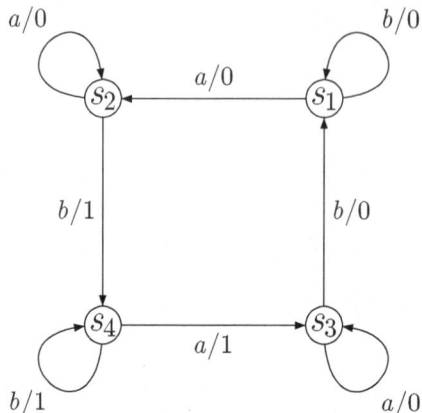

Fig. 21.1. A Mealy machine $\mathcal{M} = \langle I, O, S, \delta, \lambda \rangle$ with states $S = \{s_1, s_2, s_3, s_4\}$, input symbols $I = \{a, b\}$, and output symbols $O = \{0, 1\}$. For instance, applying a starting in s_1 produces output $\lambda(s_1, a) = 0$ and moves to next state $\delta(s_1, a) = s_2$.

The Mealy machines that we consider are **completely specified**, meaning that at every state the machine has a defined reaction to every input symbol in I, i.e., δ and λ are total. They are also **deterministic**, since for each state s and input a exactly one next state $\delta(s, a)$ and output symbol $\lambda(s, a)$ is possible.

21.2   Equivalence and Minimization

Let s and t be two states of the same Mealy machine, or two states in different machines. The states s and t are **equivalent** if $\lambda(s, x) = \lambda(t, x)$ for each input sequence $x \in I^*$. That is, for each input sequence the machine starting in s will produce the same output sequence as the machine starting in t. Two machines $\mathcal{M}$ and $\mathcal{M}'$ are **equivalent** if each state in $\mathcal{M}$ has a corresponding equivalent state in $\mathcal{M}'$ and vice versa.

If in machine $\mathcal{M}$, two states s and t are equivalent, then the machine $\mathcal{M}'$ obtained from $\mathcal{M}$ by merging s and t is clearly equivalent to $\mathcal{M}$. More generally, for each machine there is an equivalent machine with a minimal number of states, called a *reduced* or *minimized* machine. In Chapters $1 - 4$ and this appendix, we consider only minimized Mealy machines.

Given a machine $\mathcal{M}$, the minimized machine which is equivalent to $\mathcal{M}$ can be constructed by a partition refinement procedure (see, e.g., [Hop71] and [AHU74, Sec. 4.13]). A *partition* of S is a set $\{B_1, B_2, \ldots, B_r\}$ of subsets of S (sometimes called *blocks*) such that $\cup_{i=1}^{r} B_i = S$ and $B_i \cap B_j = \emptyset$ for $i \neq j$, i.e., each element of S is in exactly one of the blocks $B_1, B_2, \ldots, B_r$. Given a Mealy machine $\mathcal{M} = \langle I, O, S, \delta, \lambda \rangle$, the states of its equivalent minimized machine will be the coarsest partition (i.e., having fewest blocks) $\{B_1, B_2, \ldots, B_r\}$ of S such that whenever s and t are in the same block, then

- $\lambda(s, a) = \lambda(t, a)$ for each input symbol $a \in I$, and
- $\delta(s, a)$ and $\delta(t, a)$ are in the same block.

It is straight-forward to check that s and t are in the same block if and only if they are equivalent.

The straight-forward solution to finding this coarsest partition is to start with an initial partition of S, where two states s and t are in the same block if and only if $\lambda(s, a) = \lambda(t, a)$ for each input symbol $a \in I$. Thereafter, this initial partition is repeatedly refined by the following method. Take a block B_i of the current partition. Examine $\delta(s, a)$ for each $s \in B_i$ and $a \in I$. Partition B_i so that s and t are in the same block if and only if $\delta(s, a)$ and $\delta(t, a)$ are in the same block of the current partition. The process is is iterated until no further refinements are possible. This process yields a quadratic algorithm, since each refinement requires linear time, and there can be at most $|S|$ refinements. A more efficient algorithm has been developed by Hopcroft ([Hop71] and [AHU74, Sec. 4.13]).

21.3   Initial and Current State Uncertainty

Chapters $1 - 4$ use some basic definitions of the conclusions that can be made from observations of a machine's response to input strings.

The initial state uncertainty describes what we know about the initial state after applying an input string and observing the resulting output string.

Definition 21.2. The **initial state uncertainty** after applying input sequence $x \in I^*$ is a partition $\pi(x) \stackrel{\text{def}}{=} \{B_1, B_2, \ldots, B_r\}$ of S, such that two states s, t are in the same block B_i if and only if $\lambda(s, x) = \lambda(t, x)$.

In other words, each block in the initial state uncertainty $\pi(x)$ is the set of states from which a particular output sequence is produced in response to the input sequence x.

The current state uncertainty describes what we know about the current (final) state after having applied an input string and observed the resulting output string.

Definition 21.3. The **current state uncertainty** after applying input sequence $x \in I^*$ is the set of subsets $\sigma(x) \stackrel{\text{def}}{=} \{\delta(B_i, x) : B_i \in \pi(x)\}$ of S.

In other words, each block in the current state uncertainty $\sigma(x)$ is the set of states that the machine can end up in after generating a particular output sequence in response to the input sequence x. While the initial state uncertainty is a partition, the current state uncertainty does not need to be a partition, but just a set of nonempty blocks

21.4   Distinguishing Experiments

Chapters $1 - 4$ present algorithms that investigate the structure and current state of a Mealy machine by performing *experiments*, i.e., applying a sequence of input symbols and observing the resulting output. An experiment can be either *preset* or *adaptive*. A **preset experiment** (or preset sequence) is a fixed input sequence $x \in I^*$, and we are interested in observing the output sequence produced by the machine in response to x. In an **adaptive experiment** (or adaptive sequence), each symbol in the input sequence depends on the output produced in response to the previous input symbols. An adaptive experiment can be formalized as a decision tree, in which the internal nodes are labeled with input symbols, and the edges are labeled with output symbols, such that edges emanating from a common node have distinct output symbols. Each leaf of an adaptive experiment can be labeled with a suitable defined outcome of the experiment for the particular case that the experiment ends up in this leaf.

22   Labelled Transition Systems

Joost-Pieter Katoen

Let Act be a countable set of *actions* ranged over by $a, b, c, \ldots$. Action τ denotes the distinguished *invisible* (or, unobservable) action, i.e., $\tau \notin$ Act.

Definition 22.1. Labelled transition system A *labelled transition system* (LTS) M is a tuple $(Q, L, \rightarrow)$ with Q a countable set of states, $L \subseteq$ Act a set of observable actions called the *alphabet* of M, and transition relation $\rightarrow \subseteq Q \times (L \cup \{\tau\}) \times Q$.

We denote by $q \xrightarrow{a} q'$ that $(q, a, q') \in \rightarrow$. The main differences between a labelled transition system and a finite-state automaton are that the set of states Q and the alphabet L (and consequently $\rightarrow$) may be infinite. A state q may thus have infinitely many successors for some action a, i.e., the set $\{\, q' \mid q \xrightarrow{a} q' \,\}$ may be infinite.

Definition 22.2. A *rooted* LTS M is a tuple $(Q, L, \rightarrow, q_0)$ with $(Q, L, \rightarrow)$ an LTS with non-empty set Q of states, and an initial state $q_0 \in Q$.

Definition 22.3. LTS $M = (Q, L, \rightarrow)$ is *non-deterministic* if and only if for some $q \in Q$ we have $q \xrightarrow{\tau} q'$ for some $q' \in Q$ or for some $a \in L$ it holds: $q \xrightarrow{a} q' \wedge q \xrightarrow{a} q''$ for $q' \neq q''$. An LTS that is not non-deterministic is *deterministic*.

Let LTS $M = (Q, L, \rightarrow)$. The following abbreviations are useful:

$$q \xrightarrow{a} \quad \text{iff} \quad \exists q' \in Q.\, q \xrightarrow{a} q'$$
$$q \xnrightarrow{a} \quad \text{iff} \quad \neg(q \xrightarrow{a})$$

$q \xrightarrow{a}$ expresses that state q has an outgoing a-transition. $q \xnrightarrow{a}$ expresses that this is not the case. For σ a string of actions $a_1 \ldots a_n$ we have:

$$q \xrightarrow{\sigma} q' \text{ iff } \exists q_1, \ldots, q_{n-1}.\, q \xrightarrow{a_1} q_1 \xrightarrow{a_2} \ldots \xrightarrow{a_{n-1}} q_{n-1} \xrightarrow{a_n} q'$$
$$q \xRightarrow{\varepsilon} q' \text{ iff } \exists n \geq 0.\, q \xrightarrow{\tau^n} q'$$
$$q \xRightarrow{a} q' \text{ iff } q \xrightarrow{\tau^* a \tau^*} q'$$
$$q \xRightarrow{\sigma} q' \text{ iff } \exists q_1, \ldots, q_{n-1}.\, q \xRightarrow{a_1} q_1 \xRightarrow{a_2} \ldots \xRightarrow{a_{n-1}} q_{n-1} \xRightarrow{a_n} q'$$

The $\Longrightarrow$-notation is used for a generalized version of the transition relation that concentrates on observable behavior. Note that $q \xRightarrow{\varepsilon} q'$ notes that q can evolve into q' unobservedly, i.e., by executing zero or more τ-transitions. This includes the special case that no transitions are executed at all, and therefore $q = q'$. $q \xRightarrow{a} q'$ expresses that q may evolve into q' when executing the observable action a, possible preceded or followed by any finite number of invisible τ-transitions. $\xrightarrow{\sigma}$ and $\xRightarrow{}$ are the generalizations for strings of $\xrightarrow{a}$ and $\xRightarrow{a}$ respectively.

M. Broy et al. (Eds.): Model-Based Testing of Reactive Systems, LNCS 3472, pp. 615-616, 2005.
© Springer-Verlag Berlin Heidelberg 2005

616   Joost-Pieter Katoen

The following sets are often used:

$$traces(q) = \{\, \sigma \in L^* \mid q \xrightarrow{\sigma} \,\}$$
$$init(q) = \{\, a \in L \cup \{\tau\} \mid q \xrightarrow{a} \,\}$$
$$reach(q) = \{\, q' \mid \exists \sigma.\, q \xrightarrow{\sigma} q' \,\}$$

Note that $traces(q)$ contains sequences of actions that do not include unobservable actions. $init(q)$ is the set of actions that are possible in state q, and $reach(q)$ is the set of states that are reachable when starting from q via executing a sequence of actions (including invisible τ-actions).

For rooted LTS $M = (Q, L, \rightarrow, q_0)$ let $traces(M) = traces(q_0)$ and $init(M) = init(q_0)$ the set of observable actions that are enabled in the initial state.

Definition 22.4. State q is *stable* if and only if $q \xrightarrow{\tau}\!\!\!\!\!/\;$. State q is *unstable* if and only if q is not stable.

Definition 22.5. Trace equivalence Rooted LTSs M and M' are *trace-equivalent*, denoted $M =_{tr} M'$, if and only if $traces(M) = traces(M')$.

Definition 22.6. Bisimulation A relation $R \subseteq Q \times Q$ is a (strong) *bisimulation* if and only if for all $(q_1, q_2) \in R$ and $a \in \mathsf{Act} \cup \{\tau\}$ it is the case that:

(1) $\exists q_1'.\, q_1 \xrightarrow{a} q_1'$ implies $\exists q_2'.\, q_2 \xrightarrow{a} q_2'$ and $(q_1', q_2') \in R$
(2) $\exists q_2'.\, q_2 \xrightarrow{a} q_2'$ implies $\exists q_1'.\, q_1 \xrightarrow{a} q_1'$ and $(q_1', q_2') \in R$.

Rooted LTSs $M = (Q, L, \rightarrow, q_0)$ and $M' = (Q', L, \rightarrow', q_0')$ are bisimilar, denoted $M =_{bis} M'$ if and only if there is some bisimulation relation R such that $(q_0, q_0') \in R$.

Literature

[AB99]   Paul Ammann and Paul E. Black. A specification-based coverage met-
           ric to evaluate test sets. In *Proceedings of the 4th IEEE International
           Symposium on High-Assurance Systems Engineering (HASE 1999)*, pages
           239–248. IEEE Computer Society Press, 1999. [352]

[ABM98]   Paul Ammann, Paul E. Black, and William Majurski. Using model check-
           ing to generate tests from specifications. In *Proceedings of the 2nd IEEE
           International Conference on Formal Engineering Methods (ICFEM 1998)*,
           pages 46–54. IEEE Computer Society Press, 1998. [352]

[Abr87]   Samson Abramsky. Observation equivalence as a testing equivalence. *The-
           oretical Computer Science*, 53:225–241, 1987. [120, 123, 124, 126, 129, 131,
           132]

[Abr96]   J-R. Abrial. *The B-Book: Assigning Programs to Meanings*. Cambridge
           University Press, 1996. [343]

[ACH+95]   R. Alur, C. Courcoubetis, T. Henzinger, P. Ho, X. Nicollin, A. Olivero,
           J. Sifakis, and S. Yovine. The algorithmic analysis of hybrid systems. *Theo-
           retical Computer Science*, 138:3–34, 1995. A preliminary version appeared in
           Guy Cohen, editor, *Proceedings of 11th International Conference on Anal-
           ysis and Optimization of Systems (ICAOS 1994): Discrete Event Systems*,
           volume 199 of *Lecture Notes in Control and Information Science*, pages
           331–351. Springer-Verlag, 1994. [375]

[AD94]   Rajeev Alur and David L. Dill. A theory of timed automata. *Theoretical
           Computer Science*, 126(2):183–235, 1994. [201, 203, 204, 205, 212, 216, 360,
           367, 371]

[ADE+01]   R. Alur, T. Dang, J. Esposito, R. Fierro, Y. Hur, F. Ivančić, V. Kumar,
           I. Lee, P. Mishra, G. Pappas, and O. Sokolsky. Hierarchical hybrid mod-
           eling of embedded systems. In T. A. Henzinger and C. M. Kirsch, editors,
           *Proceedings of the 1st International Workshop on Embedded Software (EM-
           SOFT 2001)*, volume 2211, pages 14–31. Springer-Verlag, 2001. [375, 376]

[ADE+03]   R. Alur, T. Dang, J. Esposito, Y. Hur, F. Ivančić, V. Kumar, I. Lee,
           P. Mishra, G. Pappas, and O. Sokolsky. Hierarchical hybrid modeling and
           analysis of embedded systems. *Proceedings of the IEEE*, 91(1):11–28, Jan-
           uary 2003. [375, 376]

[ADG+03]   C. Artho, D. Drusinsky, A. Goldberg, K. Havelund, M. Lowry, C. Pasare-
           anu, G. Roşu, and W. Visser. Experiments with test case generation and
           run-time analysis. In E. Börger, A. Gargantini, and E. Riccobene, editors,
           *Proceedings of the 10th International Workshop on Abstract State Machines
           (ASM 2003)*, volume 2589 of *Lecture Notes in Computer Science*, pages 87–
           107, Taormina, Italy, 2003. Springer-Verlag. Invited paper. [552, 553]

[ADLU91]   A. Aho, A. Dahbura, D. Lee, and Ü. Uyar. An optimization technique for
           protocol conformance test generation based on uio sequences and rural chi-
           nese postman tours. *IEEE Transactions on Communications*, 39(11):1604–
           1615, November 1991. [70, 72, 101, 104]

[AFH94]   Rajeev Alur, Limor Fix, and Thomas A. Henzinger. Event-clock automata: A determinizable class of timed automata. In *Proceedings of the 16th International Conference on Computer-aided Verification (CAV 1994)*, volume 818 of *Lecture Notes in Computer Science*, pages 1–13. Springer-Verlag, 1994. [205, 206, 371]

[AGE]   AGEDIS homepage. http://www.agedis.de. [427]

[AGLS01]   Rajeev Alur, Radu Grosu, Insup Lee, and Oleg Sokolsky. Compositional refinement for hierarchical hybrid systems. In Maria Domenica Di Benedetto and Alberto L. Sangiovanni-Vincentelli, editors, *Proceedings of the 4th International Workshop on Hybrid Systems: Computation and Control (HSCC 2001)*, volume 2034 of *Lecture Notes in Computer Science*, pages 33–48. Springer-Verlag, 2001. [375, 376]

[AGW77]   Roy Adler, L. Wayne Goodwyn, and Benjamin Weiss. Equivalence of topological Markov shifts. *Israel Journal of Mathemtics*, 27(1):49–63, 1977. [32]

[AH97]   Rajeev Alur and Thomas A. Henzinger. Real-time system = discrete system + clock variables. *International Journal on Software Tools for Technology Transfer*, 1(1–2):86–109, 1997. [201]

[AHB03]   C. Artho, K. Havelund, and A. Biere. High-level data races. *Software Testing, Verification and Reliability*, 03(4):207–227, December 2003. Extended version of a paper in P. T. Isaías, F. Sedes, J. C. Augusto, and U. Ultes-Nitsche, editors, *New Technologies for Information Systems: Proceedings of the 3rd International Workshop on New Developments in Digital Libraries (NDDL 2003) and the 1st International Workshop on Validation and Verification of Software for Enterprise Information Systems (VVEIS 2003)*; in conjunction with the *5th International Conference on Enterprise Information Systems*, pages 82–93. ICEIS Press, 2003. [552, 553]

[AHP99]   Pavel Atanassov, Stefan Haberl, and Peter Puschner. Heuristic worst-case execution time analysis. In *Proceedings of the 10th European Workshop on Dependable Computing*, pages 109–114. Austrian Computer Society (OCG), May 1999. [383]

[AHU74]   A. V. Aho, J. E. Hopcroft, and J. D. Ullman. *The Design and Analysis of Computer Algorithms*. Addison-Wesley, 1974. [612, 613]

[Ald90]   Rudie Alderden. COOPER – the compositional construction of a canonical tester. In Son T. Vuong, editor, *Proceedings of the IFIP TC/WG6.1 2nd International Conference on Formal Description Techniques for Distributed Systems and Communication Protocols (FORTE 1989)*, pages 13–17, Vancouver, BC, Canada, 1990. North-Holland. [414, 417]

[Alu99]   Rajeev Alur. Timed automata. In Nicolas Halbwachs and Doron Peled, editors, *Proceedings of the 11th Internation Conference on Computer Aided Verification (CAV 1999)*, volume 1633 of *Lecture Notes in Computer Science*, pages 8–22. Springer-Verlag, 1999. [202, 204, 206]

[ÁMHS01]   Erika Ábrahám-Mumm, Ulrich Hannemann, and Martin Steffen. Verification of hybrid systems: Formalization and proof rules in PVS. In *Proceedings of the 7th International Conference on Engineering of Complex Computer Systems (ICECCS 2001)*, pages 48–57. IEEE Computer Society Press, 2001. [375]

[Amt00]   Peter Amthor. *Structural Decomposition of Hybrid Systems*. Number 13 in Monographs of the Bremen Institute of Safe Systems. University of Bremen, 2000. [375]

[Ang87]   D. Angluin. Learning regular sets from queries and counterexamples. *Information and Computation*, 75:87–106, 1987. [582, 594, 599]

[ASMa]   ASM homepage. http://www.eecs.umich.edu/gasm/. [412]

[ASMb]   AsmL download. http://research.microsoft.com/fse/asml/. [412]

[Aus99]   T. M. Austin. DIVA: A reliable substrate for deep submicron microarchitecture design. In *Proceedings of the 32nd Annual IEEE/ACM International Symposium on Microarchitecture (MICRO 1999)*, pages 196–207, November 1999. [527]

[BB87]   Tommaso Bolognesi and Ed Brinksma. Introduction to the ISO specification language LOTOS. *Computer Networks*, 14:25–29, 1987. [120, 163, 417, 423]

[BBHP03]   Kirsten Berkenkötter, Stefan Bisanz, Ulrich Hannemann, and Jan Peleska. HybridUML profile for UML 2.0. In *Proceedings of the Workshop on Specification and Validation of UML models for Real Time and Embedded Systems (SVERTS) in conjunction with the ⟨⟨UML⟩⟩ 2003 Conference*, October 2003. Available at http://www-verimag.imag.fr/EVENTS/2003/SVERTS. [375, 376]

[BC85]   Gérard Berry and Laurent Cosserat. The ESTEREL synchronous programming language. In Stephen D. Brookes, A. W. Roscoe, and Glynn Winskel, editors, *Proceedings of the Seminar on Concurrency, 1984*, volume 197 of *Lecture Notes in Computer Science*, pages 389–448. Springer-Verlag, 1985. [395]

[BC00]   M. Bernardo and R. Cleaveland. A theory of testing for Markovian processes. In C. Palamidessi, editor, *Proceedings of the 11th International Conference on Concurrency Theory (CONCUR 2000)*, number 1877 in Lecture Notes in Computer Science, pages 305–319. Springer-Verlag, 2000. [234, 244, 256, 257, 263, 264, 265, 267, 268]

[BCG⁺00]   Dahananjay S. Brahme, Steven Cox, Jim Gallo, Mark Glasser, William Grundmann, C. Norris Ip, William Paulsen, John L. Pierce, John Rose, Dean Shea, and Karl Whiting. The transaction-based verification methodology. Technical report, Cadence Design Systems, Inc., August 2000. [455]

[BCGM00]   Simon Burton, John A. Clark, Andy J. Galloway, and John A. McDermid. Automated V&V for high integrity systems, a target formal methods approach. In C. Michael Holloway, editor, *Proceedings of the 5th NASA Langley Formal Methods Workshop (Lfm 2000)*, number NASA/CP-2000-210100 in NASA Conference Publications, pages 129–140, 2000. [333]

[BCL92]   J. R. Burch, E. M. Clarke, and D. E. Long. Symbolic model checking with partitioned transition relations. In A. Halaas and P. B. Denyer, editors, *Proceedings of the International Conference on Very Large Scale Integration (VLSI 1991)*, volume A-1 of *IFIP Transactions*, pages 49–58, Edinburgh, Scotland, 1992. North-Holland. [567]

[BCM00]   Simon Burton, John A. Clark, and John A. McDermid. Testing, proof and automation. An integrated approach. In *Proceedings of the 1st International Workshop of Automated Program Analysis, Testing and Verification (WAP-ATV 2000)*, pages 57–63, 2000. In Conjunction with the 22nd International Conference on Software Engineering (ICSE 2000). [331]

[BCM01]   Simon Burton, John A. Clark, and John A. McDermid. Automatic generation of tests from Statechart specifications. In Ed Brinksma and Jan Tretmans, editors, *Proceedings of the 1st International Workshop on Formal Approaches to Testing of Software (FATES 2001)*, number BRICS NS-01-4 in Basic Research in Computer Science (BRICS) Notes Series, pages 31–46, 2001. [333]

[BCMD90] J. R. Burch, E. M. Clarke, K. L. McMillan, and David L. Dill. Sequential circuit verification using symbolic model checking. In *Proceedings of the 27th ACM/IEEE Conference on Design Automation Conference (DAC 1990)*, pages 46–51. ACM Press, 1990. [567]

[BCMS01] O. Burkart, D. Caucal, F. Moller, and Bernhard Steffen. Verification on infinite structures. In S. Smolka J. Bergstra, A. Pons, editor, *Handbook on Process Algebra*. North-Holland, 2001. [560]

[BDGW94] J. L. Balcázar, J. Díaz, R. Gavaldà, and O. Watanabe. The query complexity of learning DFA. *New Generation Computing*, 12:337–358, 1994. [599]

[BDGW97] J. L. Balcázar, J. Díaz, R. Gavaldà, and O. Watanabe. Algorithms for learning finite automata from queries: A unified view. In Ding-Zhu Du, Ker-I Ko, and Dingzhu Du, editors, *Advances in Algorithms, Languages, and Complexity*. Kluwer Academic, February 1997. In Honor of Ronald V. Book. [577, 590, 595]

[Bei95] B. Beizer. *Black-Box Testing*. John Wiley & Sons, 1995. [498]

[Bel57] R. Bellman. *Dynamic programming*. Princeton University Press, 1957. [206]

[BFdV+99] A. Belinfante, J. Feenstra, R. G. de Vries, J. Tretmans, N. Goga, L. Feijs, S. Mauw, and L. Heerink. Formal test automation: A simple experiment. In G. Csopaki, S. Dibuz, and K. Tarnay, editors, *Proceedings of the 12th International Workshop on Testing of Communicating Systems (IWTCS 1999)*, volume 147 of *IFIP Conference Proceedings*, pages 179–196. Kluwer Academic, 1999. [420, 424, 435, 438, 439, 443, 444, 446, 447, 448, 449, 456, 459]

[BFG+99] Marius Bozga, Jean-Claude Fernandez, Lucian Ghirvu, Susanne Graf, Jean-Pierre Krimm, and Laurent Mounier. IF: An intermediate representation and validation environment for timed asynchronous systems. In Jeannette M. Wing, Jim Woodcock, and Jim Davies, editors, *Proceedings of the World Congress on Formal Methods in the Development of Computing Systems, Volume I (FM 1999)*, volume 1708 of *Lecture Notes in Computer Science*, pages 307–327, Toulouse, France, 1999. Springer-Verlag. [419, 420]

[BFMW01] D. Bartetzko, C. Fischer, M. Moller, and H. Wehrheim. Jass – Java with assertions. In Klaus Havelund and Grigore Rosu, editors, *Runtime Verification (RV 2001)*, volume 55(2) of *Electronic Notes in Theoretical Computer Science*. Elsevier Science Publishers, 2001. [555]

[BG96] M. Bernardo and R. Gorrieri. Extended markovian process algebra. In U. Montanari and V. Sassone, editors, *Proceedings of the 7th International Conference on Concurrency Theory (CONCUR 1996)*, volume 1119 of *Lecture Notes in Computer Science*, pages 315–330. Springer-Verlag, 1996. [242]

[BGHM96] N. H. Bshouty, S. A. Goldman, T. R. Hancock, and S. Matar. Asking queries to minimize errors. *Journal of Computer and Systems Science*, 52:268–286, 1996. [599]

[BGK+02] K. Bhargavan, C. A. Gunter, M. Kim, I. Lee, D. Obradovic, O. Sokolsky, and M. Viswanathan. Verisim: Formal analysis of network simulations. *IEEE Transactions on Software Engineering*, 28(2):129–145, February 2002. [553]

[BGM91] Gilles Bernot, Marie-Claude Gaudel, and Bruno Marre. Software testing based on formal specifications: A theory and a tool. *Software Engineering Journal*, 6(6):387–405, 1991. [294, 334, 335]

[BGN+03] Mike Barnett, Wolfgang Grieskamp, Lev Nachmanson, Wolfram Schulte, Nikolai Tillman, and Margus Veanes. Towards a tool environment for model-based testing with AsmL. In *Proceedings of the 3rd International Workshop on Formal Approaches to Testing of Software (FATES 2003)*, volume 2931 of *Lecture Notes in Computer Science*, pages 252–266. Springer-Verlag, 2003. [414]

[BH89]   Ferenc Belina and Dieter Hogrefe. The CCITT Specification and Description Language SDL. *Computer Networks and ISDN Systems*, 16(4):311–341, March 1989. [1]

[BHKW03] Christel Baier, Holger Hermanns, Joost-Pieter Katoen, and Verena Wolf. Comparative branching time semantics for Markov chains. In *Proceedings of the 14th International Conference on Concurrency Theory (CONCUR 2003)*, volume 2761 of *Lecture Notes in Computer Science*, pages 492–507. Springer-Verlag, 2003. [243, 271]

[BIĆP99] Stojan Bogdanović, Balázs Imreh, Miroslav Ćirić, and Tatjana Petković. Directable automata and their generalizations. *Novi Sad Journal of Mathematics*, 29(2):29–69, 1999. [6, 31]

[Bin99]   R. Binder. *Testing Object-Oriented Systems: Models, Patterns, and Tools*. Addison Wesley, 1999. [281]

[BJLS03] Therese Berg, Bengt Jonsson, Martin Leucker, and Mayank Saksena. Insights to Angluin's learning. In *Proceedings of the International Workshop on Software Verification and Validation (SVV 2003)*, Electronic Notes in Theoretical Computer Science, December 2003. To appear. [597]

[BLL+95] Johan Bengtsson, Kim G. Larsen, Fredrik Larsson, Paul Pettersson, and Wang Yi. UPPAAL – A tool suite for automatic verification of real-time systems. In *Proceedings of the 3rd DIMACS/SYCON Workshop on Hybrid Systems: Verification and Control*, volume 1066 of *Lecture Notes in Computer Science*, pages 232–243. Springer-Verlag, October 1995. [222, 224]

[Blua]   Bluetooth Project, http://www.iti.uni-luebeck.de/Research/MUC/EKG/. [506]

[Blub]   Bluetooth Special Interest Group. *Specification of the Bluetooth System (version 1.1)*. http://www.bluetooth.com. [506]

[BPDG98] Béatrice Bérard, Antoine Petit, Volker Diekert, and Paul Gastin. Characterization of the expressive power of silent transitions in timed automata. *Fundamenta Informaticae*, 36(2–3):142–182, November 1998. [204]

[BPR93]   L. Boullier, M. Phalippou, and A. Rouger. Experimenting test selection strategies. In *Proceedings of the 6th SDL Forum, 1993*, pages 267–278. Elsevier Science Publishers, 1993. [200]

[BR87]   P. Berman and R. Roos. Learning one-counter languages in polynomial time. In *Proceedings of the 28th IEEE Symposium on the Foundations of Computer Science (FOCS 1987)*, pages 61–67, Los Alamitos, CA, 1987. IEEE Computer Society Press. [599]

[Bri89]   E. Brinksma. A theory for the derivation of tests. In S. Aggarwal and K. Sabnani, editors, *Proceedings of the 8th IFIP Symposium on Protocol Specification, Testing and Verification (PSTV 1988)*. North-Holland, 1989. [153, 154, 163, 199, 414, 415, 417]

[BRRdS96] Amar Bouali, Anni Ressouche, Valérie Roy, and Robert de Simone. The FCTOOLS user manual. Technical report, INRIA Sophia Antipolis, April 1996. [211]

[BRV95]   Ed Brinksma, Arend Rensink, and Walter Vogler. Fair testing. In Insup
          Lee and Scott A. Smolka, editors, *Proceedings of the 6th International Con-
          ference on Concurrency Theory (CONCUR 1995)*, volume 962 of *Lecture
          Notes in Computer Science*, pages 313–327. Springer-Verlag, 1995. [143,
          144, 145]
[Bry85]   R. E. Bryant. Symbolic manipulation of boolean functions using a graphical
          representation. In *Proceedings of the 22nd ACM/IEEE Design Automation
          Conference (DAC 1985)*, pages 688–694. IEEE Computer Society Press,
          June 1985. [398]
[BS01a]   Mike Barnett and Wolfram Schulte. Spying on components: A runtime
          verification technique. In *Proceedings of the OOPSLA 2001 Workshop on
          Specification and Verification of Component-Based Systems (SAVBS 2001)*,
          2001. Published as Technical Report ISU TR #01-09a, Iowa State Univer-
          sity. [531]
[BS01b]   M. Broy and K. Stølen. *Specification and Development of Interactive Sys-
          tems – Focus on Streams, Interfaces, and Refinement*. Springer-Verlag,
          2001. [286]
[Büc62]   J. R. Büchi. On a decision method in restricted second-order arithmetic. In
          E. Nagel, P. Suppes, and A. Tarski, editors, *Proceedings of the 1st Interna-
          tional Congress for Logic, Methodology, and Philosophy of Science (LMPS
          1960)*, pages 1–12. Stanford University Press, 1962. [559, 567]
[Bur00]   Simon Burton. Automated testing from Z specifications. Technical Report
          YCS-2000-329, University of York, 2000. [331, 333]
[Bur02]   Simon Burton. *Automated Generation of High Integrity Test Suites from
          Graphical Specifications*. PhD thesis, University of York, March 2002. [331,
          333]
[BvdLV95] Tommaso Bolognesi, Jeroen van de Lagemaat, and Chris Vissers, editors.
          LOTOSphere: Software Development with LOTOS. Kluwer Academic, 1995.
          [414]
[BY01]   Luciano Baresi and Michal Young. Test oracles. Technical Report CIS-TR-
          01-02, University of Oregon, Deptartment of Computer and Information
          Science, Eugene, Oregon, U.S.A., August 2001. [530]
[CC91]   Linda Christoff and Ivan Christoff. Efficient algorithms for verification of
          equivalences for probabilistic processes. In Kim Guldstrand Larsen and
          Arne Skou, editors, *Proceedings of the 3rd International Conference on
          Computer Aided Verification (CAV 1991)*, volume 575 of *Lecture Notes in
          Computer Science*, pages 310–321. Springer-Verlag, 1991. [274]
[CCG+02] A. Cimatti, E. Clarke, E. Giunchiglia, F. Giunchiglia, M. Pistore, M. Roveri,
          R. Sebastiani, and A. Tacchella. NuSMV Version 2: An opensource tool for
          symbolic model checking. In E. Brinksma and K. Guldstrand Larsen, edi-
          tors, *Proceedings of the 14th International Conference on Computer-Aided
          Verification (CAV 2002)*, volume 2404 of *Lecture Notes in Computer Sci-
          ence*, pages 359–364, Copenhagen, Denmark, July 2002. Springer-Verlag.
          [575]
[CCG+03] Sagar Chaki, Edmund M. Clarke, Alex Groce, Somesh Jha, and Helmut
          Veith. Modular verification of software components in C. In *Proceedings of
          the 25th International Conference on Software Engineering (ICSE 2003)*,
          pages 385–395. IEEE Computer Society Press, 2003. [325]
[CEP95]   CEPSCO.   GSM 11.11, Digital cellular telecommunications systems
          (phase2+); Specifications of the subscriber identity module – mobile equip-
          ment (SIM-ME) interface (GSM 11.11), 1995. [444]

[CEP00]   CEPSCO. Common electronic purse specification: Technical specification, 2000. http://www.cepsco.org. [444]

[Čer64]   Ján Černý. Poznámka k. homogénnym experimentom s konecnými automatmi. *Matematicko-fysikalny Casopis SAV*, 14:208–215, 1964. [19, 31]

[CGPT96]   M. Clatin, R. Groz, M. Phalippou, and R. Thummel. Two approaches linking test generation with verification techniques. In A. Cavalli and S. Budkowski, editors, *Proceedings of the 8th International Workshop on Protocol Test Systems (IWPTS 1996)*. Chapman & Hall, 1996. [200, 410, 411, 412]

[Che02]   Albert M. K. Cheng. *Real-Time Systems; Scheduling, Analysis, and Verification*. John Wiley & Sons, 2002. [360]

[Cho78]   Tsun S. Chow. Testing software design modeled by finite-state machines. *IEEE Transactions on Software Engineering*, 4(3):178–187, May 1978. Special collection based on the 2nd International Computer Software and Applications Conference (COMPSAC 1978). [94, 96, 108, 110, 111, 159, 220, 370, 593, 599]

[Chr90]   Ivan Christoff. Testing equivalences and fully abstract models for probabilistic processes. In *Proceedings of the 1st International Conference on Concurrency Theory (CONCUR 1990)*, volume 458 of *Lecture Notes in Computer Science*, pages 126–140. Springer-Verlag, 1990. [233, 244, 246, 249, 264, 265, 267, 268]

[CJR96]   Zhou Chaochen, Wang Ji, and Anders P. Ravn. A formal description of hybrid systems. In Rajeev Alur and Thomas A. Henzinger, editors, *Proceedings of the DIMACS/SYCON 1995 Workshop on Hybrid Systems III: Verification and Control*, volume 1066 of *Lecture Notes in Computer Science*, pages 511–530. Springer-Verlag, 1996. [375]

[CJRZ01]   Duncan Clarke, Thierry Jéron, Vlad Rusu, and Elena Zinovieva. Automated test and oracle generation for Smart-Card applications. In *Smart Card Programming and Security. Proceedings of the International Conference on Research in Smart Cards (E-smard 2001)*, volume 2140 of *Lecture Notes in Computer Science*, pages 58–70. Springer-Verlag, 2001. [424, 427, 439, 444, 446, 447, 448, 449, 450, 456, 458, 459]

[CJRZ02]   D. Clarke, T. Jéron, V. Rusu, and E. Zinovieva. STG: A symbolic test generation tool. In *Proceedings of the 8th International Conference on Tools and Algorithms for the Construction and Analysis of Systems (TACAS 2002)*, volume 2280 of *Lecture Notes in Computer Science*, pages 470–475. Springer-Verlag, 2002. [424, 426, 427]

[CJSP93]   H. Cho, S.-W. Jeong, F. Somenzi, and C. Pixley. Multiple observation time single reference test generation using synchronizing sequences. In *Proceedings of the European Conference on Design Automation (EDAC 1993) with the European Event in ASIC Design*, pages 494–498. IEEE Computer Society Press, February 1993. [7, 32]

[CKK02]   Karel Culik, Juhani Karhumäki, and Jarkko Kari. A note on synchronized automata and road coloring problem. In Werner Kuich, Grzegorz Rozenberg, and Arto Salomaa, editors, *Proceedings of the 5th International Conference on Developments in Language Theory (DLT 2001)*, volume 2295 of *Lecture Notes in Computer Science*, pages 175–185. Springer-Verlag, 2002. [6, 32]

[CL95]   Duncan Clarke and Insup Lee. Testing real-time constraints in a process algebraic setting. In *Proceedings of the 17th International Conference on Software Engineering (ICSE 1995)*, pages 51–60. ACM Press, 1995. [364]

[CL97a]   Duncan Clarke and Insup Lee. Automatic generation of tests for timing constraints from requirements. In *Proceedings of the 3rd International Workshop on Object-Oriented Real-Time Dependable Systems (WORDS 1997)*, pages 199–206. IEEE Computer Society Press, 1997. [364]

[CL97b]   Duncan Clarke and Insup Lee. Automatic test generation for the analysis of a real-time system: Case study. In *Proceedings of the 3rd IEEE Real-Time Technology and Applications Symposium (RTAS 1997)*, pages 112–124. IEEE Computer Society Press, 1997. [364, 366]

[Cla76]   Lori A. Clarke. A system to generate test data and symbolically execute programs. *IEEE Transactions on Software Engineering*, SE-2(3):215–222, September 1976. [339, 343]

[CLRS01]   Thomas H. Cormen, Charles E. Leiserson, Ronald L. Rivest, and Clifford Stein. *Introduction to Algorithms*. MIT Press and McGraw-Hill Book Company, Cambridge, MA, 2 edition, 2001. [16]

[CO00]   Rachel Cardell-Oliver. Conformance tests for real-time systems with timed automata specifications. *Formal Aspects of Computing*, 12(5):350–371, 2000. [221, 224, 228, 229, 230, 367]

[COG98]   Rachel Cardell-Oliver and Tim Glover. A practical and complete algorithm for testing real-time systems. In A. P. Ravn and H. Rischel, editors, *Proceedings of the 5th International Symposium on Formal Techniques in Real-Time and Fault-Tolerant Systems (FTRTFT 1998)*, volume 1486 of *Lecture Notes in Computer Science*, pages 251–261. Springer-Verlag, 1998. [221, 228]

[Coh]   S. Cohen. JTrek. Compaq, http://www.compaq.com/java/download/jtrek. [542]

[CPB98]   S. Barbey C. Peraire and D. Buchs. Test selection for object-oriented software based on formal specifications. In D. Gries and W. P. de Roever, editors, *Proceedings of the International Conference on Programming Concepts and Methods (PROCOMET 1998)*, volume 125 of *IFIP Conference Proceedings*, pages 385–403. Chapman and Hall, 1998. [348]

[CPHP87]   P. Caspi, D. Pilaud, N. Halbwachs, and J. A. Plaice. LUSTRE: A declarative language for programming synchronous systems. In *Conference Record of the 14th Annual ACM Symposium on Principles of Programming Languages (POPL 1987)*, pages 178–188, Munich, Germany, January 21–23, 1987. ACM SIGACT-SIGPLAN, ACM Press. [395]

[ČPR71]   Ján Černý, Alica Pirická, and Blanka Rosenauerová. On directable automata. *Kybernetika*, 7(4):289–298, 1971. [6, 31]

[CPS93]   R. Cleaveland, J. Parrow, and B. Steffen. The concurrency workbench: A semantics-based verification tool for finite state systems. *ACM Transactions on Programming Languages and Systems (TOPLAS)*, 15(1):36–72, January 1993. [575]

[CS92]   Rance Cleaveland and Bernhard Steffen. A linear-time model-checking algorithm for the alternation-free modal mu-calculus. In Kim G. Larsen and Arne Skou, editors, *Proceedings of the 3rd Conference on Computer Aided Verification (CAV 1991)*, volume 575, pages 48–58, Berlin, Germany, 1992. Springer-Verlag. [566]

[CSE96]   J. Callahan, F. Schneider, and S. Easterbrook. Specification-based testing using model checking. In *Proceedings of the 2nd SPIN Workshop 1996*, pages 193–207, 1996. [352]

[CSZ92]   R. Cleaveland, S. Smolka, and A. Zwarico. Testing preorders for probabilistic processes. In W. Kuich, editor, *Proceedings of the 19th International Colloquium on Automata, Languages and Programming (ICALP 1992)*, volume 623 of *Lecture Notes in Computer Science*, pages 708–719. Springer-Verlag, 1992. [233, 244, 246, 251, 262, 265, 267]

[DAV93]   K. Drira, P. Azéma, and F. Vernadat. Refusal graphs for conformance tester generation and simplification: A computational framework. In A. Danthine, G. Leduc, and P. Wolper, editors, *Proceedings of the 8th International Symposium on Protocol Specification, Testing and Verification (PSTV 1993)*, volume C-16 of *IFIP Transactions*, pages 257–272. North-Holland, 1993. [168, 170, 171]

[Dav02]   Gordon B. Davis. Anytime/anyplace computing and the future of knowledge work. *Communications of the ACM*, 45(12):67–73, December 2002. [525]

[DBG01]   Julia Dushina, Mike Benjamin, and Daniel Geist. Semi-formal test generation with Genevieve. In *Proceedings of the Design Automation Conference (DAC 2001)*, pages 617–622. ACM Press, 2001. [439, 443, 445, 447, 448, 449, 450, 454, 455, 456, 457, 459]

[dBORZ99]   Lydie du Bousquet, Farid Ouabdesselam, Jean-Luc Richier, and N. Zuanon. Lutess: A specification-driven testing environment for synchronous software. In *Proceedings of the 21st International Conference on Software Engineering (ICSE 1999)*, pages 267–276. ACM Press, 1999. [394, 395, 396, 398]

[dBRS+00]   L. du Bousquet, S. Ramangalahy, S. Simon, C. Viho, A. Belinfante, and R. G. de Vries. Formal test automation: The conference protocol with TGV/Torx. In H. Ural, R. L. Probert, and G. von Bochmann, editors, *Proceedings of the IFIP 13th International Conference on Testing of Communicating Systems (TestCom 2000)*, volume 176 of *IFIP Conference Proceedings*, pages 221–228. Kluwer Academic, 2000. [420, 421, 424, 435, 438, 444]

[dBZ99]   L. du Bousquet and N. Zuanon. An overview of Lutess, a specification-based tool for testing synchronous software. In *Proceedings of the 14th IEEE International Conference on Automated Software Engineering (ASE 1999)*, pages 208–215. IEEE Computer Society Press, October 1999. [435]

[Den91]   Richard Denney. Test-case generation from Prolog-based specifications. *IEEE Software*, 8(2):49–57, 1991. [334, 336]

[DF93]   Jeremy Dick and Alain Faivre. Automating the generation and sequencing of test cases from model-based specifications. In Jim C. P. Woodcock and Peter G. Larsen, editors, *Proceedings of the 1st International Symposium of Formal Methods Europe: Industrial-Strength Formal Methods (FME 1993)*, volume 670 of *Lecture Notes in Computer Science*, pages 268–284. Springer-Verlag, 1993. [328]

[DGJV01]   S. Dudani, J. Geada, G. Jakacki, and D. Vainer. Dynamic assertions using TXP. In K. Havelund and G. Roşu, editors, *Proceedings of the 1st Workshop on Run-time Verification (RV 2001)*, volume 55(2) of *Electronic Notes in Theoretical Computer Science*. Elsevier Science Publishers, 2001. [555]

[DGN02]   Z. R. Dai, J. Grabowski, and H. Neukirchen. Timed TTCN-3 – A Real-Time Extension for TTCN-3. In I. Schieferdecker, H. König, and A. Wolisz, editors, *Testing of Communicating Systems*, volume 14, Berlin, March 2002. Kluwer Academic. [505]

[DGNP04] Z. R. Dai, J. Grabowski, H. Neukirchen, and H. Pals. From design to test with UML. In R. Groz and R. Hierons, editors, *Proceedings of the 16th IFIP International Conference on Testing of Communication Systems (TestCom 2004)*, Lecture Notes in Computer Science, pages 33–49. Springer-Verlag, March 2004. [497]

[DH03a] F. Drewes and J. Högberg. Learning a regular tree language from a teacher. In Z. Ésik and Z. Fülöp, editors, *Proceedings of the 7th International Conference on Developments in Language Theory (DLT 2003)*, volume 2710 of *Lecture Notes in Computer Science*, pages 279–291. Springer-Verlag, 2003. [599]

[DH03b] F. Drewes and J. Högberg. Learning a regular tree language from a teacher even more efficiently. Technical Report 03.11, Umeå University, 2003. [599]

[DJ01] M. Ducasse and E. Jahier. Efficient automated trace analysis: Examples with morphine. In K. Havelund and G. Rosu, editors, *Proceedings of the 1st Workshop on Runtime Verification (RV 2001)*, volume 55(2) of *Electronic Notes in Theoretical Computer Science*. Elsevier Science Publishers, 2001. [555]

[DJC94] Michel Diaz, Guy Juanole, and Jean-Pierre Courtiat. Observer – a concept for formal on-line validation of distributed systems. *IEEE Transactions on Software Engineering*, 20(12):900–913, 1994. [531]

[DN84] J. Duran and S. C. Ntafos. An Evaluation of Random Testing. *IEEE Transactions on Software Engineering*, SE-10(4):438–444, July 1984. [302, 303, 306, 307, 308]

[dN87] Rocco de Nicola. Extensional equivalences for transition systems. *Acta Informatica*, 24:211–237, 1987. [127, 147]

[dNH84] Rocco de Nicola and Matthew Hennessy. Testing equivalences for processes. *Theoretical Computer Science*, 34:83–133, 1984. [123, 133, 134, 233, 258, 265]

[DS95] Jim Davies and Steve Schneider. A brief history of timed CSP. *Theoretical Computer Science*, 138(2):243–271, 1995. [360]

[DS03] D. Drusinsky and M. T. Shing. Monitoring temporal logic specifications combined with time series constraints. *Journal of Universal Computer Science*, 9(11):1261–1276, November 2003. [530]

[Duc90] M. Ducasse. Opium: An extendable trace analyser for Prolog. *The Journal of Logic Programming*, 39:177–223, 1990. [555]

[Duc99] M. Ducasse. Coca: An automated debugger for C. In *Proceedings of the 21st International Conference on Software Engineering (ICSE 1999)*, pages 504–513. ACM Press, 1999. [555]

[dVBF02] René G. de Vries, Axel Belinfante, and Jan Feenstra. Automated testing in practice: The highway tolling system. In Ina Schieferdecker, Harmut König, and Adam Wolisz, editors, *Proceedings of the IFIP 14th International Conference on Testing Communicating Systems (TestCom 2002)*, volume 210 of *IFIP Conference Proceedings*, pages 219–234. Kluwer Academic, 2002. [420, 424]

[dVT98] R. G. de Vries and J. Tretmans. On-the-fly conformance testing using Spin. In G. Holzmann, E. Najm, and A. Serhrouchni, editors, *Proceedings of the 4th Workshop on Automata Theoretic Verification with the Spin Model Checker (SPIN 1998)*, number 98 S 002 in ENST Technical Report, pages 115–128, Paris, France, November 1998. Ecole Nationale Supérieure des Télécommunications. [200, 423, 424]

[ECGN01] Michael D. Ernst, Jake Cockrell, William G. Griswold, and David Notkin. Dynamically discovering likely program invariants to support program evolution. *IEEE Transactions on Software Engineering*, 27(2):99–123, February 2001. [548, 549, 550, 554, 555]

[ECla] EClipse. http://www.eclipse.org/. [502]

[ECLb] Eclipse constraint logic programming system. http://www.icparc.ic.ac.uk/eclipse. [405]

[Eer94] E. H. Eertink. *Simulation Techniques for the Validation of LOTOS Specifications*. PhD thesis, University of Twente, Enschede, Netherlands, March 1994. [423, 424]

[EFM97] A. Engels, L. Feijs, and S. Mauw. Test generation for intelligent networks using model checking. In Ed Brinksma, editor, *Proceeedings of the 3rd International Workshop on Tools and Algorithms for Construction and Analysis of Systems (TACAS 1997)*, volume 1217 of *Lecture Notes in Computer Science*, pages 384–398. Springer-Verlag, 1997. [352]

[EGKN99] Michael D. Ernst, William G. Griswold, Yoshio Kataoka, and David Notkin. Dynamically discovering pointer-based program invariants. Technical Report UW-CSE-99-11-02, University of Washington, Seattle, WA, November 1999. [550]

[EH00] K. Etessami and G. J. Holzmann. Optimizing Büchi automata. In C. Palamidessi, editor, *Proceedings of 11th International Conference on Concurrency Theory (CONCUR 2000)*, volume 1877 of *Lecture Notes in Computer Science*, pages 153–167. Springer-Verlag, 2000. [567]

[EJ73] J. Edmonds and E. L. Johnson. Matching, Euler tours and the chinese postman. *Mathematical Programming*, 5:88–124, 1973. [92]

[EL85] E. Allen Emerson and Chin-Laung Lei. Modalities for model checking (extended abstract): Branching time strikes back. In *Conference Record of the 12th ACM SIGACT-SIGPLAN Symposium on Principles of Programming Languages (POPL 1985)*, pages 84–96. ACM Press, 1985. [565]

[Epp90] David Eppstein. Reset sequences for monotonic automata. *SIAM Journal on Computing*, 19(3):500–510, June 1990. [6, 7, 16, 25, 31, 32]

[EW92] E. H. Eertink and D. Wolz. Symbolic Execution of LOTOS Specifications. In M. Diaz and R. Groz, editors, *Proceedings of the 5th International Conference on Formal Description Techniques (FORTE 1992)*, pages 295–310. North-Holland, 1992. [423, 424]

[Fel68] W. Feller. *An Introduction to Probability Theory and Its Applications*. John Wiley and Sons, 1968. [236]

[FGK+96] J-C. Fernandez, H. Garavel, A. Kerbrat, R. Mateescu, L. Mounier, and M. Sighireanu. CADP: A protocol validation and verification toolbox. In Rajeev Alur and Thomas A. Henzinger, editors, *Proceedings of the 8th International Conference on Computer Aided Verification (CAV 1996)*, volume 1102 of *Lecture Notes in Computer Science*, pages 437–440. Springer-Verlag, 1996. [417, 419, 420, 423, 424]

[FGM+92] J.-C. Fernandez, H. Garavel, L. Mounier, A. Rasse, C. Rodriguez, and J. Sifakis. A toolbox for the verification of LOTOS programs. In *Proceedings of the 14th International Conference on Software Engineering (ICSE 1992)*, pages 246–259. ACM Press, 1992. [575]

[FHP02]   Eitan Farchi, Alan Hartman, and Shlomit Pinter. Using a model-based test generator to test for standard conformance. *IBM Systems Journal*, 41(1):89–110, 2002. [439, 444, 446, 447, 448, 449, 450, 454, 456, 457, 458, 459]

[FHS96]   A. Schmidt F. Huber, B. Schätz and K. Spies. Autofocus – A tool for distributed systems specification. In *Proceedings of the 4th International Symposium on Formal Techniques in Real-Time and Fault-Tolerant Systems (FTRTFT 1996)*, volume 1135 of *Lecture Notes in Computer Science*, pages 467–470. Springer-Verlag, 1996. [343]

[FJJV96]   J.-C. Fernandez, C. Jard, T. Jéron, and G. Viho. Using on-the-fly verification techniques for the generation of test suites. In Rajeev Alur and Thomas A. Henzinger, editors, *Proceedings of the 8th International Conference on Computer Aided Verification (CAV 1996)*, volume 1102 of *Lecture Notes in Computer Science*, pages 348–359, New Brunswick, NJ, USA, 1996. Springer-Verlag. [294, 417]

[FK00]   D. Freitag and N. Kushmerick. Boosted wrapper induction. In *Proceedings of the 17th National Conference on Artificial Intelligence (AAAI 2000) and 12th Conference on Innovative Applications of Artificial Intelligence (IAAI 2000)*, Austin, Texas, August 2000. American Association for Artificial Intelligence, The AAAI Press. Copublished and distributed by The MIT Press. [550]

[FKL99]   Lauret Fournier, Anatoly Koyfman, and Moshe Levinger. Developing an architecture validation suite – application to the PowerPC architecture. In *Proceedings of the 36th ACM Design Automation Conference (DAC 1999)*, pages 189–194. ACM Press, 1999. [439, 443, 446, 447, 448, 449, 451, 456, 457, 460]

[FKR+93]   Y. Freund, M. Kearns, D. Ron, R. Rubinfeld, R. Schapire, and L. Sellie. Efficient learning of typical finite automata from random walks. In *Proceedings of the 25th ACM Symposium on the Theory of Computing (STOC 1993)*, pages 315–324, New York, NY, 1993. ACM Press. [599]

[Fou03]   Apache Software Foundation. Byte code engineering library (BCEL). http://jakarta.apache.org/bcel/, 2003. Subproject of Jakarta. [530]

[Fra]   France Telecom R&D website. http://www.rd.francetelecom.com/. [410]

[Fri90]   Joel Friedman. On the road coloring problem. *Proceedings of the American Mathematical Society*, 110(4):1133–1135, December 1990. [6]

[FvBK+91]   S. Fujiwara, G. v. Bochmann, F. Khendek, M. Amalou, and A. Ghedamsi. Test selection based on finite state models. *IEEE Transactions on Software Engineering*, 17(6):591–603, June 1991. [96, 98, 101]

[FW88]   P. G. Frankl and E. J. Weyuker. An applicable family of data flow testing criteria. *IEEE Transactions on Software Engineering*, SE-14:1483–1498, October 1988. [297, 300]

[FW93]   P. G. Frankl and E. J. Weyuker. A formal analysis of the fault-detecting ability of testing methods. *IEEE Transactions on Software Engineering*, 19(3):202–213, 1993. [310]

[Gar98]   Hubert Garavel. OPEN/CAESAR: An open software architecture for verification, simulation, and testing. In B. Steffen, editor, *Proceedings of the 4th International Conference on Tools and Algorithms for the Construction and Analysis of Systems (TACAS 1998)*, volume 1384 of *Lecture Notes in Computer Science*, pages 68–84. Springer-Verlag, 1998. [419, 420, 423, 424]

[Gei01]   M. Geilen. On the construction of monitors for temporal logic properties. In K. Havelund and G. Roşu, editors, *Proceedings of the 1st International Workshop on Run-time Verification (RV 2001)*, volume 55(2) of *Electronic Notes in Theoretical Computer Science*. Elsevier Science Publishers, 2001. [555]

[GG75]   John B. Goodenough and Susan L. Gerhart. Toward a theory of test data selection. *IEEE Transactions on Software Engineering*, 1(2):156–173, June 1975. [88]

[GG93]   Matthias Grochtmann and Klaus Grimm. Classification trees for partition testing. *Software Testing, Verification and Reliability*, 3(2):63–82, 1993. [330]

[GGSV02]   Wolfgang Grieskamp, Yuri Gurevich, Wolfram Schulte, and Margus Veanes. Generating finite state machines from abstract state machines. In *Proceedings of the International Symposium on Software Testing and Analysis (ISSTA 2002)*, pages 112–122. ACM Press, 2002. [414]

[GH99]   A. Gargantini and C. Heitmeyer. Using model checking to generate tests from requirements specifications. In O. Nierstrasz and M. Lemoine, editors, *Proceedings of the 7th European Software Engineering Conference, held Jointly with the 7th ACM SIGSOFT Symposium on the Foundations of Software Enigneegin (ESEC/FSE 1999)*, volume 1687 of *Lecture Notes in Computer Science*, pages 146–163. Springer-Verlag, 1999. [352]

[GH03]   A. Goldberg and K. Havelund. Instrumentation of java bytecode for runtime analysis. In S. Eisenbach, G. T. Leavens, Peter Müller, A. Poetzsch-Heffter, and E. Poll, editors, *Proceedings of the 5th ECOOP Workshop on Formal Techniques for Java-like Programs (FTfJP 2003)*, pages 151–159, July 2003. Technical Report tr_408, ETH Zürich. [530]

[GHHD04]   Q. Guo, R. M. Hierons, M. Harman, and K. Derderian. Computing unique input/output sequences using genetic algorithms. In A. Petrenko and A. Ulrich, editors, *Proceedings of the 3rd International Workshop on Formal Approaches to Testing of Software (FATES 2003)*, volume 2931 of *Lecture Notes in Computer Science*, pages 164–177. Springer-Verlag, 2004. [84, 86]

[GHR93]   N. Götz, U. Herzog, and M. Rettelbach. Multiprocessor and distributed system design: The integration of functional specification and performance analysis using stochastic process algebras. In Lorenzo Donatiello and Randolph D. Nelson, editors, *Performance Evaluation of Computer and Communication Systems, Joint Tutorial Papers of Performance 1993 and Sigmetrics 1993*, volume 729 of *Lecture Notes in Computer Science*, pages 121–146. Springer-Verlag, 1993. [242]

[Gil61]   Arthur Gill. State-identification experiments in finite automata. *Information and Control*, 4(2–3):132–154, September 1961. [12, 24, 30, 36]

[Gin58]   Seymour Ginsburg. On the length of the smallest uniform experiment which distinguishes the terminal states of a machine. *Journal of the ACM (JACM)*, 5(3):266–280, July 1958. [8, 13, 30]

[GJ79]   M. R. Garey and D. S. Johnson. *Computers and Intractability. A Guide to the Theory of NP-completeness*. W. H. Freeman and Company, New York, 1979. [25, 28]

[GJL04]   O. Grinchtein, B. Jonsson, and M. Leucker. Learning of event-recording automata. Technical report, Uppsala University, 2004. [597, 599]

[GJS97]   J. Gosling, B. Joy, and G. Steele. *The Java Language Specification*. The Sunsoft Press Java Series. Addison-Wesley, New York, 1997. [444]

[GL02]   Hubert Garavel and Frédéric Lang. NTIF: A general symbolic model for communicating sequential processes with data. In Doron Peled and Moshe Y. Vardi, editors, *Proceedings on the 22nd IFIP/WG6.1 International Conference on Formal Techniques for Networked and Distributed Systems (FORTE 2002)*, volume 2529 of *Lecture Notes in Computer Science*, pages 276–291, Houston, Texas, USA, November 2002. Springer-Verlag. Full version available as INRIA Research Report RR-4666. [426, 427]

[GO01]   P. Gastin and D. Oddoux. Fast LTL to Büchi automata translation. In G. Berry, H. Comon, and A. Finkel, editors, *Proceedings of the 13th Conference on Computer Aided Verification (CAV 2001)*, volume 2102 of *Lecture Notes in Computer Science*, pages 53–65. Springer-Verlag, 2001. [567]

[Gog01]   Nicolae Goga. Comparing TorX, Autolink, TGV and UIO test algorithms. In Rick Reed and Jeanne Reed, editors, *Meeting UML – Proceedings of the 10th International SDL Forum, 2001*, volume 2078 of *Lecture Notes in Computer Science*, pages 379–402. Springer-Verlag, 2001. [433, 434]

[Göh98]   Wolf Göhring. Minimal initializing word: a contribution to Černý's conjecture. *Journal of Automata, Languages and Combinatorics*, 2(4):209–226, 1998. [6, 31]

[Gol89]   David E. Goldberg. *Genetic Algorithms in Search, Optimization & Machine Learning*. Addison-Wesley, 1989. [383]

[Gon01]   L. Gong. JXTA: A network programming environment. *IEEE Internet Computing*, 5(3):88–95, May/June 2001. [528]

[GPY02]   A. Groce, D. Peled, and M. Yannakakis. Adaptive model checking. In J.-P. Katoen and P. Stevens, editors, *Proceedings of the International Conference on Tools and Algorithms for the Construction and Analysis of Systems (TACAS 2002)*, volume 2280 of *Lecture Notes in Computer Science*, pages 357–370. Springer-Verlag, 2002. [599, 601, 602]

[GRMD01]   A. Q. Gates, S. Roach, O. Mondragon, and N. Delgado. DynaMICs: Comprehensive support for run-time monitoring. In K. Havelund and G. Rosu, editors, *Proceedings of the 1st International Workshop on Runtime Verification (RV 2001)*, volume 55(2) of *Electronic Notes in Theoretical Computer Science*. Elsevier Science Publishers, 2001. [555]

[GRR03]   A. Gargantini, E. Riccobene, and S. Rinzivillo. Using Spin to generate tests from ASM specifications. In E. Börger, A. Gargantini, and E. Riccobene, editors, *Proceedings of the 10th International Workshop on Abstract State Machines (ASM 2003)*, volume 2589 of *Lecture Notes in Computer Science*, pages 263–277. Springer-Verlag, 2003. [352]

[Gru68]   F. Gruenberger. *Computers and communication: Toward a computer utility*. Prentice-Hall, 1968. [554]

[GS97]   S. Graf and H. Saidi. Construction of abstract state graphs with PVS. In O. Grumberg, editor, *Proceedings of the 9th International Conference on Computer Aided Verification (CAV 1997)*, volume 1254 of *Lecture Notes in Computer Science*, pages 72–83, Haifa, Israel, 1997. Springer-Verlag. [287]

[GSDH97]   Jens Grabowski, Rudolf Scheuer, Zhen Ru Dai, and Dieter Hogrefe. Applying SAMSTAG to the B-ISDN protocol SSCOP. In M. Kim, S. Kang, and K. Hong, editors, *Proceedings of the 10th International Workshop on Testing of Communication Systems (IWTCS 1997)*. Chapman & Hall, 1997. [431, 433]

[GSSL99]   D. F. Gordon, W. M. Spears, O. Sokolsky, and Insup Lee. Distributed spatial control, global monitoring and steering of mobile physical agents. In *Proceedings of the IEEE International Conference on Information, Intelligence, and Systems (ICIIS 1999)*, pages 681–688. IEEE Computer Society Press, November 1999. [553]

[Gur94]   Yuri Gurevich. Evolving algebras 1993: Lipari Guide. In Egon Börger, editor, *Specification and Validation Methods*, pages 9–37. Oxford University Press, 1994. [1, 412, 414]

[Gut99]   W. Gutjahr. Partition testing versus random testing: The influence of uncertainty. *IEEE Transactions on Software Engineering*, 25(5):661–674, 1999. [302, 308]

[GW98]   Mathias Grochtmann and Joachim Wegener. Evolutionary testing of temporal correctness. In *Proceedings of the 2nd Software Quality Week Europe (QWE 1998)*, Brussel, Belgium, 1998. [383]

[Har87]   David Harel. Statecharts: A visual formalism for complex systems. *Science of Computer Programming*, 8(3):231–274, June 1987. [1]

[Har00]   Jerry J. Harrow, Jr. Runtime checking of multithreaded applications with visual threads. In K. Havelund, J. Penix, and W. Visser, editors, *SPIN Model Checking and Software Verification: Proceedings of the 7th International SPIN Workshop, 2000*, volume 1885 of *Lecture Notes in Computer Science*, pages 331–342. Springer-Verlag, 2000. [533]

[HCL+03]   Hyoung Seok Hong, Sung Deok Cha, Insup Lee, Oleg Sokolsky, and Hasan Ural. Data flow testing as model checking. In *Proceedings of the 25th International Conference on Software Engineering (ICSE 2003)*, pages 232–242. IEEE Computer Society Press, 2003. [352]

[HCRP91]   N. Halbwachs, P. Caspi, P. Raymond, and D. Pilaud. The synchronous dataflow programming language LUSTRE. *Proceedings of the IEEE*, 79(9):1305–1320, September 1991. [394, 395]

[Hen64]   F. C. Hennie. Fault detecting experiments for sequential circuits. In *Proceedings of the 5th Annual Symposium on Switching Circuit Theory and Logical Design*, pages 95–110, Princeton, New Jersey, 11–13 November 1964. IEEE Computer Society Press. [24, 101, 104]

[Hen88]   M. Hennessy. *Algebraic Theory of Processes*. MIT Press, Cambridge, 1988. [183]

[Hen96]   Thomas A. Henzinger. The theory of hybrid automata. In *Proceedings of the 11th Annual Symposium on Logic in Computer Science (LICS 1996)*, pages 278–292. IEEE Computer Society Press, 1996. [375]

[HFT00]   L. Heerink, J. Feenstra, and J. Tretmans. Formal Test Automation: The Conference Protocol with PHACT. In H. Ural, R. L. Probert, and G. von Bochmann, editors, *Proceedings of the 13th IFIP International Conference on Testing of Communicating Systems (TestCom 2000)*, pages 211–220. Kluwer Academic, 2000. [410, 435, 437, 444]

[HHK96]   R. H. Hardin, Zvi Har'El, and Robert P. Kurshan. COSPAN. In Rajeev Alur and Thomas A. Henzinger, editors, *Proceedings of the 8th International Conference on Computer Aided Verification (CAV 1996)*, volume 1102 of *Lecture Notes in Computer Science*, pages 423–427. Springer-Verlag, 1996. [575]

[HHWT97]   T. A. Henzinger, P.-H. Ho, and H. Wong-Toi. HyTech: A model checker for hybrid systems. *Sotftware Tools for Technology Transfer*, 1(1–2):110–122, 1997. [426, 427]

[Hib61]   Thomas N. Hibbard. Least upper bounds on minimal terminal state experiments for two classes of sequential machines. *Journal of the ACM (JACM)*, 8(4):601–612, October 1961. [8, 14, 21, 30]

[Hil96]   Jane Hillston. *A compositional approach to performance modelling*. Cambridge University Press, 1996. [242]

[HJGP99]   Wai-Ming Ho, Jean-Marc Jézéquel, Alain Le Guennec, and François Pennaneac'h. UMLAUT: An extendible UML transformation framework. In *Proceedings of the 14th IEEE International Conference on Automated Software Engineering (ASE 1999)*, pages 275–278, Florida, 1999. IEEE Computer Society Press. [419, 420]

[HJL96]   C. Heitmeyer, R. Jeffords, and B. Labaw. Automated Consistency Checking of Requirements Specifications. *ACM Transactions on Software Engineering and Methodology*, 5(3):231–261, July 1996. [1]

[HJL03]   John Hakansson, Bengt Jonsson, and Ola Lundqvist. Generating on-line test oracles from temporal logic specifications. *International Journal on Software Tools for Technology Transfer*, 4(4):456–471, 2003. [555]

[HK87]   Z. Har'El and R. P. Kurshan. *COSPAN User Guide*. AT&T Bell Laboratories, October 1987. [575]

[HKWT95]   Thomas A. Henzinger, Peter W. Kopke, and Howard Wong-Toi. The expressive power of clocks. In *Automata, Languages and Programming*, volume 944 of *Lecture Notes in Computer Science*, pages 417–428. Springer-Verlag, 1995. [203]

[HL02a]   Sudheendra Hangal and Monica S. Lam. Tracking down software bugs using automatic anomaly detection. In *Proceedings of the 24th International Conference on Software Engineering (ICSE 2002)*, pages 291–301. ACM Press, 2002. [551, 552, 554]

[HL02b]   R. Hightower and N. Lesiecki. *Java Tools for eXtreme Programming*. Wiley Computer Publishing. John Wiley & Sons, 2002. [501]

[HLSU02]   H. S. Hong, I. Lee, O. Sokolsky, and H. Ural. A temporal logic based theory of test coverage and generation. In J.-P. Katoen and P. Stevens, editors, *Proceedings of the 8th International Conference on Tools and Algorithms for the Construction and Analysis of Systems (TACAS 2002)*, volume 2280 of *Lecture Notes in Computer Science*, pages 327–341. Springer-Verlag, 2002. [352]

[HM80]   M. Henessy and R. Milner. Observing nondeterminism and concurrency. In J. de Bakker and M. van Leeuwen, editors, *Proceedings of the 7th International Colloquium on Automata, Languages, and Programming (ICALP 1980)*, volume 85 of *Lecture Notes in Computer Science*, pages 299–309. Springer-Verlag, 1980. [129]

[HM85]   Matthew Hennessy and Robin Milner. Algebraic laws for nondeterminism and concurrency. *Journal of the ACM*, 32(1):137–161, 1985. [271, 565]

[HME03]   Michael Harder, Jeff Mellen, and Michael D. Ernst. Improving test suites via operational abstraction. In *Proceedings of the 25th International Conference on Software Engineering (ICSE 2003)*, pages 60–71, Portland, Oregon, 2003. IEEE Computer Society Press. [548]

[HMP92]   Thomas A. Henzinger, Zohar Manna, and Amir Pnueli. What good are digital clocks? In *Proceedings of the 19th International Colloquium on Automata, Languages, and Programming (ICALP 1992)*, volume 632 of *Lecture Notes in Computer Science*, pages 545–558. Springer-Verlag, 1992. [201]

[HN83]   M. Hennessy and R. De Nicola. Testing equivalences for processes. In *Proceedings of the 10th Interantional Colloquium on Automata, Languages and Programming (ICALP 1983)*, 1983. [114, 208, 210]

[HN99]   A. Hartman and K. Nagin. TCBeans, software test toolkit. In *Proceedings of the 12th International Software Quality Week (QW 1999)*, 1999. [445, 450]

[HNS97]   Steffen Helke, Thomas Neustupny, and Thomas Santen. Automating test case generation from Z specifications with Isabelle. In Jonathan P. Bowen, Michael G. Hinchey, and David Till, editors, *Proceedings of the 10th International Conference of Z Users: The Z Formal Specification Notation (ZUM 1997)*, volume 1212 of *Lecture Notes in Computer Science*, pages 52–71. Springer-Verlag, 1997. [327, 328, 329, 330, 331]

[HNS03]   H. Hungar, O. Niese, and B. Steffen. Domain-specific optimization in automata learning. In W. A. Hunt Jr. and F. Somenzi, editors, *Proceedings of the 15th International Conference on Computer Aided Verification (CAV 2003)*, Lecture Notes in Computer Science, pages 315–327. Springer-Verlag, 2003. [595, 597]

[HNSY92]   Thomas A. Henzinger, Xavier Nicollin, Joseph Sifakis, and Sergio Yovine. Symbolic model checking for real-time systems. In *Proceedings of the 7th Symposium of Logics in Computer Science (LICS 1992)*, pages 394–406, Santa Cruz, California, 1992. IEEE Computer Scienty Press. [203]

[Hoa85]   C. A. R. Hoare. *Communicating Sequential Processes*. International Series in Computer Science. Prentice-Hall, 1985. [360]

[Hol91]   Gerard J. Holzmann. *Design and Validation of Protocols*. Prentice-Hall Software Series, 990157918X. Prentice-Hall, Englewood Cliffs, N. J., 1991. [3, 91, 92, 423]

[Hol97]   G. J. Holzmann. The model checker SPIN. *IEEE Transactions on Software Engineering*, 23(5):279–295, 1997. [575]

[Hol01]   G. Holzmann. From code to models. In *Proceedings of the 2nd International Conference on Applications of Concurrency to System Design (ACSD 2001)*, pages 3–10. IEEE Computer Society Press, 2001. [287]

[Hop71]   J. E. Hopcroft. An $n \log n$ algorithm for minimizing states in a finite automaton. In Z. Kohavi and A. Paz, editors, *Proceedings of the International Symposium on Theory of Machines and Computations, 1971*, pages 189–196, New York, 1971. Academic Press. [65, 66, 612, 613]

[How77]   W. Howden. Symbolic testing and the dissect symbolic evaluation system. *IEEE Trans. on Software Engineering*, SE-3(4):266–278, July 1977. [343]

[HPPS03a] G. Hahn, J. Philipps, A. Pretschner, and T. Stauner. Prototype-based tests for hybrid reactive systems. In *Proceedings of the 14th IEEE International Workshop on Rapid System Prototyping (RSP 2003)*, pages 78–86. IEEE Computer Society Press, 2003. [378, 379, 380]

[HPPS03b] G. Hahn, J. Phillips, A. Pretschner, and T. Stauner. Tests for mixed discrete-continuous reactive systems. Technical Report TUM-I0301, Institut für Informatik, TU München, 2003. [378]

[HR01a]   K. Havelund and G. Roşu. Monitoring Java programs with Java PathExplorer. In K. Havelund and G. Roşu, editors, *Proceedings of the 1st Workshop on Runtime Verificaton (RV 2001)*, volume 55(2) of *Electronic Notes in Theoretical Computer Science*. Elsevier Science Publishers, 2001. [555]

[HR01b]   Klaus Havelund and Grigore Roşu. Java PathExplorer – a runtime verifica-
          tion tool. In *Proceedings of the 6th International Symposium on Artificial
          Intelligence, Robotics and Automation in Space (i-SAIRAS 2001): A New
          Space Odyssey*. 2001. Montreal, Canada. [526, 533]

[HR02]   K. Havelund and G. Roşu. Synthesizing monitors for safety properties. In
          J.-P. Katoen and P. Stevens, editors, *Proceedings of the 8th International
          Conference on Tools and Algorithms for the Construction and Analysis of
          Systems (TACAS 2002)*, volume 2280 of *Lecture Notes in Computer Science*,
          pages 324–356. Springer-Verlag, 2002. [538]

[HR04]   K. Havelund and G. Roşu. An overview of the runtime verification tool
          Java PathExplorer. *Formal Methods in System Design*, 24(2):189–215, 2004.
          [536, 552]

[HSE97]   F. Huber, B. Schätz, and G. Einert. Consistent graphical specification of
          distributed systems. In *Proceedings of the 4th International Symposium
          of Formal Methods Europe (FME 1997)*, volume 1313 of *Lecture Notes in
          Computer Science*, pages 122–141. Springer-Verlag, 1997. [406]

[Hsi71]   E. P. Hsieh. Checking experiments for sequential machines. *IEEE Transac-
          tions on Computers*, C-20:1152–1166, October 1971. [69, 72]

[HT90]   D. Hamlet and R. Taylor. Partition test does not inspire confidence. *IEEE
          Transactions on Software Engineering*, 16(12):1402–1411, December 1990.
          [302, 305]

[HT92]   Dung T. Huynh and Lu Tian. On some equivalence relations for probabilis-
          tic processes. *Fundamenta Informaticae*, 17:211–234, 1992. [274]

[HU79]   J. Hopcroft and J. Ullman. *Introduction to automata theory, languages and
          computation*. Addison-Wesley, 1979. [197]

[IBM]   IBM. Gotcha users guide – release 4.0.0. [445]

[ID84]   M. Ito and Jürgen Duske. On cofinal and definite automata. *Acta Cyber-
          netica*, 6(2):181–189, 1984. [6]

[Ins03]   ETSI (European Telecommunication Standards Institute). The testing and
          test control notation version 3. In *Methods for Testing and Specification
          (MTC)*. ETSI, 2003. [467, 468, 480, 486, 497, 501]

[IS95]   Balázs Imreh and Magnus Steinby. Some remarks on directable automata.
          Acta Cybernetica, 12(1):23–35, 1995. [19, 31]

[IS99]   Balázs Imreh and Magnus Steinby. Directable nondeterministic automata.
          Acta Cybernetica, 14(1):105–115, 1999. [32]

[ISO88]   ISO/IEC. LOTOS – a formal description technique based on the temporal
          ordering of observational behaviour. International Standard 8807, Interna-
          tional Organization for Standardization – Information Processing Systems
          – Open Systems Interconnection, Genève, September 1988. [163, 417, 423]

[ISO94]   ISO/IEC. Information technology – open systems interconnection – confor-
          mance testing methodology and framework, 1994. International ISO/IEC
          multi-part standard No. 9646. [500]

[ISO02]   ISO/IEC. Information technology – Z formal specification notation – syn-
          tax, type system, and semantics. International Organization for Standard-
          ization ISO/IEC 13568, 2002. [325, 327]

[ITU99]   ITU. ITU-T recommendation Z.120: Message sequence charts (MSC). ITU
          Telecommunication Standard Sector, Geneva (Switzerland), 1999. [468]

[ITU02]   ITU. The evolution of TTCN.
          http://www.itu.int/ITU-T/studygroups/com07/ttcn.html, 2002. [465]

[JBu]   JBuilder. http://www.borland.com/jbuilder/personal/index.html. [502]

[JG90]   F. Jahanian and A. Goyal. A formalism for monitoring real-time constraints at run-time. In *Proceedings of the 20th International Symposium on Fault-Tolerant Computing Systems (FTCS 1990)*, pages 148–155, 1990. [531]

[JGL91]   Bengt Jonsson and Kim Guldstrand Larsen. Specification and refinement of probabilistic processes. In *Proceedings of the 6th IEEE International Symposium on Logic in Computer Science (LICS 1991)*, pages 266–277. IEEE Computer Society Press, 1991. [234, 269]

[JJ02]   Claude Jard and Thierry Jéron. TGV: Theory, principles and algorithms. In *Proceedings of the 6th World Conference on Integrated Design and Process Technology (IDPT 2002)*. Society for Design and Process Science, June 2002. [417, 420]

[Jon91]   Bengt Jonsson. Simulations between specifications of distributed systems. In *Proceedings of the 2nd International Conference on Concurrency Theory (CONCUR 1991)*, volume 527 of *Lecture Notes in Computer Science*, pages 346–360. Springer-Verlag, 1991. [256, 269]

[JUn]   JUnit. http://www.junit.org/. [501]

[JY95]   Bengt Jonsson and Wang Yi. Compositional testing preorders for probabilistic processes. In *Proceedings of the 10th IEEE International Symposium on Logic in Computer Science (LICS 1995)*, pages 431–441. IEEE Computer Society Press, 1995. [234, 252, 255, 265]

[JY02]   Bengt Jonsson and Wang Yi. Testing preorders for probabilistic processes can be characterized by simulations. *Theoretical Computer Science*, 282(1):33–51, 2002. [234, 244, 245, 252, 255, 256, 265, 269]

[Kar03]   Jarkko Kari. Synchronizing finite automata on eulerian digraphs. *Theoretical Computer Science*, 295(1–3):223–232, 2003. [31, 32]

[KCS98]   K. Narayan Kumar, Rance Cleaveland, and Scott Smolka. Infinite probabilistic and non-probabilistic testing. In *Proceedings of the 18th Conference on Foundations of Software Technology and Theoretical Computer Science (FSTTCS 1998)*, volume 1530 of *Lecture Notes in Computer Science*, pages 209–220. Springer-Verlag, 1998. [234, 244]

[Kel76]   Robert M. Keller. Formal verification of parallel programs. *Commun. ACM*, 19(7):371–384, 1976. [113]

[Kfo70]   Denis J. Kfoury. Synchronizing sequences for probabilistic automata. *Studies in Applied Mathematics*, 49(1):101–103, March 1970. [32]

[KGHS98]   B. Koch, J. Grabowski, D. Hogrefe, and M. Schmitt. AutoLink – a tool for automatic test generation from SDL specifications. In *Proceedings of the IEEE International Workshop on Industrial Strength Formal Specification Techniques (WIFT 1998)*, October 1998. [431, 432, 433]

[KHMP94]   Arjun Kapun, Thomas A. Henzinger, Zohar Manna, and Amir Pnueli. Proving safety properties of hybrid systems. In Hans Langmaack, Willem P. de Roever, and Jan Vytopil, editors, *Proceedings of the 3rd International Symposium on Formal Techniques in Real-Time and Fault-Tolerant Systems (FTRTFT 1994)*, volume 863 of *Lecture Notes in Computer Science*, pages 431–454. Springer-Verlag, 1994. [375]

[Kin76]   James C. King. Symbolic execution and program testing. *Communications of the ACM*, 19(7):385–394, July 1976. [338, 342]

[KJG99]   A. Kerbrat, T. Jéron, and R. Groz. Automated test generation from SDL specifications. In R. Dssouli, G. von Bochmann, and Y. Lahav, editors, *The Next Millennium – Proceedings of the 9th SDL Forum, 1999)*, pages 135–152. Elsevier Science Publishers, 1999. [419, 420]

[KKL+01] M. Kim, S. Kannan, I. Lee, O. Sokolsky, and M. Viswanathan. Java-MaC: A run-time assurance tool for Java programs. In *Proccedings of the 1st International Workshop on Run-Time Verification (RV 2001)*, volume 55(2) of *Electronic Notes in Theoretical Computer Science*. Elsevier Science Publishers, July 2001. [526, 542]

[KKL+02] M. Kim, S. Kannan, I. Lee, M. Viswanathan, and O. Sokolsky. Computational analysis of run-time monitoring. In K. Havelund and G. Roşu, editors, *Proccedings of the 2nd Workshop on Run-Time Verification (RV 2002)*, volume 70(4). Elsevier Science Publishers, 2002. [547, 553]

[KKLS01] Moonjoo Kim, Sampath Kannan, Insup Lee, and Oleg Sokolsky. Java-MaC: a run-time assurance tool for Java. In *Prodeedings of the 1st International Workshop on Run-time Verification (RV 2001)*, volume 55 of *Electronic Notes in Theoretical Computer Science*, Paris, France, July 2001. Elsevier Science Publishers. [530]

[KLS+02] M. Kim, I. Lee, U. Sammapun, J. Shin, and O. Sokolsky. Monitoring, checking, and steering of real-time systems. In K. Havelund and G. Roşu, editors, *Proceedings of the 2nd Workshop on Run-time Verification (RV 2002)*, volume 70(4) of *Electronic Notes in Theoretical Computer Science*. Elsevier Science Publishers, 2002. [547, 553, 555]

[KMP+95] W. Kelly, V. Maslov, W. Pugh, E. Rosser, T. Shpiesman, and D. Wonnacott. The Omega library interface guide. Technical Report UMIACS-TR-95-41, University of Maryland at College Park, 1995. http://www.cs.umd.edu/projects/omega/. [426, 427]

[Koh78] Zvi Kohavi. *Switching and Finite Automata Theory*. McGraw-Hill, New York, NY, second edition, 1978. [30, 31, 39, 40, 46, 67, 69, 70, 72, 160]

[Kop97] Hermann Kopetz. *Real-Time Systems – Design Principles for Distributed Embedded Applications*. Kluwer Academic, 1997. ISBN: 0-7923-9894-7. [384]

[Koz77] Dexter Kozen. Lower bounds for natural proof systems. In *Proceedings of the 18th Annual Symposium on Foundations of Computer Science (FOCS 1977)*, pages 254–266, Providence, Rhode Island, October 1977. IEEE Computer Society Press. [28, 48]

[Koz83] D. Kozen. Results on the propositional μ-calculus. *Theoretical Computer Science*, 27:333–354, December 1983. [566]

[KPN] KPN website. http://www.kpn.com/. [408]

[KPV03] Sarfraz Khurshid, Corina S. Pasareanu, and Willem Visser. Generalized symbolic execution for model checking and testing. In *Proceedings of the 9th International Conference on Tools and Algorithms for the Construction and Analysis of Systems*, 2003. [342, 349, 351]

[KRS87] A. A. Klyachko, I. K. Rystsov, and M. A. Spivak. An extremal combinatorial problem associated with the bound on the length of a synchronizing word in an automaton. *Kibernetika*, 25(2):165–171, March–April 1987. Translation from Russian. [6, 19, 31]

[KS76] J. G. Kemeny and J. L. Snell. *Finite Markov Chains*. Springer-Verlag, 1976. [237]

[KSW96] Kolyang, Thomas Santen, and Burkhart Wolff. A structure preserving encoding of Z in Isabelle/HOL. In Joakim von Wright, Jim Grundy, and John Harrison, editors, *Proceedings of the 9th International Conference on Theorem Proving in Higher Order Logics (TPHOLs 1996)*, volume 1125 of *Lecture Notes in Computer Science*, pages 283–298. Springer-Verlag, 1996. [328]

[KV94]   M. J. Kearns and U. V. Vazirani. *An Introduction to Computational Learning Theory*. The MIT Press, Cambridge, Massachusetts and London, England, 1994. [590, 595]

[KVZ98]   Hakim Kahlouche, Cesar Viho, and Massimo Zendri. An industrial experiment in automatic generation of executable test suites for a cache coherency protocol. In A. Petrenko and N. Yevtushenko, editors, *Proceedings of the 11th IFIP/TC6 International Workshop on Testing of Communicating Systems (TestCom 1998)*. Chapman & Hall, September 1998. [439, 443, 445, 447, 448, 449, 450, 455, 456, 458, 460]

[Kwa62]   Mei-Ko Kwan. Graphic programming using odd or even points. *Chinese Math*, 1:273–277, 1962. [92]

[Lai02]   Richard Lai. A survey of communication protocol testing. *Journal of Systems and Software*, 62(1):21–46, May 2002. [3]

[Lal85]   P. Lala. *Fault Tolerant and Fault Testable Hardware Design*. Prentice-Hall International, 1985. [70]

[Lan90]   Rom Langerak. A testing theory for lotos using deadlock detection. In Ed Brinksma, Giuseppe Scollo, and Chris A. Vissers, editors, *Proceedings of the IFIP/WG6.1 9th International Symposium on Protocol Specification, Testing and Verification (PSTV 1989)*, pages 87–98. North-Holland, 1990. [141, 142]

[LBGG94]   I. Lee, P. Brémond-Grégoire, and R. Gerber. A process algebraic approach to the specification and analysis of resource-bound real-time systems. *Proceedings of the IEEE*, 82(1):158–171, January 1994. [360]

[LDW03]   Tessa Lau, Pedro Domingos, and Daniel S. Weld. Learning programs from traces using version space algebra. In *Proceedings of the International Conference on Knowledge Capture (K-CAP 2003)*, Sanibel Island, FL, USA, 2003. ACM Press. [552]

[Lit]   Lite ftp and web sites. ftp://ftp.cs.utwente.nl/pub/src/lotos-tools/ and http://fmt.cs.utwente.nl/tools/lite/. [414, 417]

[LKK+99]   I. Lee, S. Kannan, M. Kim, O. Sokolsky, and M. Viswanathan. Runtime assurance based on formal specifications. In Hamid R. Arabnia, editor, *Proceedings of the International Conference on Parallel and Distributed Processing Techniques and Applications (PDPTA 1999), Volume 1*, pages 279–287. CSREA Press, 1999. [542, 546]

[LLC03]   Glen McCluskey & Associates LLC. Java^{tm} test coverage and instrumentation toolkits. http://www.glenmccl.com/, 2003. [530]

[LP81]   H. R. Lewis and C. H. Papadimitriou. *Elements of the Theory of Computation*. Prentice-Hall, Englewood Cliffs, 1981. [92]

[LP01]   B. Legeard and F. Peureux. Génération de séquences de tests à partir d'une spécification B en PLC ensembliste. In *Actes des Approches Formelles dans l'Assistance au Développement de Logiciels (AFADL 2001)*, pages 113–130, June 2001. [339, 344, 349]

[LPU02]   B. Legeard, F. Peureux, and M. Utting. Automated Boundary Testing from Z and B. In *Proceedings of the International Conference on Formal Methods Europe (FME 2002)*, volume 2391 of *Lecture Notes in Computer Science*, pages 21–40, Copenhagen, Denmark, July 2002. Springer-Verlag. [339, 344]

[LPU04]   B. Legeard, F. Peureux, and M. Utting. Controlling test case explosion in test generation from B formal models. *Software Testing, Verification and Reliability (STVR)*, 14(2):81–103, 2004. [344]

[LPY97]   Kim Guldstrand Larsen, Paul Pettersson, and Wang Yi. UPPAAL in a
nutshell. *International Journal on Software Tools for Technology Transfer*,
1(1–2):134–152, 1997. [221, 367]

[LS91]   Kim G. Larsen and Arne Skou. Bisimulation through probabilistic testing.
Information and Computation, 94:1–28, 1991. [244, 252, 270, 271, 272, 273]

[LSV01]   Nancy A. Lynch, Roberto Segala, and Frits W. Vaandrager. Hybrid I/O
automata revisited. In Maria Domenica Di Benedetto and Alberto L.
Sangiovanni-Vincentelli, editors, *Proceedings of the 4th International Workshop on Hybrid Systems: Computation and Control (HSCC 2001)*, volume
2034 of *Lecture Notes in Computer Science*, pages 403–417. Springer-Verlag,
2001. [375]

[LSW97]   K. G. Larsen, B. Steffen, and C. Weise. Continuous modelling of real time
and hybrid systems: From concepts to tools. *International Journal on Software Tools for Technology Transfer*, 1(1–2):64–85, 1997. [375]

[LT87]   N. Lynch and M. Tuttle. Hierarchical correctness proofs for distributed algorithms. In *Proceedings of the 6th ACM Symposium on Principles of Distributed Computing (PODC 1987)*, pages 137–151. ACM Press, 1987. Also:
Technical Report MIT/LCS/TM-387, Massachusetts Institute of Technology, Cambridge, U.S.A., 1987. [173, 175]

[LT89]   N. A. Lynch and M. R. Tuttle. An introduction to Input/Output Automata.
CWI Quarterly, 2(3):219–246, 1989. Also: Technical Report MIT/LCS/TM-
373 (TM-351 revised), Massachusetts Institute of Technology, Cambridge,
U.S.A., 1988. [175, 176]

[LvBP94]   G. Luo, G. von Bochmann, and A. Petrenko. Selecting test sequences for
partially-specified non deterministic finite state machines. In *Proceedings of
the 7th International Workshop on Protocol Test Systems (IWPTS 1994)*,
pages 91–106, Japan, February 1994. [191]

[LY94]   David Lee and Mihalis Yannakakis.   Testing finite-state machines:
State identification and verification. *IEEE Transactions on Computers*,
43(3):306–320, March 1994. [3, 29, 39, 40, 46, 48, 49, 50, 55, 59, 62, 63, 64,
65, 66, 67, 69, 72, 75, 79, 86, 611]

[LY96]   David Lee and Mihalis Yannakakis. Principles and methods of testing finite
state machines – a survey. *Proceedings of the IEEE*, 84(8):1090–1126, 1996.
[3, 12, 31, 40, 67, 80, 87, 88, 89, 93, 107, 611]

[MA00]   B. Marre and A. Arnould. Test sequence generation from lustre descriptions: GATEL. In *Proceedings of the 15th IEEE International Conference
on Automated Software Engineering (ASE 2000)*, Grenoble, 2000. IEEE
Computer Society Press. [402]

[Mah99]   Savi Maharaj. Towards a method of test case extraction from correctness
proofs. Presented at the *14th International Workshop on Algebraic Development Techniques (WADT 1999)*, 1999. [336, 337, 338]

[Mah00]   Savi Maharaj. Test case extraction from correctness proofs. University of
Stirling, 2000. Case for Support. [336]

[ME03]   Stephen McCamant and Michael D. Ernst. Predicting problems caused by
component upgrades. In *Proceedings of the 9th European Software Engineering Conference (ESEC 2003)*. Held jointly with the *11th ACM SIG-
SOFT International Symposium on Foundations of Software Engineering
(FSE 2003)*, pages 287–296. ACM Press, 2003. [550, 554]

[Mel88]   Thomas Melham. Abstraction mechanisms for hardware verification. In
            G. Birtwistle and P. A. Subrahmanyam, editors, *VLSI Specification, Verifi-
            cation, and Synthesis*, volume 35 of *The Kluwer International Series in En-
            gineering and Computer Science*, pages 129–157. Kluwer Academic, Boston,
            1988. [455]

[Mey79]   G. Meyer. *The Art of Software Testing*. John Wiley & Sons, Inc., 1979.
            [297]

[Mey92]   Bertrand Meyer. Design by contract. *IEEE Computer*, 25(10):40–52, Oc-
            tober 1992. [531]

[Mey01]   Oliver Meyer. *Structural Decomposition of Timed-CSP and its Application
            in Real-Time Testing*. Dissertation, University of Bremen, 2001. Number
            16 in *Monographs of the Bremen Institute of Safe Systems*. [360]

[MH99]   V. Matena and M. Hapner. Enterprise javabeans^{TM} specification. Public
            Draft version 1.1, Sun Microsystems, 1999. [528]

[Mil80]   R. Milner. *A Calculus for Communicating Processes*, volume 92 of *Lecture
            Notes in Computer Science*. Springer-Verlag, 1980. [119, 129, 145]

[Mil89]   Robin Milner. *Communication and concurrency*. Prentice-Hall, 1989. [362,
            565, 602]

[MK99]   Jeff Magee and Jeff Kramer. *Concurrency: State Models & Java Programs*.
            John Wiley & Sons, 1999. [423, 424]

[ML97]   Aloysius K. Mok and Guangtian Liu. Efficient run-time monitoring of tim-
            ing constraints. In *IEEE Real-Time Technology and Applications Sympo-
            sium*, June 1997. [531]

[Moo56]   Edward F. Moore. Gedanken-experiments on sequential machines. In C. E.
            Shannon and J. McCarthy, editors, *Automata Studies*, number 34 in An-
            nals of Mathematics Studies, pages 129–153. Princeton University Press,
            Princeton, NJ, 1956. [12, 13, 22, 30, 36, 39, 89]

[MOSS99]   M. Müller-Olm, D. Schmidt, and B. Steffen. Model checking: A tutorial
            introduction. In G. File A. Cortesi, editor, *Proceedings of the 6th Static
            Analysis Symposium (SAS'99)*, volume 1694 of *Lecture Notes in Computer
            Science*, pages 330–354, Heidelberg, Germany, September 1999. Springer-
            Verlag. [560]

[MP93]   R. Miller and S. Paul. On the generation of minimal-length conformance
            tests for communication protocols. *IEEE/ACM Transactions on Network-
            ing*, 1(1):116–129, February 1993. [72, 76]

[MP95]   O. Maler and A. Pnueli. On the learnability of infinitary regular sets.
            Information and Computation, 118(2):316–326, 1 May 1995. [599]

[MP05]   Leonardo Mariani and Mauro Pezzè. Behavior capture and test: Auto-
            mated analysis of component integration. In *Proceedings of the 10th IEEE
            International Conference on the Engineering of Complex Computer Systems
            (ICECCS 2005)*, Shanghai, China, June 2005. [551, 554]

[MRS+97]   J. R. Moonen, J. M. T. Romijn, O. Sies, J. G. Springintveld, L. G. M. Feijs,
            and R. L. C. Koymans. A two-level approach to automated conformance
            testing of VHDL designs. Technical Report SEN-R9707, CWI – Centrum
            voor Wiskunde en Informatica, Amsterdam, 1997. [410]

[MS99]   Alexandru Mateescu and Arto Salomaa. Many-valued truth functions,
            černý's conjecture and road coloring. *Bulletin of the EATCS*, 68:134–150,
            June 1999. [32]

[MSF]   Microsoft Research – Foundations of Software Engineering.
            http://research.microsoft.com/fse/. [412]

[Müh97]   H. Mühlenbein. Genetic algorithms. In E. Aarts and J. K. Lenstra, editors, *Local Search in Combinatorial Optimization*, pages 137–171. John Wiley & Sons, 1997. [84]

[Mus93]   J. D. Musa. Operational profiles in software-reliability engineering. *IEEE Software*, 10(2):14–32, March 1993. [394]

[Nai97]   K. Naik. Efficient computation of unique input/output sequences in finite-state machines. *IEEE/ACM Transactions on Networking*, 5(4):585–599, August 1997. [69, 72, 76, 77, 78, 79, 83, 84, 86]

[Nat86]   B. K. Natarajan. An algorithmic approach to the automated design of parts orienters. In *Proceedings of the 27th Annual Symposium on Foundations of Computer Science (FOCS 1986)*, pages 132–142, Toronto, Ontario, Canada, October 1986. IEEE. [7, 32]

[NdFL95]   Manuel Nuthez, David de Frutos, and Luis Llana. Acceptance trees for probabilistic processes. In Insup Lee and Scott A. Smolka, editors, *Proceedings of the 6th International Conference on Concurrency Theory (CONCUR 1995)*, volume 962 of *Lecture Notes in Computer Science*, pages 249–263. Springer-Verlag, 1995. [234]

[NH84]   R. De Nicola and M. C. B. Hennessy. Testing equivalences for processes. *Theoretical Computer Science*, 34:83–133, 1984. [179]

[Nie00]   B. Nielsen. *Speification and Test of Real-Time Systems*. PhD thesis, Department of Computer Science, Aalborg University, 2000. [371, 372]

[NPW02]   Tobias Nipkow, Lawrence C. Paulson, and Markus Wenzel. *Isabelle/HOL: A Proof Assistant for Higher-Order Logic*, volume 2283 of *Lecture Notes in Computer Science*. Springer-Verlag, 2002. [328, 331]

[NS03]   Brian Nielsen and Arne Skou. Automated test generation from timed automata. *International Journal on Software Tools for Technology Transfer*, 5:59–77, 2003. [205, 206, 212, 230]

[NT81]   S. Naito and M. Tsunoyama. Fault detection for sequential machines by transition tours. In *Proceedings of the 11th IEEE Fault Tolerant Computing Conference (FTCS 1981)*, pages 238–243. IEEE Computer Society Press, 1981. [93]

[Nta88]   S. C. Ntafos. A comparison of some structural testing strategies. *IEEE Transactions on Software Engineering*, SE-11:367–375, April 1988. [301]

[Nta98]   Simeon Ntafos. On random and partition testing. In *Proceedings of the ACM SIGSOFT International Symposium on Software Testing and Analysis (ISSTA 1998)*, pages 42–48. ACM Press, 1998. [302, 307, 441]

[OBG01]   D. Buchs O. Biberstein and N. Guelfi. Object-oriented nets with algebraic specifications: The CO-OPN/2 formalism. In Gul Agha, Fiorella de Cindio, and Grzegorz Rozenberg, editors, *Concurrent Object-Oriented Programming and Petri Nets, Advances in Petri Nets*, volume 2001 of *Lecture Notes in Computer Science*, pages 73–130. Springer-Verlag, 2001. [343]

[OMG02]   Object Management Group (OMG). *UML Testing Profile – Request For Proposal*, April 2002. OMG Document (ad/01-07-08). [497]

[OP95]   F. Ouabdesselam and I. Parissis. Constructing operational profiles for synchronous crtitical software. In *Proceedings of the 6th International Symposium on Software Reliability Engineering (ISSRE 1995)*, pages 286–293. IEEE Computer Society Press, 1995. [398]

[ORR⁺96] Sam Owre, Sreeranga Rajan, John M. Rushby, Natarajan Shankar, and
          Mandayam K. Srivas. PVS: Combining specification, proof checking, and
          model checking. In Rajeev Alur and Thomas A. Henzinger, editors, *Pro-
          ceedings of the 8th International Conference on Computer Aided Verifica-
          tion (CAV 1996)*, volume 1102 of *Lecture Notes in Computer Science*, pages
          411–414. Springer-Verlag, 1996. [325]

[ORS92]   Sam Owre, John M. Rushby, and Natarajan Shankar. PVS: A prototype
          verification system. In Deepak Kapur, editor, *Proceedings of the 11th In-
          ternational Conference on Automated Deduction (CADE 1992)*, volume 607
          of *Lecture Notes in Artificial Intelligence*, pages 748–752. Springer-Verlag,
          1992. [337]

[ORSvH95] S. Owre, J. Rushby, N. Shankar, and F. von Henke. Formal verification
          of fault-tolerant architerctures: Prolegomena to the design of PVS. *IEEE
          Transactions on Software Engineering*, 21(2):107–125, 1995. [426, 427]

[PAD⁺98] Jan Peleska, Peter Amthor, Sabine Dick, Oliver Meyer, Michael Siegel, and
          Cornelia Zahlten. Testing reactive real-time systems. Tutorial, held at
          the *5th International Symposium on Formal Techniques in Real-Time and
          Fault-Tolerant Systems (FTRTFT 1998)*, Denmark Technical University,
          Lyngby, 1998. Updated revision. Available as http://www.informatik.uni-
          bremen.de/agbs/jp/papers/ftrtft98.ps. [356, 357, 360, 375]

[Pap94]   Christos H. Papadimitriou. *Computational Complexity.* Addison-Wesley,
          New York, 1994. [28]

[Pat70]   Michael S. Paterson. Unsolvability in 3×3 matrices. *Studies in Applied
          Mathematics*, 49(1):105–107, March 1970. [32]

[Pau94]   Lawrence C. Paulson. *Isabelle: A Generic Theorem Prover*, volume 828 of
          Lecture Notes in Computer Science. Springer-Verlag, 1994. [328, 331]

[PBD93]   A. Petrenko, G. Bochmann, and R. Dussouli. Conformance relations and
          test derivation. In O. Rafiq, editor, *Proceedings of the 6th International
          Workshop on Protocol Test Systems (IWPTS 1993)*, volume C-19 of *IFIP
          Transactions*, pages 157–178, Pau, France, September 1993. North-Holland.
          [190]

[PDGN03] H. Pals, Z. R. Dai, J. Grabowski, and H. Neukirchen. UML-based modeling
          of roaming with bluetooth devices. In Chun Chen, Walter Dosch, Yuntao
          Qian, and Huaizhong Lin, editors, *First Hangzhou-Lübeck Conference on
          Software Engineering (HL-SE'03)*, 2003. [506]

[Pel02]   Jan Peleska. Formal methods for test automation – hard real-time testing of
          controllers for the airbus aircraft family. In *Proceedings of the 6th Biennial
          World Conference on Integrated Design & Process Technology (IDPT 2002)*.
          Society for Design and Process Science, June 2002. [360]

[Per98]   Cecile Peraire. *Formal testing of object-oriented software: From the method
          to the tool.* PhD thesis, École Polytechnique Fédéral de Lausanne (EPFL),
          Switzerland, 1998. [349]

[PF90]   David H. Pitt and David Freestone. The derivation of conformance tests
          from LOTOS specifications. *IEEE Transactions on Software Engineering*,
          16(12):1337–1343, December 1990. [163, 164, 165, 166]

[Pha91]   M. Phalippou. Tveda: An experiment in computer-aided test case
          generation from formal specification of protocols. Technical Note
          NT/LAA/SLC/347, France Telecom – CNET, 1991. [200]

[Pha93]   M. Phalippou. The limited power of testing. In Gregor von Bochmann, Rachida Dssouli, and Anindya Das, editors, *Proceedings of the 5th International Workshop on Protocol Test Systems (IWPTS 1992)*, volume C-11 of *IFIP Transactions*, pages 43–54, Montréal, September 1993. North-Holland. [190, 196]

[Pha94a]   M. Phalippou. Executable testers. In Omar Rafiq, editor, *Proceedings of the 6th International Workshop on Protocol Test Systems (IWPTS 1993)*, volume C-19 of *IFIP Transactions*, pages 35–50, Pau, France, September 1994. North-Holland. [200]

[Pha94b]   M. Phalippou. *Relations d'Implantation et Hypothèses de Test sur des Automates à Entrées et Sorties*. PhD thesis, L'Université de Bordeaux I, France, 1994. [173, 175, 177, 188, 412]

[Pha95]   M. Phalippou. Abstract testing and concrete testers. In S. T. Vuong and S. T. Chanson, editors, *Proceedings of the 14th IFIP/WG6.1 International Symposium on Protocol Specification, Testing and Verification (PSTV 1994)*, volume 1 of *IFIP Conference Proceedings*, pages 221–236, Vancouver, June 1995. Chapman & Hall. [200]

[Phi]   Philips website. http://www.philips.com/. [409]

[Phi87]   Iain Phillips. Refusal testing. *Theoretical Computer Science*, 50:241–284, 1987. [126, 138, 139, 140, 141]

[Pin78a]   Jean-Eric Pin. Sur les mots synchronisants dans un automate fini. *Elektronische Informationsverarbeitung und Kybernetik (EIK)*, 14:297–303, 1978. [31]

[Pin78b]   Jean-Eric Pin. Sur un cas particulier de la conjecture de černý. In Giorgio Ausiello and Corrado Böhm, editors, *Proceedings of the 5th Colloquium on Automata, Languages and Programming*, volume 62 of *Lecture Notes in Computer Science*, pages 345–352, Udine, Italy, July 1978. Springer-Verlag. [31, 32]

[Pir95]   L. Ferreira Pires. *Protocol Implementation: Manual for Practical Exercises 1995-1996*. University of Twente, the Netherlands, 1995. Lecture notes. [443]

[PJH92]   Carl Pixley, Seh-Woong Jeong, and Gary D. Hachtel. Exact calculation of synchronization sequences based on binary decision diagrams. In *Proceedings of the 29th Design Automation Conference (DAC 1992)*, pages 620–623. IEEE Computer Society Press, June 1992. [6, 32]

[PLP03]   A. Pretschner, H. Lötzbeyer, and J. Philipps. Model based testing in incremental system development. *Journal of Systems and Software*, 70(3):315–329, 2003. [289]

[PN98]   Peter Puschner and Roman Nossal. Testing the results of static worst-case execution-time analysis. In *Proceedings of the 19th IEEE Real-Time Systems Symposium (RTSS 1998)*, pages 134–143. IEEE Computer Society Press, December 1998. [383, 384]

[Pnu77]   A. Pnueli. The temporal logic of programs. In *Proceedings of the 18th IEEE Symposium Foundations of Computer Science (FOCS 1977)*, pages 46–57. IEEE Computer Society Press, 1977. [526, 529, 562]

[PO96]   I. Parissis and F. Ouabdesselam. Specification-based testing of synchronous software. In D. Garlan, editor, *Proceedings of the 4th ACM SIGSOFT Symposium on Foundations of Software Engineering (FSE 1996)*, volume 21(6) of *ACM SIGSOFT Software Engineering Notes*, pages 127–134. ACM Press, 1996. [398]

[PP04]   Wolfgang Prenninger and Alexander Pretschner. Abstractions for model-based testing. In *Proceedings of the International Workshop on Test and Analysis of Component Based Systems (TACoS 2004)*, Electronic Notes in Theoretical Computer Science. Elsevier Science Publishers, 2004. [284, 288, 452]

[PPS+03]   J. Philipps, A. Pretschner, O. Slotosch, E. Aiglstorfer, S. Kriebel, and K. Scholl. Model-based test case generation for smart cards. In *In Proceedings of the 8th International Workshop on Formal Methods for Industrial Critical Systems (FMICS 2003)*, Electronic Notes in Theoretical Computer Science. Elsivier, 2003. to appear. [286, 339, 343, 347, 406, 439, 444, 446, 447, 448, 449, 451, 453, 454, 455, 456, 457, 458, 459]

[PPW+05] Alexander Pretschner, Wolfgang Prenninger, Stefan Wagner, Christian Kühnel, Martin Baumgartner, Bernd Sostawa, Rüdiger Zölch, and Thomas Stauner. One Evaluation of Model-Based Testing and its Automation. In *Proc. ICSE'05*, 2005. To appear. [291]

[PR94]   Irith Pomeranz and Sudhakar M. Reddy. Application of homing sequences to synchronous sequential circuit testing. *IEEE Transactions on Computers*, 43(5):569–580, May 1994. [22, 32]

[Pre01]   A. Pretschner. Classical search strategies for test case generation with constraint logic programming. In E. Brinksma and J. Tretmans, editors, *Proceedings of the 3rd International Workshop on Formal Approaches to Testing of Software (FATES 2001)*, number NS/01/4 in BRICS Notes Series, pages 47–60, 2001. Satellite Workshop on CONCUR 2001. [407]

[Pre03]   A. Pretschner. Compositional generation for MC/DC test suites. In *Proceedings of the International Workshop on Test and Analysis of Component Based Systems (TACoS 2003)*, volume 82(6) of *Electronic Notes in Theoretical Computer Science*, pages 1–11. Elsevier Science Publishers, 2003. [289, 407]

[PS01]   Tatjana Petković and Magnus Steinby. On directable automata. *Journal of Automata, Languages and Combinatorics*, 6(2):205–220, 2001. [6]

[PST96]   Ben Potter, Jane Sinclair, and David Till. *An Introduction to Formal Specification and Z*. Prentice Hall, second edition, 1996. [325, 327]

[PTLP99] S. Prowell, C. Trammell, R. Linger, and J. Poore. *Cleanroom Software Engineering*. Addison Wesley, 1999. [283]

[Put94]   Martin L. Puterman. *Markov Decision Processes: Discrete Stochastic Dynamic Programming*. John Wiley and Sons, Inc, 1994. [239, 241]

[PVY99]   D. Peled, M. Vardi, and M. Yannakakis. Black box checking. In *Proceedings of the Joint International Conference on Formal Description Techniques for Distributed Systems and Communication Protocols (FORTE 1999) and Protocol Specification, Testing and Verification (PSTV 1999)*, volume 156 of *IFIP Conference Proceedings*, pages 225–240. Kluwer Academic, 1999. [599]

[Rav96]   Bala Ravikumar. A deterministic parallel algorithm for the homing sequence problem. In *Proceedings of the 8th IEEE Symposium on Parallel and Distributed Processing (SPDP 1996)*, pages 512–520, New Orleans, LA, October 1996. IEEE Computer Society Press. [31]

[Rav98]   Bala Ravikumar. Parallel algorithms for finite automata problems. In José D. P. Rolim, editor, *Proceedings of the 10 Workshops of the 12th International Parallel Processing Symposium (IPPS 1998) and 9th Symposium on Parallel and Distributed Processing (SPDS 1998)*, volume 1388 of *Lecture Notes in Computer Science*, page 373. Springer-Verlag, 1998. [31]

[RdBJ00] V. Rusu, L. du Bousquet, and T. Jéron. An approach to symbolic test generation. In W. Grieskamp, T. Santen, and B. Stoddart, editors, *Proceedings of the 2nd International Conference on Integrated Formal Methods (IFM 2000)*, volume 1945 of *Lecture Notes in Computer Science*, pages 338–357. Springer-Verlag, 2000. [174, 418, 424, 425, 426, 427]

[RG95] Anil S. Rao and Kenneth Y. Goldberg. Manipulating algebraic parts in the plane. *IEEE Transactions on Robotics and Automation (IEEETROB)*, 11(4):598–602, August 1995. [7, 32]

[RH01a] S. Rayadurgam and M.P. Heimdahl. Coverage based test case generation using model checkers. In *Proceedings of the 8th Annual IEEE International Conference and Workshop on the Engineering of Computer Based Systems (ECBS 2001)*, pages 83–91. IEEE Computer Society Press, 2001. [352]

[RH01b] S. Rayadurgam and M. P. Heimdahl. Test-sequence generation from formal requirements models. In *Proceedings of the 6th IEEE International Symposium on High-Assurance Systems Engineering (HASE 2001)*, pages 23–31. IEEE Computer Society Press, 2001. [352]

[RH01c] G. Roşu and K. Havelund. Synthesizing dynamic programming algorithms from linear temporal logic formulae. Technical report, RIACS, 2001. [534]

[RHC76] C. V. Ramamoorthy, S. F. Ho, and W. T. Chen. On the automated generation of program test data. In *Proceedings of the 2nd International Conference on Software Engineering (ICSE 1976)*, page 636. IEEE Computer Society Press, 1976. Abstract only. [343]

[Ris93] N. Risser. TVEDA V2 user guide. Technical Document DT/LAA/SLC/EVP/5, France Telecom – CNET, March 1993. [200]

[RJB99] James Rumbaugh, Ivar Jacobson, and Grady Booch. *The Unified Modeling Language Reference Manual*. Addison-Wesley, Reading, Massachusetts, USA, first edition, 1999. [1, 497]

[RKS02] Orna Raz, Philip Koopman, and Mary Shaw. Semantic anomaly detection in online data sources. In *Proceedings of the 24th International Conference on Software Engineering (ICSE 2002)*, pages 302–312. ACM Press, 2002. [526, 550, 551, 554]

[RLNS00] K. Rustan, M. Leino, G. Nelson, and J. B. Saxe. ESC/Java user's manual. Technical Report 2000-002, Compaq Systems Research Center, Palo Alto, 2000. [555]

[RNHW98] P. Raymond, X. Nicollin, N. Halbwachs, and D. Weber. Automatic testing of reactive systems. In *Proceedings of the 19th IEEE Real-Time Systems Symposium (RTSS 1998)*, pages 200–209. IEEE Computer Society Press, 1998. [399, 400]

[RP92] A. Rouger and M. Phalippou. Test cases generation from formal specifications. In *Proceedings of the 14th International Switching Symposium (ISS 1992)*, page C10.2, Yokohama, October 1992. [198]

[RS93] Ronald L. Rivest and Robert E. Schapire. Inference of finite automata using homing sequences. *Information and Computation*, 103(2):299–347, April 1993. [8, 12, 27, 586, 598]

[RSP93] June-Kyung Rho, Fabio Somenzi, and Carl Pixley. Minimum length synchronizing sequences of finite state machine. In *Proceedings of the 30th ACM/IEEE Design Automation Conference (DAC 1993)*, pages 463–468. ACM Press, June 1993. [25, 32]

[Rus02]   Vlad Rusu. Verification using test generation techniques. In L.-H. Eriksson and P. Lindsay, editors, *Getting IT Right: Proceedings of the 11th International Symposium of Formal Methods Europe (FME 2002)*, volume 2381 of *Lecture Notes in Computer Science*, pages 252–271. Springer-Verlag, 2002. [426]

[RVL+97]   Ted Romer, Geoff Voelker, Dennis Lee, Alec Wolman, Wayne Wong, Hank Levy, Brian Bershad, and Brad Chen. Instrumentation and optimization of Win32/Intel executables using Etch. In *Proceedings of the First USENIX Windows NT Workshop*, Seattle, WA, August 1997. [530]

[RW85]   S. Rapps and E. J. Weyuker. Selecting software test data using data flow information. *IEEE Transactions on Software Engineering*, SE-11:367–375, April 1985. [297, 300]

[RW88]   C. Rich and R. Waters. The programmer's apprentice: A research overview. *IEEE Computer*, 21(11):10–25, 1988. [552]

[RX96]   Bala Ravikumar and Xuefeng Xiong. Randomized parallel algorithms for the homing sequence problem. In Adam W. Bojanczyk, editor, *Proceedings of the 25th International Conference on Parallel Processing (ICPP 1996), volume 2: Algorithms & Applications*, pages 82–89. IEEE Computer Society Press, August 1996. [31]

[RX97]   Bala Ravikumar and Xuefeng Xiong. Implementing sequential and parallel programs for the homing sequence problem. In Darrell R. Raymond, Derick Wood, and Sheng Yu, editors, *Proceedings of the 1st Workshop on Implementing Automata (WIA 1996)*, volume 1260 of *Lecture Notes in Computer Science*, pages 120–131. Springer-Verlag, 1997. [31]

[Rys83]   Igor K. Rystsov. Polynomial complete problems in automata theory. *Information Processing Letters*, 16(3):147–151, April 1983. [8, 20, 27, 30, 31, 32]

[Rys92]   Igor K. Rystsov. Rank of a finite automaton. *CYBERNETICS: Cybernetics and Systems Analysis*, 28(3):323–328, May 1992. Translation of *Kibernetika i Sistemnyi Analiz*, pages 3–10 in non-translated version. [6, 30, 31, 32]

[Rys97]   Igor K. Rystsov. Reset words for commutative and solvable automata. *Theoretical Computer Science*, 172:273–279, February 1997. [6, 31]

[SA99]   Jian Shen and Jacob Abraham. An RTL abstraction technique for processor micorarchitecture validation and test generation. *Journal of Electronic Testing: Theory & Application*, 16(1–2):67–81, February 1999. [287, 439, 443, 445, 447, 448, 449, 450, 455, 456, 457, 458]

[Sad98]   Sadegh Sadeghipour. *Testing Cyclic Software Components of Reactive Systems on the Basis of Formal Specifications*, volume 40 of *Forschungsergebnisse zur Informatik*. Verlag Dr. Kovač, Hamburg, 1998. [330, 331]

[Sal02]   Arto Salomaa. Synchronization of finite automata. Contributions to an old problem. In I. Hal Sudborough T. Æ. Mogensen, D. A. Schmidt, editor, *The Essence of Computation. Complexity, Analysis, Transformation: Essays Dedicated to Neil D. Jones*, volume 2566 of *Lecture Notes in Computer Science*, pages 37–59. Springer-Verlag, 2002. [7]

[Sav70]   Walter J. Savitch. Relationships between nondeterministic and deterministic tape complexities. *Journal of Computer and System Sciences*, 4:177–192, 1970. [28]

[SBN+97]   S. Savage, M. Burrows, G. Nelson, P. Sobalvarro, and T. E. Anderson. Eraser: A dynamic data race detector for multithreaded programs. *ACM Transactions on Computer Systems*, 14(4):391–411, November 1997. [526, 532, 533]

[Sch00]   Johann M. Schumann. Automated theorem proving in high-quality software design. In Steffen Hölldobler, editor, *Intellectics and Computational Logic*, volume 19 of *Applied Logic Series*, pages 295–312. Kluwer Academic, 2000. [325]

[Sch01]   Johann M. Schumann. *Automated Theorem Proving in Software Engineering*. Springer-Verlag, 2001. [325]

[SCK⁺95] B. Steffen, A. Claßen, M. Klein, J. Knoop, and T. Margaria. The fixpoint analysis machine. In J. Lee and S. Smolka, editors, *Proceedings of the 6th International Conference on Concurrency Theory (CONCUR 1995)*, volume 962 of *Lecture Notes in Computer Science*, pages 72–87, Heidelberg, Germany, 1995. Springer-Verlag. [575]

[SCS97]   Harbhajan Singh, Mirko Conrad, and Sadegh Sadeghipour. Test case design based on Z and the classification-tree method. In Michael G. Hinchey and Shaoying Liu, editors, *Proceedings of the 1st International Conference on Formal Engineering Methods (ICFEM 1997)*, pages 81–90. IEEE Computer Society Press, 1997. [330, 331]

[SD85]   K. Sabnani and A. Dahbura. A new technique for generating protocol tests. In *Proceedings of the 9th Data Communication Symposium (SIGCOMM 1985)*, pages 36–43. IEEE Computer Society Press, 1985. Also appeared in *Computer Communication Review*, volume 15(4), September 1985. [72]

[SD88]   Krishan Sabnani and Anton Dahbura. A protocol test generation procedure. *Computer Networks and ISDN Systems*, 15(4):285–297, September 1988. [69, 72, 78, 84, 98, 99]

[SDGR03]   I. Schieferdecker, Z. R. Dai, J. Grabowski, and A. Rennoch. The UML 2.0 testing profile and its relation to TTCN-3. In D. Hogrefe and A. Wiles, editors, *Proceedings of the 15th IFIP International Conference on Testing of Communicating Systems (TestCom2003)*, volume 2644 of *Lecture Notes in Computer Science*. Springer-Verlag, May 2003. [497]

[Seg92]   R. Segala. A process algebraic view of Input/Output Automata. Technical Memo MIT/LCS/TR-557, Massachusetts Institute of Technology, Laboratory for Computer Science, Cambridge, U.S.A., 1992. [173]

[Seg96]   Roberto Segala. Testing probabilistic automata. In Ugo Montanari and Vladimiro Sassone, editors, *Proceedings of the 7th Conference on Concurrency Theory (CONCUR 1996)*, volume 1119 of *Lecture Notes in Computer Science*, pages 299–314. Springer-Verlag, 1996. [234, 244, 245, 252, 253, 255, 261, 265, 269]

[Seg97]   R. Segala. Quiescence, fairness, testing and the notion of implementation. *Information and Computation*, 138(2):194–210, 1997. [181, 182, 183]

[SEG00]   M. Schmitt, M. Ebner, and J. Grabowski. Test generation with Autolink and TestComposer. In E. Sherratt, editor, *Proceedings of the 2nd Workshop on SDL and MSC (SAM 2000)*. VERIMAG, IRISA, 2000. [430, 431, 432, 433]

[SL88]   D. Sidhu and T. Leung. Experience with test generation for real protocols. In *Proceedings of the ACM Symposium on Communications Architectures and Protocols (SIGCOMM 1988)*, pages 257–261. ACM Press, 1988. [110]

[SL89]   D. Sidhu and T.-K. Leung. Formal methods for protocol testing: A detailed study. *IEEE Transactions on Software Engineering*, 15(4):413–426, April 1989. [3, 100]

[SL94]   Roberto Segala and Nancy Lynch. Probabilistic simulations for probabilistic processes. In Bengt Jonsson and Joachim Parrow, editors, *Proceedings of the 5th Conference on Concurrency Theory (CONCUR 1994)*, volume 836 of *Lecture Notes in Computer Science*, pages 481–496. Springer-Verlag, 1994. [239, 269]

[SM93]   Sriram Sankar and Manas Mandal. Concurrent runtime monitoring of formally specified programs. *IEEE Computer*, 26(3):32–41, March 1993. [531]

[SMIM89]   F. Sato, J. Munemori, T. Ideguchi, and T. Mizuno. Test sequence generation method based on finite automata – single transition checking using W Set. *Transactions of EIC (in Japanese)*, J72-B-I(3):183–192, 1989. [93]

[Sok71]   M. N. Sokolovskii. Diagnostic experiments with automata. *Kibernetika*, 6:44–49, 1971. [40]

[Sos92]   R. Sosič. Dynascope: A tool for program directing. In *Proceedings of the SIGPLAN Conference on Programming Language Design and Implementation (PLDI 1992)*, pages 12–21, 1992. Appeared in *SIGPLAN Notices*, volume 27(7), July 1992. [531]

[SPHP02]   B. Schätz, A. Pretschner, F. Huber, and J. Philipps. Model-based development of embedded systems. In J.-M. Bruel and Z. Bellahsene, editors, *Proceedings of the Workshops of the 8th International Conference on Advances in Object-Oriented Information Systems (OOIS 2002)*, volume 2426 of *Lecture Notes in Computer Science*, pages 298–311. Springer-Verlag, 2002. [290]

[Spi92]   J. Michael Spivey. *The Z Notation*. Prentice Hall, second edition, 1992. [325, 327]

[SSD⁺03]   U. Sammapun, R. Sharykin, M. DeLap, M. Kim, and S. Zdancewic. Formalizing Java-MaC. In O. Sokolsky and M. Viswanathan, editors, *Proccedings of the 3rd Workshop on Run-Time Verification (RV 2003)*, volume 89(2) of *Electronic Notes in Theoretical Computer Science*. Elsevier Science Publishers, 2003. [526, 547]

[Sta]   Stateflow. http://www.mathworks.com/products/stateflow/. [1]

[Sta66]   Peter H. Starke. Eine Bemerkung über homogene Experimente. *Elektronische Informationverarbeitung und Kybernetic*, 2:257–259, 1966. [31]

[Sta72]   Peter. H. Starke. *Abstract Automata*. North-Holland, Amsterdam, 1972. Translation from German. [8, 15]

[Sta73]   H. Stachowiak. *Allgemeine Modelltheorie*. Springer-Verlag, 1973. [283, 288]

[Sto02]   M. I. A. Stoelinga. An introduction to probabilistic automata. In G. Rozenberg, editor, *EATCS bulletin*, volume 78, pages 176–198, 2002. [234]

[SV03]   M. I. A. Stoelinga and F. W. Vaandrager. A testing scenario for probabilistic automata. In J. C. M. Baeten, J. K. Lenstra, J. Parrow, and G. J. Woeginger, editors, *Proceedings of the 30th International Colloquium on Automata, Lnaguages, and Programming (ICALP 2003)*, volume 2719 of *Lecture Notes in Computer Science*, pages 464–477. Springer-Verlag, 2003. Also published as Technical Report of the nijmeegs instituut voor informatica en informatiekunde, number NIII-R0307. [234, 269]

[SVD01]   Jan Springintveld, Frits Vaandrager, and Pedro R. D'Argenio. Testing timed automata. *Theoretical Computer Science*, 254(1–2):225–257, March 2001. [202, 206, 212, 215, 221, 230]

[SVG02]   S. Schulz and T. Vassiliou-Gioles. Implementation of TTCN-3 test systems using the TRI. In I. Schieferdecker, H. König, and A. Wolisz, editors, *Applications to Internet Technologies and Service – Proceedings of the 14th International Conference on Testing Communication Systems (TestCom 2002)*, volume 210 of *IFIP Conference Proceedings*, pages 425–442. Kluwer Academic, 2002. [480]

[SVG03]   Ina Schieferdecker and Theofanis Vassiliou-Gioles. Realizing distributed TTCN-3 test systems with TCI. In Dieter Hogrefe and Anthony Wiles, editors, *Proceedings of the 15th International Conference on Testing of Communicating Systems (TestCom 2003)*, volume 2644 of *Lecture Notes in Computer Science*, pages 95–109. Springer-Verlag, 2003. [480]

[SVW87]   A. P. Sistla, Moshe Y. Vardi, and Pierre Wolper. The complementation problem for Büchi automata with application to temporal logics. *Theoretical Computer Science*, 49:217–237, 1987. [567]

[SW91]   Colin Stirling and David Walker. Local model checking in the modal mu-calculus. *Theoretical Computer Science*, 89(1):161–177, October 1991. [566]

[TB02]   J. Tretmans and E. Brinksma. Côte de Resyste – Automated Model Based Testing. In M. Schweizer, editor, *Progress 2002 – 3rd Workshop on Embedded Systems*, pages 246–255, Utrecht, The Netherlands, October 24 2002. STW Technology Foundation. [420, 423]

[Tel]   Telelogic website. http://www.telelogic.com/. [410]

[Tho90]   Wolfgang Thomas. Automata on infinite objects. In Jan van Leeuwen, editor, *Handbook of Theoretical Computer Science*, volume B: Formal Models and Semantics, chapter 4, pages 133–191. Elsevier Science Publishers, 1990. [203]

[TJ98]   Kevin S. Templer and Clinton L. Jeffrey. A configurable automatic instrumentation tool for Ansi C. In *Proceedings of the 13th IEEE Conference on Automated Software Engineering (ASE 1998)*, pages 249–258. IEEE Computer Society Press, October 1998. [531]

[TM95]   Ian Toyn and John A. McDermid. CADiℤ: an architecture for Z tools and its implementation. *Software – Practice and Experience*, 25(3):305–330, 1995. [331]

[Tor]   Torx website. http://www.purl.org/net/torx/. [420]

[Toy96]   Ian Toyn. Formal reasoning in the Z notation using cadiℤ. In Nicholas A. Merriam, editor, *Proceedings of the 2nd International Workshop on User Interface Design for Theorem Proving Systems (UITP 1996)*, 1996. [331]

[Toy98]   Ian Toyn. A tactic language for reasoning about Z specifications. In David Duke and Andy Evans, editors, *Proceedings of the 3rd Northern Formal Methods Workshop (NFMW 1998)*, Electronic Workshops in Computing. British Computer Society, 1998. [331]

[TP98]   Q. M. Tan and A. Petrenko. Test generation for specifications modeled by input/output automata. In A. Petrenko and N. Yevtushenko, editors, *Proceedings of the 11th International Workshop on Testing of Communication Systems (IWTCS 1998)*, volume 131 of *IFIP Conference Proceedings*, pages 83–100. Kluwer Academic, 1998. [174]

[TPvB96]   Q. M. Tan, Alexandre Petrenko, and Gregor von Bochmann. Modeling basic LOTOS by FSMs for conformance testing. In Piotr Dembinski and Marek Sredniawa, editors, *Proceedings of the 15th IFIP/WG6.1 International Symposium on Protocol Specification, Testing and Verification (PSTV 1995)*, volume 38 of *IFIP Conference Proceedings*, pages 137–152. Chapman & Hall, 1996. [156, 157, 158, 159]

[TPvB97] Q. M. Tan, A. Petrenko, and Gregor v. Bochmann. Checking experiments with labeled transition systems for trace equivalence. In *Proceedings of the 10th International Workshop on Testing Communicating Systems (IWTCS 1997)*, 1997. [160, 161, 162, 163]

[Tra02]   Avraham N. Trakhtman. The existence of synchronizing word and černý conjecture for some finite automata. In *Proceedings of the 2nd Haifa Workshop on Graph Theory, Combinatorics and Algorithms (GTCA 2002)*, June 2002. [31]

[Tre94]   Jan Tretmans. A formal approach to conformance testing. In *Proceedings of the 6th IFIP TC6/WG6.1 International Workshop on Protocol Test Systems (IWPTS 1993)*, volume C-19 of *IFIP Transactions*, pages 257–276. North-Holland, 1994. [119, 145, 146]

[Tre96a] J. Tretmans. Conformance testing with labelled transisition systems: Implementation relations and test generation. *Computer Networks and ISDN Systems*, 29:49–79, 1996. [417, 424]

[Tre96b] J. Tretmans. Test generation with inputs, outputs, and quiescence. In T. Margaria and B. Steffen, editors, *Proceedings of the 2nd International Workshop on Tools and Algorithms for the Construction and Analysis of Systems (TACAS 1996)*, volume 1055 of *Lecture Notes in Computer Science*, pages 127–146. Springer-Verlag, 1996. [173, 179, 184, 185, 187, 194]

[Tre96c] J. Tretmans. Test Generation with Inputs, Outputs and Repetitive Quiescence. *Software – Concepts and Tools*, 17(3):103–120, 1996. [175, 178, 417, 420, 421, 424]

[U2T]   U2TP Consortium. http://www.fokus.fraunhofer.de/u2tp/. [497]

[U2T04]   U2TP Consortium. *UML Testing Profile*, March 2004. Final Adopted Specification at OMG (ptc/2004-04-02). [497, 498]

[UMLa]   UML 2.0. http://www.omg.org/uml. [497]

[UMLb]   UMLAUT website. http://www.irisa.fr/UMLAUT/. [419, 420]

[UML03a] *UML 2.0 Infrastructure Specification*, November 2003. OMG Adopted Specification (ptc/03-09-15). [497]

[UML03b] *UML 2.0 Superstructure*, September 2003. OMG Adopted Specification (ptc/03-08-02). [497]

[UWZ97]   Hasan Ural, Xiaolin Wu, and Fan Zhang. On minimizing the lengths of checking sequences. *IEEE Transactions on Computers*, 46(1):93–99, 1997. [104]

[Vaa91]   F. Vaandrager. On the relationship between process algebra and Input/Output Automata. In *Proceeedings on the 6th IEEE Symposium on Logic in Computer Science (LICS 1991)*, pages 387–398. IEEE Computer Society Press, 1991. [181]

[Val84]   L. G. Valiant. A theory of the learnable. *Communications of the ACM*, 27(11):1134–1142, 1984. [307]

[Var96]   M. Y. Vardi. An automata-theoretic approach to linear temporal logic. In F. Moller and G. M. Birtwistle, editors, *Logics for Concurrency – Structure versus Automata. Proceedings of the 8th Banff Higher Order Workshop (Banff 1995)*, volume 1043 of *Lecture Notes in Computer Science*, pages 238–266. Springer-Verlag, 1996. [566, 567]

[Var01]   M. Y. Vardi. Branching vs. linear time: Final showdown. In W. Yi T. Margaria, editor, *Proceedings of the 7th International Conference on Tools and Algorithms for the Construction and Analysis of Systems (TACAS 2001)*, volume 2031 of *Lecture Notes in Computer Science*, pages 1–22. Springer-Verlag, January 2001. [562]

[Vas73]   M. P. Vasilevski. Failure diagnosis of automata. *Cybernetic*, 9(4):653–665, 1973. [101, 108, 593, 599]

[VB01]   S. A. Vilkomir and J. P. Bowen. Formalization of software testing criteria using the Z notation. In *Proceedings of the 25th International Computer Software and Applications Conference (COMPSAC 2001)*, pages 351–356. IEEE Computer Society Press, 8–12 October 2001. [297, 298]

[VB02]   S. A. Vilkomir and J. P. Bowen. Reinforced condition/decision coverage (RC/DC): A new criterion for software testing. In D. Bert, J. P. Bowen, M. Henson, and K. Robinson, editors, *Proceedings of the 2nd International Conference of B and Z Users: Formal Specification and Development in Z and B (ZB 2002)*, volume 2272 of *Lecture Notes in Computer Science*, pages 295–313. Springer-Verlag, 2002. [299]

[VCI90]   S. T. Vuong, W. Y. L. Chan, and M. R. Ito. The UIOv-method for protocol test sequence generation. In *Proceedings of the 2nd International Workshop on Protocol Test Systems (IWPTS 1990)*, pages 161–176. North-Holland, 1990. [99]

[vG01]   Rob J. van Glabbeek. The linear time – branching time spectrum I: The semantics of concrete, sequential processes. In J. A. Bergstra, A. Ponse, and S. A. Smolka, editors, *Handbook of Process Algebra*, pages 3–99. Elsevier Science Publishers, 2001. [119, 120, 127, 128, 230]

[vGSS95]   Rob J. van Glabbeek, Scott A. Smolka, and Bernhard Steffen. Reactive, generative and stratified models of probabilistic processes. *Information and Computation*, 121:59–80, 1995. [240]

[VT01]   R. G. de Vries and J. Tretmans. Towards Formal Test Purposes. In E. Brinksma and J. Tretmans, editors, *Proceedings of the 1st International Workshop on Formal Approaches to Testing of Software (FATES 2001)*, number BRICS NS-01-4 in BRICS Notes Series, pages 61–76, 2001. [422, 424]

[WBS02]   Joachim Wegener, André Baresel, and Harmen Sthamer. Suitability of evolutionary algorithms for evolutionary testing. In *Proceedings of the 26th IEEE International Computer Software and Applications Conference: Prolonging Software Life: Development and Redevelopment (COMPSAC 2002)*, pages 287–289, Oxford, England, August 2002. IEEE Computer Society Press. [384]

[Weg01]   J. Wegener. *Evolutionärer Test des Zeitverhaltens von Realzeit-Systemen*. Dissertation, Humboldt Universität zu Berlin, 2001. [383, 384]

[Wes89]   C. H. West. Protocol validation in complex systems. In *Proceedings of the ACM Symposium on Communications Architectures & Protocols (SIGCOMM 1989)*, pages 303–312, Austin, TX, September 1989. ACM Press. [421, 437]

[Wez90]   Clazien D. Wezeman. The CO-OP method for compositional derivation of canonical testers. In E. Brinksma, G. Scollo, and C. A. Vissers, editors, *Proceedings of the 9th International Symposium on Protocol Specification, Testing and Verification (PSTV 1990)*, pages 145–158. North-Holland, 1990. [166, 167, 168, 415, 417]

[Wez95]   Clazien D. Wezeman. Deriving test from LOTOS specifications. In Tommaso Bolognesi, Jeroen van de Lagemaat, and Chris Vissers, editors, *LOTOSphere: Software Development with LOTOS*, pages 295–315. Kluwer Academic, 1995. [415, 417]

[Wil01]   A. Wiles. ETSI testing activities and the use of TTCN-3. In *Proceedings of the 10th International SDL Forum, 2001*, volume 2078 of *Lecture Notes in Computer Science*, pages 123–128. Springer-Verlag, 2001. [466]

[Wol99]   Mario Wolczko. Using a tracing java^{TM} virtual machine to gather data on the behavior of java programs. Technical report, Sun Microsystems, March 1999. [531]

[WSS94]   S.-H. Wu, S. A. Smolka, and E. W. Stark. Composition and behaviors of probabilistic I/O automata. In B. Jonsson and J. Parrow, editors, *Proceedings of the 5th International Conference on Concurrency Theory (CONCUR 1994)*, volume 836 of *Lecture Notes in Computer Science*, pages 513–528, Uppsala, Sweden, August 1994. Springer-Verlag. [234]

[WVS83]   P. Wolper, M. Y. Vardi, and A. P. Sistla. Reasoning about infinite computations paths. In *Proceedings of the 24th IEEE Symposium on Foundations of Computer Science (FOCS 1983)*, pages 185–194. IEEE Computer Society Press, 1983. Extended abstract. [567]

[XP]   eXtreme Programming website. http://www.extremeprogramming.org/. [502]

[YL91]   M. Yannakakis and D. Lee. Testing finite state machines. In Baruch Awerbuch, editor, *Proceedings of the 23rd Annual ACM Symposium on the Theory of Computing (STOC 1991)*, pages 476–485, New Orleans, LS, May 1991. ACM Press. Extended abstract. An extended version appeared in the *Journal of Computer and System Sciences*, 50(2):209–227, April 1995. [98]

[ZC93]   Jinsong Zhu and Samuel T. Chanson. Fault coverage evaluation of protocol test sequences. Technical Report TR-93-19, Department of Computer Science, University of British Columbia, June 1993. [110]

[ZHM97]   H. Zhu, P. Hall, and J. May. Software unit test coverage and adequacy. *ACM Computing Surveys*, 29(4):366–427, December 1997. [297, 300, 301]

Index

Lecture Notes in Computer Science

For information about Vols. 1–3460

please contact your bookseller or Springer